Microsoft®
Office 2000
Resource Kit

PUBLISHED BY
Microsoft Press
A Division of Microsoft Corporation
One Microsoft Way
Redmond, Washington 98052-6399

Library of Congress Cataloging-in-Publication Data
Microsoft Office 2000 Resource Kit / Microsoft Corporation.
        p. cm.
    ISBN 0-7356-0555-6
    1. Microsoft Office.   2. Business--Computer programs.
    I. Microsoft Corporation.
    HF5548.4.M525M52487   1999
    005.369--dc21   99-19168
                                                                       CIP

Printed and bound in the United States of America.

 2 3 4 5 6 7 8 9   QMQM   4 3 2 1 0 9

Distributed in Canada by Penguin Books Canada Limited.

A CIP catalogue record for this book is available from the British Library.

Microsoft Press books are available through booksellers and distributors worldwide. For further information about international editions, contact your local Microsoft Corporation office or contact Microsoft Press International directly at fax (425) 936-7329. Visit our Web site at mspress.microsoft.com.

Macintosh, QuickTime, and TrueType fonts are registered trademarks of Apple Computer, Inc. Kodak and FlashPix are trademarks of Kodak and the Kodak corporate symbol is a trademark of Kodak used under license. Active Desktop, DriveSpace, FoxPro, FrontPage, IntelliMirror, IntelliMouse, JScript, Microsoft, Microsoft Press, MSDN, NetMeeting, NetShow, Outlook, PhotoDraw, Picture It!, PivotChart, PivotTable, PowerPoint, Verdana, Visual Basic, Visual C++, Visual J++, Visual SourceSafe, Visual Studio, Win32, Windows, and Windows NT are either registered trademarks or trademarks of Microsoft Corporation in the United States and/or other countries. Other product and company names mentioned herein may be the trademarks of their respective owners.

The example companies, organizations, products, people, and events depicted herein are fictitious. No association with any real company, organization, product, person, or event is intended or should be inferred.

Acquisitions Editor: Juliana Aldous
Project Editor: Maureen Williams Zimmerman

This book and its online version on the World Wide Web were produced by members of the Office Product Unit of Microsoft Corporation.

Project Lead

Randy Holbrook

Writers

Gary Ericson, Roxanne Kenison, Sonia Moore, Mark Roberts, Samantha J.W. Robertson, Rob Sanfilippo

Editors

Jennifer Morison Hendrix, Donna Johnston

Toolbox Program Managers

Darrin Hatakeda, Gordon Hardy

Designer

Lucia Enriquez

Production

Lori Fields, Phyllis Grossman, Valérie Avart Klaisner

Additional Contributors

Janet Cannon, Mike Cook, Samuel Dawson, Rob Ferrara, Ann Hoegemeier, Daniela Lammers, Anneliese Murray, Erin O'Rourke, Penny Parks, Will Sibbald, Abram Spiegelman, Debbie Uyeshiro

Toolbox Contributors

Brad Aiken, David Chicks, Gordon Church, Rob Franco, Matt Gauthier, Bill Hunter, Tim Johnson, Chris Kimmell, Zeke Koch, Jeff Larsson, Oliver Lee, Philip Melemed, Pritvinath Obla, Chris Pratley, Maithreyi Lakshmi Ratan, Robert Silver, Scott Stearns, Heather Swayne, Chris Yu

Contents

Part 2   Deploying Office 2000

Part 3   Managing and Supporting Office 2000

Part 4   Upgrading to Office 2000

Part 5   Office 2000 and the Web

Chapter 12   Integrating Office 2000 with Your Intranet   565

Contents

Part 6   Using Office 2000 in a Multinational Organization

Appendix

The Office 2000 Environment

Contents

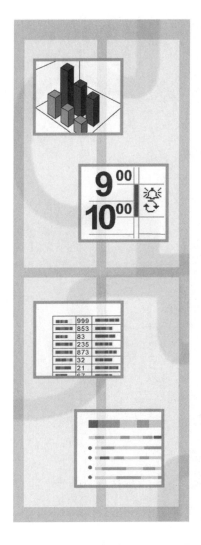

CHAPTER 1

Office 2000—What You Need to Know

Microsoft® Office 2000 offers more deployment options, configurations, and features than ever before. At the same time, Office 2000 has been designed to work efficiently and cost effectively in a broad range of network and operating system environments. The Microsoft Office 2000 Resource Kit provides comprehensive information about system requirements, upgrading strategies, and techniques for deploying and maintaining Office 2000 in your organization.

In This Chapter

The Office 2000 Resource Kit

The Microsoft Office 2000 Resource Kit brings together a comprehensive set of tools and information. These tools and information are designed to help you deploy, support, and maintain Office 2000.

Introduction to the Office 2000 Resource Kit

The Microsoft Office 2000 Resource Kit is designed for administrators, information technology (IT) professionals, and support staff who deploy and support Microsoft Office 2000. It features a comprehensive set of tools to assist you with installation, configuration, and Web services, as well as in-depth documentation of strategies and techniques that you can use to support Office 2000 in your organization.

Throughout the Office Resource Kit, a key focus is helping you to reduce the total cost of ownership. You'll find this focus in new tools such as the Office Custom Installation Wizard, as well as in the many scenarios, tips, and examples presented in the documentation.

It has never been easier to upgrade to a new version of Microsoft Office, and it has never been more efficient to manage configurations, support international users, or integrate Office with your intranet. The Office Resource Kit is a valuable tool as you work to support all of the groups and individuals within your organization.

The Microsoft Office 2000 Resource Kit is published as a printed book by Microsoft Press® and is also available in its entirety on the World Wide Web.

The printed book is available through your local bookseller, online bookstores, or directly from Microsoft Press. Included with the book is a CD-ROM that contains Office Resource Kit tools, reference information, and supplementary documents. To learn more about buying the book, visit the Microsoft Press Web site at http://mspress.microsoft.com/.

The Office Resource Kit Web site contains all of the text and graphics that make up the printed Office Resource Kit. To view the Office Resource Kit Web site, go to http://www.microsoft.com/office/ork/. To download the tools, documents, and other files included on the Office Resource Kit CD-ROM, click **Toolbox** in the left navigation pane of the Web site and follow the instructions to download the files.

Office 2000 Resource Kit Documentation

Documentation for the Microsoft Office 2000 Resource Kit is organized into six parts. The contents of each part are described in the following sections.

Part 1: The Office 2000 Environment

Part 1 provides an overview of the operating systems on which you can install Office 2000, including Microsoft Windows® 95/98, Microsoft Windows NT® Workstation 4.0, Windows NT Server 4.0, and the Windows 2000 family of products. The topics discuss hardware recommendations for running Office 2000 on these operating systems, as well as notes on using Office in a mixed-platform environment.

Server issues, which include information about service packs, security, and data access technologies, are covered separately. Also included are notes on the Microsoft BackOffice® server suites and on other supported network operating systems.

Part 2: Deploying Office 2000

Part 2 describes the tools and strategies that you can use to deploy Office 2000 throughout your organization. Basic installation methods are covered first, along with information about the new Windows installer technology.

Other topics present the Office Custom Installation Wizard, which allows you to control how users in your organization install Office on their computers, as well as the Profile Wizard, which lets you establish specific settings for toolbars, templates, and custom dictionaries. Special-case installations are also discussed, including deploying Office 2000 in a multinational setting and managing different levels of customization within one organization. Information about deploying Office 2000 with Microsoft Systems Management Server is also provided.

Part 3: Managing and Supporting Office 2000

Part 3 discusses how you can reduce the cost of supporting Office 2000 by locking down application configurations and adding your own topics and messages to the online Help system. The topics about system policies show how you can use the System Policy Editor to set configuration options such as menu commands, toolbar buttons, and dialog box options.

Other topics describe how you can add your organization's information to the online Help system, Answer Wizard, and built-in messages. A final section covers the security features supported in Office 2000 applications.

Part 4: Upgrading to Office 2000

Part 4 describes strategies that you can use to upgrade your current files to Office 2000. Information is included about the Microsoft Office Converter Pack, which enables Office 2000 applications to share files with previous versions of Office and other products. Introductory topics discuss planning your move to Office 2000, as well as special notes on year 2000 issues. An upgrading reference section lists special considerations for the core Office applications.

Part 5: Office 2000 and the Web

Part 5 presents the new Web capabilities of Office 2000, including features that allow you to publish, manage, and search Office 2000 documents on an intranet server. Also covered are the new Web Discussions feature, which allows users to collaborate on Office documents stored on a Web server, as well as other new features provided by Microsoft Office Server Extensions.

Part 6: Using Office 2000 in a Multinational Organization

Part 6 covers the built-in support provided in Office 2000 for international users. A key discussion covers the Microsoft Office 2000 MultiLanguage Pack, which allows users to change the language of the user interface and the online Help system.

Other topics cover planning for a multinational deployment, using international dictionaries and proofing tools, and taking advantage of *Unicode* support to open documents across different language versions of the product.

Conventions Used in Office 2000 Resource Kit Documentation

The following terms and text formats are used throughout the text of the Office 2000 Resource Kit.

Convention	Meaning
Bold	Indicates the actual commands, words, or characters that you type or that you click in the user interface.
Italic	In text, italic indicates new terms that are defined in the glossary.
	In procedures, command lines, or syntax, italic characters indicate a placeholder for information or parameters that you must provide. For example, if the procedure asks you to type a *file name*, you type the actual name of a file.
Path\File name	Indicates a Windows file system path or registry key—for example, the file Templates\Normal.dot. Unless otherwise indicated, you can use a mixture of uppercase and lowercase characters when you type paths and file names.
Monospace	Represents examples of code text.

Office 2000 Resource Kit Toolbox

The Microsoft Office 2000 Resource Kit contains a number of tools that help you to customize, configure, and deploy Office 2000 within your organization. You can install most of the core tools and support documents by using one integrated Setup program.

Toolbox

The Office Resource Kit Setup program is available from both the Office Resource Kit CD-ROM, which is included with the printed book, and from the download site of the Office Resource Kit Web site. For information about the Office Resource Kit Setup program, see "Overview of Tools and Utilities" on page 773.

The following table summarizes the key tools.

Tool name	Description
Custom Installation Wizard	Allows you to create a different Windows installer *transform* (MST file) for every installation scenario you need, without altering the original Windows installer *package* (MSI file).
Excel Tools	Provides a collection of Microsoft Excel utilities that can help you manage dates, files, and workbooks.
Microsoft Internet Explorer Administration Kit 5	Lets you customize, distribute, and maintain Internet Explorer 5 from one central location.
Language Version	Allows you to change the installation language of Office 2000 without reinstalling the applications.
Terminal Server Tools	Includes the Motionless Office Assistant and Setup tools for the Windows Terminal Server environment.
Profile Wizard	Helps you to create and save a default user profile, including standard locations for files and templates.
Removal Wizard	Lets you maintain a fine level of control over which files are removed from a user's system.
System Management Server Package Definition Files	Used by Microsoft Systems Management Server to install Office 2000 applications remotely.
System Policy Editor and Templates	Allows you to set and control the user interface and behavior of an application.
Unbind Binders Utility	Allows you to create separate Office documents from a binder document.
Microsoft Office 2000 Pre-Installation Pack for Windows NT	Allows you to upgrade the Microsoft Windows NT operating system so that Office 2000 can be installed without requiring Administrator privileges for end users.

In addition to these tools, the Office Resource Kit includes a collection of reference documents, spreadsheets, and sample files. Complementary tools, such as the HTML Help Workshop and the Microsoft FrontPage® 2000 Server Extensions Resource Kit, are also included.

See also

- For a list and description of all tools, utilities, and support documents included with the Office Resource Kit, see "Overview of Tools and Utilities" on page 773.

Other Sites of Interest to Administrators

In addition to the Microsoft Office 2000 Resource Kit site, there are several Web sites that feature information and tools designed to address the needs of administrators. The following sites might be of special interest to those of you who deploy and support Office 2000.

Microsoft Office

This Microsoft Office Web site, at http://www.microsoft.com/office/,serves as a gateway to dozens of specialized sites that address solutions, strategies, and support issues for the Microsoft Office family of products. You can click **Site Index** on the home page to get a complete index of all Microsoft sites related to Office 2000 products.

Microsoft TechNet

Microsoft TechNet, at http://www.microsoft.com/technet/, is a central information and community resource designed for administrators and information technology (IT) professionals. TechNet contains a wealth of information about planning, evaluating, deploying, maintaining, and supporting a range of IT systems.

Office Enterprise Information Center

The Office Enterprise Information Center, at http://www.microsoft.com/office/enterprise/, is dedicated to helping you evaluate and deploy Office 2000 as efficiently as possible within your organization. It includes articles and tools to help you analyze your business needs, deployment scenarios you can study or adapt to fit your requirements, and demos and articles about Office 2000 features that you can share with users throughout your organization.

Office Developer Forum

The Office Developer Forum, at http://msdn.microsoft.com/OfficeDev/, features articles, tools, and tips for creating programmable solutions by using Microsoft Office 2000. Many topics focus on data access technologies, automation, and developing applications by using Office 2000 components and Visual Basic® for Applications. The site also provides free downloads for controls, utilities, and demos.

Office Update

The Office Update site, at http://officeupdate.microsoft.com/, provides information about Office upgrades and service releases, as well as downloads for add-ins, templates, and utilities. The site also features links to technical support sites for Office 2000 applications.

Office Resource Kit for Office 97/98

The complete contents of the Office Resource Kit for Office 97/98 is still available through the Office Resource Kit Web site, in case you need to refer back to Office 97 or Office 98 information or tools. To view the Office Resource Kit Web site, go to http://www.microsoft.com/office/ork/.

The Office 2000 Client Platform

Systems requirements for running Microsoft Office 2000 on users' computers differ, depending on the edition of Office you install and your operating system environment. You might also need to consider additional requirements for running Office 2000 in a Windows Terminal Server environment, or for using Office Web Components to add interactive features to HTML documents created with Microsoft Excel, Microsoft Access, or Microsoft FrontPage.

Office 2000 Systems Requirements

Microsoft Office 2000 is available in five editions. Each edition installs a different set of Office applications, and each requires a different set of system requirements on users' computers.

Microsoft Office 2000 Standard

Microsoft Office 2000 Standard includes the following applications:

- Microsoft Excel 2000
- Microsoft Outlook 2000
- Microsoft PowerPoint 2000
- Microsoft Word 2000

To use Microsoft Office 2000 Standard, users' computers must meet the following requirements:

Processor   Pentium 75 MHz or higher processor

Operating system   Microsoft Windows 95/98, Microsoft Windows NT version 4.0, or Microsoft Windows 2000

Memory   For Windows 95/98, 16 MB of RAM for the operating system, plus an additional 4 MB of RAM for each application running simultaneously (8 MB for Microsoft Outlook).

For Windows NT Workstation version 4.0 or later, 32 MB of RAM for the operating system, plus an additional 4 MB of RAM for each application running simultaneously (8 MB for Outlook)

Available hard-disk space   189 MB for Microsoft Office 2000 Disc 1 (Excel, Outlook, PowerPoint, and Word).

This figure indicates a default installation; your hard-disk usage varies depending on your configuration and the options you choose to install.

Disk drives   CD-ROM drive

Monitor   VGA or higher-resolution monitor; Super VGA recommended

Pointing device   Microsoft Mouse, Microsoft IntelliMouse®, or compatible pointing device

Some Office 2000 features have additional requirements:

Modem   9600 or higher-baud modem; 14,400 baud recommended

Multimedia   Multimedia computer required for sound and other multimedia effects

E-mail   Microsoft Mail, Microsoft Exchange, Internet SMTP/POP3, IMAP4, or other MAPI-compliant messaging software

Collaboration   Microsoft Exchange Server required for certain advanced collaboration functionality in Outlook

Internet   Some Internet functionality may require Internet access and payment of a separate fee to a service provider, and local charges may apply.

Microsoft Office 2000 Small Business

Microsoft Office 2000 Small Business includes the following applications:

- Microsoft Excel 2000
- Microsoft Outlook 2000
- Microsoft Publisher 2000
- Microsoft Word 2000
- Microsoft Small Business Tools

To use Microsoft Office 2000 Small Business, users' computers must meet the following requirements:

Processor   Pentium 75 MHz or higher processor

Operating system   Microsoft Windows 95/98, Microsoft Windows NT version 4.0, or Microsoft Windows 2000

Memory   For Windows 95/98, 16 MB of RAM for the operating system, plus an additional 4 MB of RAM for each application running simultaneously (8 MB for Outlook).

For Windows NT Workstation version 4.0 or later, 32 MB of RAM for the operating system, plus an additional 4 MB of RAM for each application running simultaneously (8 MB for Outlook)

Available hard-disk space   178 MB for Office Disc 1 (Excel, Outlook, and Word); 182 MB for Office Disc 2 (Publisher and Small Business Tools).

These figures indicate a default installation; your hard-disk usage varies depending on your configuration and the options you choose to install.

Disk drives   CD-ROM drive

Monitor   VGA or higher-resolution monitor; Super VGA recommended

Pointing device   Microsoft Mouse, Microsoft IntelliMouse, or compatible pointing device

Some Office 2000 features have additional requirements:

Modem   9600 or higher-baud modem; 14,400 baud recommended

Multimedia   Multimedia computer required for sound and other multimedia effects

E-mail   Microsoft Mail, Microsoft Exchange, Internet SMTP/POP3, IMAP4, or other MAPI-compliant messaging software

Collaboration   Microsoft Exchange Server required for certain advanced collaboration functionality in Outlook

Internet   Some Internet functionality may require Internet access and payment of a separate fee to a service provider, and local charges may apply.

Microsoft Office 2000 Professional

Microsoft Office 2000 Professional includes the following applications:

- Microsoft Access 2000
- Microsoft Excel 2000
- Microsoft Outlook 2000
- Microsoft PowerPoint 2000
- Microsoft Publisher 2000
- Microsoft Word 2000
- Microsoft Small Business Tools

To use Microsoft Office 2000 Professional, users' computers must meet the following requirements:

Processor   Pentium 75 MHz or higher processor

Operating system   Microsoft Windows 95/98, Microsoft Windows NT version 4.0, or Microsoft Windows 2000

Memory   For Windows 95/98, 16 MB of RAM for the operating system, plus an additional 4 MB of RAM for each application running simultaneously (8 MB for Access or Outlook).

For Windows NT Workstation version 4.0 or later, 32 MB of RAM for the operating system, plus an additional 4 MB of RAM for each application running simultaneously (8 MB for Access or Outlook)

Available hard-disk space   217 MB for Office Disc 1 (Access, Excel, Outlook, PowerPoint, and Word); 174 MB for Office Disc 2 (Publisher and Small Business Tools).

These figures indicate a default installation; your hard-disk usage varies depending on your configuration and the options you choose to install.

Disk drives   CD-ROM drive

Monitor   VGA or higher-resolution monitor; Super VGA recommended

Pointing device   Microsoft Mouse, Microsoft IntelliMouse, or compatible pointing device

Some Office 2000 features have additional requirements:

Modem   9600 or higher-baud modem; 14,400 baud recommended

Multimedia   Multimedia computer required for sound and other multimedia effects

E-mail   Microsoft Mail, Microsoft Exchange, Internet SMTP/POP3, IMAP4, or other MAPI-compliant messaging software

Collaboration   Microsoft Exchange Server required for certain advanced collaboration functionality in Outlook

Internet   Some Internet functionality may require Internet access and payment of a separate fee to a service provider, and local charges may apply.

Microsoft Office 2000 Premium

Microsoft Office 2000 Premium includes the following applications:

- Microsoft Access 2000
- Microsoft Excel 2000
- Microsoft FrontPage 2000
- Microsoft Outlook 2000
- Microsoft PhotoDraw 2000
- Microsoft PowerPoint 2000
- Microsoft Publisher 2000
- Microsoft Word 2000
- Microsoft Small Business Tools

To use Microsoft Office 2000 Premium, users' computers must meet the following requirements:

Processor   Pentium 75 MHz or higher processor; Pentium 166 or higher required for PhotoDraw

Operating system   Microsoft Windows 95/98, Microsoft Windows NT version 4.0, or Microsoft Windows 2000

Memory   For Windows 95/98, 16 MB of RAM for the operating system, plus an additional 4 MB of RAM for each application running simultaneously (8 MB for Access, FrontPage, or Outlook; 16 MB for PhotoDraw).

For Windows NT Workstation version 4.0 or later, 32 MB of RAM for the operating system, plus an additional 4 MB of RAM for each application running simultaneously (8 MB for, Access, FrontPage, or Outlook; 16 MB for PhotoDraw)

Available hard-disk space   252 MB for Office Disc 1 (Access, Excel, FrontPage, Outlook, PowerPoint, and Word); 174 MB for Office Disc 2 (Publisher and Small Business Tools); 100 MB for Office Disc 3 (PhotoDraw).

For optimal performance, an additional 100 MB of available hard-disk space is recommended for use by the Windows swap file.

These figures indicate a default installation; your hard-disk usage varies depending on your configuration and the options you choose to install.

Disk drives   CD-ROM drive

Monitor   VGA or higher-resolution monitor; Super VGA recommended

Pointing device   Microsoft Mouse, Microsoft IntelliMouse, or compatible pointing device

Some Office 2000 features have additional requirements:

Modem   9600 or higher-baud modem; 14,400 baud recommended

Multimedia   Multimedia computer required for sound and other multimedia effects

E-mail   Microsoft Mail, Microsoft Exchange, Internet SMTP/POP3, IMAP4, or other MAPI-compliant messaging software

Collaboration   Microsoft Exchange Server required for certain advanced collaboration functionality in Outlook

Internet   Some Internet functionality may require Internet access and payment of a separate fee to a service provider, and local charges may apply.

Microsoft Office 2000 Developer

Microsoft Office 2000 Developer includes the same applications as Microsoft Office 2000 Premium, plus the following applications and tools:

- Office 2000 Developer Tools
- MSDN Library
- Visual SourceSafe 6.0
- Microsoft Access 2000 Runtime Setup
- Microsoft Answer Wizard Builder
- Microsoft Agent Character Editor
- HTML Help Workshop

Microsoft Office 2000 Developer has the same system requirements as Microsoft Office 2000 Premium, with the exception of additional hard disk space requirements. Required hard disk space varies, depending on which tools and documentation files are installed

Minimum installation

A minimum installation consists of Office 2000 Developer Tools (MSDN Library not installed) has the following hard disk space requirements.

System files   30 MB

Program files   30 MB

MSDN Library

A minimum installation plus MSDN Library has the following hard disk space requirements.

System files   35 MB

Program files   90 MB

Maximum installation

A maximum installation, which includes all of the Office 2000 Developer applications and tools, has the following hard disk space requirements.

System files   45 MB

Program files   300 MB

Toolbox

You can view a list of all the files installed for each Office 2000 feature in an Excel workbook named Filelist.xls. Filelist.xls also includes information about file sizes, installation folders, and supported versions of Windows. For information about installing this workbook, see "Office Information" on page 787.

See also

- Some of the features available to Microsoft Office 2000 users depend on which Web browser is installed on users' computers, and on which Web server components are installed on the organization's servers. For information about Web browser and Web server requirements, see "Internet and Intranet Technologies" on page 42.

- Some of the features available to Microsoft Office 2000 users depend on which messaging services are available on users' computers. For information about e-mail servers and messaging services supported by Office 2000 applications, see "Office 2000 and E-mail Servers" on page 33.

- Some data access features available to Office 2000 users depend on the data access components that are installed on users' computers. For more information about data access technologies, see "Office 2000 and Data Connectivity Technologies" on page 56.

- Some data access features available to Office 2000 users also depend on the database servers that are available on an organization's network. For more information, see "Office 2000 and Database Servers" on page 37.

- Microsoft Office 2000 provides you with the flexibility to customize and install Office in a number of different ways. For information about installation options, see "Basic Installation Methods" on page 80.

Office 2000 Requirements in a Windows Terminal Server Environment

Organizations that use Microsoft Office 2000 in cross-platform, legacy hardware, or terminal-based environments can use Microsoft Windows NT Server version 4.0, Terminal Server Edition (Windows Terminal Server). The Windows Terminal Server platform allows different types of hardware platforms to act as Windows-based terminals running Windows-based 32-bit applications from a back-end Windows NT-based server.

This configuration is a particularly compelling solution for managing the coexistence or migration period of an enterprise upgrade to Office 2000. Running Office 2000 under Windows Terminal Server can also help reduce management costs by shifting the primary hardware requirements from the user's computer to the server, which is maintained centrally. Running Office 2000 as a Windows Terminal Server application is a scalable solution that helps reduce cost of ownership without compromising productivity.

How the Windows Terminal Server platform works

Windows Terminal Server contains both server and client components. The server components can host multiple, simultaneous client sessions on Windows NT Server. The client components contain only the minimum amount of software necessary to start the client computer, establish a connection to the server, and display the user interface.

All other operating system functions run on the server, including applications such as Office 2000. Each user that runs an application on Windows Terminal Server opens a separate instance of the application on the server, and all customizations are stored in a per-user storage area.

How to run Office 2000 under Windows Terminal Server

To run efficiently on the Windows Terminal Server platform, an application must meet the following requirements.

Separate application settings and user settings

Users running applications on Windows Terminal Server must be able to customize their applications and have their settings persist between sessions, without interference from settings for other users.

In Office 2000, application-specific settings are stored in the HKEY_LOCAL_MACHINE subtree in the registry. User-specific settings can be stored as files or as registry entries. User settings stored as files are located in the Windows\Profiles\<*Username*>\Application Data folder, and user settings stored in the registry are located in the HKEY_CURRENT_USER subtree.

Flexible path names in the registry

Installation locations can change, leaving hard-coded path names pointing to invalid sources. To run well under Windows Terminal Server, an application must have the flexibility to redirect the path as necessary.

The Windows installer, which is included with all editions of Office 2000 and Windows 2000, keeps track of installation locations and installed files. If the default server is unavailable, the Windows installer redirects the connection to the next available source.

Support for environment variables

Environment variables are useful for administrators who want to create a different storage path for each user. For example, an administrator might want to store all users' Microsoft Excel files on one server by setting the path to the following:

X:\Userdata\xl**%Username%**

To work correctly, the environment variable **%Username%** must be expanded for each individual user. Because the Windows Terminal Server platform saves files using hard-coded paths, ordinarily it would not correctly expand an environment variable if the server were mapped to a different drive letter. However, Office 2000 applications use the detection capabilities of the Windows installer, which automatically detects the next recognized storage location.

Use of the Temp folder for nonpersistent data

Previous versions of Microsoft Office store some user data files in the Temp folder. Under Windows Terminal Server, however, storing user data in the Temp folder creates a security risk and can cause conflicts between user settings, because all settings are stored in the single server-based Temp folder.

To avoid this problem, Office 2000 was redesigned to use the Windows\Profiles\<*Username*>\Application Data folder and the My Documents folder as the defaults for user data storage.

Benefits of Windows Terminal Server

Office 2000 detects when it is running on the Windows Terminal Server platform and optimizes its behavior automatically. For example, when Office 2000 is running on Windows Terminal Server, it displays lower-resolution application splash screens that display more quickly.

Running Office 2000 in the Windows Terminal Server environment is a desirable option for corporations that require complete central control over the user environment, even to the level of total system lockdown. To configure and control user settings in Office 2000, administrators use systems policies. Office 2000 provides the same level of support for system policies when running on Windows and Windows Terminal Server platforms.

See also

- For information about installing Office 2000 in a Windows Terminal Server environment, see "Using Office 2000 with Windows Terminal Server" on page 92.

- For information about using system policies in Office 2000, see "Ongoing Configuration of Office on Users' Computers" on page 279.

Requirements for Office Web Components

Microsoft Office Web Components are a collection of ActiveX controls that make many of the features of Microsoft Access databases and Microsoft Excel spreadsheets, PivotTables, and charts available in HTML documents opened in Microsoft Internet Explorer.

When users open an HTML document containing Office Web Components in Internet Explorer, they can interact with information on the page. For example, they can sort, filter, and enter values for formula calculations in the Spreadsheet component. Web pages created in Access that use the Office Web Components are called *data access pages*.

Systems requirements for Office Web Components

To use HTML documents that contain the Spreadsheet, PivotTable, or Chart components, users need Microsoft Internet Explorer version 4.01 or later running on Microsoft Windows 95/98 or Windows NT Workstation 4.0 or later.

To create a data access page with Access or to browse a data access page, users need Internet Explorer 5 or later.

Note HTML documents that contain Office Web Components do not run in Netscape Navigator because Navigator does not support ActiveX controls.

License requirements for Office Web Components

Users must own an Office 2000 license in order to browse a Web page interactively using Office Web Components.

Organizations that own an Enterprise, Select, or Maintenance Agreement for Office 2000 and who plan to deploy Office 2000 in phases can allow early adopters of Office 2000 to share component-based Web pages with users who have not yet installed Office 2000. They do this by enabling auto-downloading of the Office Web Components through Internet Explorer's built-in component installer. This method of deploying Office Web Components is for internal corporate use only, and cannot be used through *firewalls* over the Internet.

Deploying Office Web Components over an intranet

Office 2000 users create interactive Web pages with the Office Web Components in Excel by saving a worksheet as a Web page (**File** menu, **Save as Web Page** command) and then making it interactive (**Publish** button).

To create a data access page in Access, users click **Pages** under **Objects** in the Database window, and then click the **New** button.

Office Web Components can also be added to Web pages created in Microsoft FrontPage by using the **Office Spreadsheet**, **Office PivotTable**, or **Office Chart** commands (**Insert** menu, **Component** submenu).

Web pages that use Office Web Components contain HTML OBJECT tags that specify which Office Web Components to load when the page is opened. If the components are already installed on the user's computer, the page opens and is interactive when the user opens the page using Microsoft Internet Explorer.

Office Web Components are automatically installed by Office 2000 Setup. If a user has not yet run Office 2000 Setup and your organization owns an Enterprise, Select, or Maintenance Agreement for Office 2000, the user can download the components from the corporate intranet the first time a Web page containing Office Web Components is opened.

Specifying the download location for Office Web Components

To specify the download location for Office Web Components, a Web page author uses the **Web Options** dialog box in Excel to specify the path to the Msowc.cab file that is used to install the Office Web Components.

▶ **To specify the Office Web Components download location**

1   On the Excel **Tools** menu, click **Options**, and then click the **General** tab.

2   Click **Web Options**, and then click the **Files** tab.

3   Select Download Office Web Components.

4   In the **Location** box, specify the path to the Msowc.cab file using the following format:

   file:*PathToOfficeInstallServer***\msowc.cab**

By default, the **Download Office Web Components** option is selected, and the path specified in the **Location** box is set to the server from which the Web page author installed Office 2000. To turn this behavior off or change the download location, set this option by using the Profile Wizard with the Custom Installation Wizard

Tip   A Web page developer can also specify the path to download Office Web Components by editing the HTML code for a page that contains an Office Web Component and setting the CODEPAGE attribute of the OBJECT tag that specifies which component to load. The CODEBASE attribute must use the same format used in the **Web Options** dialog box. For example, CODEBASE= "file:\\MyOfficeInstallServer\Office2000\msowc.cab".

Installing Office Web Components

When Internet Explorer opens a Web page that contains Office Web Components, and the components are not installed on the user's computer, Internet Explorer checks the CODEBASE attribute of the OBJECT tag that specifies the component. If the user's security settings permit, Internet Explorer downloads the Office Web Components installer file (Msowc.cab), unpacks it, and launches the Web Installer control.

The Web Installer control prompts the user to confirm that he or she owns a valid Office 2000 license and to accept the Office End User License Agreement. If the user does not confirm, the Web Installer displays the Office Web Components watermark on the page and exits. The page is not interactive. To install the Office Web Components later, the user can click the watermark, and the Web Installer runs again.

The Web Installer is an ActiveX control that runs the Windows installer. It is set to be downloaded from the root directory of an Office 2000 installation server on a network file share. If necessary, it installs or upgrades the Windows installer by running Instmsi.exe from the MSI folder on the Office installation server. Then the Web Installer calls the Windows installer and runs the Office Web Components package file, Msowc.msi, which it looks for in the same root directory. The Windows installer actually installs and registers the Office Web Components and Microsoft Data Access Components.

Redirecting users who cannot run Office Web Components

If a user opens a Web page that relies on the Office Web Components and cannot run them, the following text and a hyperlink to the Microsoft Office Web site is displayed in the page:

"To use this Web page interactively, you must have Microsoft Internet Explorer 4.01 or later and the Microsoft Office Web Components. See the Microsoft Office Web site for more information."

This text is defined in the ALT-HTML section of the OBJECT tag used to specify an Office Web Component. Both Internet Explorer and Netscape Navigator display this text if they cannot run a component on a page.

You can customize this text, by creating and setting the **MissingComponentText** value entry in the HKEY_CURRENT_USER\Software\Microsoft\Office\9.0\Common \Internet subkey in the Windows registry.

If the **MissingComponentText** value already exists, its text is written in the ALT-HTML section of the OBJECT tag for an Office Web Component when it is added to a Web page. You can embed hyperlinks in this text to direct users to other Web pages in your company by using standard HTML.

See also

- For more information about using Office Web Components, see "Adding Interactive Web Controls to Office Documents" on page 600.

- You can use systems policies to specify the download path for Office Web Components or to prevent users from downloading the Office Web Components. For more information, see "Managing Office Web Components" on page 600.

The Office 2000 Network Platform

Microsoft Office 2000 helps network administrators reduce the total cost of ownership on a broad range of operating systems and network operating systems. However, some features provided by Microsoft Windows 2000 Professional and Microsoft Windows 2000 Server or the Windows Desktop Update shell update make Office 2000 an even better total-cost-of-ownership citizen.

Network Operating Systems and Clients Supported by Office 2000

Microsoft Office 2000 supports most widely available network operating systems and network clients for file and printing services. Microsoft Office 2000 has been tested with the following network servers and clients.

Microsoft network operating systems and clients

Microsoft Office 2000 supports the following Microsoft network servers and clients.

Supported network servers

- Microsoft Windows NT Server version 4.0 with Service Pack 3 or later, including support for Microsoft Gateway Service for NetWare and Services for Macintosh

- Microsoft Windows 2000 Server, including support for Microsoft Gateway Service for NetWare and Services for Macintosh

Supported network clients

- Microsoft Windows 95 with Service Pack 1 or later and Client for Microsoft Networks

- Microsoft Windows 98 and Client for Microsoft Networks

- Microsoft Windows NT Workstation version 4.0 with Service Pack 3 or later

- Microsoft Windows 2000 Professional

Novell network operating systems and clients

Microsoft Office 2000 supports the following Novell network servers and clients:

Supported network servers

- Novell NetWare version 3.12 withyear 2000 updates
- Novell NetWare version 4.11 with year 2000 updates
- Novell intraNetWare version 4.11with Support Pack 5b and year 2000 updates

Note   Novell NetWare 5 was released late in the Microsoft Office 2000 development cycle. Due to significant changes, such as supporting TCP/IP natively, this version was not tested for full support.

Supported Novell network clients

- Microsoft Windows 95 with Service Pack 1 and Novell intraNetWare client version 2.5
- Microsoft Windows 98 with Novell intraNetWare client version 2.5
- Microsoft Windows NT 4.0 Workstation with Service Pack 3 or later and Novell intraNetWare client version 4.30.410
- Microsoft Windows 2000 Professional and Novell intraNetWare client version 4.30.410

Supported Microsoft network clients

- Microsoft Windows 95 with Service Pack 1 or later and Client for NetWare Networks with Service for NetWare Directory Services
- Microsoft Windows 98 and Client for NetWare Networks with Service for NetWare Directory Services
- Microsoft Windows NT Workstation 4.0 with Service Pack 3 or later and Client Service for NetWare
- Microsoft Windows 2000 Professional and Client Service for NetWare

Banyan network operating systems and clients

Microsoft Office 2000 supports the following Banyan network servers and clients.

Supported network servers

- Banyan VINES version 6.4
- Banyan VINES version 8.5

Note   Banyan VINES version 6.x does not support long file names. Banyan VINES 7.x or later does support long file names. Also, Banyan requires upgrading to VINES version 8.5 for year 2000 support. For this reason, Microsoft Office 2000 testing was not performed on VINES version 7.x.

Supported network clients
- Microsoft Windows 95 with Service Pack 1 or later and Banyan VINES Enterprise Client 8.52 for Windows 95
- Microsoft Windows 98 and Banyan VINES Enterprise Client 8.52 for Windows 95
- Microsoft Windows NT Workstation 4.0 with Service Pack 3 or later and Banyan VINES Enterprise Client 8.56 for Windows NT
- Microsoft Windows 2000 Professional and Banyan VINES Enterprise Client 8.56 for Windows NT

UNIX NFS clients
Microsoft Office 2000 supports the following UNIX NFS clients:

- Microsoft Windows 95 with Service Pack 1 or later and Sun Microsystems Solstice Network Client version 3.1
- Microsoft Windows 98 and Sun Microsystems Solstice Network Client version 3.1
- Microsoft Windows NT Workstation 4.0 with Service Pack 3 or later and Sun Microsystems Solstice Network Client version 3.1
- Microsoft Windows 2000 Professional and Sun Microsystems Solstice Network Client version 3.1
- Microsoft Windows 95 with Service Pack 1 or later and FTP Network Access Suite version 3.0
- Microsoft Windows 98 and FTP Network Access Suite version 3.0
- Windows NT Workstation 4.0 with Service Pack 3 or later and FTP Network Access Suite version 3.0
- Microsoft Windows 2000 Professional and FTP Network Access Suite version 3.0

Note   Microsoft Office 2000 testing is performed for Sun Microsystems Solaris 2.4 NFS services and Microsoft NT Services for NFS. Record locking in shared Microsoft Access database files (MDB) is not supported. Use of drive aliases is required for NFS client support.

IBM network operating systems and clients
Microsoft Office 2000 supports the following IBM network servers and clients.

Supported network servers
- IBM OS/2 Warp LanServer version 4.1.1

Supported network clients
- Microsoft Windows 95 with Service Pack 1 or later and IBM Network Client version 4.1
- Microsoft Windows 98 and IBM Network Client version 4.1

- Microsoft Windows NT Workstation 4.0 with Service Pack 3 or later and IBM Network Client version 4.2.2
- Microsoft Windows 2000 Professional and IBM Network Client version 4.2.2

Digital network operating systems and clients

Microsoft Office 2000 supports the following Digital network servers and clients.

Supported network servers
- Digital Pathworks version 5.0E for OpenVMS
- Digital OpenVMS v6.2 for Alpha

Supported network clients
- Microsoft Windows 95 with Service Pack 1 or later and Digital Pathworks 32 version 7.0
- Microsoft Windows 98 and Digital Pathworks 32 version 7.0
- Microsoft Windows NT Workstation 4.0 with Service Pack 3 or later and Digital Pathworks 32 version 7.0
- Microsoft Windows 2000 Professional and Digital Pathworks 32 version 7.0

Note   Record locking in shared Microsoft Access database files (MDB) is not supported.

LANtastic peer-to-peer network operating systems

Microsoft Office 2000 supports the following Artisoft LANtastic peer-to-peer networking software:

- Microsoft Windows 95 with Service Pack 1 or later and Artisoft LANtastic version 7.0
- Microsoft Windows 98 and Artisoft LANtastic version 7.0

Features Available Under Microsoft Windows 2000

If an organization deploys Windows 2000 Server and Windows 2000 Professional, including Active Directory, then Microsoft Office 2000 can take advantage of additional Windows 2000 features. Some of these features require only Windows 2000 Server or Windows 2000 Professional; most require both.

IntelliMirror support

IntelliMirror™ is a set of powerful features native to Windows 2000 for change and configuration management of users' computers. These features combine the advantages of centralized computing with the performance and flexibility of distributed computing. By leveraging different features in both the server and client operating systems, IntelliMirror allows users' data, applications, and settings to follow them to any computer on their organization's network.

All users have individual data and settings. IntelliMirror increases the availability of the user's computer and computing environment by intelligently storing information, settings, and applications based on policy definitions. IntelliMirror can recover and restore users' data, applications, and personal settings in a Windows 2000-based environment.

At the core of IntelliMirror are three features:

- User data management
- Software installation and maintenance
- User and computer settings management

Administrators can use these IntelliMirror features separately or together, depending on the requirements of their environment. Office 2000 fully supports these features.

User data management

The user data management feature of IntelliMirror supports the mirroring of user's data to the network and the local caching of selected network data. This feature ensures that data is protected, is available offline, and is available from any computer on the network.

Data follows the user only if the data is stored in a location set to roam, such as the My Documents folder. Office 2000 supports user data management by storing users Office 2000 documents in the My Documents folder by default.

Software installation and maintenance

The software installation and maintenance features in Windows 2000 allow an application to be *assigned* to a user or a computer, or *published* to a user. Office 2000 fully supports assigning and publishing applications. Assigning and publishing applications requires both Windows 2000 Professional and Windows 2000 Server.

When an application is assigned to a user, the application is advertised for that user the next time the user logs on to a Windows 2000 Professional computer. Advertising is the process of preconfiguring some Windows registry information (such as file associations, Object Linking and Embedding (OLE) activation information, and support for the Windows installer service) and application shortcuts on the client computer.

The application shortcuts allow the Windows installer to install the application the first time it is started. The application file associations and OLE activation information allow the Windows installer to install the application the first time a user attempts to open a file or activate an OLE object that requires a missing application.

When an application is assigned to a computer, the application fully installs the next time the computer is started and connects to the Windows 2000 network. The application is then available to all users of that computer.

When an application is published to users, the application is made available in the Active Directory. No *advertisement* or application information such as shortcuts are installed on user's computers; however, all published packages, such as Microsoft Office 2000, are displayed in **Add/Remove Programs** in Control Panel. Information in the Active Directory enables the application to automatically install when needed— for example, if a user who has not installed Office opens an Office 2000 document.

Microsoft Office 2000 can be assigned to either users or computers or published to users. As part of enabling applications to be assigned and published to users, Windows 2000 introduces per-user support in the HKEY_CLASSES_ROOT registry subtree. (In Windows 95, Windows 98, and Windows NT Workstation 4.0, the HKEY_CLASSES_ROOT subtree is supported on a per-machine basis.) The HKEY_CLASSES_ROOT subtree contains the file association and class registration for OLE.

In previous versions of Windows, if one user has the DOC file type set to Wordpad.exe and another user logs on to that computer, then that user's DOC files are associated with Wordpad.exe, even if the other user has DOC files associated with Winword.exe in their *roaming user profile*. Windows 2000 solves this problem by supporting the HKEY_CLASSES_ROOT subtree on a per-user basis, which allows this information to roam with the user.

These per-user associations are set up when an application is installed for a particular user. When an application is installed for all users of a computer, the per-machine version of HKEY_CLASSES_ROOT subtree is used. The per-user features of the HKEY_CLASSES_ROOT subtree require Windows 2000 Professional.

Windows 2000 has also changed OLE activation to call the Windows installer. If a user activates an OLE object, such as an embedded document, then the operating system calls the Windows installer for the required application. As long as the required application is installed by using the Windows installer and is set to **Installed on First Use**, then the Windows installer can install the application required to work with the OLE object even if the application has never been installed on the user's computer.

Note   If the required application is installed by using the Windows installer, but is set to **Not Available**, or if the application does not use the Windows installer, then an error message is displayed and the OLE object cannot be activated until the user runs Setup manually.

When the required application is set to **Installed on First Use**, the behavior of applications that use the Windows installer differ slightly, depending on the version of Windows that is running on the user's computer. When running under Windows 2000 Professional, the missing application required to open an OLE object is automatically installed without user intervention. (When running under Windows 95, Windows 98, or Windows NT Workstation 4.0, the missing application required to open an OLE object is installed, but the user is prompted first.)

Additionally, if the application has been installed, but has been damaged (for example, if a key file has been deleted), then the Windows installer repairs the application before it passes the path to the application back to OLE. This behavior gives applications that use the Windows installer install-on-demand and resiliency with OLE activation. In applications that do not use the Windows installer, OLE does not call the Windows installer and activation of the application fails.

Windows 2000 Professional is required to install an application automatically and to activate an OLE object without user intervention.

User and computer settings management

Using the Windows 2000 user and computer settings management feature allows administrators to centrally define computing environments for groups of users and computers so that those users and computers automatically get the correct environment. Administrators can add new users and computers, define settings for groups of people and computers, and apply changes for groups of people.

Furthermore, with the IntelliMirror feature enabled, administrators can restore a user's settings if a computer fails, and ensure that a user's computer settings follow the user if he or she roams to another computer on the network.

Office 2000 supports this feature by providing application policies in the form of administrative template (ADM) files that can be used to customize Office applications.

With Windows 2000, the registry policy folders (Software\Policies) under the HKEY_CURRENT_USER subtree and the HKEY_LOCAL_MACHINE subtree are volatile. When any Group Policy object that affects a user or computer changes, keys written by that Group Policy are deleted and rewritten.

This behavior allows the policy settings to change whenever the affected Group Policy objects change, such as when a user roams to a different organizational unit. Also, these registry folders are secured so that only administrators can change the entries and values. (In previous versions of Windows, any user can change policy settings in the registry.)

User and computer settings management features require Windows 2000 Professional.

Remote operating system installation

In addition to IntelliMirror features, Windows 2000 supports remote operating system installation, which simplifies the task of installing a new copy of the operating system on client computers throughout the organization.

Remote operating system installation provides a mechanism for computers to connect to a network server during initial start up, and then allows the server to drive a local installation of Windows 2000 Professional. When used with IntelliMirror, remote operating system installation reduces the costs of setting up new computers, and provides better recovery from computer failures.

If you are adding or replacing a computer, or returning a repaired computer to the network, remote operating system installation provides the services to reload the operating system. At the same time, IntelliMirror provides the services to quickly regenerate installed applications, such as Microsoft Office 2000, and to restore user data and personal computer settings.

Remote operating system installation requires Windows 2000 Server and Windows 2000 Professional.

Distributed File System

The Windows 2000 Distributed File System (DFS) provides a layer of indirection for servers. DFS permits consolidation of server and share names into a single logical directory. Using DFS, an administrator can set up a series of Office 2000 distribution servers advertised as a single DFS name. This configuration allows the administrator to provide load balancing and redundancy on the servers used to deploy Office 2000.

For example, using DFS, an administrator can publish three servers (\\Server1\Office2000, \\Server2\Office2000, and \\Server3\Office2000) as child nodes of a \\Software\Apps\Office2000 share. When a client computer gains access to the \\Software\Apps\Office2000 share, it is transparently routed to one of the three participating servers.

The Windows installer service can use a source list. If the service cannot connect to the last source it used, it searches for an available server stored in the source list. During deployment, an administrator can place other servers in the source list. If you choose to use DFS instead, you probably do not want to use the source list feature provided by the Windows installer, unless you want to have one group of servers back up another group of servers.

DFS requires Windows NT Server 4.0 or Windows 2000 Server for DFS server shares. Client computers must be running a version of Windows supported by Microsoft Office to access DFS shares. Computers running Windows 95 must install the DFS client software separately to work with DFS shares. The Windows installer source list feature works under all versions of Windows supported by Microsoft Office.

Copying, moving, and deleting HTML files and folders

When an Office 2000 application saves an HTML document that requires supporting files, it creates a file such as My Web Page.htm, and a corresponding folder that holds all of the supporting files, which is named "My Web Page files."

When a user copies, moves, or deletes an HTML file like My Web Page.htm, the Windows 2000 operating system automatically looks for a corresponding folder named "My Web Page_files." If the folder exists, Windows 2000 copies, moves, or deletes the folder along with it. If a user moves, copies, or deletes a folder named "My Web Page_files," the system automatically looks for a file named My Web Page.htm and copies, moves, or deletes that file along with the folder. (In previous versions of Windows, only the file or folder is copied, moved, or deleted.)

This feature is turned on by default when Office 2000 is running under Windows 2000. To turn this feature off, add a **DWORD** value entry named NoFileFolderConnection in the HKEY_CURRENT_USER\Software\Microsoft \Windows\CurrentVersion\Explorer subkey and set its value to **1**. Setting the NoFileFolderConnection value entry to **0** or deleting the value entry restores the default behavior.

This feature requires Windows 2000 Professional. The feature does not work when copying, moving, or deleting HTML files created with FrontPage. It also does not work when copying, moving, or deleting HTML files from the *Web Folders object*.

See also

- For more information about Windows 2000 Server, see the Windows 2000 Server Web site at http://www.microsoft.com/ntserver/windowsnt5/.

- For more information about Windows 2000 Professional, see the Windows 2000 Professional Web site at http://www.microsoft.com/windowsnt5/workstation/.

- For information about group policies in Windows 2000, search for **Windows 2000 Server group policy** to find the "Windows 2000 Server Group Policy" white paper on the Windows NT Server Web site at http://www.microsoft.com/ntserver/.

CHAPTER 2

Tools and Technologies That Work with Office

Some of the features in Microsoft Office 2000 depend on back-end servers and technologies to perform their functions. To make deploying and maintaining installations of Office 2000 more efficient, administrators can take advantage of network systems management tools, such as Microsoft Systems Management Server (SMS). The data access technologies supported by Office 2000 make sharing data simpler, and programming technologies available in Office 2000 allow developers to automate and integrate tasks across applications, and to customize and extend the features of Office 2000.

In This Chapter

Server Tools and Technologies

Microsoft BackOffice server components, as well as a variety of other server software tools and technologies, complement and extend Office 2000 applications. These server tools and technologies can make Office 2000 simpler to deploy and manage in a large organization, and can make Office 2000 users more productive by enhancing collaboration and making enterprise data readily available.

Office 2000 and Network Systems Management Tools

Network systems management tools such as Microsoft Systems Management Server allow you to manage software installation and the administration of multiple workstations from a central management point.

Microsoft Systems Management Server

Microsoft Systems Management Server is a key component in the Microsoft Zero Administration Initiative for the Microsoft Windows operating system. SMS provides tools such as hardware and software inventory, software distribution and installation, and remote diagnostics to let you better manage your computing environment.

Systems Management Server is designed to help system administrators lower their management costs by helping them install and maintain operating systems and applications, discover system configurations, and perform support staff operations. SMS is a highly scalable, WAN-compatible product that can be integrated with the major enterprise management solutions.

By using Systems Management Server, you can schedule and push installations to the users' computers, create reports about successful or unsuccessful deployments, place network bandwidth constraints on pushed installations, and store data about products installed on each computer. SMS is the ideal change and configuration management tool that can help you deploy and maintain Office 2000 in your organization.

You can use Systems Management Server to evaluate your hardware and software, and simplify Office 2000 deployment. Systems Management Server can help you distribute, install, and update Office 2000 on your servers and client computers. SMS also provides a variety of troubleshooting and network monitoring tools that help make distribution and deployment of Office 2000 a smooth and efficient process.

Systems Management Server can be used to deploy individual Office components, such as Microsoft Office Server Extensions, or Microsoft Publisher.

Other systems management tools

Other software vendors produce systems management tools that can be used to distribute and install Windows applications to client computers. These additional systems management tools include the following:

- Intel LANDesk Management Suite
- HP OpenView Desktop Administrator
- Tivoli Enterprise and Tivoli IT Director
- Computer Associates Unicenter TNG
- ON Command CCM

For information about these products, see the appropriate Web site.

See also

- For detailed information about Systems Management Server version 1.2 or 2.0 and detailed instructions for using either version to deploy Office 2000, see "Deploying Office with Systems Management Server" on page 106.

- For additional product information about Systems Management Server, see the Microsoft Systems Management Server Web site at http://www.microsoft.com/smsmgmt/default.asp.

- For information about implementing and troubleshooting Systems Management Server, see the TechNet Reference Systems Management Server Web site at http://www.microsoft.com/technet/resource/technet/servers/sms/.

Office 2000 and E-mail Servers

Microsoft Outlook 2000 can be used with a wide variety of e-mail servers and services. The primary e-mail servers and services supported by Outlook 2000 fall into two categories:

- Internet e-mail
- Corporate or workgroup servers

The Internet e-mail servers and services supported by Outlook 2000 must provide either the Simple Mail Transfer Protocol (SMTP) and Post Office Protocol version 3 (POP3), or the Internet Mail Access Protocol version 4 (IMAP4). Corporate or workgroup e-mail servers supported by Outlook 2000 must support the Messaging Application Program Interface (MAPI), which includes servers such as Microsoft Exchange Server, Lotus Domino/Notes Server, and Lotus cc:Mail server.

Outlook can also be used with a variety of other messaging and information sources, including Microsoft Mail, Microsoft Fax, Hewlett-Packard OpenMail, and CompuServe. Use of these additional service providers is made possible by the way that Outlook uses the MAPI extensibility interface. If users want to use the contacts, task, and schedule features in a stand-alone configuration, they can also use Outlook without an e-mail server.

Microsoft Exchange Server 5.5 and Outlook 2000

Microsoft Exchange Server version 5.5 is the ideal foundation for business-critical messaging and collaboration services. The following briefly describes some of the features that are available when you use Outlook with Microsoft Exchange Server:

Message Recall   Users can recall a message from recipients who have not read it yet and then replace the recalled message with a new message.

Voting   Outlook messages can contain voting buttons that are used to request and tally responses to a multiple-choice question. When used with Microsoft Exchange Server, voting notifications are consolidated in the original message.

Offline folders and offline Address Book   When users work offline (for example, when they use their laptops), Outlook folders and the Address Book at a remote location can be synchronized with folders on an Exchange Server computer to provide the latest information.

Delegate access and folder permissions   Users can give another user permission to work in their locally stored Outlook folders and to send messages on their behalf. Similarly, Outlook users can give permission to read, modify, or create items in public and private folders on Exchange Server.

Group scheduling   Users can schedule a meeting and reserve a location and equipment, and they can see the free/busy times for meeting participants and resources.

Public folders   Users can collect, organize, and share files and Microsoft Outlook items with others on their team or across their organization. Users can participate in online discussions, or they can share a contact or task list with a group.

Organize Web pages in a public folder   Outlook users can collect Web pages for a group to share, and they can keep track of how often pages are used, when pages are updated, who owns them, and more.

Out of Office Assistant   Outlook users can manage e-mail messages while they are out of the office, and they can set up an automatic response to incoming messages to let others know that they are away.

Support for Internet messaging standards

In addition to its native Messaging Application Programming Interface (MAPI), Microsoft Exchange Server 5.5 provides the Internet Mail Service, which supports the following Internet messaging standards:

- Simple Message Transfer Protocol (SMTP)
- Post Office Protocol version 3 (POP3)
- Internet Message Access Protocol version 4 (IMAP4)
- Lightweight Directory Access Protocol (LDAP) version 3
- Network News Transfer Protocol (NNTP)

These features let you choose the protocols you need to support message delivery across a variety of e-mail clients. For example, when using Microsoft Exchange Internet Mail Service, any e-mail client that supports SMTP and POP3 (such as Outlook Express, Netscape Navigator Mail, and Eudora) can be used to send and retrieve messages from an Exchange Server computer.

Support for NNTP in the Exchange News Service allows you to publish and replicate Exchange public folders as newsgroups by using Exchange or Outlook management tools. Similarly, users can use Outlook or any Web browser or newsreader to post and read messages in public folders that are published as newsgroups.

In addition to providing support for Internet messaging protocols, Microsoft Exchange also provides Exchange Active Server Components, which provide integration with Microsoft Internet Information Server using applications developed by using *Active Server Pages* (ASP) pages. Exchange Active Server Components allow users to access their private mailboxes, schedule data, public folder discussions, and directory information residing on an Exchange Server computer by using a Web browser.

Exchange Server provides the Outlook Web Access application, which is an ASP application that can be used to view e-mail messages, public folders, and the Global Address list from any browser that supports Java controls, JavaScript, and frames. Developers can also use Exchange Active Server Components features to provide Web access to Exchange e-mail, schedule, discussion, and directory information from custom applications developed by using ASP pages.

Support for connectivity and interoperability

Microsoft Exchange Server 5.5 provides broad support for connectivity and interoperability with other Exchange e-mail systems as well as other e-mail systems. To do this, Microsoft Exchange Server uses one of its built-in connectors. The family of messaging connectors that comes with Exchange Server 5.5 Enterprise can be divided into two general groups: site connectors and gateway connectors. Site connectors allow you to connect Microsoft Exchange Server sites together. Gateway connectors are used to connect Microsoft Exchange Servers to foreign messaging systems.

The following briefly summarizes the features of the Microsoft Exchange Server site connectors:

Site Connector   Requires LAN-like connections because remote procedure call (RPC) connectivity must be established between sites, therefore requiring more available network bandwidth than other connectors. You can use the Site Connector to connect Exchange sites only; you cannot use it to connect to foreign messaging systems.

X.400 Connector   Used to connect Microsoft Exchange servers to foreign X.400 systems. The X.400 Connector supports the TCP/IP, TP4, or X.25 transport stacks.

Dynamic Remote Access Service (RAS) Connector   Uses dial-up connections to transfer messages to other sites. After a dial-up connection has been established, the Dynamic RAS Connector uses RPC over the TCP/IP, SPX/IPX, or NetBEUI network protocols to transfer the data. Dial-up links such as phone lines or ISDN links are usually not as fast as other network connections. For this reason, do not use the Dynamic RAS Connector as the primary site connector unless no other network connectivity is available.

Internet Mail Service   Allows you to connect sites together through the Internet or an intranet. You can also use Internet Mail Service to connect an organization to foreign systems that support using either the Simple Message Transfer Protocol (SMTP) or the Extended SMTP (ESMTP) protocol. The SMTP and ESMTP protocols are used on top of TCP/IP to transfer messages. Dial-up and permanent connections are supported.

The following briefly summarizes the features of the Microsoft Exchange Server gateway connectors:

Microsoft Mail Connector   Provides connectivity to Microsoft Mail networks. The Microsoft Mail connector uses LAN, X.25, and dial-up connections.

Microsoft Exchange Connector for Lotus cc:Mail   Provides connectivity to one Lotus cc:Mail post office per Exchange Server computer.

Lotus Notes Connector   Provides connectivity to a single Lotus Notes/Domino server through the corresponding Lotus Notes client software. The Lotus Notes/Domino server and the Exchange Server running the connector service act as *bridgehead servers*. This way, the connector can couple your entire organization with multiple Lotus Notes domains.

OfficeVision/VM Connector   Available only with Microsoft Exchange Server 5.5 Enterprise Edition. Provides connectivity to mainframe messaging systems. The OfficeVision/VM Connector provides connectivity to IBM PROFS Version 2 Release 2 Modification Level 2, IBM OfficeVision/VM Release 2 Modification Level 0, and others. The connector requires a Microsoft SNA server in your network and an SNA client (3270 terminal emulation) installed on the Exchange Server computer.

SNA Distribution Services (SNADS) Connector   Available only with Microsoft Exchange Server 5.5 Enterprise Edition. Connects your organization to a variety of messaging systems that rely on Systems Network Architecture (SNA) Distribution Services (SNADS). Like the OfficeVision/VM Connector, the SNADS Connector uses an SNA server to provide an SNA connection to host-based messaging systems such as IBM OfficeVision/400, Verimation Memo, NB Systems TOSS, and others.

Other e-mail servers

Outlook 2000 supports sending and receiving e-mail messages through Internet e-mail servers and services that provide either the SMTP or POP3 protocols or the IMAP4 protocol. Outlook 2000 also supports servers and gateways that support the MAPI standard. See your e-mail server's product documentation for information about support for these protocols and standards.

See also

- For information about evaluating and deploying Outlook 2000 see the Microsoft Outlook Web site at http://www.microsoft.com/outlook/.

- For information about upgrading to Outlook 2000 and sharing information with other e-mail clients, see "Upgrading to Outlook 2000" on page 495.

- For information about using Outlook 2000 and other Office applications with Internet e-mail servers and clients and Web servers, see "Managing Communications on Your Intranet" on page 604.

- For additional product information about Microsoft Exchange Server, see the Microsoft Exchange Server Web site at http://www.microsoft.com/exchange/.

- For information about implementing and troubleshooting Exchange Server, see the TechNet Reference Exchange Server Web site at http://www.microsoft.com/technet/resource/technet/servers/exchange/.

- To download Exchange Server sample collaboration applications and tools, see the TechNet Exchange Application Downloads Web site at http://www.microsoft.com/technet/resource/downloads/exchange/.

Office 2000 and Database Servers

Microsoft Office 2000 support for access to data on enterprise database servers falls into three categories:

- Support for querying, importing, and data binding in native Microsoft Access databases and Microsoft Excel spreadsheets.

- Support for data binding from HTML documents that use Microsoft Office Web Components.

- Data access by using Visual Basic for Applications (VBA) and database connectivity standards.

The following sections provide an overview of the database server support in Access 2000, Excel 2000, and Office Web Components for data stored by using Microsoft SQL Server™ and other database servers.

Microsoft SQL Server

Microsoft SQL Server version 7.0 brings business advantage and improved decision making to all levels of an organization through scalable business solutions, powerful data warehousing, and integration with Microsoft Office 2000.

SQL Server 7.0 offers broad availability of tailored solutions for business operations, electronic commerce, and mobile computing. SQL Server 7.0 is scalable from a laptop running Microsoft Windows 95 or Windows 98 to multiprocessor clusters running Windows NT Server Enterprise Edition. This flexibility is achieved by using a single code base that provides full application compatibility across all editions of SQL Server 7.0. SQL Server 7.0 also provides greatly simplified administration through automatic tuning, dynamic memory management, and wizards for common tasks.

The comprehensive platform provided by SQL Server 7.0 makes it easy for you to design, build, manage, and use data warehousing solutions, allowing your organization to make effective business decisions based on timely and accurate information. Easy, seamless access to data allows desktop multidimensional analysis, and increases overall productivity by using your organization's skills and investment in Office 2000.

Microsoft Access features that work with SQL Server

Access 2000 provides a new file type called an Access project (ADP file) that lets you connect directly to database tables and other database objects stored in one of three back-end databases:

- Microsoft Data Engine (MSDE), which is available in Office
- SQL Server 7.0
- SQL Server 6.5

An ADP file can contain the same application objects available in an Access database file (*MDB file*): forms, reports, *data access pages*, macros, and modules. These objects are created and modified using tools familiar to users of earlier versions of Access. An ADP file contains no tables or queries, but instead is connected directly to the back-end MSDE or SQL Server database that contains tables, stored procedures, views and database diagrams (multiple relationships windows).

Access 2000 provides new design tools that allow users to directly create and edit the tables, views, stored procedures and database diagrams stored in the back-end MSDE or SQL Server database. These tools make it easier for Access power users and developers to extend their database knowledge to the client/server environment. Access 2000 also allows users to perform and manage common administration tasks in Microsoft SQL Server, such as replication, backup and restore, and security.

Access 2000 also supports embedding Excel PivotTable® reports in Access forms. PivotTable reports support connecting to Microsoft SQL Server OLAP Services data in Excel 2000. Additionally, Access 2000 data access pages can use Office Web Components to display and edit SQL Server data from an HTML document.

MDB files also support importing data and creating linked tables from ODBC data sources by using the **Import** and **Link Tables** commands (**File** menu, **Get External Data** submenu). Office 2000 installs ODBC drivers for SQL Server, Oracle, and other ODBC data sources.

Microsoft Excel features that work with SQL Server

Online Analytical Processing (OLAP) is an increasingly popular technology that can dramatically improve business analysis, but that has been characterized in the past by expensive tools, difficult implementation, and inflexible deployment. The OLAP features in Excel 2000 make multidimensional analysis accessible to a broader audience at a significantly lower cost of ownership.

Excel 2000 provides support for Microsoft SQL Server OLAP Services, a new feature of SQL Server 7.0 that allows users to perform sophisticated analysis on large volumes of data with exceptional performance. SQL Server OLAP Services provides server-side processing for *multidimensional data sources*. Excel 2000 users can gain access to these data sources through the OLE DB for OLAP interface.

For example, users can create dynamic PivotTable reports and PivotChart™ reports from SQL Server data by using the SQL Server OLAP Services feature. This functionality provides a new method for high-performance data analysis of large amounts of data from within the familiar interface of Excel. The benefits of analyzing large data stores and data warehouses are available to a much broader audience.

Excel 2000 also supports displaying and retrieving data with installed ODBC drivers by using the **New Database Query** command (**Data** menu, **Get External Data** submenu). Office 2000 installs ODBC drivers for SQL Server, Oracle, and other ODBC data sources.

Office Web Components that work with SQL Server

Office Web Components are a set of ActiveX® controls that can be used to provide access to SQL Server data from HTML documents created by using Access 2000 and Excel 2000. The Office Web Components consist of the following ActiveX controls:

- Microsoft PivotTable 9.0

- Microsoft Chart 9.0

- Microsoft Data Access Control 9.0

In Excel 2000, users can create HTML documents that use the Microsoft Office PivotTable and Microsoft Chart controls to display PivotTables and charts that use data from SQL Server 6.5 and 7.0 databases. The Microsoft Office PivotTable and Chart controls can also display OLAP data made available through the SQL Server OLAP Services feature of SQL Server 7.0.

In Access 2000, users can create HTML documents called data access pages that utilize the Office Web Components to display and edit data stored in SQL Server 6.5 or later. Data access pages can also use the Microsoft Office PivotTable and Microsoft Office Chart controls to display OLAP data from SQL Server 7.0.

Other database servers

Access 2000 and Excel 2000 support retrieving data from other database servers by using ODBC drivers. Access database files (MDB files) support importing data and creating linked tables from ODBC data sources by using the **Import** and **Link Tables** commands (**File** menu, **Get External Data** submenu). Excel 2000 also supports retrieving data with installed ODBC drivers by using the **New Database Query** command (**Data** menu, **Get External Data** submenu). Office 2000 installs ODBC drivers for SQL Server, Oracle, and other ODBC data sources.

All Office 2000 applications can access server data from Visual Basic for Applications (VBA) code by using ODBC drivers and OLE DB data providers. The Data Access Objects (DAO) programming model can be used to access ODBC data sources. The ActiveX Data Objects (ADO) programming model can be used to access ODBC and OLE DB data sources.

See also

- For information about Microsoft Data Engine and support for data access by using Visual Basic for Applications and database connectivity standards, see "Data Access Technologies" on page 49.

- For more information about Microsoft SQL Server, see the Microsoft SQL Server Web site, at http://www.microsoft.com/sql/, and SQL Server Books Online, which is installed with SQL Server.

- For information about implementing and troubleshooting SQL Server, see the TechNet Reference SQL Server Web site at http://www.microsoft.com/technet/resource/technet/servers/sql/.

Office 2000 and Mainframe and UNIX Server Data

Microsoft Office 2000 users might need to access data stored on mainframe or UNIX servers. Microsoft BackOffice provides Microsoft SNA Server 4.0 to provide gateway and application integration support for a broad range of desktop operating systems with IBM Host systems.

Office 2000 applications also provide support for accessing data by using the ActiveX Data Objects (ADO) programming model from Visual Basic for Applications (VBA) code and Visual Basic Scripting Edition (VBScript) script in HTML documents. ADO can use OLE DB data providers and ODBC drivers to access data.

Microsoft Systems Network Architecture Server

Organizations are increasingly employing Microsoft Windows and Microsoft Windows NT operating systems to create a variety of solutions in the enterprise including the following: sophisticated intranets, electronic commerce applications, customer services applications, and complex distributed transaction processing. Employing the latest distributed Windows and BackOffice technology ensures that these solutions can be implemented quickly and inexpensively. At the same time, businesses need to preserve their investment in existing data and applications on mainframe and AS/400 systems.

Traditionally, integration of client/server and host environments has meant employing terminal emulation to provide access to mainframe and AS/400 resources. Microsoft SNA Server 4.0 provides comprehensive gateway and application integration features such as the following:

- Support for database access that uses the Open Database Connectivity (ODBC) and Distributed Relational Database Architecture (DRDA) standards by using the StarSQL ODBC/DRDA Drivers.

- Support for record-level access to Virtual Sequential Access Method (VSAM) and other databases on mainframe and AS/400 systems by using the *OLE DB provider* for AS/400 and VSAM.

- Support for distributed transaction processing and Web-to-host integration solutions that use host Customer Information Control System (CICS) or IBM Information Management System (IMS) transactions.

You can use the StarSQL ODBC/DRDA Drivers and the OLE DB Provider for AS/400 and VSAM data provider that are installed as part of Microsoft SNA Server client software to access mainframe and AS/400 data sources from Office 2000 applications in the following ways:

- Excel 2000 supports displaying and retrieving data with installed ODBC drivers by using the **New Database Query** command (**Data** menu, **Get External Data** submenu).

- Access database files (*MDB files*) support importing data and creating linked tables from ODBC data sources by using the **Import** and **Link Tables** commands (**File** menu, **Get External Data** submenu).

- All Office 2000 applications can access server data from Visual Basic for Applications code by using ODBC drivers and OLE DB data providers. The Data Access Objects (DAO) programming model can be used to access ODBC data sources. The ActiveX Data Objects (ADO) programming model can be used to access ODBC and OLE DB data sources from VBA code and from VBScript script in HTML documents.

OLE DB providers for mainframe and UNIX server data

All Office 2000 applications can access data by using OLE DB data providers in conjunction with ADO programming model from Visual Basic for Applications code and from VBScript script in HTML documents. In addition to the OLE DB provider for AS/400 and VSAM that is installed with Microsoft SNA Server 4.0, the following vendors are currently supplying or will supply OLE DB providers to access VSAM, AS/400, HP/UX, IBM AIX, and OpenVMS data:

- Amalgamated Software of North America
- IBM Corporation
- International Software Group
- MetaWise
- Microsoft Corporation

For information about the OLE DB providers available from these vendors, see their respective Web sites.

See also

- For information about support for data access by using Visual Basic for Applications and database connectivity standards, see "Data Access Technologies" on page 49.

- For more information about Microsoft SNA Server 4.0, see the Microsoft SNA Server Web site, at http://www.microsoft.com/sna/, and SNA Server online Help, which is installed with SQL Server.

- For information about implementing and troubleshooting SNA Server, see the TechNet Reference SNA Server Web site at http://www.microsoft.com/technet/resource/technet/servers/sna/.

Internet and Intranet Technologies

Microsoft Office 2000 includes many new features that integrate Office 2000 applications with Internet and intranet technologies. In some cases, the features available to users depend on which Web browser is installed on users' computers, and on which Web server components are installed on the organization's servers.

Web Browser Support in Office 2000

Some of the features in Microsoft Office 2000 applications depend on functionality that is provided by the Web browser components that are installed on users' computers.

Web browser requirements for Office 2000

Office 2000 works best with versions of Windows that have been updated with the latest Web browsing functionality—Microsoft Internet Explorer 5 or later. If you install Office 2000 on a computer that does not include Internet Explorer 5 or later, clicking the **Install Now** button in Office 2000 Setup automatically upgrades Windows to Internet Explorer 5.

If a user's computer has a version of Windows that includes Microsoft Internet Explorer 3.0 or 4.0, users are not required to upgrade or install Web browsing functionality during Office Setup. In this case, clicking the **Customize** button in Office 2000 Setup makes upgrading Windows with Internet Explorer 5 optional.

When a user's computer has one of the following Web browsers installed, Windows must be upgraded to include the latest Web browsing functionality:

- Microsoft Internet Explorer 2.0 or earlier
- Another browser, such as Netscape Navigator
- No browser

In this case, choosing the **Customize** button in the Office 2000 Setup provides three installation options:

- Microsoft Internet Explorer 5—Standard
- Microsoft Internet Explorer 5—Minimal
- Windows Web Browsing Components Only

The Windows Web Browsing Components feature updates Windows with basic Web browsing functionality, but leaves the user's default browser unchanged. Running Office 2000 on a computer that has been updated with the Windows Web Browsing Components yields full functionality in Office 2000 applications.

Note   If Microsoft Internet Explorer 2.0 is installed before you install Microsoft Office 2000, choosing the Windows Web Browsing Components feature upgrades Internet Explorer 2.0 to Internet Explorer 5. Internet Explorer 2.0 and the updated Windows Web Browsing Components cannot coexist on the same computer.

If you do not install Microsoft Internet Explorer 5 or Windows Web Browsing Components when you install Office 2000, the available features scale to match the level of Web browsing support in Windows. An Office 2000 application determines the level of Web browsing support that is available in Windows when that application is run, and then presents users with the appropriate set of features. If users upgrade Windows to include Internet Explorer 5 or later at any time after installing Office 2000, full functionality becomes available at that time.

Tip   To upgrade to Internet Explorer 5 after installing Office 2000, run Ie5setup.exe, which is located in the \Ie\En subfolder on Microsoft Office 2000 Disc 1. Alternatively, you can download the latest version from the Internet Explorer Web site at http://www.microsoft.com/windows/ie/. The Windows Web Browsing Components can be installed only by running Office 2000 Setup.

Web features available in Office 2000

When you run Office 2000 on a version of Windows that includes Microsoft Internet Explorer 5 or later or the Windows Web Browsing Components, all Office 2000 features that depend on Microsoft Internet Explorer 5 components are available, as described in the following sections.

Application-specific Web features

In Office 2000, Word, Excel, Access, PowerPoint, and FrontPage allow users to open and save HTML documents. Access can also import and export data in several Web formats, and Excel can retrieve data from Web sources by using Web Queries. All Office 2000 applications allow users to follow hyperlinks in documents.

By using the **Open** and **Save As** dialog boxes (**File** menu), users can also open and save files on Web servers through the HTTP protocol. By using the *Web Folders object* in Windows Explorer or in the **Open** and **Save As** dialog boxes, users can also open, cut, copy, paste, or drag files to or from a Web server. These features also require that the Web server have one of the following programs installed:

- Microsoft Office Server Extensions (OSE)
- FrontPage Server Extensions
- Distributed Authoring and Versioning (DAV) protocol

Data access pages

Users can view and work with *data access pages* if they are running Windows with Internet Explorer 5 or later or the Windows Web Browsing Components. To create data access pages, Access 2000 users must have Internet Explorer 5 or later or the Windows Web Browsing Components installed.

Microsoft Office Server Extensions

In addition to using the HTTP protocol to open and save documents, OSE provides the following additional features for working with documents stored on a Web server:

- Web Discussions allows users to collaborate in threaded discussions in Word, Excel, PowerPoint, and HTML documents stored on a Web server.
- Web Subscriptions notifies users when documents on the Web server are modified.
- The OSE Start Page gives users a logical starting place for browsing or searching for documents on a Web server.

For users running Windows with Internet Explorer 5, OSE also includes offline caching and replication features.

Office online Help

Office 2000 online Help requires Microsoft Internet Explorer 3.0 or later. When running under Internet Explorer 3.0, the Show me feature and concept cards in Help are disabled and display a message prompting users to update to a later version of Internet Explorer.

Programming tools

The Microsoft Script Editor can be used to work with Visual Basic Scripting Edition (VBScript), JScript, HTML Intrinsic controls, and ActiveX controls in HTML documents. Users activate Microsoft Script Editor by clicking the **Microsoft Script Editor** command (**Tools** menu, **Macros** submenu).

Developers of Visual Basic for Applications (VBA) macros created in Word, Excel, PowerPoint, and Outlook can identify themselves to users by digitally signing the VBA project that contains their macros. When a macro is altered, the digital signature is automatically removed to indicate that the macro might have been tampered with.

Roaming user profiles

Traveling users (sometimes referred to as *roaming users*) move between different computers on a network. Through the use of *roaming user profiles*, traveling users can move between computers and take their application settings and working files with them, along with any system preferences.

Limitations under Internet Explorer 4.01

When you run Office 2000 on a version of Windows that includes Microsoft Internet Explorer 4.01, most Web features are available. However, the following Office 2000 Web features are not available to users running Office 2000 with Internet Explorer 4.01:

- Data access pages

  Viewing and working with data access pages in a Web browser requires Windows updated to Microsoft Internet Explorer 5 or later, or the Windows Web Browsing Components. To create data access pages, Access 2000 users must have Internet Explorer 5 or later or the Windows Web Browsing Components installed.

- Office Server Extensions features

  Offline features (offline caching and replication) require Windows updated to Internet Explorer 5 or later, or the Windows Web Browsing Components.

Limitations under Internet Explorer 3.0

When you run Office 2000 on a version of Windows that includes Microsoft Internet Explorer 3.0, some Web features are available. However, the following Office 2000 Web features are not available to users running Office 2000 with Internet Explorer 3.0:

- Excel Web Queries
- Data access pages

  Viewing and working with data access pages in a Web browser requires Windows updated to Microsoft Internet Explorer 5 or later, or the Windows Web Browsing Components. To create data access pages, Access 2000 users must have Internet Explorer 5 or later or the Windows Web Browsing Components installed.

- Office Server Extensions features

  Using Web Discussions and Web Subscriptions within Office applications requires Windows updated to Internet Explorer 4.01 or later. Offline features (offline caching and replication) require Windows updated to Microsoft Internet Explorer 5 or later, or the Windows Web Browsing Components.

- Office Web Components

  Office Web Components require Microsoft Internet Explorer 4.01 or later.

- Outlook 2000

  Outlook 2000 requires Microsoft Internet Explorer 4.01 or later.

- Programming tools

  Both the Microsoft Script Editor and digital signatures for VBA macros require Internet Explorer 4.01 or later.

- Roaming user profiles

Web features that require the Windows Desktop Update shell

Some features in Office 2000 require a later version of the Windows Desktop Update shell than the shell that ships with Windows NT Workstation 4.0 or Windows 95. The following Office 2000 features require the updated version of the Windows Desktop Update shell:

- Switching between files by using the Windows taskbar or by pressing ALT+TAB

- Using the Windows Installer to *advertise* a program on the Windows **Start** menu

- Sending to the Windows Desktop from Web Folders

Two versions of the shell meet the Office 2000 requirements: the version installed with Microsoft Internet Explorer 4.01, and the version installed with Window 98 or Windows 2000.

To ensure that features that depend on the Windows Desktop Update shell are available, administrators can install the Microsoft Internet Explorer 4.01 shell by using the Internet Explorer Administrator's Kit (IEAK) with the Office Custom Installation Wizard. This step is necessary only for computers running under Window 95 or Windows NT Workstation 4.0.

See also

- You can deploy, customize, and maintain Internet Explorer by using the Internet Explorer Administration Kit. For more information, see the Internet Explorer Administration Kit Web site at http://ieak.microsoft.com/.

- For more information about installing and using Office Server Extensions features, see "Using Office with a Web Server" on page 565.

- For more information about using Office 2000 with HTML documents, see "Using Office Documents in a Web World" on page 589.

- For more information about Office Web Components, see "Managing Office Web Components" on page 600 or "Adding Interactive Web Controls to Office Documents" on page 600.

- For information about roaming user profiles, see "Supporting Users Who Travel Between Computers" on page 176.

Web Server Support in Office 2000

Collaborating and sharing information are increasingly important elements of the day-to-day operations of organizations. Users must be able to find, work with, and exchange information easily with their co-workers and clients. Networks based on Web protocols are easy to install and administer, and they offer the promise of universal access to information in a heterogeneous client environment.

As a result, more organizations are relying on the Internet and corporate intranets as the infrastructure for their collaborative processes. Microsoft Office 2000 helps facilitate these trends. Office 2000 users can use HTML as a companion file format, manage files on a Web server by using Web Folders, and publish to Web servers from the **Save As** dialog box in Office 2000 applications.

Web server components in Microsoft Office Server Extensions

Some Office 2000 Web server-related features depend on a Web server that has Microsoft Office Server Extensions (OSE) installed. You can install OSE on any Web server with one of the following configurations:

- Microsoft Windows NT Server 4.0 or later and Internet Information Server 4.0 (IIS)
- Windows NT Workstation 4.0 or later and Personal Web Server 4.0.

OSE allows Office 2000 users to do the following:

- Create threaded discussions in published documents.
- Receive an e-mail notification when documents change.
- Search and navigate documents published on Web servers.

A Web site with OSE installed is called an *OSE-extended web*. When you set up an OSE-extended web, Office 2000 users can work with documents on the server by using Web features installed on their computers.

The following features work only with an OSE-extended web:

- Web Discussions
- Web Subscriptions
- OSE Start Page

Even if you do not install OSE on your Web server, users can still take advantage of some of the Web features included in Office 2000. These features work with any Web server that runs Microsoft FrontPage Server Extensions or any Web server that supports the Distributed Authoring and Versioning (DAV) Internet protocol. The following Office 2000 features do not require OSE:

- Opening and saving files on Web servers from the **Open** and **Save As** dialog boxes (**File** menu) using the HTTP protocol.

- Browsing, publishing, and managing the folders and files on Web servers from the *Web Folders object* in My Computer, Windows Explorer, and the **Save As** and **Open** dialog boxes (**File** menu) in Office 2000 applications.

Note   Microsoft FrontPage 2000 includes FrontPage Server Extensions. DAV is an Internet protocol supported by IIS version 5.0.

Other Microsoft Web server components

In addition to IIS, Microsoft Windows NT Server also provides other components that complement enterprise intranets.

Microsoft Proxy Server

Every day more and more companies connect their internal networks to the Internet for a variety of reasons, such as increased productivity, customer service, and collaboration. Some of the biggest issues these organizations face as they extend their networks to the Internet are security, manageability, and cost. Microsoft Proxy Server offers *firewall* security, content caching, and management tools that help organizations address these issues effectively.

Microsoft Certificate Server

Microsoft Certificate Server is a general-purpose, customizable server application for managing *digital certificate*s. It can be used in a variety of security applications, including verifying the identity of users and Web servers.

Microsoft Index Server

Microsoft Index Server allows users to perform full-text searches of Web server content to retrieve information in almost any format from any Web browser.

Microsoft Site Server

Designed to help you get the most out of your corporate intranet, Microsoft Site Server helps users publish, find, and share information quickly and easily. Features include extensive search capabilities and tools to perform thorough analyses of the usage and effectiveness of your intranet.

See also

- For information about installing and using OSE, see "Using Office with a Web Server" on page 565.

- For more information about Microsoft Proxy Server, see the Microsoft Proxy Server Web site at http://www.microsoft.com/proxy/.

- For more information about Microsoft Certificate Server, see the "Microsoft Certificate Server" white paper at http://www.microsoft.com/workshop/security/client/certsvr.asp.

- For more information about Microsoft Index Server, see the Microsoft Index Server technical specifications at http://www.microsoft.com/ntserver/fileprint/tech/techspec/IndexServer.asp.

- For more information about Microsoft Site Server, see the Microsoft Site Server Web site at http://www.microsoft.com/siteserver/.

Data Access Technologies

Microsoft Office applications supply a variety of data access technologies. With each release of Office, the number of features and technologies grows to address new requirements, such as enterprise data access and data access from the Web. In Office 2000, data access technology is consolidated and consistent for all Office applications.

Office 2000 and Database Engines

A *database engine* is the component of an application that provides the link between an application and its data. Microsoft Office 2000 installs Microsoft Jet version 4.0 as its primary database engine. Microsoft Access is the database application in Office 2000, and it relies on the Microsoft Jet database engine to provide data access services for Access database files (*MDB files*).

Because other Office 2000 applications can interact with data stored in Access database files, the applications also use the Jet database engine to retrieve data. For example, Microsoft Excel can retrieve data from Access databases and a variety of other data sources by creating a database query with the **New Database Query** command (**Data** menu, **Get External Data** submenu). When doing so, Excel also relies on the Jet database engine.

All Office applications that support Visual Basic for Applications (VBA) or Visual Basic Scripting Edition (VBScript) can use either the ADO programming model or the DAO programming model to retrieve and work with data that the Jet database engine manages from VBA code or VBScript script.

In addition to installing the Jet database engine, Office 2000 includes a separate program to install the Microsoft Data Engine (MSDE). MSDE is a new technology that provides local data storage compatible with Microsoft SQL Server version 7.0. Access 2000 provides tools to create and design databases that are stored by using MSDE or by using Microsoft SQL Server 6.5 or later. Access also creates a new file type called an Access project (ADP file) that stores the user interface elements, such as forms and reports that are used to work with MSDE or Microsoft SQL Server databases.

Microsoft Jet database engine

Access 2000 and the other Office 2000 applications rely on the Jet database engine to provide data access services to the Access database file format. The Jet database engine also provides access to data that is stored in tables in a variety of formats, including the following:

- Microsoft Excel workbooks
- Microsoft Outlook folders
- Microsoft SQL Server databases
- HTML tables
- dBASE files
- Lotus 1-2-3 spreadsheets
- Tabular text files

Toolbox

The Office Resource Kit includes information about the data formats and drivers that are supported by the Jet database engine, as well as other data access components that are installed by Office, in a Word document named Formats.doc. For more information about installing this document, see "Office Information" on page 787.

The following sections describe the many improvements and new features in Microsoft Jet version 4.0.

Unicode support for character data

All character data that is stored in the Text and Memo fields in Access are now stored in the *Unicode* two-byte character representation format. Unicode storage replaces ANSI character sets and the Multibyte Character Set (MBCS) format used in previous versions of the Microsoft Jet database engine to store character data for languages such as Japanese and Chinese.

To accommodate the change to Unicode, and to enable all existing data to be converted successfully, page size (the internal unit of storage) is increased from 2 kilobytes (KB) to 4 KB. This larger page size allows an increase in the maximum database size from 1.07 gigabytes (GB) to 2.14 GB. Although the Unicode representation of character data requires more space to store each character (two bytes instead of one byte), columns with string data types can be defined to automatically compress the data, whenever it is possible.

Support for standardized sorting

The Unicode representation for the storage of character data enables the Microsoft Jet database engine to use a new sorting mechanism that is based on the native Microsoft Windows NT sorting functionality. This sorting mechanism uses the same *locale IDs* (LCID), and supports all Windows NT 4.0 and Windows 2000 sort orders.

Microsoft Jet uses the new sorting mechanism when running on all supported versions of Windows—Windows 2000, Windows NT 4.0, and Windows 95/98. This sorting mechanism standardizes sorting and ensures sorting consistency across operating systems. Microsoft SQL Server 7.0 and Microsoft Visual Basic 6.0 also use the sorting mechanism to provide cross-product consistency.

Compatibility with SQL Server data types

To make it easy to upsize Access databases to Microsoft SQL Server databases, and for better compatibility between Microsoft Jet database engine and Microsoft SQL Server replication, data types used by the Jet database engine are more closely aligned with Microsoft SQL Server data types. In some instances, this data type consistency also provides greater compatibility with Open Database Connectivity (ODBC) data sources that you can access by using the Jet database engine.

New SQL commands and syntax

The SQL commands, syntax, and query processor used by the Microsoft Jet 4.0 database engine have been enhanced to support Unicode, and to conform more closely to the *ANSI SQL-92* specification. Because Microsoft SQL Server 7.0 and SQL Server 6.5 also support Unicode and much of the ANSI SQL-92 specification, these enhancements make it easy to write SQL statements that are compatible with both native Access databases (MDB files) and Microsoft SQL Server databases. The enhancements also simplify converting Visual Basic for Applications code that contains SQL statements to Microsoft SQL Server.

Important   The new Microsoft Jet 4.0 SQL commands and syntax are available only from VBA code written by using the ADO programming model.

Connection control

The Jet database engine provides a new connection control feature that allows you to deny access to all new user connections and current users after they close the database. This connection control is useful for an administrator who needs exclusive access to a database to perform maintenance tasks such as compacting the database or making design changes to the database.

User list

The user list feature allows you to view a table of user information in a multiuser database. You can use Visual Basic for Applications code and the ADO **OpenSchema** method to obtain the user list. The user list returns the following information for each user:

- Network name of the user's computer.
- The user's security ID when the user is connected.
- Whether a connection was terminated normally after a user disconnects.

Record-level locking

With the increased page size required to support Unicode, performance might decrease, and *concurrency* might diminish, which means that the same sets of data and objects might not be available to multiple users. However, the record-level locking feature in the Jet database engine minimizes the impact of the increased page size, and increases performance and concurrency. Instead of locking an entire data page or multiple records, an application can be programmed to lock only a single record at a time.

Lock promotion

When an SQL statement is carried out, or when a transaction that modifies a large number of records in a table is carried out, the Jet database engine places individual write locks on all corresponding index and data pages in the database. The individual write lock feature maximizes concurrency, but it might significantly decrease performance because the locks need to be set and maintained. This is particularly true when the database is on a server, and the database is being accessed over a local area network (LAN).

The new table lock feature permits a user to open a table exclusively and then to modify records in the table without locks being placed on either the corresponding index pages or data pages. This reduces concurrency because only one user can update the table, but it increases performance when large numbers of records are being modified.

The Jet database engine provides an option to automatically attempt to promote the page locks on a table to an exclusive table lock when large numbers of page locks are being placed on a table. This option is controlled by the value entry **PagesLockedToTableLock**, which is located in the HKEY_Local_Machine\Software \Microsoft\Jet\4.0\Engines\Jet 4.0 subkey in the Windows registry. The default value is **0**, which disables the capability. A value greater than **0** specifies the page lock count at which promotion to an exclusive table lock should be attempted.

For example, if **PagesLockedToTableLock** is set to a value of **50**, then on the fifty-first data page lock, Microsoft Jet tries to escalate the user's shared table read lock to an exclusive table read lock. If the promotion is unsuccessful, the Jet database engine retries on the 101st data page lock and so on. The lock count is maintained on a per-table basis, and it is reset when the transaction level reaches 0 (zero).

New replication features

Database replication is the process of sharing data or database design changes between copies of an Access database in different locations without having to redistribute copies of the entire database. Replication involves producing one or more copies, (*replicas*) of a single original database (the *Design Master*). Together, the Design Master and its replicas are called a *replica set*. By performing a process called synchronization, changes to objects and data are distributed to all members of the replica set. You can make changes to the design of objects only in the Design Master, but you can make changes to data from any member of the replica set.

Note   Microsoft SQL Server also provides replication features that use a different publish-and subscribe-model.

In previous versions of Microsoft Jet, Microsoft SQL Server data is replicated to an Access database; but changes to the Access database cannot be used to update the Microsoft SQL Server database because replication is unidirectional—that is, replication goes from a SQL Server publisher to an Access subscriber. However, Microsoft Jet 4.0, and Microsoft SQL Server 7.0 support bidirectional replication between Access and Microsoft SQL Server databases.

The bidirectional replication feature ensures that changes to data in a Microsoft SQL Server database can be replicated to an Access database and that changes to the data in Access can be synchronized to and reconciled with the SQL Server database.

In previous versions of Microsoft Jet, replication differentiates between synchronization conflicts and synchronization errors. Synchronization conflicts occur when two users update the same record in two different databases in a replica set. Synchronizing the two databases succeeds when one of the two sets of changes is applied to both databases. Thus, only one set of changes is made. Synchronization errors occur when a change to data in one database in a replica set cannot be applied to another database in the replica set because the change violates a constraint such as referential integrity or uniqueness.

In Microsoft Jet 4.0, replication events that cause synchronization conflicts and synchronization errors are identified as synchronization conflicts, and a single mechanism is used to record and resolve the conflicts, making conflict resolution easy. When a conflict occurs, an acceptable change is selected and applied, and the conflicting change is recorded as a conflict in all replicas. You can use the new Conflict Resolution Wizard to reconcile and resolve synchronization conflicts either with Microsoft SQL Server 7.0 or with Microsoft Jet 4.0 replicated databases.

In Microsoft Jet 3.5, conflicts are determined at the record level. In other words, when two users in two different replicas change the same customer record, but each user changes a different field in the record, the two records conflict when the replicas are synchronized because conflicts are determined at the record level.

In Microsoft Jet 4.0, field-level conflict resolution means that changes to the same record in two different replicas causes a synchronization conflict only when the same field in the same record is changed. Field-level change tracking and conflict resolution significantly do the following:

- Reduce the potential for conflicts.
- Simplify the maintenance of replicated databases.

Microsoft Data Engine

Microsoft Data Engine (MSDE) is a new technology that provides local data storage compatible with Microsoft SQL Server 7.0. You can use MSDE as a small workgroup database server, and because Access now provides the Access project file (ADP file) to connect to SQL Server databases, you can use MSDE as an alternative to the Microsoft Jet database engine. MSDE runs on Windows NT Workstation 4.0, Windows 2000, and Windows 95 or later. It is designed and optimized for use on smaller computer systems such as a single-user computer or small workgroup server.

MSDE does not limit the number of users who can connect to its database, but MSDE is optimized for five users. For a larger number of users, use Microsoft SQL Server 7.0. Databases created with MSDE are fully compatible with SQL Server 7.0, and they support many of the features of SQL Server 7.0, including most Transact-SQL commands.

MSDE also logs transactions, which means that if anything goes wrong while writing to an MSDE database, such as a disk error, network failure, or power failure, then MSDE recovers from its transaction log and reverts to its last consistent state. This gives MSDE databases better reliability than Microsoft Jet databases (MDB files), which do not log transactions.

Because MSDE is based on the same database engine as Microsoft SQL Server, most Access projects can run unchanged on either version. However, MSDE has a 2-gigabyte database size limit and supports up to two processors for Symmetrical Multiprocessing (SMP). In a replicated database environment, MSDE can act as a replication subscriber for both transactional and merge replication and as a replication publisher for merge replication. However, unlike SQL Server, MSDE cannot be a replication publisher for transactional replication.

Compared with using Access with a Microsoft Jet database (MDB file), using MSDE does require more memory. The minimum supported configuration for running MSDE is a computer with a Pentium 166 processor and 32 megabytes (MB) of RAM. MSDE does manage its memory usage dynamically; so MSDE reacts to operating system pressure on memory resources to allocate as much memory as it can effectively use, but it stops allocating memory and even, if needed, gives back memory to ensure that other applications have memory available. However, if your solution requires the minimum usage of memory resources, use Access with a Microsoft Jet database.

You can install MSDE from Microsoft Office 2000 Disc 1 by double-clicking **Setupsql.exe** in the SQL\x86\Setup folder.

See also

- For more information about the Microsoft Jet database engine, see *Microsoft Jet Database Engine Programmer's Guide, Second Edition.*

- For more information about replicating data between Microsoft SQL Server and Microsoft Access, see *SQL Server Books Online*, which is installed with SQL Server 7.0.

Office 2000 and Database Files

Microsoft Access 2000 makes it easier than ever to work with Microsoft SQL Server databases. When working with an Access project file (ADP file), Access provides a variety of tools that you can use to work with SQL Server 7.0 and 6.5 databases. These tools allow you to work with existing databases, create entirely new databases, and to work with the design of database objects. Access also provides the Upsizing Wizard, which helps you convert an existing Access database into an Access project file connected to a SQL Server database.

By isolating all database files under the control of a database server, SQL Server can provide advanced features that cannot be furnished by the Jet database engine. For example:

Online backup   Use an automatic scheduler to back up your database without having to exclude users from the database.

Durable transactions   SQL Server logs transactions so that updates made within a transaction can always be recovered or rolled back if either the client or the server computer fails.

Better reliability and data protection   If either a workstation or file server fails while an Access database (*MDB file*) is being written to, the database might be damaged. You can usually recover a damaged database by compacting and repairing the database, but you must have all users close the database before doing so. This rarely happens with a Microsoft SQL Server database.

Faster query processing   Because an Access database is a file-server system, it must load the Jet database engine locally to process queries on the client workstation. For large databases, this can involve moving a lot of data over the network. In contrast, SQL Server runs queries on the server, which is typically a much more powerful computer than client workstations. Running queries on the server increases the load on the server, but this can reduce the network traffic substantially—especially if the database application is designed so that users can select only a small subset of the data at a time.

Advanced hardware support   Uninterruptible power supplies, hot-swappable disk drives, and multiple processors can all be added to the server with no changes to the client workstations.

See also

- For more information about Microsoft SQL Server, see the Microsoft SQL Server Web site, at http://www.microsoft.com/sql/, and *SQL Server Books Online*, which is installed with SQL Server 7.0.

Office 2000 and Data Connectivity Technologies

In the past, Microsoft Office applications have supported a broad variety of data formats and data access technologies. Microsoft Office 2000 is no exception to this trend. However, all Microsoft products that support data access are converging on a new data access strategy called Universal Data Access.

The primary technologies that are used to implement Universal Data Access are the low-level data access component architecture, called OLE DB, and the higher level programming interface to OLE DB, ActiveX Data Objects (ADO). ADO can be used from any programming language that complies with the *Component Object Model* (COM). For Office solution development, COM compliance includes Visual Basic for Applications (VBA), Visual Basic Scripting Edition (VBScript), Microsoft JScript®, Microsoft Visual C++® and Microsoft Visual J++®.

You can install the OLE DB components and ADO 2.1 with Office 2000. ADO supports a broader array of data sources than the Data Access Objects (DAO) programming model. However, Office 2000 applications continue to provide support for DAO through the Microsoft DAO 3.6 object library, so users can continue to run existing solutions that were developed by using DAO, and developers can continue to create new solutions that use DAO as well. You can also use both ADO and DAO code in your solution if you want.

OLE DB

OLE DB is an interface with an open specification designed to build on the success of Open Database Connectivity (ODBC) by providing an open standard for accessing an even broader variety of data. Whereas ODBC was created to access only relational databases, OLE DB is designed for both relational and nonrelational data sources, including mainframe and hierarchical databases; e-mail and file system stores; text, graphical, and geographical data; custom business objects; and more.

OLE DB consists of a collection of COM interfaces to various database management system services. OLE DB provides access to a particular data source by using a COM component called a data provider, which is often referred to as an *OLE DB provider*. If the system an Office solution is running on has the appropriate OLE DB provider installed (as well as the core ADO and OLE DB components, which you install with Office), that solution can use ADO code to work with the data exposed by that provider.

The primary providers used by Office solution developers are the Microsoft Jet 4.0 OLE DB Provider and the Microsoft OLE DB Provider for SQL Server.

Microsoft Jet 4.0 OLE DB Provider   Works with the Microsoft Jet database engine, which provides access to data in Microsoft Access databases; also provides database access to the installable Indexed Sequential Access Method (I-ISAM) data supported by Jet tabular data stored in Microsoft Excel workbooks, Microsoft Outlook or Microsoft Exchange mail stores, dBASE tables, Paradox tables, Lotus 1-2-3 spreadsheets, text, and HTML files.

Microsoft OLE DB Provider for SQL Server   Provides access to databases stored on Microsoft SQL Server versions 6.5 and 7.0.

Toolbox

For data sources that do not have OLE DB providers, you can use the Microsoft OLE DB Provider for ODBC. The Office Resource Kit includes information about the data formats and drivers that are supported by the Jet database engine, as well as other data access components that are installed by Office, in a Word document named Formats.doc. For more information about installing this document, see "Office Information" on page 787.

ActiveX Data Objects

ADO is an easy-to-use, application-level programming interface to the new and powerful data access technology, OLE DB. The ADO programming model supports key features for building desktop, client/server, and Web-based solutions, including the following:

- Support for independently created objects. Unlike DAO or Remote Data Objects (RDO), you no longer have to navigate through a hierarchy to create objects because most ADO objects can be independently created. This allows you to create and track only the objects you need and also results in fewer ADO objects and thus a smaller memory footprint.

- Batch updating, which helps improve performance by locally caching changes to data, and then writing all the changes to the server in a single update.

  Note   Although the Microsoft Jet 4.0 OLE DB Provider supports batch updating, there is no need to use batch updating with Access databases to improve performance because the Jet database engine runs locally. However, you are probably going to have a performance gain when performing batch updates against a SQL Server database.

- Support for stored procedures with in/out parameters and return values against a Microsoft SQL Server database.

- Different cursor types, including the potential for support of cursors specific to back ends.

- Support for limits on the number of returned records and other query goals for performance tuning.

  Tip   The ADO **MaxRecords** property of a **Recordset** object, which is designed to limit the number of returned records, is not supported by the Microsoft Jet 4.0 OLE DB Provider or the Microsoft Access ODBC driver. However, if you require this functionality, you can use the TOP *n* predicate in a Microsoft Jet SQL statement, or you can set the **TopValues** property of a query that is saved in an Access database.

- Support for multiple **Recordset** objects returned from stored procedures or batch statements.

  Note   Multiple **Recordset** objects can be returned for SQL Server databases. Access databases cannot return multiple **Recordset** objects because Microsoft Jet SQL statements do not support multiple SELECT statements.

- Free-threaded objects for efficient Web server applications.

Support for older data access technologies

Office 2000 and Access 2000 continue to support data access solutions that use the older DAO programming model and ODBC drivers.

Data Access Objects

When you install Office 2000 or Access 2000, you get DAO version 3.6. When an Access database (*MDB file*) is converted from an earlier version of Access to Access 2000 format, a reference is established to the DAO 3.6 Object Library, which is used to work with any DAO code in the database. DAO code written in previous versions of Access that use the DAO 3.5 programming model continue to work in a database converted to Access 2000 format. However, DAO code written by using DAO 3.0 or earlier might need to be recompiled or rewritten to work in Access 2000.

Apart from conversion issues, there are a number of reasons to continue to use DAO when writing Visual Basic for Applications code to work with new Access databases. Although ADO provides access to a broader variety of data sources than DAO, and even exposes some features of the Microsoft Jet 4.0 database engine that are not available from DAO, there are a number of limitations to using ADO against Access databases:

- In the Access *object model*, the new **Recordset** property of a **Form** object can be used to request or specify a **Recordset** object for the data being browsed in a form. If you request the **Recordset** object for the current form in an Access database, Access always returns a DAO **Recordset** object. Therefore, you must continue to use DAO code to work with the **Recordset** object that is returned.

- When you use the **Recordset** property to set the **Recordset** object of a **Form** object to a **Recordset** object you created, if you set the **Form** object to an ADO **Recordset** object, the data is read-only. If you want the data to be writable, you must set the **Form** object to a DAO **Recordset** object.

- To read and set database properties in an Access database, and to read and set certain table properties, such as the **Description** and **Filter** properties, you must continue to use DAO code.

- It is not possible to exchange information between ADO and DAO code. For example, if a DAO procedure returns a **Recordset** object, there is no way to translate or pass that DAO **Recordset** object to ADO code, and vice versa—an ADO **Recordset** object cannot be read by or translated to DAO. However, this does not mean that ADO cannot work with saved database objects, such as tables and queries, that were created with DAO, and vice versa. But it does mean that although ADO and DAO can coexist in the same project, you cannot use ADO code to work with objects returned by preexisting DAO code. You must continue to use DAO code, or you must rewrite those procedures by using ADO code.

If you are updating an existing DAO data access component, or developing new data access components that work only with Access databases or other data sources supported by the I-ISAM drivers of the Jet database engine, you can continue to use DAO by establishing a reference to the Microsoft DAO 3.6 object library. All DAO code written for DAO 3.5 (with the exception of code that defines *user-level security* for code modules in Access 2000 databases) will continue to work with DAO 3.6.

Only the following Jet database engine features require ADO:

New Jet SQL commands and syntax   Additional SQL commands and syntax were added to make Jet SQL conform more closely to the ANSI SQL-92 specification.

Connection control   A setting that allows you to exclude all new connections and exclude current users after they close the database.

User list   Programmatically displaying a list of information about all the users who are currently logged on to the database.

Programmatic control over page-level or record-level locking   You can use ADO to control whether the Jet database engine uses page-level or record-level locking when records are being added, deleted, or modified from Visual Basic for Applications code.

If you do not require access to these Jet database engine features and do not require other ADO-specific features, you can continue to write code that uses DAO until you encounter these requirements.

Open Database Connectivity

Versions of Office earlier than Office 2000 included features that use ODBC drivers and components to connect to data, such as viewing and importing data from ODBC data sources in Access and Excel. Office 2000 continues to support features that use ODBC data sources. Office 2000 installs updated versions of ODBC drivers for Access, Excel, Microsoft Visual FoxPro®, Microsoft FoxPro®, dBASE, Paradox, and text files; and also installs ODBC drivers for Microsoft SQL Server and Oracle databases.

In most cases, DAO code written to use ODBC data sources in versions of Office earlier than Office 2000 do continue to work. Code that uses 16-bit versions of ODBC drivers do not work until you recreate data source names by using the **ODBC Data Sources (32bit)** icon in Control Panel. ODBC data sources can also be used from code written by using the new ADO programming model.

Sharing databases by using Web technologies

Office 2000 provides features to share databases from Web browsers by using Microsoft Office Web Components, which can be used in HTML documents displayed in Microsoft Internet Explorer 5 or later. Office 2000 also continues to support other technologies for sharing databases, such as *Active Server Pages* (ASP) pages, which can be used from Internet Explorer as well as from other Web browsers, such as Netscape Navigator.

Using Office Web Components

Office 2000 installs Microsoft Office Web Components to enable publishing Office documents to the Web while preserving the interactivity that the documents have when they are viewed in their native applications. The Office Web Components are a collection of ActiveX controls designed to let you publish fully interactive worksheets, charts, PivotTable reports, and databases to the Web.

When users view a Web page that contains an Office Web Component, they can interact with the data displayed while in Internet Explorer. Users can sort, filter, add, or change data, expand and collapse detail views, work with PivotTable lists, and chart the results of their changes. In addition, the Office Web Components are fully programmable by using Visual Basic for Applications within an Office application or by using Visual Basic Scripting Edition or Microsoft JScript code in a Web page.

Office Web Components include the Microsoft Office Data Source Control, which manages communication between other controls on the page and the source of data for the page. The Microsoft Office Data Source Control can be used to work with either Access or Microsoft SQL Server databases. The Microsoft Office Data Source Control uses OLE DB and ADO components to work with the source of data for the page. HTML documents authored by using the Microsoft Office Data Source Control in conjunction with other Office Web Components are created in Access and are called *data access pages.*

Important   Office Web Components work only in Internet Explorer 4.01 or later. Office Web Components on Access data access pages work only in Internet Explorer 5 or later. You get the most complete functionality with all of the Office Web Component controls in Internet Explorer 5 or later. To view and work with any of the Office Web Components, either users must have Office 2000 installed or you can set up Office Web Components so that they can be installed from your corporate intranet (a site license is required).

Using other Web data access technologies

Access 2000 continues to support the following features for sharing databases from Web pages that can be viewed in Internet Explorer, as well as in other Web browsers:

- Saving data from tables, queries, reports, and form datasheets as static HTML documents.

- Creating Internet Database Connector/HTML extension (IDC/HTX) files to query data from a table, query, or form datasheet in a database on a Web server and display it in a Web page.

- Saving an Access form as an ASP page that allows users to view, enter, and update information in a database on a Web server.

- Creating an ASP page to query data from a table, query, or form datasheet in a database on a Web server and display it in a Web page.

- Saving Access reports to a special graphics format called a snapshot file, and publishing them from Web pages.

See also

- When converting databases created in earlier versions of Access, in some cases DAO code must be recompiled or altered before conversion is successful. For information about troubleshooting code problems in converted databases, see "Upgrading to Access 2000" on page 455.

- For more information about the Microsoft Universal Data Access strategy, OLE DB components, and the ADO programming model, see the Microsoft Universal Data Access Web site at http://www.microsoft.com/data/.

- For more information about working with Microsoft Office Web components, see "Adding Interactive Web Controls to Office Documents" on page 600 and "Managing Office Web Components" on page 600.

Programming Technologies

Microsoft Office 2000 includes powerful new technologies and programming models that help developers build custom Office solutions. Each new version of Office contains new tools and technologies that make it easy to develop and deliver custom Office-based solutions. These new tools and technologies improve the ability of users to gather, analyze, customize, publish, and share information.

Office 2000 and Visual Basic for Applications

Automation is the *Component Object Model* (COM) technology that makes Microsoft Office 2000 applications programmable, which makes creating an integrated Office solution possible. Automation (formerly called OLE Automation) includes the following features.

Automation exposes features in a hierarchy of programmable objects Applications, dynamic-link libraries (DLLs), and ActiveX controls that support the appropriate Automation interfaces expose their features as a set of programmable objects. Any application or service that supports these interfaces is called a COM component. The set of programmable objects that a COM component exposes is organized into a set of hierarchical relationships that is called an *object model*, or a programming model.

Automation allows applications to share features with other applications A COM component can be either an Automation server that shares its component objects with other applications or an Automation client that uses the component objects of other applications.

Visual Basic for Applications provides features that make it easy to use Automation

When you use Visual Basic for Applications (VBA) code, you can establish a reference to the programming model of an Automation server by using the **References** dialog box (**Tools** menu). The reference allows your solution to allocate memory efficiently to work with the objects that the Automation server exposes. The reference also allows the Visual Basic Editor to assist you when you enter VBA statements by automatically listing relevant objects, properties, and methods from the referenced programming model. And you can use the **Object Browser** command (**View** menu) to examine how the objects that are exposed by the Automation server are related to each other, and to find more information about how to program the objects.

Automation servers and Automation clients

Office 2000 developers can take advantage of all Automation features when developing custom solutions. Office applications can function as COM components that expose most of their features to other applications that support Automation as programmable objects. Office applications serve as both Automation servers and Automation clients. And most Office applications incorporate the VBA programming environment that makes working with Automation easy.

Programmable applications

The Visual Basic for Applications programming language and the Visual Basic Editor can be incorporated into applications that support Automation to make the applications programmable. The following Office 2000 applications support the VBA programming language and the same version of the Visual Basic Editor:

- Microsoft Access 2000
- Microsoft Excel 2000
- Microsoft FrontPage 2000
- Microsoft Outlook® 2000
- Microsoft PowerPoint® 2000
- Microsoft Word 2000

In addition, many other applications incorporate the Visual Basic for Applications programming environment and are written to expose their functionality to VBA programmers through Automation interfaces. This means that developers can use Visual Basic for Applications to create solutions that integrate not only Office 2000 applications, but also other applications that support VBA and Automation.

Programming individual Office applications

Visual Basic for Applications and Automation allow you to program individual Office applications. For example, you can create procedures (macros) to automatically create and format documents in Word 2000. Developers can also use Automation to run other applications from within a client application. For example, a VBA solution developed in Access can run a hidden instance of Excel to perform mathematical and analytical operations on Access data.

Working with programmable services

Automation also allows developers to use Visual Basic for Applications code to work with programming models that do the following:

- Function as free-standing services.

- Are independent of individual applications.

For example, Office 2000 installs the Microsoft Data Access Components (MDAC), which consist of OLE DB components that provide low-level access to a variety of data sources and components that make up the ActiveX Data Objects (ADO) programming model. Because the ADO programming model supports Automation, you can use ADO from Visual Basic for Applications code running in any Office application to gain access to, and work with, any data source that is available through an *OLE DB provider* or an ODBC driver.

New programming features

The programming models of the Office 2000 applications expose new objects, methods, properties, and events. The Visual Basic for Applications language also has new features.

Expanded event model

The Office 2000 event model has been greatly expanded. Word, PowerPoint, and FrontPage now expose more than two dozen new events, primarily associated with window and document objects.

In addition, all Office applications now expose three command bar events: The **CommandBarButton** object has a click event, the **CommandBarComboBox** object has a change event, and the **CommandBars** collection object has an update event.

New VBA functions

Several new features make it easier to format data or to parse and manipulate strings. New Visual Basic for Applications features include the following:

- Use **FormatCurrency**, **FormatDateTime**, **FormatNumber**, and **FormatPercent** functions to format data.

- Use the **Split**, **Join**, and **Filter** functions to parse strings.

  The **Split** function parses a string into an array of substrings. The **Join** function is the opposite of the **Split** function; it creates a string from an array of substrings. The **Filter** function filters an array and returns an array containing the elements that match the specified criteria.

- Use the new **Replace** and **InStrRev** functions to manipulate strings.

- Use the **Round** function to round a number to a specified number of decimal places.

In this latest version of Visual Basic for Applications, you can also write functions that return arrays, and you can assign one array to another.

New VBA objects

Also new to Visual Basic for Applications in Office are the **FileSystemObject** and **Dictionary** objects. The **Dictionary** object is analogous to a VBA collection, except that the **Dictionary** object can hold objects of different data types. You can use the **FileSystemObject** object to work with the drives, directories, and files on your computer as if they were objects and collections of objects with methods and properties you can use to return information about your file system.

New custom object features

Visual Basic for Applications also allows you to create your own objects. New to VBA in Office 2000 is the ability to add custom events to objects that you create. In addition, you can now extend your custom objects by implementing interfaces.

See also

- For more information about the Visual Basic for Applications programming language and applications that support it, see the Microsoft Visual Basic for Applications Web site at http://msdn.microsoft.com/vba/.

- For more information about developing custom solutions by using Office applications and the Visual Basic for Applications programming language, see the Microsoft Office Developer Web site, at http://www.microsoft.com/officedev/, and the *Microsoft Office 2000/Visual Basic Programmer's Guide*.

- For more information about ADO and the data access technologies that Office 2000 supports, see "Data Access Technologies" on page 49.

Office 2000 and Microsoft Script Editor

Microsoft Office developers are accustomed to using the Visual Basic Editor to add Visual Basic for Applications (VBA) code to Office documents. However, now that Office 2000 documents support HTML as a native document format, developers need to work with objects and *scripts* in an Office 2000 document that can be displayed on the Web.

To help developers work with HTML documents, Microsoft Word 2000, Microsoft Excel 2000, Microsoft PowerPoint 2000, Microsoft Access 2000, and Microsoft FrontPage 2000 provide the Microsoft Script Editor. The Script Editor is a new and powerful integrated development tool that allows developers to work with Office 2000 documents as Web pages.

The Script Editor allows you to do the following:

- Edit HTML in a document.
- Add script, ActiveX, and HTML intrinsic controls.
- View a document as a Web page.

▶ **To open the Microsoft Script Editor in Word, Excel, PowerPoint, or FrontPage**

1   On the **Tools** menu, point to **Macro**.

2   Click **Microsoft Script Editor**.

In Access, the Microsoft Script Editor is available from the **Tools** menu only when you are working with *data access pages*.

Note   FrontPage supports entering script from the **HTML** tab in Page view, and automatically generates HTML when using other tools such as the **DHTML Effects** tool. Microsoft Outlook 2000 does not support the Microsoft Script Editor. However, you can write Visual Basic Scripting Edition (VBScript) to customize Outlook by using the scripting environment available within the Outlook forms, which are used to display items such as messages and appointments.

The Microsoft Script Editor supports working with the scripting languages provided by the scripting engines that are installed on a user's computer. Office 2000 installs Microsoft Internet Explorer 5, which installs scripting engines for Microsoft Visual Basic Scripting Edition version 5.0, and Microsoft JScript version 5.0 scripting languages.

VBScript

Visual Basic Scripting Edition provides a subset of the Microsoft Visual Basic programming language features, and as a result, VBScript is very easy to use for developers who are familiar with Visual Basic. VBScript can be used with Internet Explorer to work with the following:

- Dynamic HTML
- ActiveX controls
- Automation servers
- Java applets

Visual Basic Scripting Edition can also be used for server-side script that runs on Microsoft Internet Information Server (Windows NT 4.0) or Internet Information Services (Windows 2000), and for working with Windows Scripting Host.

JScript

JScript is the Microsoft implementation of the ECMA 262 language specification. JScript is a full implementation, with some additional enhancements that take advantage of capabilities of Internet Explorer. JScript is a general-purpose scripting language that appeals to the programmers who use C, C++, and Java. JScript can also be used with Internet Explorer to work with the following:

- Dynamic HTML
- ActiveX controls
- Automation servers
- Java applets

JScript can also be used for scripting in Web pages that are viewed in Netscape Navigator.

See also

- For more information about using VBScript and JScript, see the Microsoft Scripting Technologies Web site at http://msdn.microsoft.com/scripting/.

New Architecture for Office 2000 Add-ins

One way to provide users with a custom Microsoft Office solution is to develop and distribute an *add-in*. An add-in extends an Office application by adding functionality that is not in the core product. For example, an add-in might add new menu commands or toolbar buttons that display custom forms to add new features to an Office application.

If you are a frequent user of Microsoft Excel or Microsoft Access, you might already be familiar with some of the add-ins that these applications include. The Linked Table Manager in Access is an example of an add-in that uses Visual Basic for Applications (VBA). Many of the wizards that are available in other Office applications are also add-ins.

All Office 2000 applications support the new add-in architecture called COM add-ins that allows developers to create a single add-in that can run in any application. VBA developers can create COM add-ins by using Office 2000 Developer. COM add-ins can also be created by developers who are using one of the following programming languages:

- Microsoft Visual Basic versions 5.0 or later
- Microsoft Visual C++
- Microsoft Visual J++
- Any language that can create COM components

This wide support for COM add-ins means that developers can now use multiple development environments to create custom solutions in Office 2000. The only requirement to connect COM add-ins to an Office application is for the add-in to implement the IDExtensibility2 interface. COM add-ins can be loaded when the host application starts, or they can be loaded on demand. Support has also been added to allow the **OnAction** property of a custom command bar button to load a COM add-in.

See also

- For more information about creating COM add-ins, see the *Microsoft Office 2000/Visual Basic Programmer's Guide*.

Deploying Office 2000

Contents

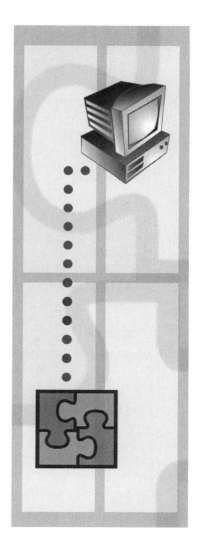

CHAPTER 3

Installing Office 2000 in Your Organization

Whether you administer Microsoft Office 2000 for a few users on a small local area network or for departments spread out across continents, you can use the information presented here to customize and install Office 2000. These topics cover a powerful and flexible set of tools and procedures that make your job of deploying Office 2000 a much easier task.

In This Chapter

What's New in Office 2000 Installation

The installation process for Microsoft Office 2000 has been significantly improved over previous versions of Office.

Windows Installer Replaces Acme Setup

Previous versions of Microsoft Office used *Acme Setup* to install Microsoft Office. Acme Setup relied on tables of information in text files to copy program files, set registry entries, and perform other tasks necessary for installing Office on a user's computer.

Office 2000 Setup uses the new Windows installer technology to install Office. This technology provides a number of benefits over Acme Setup.

Logically grouped features and components   When a user selects a feature to install during Office Setup, the installer identifies a corresponding set of components to copy to the user's computer. Each component consists of files, programs, dynamic-link libraries, and registry entries that work together as a unit. This more efficient management of resources also makes customizing installations a simpler task for an administrator.

Install features when required   When you select this option for a feature or application, the installer does not copy the corresponding components during installation. However, the first time that a user starts the feature or application, the installer automatically copies the necessary components to the user's computer. This option saves disk space on the user's computer until features are actually needed.

Resilient components   The installer maintains a record of all components installed on the computer. If a file or registry entry is deleted or corrupted after installation, then the installer automatically reinstalls the component from the installation source.

Efficient customization process   All the data and instructions used during Setup are stored in a Windows installer *package* (MSI file). To customize the installation process, you use the Office Custom Installation Wizard to record changes to the master installation in a Windows installer *transform* (MST file). Because the original package is never altered, you can create a different transform for every installation scenario you need.

Installing Office more efficiently with a Windows installer package

The Windows installer package is a relational database that replaces the Acme Setup STF and INF text files. The package contains all the information necessary to install Office 2000. The database associates product components with features and contains information about the installation process itself, such as installation sequence, destination folder paths, system dependencies, and installation options.

After installation, the installer continues to use the package to add or remove components, replace missing or damaged files, or install new components on first use.

Customizing Office with a Windows installer transform

The Windows installer transform describes how to transform the package so that Setup installs Office the way you want. Like the package, the transform is a relational database with information about components, features, and Setup properties. But the transform contains only the changes that you want to apply to the package.

To customize the Office installation, you no longer need to directly edit the MSI file the way you had to edit the Acme STF file. Instead, you use the Custom Installation Wizard to create a new transform with all the changes you want to make to the Office installation. When you run Setup with both the package and the transform, the installer applies the transform to the original package, and Setup uses your altered configuration to perform the installation.

The installer does not change the package itself; but only temporarily applies the changes in memory before carrying out the package instructions. There's no worry about corrupting the original file. The transform is typically much smaller than the package, so you can easily create multiple custom installations by creating multiple transforms to use with the default package.

See also

- Office 2000 Setup takes full advantage of the improved features of the Windows installer. For more information about Office Setup, see "Office Setup Program" on page 241.

- The Custom Installation Wizard provides great flexibility in customizing the Office installation process. For more information about the changes that you can make during Office Setup, see "Office Custom Installation Wizard" on page 250.

Intelligent Installation—Office 2000 Setup Improvements

In Microsoft Office 97, you had three options when deploying Office throughout an organization:

- Install Office on users' computers so that users can run the applications locally.
- Leave Office on the source (network or CD-ROM), and run the applications over the network.
- Omit rarely needed components from the installation.

Office 2000 Setup offers much more flexibility. You can install exactly what you need—exactly when you need it.

Installing the features you want

In Office 97, you had to install all of the Office applications in the same way. For example, you could not install Microsoft Word on users' computers and run Microsoft PowerPoint from the server—even if most of your users rarely needed PowerPoint.

In Office 2000, the Windows installer technology allows you to choose different installation states for different features. Not only can you install Word locally and leave PowerPoint on the server, but you can also install Word program files locally and leave Word Help files on the server.

Installing files when you need them

In Office 2000, you can select an additional installation option: **Installed on First Use**. If you select this option, the files that make up a feature are not physically installed on a user's computer until the user actually needs the feature.

For example, you can install Word program files to run from the user's hard disk, and you can set the Word Help files to be installed on first use. Setup does not copy the Word Help files to the user's computer during installation, but instead the installer records where the Help files are located if they are ever needed.

The first time that the user clicks **Help** to look for information, Office prompts the installer to copy the Help files to the user's hard disk. After the files are installed, the command proceeds normally. The user might notice a small delay the first time that the command is used.

The main advantage of this option is that you do not need to configure the installation ahead of time with exactly the features your users might need. Instead, this option leaves open multiple possibilities. Installing features on first use not only saves disk space on users' computers but also makes your initial Office installation run much more quickly.

Reinstalling files automatically

Because Office 2000 Setup uses the new Windows installer technology, Office works with the installer to keep track of files on the user's computer. When a user runs an Office application or chooses an Office command, the installer finds the files in the original source location (on the CD-ROM or the network) and runs them.

If a file is accidentally deleted or becomes corrupt, the installer detects this condition and retrieves a new copy of the file from the installation source on the network or Office CD-ROM. This repair process happens automatically, without the user's intervention and without the application failures that might otherwise occur.

Users can also perform this function manually by using the **Detect and Repair** command (**Help** menu) in any Office 2000 application. This command checks all Office files associated with the application. If any files are missing or corrupted, new copies of the files are restored from the installation source.

See also

* Office 2000 Setup has a number of features that make installing Office easier and more flexible than previous versions of Office. For more information about Office Setup, see "Office Setup Program" on page 241.

Custom Installation Wizard Replaces Network Installation Wizard

To customize the installation process in previous versions of Microsoft Office, you used the Network Installation Wizard to modify the text files used by *Acme Setup*—a complex and labor-intensive undertaking. In Office 2000, new tools make this process much more efficient and flexible.

The Office Custom Installation Wizard works with the new Windows installer technology. The choices you make in the Custom Installation Wizard are recorded in a Windows installer *transform* (MST file). When you run the transform with the Windows installer *package* (MSI file), your modifications to the standard installation process are carried out.

Because the original package file remains unchanged, you can create as many different transforms as you wish—which means you can use the wizard to create unique installations of Office 2000 for every department in your organization.

Customizing Office more precisely

The functionality, flexibility, and user interface of the Custom Installation Wizard represent a great improvement over the Network Installation Wizard. The Custom Installation Wizard has been expanded to include new features and extensive online Help.

Unlike the Network Installation Wizard, the new installation technologies in Office 2000 allow you to customize many more aspects of the installation process. By using the Custom Installation Wizard, you can:

- Set installation options for individual Office features, rather than having to set one option for the entire product.
- Hide selected options from users during Setup.
- Add custom files and registry keys to the installation.
- Customize desktop shortcuts for each Office application.
- Set default user options.

Customizing applications beyond Office

Although the Custom Installation Wizard is designed especially for customizing Office 2000 Setup, it can also be used with the broader family of Office-compatible applications—any product that uses the Windows installer technology.

For example, you can use the Custom Installation Wizard to perform any of the following tasks:

- Customize installation of the Microsoft Office 2000 MultiLanguage Pack.
- Customize installation of Microsoft Publisher 2000.
- Specify other applications to run on the user's computer after Office Setup is completed.

The Custom Installation Wizard takes advantage of other Office customization tools as well. For example, you can include an Office profile settings (OPS) file that you create with the Profile Wizard to preset user options in Office applications. You can also run the Microsoft Internet Explorer Administration Kit from within the Custom Installation Wizard to customize the way that Office Setup installs Internet Explorer 5.

See also

- The Custom Installation Wizard makes it easy to customize the Office installation process as well as the user's computer. For more information about the Custom Installation Wizard, see "Office Custom Installation Wizard" on page 250.

New Profile Wizard Collects User Settings

The new Microsoft Profile Wizard helps you upgrade your users to Office 2000 with standard settings across your organization.

Specifying standard user settings

When you upgrade to a new version of a software application, it helps if everyone in your organization can begin learning the application with the same options and settings. Having a consistent base for training can cut down on support costs, especially in the early stages of the conversion process.

There has never been an easy way to install Office with standard settings across an entire organization. Until now. In Office 2000, the Profile Wizard helps you create and distribute a default user profile, including standard locations for files and templates. You can preset options so that users don't have to customize anything.

By using the Profile Wizard, you can also change default values to match your organization's needs or to ensure that users have access to shared templates. When you deploy a standard user profile, all of your users start with the same Office configuration, and you can be sure of a smoother transition.

Storing and retrieving user settings

Organizations today face the challenge of keeping users up and running, with a minimum of downtime. One way that you can dull the pain of events like a computer upgrade or a hardware failure is by using user profiles.

By using the new Profile Wizard, you can store most Office 2000 user settings. Users can back up their settings and restore them to a new computer—and get back to work more quickly, without any noticeable change in their work environment.

See also

- You can use the Profile Wizard with the Office Custom Installation Wizard to distribute a standard *Office user profile* to your users during installation. For more information about creating a standard user profile, see the "Profile Wizard" on page 255.

- To minimize the amount of tweaking that users can do, consider using system policies to lock down certain Office 2000 options. For more information, see "Managing Users' Options with System Policies" on page 279.

Better Design for Deploying Office Internationally

Microsoft Office 2000 combines support for all languages in a single product. Previously, international organizations had to install a separate version of Office in each country. When you use Office 2000, you can now deploy Office 2000 with MultiLanguage Pack around the world and use *plug-in language features* to run applications in local languages.

Installing a single version of Office across your multinational organization simplifies the tasks of deploying, administering, and supporting Office. This design also benefits users by letting them choose a familiar language when they create documents, view online Help, or work with the user interface.

Administering one multilingual installation

Installations of Office 2000 look and behave alike, no matter where they are installed. Anyone, anywhere in your international organization can open, display, edit, or print documents created by anyone else in the organization, provided the operating system supports display and input of the language.

For example, you can standardize your organization on English as the user interface language. If some users need to edit text in Japanese, however, the user interface can provide tools for Asian text layout. Users can also view online Help in their own language, even if the user interface is displayed in English to match the product documentation.

A single multilingual installation of Office 2000 offers new flexibility to users who travel or who work in more than one language:

- Users who travel to an office in another country can run Office in their own language.

- Multilingual users or users who share a computer with someone who speaks a different language can switch the user interface or online Help language.

Customizing for local environments

You can customize Office at deployment by specifying languages for the Office user interface, online Help, and editing tools. Language-specific features in Office 2000 are available according to the languages that you specify during installation or that users specify after installation.

In addition to specifying languages in Office, you must also install the Microsoft Office 2000 MultiLanguage Pack. The MultiLanguage Pack contains the files necessary to run the Office user interface and online Help in a number of languages. It also includes tools, such as spelling and grammar checkers, for many languages.

The MultiLanguage Pack has a Setup program separate from Office, and the installation can be customized to meet the needs of different international users.

Localized versions of Office 2000 are still available

Office 2000 with MultiLanguage Pack is an international core on top of which you can run language features from the MultiLanguage Pack. However, the MultiLanguage Pack does not include plug-in language features for all languages—for example, Excel add-ins are supported only in English.

If your users need to run completely localized software, you can deploy localized versions of Office 2000 and still have the advantage of a shared file format. Users can share documents seamlessly between the localized versions and Office 2000 with MultiLanguage Pack.

See also

- If your organization is international, you can to take advantage of the international features of Office 2000. For more information, see "Overview of International Features in Office 2000" on page 725.

- It is easy to deploy Office to international groups of users. To learn how, see "Deploying Office in a Multinational Setting" on page 151.

Basic Installation Methods

Microsoft Office 2000 provides you with the flexibility to customize and install Office in a number of different ways. The simplest methods of installing a customized version of Office include creating an administrative installation point on the network, or distributing a customized version of Microsoft Office 2000 Disc 1.

How to Install Office from a Network Server

The most common method of deploying a customized version of Microsoft Office 2000 to a large number of users is to create a central copy of Office on a network server. Then users can install Office on their computers over the network. This method provides a number of advantages over having users install Office individually from Microsoft Office 2000 Disc 1:

- You can manage one set of Office files from a central location.
- You can create a standard set of Office features and options for all users.
- You can take advantage of flexible installation options, such as setting features to be installed on first use.
- You have more control when you upgrade Office in the future.

When you install Office from a network server, you first create an *administrative installation point* and customize your version of Office Setup. Then you run Setup on users' computers.

Create an administrative installation point

The administrative installation point is a server share that contains all of the Office files. Users connect to the share and run Setup to install Office on their computers.

▶ **To create an administrative installation point for Office**

1   Create a share on a network server for the administrative installation point.

  The network share must have at least 550 megabytes (MB) of available disk space.

2   On a computer running Microsoft Windows 95/98 or Microsoft Windows NT that has write access to the share, connect to the server share.

3   On the **Start** menu, click **Run**, and then click **Browse**.

4   On Office Disc 1 in the CD-ROM drive, select **setup.exe** and click **Open**.

5   On the command line following **setup.exe**, type **/a data1.msi** and click **OK**.

  For example:

  e:\setup.exe /a data1.msi

6   When prompted by Setup, enter the organization name that you want to define for all users who install Office from this location.

7   When prompted for the installation location, enter the server and share you created.

Setup copies all the files from Office 2000 Disc 1 to the network server, creating a hierarchy of folders in the root folder of the share. Setup also modifies the Windows installer package for Office (Data1.msi), identifying the network share as an administrative installation point. After you create the administrative installation point, you make the share available to users by providing them with read access.

If you need multiple administrative installation points from which users can install Office, then you can run Setup again for each administrative installation point. Alternatively, you can copy the complete folder hierarchy and files from one administrative installation point to multiple servers. If you copy the folders, then each new administrative installation point you create has the same default organization name that you specified in Setup.

When users run Setup to install Office, any Office features that are installed to run from the network use this administrative installation point as the source of Office files, and Office runs the features over the network from this server. Similarly, for features that are set to be installed on first use, Office copies files from this server when needed. If you install features in one of these two states, then you must keep this network server available to your users.

Customize Setup

Before users run Setup to install Office, you can modify the administrative installation point to customize the installation process and default settings. You have three options for customizing Setup:

- Create a custom command line.
- Edit the *Setup settings file*.
- Create a Windows installer *transform* (MST file) by using the Microsoft Custom Installation Wizard.

Create a custom command line

Setup command-line options allow you to define properties that Setup uses to control the installation process. You can also specify whether Setup runs interactively or in quiet mode (without user interaction). Users install Office on their computers by running Setup with your command-line options.

You have several options for distributing command-line options to users:

- You can document the command-line options and have users enter them on the command line when they run Setup.
- You can create a batch file that runs Setup with the options you choose.
- You can run Setup for your users (for example, through a network logon script or through a systems management service) and specify your own command-line options.

For example, you can run Setup in quiet mode, specify a unique organization name, and restart when the installation is complete by entering the following command line:

setup /qn REBOOT="Force" COMPANYNAME="Northwind Traders"

Edit the Setup settings file

The Setup settings file (Setup.ini) is a text file in which you enter properties and values. You can edit the Setup settings file to specify the same properties as you do on the Setup command line—every command-line option has a corresponding setting in the settings file.

The advantage of modifying the Setup settings file is that your custom values are used whenever a user runs Setup from the administrative installation point with no command-line options.

For example, you can run Setup quietly, specify a unique organization name, and restart when the installation is complete by adding these lines to the settings file:

```
[MSI]
MSI=Data1.msi

[Display]
Display=None

[Options]
REBOOT=Force
COMPANYNAME=Northwind Traders
```

You can create more than one settings file with different values, and then you can specify which settings file you want to use with the **/settings** command-line option. For example:

setup.exe /settings newsetup.ini

Create a transform by using the Custom Installation Wizard

The Custom Installation Wizard allows you to specify the same property settings that you can define on the command line or in the settings file, but the wizard also allows you to make many more customizations.

For example, you can select the Office features that you want to install, modify shortcuts, customize options for Microsoft Internet Explorer 5 and Microsoft Outlook, and even add your own custom files to the installation. The wizard saves your selections in a transform.

When you run Setup, you need to specify the transform that you want Setup to use. You can specify an MST file on the Setup command line, or you can set the TRANSFORMS property in the Setup settings file.

For example, this command line specifies the transform Custom.mst:

setup.exe TRANSFORMS="Custom.mst"

In the settings file, these lines specify the same transform:

```
[Options]
TRANSFORMS=Custom.mst
```

Caution Do not alter anything in the administrative installation point other than editing the settings file or adding a transform. Setup relies on the folder hierarchy and files to remain as they are when the administrative installation point is created.

Run Setup on users' computers

After you create and customize the administrative installation point, users can install Office by running Setup from the root folder of the server share. Users can run Setup themselves by using the command-line options, settings file, or transform that you have chosen. For a more controlled installation, you can run Setup for them through a network logon script or systems management software, such as Microsoft Systems Management Server.

See also

- For a complete description of how to use Office Setup to create an administrative installation point from which users can install Office, see "How to Create an Administrative Installation Point" on page 243.

- Office Setup allows you to customize how Office is installed by modifying the command line or the settings file. For more information, including a complete description of command-line options and the settings file, see "Customizing How Setup Runs" on page 215.

- For more advanced customizations, use the Office Custom Installation Wizard to alter the installation process. For more information, see "Customizing How Office Features Are Installed" on page 224.

- Office Setup works well with systems management software, giving you greater flexibility in deploying Office in your organization. For information about using Microsoft Systems Management Server to install Office, see "Deploying Office with Systems Management Server" on page 106.

How to Install Office from a Custom CD-ROM

If you have users who cannot install or run Microsoft Office over the network, you can still create a customized version of Office for them by modifying and distributing a custom copy of Microsoft Office 2000 Disc 1. This option requires that you have the capability to create and distribute CD-ROMs.

Important   You must obtain the proper user licenses before copying, modifying, or distributing a customized version of Office Disc 1. For more information about licensing, see your Microsoft reseller.

The process of customizing Office Disc 1 is similar to the process of customizing an *administrative installation point*. First, you edit the *Setup settings file* or create a Windows installer *transform* (MST file) to use with Setup. However, instead of customizing an administrative installation point on the network, you copy the contents of Office Disc 1 to your hard disk. After modifying the Office installation with your settings, you save and distribute copies of your custom CD-ROM to your users.

Copy Office Disc 1 to your hard disk

Select a folder on your hard disk with at least 496 MB of free space, and copy the complete folder hierarchy and files from Office Disc 1 to the folder. This step creates an exact copy of the CD-ROM contents. You can customize this copy before using it to create custom copies of Office Disc 1.

Note   The folder structure that you copy from Office Disc 1 to your hard disk is nearly identical to the folder structure created by Setup when you create an administrative installation point. However, users cannot perform a network installation from the CD-ROM image. To create a valid administrative installation point, you must use Setup with the **/a** option.

Customize Setup

When users insert Office Disc 1 into a CD-ROM drive, Microsoft Windows uses the Autorun.inf file to run Setup.exe from the CD-ROM. Users can also double-click Setup.exe on the CD-ROM. You can modify your copy of the CD-ROM files on disk to customize the way that Setup.exe installs Office.

You have two options for customizing the way that Office is installed when users run Setup from your custom Office CD-ROM:

- Edit the Setup settings file.
- Create a transform by using the Office Custom Installation Wizard.

Edit the Setup settings file

You edit the Setup settings file (Setup.ini) to define properties that Office Setup uses to control the installation process. You can also specify whether Setup runs interactively or quietly. Setup uses the property values that you define in the settings file and alters the installation process accordingly.

For example, you can run Setup quietly, specify a unique organization name, and restart when the installation is complete by adding these lines to the settings file:

```
[MSI]
MSI=Data1.msi

[Display]
Display=None

[Options]
REBOOT=Force
COMPANYNAME=Northwind Traders
```

Create a transform by using the Custom Installation Wizard

The Custom Installation Wizard allows you to specify the same property settings that you can define on the command line or in the settings file, but the wizard also allows you to make many more customizations.

For example, you can select the Office features that you want to install, modify shortcuts, customize options for Microsoft Internet Explorer 5 and Microsoft Outlook, and even add your own custom files to the installation. The wizard saves your selections in a transform.

When you run Setup, you specify the transform that you want Setup to use by setting the TRANSFORMS property in the Setup settings file. For example, these lines specify the transform Custom.mst:

```
[Options]
TRANSFORMS=Custom.mst
```

Caution   Do not alter anything in the files that you copied from Office Disc 1 to the hard disk other than editing the settings file or adding a transform. Setup relies on the folder hierarchy and files to remain as they are on Office Disc 1.

Copy and distribute your custom CD-ROM

After you have customized your copy of the CD-ROM on disk, you can use this copy to create CD-ROMs for your users. The CD-ROM that you create can be used in the same way as the original Office Disc 1, except that Setup runs with your modifications.

See also

- Office Setup allows you to customize how Office is installed by modifying the Setup settings file. For more information, including a complete description of settings file options, see "Customizing How Setup Runs" on page 215.

- For more advanced customizations, use the Office Custom Installation Wizard to create a transform to alter the installation process. For more information, see "Customizing How Office Features Are Installed" on page 224.

How to Include Office on a Hard Disk Image

Some organizations deploy a complete user system at one time, including Microsoft Windows software, device drivers, application software, and custom configurations. In this scenario, you install the entire system onto a test computer, and then you create an image of the hard disk to copy to users' computers.

You can deploy a customized version of Microsoft Office with the system. Before you make the hard disk image, you install and configure Office on the test computer. You can select the Office features you want users to have, and you can preset any Office application options your users need. Users who receive the disk image begin with Office preconfigured based on your test installation.

Install Office

After you have installed and configured all the system software on the test computer, run Office Setup to install Office. Set the **NOUSERNAME** property on the Setup command line so that a user name is not defined during installation. This step allows users to enter their own user names the first time they run an Office application.

▶ **To install Office on the test computer**

1 On the **Start** menu, click **Run**.

2 Enter the file name and path of Office Setup, and set the NOUSERNAME property on the command line.

   For example, to run Setup from Microsoft Office 2000 Disc 1 in drive E, enter the following command:

   e:\setup.exe NOUSERNAME=True

If you plan to install all Office features to run from the local hard disk, except for those features you choose to make unavailable, you can install Office directly from Office Disc 1. However, if you want to install some features to run from the network, or if you want to set some features to be installed on first use, then you must install Office from an *administrative installation point*. All users who receive the disk image use this administrative installation point as their primary server.

Configure Office

After you install Office on the test computer, you can customize the Office configuration for your users. For example, you can set the default file save format for Word or Excel, or you can customize the toolbars and menus. After you configure Office and distribute the disk image, your users have the customized version of Office ready to run on their computers.

There are two methods you can use to configure Office on the test computer. If you want to set only simple options for Office applications, use the System Policy Editor with the Office policy templates. If you want to customize options that are not available in the policy templates, such as custom toolbar items or custom menu items, run the Office applications on a second test computer, configure Office directly, and save the configuration with the Profile Wizard.

Configure Office with the System Policy Editor

To customize user settings in Office applications, you can use the Office policy templates included with the Microsoft Office 2000 Resource Kit. In addition to creating a system policy file to control user options across a network, the System Policy Editor also allows you to use the policy templates to modify the Windows registry on the local computer.

▶ **To set Office application options with the System Policy Editor**

1   Start the System Policy Editor on the test computer.

2   On the **Options** menu, click **Policy Template**, and then select the templates that you want to use.

3   On the **File** menu, click **Open Registry** to open the local Windows registry.

4   Modify policy values to set Office application options on the test computer.

5   On the **File** menu, click **Save**.

The values that you modify are written to the Windows registry on the test computer.

6   On the **File** menu, click **Exit**.

Configure Office with the Profile Wizard

To configure Office options that are not available through policy templates, you can configure Office on a second test computer and then use the Profile Wizard to copy your Office configuration to the original test computer on which you are building the hard disk image. Your choices are replicated for every user who installs Office from the hard disk image.

Note Do not run Office on the test computer on which you are building the hard disk image. The first time you run an Office application after installing Office, you are prompted for a user name, which is then used by all Office applications. If you run an Office application on the original test computer, the user name you enter is saved in the disk image you create from that computer. By default., all users who run Office from the disk image are given the name you enter.

▶ **To configure Office with the Profile Wizard**

1 On a second test computer, install Office 2000 in the same way you installed Office on the original test computer.

2 Run Office applications on the second test computer to set options, customize toolbars and menus, customize default templates, and so forth.

3 Run the Profile Wizard on the second test computer and select **Save the settings from this machine** on the **Save or Restore Settings** panel.

4 Enter a file name and path for the *OPS file* you want to create, and click **Finish**.

5 Run the Profile Wizard on the original test computer and select **Restore previously saved settings** on the **Save or Restore Settings** panel.

6 Enter the file name and path for the OPS file, and click **Finish**.

After the Profile Wizard copies the Office configuration to the original test computer, you can create the hard disk image from that computer. Your Office configuration is replicated to every user who runs Office from the hard disk image.

Create multiple hard disk images

If you need to create a set of different disk images, but you want to use the same Office configuration for each image, you can install and configure Office separately on each test computer. Or you can use the following method to duplicate your original Office installation.

▶ **To create identical Office installations for multiple hard disk images**

1 Create an administrative installation point on the network.

2 By using the Office Custom Installation Wizard, customize the administrative installation point and record your settings in a Windows installer *transform* (MST file).

3 Install Office on one test computer from the administrative installation point.

4 On the test computer, run the Office applications and modify application settings.

5 By using the Profile Wizard, save your application settings in an Office profile settings (OPS) file.

6 By using the Custom Installation Wizard, include the OPS file in the transform on the administrative installation point.

7 Run Setup on each test computer with the modified transform.

   For example, to run Setup quietly with the transform Newsetup.mst, enter the following command line:

   setup.exe /qb TRANSFORMS=Newsetup.mst

Each computer on which you run Setup in this way has an identical installation of Office.

See also

- For a complete description of how to use Office Setup to create an administrative installation point from which users can install Office, see "How to Create an Administrative Installation Point" on page 243.

- Office Setup allows you to customize how Office is installed by modifying the *Setup settings file*. For more information, including a complete description of settings file options, see "Customizing How Setup Runs" on page 215.

- For more advanced customizations, use the Office Custom Installation Wizard to alter the installation process. For more information, see "Customizing How Office Features Are Installed" on page 224.

Installing Office in a Windows Terminal Server Environment

Microsoft Office 2000 has been designed to work effectively with Microsoft Windows NT Server version 4.0, Terminal Server Edition. Terminal Server allows users to run Windows-based programs on computers that cannot run the latest versions of Windows. With Terminal Server, you can deploy Office 2000 on the server and have users run Office applications over the network.

Using Office 2000 with Windows Terminal Server

Microsoft Windows NT Server version 4.0, Terminal Server Edition provides a thin-client solution in which Windows-based programs are executed on the server and remotely displayed on the client. If your users have computers with limited disk space, memory, or processing speed, you can install Microsoft Office 2000 to run in this environment.

Important   You must install Microsoft Windows NT 4.0 Terminal Server, Service Pack 4 on the Terminal Server computer before installing Office 2000. You can obtain Service Pack 4 from the Microsoft Web site at http:// www.microsoft.com.

With Terminal Server, you install a single copy of Office on the Terminal Server computer. Instead of running Office locally on their hard disks, multiple users can connect to the server and run Office from there.

Toolbox

Because of the special requirements for running Office in a Windows Terminal Server environment, you must use the transform provided in the Office Resource Kit to install Office on the Terminal Server computer. Office Setup does not install Office on the Terminal Server computer without this transform. For information about installing TermSrvr.mst, see "Terminal Server Tools" on page 778.

The following is an overview of how you use Office with Terminal Server:

1   The administrator installs a single copy of Office on the Terminal Server computer.

2   Users install Windows Terminal Client on their computers.

3   Users log on to the Terminal Server computer, start Windows, and run Office from within the Windows session.

   The Office applications run on the Terminal Server computer, and only the Windows display is transmitted to users' computers.

In the Terminal Server environment, Office 2000 separates application and user data, and uses environmental information supplied by Terminal Server. This arrangement allows multiple Terminal Client users to run from the same Office installation.

To improve performance in the Terminal Server environment, Office optimizes certain functions in the Office applications to reduce the amount of network traffic necessary to update the user's display. For example, in the Terminal Server environment, Office applications display a text-based splash screen, rather than the standard graphics-based screen—the text-based screen is faster to display.

Tip You can improve the performance of Office in a Terminal Server environment even more by reducing the amount of incidental display information transmitted over the network. For example, select the Office Logo Office Assistant, which uses the least amount of animation, and set application options that eliminate menu or cursor animations. Or install the Motionless Office Assistant from the Office Resource Kit.

How to Install Office Disc 1 on a Windows Terminal Server

You install Microsoft Office 2000 from Microsoft Office 2000 Disc 1 on a Microsoft Windows Terminal Server computer in much the same way you install Office on a client computer. With some careful planning and a few modifications, Office performs well in the Windows Terminal Server environment.

To run Office 2000 in this environment, follow these steps:

1   Customize the Terminal Server *transform* (MST file).

2   Install Office on the Terminal Server computer.

3   Set default Office application settings for Windows Terminal Client users.

4   Configure Microsoft Outlook 2000.

Running Office on individual users' computers is different from running it in a Terminal Server environment. When you install Office on a Terminal Server computer, the users who connect to the server are limited to your Office configuration and cannot install or remove features.

In other words, all users running Office from the Terminal Server computer inherit the features you select during installation. If your users need different sets of Office functionality, you might need several Terminal Server computers—one for each unique Office configuration.

Because of the multiuser nature of the Terminal Server computer, and users' restricted access to the server, you cannot select the following installation options for any Office features:

- **Run from CD** or **Run from Network**
- **Run all from CD** or **Run all from Network**
- **Installed on First Use**

Instead, you must predetermine which Office features your users need and select one of the following installation options for each feature:

- **Run from My Computer**
- **Run all from My Computer**
- **Not Available**

Customize the Terminal Server transform

The Microsoft Office 2000 Resource Kit includes a Windows installer transform that you must use when installing Office on the Terminal Server computer—Setup does not install Office on the Terminal Server computer without the transform. This transform, named TermSrvr.mst, is configured to install all Office features to run from the local computer or not be installed at all.

Toolbox

Because of the special requirements for running Office in a Windows Terminal Server environment, you must use the transform provided in the Office Resource Kit to install Office on the Terminal Server computer. Office Setup does not install Office on the Terminal Server computer without this transform. For information about installing TermSrvr.mst, see "Terminal Server Tools" on page 778.

What the TermSrvr.mst file does

The Windows installer transform included in the Office Resource Kit, TermSrvr.mst, is configured to install Office correctly on the Terminal Server computer. Office Setup does not install Office on the Terminal Server computer without this transform.

The primary function of the TermSrvr.mst file is to modify the feature tree so that all Office features are installed to run from the local computer. There are a few exceptions—those features that are not recommended or that do not perform well in the Terminal Server environment are set to not be installed at all.

In addition, the **NOUSERNAME** property is set so that Setup does not supply a default user name when you install Office on the Terminal Server computer. This setting ensures that users who log on to the Terminal Server computer are asked to provide a user name when they run an Office application for the first time. This property is set internally in the transform—if you examine the transform with the Custom Installation Wizard, you do not see the **NOUSERNAME** property listed on the **Modify Setup Properties** panel.

The TermSrvr.mst file also sets a property to increase the amount of registry space allocated for Office on the Terminal Server computer. This setting allows Office to store necessary information in the registry for each Office user. Again, this property is not listed on the **Modify Setup Properties** panel.

In the TermSrvr.mst file, all Office features are set to one of the following installation states:

- Most features are set to **Run from My Computer**.

  These are features that work well in the Terminal Server environment.

- A few features are set to **Not Available**.

  These are features that do not perform well in the Terminal Server environment, typically because they use additional animation that generates excess data traffic between the Terminal Server computer and the Terminal Client computer. Consider leaving these features set to **Not Available** so that they are not installed.

- A few features are set to both **Not Available** and **Hidden**.

  These features do not work under Terminal Server because they rely on capabilities not available in this environment or they require write access to restricted areas of the Terminal Server computer. Leave these features set to **Not Available** so that they are not installed on the Terminal Server computer.

- Some features are set to **Run from My Computer** and **Hidden**.

  These are features that are normally hidden in the Office Setup feature tree, but they have been exposed in the Custom Installation Wizard so that you can choose whether you want to install them.

Toolbox

A number of Outlook features, normally hidden in the Office Setup feature tree, are exposed in the Terminal Server transform. This arrangement allows you to choose whether to install these features. The Office Resource Kit includes an Excel workbook named OutlFeat.xls that describes these Outlook features. For information about installing OutlFeat.xls, see "Terminal Server Tools" on page 778.

If you want to accept the default Office configuration, you do not need to modify TermSrvr.mst. However, if there are Office features that are not needed by your users, you can improve overall performance and conserve disk space by customizing TermSrvr.mst so that Office Setup does not install these features on the Terminal Server computer.

Installing nonEnglish versions of Office

The TermSrvr.mst file was created using the Windows installer *package* (Data1.msi) for the US English version of Office 2000. Some other language versions of Office have additional features that are not present in the US English version, and the TermSrvr.mst file does not change the installation states of those features. If any of these additional features are set to **Run from Network** or **Installed on First Use**, then they do not function correctly on the Terminal Server computer.

To install a nonEnglish version of Office on a Terminal Server computer, use the Office Custom Installation Wizard to make sure that all features in the transform are set to either **Run from My Computer** or **Not Available**.

▶ **To customize the Terminal Server transform**

1 Start the Office Custom Installation Wizard.

2 On the **Open the MSI File** panel, specify the Office MSI file, Data1.msi.

3 On the **Open the MST File** panel, select **Open an existing MST file** and enter the file name and path of the TermSrvr.mst file.

4 On the **Select the MST File to Save** panel, enter the file name and path of the TermSrvr.mst file.

   If you do not want to modify the original MST file, then you can enter a new file name for the wizard to create.

5 On the **Set Feature Installation States** panel, set unneeded features to **Not Available**.

   Make sure that all features that you want to install are set to **Run from My Computer**.

6 If you are installing Outlook, under **Microsoft Outlook for Windows\OutlookMessaging**, select either **OutlookMAPI** or **OutlookOMI**; set one feature to **Run from My Computer** and the other feature to **Not Available**.

7 On the **Customize Outlook Installation Options** panel, select **Customize Outlook profile and account information** and set **Configuration Type** to either **Corporate or Workgroup Settings** or **Internet Only Settings**.

   This choice must match your choice in Step 5. If you select **OutlookMAPI**, you must select **Corporate or Workgroup Settings**; if you select **OutlookOMI,** you must select **Internet Only Settings**. Because users are restricted in how they can configure the Terminal Server computer after installation, you must make this selection during installation.

8 On the remainder of the panels, make additional customizations to tailor the Office installation on the Terminal Server computer.

   For example, to fully customize how Internet Explorer 5 is installed, click **Customize** on the **Customize IE5 Installation Options** panel.

Toolbox

By default, the Terminal Server transform (TermSrvr.mst) does not install any Office Assistants. However, after running Office Setup you can install the Motionless Office Assistant (Stillogo.acs) included in the Office Resource Kit. This Office Assistant uses no animation, so there is minimal network traffic between the Terminal Server computer and the Terminal Client computer. For information about installing the Motionless Office Assistant, see "Terminal Server Tools" on page 778.

Install Office on the Terminal Server computer

To install Office, run Office Setup on the Terminal Server computer. You can run Setup from a network *administrative installation point* or from the Office Disc 1. You must specify the Terminal Server transform (TermSrvr.mst) and additional command-line options.

Note   Before you install Office on a Terminal Server computer, log on to the server with *administrator privileges*.

▶ **To install Office Disc 1 on the Terminal Server computer**

1   In Control Panel, double-click **Add/Remove Programs**, click **Install,** and then click **Next**.

2   Click **Browse**.

3   In the root folder of the Office Disc 1, select **setup.exe** and click **OK**.

   Setup.exe is added to the **Command line for installation program** box.

4   On the command line, add the following two commands after **setup.exe**, separated by spaces:

   TRANSFORMS="*path***\TermSrvr.mst"**

   This command identifies the Terminal Server transform for Setup to use during installation. Specify the correct *path* to the MST file.

   /l* "%WINDIR%\Office 2000 Setup(0001).txt"

   This optional command places the Setup log file in the Windows folder, rather than in the %TEMP% folder, so that it is not deleted automatically by Windows.

5   Click **Next**

6   In **Add/Remove Programs**, select **All users begin with common application settings**, and then click **Next** to run Office Setup.

Important   You must use **Add/Remove Programs** in Control Panel with the **All users begin with common application settings** option selected. This setting runs Setup in *Install mode*, which installs Office for all Terminal Client users who connect to the Terminal Server computer. If you run Setup directly from Office Disc 1, then Setup runs in *Execute mode*, which installs Office only for the user running Setup.

Set default Office application settings

You can use the Profile Wizard to customize the default Office user settings for all users logging on to the Terminal Server computer. For best performance in this environment, consider setting the following options in Office applications.

Microsoft Access 2000

- On the **Tools** menu, click **Customize**, and then click the **Options** tab. Set the **Menu animations** option to **None**.

- On the **Tools** menu and then click **Customize**. Remove the **Detect and Repair** command from the **Help** menu.

- On the **Tools** menu, click **Options,** and then click the **General** tab. Clear the **Provide feedback with sound** check box.

Microsoft Excel 2000

- On the **Tools** menu, click **Customize** and then click the **Options** tab. Set the **Menu animations** option to **None**.

- On the **Tools** menu and then click **Customize**. Remove the **Detect and Repair** command from the **Help** menu.

- On the **Tools** menu, click **Options,** and then click the **Edit** tab. Clear the **Provide feedback with animation** check box.

- On the **Tools** menu, click **Options,** and then click the **General** tab. Clear the **Provide feedback with sound** check box.

Microsoft FrontPage 2000

- On the **Tools** menu, click **Customize,** and then click the **Options** tab. Set the **Menu animations** option to **None**.

Microsoft Outlook 2000

- On the **Tools** menu, click **Customize**, and then click the **Options** tab. Set the **Menu animations** option to **None**.

- On the **Tools** menu, click **Customize**, and then click the **Commands** tab. Remove the **Save as Web Page** command from the **File** menu, and remove the **Detect and Repair** command from the **Help** menu.

- On the **Tools** menu, click **Options**, and then click the **Other** tab. Click **Advanced Options** and clear the **Provide feedback with sound** check box.

- On the **Tools** menu, click **Options**, and then click the **Preferences** tab. Click **E-mail Options** and clear the **Display a notification message when new mail arrives** check box.

- On the **Tools** menu, click **Options**, and then click the **Preferences** tab. Click **E-mail Options**, click **Advanced E-mail Options**, and clear the **Play a sound** and **Briefly change the mouse cursor** check boxes.

- On the **Tools** menu, click **Options**, and then click the **Preferences** tab. Click **Calendar Options** and clear the **Use Microsoft Schedule+ as my primary calendar** check box.

Microsoft PowerPoint 2000

- On the **Tools** menu, click **Customize** and then click the **Options** tab. Set the **Menu animations** option to **None**.

- On the **Tools** menu and then click **Customize**. Remove the **Detect and Repair** command from the **Help** menu.

- On the **Tools** menu, click **Options,** and then click the **General** tab. Clear the **Provide feedback with sound to screen elements** check box.

- On the **Tools** menu, click **Options**, and then click the **Spelling and Style** tab. Clear the **Check spelling as you type** check box.

- On the **Tools** menu, click **Options**, and then click the **General** tab. Click **Web Options**, click the **General** tab, and clear the **Show slide animation while browsing** check box.

Microsoft Word 2000

- On the **Tools** menu, click **Customize** and then click the **Options** tab. Set the **Menu animations** option to **None**.

- On the **Tools** menu and then click **Customize**. Remove the **Detect and Repair** command from the **Help** menu.

- On the **Tools** menu, click **Options**, and then click the **General** tab. Clear the **Provide feedback with animation** and **Provide feedback with sound** check boxes.

- On the **Tools** menu, click **Options**, and then click the **Spelling and Grammar** tab. Clear the **Check grammar as you type** check box.

After you customize all the application settings you want, run the Profile Wizard and save your settings in an *OPS file*. Store the OPS file in a folder that is accessible to users running Office from the Terminal Server computer.

▶ **To point users to your customized settings**

1   On the **Start** menu, click **Run**, and type **regedit.exe** to open the Windows Registry Editor.

2   Create a new subkey named RunOnce in the following subkey:

HKEY_LOCAL_MACHINE\SOFTWARE\Microsoft\Windows NT\CurrentVersion \Terminal Server\Install\Software\Microsoft\Windows\Current Version

3   In the RunOnce subkey, create a new entry with a string value and any value name.

4   Set the value of the new entry to the following:

path**Proflwiz.exe** /r *file* /**q**

where *path* is the fully qualified path to the Profile Wizard, and *file* is the file name and fully qualified path to the OPS file you created.

When users log on to the Terminal Server computer, Windows runs the Profile Wizard using the command line in the RunOnce subkey and restores the settings you saved in the OPS file. This command runs one time for each user the first time the user logs on to the Terminal Server computer.

Configure Microsoft Outlook 2000

To complete the installation of Outlook 2000, you need to perform two additional steps after running Office Setup. First: run Outlook 2000 once; and second, optionally provide write access to a portion of the Windows registry.

Outlook 2000 performs a number of initialization tasks when it runs for the first time on the Terminal Server computer. These tasks complete the Outlook installation and require write access to system areas on the Terminal Server computer.

▶ To allow Outlook to finish installing

1   Before any user runs Outlook on the Terminal Server computer, log on to the Terminal Server computer as the administrator.

2   Run Outlook.

    Outlook completes any remaining installation tasks.

3   Exit Outlook.

By default, users have write access to all portions of the Windows registry on the Terminal Server computer. However, if you have any custom Outlook forms installed on the computer, and you have configured the Windows registry on the Terminal Server computer to restrict user access, then you need to make sure that users have write access to the HKEY_CLASSES_ROOT\CLSID key in the Windows registry.

Outlook registers custom forms the first time that they are opened, and this requires that the user have write access to this portion of the registry.

▶ To give users write access to the CLSID key

1   Log on to the Terminal Server computer as the administrator.

2   On the **Start** menu, click **Run**.

3   Type **regedt32.exe** and click **OK**.

4   In the **HKEY_CLASSES_ROOT** window, select **CLSID**.

5   On the **Security** menu, click **Permissions**.

6   In the **Registry Key Permissions** dialog box, select the **Replace Permission on Existing Subkeys** check box, and then click **Add**.

7   In the **Name** box, click **Everyone,** click **Add**, and then click **OK**.

    If you do not want to give all users this access, you can add specific users or groups of users in the **Names** box, rather than selecting **Everyone**.

8   In the **Type of Access** box, select **Special Access**, and then select the **Query Value**, **Set Value**, and **Create Subkey** check boxes.

9   Click **OK** and close the Registry Editor.

See also

- Office 2000 Setup contains other options that you may want to take advantage of, such as installing Microsoft Internet Explorer 5 and removing previous versions of Office. For more information about Office 2000 Setup, see "Office Setup Program" on page 241.

- By using the Office 2000 Custom Installation Wizard, you can modify TermSrvr.mst to further customize your Terminal Server installation. For more information about the Custom Installation Wizard, see "Office Custom Installation Wizard" on page 250.

- For more information about the user settings that the Profile Wizard saves and restores, see "Profile Wizard" on page 255.

How to Install Office Disc 2 on a Windows Terminal Server

You install Microsoft Publisher 2000 and other applications from Microsoft Office 2000 Disc 2 on a Windows Terminal Server computer in much the same way you install Microsoft Office 2000 Disc 1 on a Terminal Server computer, except that no special *transform* (MST file) is needed.

Running Publisher on individual users' computers is different than running it in a Windows Terminal Server environment. When you install Publisher on a Terminal Server computer, the users who connect to the server are limited to your Publisher configuration.

In other words, all users running Publisher from the Terminal Server computer inherit the features you select and the options you set during installation. If your users need different sets of Publisher functionality, you might need several Terminal Server computers—one for each unique Publisher configuration.

Important   To run Setup, you must use **Add/Remove Programs** in Control Panel with the **All users begin with common application settings** option selected. This setting runs Setup in *Install mode*, which installs Office for all Terminal Client users who connect to the Terminal Server. If you run Setup directly from Office Disc 2, then Setup runs in *Execute mode,* which installs Office only for the user running Setup.

▶ **To install Office Disc 2 on a Terminal Server computer**

1   In Control Panel, double-click **Add/Remove Programs**, click **Install,** and then click **Next**.

2   Click **Browse**.

3   In the root folder of Office Disc 2, select **setup.exe** and click **OK**.

   Setup.exe is added to the **Command line for installation program** box.

4   On the command line, add the following command after Setup.exe, separated by a space:

   NOUSERNAME=True

   With this property setting, Office prompts each user for a user name when the user runs an Office application for the first time.

5   Select **All users begin with common application settings**, and then click **Finish** to run Office Setup.

6   On the **Ready to Install** panel in Office Setup, click **Customize**.

7   On the **Selecting Features** panel, select Microsoft Office and click **Run all from My Computer**.

8   Expand the feature tree and select **Not Available** for each feature you do not want to install.

Note If you install all the clip art files on the Terminal Server computer, you need approximately 400 MB of available disk space.

The following Office Disc 2 features do not perform well in the Terminal Server environment, so consider setting them to **Not Available**:

- All individual Office assistants

Leave the **Office Assistant** feature itself set to **Run from My Computer**. This setting installs the files necessary to support an Office assistant you might want to install later (such as the Motionless Office Assistant, which is included in the Office Resource Kit).

In addition, the following Office Disc 2 features are not supported in the Terminal Server environment, so set them to **Not Available**:

- **Microsoft Small Business Tools**
- **Scanner and Camera Add-In**
- **System Information**

Toolbox

After running Office Disc 2 Setup, you can install the Motionless Office Assistant (Stillogo.acs) included in the Office Resource Kit. This Office Assistant uses no animation, so there is minimal network traffic between the Terminal Server computer and the Terminal Client computer. For information about installing the Motionless Office Assistant, see "Terminal Server Tools" on page 778.

See also

- The procedure for installing Office Disc 2 is very similar to the procedure for installing Office Disc 1, except that the use of a transform is not required. For more information, see "How to Install Office Disc 1 on a Windows Terminal Server" on page 93.

Deploying Office with Systems Management Server

Microsoft Systems Management Server (SMS) is a powerful software package that can be used to assess your computing environment and to deploy new software. You can deploy Microsoft Office 2000 and many other applications with SMS by creating Systems Management Server packages and distributing them to selected clients. New wizards and other enhancements make it easy to deploy multiple applications with Systems Management Server version 2.0.

This topic presents a high-level overview of using Systems Management Server to deploy Office 2000. For more information about installing SMS and detailed procedures for using SMS to deploy Office 2000, see updated information about SMS on the Office Resource Kit Web site at http://www.microsoft.com/office/ork/.

Assessing Your Network Resources

Before you deploy Microsoft Office 2000 in your organization, you must use the software inventory, hardware inventory, and query features of Systems Management Server to determine which client computers in your organization can receive an upgrade and which client computers need a hardware upgrade before you install Office 2000.

You can also use the SMS Network Monitor tool to assess your network environment to determine the impact that deployment will have on your current network resources. Finally, you must determine which servers in your network will host Microsoft Office Server Extensions (OSE).

The network can be used in two ways to deploy Office 2000. You can install Office 2000 on client computers from a network server, or you can run Office 2000 applications over the network from a server. You might need different configurations for the different levels of network connectivity within your organization.

Wide area network (WAN) connections   For client computers connected over a slow-link network, installing or running Office 2000 remotely over the network might not be practical.

Network operating systems in use   Your particular network operating system might affect your plans for deploying Office 2000. Some issues to consider include server file sharing methods and client-server permission schemes.

Network bandwidth   Installing Office 2000 over the network or running Office 2000 applications over the network place different demands on network bandwidth, both in response time and in length of time connected. You can use Network Monitor, a Systems Management Server utility, to help identify network traffic patterns and network problems.

Collecting hardware inventory

Before you run queries, you must first collect hardware inventory. When you collect hardware inventory for the computers in your network, Systems Management Server automatically gathers a wide variety of information about each computer. Some of the most important information collected includes the following:

- Processor type and speed
- Memory capacity
- BIOS
- Hard disk space

This information helps determine whether a user's computer is capable of running Office 2000. Queries, collections, and reports that ship with Systems Management Server can help you categorize your systems. A basic query for Office 2000 checks the amount of RAM, disk space, and processor type and speed on users' computers. You can also use reports generated from this information to plan for future upgrades.

Collecting software inventory

Before you upgrade to Office 2000, you need accurate software inventory for existing servers and client computers. Then you can use a query to determine what operating system and application software programs are running when you plan your Office 2000 deployment.

You can use Systems Management Server software inventory capabilities to collect information about the software running on client computers, including installed user configurations and operating environments and installed versions of Office. This information helps you determine which computers are ready for the Office 2000 upgrade.

See also

- For more information about creating queries in Systems Management Server 1.2, see the *Microsoft Systems Management Server 1.2 Resource Guide* in the *Microsoft BackOffice Resource Kit, Second Edition*.

Targeting Client Computers for Upgrade

Running queries on hardware and software inventory data produces a list of target computers that can be upgraded to Microsoft Office 2000. Depending on the number of computers in this inventory, you can divide the computers into groups and stagger the distribution of Office 2000. These subsets are known as machine groups in Microsoft Systems Management Server version 1.2, and collections in Microsoft Systems Management Server version 2.0.

Preparing for Distribution of Office 2000

Microsoft Systems Management Server (SMS) uses *distribution points* to store the files needed to distribute programs to client computers. Distribution points are servers on your site to which client computers connect to download applications or files. The software distribution process places the files required for Office Setup on previously defined distribution points.

The following steps are required for preparing an Office 2000 deployment with Systems Management Server:

- Select distribution points for the installation.

  You can use the Manage Distribution Points Wizard in the SMS Administrator to select distribution points (SMS 2.0 only).

- Create an administrative installation point and copy it to the package source directory on your site server.

  Software distribution replicates these files to each distribution point.

- Use the Office Custom Installation Wizard to add the Off9spec.ini file to a Windows installer *transform* (MST file) when you deploy Office (SMS 1.2 only).

  This step is required to properly inventory Office 2000 after deployment. It is not required for SMS 2.0.

- Modify the package definition files (PDFs) as needed for your installation.

  If you are installing Office 2000 Premium, the PDF files are named Off9pre.pdf (SMS 1.2) and Off9pre.sms (SMS 2.0). When you modify a PDF, you can add a custom transform, or change the Setup command line.

- Copy the PDFs that are included in the packages into the root directory of the administrative installation point.

  You must also copy any auxiliary files created by the Custom Installation Wizard or the SMS Installer.

See also

- For more information about creating and modifying PDF files in Systems Management Server 2.0, see the *Microsoft Systems Management Server 2.0 Resource Guide* in the *BackOffice 4.5 Resource Kit.*

- For more information about creating software distributions in Systems Management Server 2.0, see the *Microsoft Systems Management Server 2.0 Administrator's Guide*, which comes with SMS 2.0.

- The Office Resource Kit includes step-by-step instructions for creating an administrative installation point. For more information, see "How to Install Office from a Network Server" on page 80.

- The new Windows installer technology uses Windows installer transforms (MST files) to apply changes to the standard Office installation. For more information, see "Office Setup Program" on page 241.

Using Systems Management Server to Deploy Office Applications Separately

Microsoft Office 2000 Setup installs a number of applications and features in addition to the standard Office 2000 suite. For example, using Office Setup, you can install Microsoft Outlook 2000, Microsoft Internet Explorer 5, and Microsoft PhotoDraw™ 2000 separately from your main Office installation.

You can leverage Microsoft Systems Management Server (SMS) to install specific Office applications or features and to ensure that any prerequisite applications are installed prior to your deployment of Office 2000.

Systems Management Server can perform the standard installation for a number of Office configurations. The following table lists the choices that are available, as well as the corresponding package definition files and INI files.

Software	PDFs and INIs (SMS 1.2)	PDFs (SMS 2.0)
Office Premium	Off9pre.pdf, Off9spec.ini	Off9pre.sms
Office Professional	Off9pro.pdf, Off9spec.ini	Off9pro.sms
Office Small Business	Off9sbe.pdf, Off9spec.ini	Off9sbe.sms
Office Standard	Off9std.pdf, Off9spec.ini	Off9std.sms
Access	Acc2000.pdf, Accspec.ini	Acc2000.sms
Excel	Xl2000.pdf, Xlspec.ini	Xl2000.sms
FrontPage	Fp2000.pdf, Fpspec.ini	Fp2000.sms
Outlook	Outl2000.pdf, Outlspec.ini	Outl2000.sms
PowerPoint	Ppt2000.pdf, Pptspec.ini	Ppt2000.sms
Word	Word2000.pdf, Wordspec.ini	Word2000.sms
Publisher	Pub2000.pdf, Pubspec.ini	Pub2000.sms
Office Disc 2	Off9cd2.pdf, Off9cd2.ini	Off9cd2.sms

Note   Each of these PDF files can be used only with the corresponding Office application or set of applications. For example, Fp2000.pdf can be used to deploy the standalone FrontPage 2000 application; it cannot be used to deploy FrontPage 2000 with Office 2000 Premium. Only SMS 1.2 requires INI files.

Installing PhotoDraw 2000 separately

In addition to using the package definition files and INI files to install specific Office applications, Systems Management Server can be used to facilitate these separate installations in other ways. The following example of the PhotoDraw installation highlights a common strategy.

For PhotoDraw to work properly, users must be running Microsoft Windows 95/98 or Microsoft Windows NT 4.0 with Service Pack 3 or later. In addition, the following software must be installed:

- Microsoft Internet Explorer version 4.0 or later.
- Microsoft DirectX® version 6.0 (Windows 95/98 only).

When you install PhotoDraw from the command line or from a network location, Setup does not detect the existence of the prerequisite applications. If you plan to use either of these network strategies to install PhotoDraw, consider using Systems Management Server to facilitate the process.

You can use the software inventory capabilities of Systems Management Server to create a machine group or collection that meets the required criteria. Not only can Systems Management Server detect the existence of the prerequisite applications, but it can also trigger their installation if the software is not found.

See also

- For more information about installing PhotoDraw, see "Using Acme Setup to Install PhotoDraw" on page 202.
- For more information about installing Outlook 2000 separately from Office, see "Installing Outlook 2000 After Installing Office 2000" on page 201.

How to Create Systems Management Server Packages for Your Office Installation

To begin Microsoft Office deployment with Microsoft Systems Management Server (SMS), you need to create a Systems Management Server *package*. Systems Management Server packages define both the files required to install the software, as well as configuration and identification information for the package itself. When you create a package, you must specify a Setup command line.

Use a package definition file

In Systems Management Server 1.2 and 2.0, you use package definition files (PDFs) to deploy Office. A PDF is an ASCII text file that contains predefined **Workstations**, **Sharing**, and **Inventory** property settings for a package. When you import a PDF, the properties of the package are automatically entered for you.

You can import the PDFs into the Distribute Software Wizard to complete the entire distribution in a single step, or you can import them into the Create Package from Definition Wizard to create just the software package. The Distribute Software Wizard is available only in Systems Management Server 2.0.

When the wizard is completed, Systems Management Server displays the new package in the SMS Administrator . By default, the User and Guest accounts are granted Change *permissions* to the package share on distribution points. You can modify the packages and programs by using the SMS Administrator.

Toolbox

Systems Management Server includes package definition files for a number of software applications and operating systems. The Office Resource Kit includes PDFs for Office 2000. For information about installing these PDFs, see "Systems Management Server Package Definition Files" on page 780.

See also

- For more information about deploying software with Systems Management Server 1.2, see the Microsoft Systems Management Server 1.2 Resource Guide in the Microsoft BackOffice Resource Kit, Second Edition.

- For more information about deploying software with Systems Management Server 2.0, see the *Microsoft Systems Management Server 2.0 Administrator's Guide,* which comes with SMS 2.0. Information is also available in the *Microsoft Systems Management Server 2.0 Resource Guide* in the *Microsoft BackOffice 4.5 Resource Kit.*

- For information about new developments and tools for Systems Management Server, see the Microsoft Systems Management Server Web site at http://www.microsoft.com/smsmgmt/.

How to Distribute Systems Management Server Packages

When you distribute a Microsoft Systems Management Server (SMS) package, you must specify which computers receive the package, where the source files for the installation are located, and when the installation occurs.

In Systems Management Server 2.0, the distribution of packages to clients is a two-step process. First you create the package and send it to the *distribution points*; then you create an *advertisement*.

Systems Management Server 2.0 uses distribution points to store the files needed to distribute programs to clients. To run advertised programs, clients must have access to at least one distribution point. To send packages to distribution points, you use the Manage Distribution Points Wizard.

Like a job in Systems Management Server 1.2, a Systems Management Server 2.0 advertisement specifies the program to run on the client, the target collection that receives the package, and the schedule of when the program is available to clients.

Deploying Multiple Applications with Systems Management Server

By using Microsoft Systems Management Server (SMS), you can install Microsoft Office 2000 features individually or in sets. For example, you can distribute Office 2000 to all clients but deploy Microsoft Outlook and Microsoft Publisher on only a subset of those clients. Both Systems Management Server version 1.2 and Systems Management Server version 2.0 provide the flexibility to let you choose which Office features are installed.

Deploying multiple applications by using SMS 1.2

Although Systems Management Server 1.2 does not natively support consecutive installation of multiple applications, you can use a batch file to control Systems Management Server application distribution. By enclosing the Setup command between **START** and **/w** on the command line, you can control the chronological installation of applications. This method halts the batch file until Setup is complete. When Setup is done, the batch file continues processing. Alternatively, you can use simple logic in the batch file to check for files prior to starting Office Setup.

Note When Package Command Manager (PCM) runs an installation program, it maps an available drive to the Systems Management Server Distribution server package share. Because this drive letter is dynamic, batch files created to install applications through Systems Management Server cannot depend on specific drive letters. The batch file created to perform the customized installation must be placed in the source directory of the Systems Management Server package.

See also

- You can customize many aspects of your Office installation, include specifying which Office programs or features are installed on users' computers. For more information, see "Customizing How Office Features Are Installed" on page 224.

Managing a Successive Deployment of Office Premium and Related Products

The applications and tools included with Microsoft Office 2000 Premium provide a wide range of functionality for users. Office-related products include security enhancements for Microsoft Outlook 2000 and plug-in language features in the Microsoft Office 2000 MultiLanguage Pack. You can install these Office-related applications and tools on users' computers at the same time that you deploy Office, or you can stagger the deployment and install them when and where you need them.

Software That You Can Install with Office 2000 Premium

Microsoft Office 2000 Premium contains the following software:

- Microsoft Access 2000
- Microsoft Excel 2000
- Microsoft FrontPage 2000
- Microsoft Outlook 2000
- Microsoft PowerPoint 2000
- Microsoft Word 2000
- Microsoft Internet Explorer 5
- Microsoft Publisher 2000
- Microsoft PhotoDraw 2000
- Microsoft Office Server Extensions
- Microsoft Office Web Components
- Other applications and tools for Office

You install the software from the following Office 2000 Premium CD-ROMs:

Disc 1   Office (Access, Excel, FrontPage, Outlook, PowerPoint, and Word), Microsoft Data Engine, and Internet Explorer 5

Disc 2   Publisher, Small Business Tools, and shared clip art

Disc 3 (PhotoDraw Disc 1)   PhotoDraw, Office Server Extensions, Internet Explorer 4.01 with Service Pack 1a, Windows NT 4.0 Service Pack 4, and Windows NT Server 4.0 Option Pack.

Disc 4 (PhotoDraw Disc 2)   PhotoDraw content

If you purchase Microsoft Office 2000 Premium with MultiLanguage Pack, then you have access to user interface language modules for Office and Internet Explorer 5, including Internet Explorer menu and dialog box languages, and localized files for the Excel object library, Microsoft Jet 4.0, and Electronic Forms Designer.

The following software, which works with Office 2000, is available separately:

Internet Explorer 128-bit upgrade   Upgrades Windows and Internet Explorer to *128-bit encryption*, which enhances data encryption for Internet Explorer 4.0 and Internet Explorer 5. You can download the 128-bit encryption upgrade from the Internet Explorer area on the Microsoft Windows Update Web site at http://www.microsoft.com/windows/ie/download/windows.htm. For more information, see the Microsoft Internet Explorer Security Updates Web site at http://www.microsoft.com/windows/ie/security/.

Outlook 2000 Domestic Security Patch   Upgrades Windows and Outlook to 128-bit encryption, which enhances data encryption for Internet Explorer 4.0, Internet Explorer 5, and Outlook 2000. For more information, see the Outlook 2000 high encryption page on the Office Update Web site at http://officeupdate.microsoft.com/info/outlook2000highencrypt.htm.

Each of the Office 2000 applications and related products included in Office 2000 Premium or available separately has a unique set of installation requirements. The methods you use to install each of these products differ based on the following conditions:

- Installation technology used to install the software.
- Whether the software requires *elevated privileges* when you install it on a computer running under Windows NT 4.0.
- Prerequisite software that must already be installed on the computer.
- Whether you must reboot the computer after installation.

These product-specific installation requirements are described on the following pages.

Installing Office with Elevated Privileges on Windows NT 4.0

Some of the installation programs for Microsoft Office 2000 and Office-related applications must make changes to system areas of the user's computer. These programs might update system files or make changes to system areas of the Windows registry.

Under Microsoft Windows 95 and Windows 98, any user logged on to the computer has access to these system areas and can run the installation programs. On the Microsoft Windows NT 4.0 operating system, however, system areas are protected from users running under normal user accounts. To install on Windows NT 4.0, the installation program must have elevated privileges. A program running with elevated privileges has access to the protected areas of the system.

There are several methods you can use to run an installation program with elevated privileges.

Logging on as an administrator

If you log on to the computer with a user account that has *administrator privileges*, then all programs that you run have elevated privileges. This method is the simplest way to install Office applications on Windows NT 4.0.

Advertising the Windows installer package

If the installation program uses the Windows installer, as Office Setup and Microsoft Publisher Setup do, then you can use the **/jm** *msifile* command-line option to *advertise* the installer *package* (MSI file) on computers running under Windows NT 4.0. For example, to advertise Office you can use the following command line:

setup.exe /jm data1.msi

If you also include a Windows installer *transform* (MST file) to customize the installation, use the **/t** command-line option to specify the transform. For example,

setup.exe /jm data1.msi /t office.mst

When you advertise a package, the package is configured to be installed the first time the user attempts to use the application. You must be logged on with administrator privileges to advertise a package.

Advertising a package is much faster than installing a package. When the user attempts to use the application for the first time, the installer completes the installation under administrator privileges, including rebooting the system if necessary. The user can also run Setup to install specific features, and Setup runs under administrator privileges regardless of how the user is logged on.

Note   You cannot install Microsoft Internet Explorer 5 by advertising it. You can, however, install Internet Explorer 5 on the user's computer first, and then advertise Office.

Windows NT 4.0 with Internet Explorer 4.01 and Active Desktop supports Windows installer shortcuts. In this scenario, the installer adds application icons to the **Start** menu when you advertise the package. When the user clicks one of these icons, the Windows installer installs that application on the computer before running it. When installing the advertised package, the Windows installer runs under administrator privileges, regardless of how the user is logged on, so it can make any needed system modifications.

Windows NT 4.0 without Active Desktop does not support Windows installer shortcuts. In this case, you can advertise the package, but the user must run Setup to install the program. When the user runs Setup after Office has been advertised, the Windows installer performs the installation with administrator privileges.

Note   If you advertise a package, and the user later runs Setup to install Office, then the user must specify the option **/q**, **/qn**, or **/qb** on the Setup command line. Setup cannot install an advertised package unless one of these command-line options is used.

Using Windows system policies

If the installation program uses the Windows installer, as Office Setup and Publisher Setup do, then you can set a Windows system policy on the user's computer. The policy allows all Windows installer packages to be installed with administrator privileges.

Caution   When you set these system policies, any Windows installer package run by any user can make changes to the system. This arrangement makes the system vulnerable to viruses.

▶ **To enable elevated privilege on a user's computer by using policies**

1   On the **Start** menu, click **Run**.

2   Type **regedit** and click **OK**.

3   Locate the following subkey in the Windows registry:

HKEY_LOCAL_MACHINE\Software\Microsoft\Windows\Installer

4   In the Installer subkey, set the value of **AlwaysInstallElevated** to **1**.

5   Locate the following subkey in the Windows registry:

HKEY_CURRENT_USER\Software\Microsoft\Windows\Installer

6   In the Installer subkey, set the value of **AlwaysInstallElevated** to **1**.

7   Repeat steps 5 and 6 for each user

Using Systems Management Server

If you are using Microsoft Systems Management Server to install Office, you can run the Package Command Manager as a service on the user's computer so that it runs with administrator privileges.

See also

- You can use a software management system such as Systems Management Server to deploy Office in your organization. For more information, see "Deploying Office with Systems Management Server" on page 106.

Installation Requirements for Office and Internet Explorer

Microsoft Office 2000 Premium resides on Office 2000 Premium Disc 1 and includes Microsoft Internet Explorer 5. The Office Setup program allows you to install both Office and Internet Explorer together, or you can use the Internet Explorer Setup program to install Internet Explorer separately. If you deploy Office or Internet Explorer with other Office-related products and components, keep in mind the following installation requirements.

Product	Installation technology	Elevated privileges	Reboot
Office 2000	Windows installer	Partial	Yes
Internet Explorer 5	Active Setup	Yes	Yes

Office 2000

To install Office, run Setup.exe from the root folder of Office Disc 1. Using the **/a** command-line option, you can create an administrative installation point from which users can install Office over the network. You can then run Setup.exe from the root folder of the administrative installation point to install Office on users' computers.

Software prerequisites

Some Office applications require that other software be preinstalled or preconfigured on the user's computer before you install Office.

Windows NT 4.0 Service Pack 3   Required by most Office applications under Microsoft Windows NT 4.0.

Windows NT 4.0 Service Pack 4   Required by NetMeeting.

Internet Explorer 3.0 or later   Required by Microsoft Access, Microsoft Excel, Microsoft PowerPoint, and Microsoft Word.

Internet Explorer 4.01 or later   Required by Microsoft Outlook.

Internet Explorer 5 or later   Required by NetMeeting.

Toolbox

You can find a complete list of the Office features that require Internet Explorer in the Internet Explorer 5 Dependent Features workbook (IE5Feats.xls). This workbook includes a description of how each feature behaves when the required version of Internet Explorer is not installed. For information about installing IE5Feats.xls, see "Office Information" on page 787.

Elevated privileges

To install Office on Windows NT 4.0, you must run Setup with *elevated privileges*. If Office Setup requires you to reboot the user's computer, then you must be logged on with elevated privileges both before and after reboot.

If you install Microsoft PhotoDraw 2000 with Office and you want to minimize the number of times you have to reboot the user's computer, you must install PhotoDraw first, install Office, and then reboot the computer. If you want to install PhotoDraw after Office, you must reboot the computer after you install Office and allow Office Setup to finish installation tasks before you install PhotoDraw.

Important   If you install Office before you install PhotoDraw, and you do not reboot the computer after installing Office and before installing PhotoDraw, then Office may not function correctly.

If your users run Outlook in a secure Windows NT environment that restricts user access to the Windows registry, you must specify the Outlook configuration type in a *transform* because users cannot select or change this configuration. In the **Customize Outlook Installation Options** panel of the Custom Installation Wizard, select and configure either **Corporate and Workgroup Settings** or **Internet Only Settings**.

Tip   You can enable Outlook encryption features even if the user installs Office without elevated privileges. Just install the Outlook 2000 Domestic Security Patch with elevated privileges before the user installs Office.

Reboot requirements

Office Setup requires you to reboot the computer if you install Internet Explorer 5, or if Setup needs to update system files that are in use during installation. If Setup requires you to reboot the computer, then you must log on again using the same account so that Setup can finish the installation.

Internet Explorer 5

To install Internet Explorer separately from Office, run IE5Setup.exe from the IE5 folder of Office Disc 1. If you perform an administrative installation of Office, you can also find IE5Setup.exe in the IE5 folder in the root of the administrative installation point.

You can customize how Setup installs Internet Explorer by running the Internet Explorer Administration Kit (Ieak5.exe) from the IE5*Language* folder located in the root of Office Disc 1 or in the root of the Office administrative installation point.

Software prerequisites

No other software needs to be installed before you install Internet Explorer. If an earlier version of Internet Explorer exists on the user's computer, IE5Setup upgrades it to Internet Explorer 5.

Elevated privileges

To install Internet Explorer on Windows NT 4.0 you must run IE5Setup with elevated privileges. You must be logged on with elevated privileges both before and after reboot.

Note   Because IE5Setup is not a Windows installer application, you cannot advertise Internet Explorer 5, and the **/j** command-line option is not recognized.

Reboot requirements

IE5Setup requires you to reboot the computer after you install Internet Explorer. You must log on again using the same account so that IE5Setup can finish the installation.

See also

- Office 2000 Setup gives you many options when you install Office on users' computers. For more information, see "Office Setup Program" on page 241.

- The Custom Installation Wizard provides great flexibility for customizing the Office installation process. For more information about the changes that you can make during Office Setup, see "Office Custom Installation Wizard" on page 250.

Installation Requirements for Other Office Applications and Related Products

In addition to the core applications, Microsoft Office 2000 Premium includes the following Office applications and related products and features, which you can deploy with Office:

- Microsoft Publisher 2000
- Microsoft PhotoDraw 2000
- Microsoft Data Engine
- Microsoft Office Server Extensions
- Microsoft Office 2000 Web Components

If you install these products with Office or other related products, keep in mind the following installation requirements.

Product	Installation technology	Elevated privileges	Reboot
Publisher 2000	Windows installer	Partial	Yes
PhotoDraw 2000	ACME Setup	Yes	No
Microsoft Data Engine	InstallShield	Yes	No

Note   Office Server Extensions and Office Web Components are included on the Office Premium discs. Installation requirements for these products are described in detail in the Microsoft Office 2000 Resource Kit. For more information about installing Office Server Extensions, see "Installing Office Server Extensions" on page 637. For more information about installing Web Components, see "Requirements for Office Web Components" on page 18.

Publisher 2000

To install Publisher, run Setup.exe from the root folder of Office Disc 2. Using the **/a** command-line option, you can create an administrative installation point from which users can install Publisher over the network. You can then run Setup.exe from the root folder of the administrative installation point to install Publisher on users' computers.

Software prerequisites

Publisher requires that other software be preinstalled on the user's computer.

Windows NT 4.0 Service Pack 3   Must be installed before you install Publisher..

Elevated privileges

To install Publisher on Windows NT 4.0, you must run Setup with *elevated privileges*.

If Setup requires you to reboot the user's computer, then you must be logged on with elevated privileges both before and after reboot.

Reboot requirements

Setup requires you to reboot the computer if you install Microsoft Internet Explorer 5, or if Setup needs to update system files that are in use during installation. If Setup requires you to reboot the computer, then you must log on again using the same account so that Setup can finish the installation.

PhotoDraw 2000

To install PhotoDraw, run Setup.exe from Office Disc 3 (PhotoDraw Disc 1).

Office Disc 3 also includes installation programs for the following software.

To install this component	Run this Setup program
Internet Explorer 4.01 with Service Pack 1a	IE401\ie4setup.exe
DirectX 6.0	DirectX\dxsetup.exe
Windows NT 4.0 Service Pack 4	NT4SP4\SP4I386.exe

Software prerequisites

PhotoDraw requires that other software be preinstalled on the user's computer.

Internet Explorer 4.0 or later   Must be installed before you install PhotoDraw.

DirectX 6.0   Must be installed before you install PhotoDraw on Windows 95/98.

Windows NT 4.0 Service Pack 3   Must be installed before you install PhotoDraw on Windows NT 4.0.

Elevated privileges

To install PhotoDraw on Windows NT 4.0, you must log on as an administrator when you run Setup.

Reboot requirements

Setup may require you to reboot the computer, depending on whether system files are updated during installation. You do not need elevated privileges to finish the installation after rebooting.

If you install PhotoDraw 2000 with Office and you want to minimize the number of times you have to reboot the user's computer, you must install PhotoDraw first, install Office, and then reboot the computer. If you want to install PhotoDraw after Office, you must reboot the computer after you install Office and allow Office Setup to finish installation tasks before you install PhotoDraw.

Important   If you install Office before you install PhotoDraw, and you do not reboot the computer after installing Office and before installing PhotoDraw, then Office may not function correctly.

Microsoft Data Engine

Microsoft Data Engine (MSDE) is installed silently with Office Server Extensions, but you can also install it separately. You can install MSDE from Office Disc 1 by double-clicking **Setupsql.exe** in the SQL\x86\Setup folder.

Software prerequisites

MSDE requires that other software be preinstalled on the user's computer.

Internet Explorer 4.01 Service Pack 1 or later   Must be installed before you install MSDE.

Microsoft Access 2000 or Office Server Extensions   Must be installed before you install MSDE.

DCOM 95   Must be installed before you install MSDE on Windows 95/98.

Windows NT 4.0 Service Pack 4   Must be installed before you install MSDE on Windows NT 4.0.

Elevated privileges

To install MSDE on Windows NT 4.0, you must log on as an administrator when you run Setup. You do not need elevated privileges to run MSDE.

Reboot requirements

Setup might require you to reboot the computer, depending on whether system files are updated during installation.

See also

- PhotoDraw 2000 is included with Office 2000 Premium. For more information about how to install and configure PhotoDraw, see "Installing PhotoDraw with Office" on page 202.

- When you install PhotoDraw, you can use command-line options to install quietly or to otherwise customize the installation. For more information, see "Using Command-Line Options with Acme Setup" on page 212.

- Using Office Server Extensions (OSE), users can publish documents, participate in discussions, and collaborate on team projects. For more information about how to install and configure OSE, see "Installing Office Server Extensions" on page 637.

- Using Office Web Components, users can interactively manipulate data from within a Web browser. For more information about installing and using Office Web Components, see "Managing Office Web Components" on page 600.

Installation Requirements for International Components

If you install the international features included in Microsoft Office 2000 Premium with MultiLanguage Pack, keep in mind the following installation requirements.

Product	Installation technology	Elevated privileges	Reboot
Microsoft Office 2000 MultiLanguage Pack	Windows installer	No	No
Localized Microsoft Excel add-ins	File copy	No	No
Localized Excel object library files	File copy	No	No
Microsoft Internet Explorer user interface languages	IExpress	Yes	No
Japanese Input Method Editor	Windows installer	Yes	No
Chinese Input Method Editors	ACME Setup	Yes	No
Microsoft Jet 4.0 user interface language files	File copy	No	No
Microsoft Outlook At Work fax patch	IExpress	No	No
Outlook forms	IExpress	No	No

Office 2000 MultiLanguage Pack

The Office 2000 MultiLanguage Pack is included in Office 2000 Premium with
MultiLanguage Pack. To install the MultiLanguage Pack, run Setup.exe from the
MultiLanguage Pack CD-ROM. You can use the **/a** command-line option to create an
administrative installation point for the MultiLanguage Pack on a network server.

Software prerequisites

The MultiLanguage Pack requires that other software be preinstalled on the user's
computer.

Office 2000   Must be installed before you install the MultiLanguage Pack.

Elevated privileges

You do not need *elevated privileges* to install the MultiLanguage Pack.

Reboot requirements

The MultiLanguage Pack does not require you to reboot the user's computer after
installation.

Localized Excel add-ins

The MultiLanguage Pack includes several localized Excel add-ins. You can install
these add-ins on a user's computer by copying the contents of the Extras\XLAddins
folder on the MultiLanguage Pack CD-ROM to Program Files\Microsoft
Office\Office\Library on the user's computer.

Software prerequisites

If you plan to install the localized add-ins, do not install English add-ins.

Elevated privileges

You do not need elevated privileges to install the Excel add-ins.

Reboot requirements

You do not need to reboot the computer after installing the Excel add-ins.

Localized Excel object library files

The MultiLanguage Pack contains localized Excel object libraries that you can use to translate nonEnglish Excel 95 or Excel 5.0 macros to English so that you can run them. You must install an object library for each language used in a macro.

To install the object libraries, run Instolb.exe in the Extras\95olbs folder on the MultiLanguage Pack CD-ROM.

Software prerequisites

No other software needs to be installed before you install the Excel object libraries.

Elevated privileges

You do not need elevated privileges to install the Excel object libraries.

Reboot requirements

You do not need to reboot the computer after installing the Excel object libraries.

Internet Explorer user interface languages

The Internet Explorer user interface language files allow you to change the language of the Internet Explorer 5 user interface. To install the files, run the IExpress file Ieui*xx*.exe, where *xx* is a two-letter language code from the Extras\Ie5*language* folder on the MultiLanguage Pack CD-ROM.

Software prerequisites

Internet Explorer user interface language files require that other software be preinstalled on the user's computer.

Internet Explorer 5   Must be installed on the computer before you install the user interface languages.

Elevated privileges

To install Internet Explorer user languages under Microsoft Windows NT 4.0, you must run Setup with elevated privileges.

Reboot requirements

You do not need to reboot the computer after installing Internet Explorer user interface languages.

Input Method Editors

Input Method Editors (IMES) for Japanese, Korean, Simplified Chinese, and Traditional Chinese allow users to type Asian characters regardless of the language of their operating system. The installation program that you run to install an IME depends on the language of the user's operating system. You either run a self-extracting executable file located in the Extras\Ime*language*\Global folder of the MultiLanguage Pack CD-ROM, or you run Setup.exe in the Extras\Ime*language*\Regular folder.

You can run the Setup program for an IME quietly by using the **/q** command-line option with the Japanese version, or the **/n** command-line option with the Chinese versions.

Note   IME Setup does not support the **/j** command-line option to advertise an IME.

Localized editions of Office Setup install the IME associated with the language of the Office product. If you run Setup silently, Setup does not install the IME.

Tip   You can disable the installation of an IME in Office Setup by setting the property **INSTALLIME** to **False** on the Setup command line, in the Setup settings file, or in a transform (MST file).

Software prerequisites

No other software needs to be installed before you install the IMEs.

Elevated privileges

To install the Japanese and Chinese IMEs under Windows NT 4.0, you must run the installation program with elevated privileges.

Reboot requirements

The Japanese IME prompts you to reboot the computer after installation. You can use the **/qn** command-line option to suppress this prompt, just as you can with Office Setup.

The Chinese and Korean IMEs do not require you to reboot the computer after installation.

Microsoft Jet 4.0 user interface language files

The Microsoft Jet 4.0 user interface language files are dynamic-link library (DLL) files that allow you to change the Jet 4.0 user interface language. Users install the appropriate language files for the language they want to use.

To install the files, copy Msjint40.dll and Mswstr10.dll from the Extras\Jet*language* folder on the MultiLanguage Pack CD-ROM to the user's Windows System folder.

Software prerequisites

No other software needs to be installed before you install the Jet 4.0 user interface files.

Elevated privileges

You do not need elevated privileges to install the Jet 4.0 user interface files.

Reboot requirements

You do not need to reboot the computer after installing the Jet 4.0 user interface files.

Outlook At Work fax patch

If your users are running a nonEnglish language version of Windows 95/98 and are using the Outlook At Work fax feature, they must install the localized patch file.

Note   If users are upgrading from Outlook 98, they do not need to install the patch.

To install the patch on the user's computer, run Awfaxpch.exe from the Extras\AWFAXpat*language* folder on the MultiLanguage Pack CD-ROM.

Software prerequisites

No other software needs to be installed before you install the Outlook At Work fax patch.

Elevated privileges

You do not need elevated privileges to install the Outlook At Work fax patch.

Reboot requirements

You do not need to reboot the computer after installing the Outlook At Work fax patch.

Outlook forms

If your organization uses 16-bit Electronic Forms Designer (EFD) forms and your users are running nonEnglish language versions of Windows 95/98 or Windows NT, then you must install the localized version of EFD. Using the localized version allows users to open 16-bit forms supported by Microsoft Outlook and Microsoft Exchange Client.

You can install the Microsoft Outlook for Windows/Electronic Forms Designer Runtime feature during Office Setup by changing its installation state from **Not Available** to another setting. However, because EFD Runtime does not change languages when you switch the language versions of Office, you can also install a localized version of EFD Runtime separately from Office.

Note   If users are upgrading from a previous version of Outlook, they do not need to install the localized EFD files.

To install a localized version of EFD Runtime, run Efd.exe from the \Extras\EFDSupp*language* folder of the MultiLanguage Pack CD-ROM. You can use the **/q** command-line option to run the Setup program quietly.

Software prerequisites

No other software needs to be installed before you install EFD Runtime.

Elevated privileges

You do not need elevated privileges to install EFD Runtime.

Reboot requirements

You do not need to reboot the computer after installing EFD Runtime.

See also

- The MultiLanguage Pack allows users all over the world to run the Office 2000 user interface and online Help in their own languages and to create documents in many other languages. For more information, see "How to Deploy Office Internationally" on page 155.

- The MultiLanguage Pack contains a number of extra features that you can install with Office. For more information, see "MultiLanguage Pack Extras" on page 160.

- The Custom Installation Wizard provides great flexibility for customizing the Office installation process. For more information about the changes that you can make during Office Setup, see "Office Custom Installation Wizard" on page 250.

Installation Requirements for Encryption Components

If you install encryption components with Microsoft Office 2000 Premium or related products, keep in mind the following installation requirements.

Product	Installation technology	Elevated privileges	Reboot
Microsoft Internet Explorer 128-bit upgrade	IExpress	Yes	No
Microsoft Outlook Domestic Security Patch	IExpress	Yes	No

Internet Explorer 128-bit upgrade

By default, Internet Explorer uses *40-bit encryption* technology for secure communications. The Internet Explorer 128-bit upgrade modifies Microsoft Windows and Internet Explorer so that they can use *128-bit encryption*.

You can download the 128-bit encryption upgrade from the Internet Explorer area on the Microsoft Windows Update Web site at http://www.microsoft.com/windows/ie/download/windows.htm. For more information, see the Microsoft Internet Explorer Security Updates Web site at http://www.microsoft.com/windows/ie/security/.

Note   128-bit encryption is available only to users in the United States and Canada, and is limited by US export license. For more information, see the Microsoft Security Advisor Web site at http://www.microsoft.com/security/.

Software prerequisites

The Internet Explorer 128-bit upgrade requires that other software be preinstalled on the user's computer.

Internet Explorer   To install the upgrade, you must have Internet Explorer 4.0 or later installed. As an alternative, you can download the complete 128-bit version of Internet Explorer 3.02 or higher.

Elevated privileges

To install the 128-bit upgrade under Windows NT 4.0, you must run Setup with *elevated privileges*.

Reboot requirements

You do not need to reboot the computer after installing the 128-bit upgrade.

Outlook Domestic Security Patch

When you install Office 2000, Setup configures Outlook with the same encryption level as Internet Explorer on the user's computer. If Internet Explorer is installed with 40-bit or 128-bit encryption, Setup configures Outlook with 40-bit or 128-bit encryption, respectively. If Internet Explorer is not installed, or if you install Office on Windows NT 4.0 without elevated privileges, Setup configures Outlook with no encryption.

Tip You can enable Outlook security features even when a user installs Office without elevated privileges. Remove Outlook 97/98 from the user's computer and then install the Outlook 2000 Domestic Security Patch with elevated privileges before the user installs Office.

After you install Office, you can upgrade Outlook to 128-bit encryption by installing the Outlook Domestic Security Patch. The patch also upgrades Windows and Internet Explorer to 128-bit encryption—so if you install the Outlook Domestic Security Patch, then you do not need to install the Internet Explorer 128-bit upgrade.

The Outlook 2000 Domestic Security Patch consists of an IExpress file (O2kdom.exe) that contains domestic security patches for Internet Explorer 4.0, Internet Explorer 5, and Outlook 2000. To install the Outlook 2000 Domestic Security Patch, download the file from the Outlook 2000 high encryption page on the Office Update Web site at http://officeupdate.microsoft.com/info/outlook2000highencrypt.htm.

When you run O2kdom.exe on a user's computer, the program determines which version of Internet Explorer is installed, updates it to 128-bit security, and then updates Outlook 2000. You can use the **/q** command-line option to perform the installation quietly and the **/r** command-line option to suppress automatic reboot.

Note 128-bit encryption is available only to users in the United States and Canada, and is limited by US export license. For more information, see the Microsoft Security Advisor Web site at http://www.microsoft.com/security/.

Software prerequisites

Before the security patch can update Outlook, Outlook requires that other software be preinstalled on the user's computer.

Internet Explorer 4.0 or Internet Explorer 5 Must be installed before installing the Outlook Domestic Security Patch. If Internet Explorer is not already upgraded to 128-bit encryption, the security patch upgrades Internet Explorer first and then upgrades Outlook.

Outlook 2000 Must be installed on the computer before installing the Outlook Domestic Security Patch.

Elevated privileges

To install the Outlook Domestic Security Patch on Windows NT 4.0, you must run Setup with elevated privileges.

Reboot requirements

You must reboot the computer after installing the Outlook Domestic Security Patch. The patch prompts the user to reboot the computer unless you use the **/r** command-line option.

See also

- Outlook 2000 provides enhanced security features for sending and receiving secure e-mail messages over the Internet or your intranet. For more information, see "Using Security Features in Outlook" on page 414.

How to Install Office and Related Products in the Correct Sequence

Microsoft Office 2000 Premium contains Office applications plus a number of related products. Each of these products has a unique set of installation requirements, including what software must already be installed, whether *elevated privileges* are required during installation, and whether you must reboot the computer after installation.

The following table summarizes the required software that must be installed before you install the corresponding Office features and applications. Use this table to help decide which products to install and in what order.

This product	Is required by these features and applications
Microsoft Windows NT 4.0 with Service Pack 3	Most Office applications, including Microsoft Publisher and Microsoft PhotoDraw
Windows NT 4.0 with Service Pack 4	NetMeeting, Microsoft Data Engine
DirectX 6.0	PhotoDraw (Windows 95/98)
DCOM 95	Microsoft Data Engine (Windows 95/98)
Microsoft Internet Explorer 3.0 or later	Microsoft Access, Microsoft Excel, Microsoft PowerPoint, Microsoft Word
Internet Explorer 4.01 or later	Microsoft Outlook, PhotoDraw, Internet Explorer 128-bit upgrade
Internet Explorer 4.01 with Service Pack 1 or later	Microsoft Data Engine, Outlook Domestic Security Patch
Internet Explorer 5 or later	NetMeeting, Internet Explorer user interface languages
Microsoft Office 2000	Microsoft Office 2000 MultiLanguage Pack, Outlook Domestic Security Patch
Access 2000 or Microsoft Office Server Extensions	Microsoft Data Engine

For example, if you plan to install Microsoft Data Engine (MSDE) on a computer running under Windows NT 4.0, then you must first install the following software:

- Windows NT 4.0 Service Pack 4

- Internet Explorer 4.01 with Service Pack 1 or Internet Explorer 5

- Access or Office Server Extensions

The following procedures outline the optimal sequences you can use to install Office and related products on users' computers, taking into account the necessary software prerequisites and the elevated privileges and reboot requirements.

Note   When installing on Windows NT 4.0, you can choose whether to perform the entire installation under elevated privileges, or whether to allow your users to perform part of the installation process.

Installing on Windows 95

To install Office 2000 Premium and all related products on a computer running Microsoft Windows 95, use the following sequence.

▶ **To install Office and related products on Windows 95**

1 If you want to standardize on a previous version of Internet Explorer, install Internet Explorer 3.0 or 4.0 and reboot the computer.

2 If you plan to work with Japanese or Chinese files, install the appropriate Japanese or Chinese Input Method Editor (IME).

3 Install DirectX 6.0 for PhotoDraw.

4 If you want to upgrade Windows and Internet Explorer to *128-bit encryption*, install the Internet Explorer 128-bit upgrade.

5 Install Office 2000.

   If you want to install Internet Explorer 5, install it at the same time you install Office.

6 If you need to change the user interface language of Internet Explorer 5, install Internet Explorer user interface languages.

7 Reboot the computer.

   Office Setup must complete its work after rebooting before you can install any other software.

8 Install PhotoDraw.

9 Install the Microsoft Data Engine.

10 If you did not enable 128-bit encryption before installing Office, and you want to upgrade to 128-bit encryption now, then install the Outlook 2000 Domestic Security Patch.

11 If you have Office 2000 Premium with MultiLanguage Pack and you want to install *plug-in language features*, install the MultiLanguage Pack.

12 Install Microsoft Publisher.

13 Reboot the computer.

Installing on Windows 98

To install Office 2000 Premium and all related products on a computer running Microsoft Windows 98, use the following sequence.

▶ **To install Office and related products on Windows 98**

1   If you plan to work with Japanese or Chinese files, install the appropriate Japanese or Chinese Input Method Editor (IME).

2   Install DirectX 6.0 for PhotoDraw.

3   Install PhotoDraw.

4   If you want to upgrade Windows and Internet Explorer 4.0 or Internet Explorer 5 to 128-bit encryption, install the Internet Explorer 128-bit upgrade.

5   Install Office 2000.

   If you want to install Internet Explorer 5, install it at the same time you install Office.

6   If you need to change the user interface language of Internet Explorer 5, install Internet Explorer user interface languages.

7   Reboot the computer.

   Office Setup must complete its work after rebooting before you can install any other software.

8   Install the Microsoft Data Engine.

9   If you did not enable 128-bit encryption before installing Office, and you want to upgrade to 128-bit encryption now, then install the Outlook 2000 Domestic Security Patch.

10   If you have Office 2000 Premium with MultiLanguage Pack and you want to install plug-in language features, install the MultiLanguage Pack.

11   Install Publisher.

12   Reboot the computer.

Installing on Windows NT 4.0 with elevated privileges

To install Office 2000 Premium and all related products on a computer running Windows NT 4.0, use the following sequence. This procedure requires that you have elevated privileges on the user's computer.

▶ **To install Office and related products on Windows NT 4.0 with elevated privileges**

1 Log on to the computer using an account that has administrator privileges.

2 For Office, PhotoDraw, and most other products, install Windows NT 4.0 Service Pack 3.

   −or−

   For Net Meeting and Microsoft Data Engine, install Windows NT 4.0 Service Pack 4.

3 Reboot the computer.

4 If you want to standardize on a previous version of Internet Explorer, install Internet Explorer 3.0 or 4.0 and reboot the computer.

5 If you plan to work with Japanese or Chinese files, install the appropriate Japanese or Chinese Input Method Editor (IME).

6 If you want to upgrade Windows and Internet Explorer 4.0 or Internet Explorer 5 to 128-bit encryption, install the Internet Explorer 128-bit upgrade.

7 Install Office 2000.

   If you want to install Internet Explorer 5, install it at the same time you install Office.

8 If you need to change the user interface language of Internet Explorer 5, install Internet Explorer user interface languages.

9 Reboot the computer.

   Office Setup must complete its work after rebooting before you can install any other software.

10 Install PhotoDraw.

11 Install the Microsoft Data Engine.

12 If you did not enable 128-bit encryption before installing Office, and you want to upgrade to 128-bit encryption, then install the Outlook 2000 Domestic Security Patch.

13 If you have Office 2000 Premium with MultiLanguage Pack and you want to install plug-in language features, install the MultiLanguage Pack.

14 Install Publisher.

15 Reboot the computer.

Installing on Windows NT 4.0 without elevated privileges

To install Office 2000 Premium and all related products on a computer running under Windows NT 4.0, use the following sequence. This procedure allows you to install Office, Publisher, and the MultiLanguage Pack from a user account that does not have elevated privileges.

▶ To install Office and related products on Windows NT 4.0 without elevated privileges

1   Log on to the computer using an account that has administrator privileges.

2   For Office, PhotoDraw, and most other products, install Windows NT 4.0 Service Pack 3.

   –or–

   For Net Meeting and Microsoft Data Engine, install Windows NT 4.0 Service Pack 4.

3   Reboot the computer and then log on again with administrator privileges.

4   Install Internet Explorer 3.0, Internet Explorer 4.0, or Internet Explorer 5; reboot the computer and log on again with administrator privileges.

5   If you plan to work with Japanese or Chinese files, install the appropriate Japanese or Chinese Input Method Editor (IME).

6   If you want to upgrade Windows and Internet Explorer 4.0 or Internet Explorer 5 to 128-bit encryption, install the Internet Explorer 128-bit upgrade.

7   If you need to change the user interface language of Internet Explorer 5, install Internet Explorer user interface languages.

8   Advertise Office using the **/jm** Setup command-line option.

9   Install PhotoDraw.

10   Reboot the computer and log on with a user account.

11   Install Office.

12   If you have Office 2000 Premium with MultiLanguage Pack and you want to install plug-in language features, install the MultiLanguage Pack.

13   Install Publisher.

14   Reboot the computer and log on with administrator privileges.

15   If you did not enable 128-bit encryption before installing Office, and you want to upgrade to 128-bit encryption, then install the Outlook 2000 Domestic Security Patch.

16   Install Microsoft Data Engine.

17   Reboot the computer.

See also

- When you install products on a computer running under Windows NT 4.0, there are a number of ways to give the installation program elevated privileges. For more information, see "Installing Office with Elevated Privileges on Windows NT 4.0" on page 117.

Staging Your Deployment of Office Premium

When you deploy Microsoft Office 2000 Premium, the simplest method is to deploy all the Office applications together. However, in some circumstances, you might find it necessary to deploy different Office applications or features at different times or by using different methods.

For example, you might have one group in your organization that deploys desktop applications, such as Microsoft Word and Microsoft Excel, and another group that deploys mail applications, such as Microsoft Outlook. The desktop applications group might be ready to deploy Word and Excel immediately, but the mail applications group might need to wait until other mail-related services are ready. In this scenario, you can deploy most Office applications together at one time, and then deploy Outlook later.

Note   This discussion assumes that you are deploying Office by creating an administrative installation point and installing Office on users' computers over the network. When you run Setup with the **/a** command-line option, Setup creates a hierarchical folder structure into which it copies all the product files. Users run Setup from the administrative installation point to install Office on their computers.

There are three methods that you can use to deploy Office applications in stages.

Deploy Office applications from separate administrative installation points   Install Office Premium on one *administrative installation point*, and install each separate application on its own administrative installation point. You can deploy some applications from the Office administrative installation point, and then deploy the rest as standalone products.

This method is the most straightforward, and it gives you the most flexibility in configuring the individual applications. However, it uses the greatest amount of disk space on the server computers.

Deploy Office applications from a single administrative installation point   Install Office Premium and each standalone application on a single administrative installation point. You can deploy some applications by using Office Setup from the administrative installation point, and then deploy the rest by using the Setup program specific to the individual application.

This method takes a little more planning to prevent overwriting of duplicate files, but it gives you flexibility in configuring the individual applications and reduces disk space usage considerably on the server computers.

Deploy all Office applications from Office Premium, but use installation options to delay installation of some applications   Install Office Premium on one administrative installation point but set certain features to **Not Available**. Later, using Setup properties, change the installation state of these features to make them available to users.

This method requires more detailed knowledge of how to customize the installation process, and there are limitations on how you can customize the applications installed later. But with this method you do not have to worry about file duplication issues, and you can manage your applications more efficiently.

Tip   If you use the Profile Wizard to preconfigure Office application settings on users' computers when you install Office, then you need to preconfigure these settings in stages as well. For more information about how to customize the Profile Wizard when you deploy Office in stages, see "Customizing the Profile Wizard" on page 263.

Deploying Office applications from separate administrative installation points

To deploy Office and selected Office applications separately, you can purchase Microsoft Office 2000 Premium plus the individual products you need, such as Microsoft Outlook 2000. Then you can create multiple administrative installation points—one for Office and one for each individual application.

These administrative installation points can be in different folders on one network server, or they can be on separate servers. Files that are common among all Office applications are duplicated on each administrative installation point.

You install Office on users' computers by running Setup from the Office administrative installation point. Using the Office Custom Installation Wizard, create a transform in which you set those applications that you are installing separately to **Not Available** and **Hide**. Later you can install the individual applications from their own administrative installation points.

▶ **To create separate administrative installation points for Office and individual applications**

1 Run Setup from Office Premium Disc 1with the **/a** command-line option; when prompted for the server location, enter a folder on a network server. For example:

\\server1\software\office

2 Using the Office Custom Installation Wizard, create a transform in which you set the installation state for any application that you want to deploy separately to **Not Available** and **Hide**.

For example, if you are deploying Outlook separately, click the Microsoft Outlook for Windows feature in the **Set Feature Installation States** panel and select **Not Available**. Right-click the same feature and select **Hide**.

3 Edit the *Setup settings file* (Setup.ini) to specify the transform that you created.

For example, if the name of your custom transform is Officemain.mst, add the following line under the [MST] section of Setup.ini:

MST1=Officemain.mst

4 Run Setup with the /a command-line option from the CD-ROM for each standalone application that you want to deploy; when prompted for the server location, enter a unique folder for each product. For example:

\\server1\software\outlook

You can install each product in a separate folder, or you can create a single network share and designate a subfolder for each application.

Tip   In the Setup settings file, the [MST] section is included by default, but the line is commented out. When you specify a transform, be sure to remove the semicolon (;) from the beginning of the [MST] section.

After you create the administrative installation point for Office, users can install Office by running Office Setup from that administrative installation point. Users can then install each individual application by running Setup from that application's administrative installation point.

When you maintain separate administrative installation points, keep in mind the following.

Common Office application files duplicated on the server

Because Office applications are highly integrated, they share a number of files in common. For example, all Office applications use the same set of Office Assistant files. When you create an administrative installation point for Office, Office Setup copies all of these common files to a single location on the server where the applications can share them.

When you create a separate administrative installation point for an Office application, the Setup program for that application copies many of the same files to a different location, duplicating the files on the server.

Duplicate copies of Mso9.dll loaded into memory

All Office applications share the dynamic-link library (DLL) Mso9.dll. When you run an Office application, it loads Mso9.dll into memory. When you run an Office application from the network server, the application attempts to load Mso9.dll from the administrative installation point.

When you run two Office applications simultaneously, they each attempt to load Mso9.dll into memory. If they load the DLL file from the same folder, Windows detects that they are loading the same file and only loads it once.

When you run two Office applications from separate administrative installation points, however, the applications attempt to load Mso9.dll from different folders. In this case, Windows assumes that they are requesting different files and it loads both copies of Mso9.dll into memory. Because Mso9.dll uses approximately 5 MB of memory when loaded, running more than one Office application in this configuration uses memory needlessly.

Note   When you install the Office applications locally to the same location on the user's computer, then the Setup program for each application installs Mso9.dll to the same folder. When you run two applications simultaneously, Windows loads only one copy of Mso9.dll into memory, even if the applications were installed from different locations on the server.

Deploying Office applications from a single administrative installation point

A more advanced method for deploying some Office applications separately is to create a single administrative installation point on a network server that includes both Office and the separate Office applications. You create the initial administrative installation point using Office Setup, and then you install each individual application into the same folder structure.

This method saves disk space because files that are common among all Office applications are shared on the single administrative installation point. However, Office and each individual application use the same names for Setup files—namely, Setup.exe, Setup.ini, Setup.hlp, Data1.msi, and Autorun.inf. So you must take steps to avoid overwriting Setup files when you install the individual applications after installing Office on the administrative installation point.

Creating an initial administrative installation point for Office

You begin by creating an administrative installation point for Office on a network share and providing unique names for the Setup files.

▶ **To create an initial administrative installation point for Office**

1   Run Setup from Office Disc 1with the **/a** command-line option; when prompted for the server location, enter a folder on a network server. For example:

    \\server1\software\office

2   Using the Office Custom Installation Wizard, create a transform in which you set the installation state for any application you want to deploy separately to **Not Available** and **Hide**.

    For example, if you are deploying Outlook separately, click the Microsoft Outlook for Windows feature in the **Set Feature Installation States** panel and select **Not Available**. Right-click the same feature and select **Hide**.

3   In the root folder of the administrative installation point, rename Setup.exe, Setup.ini, Data1.msi, and Autorun.inf to prevent these files from being overwritten when you install the separate applications.

    Use similar file names and include the appropriate file name extensions. For example:

    OffSetup.exe, **OffSetup.ini**, **OffInst.msi**, and **OffAuto.inf**.

4   Edit the Setup settings file (Setup.ini) to specify the transform that you created plus the new names for the MSI and Autorun.inf files.

    For example, add or edit the following lines in the settings file to indicate the new file names:

    [MSI]

    MSI=OffInst.msi

    [MST]

    MST1=Officemain.mst

    [Autorun]

    autorun.inf=OffAuto.inf

To install Office from this administrative installation point, run Office Setup by using the Setup program file name you created. Setup automatically searches for the Setup settings file with the same file name as the Setup program. For example, if you renamed Setup.exe to OffSetup.exe, Setup looks for OffSetup.ini. Setup uses this settings file to find the correct MSI, MST, and Autorun.inf files.

Installing individual applications on the Office administrative installation point

When you are ready to deploy an individual Office application separately, you can install the application on the same administrative installation point that you created for Office.

▶ To install an individual application on the Office administrative installation point

1 Temporarily rename Setup.hlp to prevent it from being overwritten.

   For example, rename **Setup.hlp** to **OffSetup.hlp**.

2 Run Setup with the **/a** command-line option from the standalone product CD-ROM. When prompted for the server location, enter the same folder on the server where you installed Office. For example:

   \\server1\software\office

3 In the root folder of the administrative installation point, rename Setup.exe, Setup.ini, Setup.hlp, Data1.msi, and Autorun.inf to prevent these files from being overwritten when you install the separate applications.

   Use similar file names and include the appropriate file name extensions. For example:

   OlkSetup.exe, **OlkSetup.ini**, **OlkSetup.hlp**, **OlkInst.msi**, and **OlkAuto.inf**.

4 Edit the Setup settings file (Setup.ini) to specify the transform that you created plus the new names of the MSI and Autorun.inf file.

   For example, add or edit the following lines in the settings file to indicate the new file names:

   [MSI]

   MSI=OlkInst.msi

   [Autorun]

   autorun.inf=OlkAuto.inf

5 In the root folder of the administrative installation point, rename the original Office Setup.hlp file back to Setup.hlp.

   For example, rename **OffSetup.hlp** to **Setup.hlp**.

To install an application from this administrative installation point, run Setup by using the Setup program file name that you created. Setup automatically searches for the Setup settings file with the same file name as the Setup program. For example, if you renamed Outlook Setup.exe to OlkSetup.exe, Setup looks for the settings file named OlkSetup.ini. Setup uses this settings file to find the correct MSI and Autorun.inf files. (Setup uses the Office version of Setup.hlp for the **Help** command.)

Changing installation states after Office installation

Another method for deploying Office applications separately involves creating a single Office administrative installation point, installing Office with specific features set to **Not Available**, and later adding those features to the user's computer by rerunning Office Setup to change the installation states.

Rerunning Setup interactively on users' computers

After you install Office on a user's computer, you can run Setup interactively again to change the installation state of the Office features that you set to **Not Available** during your initial installation. When you rerun Setup after Office is installed, Setup runs in maintenance mode.

Depending on the new installation state you choose for a feature, Setup uses the source files on the original administrative installation point and copies the appropriate files to the user's computer, creates shortcuts, or prepares the feature to be installed on first use.

For example, if you set the installation state for Microsoft Outlook for Windows to **Not Available** in your initial Office deployment, but you have now upgraded your e-mail services and want to deploy Outlook 2000, you can rerun Setup in maintenance mode. Now you can set Microsoft Outlook for Windows to **Run from My Computer**, and Setup installs Outlook on users' computers.

Using the Setup command line or settings file

As an alternative to running Setup interactively on users' computers, you can also change the installation state of any feature by using Setup properties in the Setup command line or settings file (Setup.ini).

For example, to set Outlook to **Run from My Computer**, you can use the following command line:

setup.exe ADDLOCAL="OUTLOOKFiles"

Or you can add these lines to the Setup settings file:

**[Options]
ADDLOCAL=OUTLOOKFiles**

In the Setup command-line or in Setup.ini, you can use the following Setup properties to change the installation states of features after Office is installed.

Setup property	Corresponding installation state
ADDLOCAL	**Run from My Computer**
ADDSOURCE	**Run from CD** or **Run from Network** (depending on the location of the source files)
ADVERTISE	**Installed on First Use**
REMOVE	**Not Available**

For each Setup property that you set, you must specify a list of feature IDs, separated by commas and no spaces. Each feature displayed in the Setup feature tree is defined in the MSI file with a unique feature ID. For example, the feature Microsoft Binder is defined in the MSI file as BinderFiles. You must use the feature ID and not the feature title that is displayed in Setup. (You can also use the keyword **ALL**, without a list of feature IDs, to specify all features.)

Feature IDs are case-sensitive and must be entered exactly as they appear in the MSI file. If you misspell a feature ID, or insert a space between feature IDs, Setup displays an error message and terminates. In this case, you can just correct the feature IDs you specified and try again.

Toolbox

The Office Resource Kit includes a workbook named FileList.xls that contains information for all Office features, including the feature ID associated with each feature. In the workbook, the Feature Title column shows the text displayed by Setup in the feature tree, and the Feature Name column shows the feature ID defined in the MSI file. For information about installing FileList.xls, see "Office Information" on page 787.

You can set any combination of these properties in the Setup command line or settings file. For example, you can use the following command line to change the states of Microsoft Binder and Microsoft Binder Help to **Installed on First Use** and Office Assistant Dot to **Run from My Computer**:

setup.exe ADVERTISE="BinderFiles,BinderHelpFiles" ADDLOCAL="ASSISTANTDot"

You can accomplish the same thing with the following lines in the settings file:

[Options]
ADVERTISE=BinderFiles,BinderHelpFiles
ADDLOCAL=ASSISTANTDot

Tip Use the settings file if you want to set several property values. The settings file does not have the same length restrictions as the Setup command line (which is limited to 255 characters on some systems). The settings file also allows you to organize the list of properties and feature names more easily. Remember to remove the default semicolon (;) preceding the [Options] section name.

Differences between using Setup properties and running Setup interactively

Setting a Setup property on the command line or in the Setup settings file is equivalent to running Setup interactively and selecting the corresponding installation option in the feature tree. However, there are some exceptions.

When you run Setup interactively, Setup does not allow you specify an installation state that the feature does not support. However, when you use Setup properties, you can specify a state that the feature does not support. In this case, Setup ignores your setting.

When you run Setup interactively and change the installation state of a feature, Setup usually changes the state of any *child features* to match. However, when you use Setup properties, Setup changes only the state of the feature. (In a few cases, when the child feature is tightly dependent on the feature that contains it, Setup does change the child feature.) To ensure that all features are installed the way you want, you must specify every feature and child feature whose state you want to change.

Example: changing installation states for selected Outlook features

Suppose you are ready to deploy Office 2000, but you want to delay your deployment of Outlook so that you can synchronize with the department that handles e-mail systems. In this scenario, you can deploy Office to users' computers without Outlook. Later, when the mail system has been upgraded and you are ready to deploy Outlook, you can rerun Setup on users' computers. At that stage, you can finetune your Outlook deployment to install a subset of Outlook features in the following installation states.

Outlook feature	Installation state
Outlook	**Run from My Computer**
Outlook Help	**Run from My Computer**
Importers and Exporters	**Installed on First Use**
Stationery	**Run from Network**
Junk E-mail	**Installed on First Use**
Net Folders	**Run from My Computer**
All remaining features	**Not Available**

You can run Office Setup on each user's computer to modify the installation states of these Outlook features. A more efficient alternative, however, might be to change the installation states of Outlook features by using the following procedure.

▶ **To deploy selected Outlook features after installing Office**

1   When you install Office on the user's computer, set the installation state for the Microsoft Outlook for Windows feature to **Not Available**.

This step removes Outlook and all its child features from the installation.

2   When you are ready to deploy Outlook, copy the Setup.ini file on the administrative installation point to Outlook.ini.

3   Edit the new Outlook.ini file and add the following lines:

[Options]

ADDLOCAL=OUTLOOKFiles,OutlookHelpFiles,OutlookFolderPublishing

ADDSOURCE=OutlookStationeryFiles

ADVERTISE=OutlookImportExportFiles,AntiSpam

4   Run Setup on the user's computer, specifying the new INI file with the **/settings** command-line option.

For example,

setup.exe /q+ /settings Outlook.ini

Setup updates the installation states of the features you specified on the user's computer. Setup copies the Outlook program files and Help files to the user's computer, configures the system to access the stationery files from the administrative installation point, and prepares the import/export files and junk e-mail files to be installed the first time they are used.

To verify that the changes occurred correctly, run Setup interactively, click **Add or Remove Features**, and examine installation states for these features in the feature tree.

See also

- Office 2000 Setup provides you with a lot of flexibility for installing Office. For more information, see "How to Install Office on Client Computers" on page 245.

- By installing Office on an administrative installation point on a network server, you can more easily customize and manage your Office deployment. For more information, see "How to Create an Administrative Installation Point" on page 243.

- For more information about how to distribute a customized Setup command line or settings file to your users, see "Customizing How Setup Runs" on page 215.

- The Office Custom Installation Wizard allows you to fully customize your Office installation. For more information, see "Office Custom Installation Wizard" on page 250.

CHAPTER 4

Installing Special Configurations of Office 2000

Microsoft Office 2000 gives you considerable flexibility when you are installing Office in unique environments or special configurations. You can deploy Office 2000 internationally across multiple languages. You can configure Office to maintain the same working environment for users on different computers. And you can control how applications such as Microsoft Outlook and Microsoft PhotoDraw are deployed with Office.

In This Chapter

Deploying Office in a Multinational Setting

You can deploy and maintain a single version of Microsoft Office 2000 throughout your multinational organization. The plug-in language features of Office allow users in foreign subsidiaries to continue working in their own languages.

Planning an International Deployment

The core functionality of Microsoft Office 2000 and the *plug-in language features* of the Microsoft Office 2000 MultiLanguage Pack allow users all over the world to run the Office 2000 user interface and online Help in their own languages and create documents in many other languages.

For administrators, this core functionality means that you can deploy a single version of Office to all users, regardless of their language-speaking area. Then you can customize the installation to include local language capabilities or allow users to select their own language settings.

Office language versions and editing tools

Microsoft Office 2000 with MultiLanguage Pack includes files for displaying the Office user interface and online Help in several languages. The MultiLanguage Pack is based on the English version of Office 2000; it does not work with localized versions of Office 2000. The MultiLanguage Pack is included in the following Office configurations:

- Microsoft Office 2000 Premium with MultiLanguage Pack
- Microsoft Office 2000 Professional with MultiLanguage Pack
- Microsoft Office 2000 Standard with MultiLanguage Pack

The Microsoft Office 2000 Proofing Tools, which provide editing tools for many languages, are included in the MultiLanguage Pack and are also available separately. The Proofing Tools do work with localized versions of Office 2000.

Note   The MultiLanguage Pack Setup program is available in English only. However, the Setup program for the Proofing Tools is available in Brazilian Portuguese, English, French, German, Italian, Japanese, and Spanish.

In addition to the multilingual capabilities of Office 2000 with MultiLanguage Pack, Office 2000 is also localized in many different languages. The localized versions are based on the same international core as Office 2000 with MultiLanguage Pack, but they provide more language-specific functionality.

You can install different combinations of Office language versions and language-specific tools, based on the needs of your international organization, as described in the following table.

If you want to do this	Install this language version and tools
Deploy a single version of Office internationally, but allow users to work in their own language.	Office 2000 with MultiLanguage Pack
Standardize on an English user interface, but allow users to edit documents in a variety of languages.	English Office 2000 only
Standardize on an English user interface, but provide proofing tools for editing in other languages.	Office 2000 and the Proofing Tools

If you want to do this	Install this language version and tools
Provide users with fully localized functionality in all Office applications.	Localized versions of Office 2000
Provide users with fully localized functionality in all Office applications, and provide proofing tools for editing in additional languages.	Localized versions of Office 2000 and the Proofing Tools

International deployment strategies

Depending on the structure of your organization and the languages that you need, you can adopt one of several different strategies for deploying Office internationally. For example, you can deploy language-specific custom installations from a centralized administrative source. Or you can deploy Office across your international administrative departments and allow each department to customize the installation for its own language-speaking area.

Deploying Office from international headquarters

If your organization is centralized, where one administrative group deploys Office to the entire organization, you can make all the customizations your users need at your headquarters and deploy directly to users internationally. In this scenario, you customize the MultiLanguage Pack and create a custom installation of Office for each language-speaking area.

For example, if you were deploying Office and the MultiLanguage Pack to users in the United States and Canada, you might deploy Office as follows:

- For English-speaking users in the United States, install only proofing tools from the MultiLanguage Pack, and enable languages for editing as needed.

- For Spanish-speaking users in the United States, install Spanish language features from the MultiLanguage Pack, leave the *installation language* set at U.S. English, set the user interface and online Help language to Spanish, and enable Spanish for editing (English is automatically enabled for editing if the installation language is English).

- For users in English-speaking Canadian provinces, set the installation language to Canadian English, and enable Canadian French and Canadian English for editing.

- For users in Québec, install French language features from the MultiLanguage Pack, set the installation language to Canadian French, set the user interface and online Help language to French, and enable Canadian French and Canadian English for editing.

Deploying Office at local subsidiaries

If your organization's administrative resources are distributed internationally, each local subsidiary can modify the standard installation for local users.

In this case, a central corporate administrative group supplies each local office with a standard Windows installer *transform* (MST file) with the installation language set to English. Local administrators customize the MultiLanguage Pack, select language settings, and modify the transform for their language-speaking area.

For example, if you are a site administrator in Hong Kong, you might customize the corporate deployment as follows:

- Install Traditional Chinese language features on users' computers and set Simplified Chinese language features so that they are installed the first time users activate the features.

- Set English or Traditional Chinese as the language for the user interface and online Help, set the installation language to Pan-Chinese, enable Simplified Chinese and Traditional Chinese and U.K. English for editing, and select Traditional Chinese as the preferred language (for *executable mode* in Microsoft Excel and Microsoft Access).

- Customize Office applications for Hong Kong users.

   For example, add a button to the toolbar in Microsoft Word for converting between Simplified Chinese and Traditional Chinese.

Note   For Traditional Chinese user interface and executable mode, users must be running a Traditional Chinese version of Microsoft Windows, or Windows 2000 with the *system locale* of Hong Kong or Taiwan.

See also

- Office 2000 has many features designed to fit the needs of international organizations. For more information, see "Overview of International Features in Office 2000" on page 725.

- The language features you install must be supported by the user's operating system. For more information, see "Configuring Users' Computers in an International Environment" on page 732.

- Office 2000 migrates settings from and can share files with previous localized versions of Office. For more information, see "Planning an International Move to Office 2000" on page 745.

How to Deploy Office Internationally

The following general steps apply to all international deployments of Microsoft Office 2000:

1 Create an *administrative installation point* for the Microsoft Office 2000 MultiLanguage Pack.

2 Customize the MultiLanguage Pack installation.

3 Install Office and the MultiLanguage Pack on a test computer, and specify language settings.

4 Customize the Office installation for different language-speaking areas.

Note When you customize the installation of Office and the MultiLanguage Pack, you create separate Windows installer *transforms* (MST files) for Office and for the MultiLanguage Pack. You must distribute the MultiLanguage Pack transform to users after Office is installed on their computers.

Create an administrative installation point for the MultiLanguage Pack

You run the Setup program for the MultiLanguage Pack in administrative mode to install the MultiLanguage Pack on a server.

Note The MultiLanguage Pack consists of sets of languages on multiple CD-ROMs. If you want to use languages on different CD-ROMs, you must run Setup separately for each CD-ROM you need and create a separate *administrative installation point* for each CD-ROM.

▶ **To create administrative installation point for the MultiLanguage Pack**

1 Create a share on a network server for the administrative installation point.

The share must be large enough to store the resources for the languages that you need. Each CD-ROM requires approximately 650 megabytes (MB) of server space.

2 On a computer running Windows 95/98 or Microsoft Windows NT with write access to the share, connect to the server share.

3 On the **Start** menu, click **Run**, and then click **Browse** to locate the MultiLanguage Pack CD-ROM.

4 On the MultiLanguage Pack CD-ROM in the CD-ROM drive, select **setup.exe** and click **Open**.

5 On the command line following **setup.exe**, type **/a** and click **OK**.

6 When prompted by Setup, enter the organization name you want to define for all users who install the MultiLanguage Pack from this location.

7 When prompted for the installation location, enter the server and the share that you created.

Note   When you run the Setup program for the MultiLanguage Pack in administrative mode, it behaves in the same way as the administrative mode of Office Setup.

Customize the MultiLanguage Pack installation

After you create an administrative installation point, you can use the Office Custom Installation Wizard to create a customized installation of the MultiLanguage Pack for users in different language-speaking areas.

Important   If you are installing the MultiLanguage Pack on computers running a non-Western European language version of Windows, use only ASCII characters for the text you type to create the MST file in the Custom Installation Wizard. Otherwise, the Windows installer *package* (MSI file) for the MultiLanguage Pack, which is based on the Western European *code page*, might not correctly interpret data in the transform.

▶ **To customize the MultiLanguage Pack installation**

1   Start the Custom Installation Wizard.

2   On the **Open the MSI File** panel, open Langpack.msi, the installer package for the MultiLanguage Pack.

3   On the **Open the MST File** panel, click **Do not open an existing MST file**.

4   On the **Select the MST File to Save** panel, specify a name for your custom MST file.

5   On the **Set Feature Installation States** panel, select the features you want to install on users' computers and specify the installation states.

Install Office and the MultiLanguage Pack and specify language settings

On a test computer, set **Regional Settings** (*user locale*) in Control Panel to match those of the target computer. Doing so allows Office to configure itself for a particular locale when it is installed. If the user is running Microsoft Windows NT, you can also set the test computer's default code page and fonts (*system locale*) to match the target computer.

Note   In Windows NT 4.0, if you change the system locale, you must reinstall Windows NT Server 4.0 with Service Pack 3 to restore the operating system's user interface.

After the system and user locales are set, run Office Setup from either the administrative installation point or from Microsoft Office 2000 Disc 1. Then install the MultiLanguage Pack from its administrative installation point by using a Windows installer *transform* (MST file) that installs resources for the language settings you want.

Note If you are using one computer to create more than one custom installation of Office, be sure to remove one installation of the MultiLanguage Pack before you run the MultiLanguage Pack Setup program with another MST file.

You can also install other MultiLanguage Pack features not installed by the MultiLanguage Pack Setup program on your test computer at this time. These features are in the Extras folder of the MultiLanguage Pack CD-ROMs. The CD-ROMs include files for displaying the Microsoft Internet Explorer 5 user interface in different languages, Input Method Editors (IMEs) for Asian languages, and other features.

When you run Office to specify language settings and user preferences, you can use the Profile Wizard to store the settings in an Office profile settings (OPS) file. The *OPS file* becomes part of a customized installation of Office. Because the choice of editing languages affects the functionality of certain applications, you can create unique OPS files for different groups of users based on the languages they are using.

Typically, most users creating multilingual documents rarely work with more than three languages. Limiting the number of editing languages results in a user interface that is less cluttered and allows Office applications to run optimized for particular languages.

If you want the custom installation of Office to behave like a localized version of Office, run the Language Version utility before specifying language settings. Running this utility switches the *installation language*, setting your choices of language-related features to only those appropriate for a particular language.

Toolbox

The installation language is set when you install Office. The Office Resource Kit includes the Language Version utility, which allows you to change the installation language after Office is installed. For information about installing this utility, see "Language Version" on page 777.

▶ To switch the language version of Office

1 Start the Language Version utility.

2 In the **Use default for** box, select the language that you want to switch to.

Important Running the Language Version utility replaces existing language-related settings and some other custom settings for several applications, so run the utility before you create any custom settings. When you're finished making settings for one language version, you can rerun the utility and make settings for another language version.

After Office and the MultiLanguage Pack are installed, specify language settings in the Office applications.

▶ **To create and store language settings**

1   On the **Start** menu, point to **Programs**, point to **Microsoft Office Tools**, and then click **Microsoft Office Language Settings**.

2   Select languages to use for the user interface, online Help, and editing.

   Users can change these default settings later by running the Language Version utility themselves.

3   Start Office, and specify additional user settings.

4   Start the Profile Wizard to save your settings in an OPS file.

Tip   Even though you include default language settings as part of the custom installation of Office, users can switch languages by running the Microsoft Office Language Settings utility themselves. To prevent users from switching languages, customize the Office installation by using the Custom Installation Wizard and make the feature Microsoft Office\Office Tools\Language Settings Tool unavailable to users.

Customize Office installation for different language-speaking areas

You run the Custom Installation Wizard to create customized installations of Office for users in different language-speaking areas. Create a separate Windows installer *transform* (MST file) for each language-speaking area.

Important   If you are installing Office on computers running a non-Western European language version of Windows, use only ASCII characters for the text you type to create the MST file in the Custom Installation Wizard. Otherwise, the installer package (MSI file) for the Office, which is based on the Western European code page, might not correctly interpret data in the transform.

▶ **To customize the Office installation for different language-speaking areas**

1   Start the Custom Installation Wizard.

2   On the **Set Feature Installation States** panel, expand the Microsoft Office\Office Tools\International Support portion of the feature tree.

3   Select the Core Support Files feature, and select an installation option.

   This set of files accommodates all commonly used code pages.

4   Select the Extended Support Files feature, and select an installation option.

   This set of files accommodates code pages rarely used in Windows, such as EBCDIC, Macintosh®, MS-DOS® Multilingual (Latin 1), and IBM Cyrillic.

5 Set the installation state for language-specific features, such as for an Asian language or a right-to-left language (Arabic, Hebrew, Farsi, or Urdu).

6 On the **Customize Default Application Settings** panel, click **Get values from an existing settings profile**, and enter the path to the OPS file that contains your custom language settings.

7 On the **Add Installations and Run Programs** panel, include any batch files you created to install extra language utilities from the MultiLanguage Pack CD-ROM.

8 On the **Modify Setup Properties** panel, double-click **INSTALLLANGUAGE**, and select a language.

The installation language setting determines default behavior of Office applications. For example, if the installation language is German, Word bases its Normal.dot template on German settings and automatically enables German features, such as not tracking editing time.

When you select language-specific features on the **Set Feature Installation States** panel, keep in mind the following:

- If your users work with languages that use more than one code page, install the Core Support Files feature on users' computers.

- If your users work with a right-to-left language (Arabic, Hebrew, Farsi, or Urdu) and their operating system can support right-to-left text, install the Bidirectional Support feature on users' computers.

- If your users work with Asian text and they are not running a matching language version of Windows, install the Japanese, Korean, Traditional Chinese, or Simplified Chinese fonts on users' computers.

- If your users need a full *Unicode* font—for example, if they are working with Access datasheets that include languages that use more than one code page—install the Universal font on users' computers.

Note For users running a non-Asian version of Windows NT version 4.0, do not install more than two of the Asian or Universal font choices. These fonts include many characters and might not display properly if more than two of them are installed on a computer running Windows NT version 4.0.

See also

- The steps for customizing and distributing Office and the MultiLanguage Pack are part of the larger process of deploying Office. For more information, see "Managing a Successive Deployment of Office Premium and Related Products" on page 115.

- In addition to specifying language features and providing support for international users, you can customize many other aspects of your Office installation. For more information, see "Customizing How Office Features Are Installed" on page 224 and "Customizing How Office Options Are Set" on page 233.

- You can use the Office Custom Installation Wizard to customize international installations of Office. For more information, see "Office Custom Installation Wizard" on page 250.

- You can use the Profile Wizard to save language-related settings to a file you distribute as part of a custom installation of Office. For more information, see "Profile Wizard" on page 255.

MultiLanguage Pack Extras

In addition to the features that are installed with the Microsoft Office 2000 MultiLanguage Pack Setup program, you can install other features from subfolders in the Extras folder on the MultiLanguage Pack CD-ROM. These MultiLanguage Pack extras are described in the following table.

MultiLanguage Pack Extra	Description
Excel add-ins	Users can run certain localized add-ins, such as Update Add-in Links.
Excel object libraries	Microsoft Excel 2000 users can run multilingual macros created in Excel 95 or Excel 5.0.
Microsoft Internet Explorer user interface languages	Users can change the language of the user interface in Microsoft Internet Explorer 5.
Input Method Editors (IMEs)	Users can enter Asian text.
Microsoft Jet 4.0 user interface languages	Users can change the language of the user interface for the Microsoft Access 2000 database engine and other applications that use Microsoft Jet 4.0.
Outlook forms	Users can open forms by using localized Electronic Forms Designer files.
Outlook At Work fax patch	Users can install a localized patch for the Outlook At Work fax feature.

You can install some of these features by running the Office Custom Installation Wizard and adding the feature's Setup program to the Windows installer *transform* (MST file) for the MultiLanguage Pack. Other features, however, already use the installer in their own Setup programs. These features cannot be added to the MultiLanguage Pack transform; they must be deployed separately.

You can install other MultiLanguage Pack extras by copying the files from the MultiLanguage Pack CD-ROM to users' hard disks and changing the related registry settings. In this case, you can add the files and registry entries to the MultiLanguage Pack transform by using the Custom Installation Wizard. Alternatively, you can create a batch file that copies the files and creates the registry settings and then add the batch file to the MultiLanguage Pack transform.

Excel add-ins

The MultiLanguage Pack provides several localized Excel add-ins. Other than these localized add-ins, users cannot change the user interface language of Excel add-ins. You can load localized Excel add-ins on users' computers as part of a custom deployment of the MultiLanguage Pack. Use the Custom Installation Wizard to add the necessary files to the MultiLanguage Pack transform.

▶ **To include localized Excel add-ins in the MultiLanguage Pack transform**

1   Copy the folders in the Extras\XLAddins folder from the MultiLanguage Pack CD-ROM to the *administrative installation point* for the MultiLanguage Pack.

2   Start the Custom Installation Wizard.

3   On the **Add Files to the Installation** panel, click **Add**.

4   In the **Add Files to MST File** dialog box, open the folder for the language you want from the administrative installation point, select the files that you want to install, and click **Add**.

5   In the **File Destination Path** dialog box, enter a path for the localized file in the **Destination path on the user's computer** box. (This path is usually Program Files\Microsoft Office\Office\Library.)

Important   If you plan to install the localized add-ins, do not install English add-ins. For each localized add-in you want to install, set the English equivalent to **Not Available** when you customize the Office installation. If English add-ins are already installed, remove them before you install the localized add-ins.

Excel object library files

When Excel 2000 users open an Excel 95 or Excel 5.0 workbook that contains non-English macros, Excel 2000 must translate the macros to English in order to run them. To translate the macros, Excel 2000 users must have Excel object libraries installed.

If users are upgrading to Excel 2000 from a localized version of Excel 95 or Excel 5.0 and they run non-English macros, they must install object libraries for the localized language. If the Excel 95 or Excel 5.0 macro includes procedures written in more than one language, Excel 2000 users must install an object library for each language used in the macro.

Note   All Excel 97 macros are compiled in English, so Excel 2000 does not need to translate them.

Users can install the object libraries they need after they install Excel 2000, or you can install object libraries on users' computers when you deploy the MultiLanguage Pack.

Distributing Excel object libraries

You can make the Excel object libraries and the object library installation program available to users so that they can install the object libraries they need.

▶ **To make object libraries available on a network share**

1   Copy the contents of the Extras\95olbs folder from the appropriate MultiLanguage Pack CD-ROM to a network share.

If you want to use Excel object libraries from more than one MultiLanguage Pack CD-ROM, copy the subfolders of the Extras\95olbs folder from each CD-ROM to the same network share.

2   At the root level of the folder on the network share, users run InstOLB.exe.

3   In the **Object Library Installer** dialog box, users select the languages for which they want to install object libraries.

Installing Excel object libraries

You can install Excel object libraries on users' computers as part of a custom deployment of the MultiLanguage Pack. Use the Custom Installation Wizard to create a transform that instructs Setup to copy the files and create registry settings on users' computers.

▶ **To add object library files to the MultiLanguage Pack transform**

1   Copy the folders in the Extras\95olbs folder from the MultiLanguage Pack CD-ROM to the administrative installation point for the MultiLanguage Pack.

2   Start the Custom Installation Wizard.

3 On the **Add Files to the Installation** panel, click **Add**.

4 For each language for which you want to deploy object libraries, open the appropriate folder, select the files Xl5en32.olb and Xl5*x*32.olb, where *x* is the language of the OLB file name, and then click **Add**.

5 In the **File Destination Path** dialog box, enter the path to the location of Excel.exe in the **Destination path on the user's computer** box, and then click **OK**.

The default location for Excel.exe is \Program Files\Microsoft Office\Office.

6 On the **Add Files to the Installation** panel, click **Add** again.

7 For each language for which you added object library files, open the appropriate folder, select the files Vbaen32.olb and Vba*x*32.olb, where *x* is the language of the OLB file name, and click **Add**.

8 In the **File Destination Path** dialog box, enter **<System>** in the **Destination path on the user's computer** box.

After you add the object library files to the transform, you add the corresponding registry settings in the Custom Installation Wizard.

▶ **To add object library registry settings to the MultiLanguage Pack transform**

1 On the **Add Registry Entries** panel of the Custom Installation Wizard, click **Add**, enter the following values, and click **OK**:

In the **Root** box, select **HKEY_LOCAL_MACHINE**.

In the **Data type** box, select **REG_SZ**.

In the **Key** box, enter **\Software\Classes\TypeLib\{000204F3-0000-0000-C000-000000000046}\1.0*n*\win32**, where *n* is the language of the subkey number.

In the **Value name** box, enter **Default**.

In the **Value data** box, enter *System***\VBA*x*32.olb**, where *System* is the path to the user's System folder.

2 On the **Add Registry Entries** panel, click **Add** again, enter the following values, and click **OK**:

In the **Root** box, select **HKEY_LOCAL_MACHINE**.

In the **Data type** box, select **REG_SZ**.

In the **Key** box, enter **\Software\Classes\TypeLib \{00020813-0000-0000-C000-000000000046}\1.0*n*\win32**, where *n* is the language of subkey number.

In the **Value name** box, enter **Default**.

In the **Value data** box, enter *ExcelFolder***\XL5*x*32.olb**, where *ExcelFolder* is the path to Excel.exe.

The alphabetical (*x*) and numeric (*n*) placeholders in the OLB file names and registry subkeys identify the language used in the macro, as described in the following table.

Language	OLB file name	Subkey number
Arabic	AR	1
Brazilian (Portuguese)	PTB	416
Chinese (Simplified)	CHS	804
Chinese (Traditional)	CHT	404
Danish	DA	6
Dutch	NL	13
Finnish	FI	B
French	FR	C
German	DE	7
Hebrew	HE	D
Italian	IT	10
Japan	JP	11
Korean	KO	12
Norwegian	NO	14
Portuguese	PTG	16
Spanish	ES	A
Swedish	SV	1d

Installing specialized English libraries for some languages

In some language versions of Excel 95 and Excel 5.0, notably Asian and right-to-left (Arabic or Hebrew) languages, the object libraries include specialized English libraries, which you must install in addition to the non-English library.

Because each non-English object library has a different file name, you can install libraries for multiple languages. However, all the English library files have the same name, so if you install libraries for multiple languages, the English library that is installed last overwrites any previously installed English libraries.

Therefore, if users need libraries for more than one language, install the primary language libraries last. For example, if your users are upgrading from the Arabic language version of Excel 95, but sometimes run macros created in French, install the object libraries for the Arabic language version last.

Internet Explorer user interface languages

If users want to change the language of the user interface of Internet Explorer 5, they must have the appropriate language files installed. You can include these files in the MultiLanguage Pack transform.

Note   Users must have Internet Explorer 5 installed before they can install the language files for a different user interface language.

▶ **To add Internet Explorer user interface languages to the transform**

1   Copy the folders in the Extras\Ie5 folder from the MultiLanguage Pack CD-ROM to the administrative installation point for the MultiLanguage Pack.

2   Start the Custom Installation Wizard.

3   On the **Add Installations and Run Programs** panel, click **Add**.

4   In the **Add/Modify Program Entry** dialog box, click **Browse**.

5   For each language that you want, open the language folder from the administrative installation point, and then double-click the *file name*.exe file.

Input Method Editors

Input Method Editors (IMEs) are software utilities that convert keystrokes to characters in an *ideographic script*. The MultiLanguage Pack includes IMEs for Japanese, Korean, Simplified Chinese, and Traditional Chinese.

For Japanese, Simplified Chinese, and Traditional Chinese, you install either a locale-specific IME or a Global IME, depending on the language version of the user's operating system. Install the locale-specific IME if the language of the IME matches the language of the user's operating system; otherwise, install the appropriate Global IME. Global IMEs allow users to enter Asian text regardless of the language version of their operating system. (For Korean, only the Global IME is available.)

Note   Global Input Method Editors (Global IMEs) allow users running non-Asian versions of the Microsoft Windows operating system to type Asian text in Microsoft Word, Microsoft Outlook, and Internet Explorer.

You can add the Setup programs for Global IMEs to the MultiLanguage Pack transform. However, the Setup program for locale-specific IMEs uses the Windows installer; these installations cannot be added to the MultiLanguage Pack transform.

Chinese Input Method Editors

If users who want to enter Chinese text are running a language version of the operating system that matches the language of the IME they want to use, they must install the locale-specific IME. Otherwise, they must install the Global IME.

▶ **To add the Setup program for a Chinese Global IME to the transform**

1   For Simplified Chinese, copy the contents of the folder Extras\Ime\ChinSimp\Global from the MultiLanguage Pack CD-ROM to the administrative installation point for the MultiLanguage Pack.

−or−

For Traditional Chinese, copy the contents of the folder Extras\Ime\ChinTrad\Global to the administrative installation point.

2   Start the Custom Installation Wizard.

3   On the **Add Installations and Run Programs** panel, click **Add**.

4   In the **Add/Modify Program Entry** dialog box, click **Browse**.

5   Go to the administrative installation point, and double-click **msscaime.exe** for the Simplified Chinese IME.

−or−

Double-click **mstcaime.exe** for the Traditional Chinese IME.

Users can install locale-specific Chinese IMEs from a network share. They can perform the installation manually, or you can incorporate the procedure either into a logon script or into a batch file that you distribute in e-mail to your users. The Setup program for the locale-specific Chinese IMEs are in the \ChinSimp\Regular folder (for Simplified Chinese) and the \ChinTrad\Regular folder (for Traditional Chinese).

Japanese Input Method Editors

If users who want to enter Japanese text are running a Korean, Simplified Chinese, or Traditional Chinese language version of the operating system, they must install the Japanese Global IME. You can add the installation of the Japanese Global IME to the MultiLanguage Pack transform.

▶ **To add the Setup program for the Japanese Global IME to the transform**

1   Copy the folder Extras\Ime\Japanese\Global\Asianwin from the MultiLanguage Pack CD-ROM to the administrative installation point for the MultiLanguage Pack.

2   Start the Custom Installation Wizard.

3   On the **Add Installations and Run Programs** panel, click **Add**.

4   In the **Add/Modify Program Entry** dialog box, click **Browse**.

5   Go to the administrative installation point, and double-click **msjaime.exe**.

If users who want to enter Japanese text are running a Japanese or non-Asian language version of the operating system, they must run a separate Setup program that installs the appropriate Japanese IME. This Setup program uses the Windows installer, so you cannot add the installation to the MultiLanguage Pack transform. However, you can create an *administrative installation point* so that users can install the Japanese IME from a network share.

▶ **To create an administrative installation point for Japanese IMEs**

1   Create a share on a network server for the administrative installation point, with at least 40 megabytes (MB) available.

2   On a computer running Microsoft Windows 95/98 or Microsoft Windows NT with write access to the share, connect to the server share.

3   On the **Start** menu, click **Run**, and then click **Browse**.

4   Insert the MultiLanguage Pack CD-ROM in the CD-ROM drive, and then open the Extras\Ime\Japanese\Regular folder, and click **setup.exe**.

5   On the command line following **setup.exe**, type **/a**.

6   When prompted for the installation location, enter the path to the administrative installation point.

Users can install the Japanese IME from the network share by running Setup.exe manually, or you can incorporate the procedure into a logon script or batch file distributed in e-mail. Because the installation uses the Windows installer, users must have Office 2000 installed before installing the Japanese IME.

Note   The user interface of the installation program for the Japanese IME is in English.

Korean Input Method Editor

If users who want to enter Korean text are running a non-Korean version of the operating system, they must install the Korean Global IME. You can add the installation of the Korean Global IME to the MultiLanguage Pack transform.

▶ **To add the Setup program for the Korean Global IME to the transform**

1   Copy the contents of the folder Extras\Ime\Korean\Global from the MultiLanguage Pack CD-ROM to the administrative installation point for the MultiLanguage Pack.

2   Start the Custom Installation Wizard.

3   On the **Add Installations and Run Programs** panel, click **Add**.

4   In the **Add/Modify Program Entry** dialog box, click **Browse**.

5   Go to the administrative installation point, and double-click **mshaime.exe**.

Microsoft Jet 4.0 user interface language files

The Microsoft Jet 4.0 user interface files are dynamic-link library (DLL) files that are installed on top of a user's existing installation of Access 2000. When users install one of these DLL files, they can change the Microsoft Jet 4.0 user interface language. Users must install the appropriate DLL file for the language they want to use.

You can install Microsoft Jet 4.0 user interface files on users' computers as part of a custom deployment of the MultiLanguage Pack. Use the Custom Installation Wizard to add the necessary files to the MultiLanguage Pack transform.

▶ **To include Microsoft Jet 4.0 user interface files in the MultiLanguage Pack transform**

1   Copy the folders in the Extras\Jet folder from the MultiLanguage Pack CD-ROM to the administrative installation point for the MultiLanguage Pack.

2   Start the Custom Installation Wizard.

3   On the **Add Files to the Installation** panel, click **Add**.

4   In the **Add Files to MST File** dialog box, open the folder for the language you want from the administrative installation point, select Msjint40.dll and Mswstr10.dll, and click **Add**.

5   In the **File Destination Path** dialog box, enter **<System>** in the **Destination path on the user's computer** box.

Outlook At Work fax patch

If your users are running a non-English language version of Windows 95/98 and are using the Outlook At Work fax feature, they must install the localized patch file. You can add this file to the MultiLanguage Pack transform.

Note   If users are upgrading from Outlook 98, they don't need to install the patch.

▶ **To add a localized Outlook At Work fax patch to the transform**

1   Copy the folders in the Extras\AWFAXpat folder from the MultiLanguage Pack CD-ROM to the administrative installation point for the MultiLanguage Pack.

2   Start the Custom Installation Wizard.

3   On the **Add Installations and Run Programs** panel, click **Add**.

4   In the **Add/Modify Program Entry** dialog box, click **Browse**.

5   Open the folder for the language you want from the administrative installation point, and then double-click **Awfaxpch.exe**.

Outlook forms

If your organization uses 16-bit Electronic Forms Designer forms and your users are running non-English language versions of Windows 95/98 or Windows NT, you must deploy localized Visual Basic support files. These files allow users to open 16-bit forms that are supported by Microsoft Outlook and the Microsoft Exchange client. You can add these files to the MultiLanguage Pack transform.

Note   If users are upgrading from a previous version of Outlook, they don't need to install the localized files.

▶ **To add localized files for the Electronic Forms Designer to the transform**

1   Copy the folders in the Extras\EFDSupp folder from the MultiLanguage Pack CD-ROM to the administrative installation point for the MultiLanguage Pack.

2   Start the Custom Installation Wizard.

3   On the **Add Installations and Run Programs** panel, click **Add.**

4   In the **Add/Modify Program Entry** dialog box, click **Browse.**

5   Open the folder for the language you want from the administrative installation point, and then double-click **efd.exe.**

See also

• You can use the Office Custom Installation Wizard to customize international installations of the MultiLanguage Pack. For more information, see "Office Custom Installation Wizard" on page 250.

• The MultiLanguage Pack includes other features in addition to those in the Extras folder of the MultiLanguage Pack CD-ROM. For more information, see "Features of the MultiLanguage Pack" on page 727.

Customizing Language Features

You can customize language settings when you deploy Microsoft Office 2000 by using the Office Custom Installation Wizard and the Profile Wizard. These wizards record your settings and modify the Windows registry on users' computers when users install your customized version of Office.

When Office is installed, Office Setup creates the following registry subkey:

HKEY_CURRENT_USER\Software\Microsoft\Office\9.0\Common\LanguageResources

When Office applications run, they look up entries in the LanguageResources subkey to determine language-related default behavior. For example:

- Microsoft Word checks **LCID** entries and turns on its language auto-detection feature for languages that are enabled for editing.

- Microsoft Excel and Microsoft Access check the **ExeMode** entry to determine which Asian or right-to-left language to provide full support for.

- Word checks the **InstallLanguage** entry to determine how to create its initial Normal.dot file.

Customizing the installation language

When you install Office 2000, an *installation language* setting is added to the Windows registry. When users start an Office application, the application reads this setting to determine default behavior, such as how to create the initial Normal.dot file for Word and whether to display language-specific capabilities.

In the Language Resources subkey, Office Setup creates an entry named **InstallLanguage** with a value equal to the *locale ID* (LCID) for the installation language of Office. For example, if the value of **InstallLanguage** is **1041**, the installation language is Japanese. In this case, Normal.dot in Word is based on Japanese settings, and Office applications run with Japanese settings as their default.

Office Setup automatically sets the installation language to correspond to the language version of Office that you purchased. You can customize the installation language for foreign offices, however, so that Office runs with defaults that match foreign locations.

To customize the installation language during deployment, double-click **INSTALLLANGUAGE** on the **Modify Setup Properties** panel of the Office Custom Installation Wizard, and select a language in the **Value** box.

Toolbox

The installation language is set when you install Office. The Office Resource Kit includes the Language Version utility, which allows you to change the installation language after Office is installed. For information about installing this utility, see "Language Version" on page 777.

Set the language for spelling checking in Microsoft Excel

When you use the Custom Installation Wizard to modify the value of **InstallLanguage**, the spelling checking language in Excel is not reset to match. To change the installation language and also set the spelling checking language in Excel, use the Language Version utility to set the language.

Alternatively, if you use the Custom Installation Wizard to modify the **InstallLanguage** setting, you can set the language for spelling checking in Excel manually. In the HKEY_CURRENT_USER\Software\Microsoft\Office \9.0\Excel\Spell Checker subkey, set the value of **Speller** to the locale ID (LCID).

Configuring language-specific defaults

In addition to using the installation language setting, Office 2000 also configures language-related defaults, such as number format, to match the *user locale* of the operating system. If you want Office to use defaults based on the installation language regardless of the user locale, you can set the value of **Pure** entry in the Language Resources subkey to **ON**.

System Policy Tip   You can use system policies to prevent Office from adjusting defaults to the user locale for any group of users in your organization. In the System Policy Editor, set the **Microsoft Office 2000\Language Settings\Other\Do not adjust defaults to user's locale** policy. For more information about the System Policy Editor, see "Using the System Policy Editor" on page 296.

For example, if your organization is based in the United States and you want to standardize settings internationally, you can deploy Office with the **InstallLanguage** entry set to **1033** (U.S. English) and the **Pure** entry set to **ON**. Users would get the same set of defaults regardless of their user locale.

An advantage of preventing Office from configuring to the user locale is that macros are more compatible internationally when all settings are consistent. A disadvantage of setting the **Pure** entry to **ON** is that, if you are upgrading from a previous localized version of Office, you cannot migrate user settings from a language version that differs from the Office 2000 installation language.

Note   Because Office requires default Asian fonts when you set Asian user locales, do not set the value of **Pure** to **ON** for Asian user locales.

Customizing the executable mode for Access and Excel

If an Asian or right-to-left language (Arabic, Hebrew, Farsi, or Urdu) is enabled for editing, Access and Excel must run in a mode that supports Asian or right-to-left text. This mode is known as the *executable mode*. When you deploy Office, you can specify the executable mode for a group of users.

Note   For users running an Asian or right-to-left language version of Microsoft Windows, Access and Excel work best when the executable mode is set to match the language of the operating system.

To customize the executable mode during deployment, use the Microsoft Office Language Settings utility to set the executable mode, and then capture the setting by using the Profile Wizard.

▶ To set the executable mode

1   On the **Start** menu, point to **Programs**, and then point to **Microsoft Office Tools**.

2   Click **Microsoft Office Language Settings**.

3   On the **Enabled Languages** tab, select the Asian or right-to-left languages you want to be available for editing documents.

4   In the **Preferred Language** box, select the preferred Asian or right-to-left language; this is the language that determines the executable mode.

In Excel, if you select one Asian language as the executable mode, you can still work in other Asian languages. However, some features (such as number formats) might be supported only by the preferred language. In both Access and Excel, if you want the applications to support right-to-left text, you must select a right-to-left language as the preferred language.

Customizing languages for user interface, online Help, and editing

Office 2000 allows users to choose different languages for displaying menus and dialog box text, Help text, and for editing documents. To customize users' default language choices during deployment, use the Microsoft Office Language Settings utility to select languages, and then capture the settings by using the Profile Wizard.

▶ To select language settings

1   On the **Start** menu, point to **Programs**, and then point to **Microsoft Office Tools**.

2   Click **Microsoft Office Language Settings**, and then click the **User Interface** tab.

   The **User Interface** tab is available only if the MultiLanguage Pack has been installed.

3   In the **Display menus and dialogs in** box, select the user interface language.

4   In the **Display Help in** box, select a language for online Help.

   If you don't specify a language in the **Display Help in** box, the online Help language defaults to the language that you selected as the user interface language.

5   Click the **Enabled Languages** tab, and select languages that you want to be available for editing documents.

6   In the **Installed version of Microsoft Office** box, select a subset of the Office installation language, such as Canadian or U.S. English (optional).

   If the installation language of Office is English, French, German, Norwegian, or Serbian, selecting the local variety of the language makes utilities such as spelling checkers more useful.

Enabling languages without the MultiLanguage Pack

The options on the **User Interface** tab in the **Microsoft Office Language Settings** dialog box include all the languages installed from the Microsoft Office 2000 MultiLanguage Pack. However, the options on the **Enabled Languages** tab include all the languages supported by Office, regardless of what is installed from the MultiLanguage Pack.

Consequently, you can enable functionality for working with certain languages regardless of whether the MultiLanguage Pack is installed. For example, by selecting Korean as an editing language, you enable Asian and Korean features in Word regardless of whether Korean proofing tools from the MultiLanguage Pack are available.

If you installed the Microsoft Office 2000 Proofing Tools instead of the MultiLanguage Pack, Office uses those proofing tools for the languages you enable for editing.

System Policy Tip   You can use system policies to specify default language settings for any group of users in your organization. In the System Policy Editor, set the **Microsoft Office 2000\Language Settings\User Interface** policies to determine user interface languages. To determine editing languages, set the **Microsoft Office 2000\Language Settings\Enabled Languages\Show controls and enable editing for** policies. For more information about the System Policy Editor, see "Using the System Policy Editor" on page 296.

When you set system policies for the user interface and online Help, be sure the languages you select are supported by users' operating system, as follows:

- In English and European versions of Windows 95/98 and Windows NT 4, users can run the user interface and online Help in English and all European languages.

- In Greek, Asian and right-to-left language (Arabic, Hebrew) versions of Windows 95/98 and Windows NT 4, users can run the user interface and online Help in English or the language of their operating system.

Note   Users running an Arabic version of Windows 95/98 and Windows NT 4 can also select French as their user interface and online Help language.

Deploying Localized Versions of Office 2000

Deploying Microsoft Office 2000 with MultiLanguage Pack gives you the advantage of having a single installation of Office for your entire international organization. However, due to limitations of some *plug-in language features*, you might decide to deploy localized versions of Office 2000 in some language-speaking areas.

Advantages of installing localized versions of Office

Some features in Office 2000 with MultiLanguage Pack cannot switch the language of their user interface. If it is important that users run these features in their own language, you can deploy a localized version of Office to these users. Localized versions of Office 2000 are based on the same international core as Office 2000 with MultiLanguage Pack, so users can exchange documents between language versions of Office 2000 with no loss of data.

There are some differences between running Office 2000 with MultiLanguage Pack and running a localized version of Office. For example:

- The Office 2000 with MultiLanguage Pack cannot switch the user interface language of Microsoft Map in Microsoft Excel, Excel add-ins, some OCX controls, and some Help elements (such as dialog boxes and the **Contents** tab).

- In Office 2000 with MultiLanguage Pack, shortcuts on the **Start** menu are not localized.

- Localized versions of Office include more localized templates and wizards than are provided in the MultiLanguage Pack.

Toolbox

You can look up information about which Office features cannot switch the language of their user interface in an Excel workbook named Intlimit.xls. For more information about installing this workbook, see "International Information" on page 786.

Disadvantages of installing localized versions of Office

There are some drawbacks to deploying localized versions of Office rather than standardizing on a single version. With separate versions, you need separate procedures for deployment, support, and administration. Also, localized versions do not usually support the ability to switch the language of the user interface.

However, some localized versions of Office 2000 provide limited ability to switch the language of the user interface. You can switch the language of the user interface to English in the following localized versions of Office 2000:

- Arabic
- Hebrew
- Pan-Chinese
- Simplified Chinese
- Traditional Chinese
- Japanese
- Korean
- Thai

In the Arabic version of Office 2000, you can also switch the user interface to French. In the Pan-Chinese (Hong Kong) version, you can switch most Office 2000 applications to Simplified Chinese (except for Microsoft Outlook and Microsoft FrontPage) if the user is running Microsoft Windows NT.

Depending on your needs, you can deploy a localized version of Office 2000 in selected language-speaking areas. For example, you might deploy Office 2000 with MultiLanguage Pack everywhere except Japan, where you deploy the Japanese version of Office 2000.

Supporting Users Who Travel Between Computers

Microsoft Office 2000 makes it easier than ever to support users who travel between computers on a network. With new installation options and an improved model for storing user preferences, users can travel and take their Office 2000 documents and settings with them.

Taking Your Office with You

Traveling users (sometimes referred to as *roaming users*) move between different computers on a network. By using Microsoft Office 2000, traveling users can move between computers without changing the way that they work. Their application settings and working files travel with them, along with any system preferences.

Traveling users are possible because of *roaming user profiles*. Microsoft Windows 95/98, Windows NT Workstation version 4.0, and Windows 2000 Professional support roaming user profiles, as do Windows NT Server 4.0, Windows 2000 Server, and third-party servers. Office 2000 takes advantage of the operating systems' features to make Office settings travel with your users.

When you turn on roaming user profiles, you can keep employees working no matter where they happen to be. Users can switch between computers in a lab, in different buildings, or in different offices around the world, as long as they log on to the same network and retrieve their user information from that network. This flexibility helps you make the most of your computer resources.

Traveling between international offices

When your users travel to offices in other regions, you can make sure that their Office 2000 environments travel with them.

For example, if your U.S.-based customer representative handles accounts in different countries, she can customize Office 2000 to include a custom dictionary that contains the names of the people and companies she corresponds with often.

When your customer representative travels overseas to meet with customers, she can log on to the network from any foreign office and download her user profile. The profile allows her to work as if she were at her home computer. If she sends a memo to one of her customers and checks the spelling, her customized version of Office 2000 automatically skips any names already in her custom dictionary.

Traveling within a regional site

If your company has several offices in one region, you can take advantage of roaming user profiles to make these offices work like one office.

For example, you might have a manager who is currently working on a memo detailing budget requests for the next year, which includes hidden text to remind him of important points that need to be made face to face. He customizes his toolbar to include the **Show All** button for easy access to his hidden text.

He is called to a meeting with the Finance group to go over the information he's just been working on. He logs off of his computer, thus updating his user profile; and then during the meeting, he logs on to a computer in the conference room and retrieves his memo, and then he uses his customized toolbar to display hidden text. He's able to review his arguments as the meeting goes along and make his arguments to the Finance group.

Sharing computers among multiple users

If your company doesn't fit the typical "one user to one computer" scenario, you can use roaming user profiles to make sure that your users always have access to their information on whatever computer they are using that day.

For example, several users might take advantage of computers in your lab on an as-needed basis. One user logs on to work on a report in Microsoft Word. He saves his report as a template so that he can use it again to create his next report. When he logs off, his user profile is updated with the change.

Later that same day, another user logs on to the same computer and opens Word to create a memo. She uses the **New** command (**File** menu) and selects from the standard list of available templates. The template that her co-worker created does not appear in her list. She goes on to perform her work as usual.

System Requirements for Traveling Users

To set up roaming user profiles for your *traveling users*, your server and client computers must have the following software installed.

Server requirements

- Microsoft Windows NT Server version 4.0 or Microsoft Windows 2000 Server

  –or–

  Novell NetWare version 3 or higher

  –or–

  Other third-party servers that support roaming user profiles

Note   The server must support long file names for user profiles to travel successfully.

Client requirements

- Windows NT Workstation version 4.0 or Windows 2000 Professional

  –or–

  Windows 98 with user profiles turned on

  –or–

  Windows 95 including Microsoft Internet Explorer version 4.01 with Service Pack 1 with the Active Desktop™ and user profiles turned on

Note   Roaming user profiles are platform-specific. Because of differences between the Windows registry and the Windows NT registry, users cannot travel between Windows 95/98 and Windows NT or Windows 2000.

Other requirements

- Administrator or User privileges for all user and computer accounts. Accounts with Guest privileges do not travel.

See also

- For additional information about setting up roaming user profiles on your Windows NT network, see the *Windows NT Server 4.0 Resource Kit*.

- For additional information about user profiles and your client operating system, see the product documentation for Windows 95, Windows 98, Windows NT Workstation 4.0, or Windows 2000 Professional.

Preparing Office for Traveling Users

Users are able to travel easily between computers when their documents and application preferences travel with them. This requires both configuring the Microsoft Office 2000 installation to make it easier for users to travel and configuring the operating system to support users who travel.

A uniform configuration of operating system and application software throughout your network simplifies the task of supporting *traveling users*. In addition, it helps to install Office 2000 to the same place on each computer.

Flexible application shortcuts with the Windows installer

Standard shortcuts to an application contain a path to the program file. With the new Windows installer, however, you can take advantage of a more flexible type of shortcut. *Windows installer shortcuts* use a globally unique identifier (GUID) to point to the application, so they are not dependent on a particular application path.

Windows installer shortcuts make it easy to support traveling users. When you use Windows installer shortcuts, you don't have to worry about installing Office to the same place on each computer. When users click a Windows installer shortcut, the shortcut tracks down the Office application. If the application isn't installed, the installer automatically installs the missing application, and users can resume their work.

Windows installer shortcuts work with Office 2000 running on Microsoft Windows 2000 and Windows 98. You can also use them with Microsoft Windows NT 4.0 or Windows 95 including Microsoft Internet Explorer 4.01 with Service Pack 1 and Active Desktop turned on. Windows installer shortcuts are created automatically when you install Office 2000 on one of these operating systems.

The following guidelines can help you make your environment work well for traveling users:

Install Office 2000 to the same folder on each computer   If users travel from a computer that has Office installed on drive C to a computer that has Office installed on drive D, their shortcuts and customized settings might not work correctly.

Install Office on a per-computer, rather than per-user, basis   Traveling users rely on user profiles to transfer their individual settings. However, you can save both hard disk space and download time by installing Office 2000 on a per-computer basis. For Windows NT, log on as an administrator of the computer and then install Office 2000. For Windows 95/98, install Office before you turn on user profiles. Installing on a per-computer basis ensures that the installation information is shared between all users on that computer, so it does not need to be stored separately for each user.

Note   Installing Office 2000 before enabling user profiles on Windows 95/98 gives you a per-computer installation of Office 2000. Be aware, however, that using this method for Windows 95/98 can cause Windows installer shortcuts to display a generic image, rather than the application icon. The shortcuts continue to function correctly; only the image is affected.

Install Office applications to run from the network   If you install the Office applications on the network, these applications are always available to traveling users, as long as your network is running. With the applications on the network, you also cut down on the number of files and other objects that must be copied to each hard disk when users travel to a new computer.

Install crucial Office applications to run from the local hard disk   You can install the Office applications that users need most to run from the local hard disk. For example, if everyone uses Word on a daily basis to work on reports, memos, and other documents, you can ensure that their work is not interrupted by server problems by installing Word on the local hard disk.

Store user information on the network   When you configure a user profile to roam, it is copied to the network, and then downloaded when a user travels to a new computer. To make roaming even easier, you can also store other information, such as your users' My Documents or Personal folders on a server, so that users can open their documents from the server, no matter which computer they are using.

Tip   If you store user information on a file server, rather than your Primary Domain Controller (PDC), you can also balance the load on your servers more efficiently. For more information about load balancing, see your network documentation.

Create a default Office user profile   Office 2000 includes the Profile Wizard that you can use to save a set of Office options. This set of options is called an *Office user profile*. You can start all of your users off with the same configuration by creating and deploying a default Office user profile when you deploy Office 2000.

Set system policies   You can protect or enforce important settings through system policies. For example, if you want all users to save files in a particular format, you can set the file type to use through a system policy.

Tip   Do not lock down the system entirely if you are supporting traveling users. Make sure that user profiles and system policies allow users to install the applications they need when they travel to a new computer. You can also set the **Always install with** *elevated privileges* policy for the Windows installer. This policy allows any user to install Office 2000 features as if the user were an administrator for that computer.

See also

- You can use the Profile Wizard to create an Office profile and give your traveling users a standard environment to start from. For more information about using the Profile Wizard, see "Profile Wizard" on page 255.

- You can set system policies to control which options are available to your traveling users. For more information about system policies and Office options, see "Managing Users' Options with System Policies" on page 279.

- Traveling users rely on roaming user profiles to track their user information. For more information about roaming user profiles in Windows NT 4.0, see the "Guide to Microsoft Windows NT 4.0 Profiles and Policies." To find the guide, search for **Windows NT 4.0 Profiles** on the Microsoft Web site at http://www.microsoft.com/.

How to Customize Office Installation for Traveling Users

There are several settings that you can change in the Office Custom Installation Wizard to make it easier to set up Microsoft Office 2000 for *traveling users*.

▶ To customize the Office 2000 installation for traveling users

1 Start the Office Custom Installation Wizard.

2 On the **Specify Default Path and Organization** panel, verify that **<Program Files>\Microsoft Office** appears in the **Default installation path** box.

3 On the **Set Feature Installation States** panel, click the down arrow next to Microsoft Office and select **Run from Network**.

4 To set a mission-critical application to run from the local hard disk, click the down arrow next to the application name and select **Run from My Computer**.

5 On the **Customize Default Application Setting** panel, click **Get values from an existing settings profile** and then type the path to your Office profile settings (OPS) file.

6 On the **Modify Setup Properties** panel, click **TRANSFORMSATSOURCE** in the **Property Name** box, and then click **Modify**.

7 In the **Modify Property Value** box, select **Set property to 'True'** in the **Value** box.

Packing for the Trip with User Profiles

Traveling users rely on user profiles to track their user information, and on servers to make sure that the user profile information travels with them. Microsoft Office 2000 helps traveling users by storing all application data (such as user information, working files, and settings and preferences) in the Application Data folder for easy retrieval by the profile.

The Application Data folder is stored in different places, depending on your operating system installation. The following table identifies the default locations for the Application Data folder for each installation.

Installation scenario	Default location for Application Data folder
Installing Windows 98 or Windows 95	\Windows\Profiles*Username*
Upgrading to Windows 2000 from Windows 95/98	%Systemdrive%\Documents and Settings*Username*
Installing Windows NT 4.0	\Winnt\Profiles*Username*
Upgrading to Windows 2000 from Windows NT 4.0	\Winnt\Profiles*Username*
Installing Windows 2000	%Systemdrive%\Documents and Settings*Username*

Note   In the beta 2 version of Windows 2000, the Application Data folder is stored in \Winnt\Profiles*Username*. When you upgrade from beta 2 to the final version of Microsoft Windows 2000, the Application Data folder remains in the beta 2 folder.

Office 2000 stores all user-specific settings in the HKEY_CURRENT_USER subtree in the Windows registry. (Previous versions of Office stored these settings in both the HKEY_CURRENT_USER and HKEY_LOCAL_MACHINE subtrees.) With all the Office 2000 settings in one place, it's easier to retrieve settings and keep the user profile up to date.

To support traveling users, you must set up both client and server computers with *roaming user profiles* (profiles that travel with the user account). Roaming user profiles are stored on the server and automatically downloaded to the client computer when users log on.

Note   Roaming user profiles are platform-specific. Because of differences between the Windows registry and the Windows NT registry, users cannot travel between Windows 95/98 and Windows NT or Windows 2000.

With roaming user profiles, traveling users can log on to any computer on the network and download their user profile information. When users change any of their settings, the profile is automatically updated on the server when they log off and their new information is automatically updated, too.

Note   During Setup, the Windows installer lets you set Office 2000 applications to **Installed on First Use**. This installation option works on a per-computer basis rather than on a per-user basis, so the Windows installer cannot track which applications your users have installed as they travel between computers. Your users' application settings travel, but not the specific applications that have been installed on a particular computer. When users log on to the new computer and attempt to open an application, they might have to wait while the application is installed.

How to Configure Windows NT Servers for Traveling Users

Setting up roaming user profiles for a Windows NT network involves two steps on the server side:

1   Create a shared Profiles folder on the server to store roaming user profiles.

2   Update client user profiles to point to the shared Profiles folder.

Tip   Use a file server, rather than your Primary Domain Controller (PDC), to store user profiles. Using a file server helps you balance the workload without straining the resources on your PDC.

After you update the profile information to point to that shared folder, the profile is retrieved automatically when the user logs on, and updated automatically when the user logs off. This retrieving and updating process is called *reconciling* the user profile.

Create a Profiles folder on the server

The Profiles folder stores all your roaming user profiles on an *NTFS* drive on the server. Make sure your *traveling users* have full control *permissions* to their subfolders so they can update their profiles whenever they change. However, do not give users access to any subfolders other than their own.

Note   Do not create the Profiles folder in the %Systemroot% directory on your server. If you use %Systemroot%\Profiles, the client computer uses the local profile instead of the server copy.

Update client user profiles to point to the Profiles folder

You update all your client user profiles on the PDC server.

▶ **To update user profile information for each traveling user**

1   On the PDC server, click **Start**, point to **Programs**, point to **Administrative Tools (Common)**, and then click **User Manager for Domains**.

2   In the list of user names, double-click a user name.

3   In the **User Properties** box, click **Profile**.

4   In the **User Profile Path** box, type the full path to the Profiles folder you created (Windows NT Workstation client).

– or –

Under **Home Directory**, in the **Local Path** box, type the full path to the Profiles folder you created (Windows 95/98 client).

For example, \\Servername\Subfoldername\Profiles.

Note   These steps are different for Windows 2000 Server. For information about updating user profile information for each user on Windows 2000 Server, see the Windows 2000 Server documentation.

See also

• For additional information about setting up roaming user profiles on your Windows NT network, see the *Windows NT Server 4.0 Resource Kit*.

• You can set profile information for all of the users in your organization at once by using a system policy. For more information about system policies, see "Managing Users' Options with System Policies" on page 279.

How to Configure Windows Clients for Traveling Users

Setting up roaming user profiles for a Windows client involves different steps, depending on the client you are supporting. Microsoft Windows NT Workstation clients are automatically set up for roaming user profiles. Microsoft Windows 98 and Windows 95 clients must be configured to support roaming before your user profiles can roam.

For roaming user profiles to work, you must use the same drive and directory names for the Windows client on each computer that the user travels to. For example, if you install Windows in C:\Windows on one computer, and in C:\Win or D:\Windows on other computers, some components of the user profile are not transferred successfully between the computers.

Note   Roaming user profiles are platform-specific. Because of differences between the Windows registry and the Windows NT registry, users cannot travel between Windows 95/98 and Windows NT or Windows 2000.

Configure Windows NT Workstation clients for traveling users

Windows NT clients support roaming user profiles and *traveling users* with the least amount of administrative cost. Windows NT Workstation version 4.0 and Windows 2000 Professional are both automatically set up for traveling users. Both operating systems have user profiles turned on by default, and both store user files in the user profile. All you need to do is to configure the user account on the domain server.

Note   Users' data for digital identification does not roam to other computers. Instead, users with digital identification must store their *encryption* keys on a diskette and copy them to a new computer at their destination.

Configure Windows 98 clients for traveling users

Windows 98 was designed with traveling users in mind. Windows 98 stores files in the Application Data folder, where they can be retrieved and replicated easily. User profiles are available, although they are not turned on by default.

▶ **To enable traveling users for Windows 98**

1   On the client computer, click **Start**, point to **Settings**, and then click **Control Panel**.

2   Double-click the **Passwords** icon.

3   Click the **User Profiles** tab, and then click **Users can customize**.

Configure Windows 95 clients for traveling users

You can modify Windows 95 to support traveling users by installing Microsoft Internet Explorer version 4.0 or later and by turning on user profiles. When you install Internet Explorer 4.0, you mimic the environment found in Windows 98. Internet Explorer Setup creates the Application Data folder and stores files there, making it easy to retrieve them as part of the user profile.

▶ **To enable traveling users for Windows 95**

1   Install Internet Explorer 4.0 or later on the client computer.

2   On the client computer, click **Start**, point to **Settings**, and then click **Control Panel**.

3   Double-click the **Passwords** icon.

4   Click the **User Profiles** tab, and then click **Users can customize**.

See also

- You can set profile information for all of the users in your organization at one time by using a system policy. For more information about system policies, see "Managing Users' Options with System Policies" on page 279.

Special Considerations for International Travelers

Because operating systems differ in their support of some languages, users who are traveling internationally can take their roaming user profiles to another computer only when both the source and destination computers use the same *code page*.

Note   You must have a consistent level of security in your operating system to travel successfully between computers. For example, if you are using a Microsoft Windows NT 4.0 computer with *128-bit encryption* capabilities, you must travel to another Windows NT 4.0 computer with 128-bit encryption in order for all of your security settings to work as expected.

Within the limitations of multilingual support in various operating systems, you can make accommodations for users who travel internationally. The following operating systems allow users to take roaming user profiles from one computer to another:

- Windows NT Workstation version 4.0 or Windows 95 or Windows 98. In this case, both the destination computer and the source computer must use the same language version of the operating system.

    –or–

- Windows 2000 Professional with support for multiple languages.

For example, if your organization is based in the United States, but your users travel frequently to Europe and Asia, you can install the English version of Windows NT Workstation 4.0 or Windows 98 on all computers available to *traveling users*. This arrangement allows traveling users to take their Microsoft Office settings and files with them.

Alternatively, if you do not want to use the English version of the operating system in foreign subsidiaries, you can install Windows 2000 Professional configured with the Multilingual UI (MUI). Traveling users can set the locale of their operating system, travel to any other computer running Windows 2000 Professional, and take their roaming user profiles with them.

If international users need the Microsoft Office 2000 MultiLanguage Pack to display the user interface and online Help in another language, install the MultiLanguage Pack on computers that will be used by traveling users. Just as with Office, install the MultiLanguage Pack on a per-computer basis, and install it on the same drive (such as drive C or D) throughout your organization.

Tip   When traveling users log on to the network, their roaming user profiles are downloaded to their new location. For users who travel abroad, it might be more efficient to set them up to use a local server at their destination, rather than downloading large amounts of data from their original domain.

See also

- If all traveling users have Office 2000 with MultiLanguage Pack, they can use the MultiLanguage Pack to run the user interface and online Help in any supported language. For information about the plug-in language capability of Office, see "Overview of International Features in Office 2000" on page 725.

- Office does not automatically uninstall MultiLanguage Pack files. If a traveling user leaves behind a set of languages, you might want to delete the associated language files. For more information, see "How to Remove MultiLanguage Pack Files" on page 730.

Deploying Outlook 2000

Microsoft Outlook 2000, like other Microsoft Office 2000 applications, takes advantage of the new Windows installer and Office Custom Installation Wizard technologies. With these new technologies, you control exactly how Outlook 2000 is installed for your users.

Customizing Outlook 2000 Installation

Microsoft Outlook 2000 uses the same installation tools as your other Microsoft Office 2000 applications, including the Windows installer and the Microsoft Office Custom Installation Wizard. When you customize Outlook 2000 installation, you can do the following:

- Specify installation states for the Outlook features.
- Set Outlook configuration options.
- Configure Outlook profile settings.
- Specify other settings to apply during the installation process.

Note To function correctly, Outlook 2000 requires that Internet Explorer version 4.01 or later is installed on the client computers.

Specifying feature installation states

As with the other Office 2000 applications, you can specify where and when specific features of Outlook 2000 or all of Outlook 2000 is installed. On the **Set Feature Installation States** panel in the Office Custom Installation Wizard, set the Outlook 2000 features to one of the following installation states:

- **Run from My Computer**

  The feature is installed on the local hard disk.

- **Run from CD** or **Run from Network**

  The feature is run from Microsoft Office 2000 Disc 1 or from a network server.

- **Installed on First Use**

  The feature is installed the first time a user tries to activate it.

- **Not Available**

  The feature is not available for installation.

Specifying Outlook configuration options

Outlook 2000 can be installed in two configurations:

- Corporate/Workgroup configuration

  The Corporate/Workgroup configuration works with Microsoft Exchange Server and other corporate and workgroup e-mail servers across a local area network (LAN).

- Internet Only configuration

  The Internet Only configuration connects Outlook 2000 users to Simple Mail Transfer Protocol (SMTP), Post Office Protocol version 3 (POP3), Internet Mail Access Protocol version 4 (IMAP4), and Lightweight Directory Access Protocol (LDAP) Internet mail servers.

By default, the first time a user starts Outlook 2000, the application analyzes the user's computer to determine the best configuration for that user. As an administrator, you can determine which configuration is used at deployment by choosing a configuration in the Office Custom Installation Wizard.

If you are in a corporate or workgroup environment and you work primarily with Microsoft Exchange Server, Microsoft Mail, or another third-party LAN-based mail system (such as cc:Mail), but might also use Internet mail, choose the Corporate or Workgroup configuration. If you use an Internet service provider (ISP) only for e-mail messaging or for an Internet-standard (such as a POP3/SMTP or IMAP) server in your enterprise, choose the Internet Only configuration.

You can have Internet e-mail service even if Outlook 2000 is configured for Corporate/Workgroup e-mail support.

▶ **To add Internet e-mail support**

1 On the **Tools** menu, click **Service**, and then click **Add**.

2 In the **Add Service to Profile** box, click **Internet E-mail**, and then click **OK**.

3 In the **Mail Account Properties** box, enter the user, server, and connection information.

See also

- You can use the Office Custom Installation Wizard to tailor your Office 2000 installation for your users. For more information, see "Office Custom Installation Wizard" on page 250.

- If you are upgrading from a previous version of Outlook or Microsoft Exchange Client, there are a few upgrading and migration issues that you must be aware of. For more information, see "Upgrading to Outlook 2000" on page 495.

Configuring Outlook Profile Settings

Microsoft Outlook 2000 uses profiles to store information about users' e-mail servers, where their Outlook information is stored (on the server or in a local file), and other options.

Using default Outlook profiles

When users install Outlook 2000 on a clean computer, the Outlook Profile Wizard assists them in creating a profile the first time they start Outlook. If a user is upgrading from a previous version of Outlook or Microsoft Exchange Client, Outlook 2000 detects the existing profile on the user's computer and uses that profile instead of creating a new one.

Creating Outlook profiles by using the Custom Installation Wizard

Outlook profile configuration is critical in sending and receiving e-mail messages. Because profiles are so important, you might prefer to automate profile creation, rather than allowing users to create their own by using the Outlook Profile Wizard. You can use the Office Custom Installation Wizard to create profiles automatically for your users during installation.

All Outlook profile information entered in the Custom Installation Wizard is stored in the *transform* (MST file) that the wizard creates. When you install Office 2000, this information is written to the HKEY_LOCAL_MACHINE\Software\Microsoft\Newprof subkey on the target computer. When Outlook 2000 is started for the first time, it determines whether any Outlook profiles already exist on the computer. If there are no existing profiles, Outlook reads the customized information from the registry to create a new Outlook profile.

Note   You can force Outlook to create a new Outlook profile even if a user already has an existing profile by using the Newprof.exe file.

The **Custom Outlook Installation Options** panel in the Office Custom Installation Wizard provides a simplified interface for creating Outlook profiles.

▶ **To create Outlook profiles in the Custom Installation Wizard**

1   Start the Custom Installation Wizard.

2   On the **Custom Outlook Installation Options** panel, click **Customize Outlook profile and account information**.

3 In the **Configuration type** box, select the configuration you want to use, either **Corporate or Workgroup Settings** or **Internet Only Settings**.

4 Click a setting in the left pane, and then enter the corresponding option you want to use in the right pane.

Configuring Corporate or Workgroup settings

As you configure the Corporate or Workgroup settings, keep in mind the following items:

- The **General** settings under **Corporate or Workgroup Settings** include an **Enter Profile Name** box. You must type a profile name in this box for a profile to be created.

- After you choose the services in the **Services List** section, you must configure options for each service in the appropriate settings section.

- When you configure an Internet E-mail service, you must enter information in both the **Internet E-mail Settings** and **POP3 Account Settings** sections. Make sure you type exactly the same account name in each of these two sections.

- When you configure an Internet E-mail service, you must also type **Internet E-mail**—before the account name in the **Enter long account name** box in the **Internet E-mail Settings** section. For example, if the account name is Microsoft, then you must enter the long account name as **Internet E-mail—Microsoft**.

Configuring Internet Only settings

When you configure the Internet Only settings, keep in mind the following item:

- After you select the accounts you want to create in the **General** section, you must configure options for the account in the appropriate settings section.

Creating an Outlook profile automatically by using Newprof.exe

Newprof.exe is the tool that Outlook uses to create Outlook profiles. Usually, Outlook uses Newprof.exe only to create a new Outlook profile when no Outlook profile exists. If you want to create a new Outlook profile regardless of whether a profile already exists, you can use the Custom Installation Wizard to include Newprof.exe as an application to run after installation.

When you include Newprof.exe as a standalone application, you must also include a reference to a PRF file, a text file that contains Outlook profile settings information.

Toolbox

The Office Resource Kit includes a sample Outlook.prf file. This sample file contains an example and instructions for modifying the file to create various Outlook profiles. For information about installing Outlook.prf, see "Outlook Information" on page 788.

After you have created or modified a PRF file, you are ready to include Newprof.exe as part of the customized Office 2000 installation.

▶ **To add Newprof.exe to an Office 2000 installation**

1   Start the Custom Installation Wizard.

2   On the **Add Installations and Run Programs** panel, click **Add**.

3   In the **Command line** box, type the following:

*<path1>***Newprof.exe –p** *<path2>***outlook.prf**

where *path1* and *path2* specify the path to Newprof.exe and Outlook.prf, respectively.

Creating an Outlook profile by using environment variables

Both the **Custom Outlook Installation Options** panel in the Custom Installation Wizard and the PRF file now support user environment variables. This support means that you can use one set of Outlook profile settings to configure unique profiles for many different users.

Using logon scripts or batch files, you can set user environment variables on users' computers. You can then refer to these variables in the Outlook profile settings as "*%variable%*". For example, on computers running under Windows NT and Windows 2000, a user's logon name is stored as the default user environment variable **%USERNAME%**. When configuring Outlook profile settings, you can use this variable in several ways. For example:

- Name of the profile—**ProfileName = Microsoft - %USERNAME%**

- Exchange mailbox name—**MailboxName = %USERNAME%**

- Name of a Personal Folders file—**PathToPersonalFolders = C:\%USERNAME%.pst**

How to Customize Outlook 2000 Installation

As part of Microsoft Office 2000, Microsoft Outlook 2000 installation is highly customizable. By using the Office Custom Installation Wizard, you can specify which features you want installed, whether they should run from the local hard disk or the network, which configuration to use, and so on.

Specify installation states for Outlook 2000 features

You can specify installation states for many features in Outlook 2000 when you customize the Office 2000 installation.

▶ **To set installation states for Outlook 2000 features**

1 Start the Custom Installation Wizard.

2 On the **Set Feature Installation States** panel, click the plus sign (+) next to **Microsoft Outlook for Windows** to expand the feature tree.

3 Click the down arrow next to the feature you want to set, and then select the installation state to use for that feature.

Specify Outlook 2000 configuration options

You can specify the Outlook 2000 configuration for all of your users when you customize the Office 2000 installation.

▶ **To specify the Corporate or Workgroup e-mail configuration**

1 Start the Custom Installation Wizard.

2 On the **Customize Outlook Installation Options** panel, click **Customize Outlook profile and account information**.

3 In the **Configuration type** box, select **Corporate or Workgroup Settings**.

4 Click an item in the left pane of the Settings area, and enter the settings you want to use in the right pane.

For a Corporate or Workgroup configuration, you can supply settings for profile information, services, forms, Exchange server, personal folders, and so on.

▶ **To specify the default Internet Only e-mail configuration**

1 Start the Custom Installation Wizard.

2 On the **Customize Outlook Installation Options** panel, click **Customize Outlook profile and account information**.

3 In the **Configuration** type box, select **Internet Only Settings**.

4 Click an item in the left pane of the Settings area, and enter the settings you want to use in the right pane.

For an Internet Only configuration, you can supply settings for a POP3 or LDAP account, such as account settings, dial-up networking settings, security settings, and so on.

You can also select a configuration on the **Modify Setup Properties** panel in the Office Custom Installation Wizard.

▶ **To specify an Outlook configuration with Setup properties**

1 Start the Custom Installation Wizard.

2 On the **Modify Setup Properties** panel, select the **OutlookConfiguration** property, and click **Modify**.

3 In the **Value** box, select one of the following:

   Corporate or Workgroup

   Internet Only

   Ask user when Outlook first runs.

   The **Ask user when Outlook first runs** setting is the default for Outlook 2000.

Note   Options set on the **Modify Setup Properties** panel take precedence over those set on the **Customize Outlook Installation Options** panel.

Set Outlook as the default mail, calendar, contacts, and news application

Outlook 2000 can be registered with Windows as the default application for e-mail messages, calendar information, contact information, and news. In this scenario, Outlook handles the basic functional tasks that other applications request. For example, as the default e-mail application, Outlook creates e-mail items when a user click a mail-to URL in a Web browser, or when a user sends an e-mail message from another application, such as Microsoft Word.

When Outlook 2000 is started the first time, if it is not already the default application, the user is prompted to make Outlook the default. You can also automatically set Outlook as the default application by using the Office Custom Installation Wizard. You can choose to make Outlook the default application for only e-mail messaging; for e-mail messages, calendar, and contacts information; or for all such information, including news.

▶ **To set Outlook as the default mail, calendar, contacts, or news application**

1 Start the Custom Installation Wizard.

2 On the **Modify Setup Properties** panel, click the **OUTLOOKASDEFAULTAPP** property, and then click **Modify**.

3 In the **Value** box, select one of the following values:

   All (the default setting)

   Mail Only

   Mail, Calendar, Contacts

   Ask user when Outlook first runs

How to Perform a Quiet Installation of Outlook 2000

Like the other Microsoft Office 2000 applications, Microsoft Outlook 2000 prompts users for information during installation (for example, for the installation location). In addition, Outlook 2000 prompts users for information the first time that a user starts the application (for example, for Outlook profile information, an Outlook configuration, and so on).

If you prefer to install Outlook 2000 without any user prompts, you can use a quiet installation. If you want to avoid user prompts when Outlook is started for the first time, you can preset several settings in the Office Custom Installation Wizard.

Specify Outlook 2000 configuration options

You use the Office Custom Installation Wizard to specify Outlook 2000 configuration options for your users. You can use the options on either the **Customize Outlook Installation Options** panel or the **Modify Setup Properties** panel.

Note   Options set on the **Modify Setup Properties** panel take precedence over those set on the **Customize Outlook Installation Options** panel. Do not specify configuration options on both panels in the Custom Installation Wizard.

▶ **To specify Outlook 2000 configuration options on the Customize Outlook Installation Options panel**

1   Start the Custom Installation Wizard.

2   On the **Customize Outlook Installation Options** panel, click **Customize Outlook profile and account information**.

3   In the **Configuration type** box, select a configuration.

▶ **To specify Outlook 2000 configuration options on the Modify Setup Properties panel**

1   Start the Custom Installation Wizard.

2   On the **Modify Setup Properties** panel, select the **OutlookConfiguration** property.

3   Click **Modify**, and in the **Value** box, select either **Corporate or Workgroup** or **Internet Only**.

Note   If you don't want users to see any prompts when they run Outlook for the first time, do not use the **Ask user when Outlook first runs** value for the **OutlookConfiguration** property.

Set Outlook as the default application for mail, calendar, contacts, and news

Outlook can be registered as the default manager of e-mail, calendar, contacts, and news items using **OUTLOOKASDEFAULTAPP** property in the Custom Installation Wizard.

▶ **To set Outlook as the default mail, calendar, contacts, and news application**

1 Start the Custom Installation Wizard.

2 On the **Modify Setup Properties** panel, click the **OUTLOOKASDEFAULTAPP** property, and then click **Modify**.

3 In the **Value** box, select one of the following values:

All (the default setting)

Mail Only

Mail, Calendar, Contacts

Note If you don't want users to see any prompts when they run Outlook for the first time, do not use the **Ask user when Outlook first runs** value for the **OUTLOOKASDEFAULTAPP** property.

See also

- To perform a quiet installation of Outlook 2000, you must also create or configure Outlook profiles for your users. If an Outlook profile already exists, Outlook does not prompt users to create a new one. If users do not already have Outlook profiles, you can set up Outlook profiles by using the Office Custom Installation Wizard. For more information, see "Configuring Outlook Profile Settings" on page 190.

- Because Outlook 2000 uses the Microsoft Windows installer, it supports the same Setup command-line options that the other Office 2000 applications support. These options can be set to prevent any prompts from appearing during installation. For more information about these options, see "Customizing How Setup Runs" on page 215.

Outlook 2000 and Internet Explorer 5

Many Microsoft Outlook 2000 features, including HTML-based e-mail messaging, high *encryption*, and Help, use Microsoft Internet Explorer functionality. To use all of the features of Outlook 2000, it is best to install Internet Explorer 5, which ships with Office 2000.

If you don't want to use Internet Explorer 5, you can change some settings in the Office Custom Installation Wizard to control how Internet Explorer 5 is used in your Office 2000 installation.

Deploying Outlook 2000 without Internet Explorer 5

By default, Internet Explorer 5 is installed with Office 2000. However, you can use the Office Custom Installation Wizard to prevent Internet Explorer 5 from being installed on users' computers.

▶ **To prevent Internet Explorer 5 from being installed with Office 2000**

1   Start the Custom Installation Wizard.

2   On the **Customize IE 5 Installation Options** panel, click **Do not install Internet Explorer 5**.

Important   Outlook 2000 requires at least Internet Explorer 4.01 to be installed in order to function properly. If you choose not to install Internet Explorer 5 when you deploy Outlook 2000, you must install at least Internet Explorer 4.01.

Using Outlook 2000 with another Web browser

By default, Outlook 2000 installs Internet Explorer 5 and sets it as the default Web browser. If you prefer to use Netscape Navigator or another Web browser as the default Web browser in your organization, then you can use the Office Custom Installation Wizard to prevent Internet Explorer 5 from being registered as the default Web browser.

▶ **To prevent Internet Explorer 5 from being registered as the default Web browser**

1   Start the Custom Installation Wizard.

2   On the **Customize IE 5 Installation Options** panel, clear the **Make Internet Explorer 5 the default browser** check box.

Installing new versions of Internet Explorer

It is easy to deploy a new version of Internet Explorer 5 throughout your organization (for example, by installing a service pack) without changing your existing Outlook 2000 installation. If you deployed Office 2000 over the network, all of the Internet Explorer installation files are located in the \IE5 folder on the *administrative installation point*. You can remove the files and replace them with a new version of Internet Explorer 5.

Any user who installs Outlook 2000 from the updated administrative installation point receives the new version of Internet Explorer. Users who have previously installed Outlook 2000 have two options. They can uninstall and reinstall Office 2000 to receive the new Internet Explorer installation, or they can install the updated version of Internet Explorer 5 separately.

Preventing the Internet Explorer icon from appearing on the desktop

By default, the Internet Explorer installation included with Office 2000 creates an Internet Explorer icon on the desktop. You can prevent this icon from appearing on users' desktops by using the Office Custom Installation Wizard.

▶ **To prevent the Internet Explorer 5 icon from appearing on the desktop**

1   Start the Custom Installation Wizard.

2   On the **Customize IE 5 Installation Options** panel, clear the **Show Internet Explorer 5 icon on the user's computer** check box.

How to Install Outlook 2000 on a Locked Down System

If you want a secure system, you can lock down system folders and areas of the Windows registry using an *access-control list* (ACL). With this type of locked-down system, you can be sure that your users cannot accidentally uninstall crucial items, or corrupt their Windows registry data.

However, there are some drawbacks to this level of security. Although most system files now reside in other locations, Microsoft Outlook 2000 still installs some files in the System folder. Subsequently, only a user with *administrator privileges* can install Outlook on computers with a locked-down System folder.

Outlook 2000 uses the HKEY_LOCAL_MACHINE registry subtree to record which Outlook configuration (Corporate/Workgroup or Internet Mail Only) to use and whether Outlook 2000 is the default application for mail, calendar, contacts, and news. On a locked down system, a user cannot run Outlook 2000 without a customized installation that includes these settings, or unless an administrator of that computer installs and runs Outlook 2000.

In other words, if the HKEY_LOCAL_MACHINE subtree is locked, the administrator must either specify configuration settings for each computer in the Office Custom Installation Wizard, or the administrator must run Outlook 2000 once on each computer to configure settings.

To configure Outlook 2000 to install and run on a locked-down system, perform the following tasks before installation:

- Specify Outlook 2000 configuration options
- Set Outlook as the default application for mail, calendar, contacts, and news

Specify Outlook 2000 configuration options

You use the Office Custom Installation Wizard to specify Outlook 2000 configuration options for your users. You can use the options on either the **Customize Outlook Installation Options** panel or the **Modify Setup Properties** panel.

▶ **To specify Outlook 2000 configuration options on the Customize Outlook Installation Options panel**

1 Start the Custom Installation Wizard.

2 On the **Customize Outlook Installation Options** panel, click **Customize Outlook profile and account information**.

3 In the **Configuration type** box, select a configuration.

▶ **To specify Outlook 2000 configuration options on the Modify Setup Properties panel**

1 Start the Custom Installation Wizard.

2 On the **Modify Setup Properties** panel, select the **OutlookConfiguration** property.

3 Click **Modify,** and in the **Value** box, select either **Corporate or Workgroup** or **Internet Only**.

Note If you don't want users to see any prompts when they run Outlook for the first time, do not use the **Ask user when Outlook first runs** value for the **OutlookConfiguration** property.

Set Outlook as the default application for mail, calendar, contacts, and news

Outlook can be registered as the default manager for mail, calendar, contacts, and news items. On a locked down system, Outlook must be registered as the default application for all of these items using the Custom Installation Wizard.

▶ **To set Outlook as the default mail, calendar, contacts, and news application**

1   Start the Custom Installation Wizard.

2   On the **Modify Setup Properties** panel, click the **OUTLOOKASDEFAULTAPP** property, and then click **Modify**.

3   In the **Value** box, select **All**.

Move storage files from previous versions of Outlook

Users upgrading from previous versions of Outlook may have one or more PST, OST, PAB, or OAB data storage files on their system. Previous versions of Outlook place these files in the Windows folder, but Outlook 2000 places new storage files in the user's Application Data folder.

The Outlook 2000 upgrade process does not migrate existing storage files from the Windows folder to the Application Data folder. This behavior can cause problems if the Windows folder is locked down, because Outlook 2000 does not have write access to the files. If you want to be able to write to the following files in a locked-down system, make sure that they are stored in the Application Data folder, rather than the Windows folder.

File	Description
PST	Personal Folders storage file
PAB	Personal Address Book storage file
OAB	Offline Address Book storage file
OST	Offline storage file

See also

- You can include registry information to be installed with Outlook by adding the registry entries and values in the Office Custom Installation Wizard. For more information, see "Office Custom Installation Wizard" on page 250.

- For more information about migration issues when upgrading from previous versions of Outlook or other e-mail and scheduling applications, see "Upgrading to Outlook 2000" on page 495.

Installing Outlook 2000 After Installing Office 2000

By default, Microsoft Outlook 2000 is included in each of the following Microsoft Office 2000 editions:

- Office 2000 Premium
- Office 2000 Professional
- Office 2000 Standard
- Office 2000 Small Business

If you do not want to install Outlook 2000 when you install the rest of Office 2000, however, you can use the Office Custom Installation Wizard to remove Outlook from the installation. Then, when you are ready to deploy Outlook 2000, you can add it back in to your installation and deploy Office 2000 again.

▶ **To deploy Office 2000 without Outlook 2000**

1   Start the Office Custom Installation Wizard.

2   On the **Set Feature Installation States** panel, click the down arrow next to **Microsoft Outlook for Windows**, and then click **Not Available**.

3   Right-click the down arrow, and then click **Hide**.

4   Configure the rest of Office 2000 and deploy Office 2000.

▶ **To deploy Outlook 2000 after Office 2000**

1   Start the Office Custom Installation Wizard.

2   On the **Open the MST File** panel, click **Open an existing MST file**.

3   Click **Browse** to select the *transform* (MST file) from your original Office 2000 deployment.

4   On the **Set Feature Installation States** panel, click the down arrow next to **Microsoft Outlook for Windows**, and then select the installation option you want to use.

5   Right-click the down arrow, and then click **Unhide**.

6   Uninstall the previous Office 2000 with no user prompts or user interface displayed.

7   Configure the rest of the Outlook 2000 options in the Custom Installation Wizard.

8   Deploy Office 2000 again with your modified *transform* (MST file).

See also

- The Office 2000 Setup program can be run quietly, with no user prompts or with no user interface whatsoever, by using command-line options. Using the same settings, you can uninstall Office 2000 and reinstall it with Outlook 2000. For more information, see "Customizing How Setup Runs" on page 215.

Installing PhotoDraw with Office

Microsoft PhotoDraw 2000 is part of Microsoft Office 2000 Premium. Office users can use the photo-editing and drawing features in PhotoDraw to quickly create professional-looking graphics for use on Web sites or in printed materials.

Using Acme Setup to Install PhotoDraw

Microsoft PhotoDraw uses *Acme Setup* as its underlying setup technology. Unlike the new Windows installer, which stores installation instructions in a relational database, Acme Setup relies on tables of information in STF and INF text files to copy program files and perform other tasks that are necessary for installing PhotoDraw.

You'll find all the PhotoDraw program files on two CD-ROMs included with Microsoft Office 2000 Premium. These discs are labeled Microsoft Office 2000 Disc 3 (PhotoDraw Disc 1) and Microsoft Office 2000 Disc 4 (PhotoDraw Disc 2). Office Disc 3 (PhotoDraw Disc 1) contains the PhotoDraw Setup program (Setup.exe) and other program files. Office Disc 4 (PhotoDraw Disc 2) contains graphical content such as PhotoDraw clip art and template files.

If you have a license to install PhotoDraw on more than one client computer, there are two ways that you can deploy PhotoDraw throughout your organization. You can distribute the PhotoDraw discs to users, or you can install PhotoDraw on a network so that users can install it from there.

Installing PhotoDraw over the network

You install PhotoDraw separately from the rest of Office 2000. A network installation for PhotoDraw involves the following two-step process:

- First, create an *administrative installation point* on the network that contains all the PhotoDraw program files. Run PhotoDraw Setup from the PhotoDrw folder on Office Disc 3 (PhotoDraw Disc 1) with the **/a** command-line option to create the administrative installation point.

   The administrative installation point must be located on a server to which users can connect.

- Second, have users run PhotoDraw Setup from the administrative installation point to install PhotoDraw on their computers.

Customizing PhotoDraw Setup

When you create the administrative installation point, you can customize several aspects of the client installation process. For example, you can change the PhotoDraw installation path or shortcut location.

Acme Setup does not support the new Windows installer technology. For example, Acme Setup does not automatically find and repair errors in the PhotoDraw installation or install features on first use. Also, because PhotoDraw doesn't store Setup data and instructions in a Windows installer package (MSI file), you can't use the Office Custom Installation Wizard to customize client installations.

Special installation requirements for PhotoDraw

There are special installation requirements that you need to consider before you roll out Microsoft PhotoDraw in your organization. For example, for three-dimensional (3-D) features to work in PhotoDraw, Microsoft DirectX version 6.0 must be installed on client computers running Microsoft Windows 95/98.

To use PhotoDraw, users must be running operating systems with the following functionality:

- Microsoft Windows 95/98 with DirectX 6.0

  −or−

  Microsoft Windows NT 4 with Service Pack 3 or later
- Microsoft Internet Explorer version 4.0 or later

PhotoDraw comes with DirectX 6.0, Internet Explorer 4.01 Service Pack 1a, and Windows NT 4.0 Service Pack 4. You can find the Setup utility for the software on Office Disc 3 (PhotoDraw Disc 1).

When you run client Setup directly from the root level of the PhotoDraw CD-ROM, Setup searches for these applications on your computer and then installs or upgrades them if necessary. However, Setup does not search for these applications when you run Setup in administrative mode or when users install PhotoDraw from an administrative installation point. For this reason, you must make sure that the necessary applications are installed on client computers before you deploy PhotoDraw.

See also

- You can install PhotoDraw at the same time as the other Office 2000 applications. For more information about this process, see "Managing a Successive Deployment of Office Premium and Related Products" on page 115.
- On Windows NT 4.0 and Windows 2000, users must have administrative privileges to install and uninstall PhotoDraw. For more information about administrative privileges, see the documentation for Windows NT 4.0 or Windows 2000.
- For a complete list of the system requirements for PhotoDraw and the other Office 2000 applications, see "The Office 2000 Client Platform" on page 9.

How to Create an Administrative Installation Point for PhotoDraw

If you want users in your organization to install Microsoft PhotoDraw from a network location, you must run PhotoDraw Setup in administrative mode to install all files from Office Disc 3 (PhotoDraw Disc 1) to an *administrative installation point* on a network server. You must also copy the contents of Office Disc 4 (PhotoDraw Disc 2) to a network location.

The procedure for creating an administrative installation point for Microsoft PhotoDraw differs from the one for Microsoft Office 2000. For example, you do not use the Office Custom Installation Wizard to modify client installation features for PhotoDraw. Instead, you modify installation features while running Setup in administrative mode.

Copy the contents of Office Disc 4 (PhotoDraw Disc 2)

Before you create an administrative installation point, you must copy the contents of Office Disc 4 (PhotoDraw Disc 2) to a network share. PhotoDraw looks for the contents of Office Disc 4 (PhotoDraw Disc 2) on this share whenever a user accesses PhotoDraw templates, clip art, or other graphical content in the user interface. The network share must have at least 430 megabytes (MB) of available disk space.

Run Setup in administrative mode

After you copy the contents of Office Disc 4 (PhotoDraw Disc 2), you create the administrative installation point by running Setup from Office Disc 3 (PhotoDraw Disc 1) by using the **/a** command-line option.

Note   PhotoDraw comes with two Setup.exe files. One file is located at the root level of Office Disc 3 (PhotoDraw Disc 1) and the other is located in the PhotoDrw folder. For administrative Setup to work properly, you must run Setup from the PhotoDrw folder instead of from the root level location.

▶ To run Setup in administrative mode

1   Create a share on a network server for the administrative installation point.

   The network share must have at least 300 MB of available disk space.

2   On a computer running Microsoft Windows 95/98 or Microsoft Windows NT version 4.0 with write access to the share, connect to the server share.

3   On the **Start** menu, click **Run**, and then click **Browse**.

4 On Office Disc 3 (PhotoDraw Disc 1) in the CD-ROM drive, select **Setup.exe** in the PhotoDrw folder, and then click **Open**.

5 On the command line following **setup.exe**, type **/a**.

For example:

E:\Photodrw\Setup.exe /a

Enter organization name and CD key

Before you enter the CD key, Setup allows you to specify your organization name. This organization name appears on users' computers in the **About Microsoft PhotoDraw** box (**Help** menu) in PhotoDraw.

When users run Setup from the CD-ROM, they are prompted for an organization name. However, when users run Setup from the administrative installation point, the organization name that you specified is used.

Specify folder and server locations for PhotoDraw files

Next, enter the location for the PhotoDraw folders on the administrative installation point. Setup prompts you to create two folders. One folder contains the main program files, and the other one contains the shared program files.

You must also verify the server connection and specify the way in which users connect to the administrative installation point.

▶ **To specify folder and server locations**

1 On the **Microsoft PhotoDraw Setup** panel, enter the name and path for the folder on the administrative installation point in which you want to store the main PhotoDraw program files.

2 Enter the name and a path for the folder in which you want to store the shared program files.

You can store these files on the same server as the folder that contains the main program files or on a different server altogether.

3 On the **Network Server Confirmation** panel, under **Network location**, verify that the server name and path for the shared applications folder are correct.

Type the exact path that users must type when they install PhotoDraw.

4 Under **Connect to server using**, click **Server Name** if you want users to reference the shared applications folder with a universal naming convention (UNC) path.

–or–

If you want users to connect to the server by using a drive letter, click **Drive Letter** and enter a drive letter in the **Drive** box.

Setup verifies the server by connecting to it as specified. If Setup cannot connect to the server, an error message is displayed. Errors can occur for several reasons. The following table explains what to do to correct these errors.

If the error is caused by this	Do this
Misspelled server or share name	Click **Edit** and correct the name.
Share not yet created	Click **Continue,** and create the share before users begin installing Office.
Cannot connect to a local share on the server. (Some networks do not allow you to do this if you run PhotoDraw directly from the server.)	Click **Continue**; you can verify the share later from another computer on the network.
Invalid UNC path	Click **Continue**; verify that the share is accessible before users try to install from this server.

Specify an installation option for shared applications

After you verify the path for the shared applications folder, you must specify how you want users to access shared applications. The option you select here controls the choices that users have during client Setup.

Note For PhotoDraw, shared applications include graphics filters. These filters require 10 MB of available disk space.

▶ To select an installation option for shared applications

- To have users run shared applications over the network, click **Server**.

  –or–

  To install shared applications on each user's hard disk, click **Local Hard Drive**.

  –or–

  To allow users to choose where to install shared applications during client Setup, click **User's Choice**.

Accept end-user license agreement

Setup displays the end-user license agreement. By accepting the agreement here, you are accepting on behalf of the users who install PhotoDraw from this administrative installation point.

Customize the client installation process

The final panel in PhotoDraw Setup is **Microsoft PhotoDraw Administrator Setup**, where you can override default installation options on users' computers with your own settings.

▶ **To customize the client installation process**

1   On the **PhotoDraw Administrator Setup** panel, type the name and path for the folder where you copied the contents of Office Disc 4 (PhotoDraw Disc 2).

Be sure to specify whether users gain access to the server by using a drive letter or a UNC path. If you select a drive letter, your users must map the drive letter to the network server in order to run PhotoDraw.

2   To change the installation location for PhotoDraw, type a name, path, and drive letter for the new installation folder.

By default, PhotoDraw is installed in the same place as Microsoft Office on users' computers.

Important   The new installation folder and path must exist on the computer that you are using to run administrative Setup.

3   To specify a different name for the PhotoDraw application shortcut, type the name in the **Shortcut Name** box.

4   To specify where the PhotoDraw application shortcut is installed, click an option in the **Shortcut Location** box.

Note   To use the PhotoDraw shortcut in the Quick Launch bar, users must have the Microsoft Internet Explorer 4.01 Windows Desktop Update installed on their computers.

Setup copies the PhotoDraw files from Office Disc 3 (PhotoDraw Disc 1) to the administrative installation point along with the customizations that you just made. Users can now run client Setup from this administrative installation point and install PhotoDraw on their computers.

See also

- Using command-line options gives you more control over Setup choices. For more information, see "Using Command-Line Options with Acme Setup" on page 212.

- After you create an administrative installation point, users can install PhotoDraw from that location. For more information about the client installation process, see "How to Run PhotoDraw Setup on Client Computers" on page 208.

- You can install PhotoDraw at the same time as the other Office 2000 applications. For more information about this process, see "Managing a Successive Deployment of Office Premium and Related Products" on page 115.

How to Run PhotoDraw Setup on Client Computers

After you create the *administrative installation point*, users can connect to that location, run client Setup, and install Microsoft PhotoDraw. The following procedures describe an interactive client Setup, which means the user selects options presented by Setup. Client Setup can also be run in batch mode, in which Setup options are determined by the client Setup script.

▶ **To start PhotoDraw Setup on a client computer**

1   Connect to the administrative installation point, and then open the folder containing the main PhotoDraw program files.

2   Double-click **Setup.exe**.

3   Enter a user name.

Setup automatically enters the organization name from the administrative installation point.

4   Enter a name for the destination folder for the main PhotoDraw program files.

This folder can be on your hard disk, or it can be a network drive to which you have read, write, and delete *permissions*.

After you specify a location for the PhotoDraw folder, Setup might prompt you for a destination location for shared applications (depending on the selections made during administrative Setup).

▶ **To select a location for shared applications**

- To run shared applications over the network, click **Server**. Setup configures your system to point to the server share.

  −or−

  To install shared applications on your hard disk, click **Local Hard Drive**, and then enter a folder name. Setup copies shared program files to that folder.

Next, Setup prompts you for the installation to use.

▶ **To select the type of installation**

- To install a predefined set of the commonly used PhotoDraw components, click **Typical**.

  −or−

  To select from a list of all the available PhotoDraw features and components, click **Custom**.

After you select the installation options you want, Setup checks for available disk space and begins copying files to the client computer.

See also

- You can use *Acme Setup* to create an administrative installation point for PhotoDraw. For information, see "How to Create an Administrative Installation Point for PhotoDraw" on page 204.

- You can install PhotoDraw at the same time as the other Office 2000 applications. For more information about this process, see "Managing a Successive Deployment of Office Premium and Related Products" on page 115.

How to Install PhotoDraw from the PhotoDraw CD-ROM

To deploy Microsoft PhotoDraw 2000 throughout your organization, you must either purchase a copy of PhotoDraw for each user in your organization or (if you have multiple licenses) copy the contents of Office Disc 3 (PhotoDraw Disc 1) and Office Disc 4 (PhotoDraw Disc 2) to a server and have users run Setup from there.

When you run PhotoDraw Setup from the PhotoDraw CD-ROM, you might be prompted to install or upgrade to Microsoft Internet Explorer version 4.01. If you are running Microsoft Windows NT version 4.0 without Service Pack 3 or later, you might be prompted to upgrade.

If you have a large number of users and multiple licenses, you can also copy the files from Office Disc 3 (PhotoDraw Disc 1) and Office Disc 4 (PhotoDraw Disc 2) to a server. Users can then run Setup from the server; Setup functions the same as it does when run from the CD-ROM.

The advantage of sharing the CD-ROM on a server, instead of creating an *administrative installation point*, is that this method takes less server disk space because the shared files are not duplicated. However, this method is less flexible and provides less opportunity for customizing.

The server must have sufficient disk space for the entire contents of both CD-ROMs. The PhotoDraw program files on Office Disc 3 (PhotoDraw Disc 1) require 300 megabytes (MB); the content files on Office Disc 4 (PhotoDraw Disc 2) require 430 MB.

▶ To copy CD-ROM contents to a server

1 Create two folders on a network server, one to hold the contents of Office Disc 3 (PhotoDraw Disc 1) and the other to hold the contents of Office Disc 4 (PhotoDraw Disc 2).

2 Copy the folders PhotoDrw, IE401, NT4SP4, and DirectX from Office Disc 3 (PhotoDraw Disc 1) to the first folder.

3 Copy the files Setup.exe, Netwrk.wri, Readme.wri, Autorun.exe, and Autorun.inf from the root directory of Office Disc 3 (PhotoDraw Disc 1) to the first folder.

4 Copy all files from Office Disc 4 (PhotoDraw Disc 2) to a second folder on the server.

5 Specify network folder locations for Office Disc 4 (PhotoDraw Disc 2) by creating the following entry in a file called Pdsetup.ini:

   [CD Locations]

   CD2=<*network share*>\<*path to Office Disc 4 folder*>

6 Copy Pdsetup.ini to the following location:

   <*network share*>\<*path to Office Disc 2 folder*>**Photodrw\Pdsetup.ini**

   where <*network share*> is the network share that contains the copy of Office Disc 3 (PhotoDraw Disc 1), and <*path to Office Disc 2 folder*> is the full path of the folder that contains the copy of Office Disc 3 (PhotoDraw Disc 1).

Users can then connect to the server, open the folder, and run Setup as if they were installing directly from the PhotoDraw CD-ROM.

See also

- You can use *Acme Setup* to create an administrative installation point for PhotoDraw. For information, see "How to Create an Administrative Installation Point for PhotoDraw" on page 204.

- Office Disc 3 (PhotoDraw Disc 1) also contains the Setup program for Microsoft Office Server Extensions (OSE). For more information, see "Installing Office Server Extensions" on page 637.

Installing the Latest FPX/MIX Graphics Filter

Microsoft PhotoDraw creates and saves picture files in the MIX file format. The FPX/MIX graphics filter (Fpx32.flt) that PhotoDraw installs is newer than the one that comes with Microsoft Office 2000.

If you want users to install the latest filter but you don't want them to install PhotoDraw, you can choose to upgrade the version of Fpx32.flt that comes with Office 2000. Doing so can prevent error messages from appearing when users insert PhotoDraw MIX files into their Office 2000 documents or presentations.

You can install or upgrade the filter in one of three ways:

- By replacing the existing filter on the Office *administrative installation point*. When you set Fpx32.flt to be installed on first use, Setup automatically installs and registers the filter the first time a user inserts a MIX file into an Office document.

- By replacing the existing filter on a client computer. You can create a batch file that copies the latest version of Fpx32.flt to C:\Program Files\Common Files\Microsoft Shared\Graphflt on users' hard disks. After replacing the filter, you must instruct the batch file to register the filter by running Regsvr32.

- By running client Setup for PhotoDraw on users' computers. You can install the filter locally without installing the rest of PhotoDraw by clearing all installation options in Setup except for **FPX/MIX File Format** under **Graphics Filters**.

You can find the latest version of the filter in the following location on Office Disc 3 (PhotoDraw Disc 1):

\Photodrw\Shared\Graphflt\Fpx32.flt

Using Command-Line Options with Acme Setup

You can run the Microsoft PhotoDraw Setup program from a command line. If you run Setup from a command line, you can add parameters that allow you to specify certain options. For example, you can use a command-line option to limit the amount of interaction that users have with Setup when they install PhotoDraw.

▶ To run Setup from a command line

1   On the **Start** menu, click **Run**.

2   Type the location from which you are installing, and then type **setup**. For example:

   E:\Photodrw\Setup

If you want to add a command-line option, type it after the command. For example, to run Setup in administrative mode, type the following command line:

E:\Photodrw\Setup /a

Definitions of Acme Setup command-line options

The following list shows the command-line options recognized by the PhotoDraw *Acme Setup* program.

/a   Creates an *administrative installation point.*

/b "number"   Bypasses the **Microsoft PhotoDraw Setup** dialog box by preselecting the type of installation.

Option	Description
1	Typical
2	Custom

/g[+] "file"   Generates a log file that records details of the Setup process. When you specify a plus sign (+), Setup appends new information to the log file instead of overwriting it.

/gc[+] "file"   Does the same as **/g**, except all calls and returns from custom actions are also logged, which can make the log file very large.

/k "number"   Bypasses the **Setup** panel for entering and validating the 10-digit CD key from the CD-ROM sticker by entering the number you specify.

/n ""   Prompts for a user name if no default user name exists in the Windows registry.

/n "name"   Specifies the user name if no default user name exists in the Windows registry.

/o ""   Prompts for an organization name if no default organization name exists in the Windows registry.

/o "organization"   Specifies the organization name if no organization name exists in the Windows registry.

/q[option]   Specifies the level of user interaction for batch mode installation:

Option	Description
0	Suppresses all Setup panels except the final one. Using **0** is the same as using no argument.
1	Suppresses all Setup panels, including the final one.
t	Suppresses all Setup user interface elements.

/qn[option]   Does the same as **/q**, except that the system is not rebooted and **0** is not a valid value. To suppress all dialog boxes except the final one, use **/qn** with no argument.

/r   Reinstalls PhotoDraw. Use in maintenance mode only.

/s "folder"   Overrides the default source (the folder containing Setup.exe or the source specified in the maintenance mode STF file) with the specified folder.

/u[a]   Removes PhotoDraw. If **a** is specified, shared components are removed without prompting the user; otherwise, the user is prompted before removing shared components. Use in maintenance mode only.

/x "file"   Creates a network installation log file for tracking the number of installations made from an administrative installation point.

/y   Proceeds normally, including setting registry entries, but does not copy any files to the user's disk. Use this option to restore registry values or to track down processing problems.

Note   If you enter any invalid parameter, Setup displays a partial list of valid command-line options.

The following are special considerations when combining options on the same command line:

- The **/a** and **/q** options are mutually exclusive; using both results in an error message.

- The **/n** option is ignored if **/a** is used.

- The **/u** and **/r** options are mutually exclusive; using both results in an error message.

- The prompt elicited by the **/u** option is suppressed if **/q** is used, and the shared components are not removed.

- If you use the **/q** option during administrative Setup, you must also use the **/k** option.

ERRORLEVEL values

In Microsoft Windows 95/98, Setup returns one of the following values as the MS-DOS ERRORLEVEL value used to control batch file processing.

This ERRORLEVEL value	Indicates this condition
0	Success
1	User quit
2	Parsing Command Line error
3	Default user or organization name error
4	External error
5	Internal error
6	Out of memory
7	Partly installed
8	Restart failed
9	Failed to run Acmeseup.exe

CHAPTER 5

Customizing Your Office 2000 Installation

By using the functionality of Microsoft Office 2000, and the tools available in the Microsoft Office 2000 Resource Kit, you can customize Office to suit the needs of your users. This section provides the information you need to deploy a custom installation of Office effectively and efficiently in your organization.

In This Chapter

Customizing How Setup Runs

You can always run Office Setup interactively to install Microsoft Office—or allow users to run Setup interactively. However, Office Setup offers you many opportunities to customize Office installations throughout your organization by using command-line options or by modifying the *Setup settings file*.

Modifying Setup Options

You can customize the way Office Setup installs Microsoft Office by modifying Setup options. You can specify whether to perform a user or administrative installation, or you can initiate the repair or reinstallation of Office.

Other Setup options allow you to do the following:

- Control the degree to which users interact with Setup, even running Setup in quiet mode.
- Enable logging.
- Specify values for Setup properties that further customize the installation process.

You can specify values for these Setup options in three ways:

- On the Setup command line.
- In the *Setup settings file*.
- In a Windows installer *transform* (MST file).

Each method provides unique advantages in terms of what you can customize and how you give users access to the custom installation. You can implement one or more of these methods, depending on the level of customization you need.

Resolving conflicting Setup options

If you specify the same Setup options, but use different values, in the Setup command line, settings file, and transform, then Setup uses the following rules to determine which settings to use:

- If you set an option in the Office Custom Installation Wizard that corresponds to a Setup property, the wizard sets the corresponding property automatically in the MST file.
- If you modify a Setup property on the **Modify Setup Properties** panel of the Custom Installation Wizard, this setting overrides any corresponding options that you set on previous panels of the wizard. Your modified Setup property is written to the MST file.
- If you set options, including Setup properties, in the settings file that conflict with options in the transform, then the values in the settings file take precedence.
- If you set options on the command line, those settings take precedence over any conflicting values in either the settings file or the transform.

Managing the installation process with Setup properties

Many of the customizations that you make to the installation process are done through Setup properties. Setup uses these properties to control different aspects of the installation process. For example, the **COMPANYNAME** property defines the default organization name that Setup uses during installation, and the **REBOOT** property determines whether Setup reboots after the installation is complete. By modifying these property values, you can customize the way that Setup installs Office.

The default values for Setup properties are defined in the Windows installer *package* (MSI file). You can modify Setup properties in the transform, in the Setup settings file, or on the command line.

There are two types of Setup properties:

- *Public property* names are all uppercase and can be specified in the Setup command line, in the settings file, or on the **Modify Setup Properties** panel of the Custom Installation Wizard.

- *Private property* names are a mix of uppercase and lowercase letters and can be specified only on the **Modify Setup Properties** panel of the Custom Installation Wizard.

If you enter a property name in the Setup command line or settings file, Setup assumes that it is a public property and the name is converted to all uppercase letters. If you enter a property name in the Custom Installation Wizard, you must enter the name exactly as it is defined, in all uppercase letters or in mixed-case letters. With few exceptions, all properties that you can use for managing the installation process are public properties.

Consider the following when setting properties:

- String properties are not validated for proper syntax. Any value entered for a string property is considered valid.

- Leading and trailing blanks are removed from property values.

- Property values cannot contain environment variables.

Toolbox

You can find detailed information about Setup command-line options and Setup properties in separate worksheets in the Setup Reference workbook (SetupRef.xls). An additional worksheet in this workbook describes the format of the Setup settings file. For information about installing the Setup Reference workbook, see "Office Information" on page 787.

See also

- For a complete description of the features available in the Office Setup program, including information about how to perform administrative and client installations, see "Office Setup Program" on page 241.

- The Office Custom Installation Wizard allows you to fully customize the installation process, from modifying Setup properties to adding custom files and registry entries to the installation. For more information about the Office Custom Installation Wizard, see "Office Custom Installation Wizard" on page 250.

Specifying Values on the Setup Command Line

When you run Setup, you can use command-line options to change some of the parameters that Setup uses to install Office. By using command-line options, you can do the following:

- Identify the MSI and MST files to use
- Direct Setup to run in quiet mode
- Initialize Windows installer logging
- Alter Setup property values

For example, you can enter the following options on the command line:

setup.exe /qb+ /l*+ c:\office9.txt companyname="Northwind Traders"

This command line customizes Setup in the following ways:

- Setup does not prompt the user for information, but it displays progress indicators and a completion message as it installs Office. Setup installs the same Office features as it would if the user ran Setup and clicked **Install Now**.
- The Windows installer logs all information and any error messages, appending this information to the file C:\Office9.txt on the user's computer.
- Setup sets the default organization name to Northwind Traders.

Toolbox

You can find detailed information about Setup command-line options in a worksheet in the Setup Reference workbook (SetupRef.xls). For information about installing the Setup Reference workbook, see "Office Information" on page 787.

How to distribute Setup command-line options

If users double-click Setup.exe, Setup runs with no command-line options. To use your custom command-line options, users must click **Run** on the Windows **Start** menu and enter the path to Setup.exe, along with your command-line options.

To simplify this process for your users, you can create in MS-DOS a batch file that runs Setup.exe with your command-line options. Or you can create a Windows shortcut and add your custom options to the command-line box. Users double-click the batch file or shortcut to run the Setup command line that you have defined. You can store the batch file or shortcut in the main folder of the *administrative installation point*.

If you run Setup from a network logon script or through a systems management tool (such as Microsoft Systems Management Server), you can add your custom options to the Setup command line in the script or deployment package.

When to use Setup command-line options

The Setup command line is most useful when you have few customizations to make or when you want to create several different installations quickly. You do not need to edit any Office files (such as the Setup settings file) or run any special tools (such as the Office Custom Installation Wizard).

You can create multiple custom installations by defining different command lines for different users or by creating multiple batch files or shortcuts. This method is especially useful if you need to create multiple deployment packages by using a systems management tool—and each package requires a different command line.

For example, you can have your Engineering and Accounting departments install the same version of Office but use unique organization names. In the administrative installation point, you create two shortcuts that have the following command lines:

- **setup.exe /q companyname="Engineering Department"**
- **setup.exe /q companyname="Accounting Department"**

See also

- For a complete description of the features available in the Office Setup program, including information about how to perform administrative and client installations, see "Office Setup Program" on page 241.

Specifying Values in the Setup Settings File

In addition to using options specified on the command line, Setup also reads the options specified in the *Setup settings file*, Setup.ini. The settings file allows you to set the same options as the command line.

Note   Some logging options behave differently in the Setting file and on the command line. The /l command-line option enables only Windows installer logging. By contrast, the Logging section of the settings file enables both Setup and Windows installer logging and provides you with more flexibility in naming the log file.

The settings file is divided into five sections that contain keyword and value pairs, much like a standard Microsoft Windows INI file. The five sections are as follows:

- MSI section

  Specify an alternative Windows installer *package* (MSI file). The file must be in the same folder as Setup.exe.

- MST section

  Specify the full path to a Windows installer *transform* (MST file).

- Display section

  Specify the level at which Setup interacts with the user. You can specify levels from full user interaction (the default) to a completely quiet installation.

- Logging section

  Specify log files and options for Setup and the Windows installer.

- Options section

  Specify values for one or more Setup properties.

For example, you can include the following entries in the settings file:

```
[Display]
Display=Basic
CompletionNotice=Yes

[Logging]
Path=c:\
Template=office9.txt
Type=*+

[Options]
COMPANYNAME=Northwind Traders
```

These entries customize Setup in the following ways:

- Setup does not prompt the user for information, but displays progress indicators and a completion message as it installs Office. Setup installs the same Office features as it would if the user ran Setup and clicked **Install Now**.

- The Windows installer logs all information and any error messages, appending this information to the file C:\Office9.txt on the user's computer.

- Setup sets the default organization name to Northwind Traders.

Toolbox

You can find a description of the format of the Setup settings file in a worksheet in the Setup Reference workbook (SetupRef.xls). For information about installing the Setup Reference workbook, see "Office Information" on page 787.

How to distribute the Setup settings file

When you edit the default settings file (Setup.ini), users can run Setup without using command-line options to install Office with your customizations. (Be sure to back up the original Setup.ini file before modifying it.)

To create multiple custom installations that use different Setup options, you can create several custom settings files that have different names and store them in the main folder of the *administrative installation point*. Users must specify the name of a settings file by using the **/settings** Setup command-line option. You can simplify this process for your users by creating an MS-DOS batch file or Windows shortcut that contains the appropriate **/settings** command-line option.

If you run Setup from a network logon script or through a systems management tool (such as Microsoft Systems Management Server), then you must edit the Setup command line in the script or deployment package to refer to the appropriate settings file using the **/settings** option.

When to use the Setup settings file

When a user double-clicks Setup.exe, Setup reads your customizations from the Setup.ini file automatically. Use the Setup settings file when you do not want to require users to enter a complicated command line when they run Setup or when you do not want to create a batch file or shortcut.

The settings file is also useful when you want to set options that are awkward to include in a command line. The settings file organizes Setup options in an easy-to-read format that you might find more helpful than creating a long command line.

The settings file also differs from the Setup command line in that the settings file provides more flexibility for installation logging. The Setup **/l** command-line option initializes only Windows installer logging. By contrast, the Logging section of the settings file initializes both Windows installer and Office Setup logging. The settings file also provides you with more flexibility in naming the log file.

You can create multiple settings files for different groups of users. Users specify the settings file they want to use by using the **/settings** Setup command-line option. You can also specify Setup command-line options along with a custom Setup settings file. If you specify a command-line option that conflicts with a value in the settings file, Setup uses the command-line option.

For example, you can create two settings files for your Engineering and Accounting departments. Users in each department run Setup by using one of the following command lines:

- **setup.exe /settings off9engr.ini**
- **setup.exe /settings off9acct.ini**

Suppose, however, that you want these two departments to use a common set of custom options, except that each needs a different organization name. You can customize the default settings file (Setup.ini) with the standard options, and then you can have your Engineering and Accounting departments use the following command lines to run Setup:

- **setup.exe companyname="Engineering Department"**
- **setup.exe companyname="Accounting Department"**

Setup uses the options defined in the settings file and sets the organization name according to the command line.

See also

- For a complete description of the features available in the Office Setup program, including information about how to perform administrative and client installations, see "Office Setup Program" on page 241.

Storing Values in a Windows Installer Transform

You can make extensive modifications to the installation process by using a Windows installer *transform* (MST file), including many modifications that you cannot make in the Setup command line or settings file. These modifications include specifying the following:

- Where Microsoft Office is installed
- Which Office features are installed
- Where Office shortcuts are installed
- What previous versions of Office are removed
- How Setup property values are set

In the MST file, you can also add custom files and registry entries to the installation to distribute company templates or custom applications.

You create a Windows installer transform by using the Office Custom Installation Wizard. The Windows installer transform contains the changes that you want to make to the installation process. The Windows installer applies your changes to the Windows installer *package* (MSI file) before installing Office.

How to distribute a transform

For users to install Office with your customizations, you must specify the name and path to the transform by using the Setup **TRANSFORMS=** command-line option or by using an entry in the MST section of the *Setup settings file*.

For example, to direct Setup to use the transform Custom.mst (in the same folder as Setup.exe), you use the following Setup command line:

setup.exe transforms=custom.mst

You can also use the following entry in the settings file:

```
[MST]
MST1=Custom.mst
```

When to use a transform

The Windows installer transform is most useful when you want to make extensive customizations, especially customizations that you cannot make by using the Setup command line or settings file.

For example, in the MST file you can set the installation state of Office features. For each Office feature, the Office Custom Installation Wizard allows you to specify whether you want to copy the feature to the user's computer, run the feature from the network, install the feature on first use, or not install the feature at all. You can even hide features that you do not want users to modify during Setup.

You can create more than one transform for different groups of users, and then specify—on the command line or in the settings file—which transform to use. For example, to have your Engineering and Accounting departments use two different transforms, you can create two shortcuts in the *administrative installation point* by using the following command lines:

- **setup.exe transforms=off9engr.mst**
- **setup.exe transforms=off9acct.mst**

See also

- The Office Custom Installation Wizard allows you to fully customize the installation process, from modifying Setup properties to adding custom files and registry entries to the installation. For more information about the Office Custom Installation Wizard, see "Office Custom Installation Wizard" on page 250.

Customizing How Office Features Are Installed

Microsoft Office 2000 and the Windows installer provide you with a lot of flexibility in customizing what you install on the Office user's computer. You have complete control over which features Office Setup installs and how they are installed, including customizing the way that Setup creates shortcuts for these features. You can even add your own custom files to the Office installation.

How to Use a Transform with Office Setup

To customize how Setup installs Microsoft Office on the user's computer, you can use the Office Custom Installation Wizard to create a Windows installer *transform* (MST file). The transform contains the changes that you want to make to the installation process. Users can run Setup with the transform to install your customized version of Office.

To create and use a transform, follow these general steps:

1   Create an administrative installation point. This is a location on a server that contains copies of all Office files; users install Office from the administrative installation point.

2   Create a transform. By using the Office Custom Installation Wizard, create an MST file that contains your customizations.

3   Have users run Setup with the transform. Users specify the name of the transform when they run Office Setup.

Create an administrative installation point

Run Setup from Microsoft Office 2000 Disc 1 with the **/a** command-line option to create an *administrative installation point* on a network server. The administrative installation point contains copies of all Office files, and users can install Office from this location. By customizing the files here, you can control how Setup installs Office for your users.

▶ **To create an administrative installation point**

1   Create a network share.

The share must be accessible by all users who need to install Office, and you must have write access to it.

2   Run Setup from Office Disc 1 by using the **/a** command-line option. Use the **Run** command in the **Start** menu to add the **/a** option to the Setup.exe command line. For example:

e:\setup.exe /a

When Setup prompts you for the installation location, enter the network share that you created.

Setup copies all of the files from Office Disc 1 to the network share.

Create a custom transform

Use the Microsoft Office Custom Installation Wizard to open the Windows installer *package* (MSI file) for Office. Then use the wizard to select the features you want, and save your selections in a custom MST file.

▶ **To create a custom transform**

1   Start the Custom Installation Wizard.

2   On the **Open the MSI** panel, enter the file name and path of the MSI file for Office.

The package is located in the root folder of the administrative installation point. For example:

\\Server1\Office\Data1.msi

3   On the **Open the MST** panel, select **Do not open an existing MST file** to create a new transform.

   −or−

To open and modify an existing transform, select **Open an existing MST file** and enter the file name and path of the transform.

4   On the **Select the MST File to Save** panel, enter the name and path of the MST file you want to create.

Place the MST file in the same folder as the MSI file to make it easier for users to find. For example:

\\Server1\Office\Custom.mst

5   On the subsequent panels of the wizard, customize facets of the installation process that affect your organization, including selecting which features are installed and customizing installation options for Microsoft Internet Explorer 5 and Microsoft Outlook.

6   When you have finished making all your selections, click **Finish**.

The Custom Installation Wizard creates a transform that contains your customizations.

Toolbox

You can customize Office Setup with the Custom Installation Wizard. The wizard includes extensive online assistance that you can view by clicking the **Help** button on any panel. For information about installing the wizard, see "Custom Installation Wizard" on page 774.

Run Setup with your custom transform

To use your custom transform when you install Office on a user's computer, you must provide Setup with the file name and path of the MST file. You can do this by including the information on the Setup command line or in the *Setup settings file* (Setup.ini).

Use the Setup command line

When you run Setup to install Office on the user's computer, add the **TRANSFORMS=** option to the Setup.exe command line to specify the file name and path of the MST file.

For example (assuming that the MST file is in the same folder as the MSI file), type the following command:

\\server1\office\setup.exe transforms="Custom.mst"

Use the Setup settings file

Setup uses a settings file (Setup.ini) for installation options. Add the **MST1=** key to the MST section of the settings file to specify the file name and path of the MST file. For example:

```
[MST]
MST1=Custom.mst
```

You can add the key directly to the default settings file (Setup.ini), or you can create a copy of Setup.ini with a different file name and add the key to the duplicate file. If you create a duplicate settings file, you also need to specify the name of the settings file with the **/settings** command-line option. For example, type the following command to specify a settings file:

\\server1\office\setup.exe /settings newsetup.ini

See also

- Creating the administrative installation point on a network server is the first step in deploying a customized version of Office over the network to your users. For detailed information about how to create an administrative installation point, see "How to Create an Administrative Installation Point" on page 243.

- You can also customize how Office Setup runs by using the command line and settings file. For more information, see "Customizing How Setup Runs" on page 215.

- You can use the Office Custom Installation Wizard to customize many aspects of your Office installation. For more information, see "Office Custom Installation Wizard" on page 250.

How to Select Office Features

When running Office Setup interactively, users can choose which Microsoft Office features are installed by selecting from a list that Setup displays. Users can choose to install a particular feature in one of several ways:

- On the local hard disk

- On the network server, from where the user runs the feature

- On first use, meaning that Setup does not install the feature until the first time it is used.

- Not installed at all.

By using the Office Custom Installation Wizard, you can make these choices ahead of time for users. When users run Setup interactively, your choices become the default. When users run Setup quietly, your choices determine how the features are installed.

Set the installation state for features

On the **Set Feature Installation States** panel of the Custom Installation Wizard, you can click any feature to select the installation state. You can choose from the following options:

- **Run from My Computer**

  Components for the feature are copied to the local hard disk, and the feature is run from there.

- **Run all from My Computer**

  Same as **Run from My Computer**, except that all of the *child features* belonging to the feature are also set to this state.

- **Run from CD** or **Run from Network**

  Components for the feature are left on Microsoft Office 2000 Disc 1 or on the network server (depending on how users are installing Office). The feature is run from Office Disc 1 or the network server.

- **Run all from CD** or **Run all from Network**

  Same as **Run from CD** or **Run from Network**, except that all of the child features belonging to the feature are also set to this state.

- **Installed on First Use**

  Components for the feature and all its child features are left on Office Disc 1 or on the network server (depending on how users are installing Office). When the user attempts to use the feature for the first time, the components are automatically copied to the local hard disk, and the feature is run from there just as if it had been installed with the option **Run from My Computer**.

- **Not Available**

  The components for the feature, and all of the child features belonging to this feature, are not installed on the computer, and the feature is unavailable to the user.

Not all installation states are available for every feature. For example, if a feature contains a component that cannot be run over the network, then the feature does not have **Run from CD** or **Run from Network** as a choice in its list of installation states.

Tip   If you run the Custom Installation Wizard with the **/x** command-line option, the wizard displays the feature tree fully expanded on this panel.

Hide features from users during Setup

In addition to setting the installation state, you can right-click any feature on the **Set Feature Installation States** panel of the Custom Installation Wizard to hide the feature from the user. If you select **Hide**, then Setup does not display the feature when the user runs Setup interactively; instead, the feature is installed behind the scenes according to the installation state that you have specified.

To reverse this setting, right-click the feature and select **Unhide**. If you hide or unhide a feature, all of the child features belonging to the feature are hidden or not hidden accordingly.

See also

- When you change the installation state of an Office feature, the installation states of the child features change in various ways. For more information, click **Help** on the **Set Feature Installation States** panel of the Custom Installation Wizard.

- Creating the *administrative installation point* on a network server is the first step in deploying a customized version of Office over the network to your users. For more information, see "How to Create an Administrative Installation Point" on page 243.

- You can use the Office Custom Installation Wizard to customize many aspects of your Office installation. For more information, see "Office Custom Installation Wizard" on page 250.

How to Customize Office Shortcuts

By using the Office Custom Installation Wizard, you can customize the shortcuts that Setup creates for Microsoft Office applications. You can control what shortcuts are installed, and you can also customize settings such as what folder the shortcut is installed in and what command-line options to use with the shortcut.

On the **Add, Modify, or Remove Shortcuts** panel of the Custom Installation Wizard, the wizard displays all of the shortcuts that correspond with the features that you selected on the **Set Feature Installation States** panel.

Modify an existing shortcut

On the Custom Installation Wizard panel, you modify any existing shortcut by selecting the shortcut and clicking **Modify**. In the **Add/Modify Shortcut Entry** dialog box, you can make the following modifications:

- **Target**

  Change the application associated with the shortcut. The names in the list correspond to features that you selected on the **Set Feature Installation States** panel of the wizard, plus any custom files that you added to the installation on the **Add Files to the Installation** panel. You can also add command-line options by appending a space and a list of options to the target name.

  For example, to customize the Microsoft Word shortcut to open a Word document as a template, select **<Microsoft Word>** and append the **/t** option as follows:

  <microsoft word> /t "c:\Tools\Accounting Forms.doc"

- **Location**

  Change the folder in which the shortcut is created by selecting a location from the list. You can specify a subfolder by appending a backslash (\) followed by the subfolder name.

  For example, to install the Microsoft Word shortcut in the subfolder Office 2000 in the Programs folder in the **Start** menu, select **<StartMenu\Programs>** and append the subfolder name as follows:

  <startmenu\programs>\Office 2000

- **Name**

  Change the name of the shortcut by entering any string.

- **Start in**

  Change the starting folder for the application by entering a path. The path must be a valid path on the user's computer. If it is not, the user gets an error message when trying to use the shortcut.

- **Shortcut key**

  Associate a shortcut key with this shortcut by entering the shortcut key string in this box. Click the **Help** button in the wizard for a description of how to specify a shortcut key.

- **Run**

  Select how you want the application to run when the user double-clicks this shortcut. For example, if you want the application to run in a maximized window by default, then select **Maximized**.

- **Change Icon**

  Select a new icon for the shortcut.

Add or remove shortcuts

You can also click **Add** to add a new shortcut for any file being installed by Setup. This step allows you to create duplicate shortcuts for the most-used Office applications on the user's computer. It also allows you to create shortcuts for custom files or applications you add to the installation.

To remove a shortcut from the list, select the shortcut and click **Remove**.

See also

- You can use the Office Custom Installation Wizard to customize many aspects of your Office installation. For more information, see "Office Custom Installation Wizard" on page 250.

How to Add Files to the Installation

In addition to selecting what Office files are installed, Microsoft Office 2000 Setup allows you to add your own files to the Office installation. You can deploy corporate templates, images, custom applications, or other files along with Office.

On the **Add Files to the Installation** panel of the Office Custom Installation Wizard, click **Add** to add a new file to the installation. After you select one or more files to add, enter the destination path for the file or files in the **File Destination Path** dialog box. You can enter an absolute path on the user's computer, or you can select a path from the list. If you select a path, you can add a subfolder to it by appending a backslash (\) followed by the subfolder name.

When you click **OK**, the wizard adds the file to the transform. Setup installs the file on the user's computer, in the folder you specified, when the user installs Office.

After you add the file, you can add a shortcut for the file on the **Add, Modify, or Remove Shortcuts** panel of the wizard. On that panel, click **Add**—the file you added appears in the **Target** box.

Because the file is copied into the transform, you must update the transform if the file changes later on.

▶ To update the installation with modified files

1 On the **Create or Open the MST File** panel, enter the name of the Windows installer transform (MST file).

2 On the **Select the MST File to Save** panel, enter the name of the MST file again.

3 Click **Next** until you reach the **Add Files to the Installation** panel.

4 Select the file that has changed, and click **Remove**.

5 Click **Add**, and then enter the information for your modified file.

See also

- You can use the Office Custom Installation Wizard to customize many aspects of your Office installation. For more information, see "Office Custom Installation Wizard" on page 250.

Customizing How Office Options Are Set

Microsoft Office 2000 and the Windows installer provide you with a lot of flexibility for configuring Office when you deploy it throughout your organization. You can preset options and settings for all Office applications, and you can set specific registry entries on users' computers.

Customizing User Options

When you install Microsoft Office on users' computers, you can use several methods to customize user options. You can use the Profile Wizard to preset Office application options, or you can customize specific registry settings on users' computers.

If you define duplicate options by using a combination of the following methods, the user's computer determines which settings to use according to where the method falls in the following order of precedence (a given method overrides any preceding methods):

- Settings in an *OPS file* included in a *transform*
- Registry values specified in a transform
- Settings in an OPS file included in the Profile Wizard
- Settings that migrate from a previous version of Office
- Settings modified through system policies

Specifying settings in an OPS file included in the MST file

By using the Profile Wizard, you can customize users options and save your settings in an OPS file. By using the **Customize Default Application Settings** panel of the Office Custom Installation Wizard, you can include the OPS file in the Windows installer transform (MST file). The OPS file contains registry values corresponding to option settings in Office applications; these registry values are set on users' computers by Setup during installation.

Setting registry entries in the MST file

By using the **Add Registry Entries** panel of the Custom Installation Wizard, you can define registry values that are set on users' computers by Setup during installation. These values override duplicate values in the OPS file included in the transform.

Specifying settings in an OPS file and running the Profile Wizard

By using the **Add Installations and Run Programs** panel of the Custom Installation Wizard, you can create a command line for running the Profile Wizard with an OPS file to restore default Office application settings. This command line runs immediately after Office Setup is completed. Values in this OPS file override duplicate values that you added by using the **Add Registry Entries** panel of the Custom Installation Wizard and duplicate values in the OPS file included in the transform.

Migrating user settings

If a previous version of Office is installed on a user's computer, Setup copies the former application settings for that version of Office to Office 2000. Migrated settings override duplicate settings contained in any OPS file or added to the registry during installation.

Note   If you want to prevent migrated settings from overriding the OPS file, set the **DONOTMIGRATEUSERSETTINGS** property to TRUE, or clear the **Migrate user settings** check box on the **Customize Default Application Settings** panel of the Custom Installation Wizard.

Modifying settings through system policies

After installation is complete, you can modify registry values by using Windows system policies. System policy settings take effect when the user logs on to the network, and they override any duplicate values you set during installation.

See also

- By using the Profile Wizard, you can create an OPS file that contains default Office application settings that you can use to configure your users' computers. For more information, see "Profile Wizard" on page 255.

- By using the Custom Installation Wizard, you can create a transform that contains an OPS file, or you can create a transform that runs the Profile Wizard. For more information about how to create and use a transform, see "Storing Values in a Windows Installer Transform" on page 223.

- You can use the Custom Installation Wizard to customize many aspects of your Office installation, including selecting which features are installed and customizing installation options for Microsoft Internet Explorer 5 and Microsoft Outlook. For more information, see "Office Custom Installation Wizard" on page 250.

How to Preset User Options in an OPS File

A Microsoft Office 2000 user can configure Office applications by customizing a broad array of options. Users can select options such as toolbar settings, custom dictionaries, the location of templates, and the default format for saving files.

By using the Profile Wizard and the Office Custom Installation Wizard, you can change the default settings for these options and set new defaults on users' computers. Your changes are implemented when users install Office 2000 on their computers.

To customize default options for users, follow these general steps:

1 By using the Profile Wizard, create an *OPS file* that contains your default settings for Office application options.

2 By using the Custom Installation Wizard, create a Windows installer *transform* (MST file) that contains your OPS file.

 −or−

 Run the Profile Wizard during Office Setup to implement your default settings. You can create an MST file that runs the Profile Wizard immediately after Office 2000 is installed.

Create an OPS file that contains your settings

Before you create your OPS file, you must start each Office application and set all the options you want for your users. You can set most options by using the **Options** command (**Tools** menu). To customize toolbars and menus, use the **Customize** command (**Tools** menu).

You can even add words to the custom dictionary by using the **Spelling and Grammar** command (**Tools** menu) or by clicking the **Dictionaries** button on the **Spelling & Grammar** tab in the **Options** dialog box.

After you have customized the Office applications, run the Profile Wizard to save the settings to an OPS file.

▶ **To save settings to an OPS file**

1 Run the Profile Wizard.

2 On the **Save or Restore Settings** panel, select **Save the settings from this machine**, and type the name and path for the OPS file.

3 Click **Finish**.

The Profile Wizard saves all the Office application settings on your computer to the OPS file.

Toolbox

The Profile Wizard allows you to save and restore Office application settings on a user's computer. For information about installing the wizard, see "Profile Wizard" on page 779.

Create a transform that contains your OPS file

You use the Custom Installation Wizard to create an MST file that customizes the Office 2000 installation process. By using the wizard, you can customize many aspects of the installation that affect your organization. On the **Customize Default Applications Settings** panel of the wizard, you can add your OPS file to the transform.

▶ **To create a custom transform that contains the OPS file**

1   Run the Custom Installation Wizard.

2   On the **Customize Default Application Settings** panel, select **Get values from an existing settings profile**, and type the file name and path of the OPS file you created.

3   On the same panel, select the **Migrate user settings** check box if your users are upgrading from a previous version of Office and you want to apply their former application settings to Office 2000.

The Custom Installation Wizard creates a transform that contains your OPS file and any other customizations you have made.

Toolbox

The Custom Installation Wizard includes extensive online assistance that you can view by clicking the **Help** button on any panel of the wizard. For information about installing the wizard, see "Custom Installation Wizard" on page 774.

Run the Profile Wizard during Office Setup

Instead of including an OPS file in the MST file, you can run the Profile Wizard during Setup to restore the settings from the OPS file. This alternative gives you the flexibility to place the OPS file in a common location, such as a network server, so that the OPS file can be modified without having to update the MST file.

To run the Profile Wizard during Setup, run the Custom Installation Wizard to add a command line for the Profile Wizard on the **Add Installations and Run Programs** panel.

▶ **To run the Profile Wizard during Setup**

1 Copy the Profile Wizard executable file (Proflwiz.exe) and your customized OPS file to the Office *administrative installation point.*

   You can place the files in the same folder as Office Setup.exe, or you can create a subfolder for them.

2 Run the Custom Installation Wizard.

3 On the **Add Installations and Run Programs** panel, click **Add**.

4 In the **Command line** box, type the file name and path to Proflwiz.exe, or click **Browse** to select the file.

5 In the **Command line** box, add command-line options directing the Profile Wizard to restore the OPS file to the user's computer, and then click **OK**.

   For example, to run the Profile Wizard from the Profile subfolder in the Office administrative installation point and restore settings from the file Newprofile.ops, type the following command line:

   profile\proflwiz.exe /q /r profile\newprofile.ops

After Office is installed, the Windows installer starts all the applications you specify on the **Add Installations and Run Programs** panel in the order in which you specify them.

See also

- You can run the Profile Wizard interactively, or you can use command-line options to run it in quiet mode (without user interaction) to save or restore settings. For more information, see "Profile Wizard" on page 255.

- By using the Custom Installation Wizard, you can create a Windows installer transform that contains an OPS file or that runs the Profile Wizard during Setup. For more information about how to create and use a transform, see "Storing Values in a Windows Installer Transform" on page 223.

- You can use the Custom Installation Wizard to customize many aspects of your Office installation, including selecting which features are installed and customizing installation options for Internet Explorer 5 and Microsoft Outlook. For more information, see "Office Custom Installation Wizard" on page 250.

How to Set Registry Entries

You can include custom applications in Office Setup that require custom Windows registry settings. You can also customize certain Microsoft Office options by changing registry settings. In these situations, you can use the Office Custom Installation Wizard to define registry values that are set on users' computers during Office installation.

To set registry values during Office installation, you add individual registry entries to a Windows installer *transform* (MST file). You can also import a registry file containing multiple registry entries.

Add registry entries to a transform

By using the Custom Installation Wizard, you can customize many aspects of the Office installation process that affect your organization. To add registry entries to a Windows installer transform, you use the **Add Registry Entries** panel of the wizard. You need to know the complete path for each registry entry, as well as the value name and the data type for that entry.

▶ **To add Windows registry entries to a transform**

1   Run the Custom Installation Wizard.

2   On the **Add Registry Entries** panel, click **Add**.

3   Enter the full path for the registry entry you want to add, enter the value name and data, and click **OK**.

For more information about how to enter these values, click the **Help** button.

Import a registry file into a transform

To add multiple registry entries to a Windows installer transform, first you create a registry (.reg) file, and then you use the **Add Registry Entries** panel of the Custom Installation Wizard to import the registry file.

A registry file is a text file that contains a copy of a section of the Windows registry. If your computer already has the registry entries you want to copy to users' computers, then creating a registry file is an efficient way of copying those entries.

▶ To create a registry file

1   On the computer that has the registry entries you want to add to the installation, click **Run** on the **Start** menu and type **regedit**.

2   In the registry editor, select the portion of the registry tree that you want to copy.

3   On the **Registry** menu, click **Export Registry File**, and follow the instructions to export the selected portion of the registry tree to a registry file.

▶ To import a registry file to a transform

1   Run the Custom Installation Wizard.

2   On the **Add Registry Entries** panel, click **Import**.

3   Select the registry file you created, and click **Open**.

The wizard adds the registry entries from the registry file to the list on the **Add Registry Entries** panel.

If the wizard encounters an entry in the registry file that is a duplicate of an entry already in the list and the two entries contain different value data, then the wizard prompts you to select the entry you want to keep.

After Office Setup is completed, the Windows installer copies the registry entries that you added to the transform to users' computers.

CHAPTER 6

Behind the Scenes—Office 2000 Installation Tools

The Setup program for Microsoft Office 2000 provides you with considerable flexibility when you install Office on users' computers. In addition, the Microsoft Office 2000 Resource Kit contains a number of tools that allow you to customize the installation process. These topics provide a comprehensive reference to the Office Setup program and to the Office Resource Kit customization tools.

In This Chapter

Office Setup Program

You use the Setup program for Microsoft Office 2000 to install Office on users' computers or to create an administrative installation point for users to install Office over the network.

Working with Office Setup Components

The Office 2000 Setup program, Setup.exe, installs Microsoft Office 2000. Behind the scenes, however, Setup uses the new Windows installer technology to perform installation tasks. Improvements in this process have made installing Office more flexible and more reliable.

Setup.exe bootstrap program

The executable file Setup.exe is a bootstrap program. That is, it performs a few preliminary tasks and then calls the Windows installer program, Msiexec.exe, to perform the actual installation. All command-line options documented in the Microsoft Office 2000 Resource Kit are defined for Setup.exe, which passes appropriate options to Msiexec.exe.

You run Office Setup by double-clicking **setup.exe**. If Office 2000 is not currently installed on the computer, you can also run Office Setup by inserting Microsoft Office 2000 Disc 1 in the CD-ROM drive. When Setup.exe starts, it performs the following functions:

- If the Windows installer is not installed on the computer, Setup installs it from Office Disc 1.
- If Office is installed, Setup allows the user to add or remove Office features.
- If Office is not installed, Setup runs the Windows installer (Msiexec.exe) to perform the Office installation.

Office Setup automatically installs the Windows installer on computers running Microsoft Windows 95/98. If you are running Setup on Microsoft Windows NT 4.0, you must have administrative *permissions* for Setup to install the Windows installer components.

Note Throughout the Office Resource Kit, the terms *Setup* and *Setup.exe* refer to both the bootstrap Setup program and the Windows installer program.

Msiexec.exe installer program

The Msiexec.exe program is a component of the Windows installer. When called by Setup.exe, Msiexec.exe uses a dynamic-link library, Msi.dll, to read the Windows installer *package* (*MSI file*), apply the Windows installer *transform* (MST file), incorporate command-line options supplied by Setup.exe, and install the Office applications.

Important Do not run Msiexec.exe directly. Instead, always run Setup.exe to perform Office installations. Running Setup.exe ensures that all system verifications are performed.

When Windows installer is installed on a computer, it changes the registered file type of MSI files, so double-clicking the MSI file runs Msiexec.exe with that file. You can change the default file types on your users' computers to prevent them from inadvertently running Msiexec.exe with the Office MSI file, rather than Setup.exe. You change default file types by using the **Folder Options** command on the **View** menu in Windows Explorer.

See also

- You can run Office Setup interactively to install Office—or allow users to run Setup interactively. However, Office Setup offers you many opportunities to customize Office installations throughout your organization. For more information, see "Customizing How Setup Runs" on page 215.

How to Create an Administrative Installation Point

To create an *administrative installation point* for Microsoft Office, run Setup with the **/a** command-line option and specify a Windows installer *package* (*MSI file*). For example:

setup.exe /a data1.msi

Administrative Setup guides you through the steps that are necessary to install Office on your administrative installation point.

Enter CD key and organization name

After you enter the CD key, Setup allows you to specify your organization name. The organization name is stored in the MSI file for use by Setup during client installation. This organization name appears on users' computers in the **About** box (**Help** menu) in Office applications.

When users run Setup from Microsoft Office 2000 Disc 1, they are prompted for an organization name. However, when users run Setup from the administrative installation point, the organization name that you specified is used by default.

In the Office Custom Installation Wizard, you can create a Windows installer *transform* (MST file) that modifies the organization name during installation. This flexibility allows you to create different organization names for different groups of users in your organization. Set the organization name on the **Specify Default Path and Organization** panel, or set the **COMPANYNAME** property on the **Modify Setup Properties** panel. You can also set the organization name in the Setup command line or *settings file* when users run Setup, but to do this you must leave the organization name blank when you create the administrative installation point.

Accept end-user license agreement

Setup displays the end-user license agreement. By accepting the agreement here, you are accepting on behalf of the users who install Office from this administrative installation point.

Specify installation location

Enter the path where you want to create the administrative installation point for Office. Setup requires approximately 550 megabytes (MB) of disk space in this folder to copy all of the Office files. Setup installs a hierarchy of folders in the folder that you specify.

Note   When you specify the location of the administrative installation point during administrative Setup, do not include extended characters in the folder name. Setup does not allow you to install Office from this location if the folder name contains extended characters.

After installing Office, share this folder and provide read access for all users who need to run Setup from this server.

Install Office

When you click **Install Now**, Setup copies the Office files from Office Disc 1 to the network server, customizing the organization name and installation location according to the responses that you have given.

The administrative installation point uses short file names

When you run Setup with the **/a** command-line option, Setup sets the property **SHORTFILENAMES=Yes** in the command line when it calls Msiexec.exe to create the administrative installation point. This setting directs Msiexec.exe to create all files and folders with the MS-DOS-compatible file names used on Office Disc 1.

You can disable this option by setting the property **SHORTFILENAMES=""** in the Setup command line or settings file. If the network server supports long file names, then Msiexec.exe uses long folder and file names where appropriate. For example, with this option disabled, Setup creates the wizard **agenda.wiz** using the name **Agenda Wizard.wiz**.

However, if you create the administrative installation point with long file names, then Office Disc 1 cannot be used as an alternate source if the server becomes unavailable. This is because some file and folder names on the administrative installation point do not match the short file and folder names used on Office Disc 1.

See also

- For more information about the Setup command line, the Setup settings file, and Setup properties, see "Customizing How Setup Runs" on page 215.

- The Office Custom Installation Wizard allows you to fully customize the installation process, from modifying Setup properties to adding custom files and registry entries to the installation. For more information about the Office Custom Installation Wizard, see "Office Custom Installation Wizard" on page 250.

How to Install Office on Client Computers

Users install Microsoft Office by running Setup from Microsoft Office 2000 Disc 1 or from an *administrative installation point* that you create. Client Setup guides users through the steps necessary to install Office on their computers.

Enter name and organization

This name and organization appears on users' computers in the **About** box (**Help** menu) in Office applications. If a user is installing Office from the administrative installation point, Setup uses the organization name you specified without prompting the user.

Accept end-user license agreement

Setup displays the end-user license agreement. If a user is installing Office from the administrative installation point, the license agreement you agreed to when creating the administrative installation point applies here.

Select installation mode

On the third panel in Setup, users click **Install Now** to perform an automatic installation of Office, or they click **Customize** to select Office features and specify how they are installed.

Install a predefined set of Office features

When a user clicks **Install Now**, Setup skips the remaining panels and installs a predefined set of the most frequently used features of Office in the default installation location.

In the Custom Installation Wizard, you can create a Windows installer *transform* (MST file) that specifies the default features installed by Setup when the user clicks **Install Now**. You specify the default features on the **Set Feature Installation States** panel of the wizard.

You can change the label of the **Install Now** button and the accompanying text by setting the **TYPICALINSTALLTEXT, TYPICALINSTALLDESCRIPTION, TYPICALINSTALLHEADER, TYPICALUPGRADEHEADER,** or **TYPICALUPGRADETEXT** properties on the **Modify Setup Properties** panel. You can also set these properties on the Setup command line or in the *Setup settings file*.

Select Office features to install

If a user clicks **Customize**, Setup prompts the user for the installation location and then displays a hierarchy of Office features. The user can select an installation state for each feature.

In the Custom Installation Wizard, you can change the label of the **Customize** button and the accompanying text by setting the **CUSTOMINSTALLTEXT, CUSTOMINSTALLDESCRIPTION,** and **CUSTOMINSTALLHEADER** properties on the **Modify Setup Properties** panel. You can also set these properties on the Setup command line or in the Setup settings file.

Enter installation location

Users enter the path where they want Setup to install Office. The default location is the Program Files\Microsoft Office folder.

In the Office Custom Installation Wizard, you can specify a default value for the installation location on the **Specify Default Path and Organization** panel of the wizard. You can also specify the location by setting the **INSTALLLOCATION** Setup property on the **Modify Setup Properties** panel of the wizard, or you can set the property on the Setup command line or in the Setup settings file.

Select previous versions of Office to keep

If the user is upgrading from a previous version of Office, Setup displays a list of all the Office applications currently installed—applications that Setup removes when it installs Office 2000. If the user installs Office 2000 in a folder that is different from the folder in which the previous version of Office is installed, however, then the user can choose to keep these applications.

If a user chooses to keep programs from a previous version of Office, Setup does not remove these applications. However, Setup does redefine system settings, such as file types, to point to the Office 2000 applications.

Tip   In the Office Custom Installation Wizard, you can create an MST file that specifies the default behavior of this Setup panel, including hiding the panel from users. Set these options on the **Keep Previous Versions** panel of the wizard.

Upgrade Microsoft Internet Explorer

The user can choose to upgrade to Microsoft Internet Explorer 5 if a previous version of Internet Explorer is installed on the user's computer. Several features of Office require Internet Explorer 5 support in order to fully function. If the user chooses not to install Internet Explorer 5, the basic support components of Internet Explorer 5 are installed, but not the entire browser.

Toolbox

The Microsoft Internet Explorer Administration Kit describes many different ways that Setup allows you to install Internet Explorer 5 on users' computers. You can run the Microsoft Internet Explorer Administration Kit from the **Customize IE 5 Installation Options** panel of the Office Custom Installation Wizard. For information about the kit, see "Microsoft Internet Explorer 5 Administration Kit" on page 776.

Select installation options for Office features

If users choose the **Customize** installation mode, Setup displays Office features on the **Selecting Features** panel, and users can set an installation state for each feature.

In the hierarchical feature tree, features can contain any number of subordinate *child features*. A child feature might also contain additional child features. For example, the **Microsoft Word for Windows** feature includes the child feature **Help**. The **Help** feature includes the child feature **Help for WordPerfect Users**.

To expand the tree and display the child features belonging to that feature, click the plus sign (+) to the left of a feature. To collapse the tree, click the minus sign (–).

Users select the installation state for each feature by clicking the icon to the left of the feature and selecting one of six settings.

When you change the installation state of a feature, Setup sometimes automatically changes the state of other features in the feature tree to match. Setup makes this change to ensure that child features are installed in a state that is consistent with the feature that contains them. If, as a result of your changes, Setup attempts to change a feature to an installation state that the feature does not support, then Setup selects another supported state for that feature.

Note   Changes that you make to the installation state of a child feature might also cause Setup to change the installation state of the feature that contains that child feature. Specifically, if a feature is set to either **Installed on First Use** or **Not Available**, and you set one of its child features to **Run from My Computer**, **Run from CD**, or **Run from Network**, then Setup changes the feature to the same state as the child feature.

Run from My Computer

Setup copies files to the user's hard disk, and the application runs the feature locally. Use this option if the user does not have a persistent network connection, to reduce network usage, or to run the feature with the highest performance.

When you select this option for a feature, Setup automatically changes all associated child features to **Run from My Computer**, unless the child feature is already set to **Installed on First Use** or **Not Available**.

Run all from My Computer

Setup installs this feature and all its child features on the user's hard disk, and the application runs the feature locally.

When you select this option for a feature, Setup automatically changes all associated child features to **Run from My Computer**, regardless of the current installation state of the child features.

Run from CD or Run from Network

Setup leaves files on Office Disc 1 or on the administrative installation point, and the application runs the feature from there. Use this option to minimize the amount of local disk space used by the application, provided the user has a CD-ROM drive or a reliable network connection.

When you select this option for a feature, Setup automatically changes all associated child features to **Run from CD** or **Run from Network**, unless the child feature is already set to **Not Available**.

Run all from CD or Run all from Network

Setup leaves this feature and all of its child features on Office Disc 1 or on the administrative installation point, and the application runs the feature from there.

When you select this option for a feature, Setup automatically changes all associated child features to **Run from CD** or **Run from Network**, regardless of the current installation state of the child features.

Installed on First Use

Setup does not install the files associated with the feature until the user tries to use the feature through a menu command or shortcut. When the user activates the feature for the first time, the Windows installer copies the files to the local hard disk and runs the feature locally. The feature then remains on the user's hard disk. Use this option to minimize the use of local disk space by installing only necessary features on the computer.

Important   Installed on First Use is supported only on operating systems that support *Windows installer shortcuts*, including Windows 98; Windows 95 with Internet Explorer 4.01 with Service Pack 1 or later; and Windows NT 4.0 with Service Pack 3 and Internet Explorer 4.01 with Service Pack 1 or later. On Windows 95 and Windows NT 4.0, you must also have Active Desktop installed (but not necessarily enabled) before you install Office. If you install Office on an operating system that does not support Windows installer shortcuts, then features set to **Installed on First Use** are set to **Run from My Computer** instead.

When you select this option for a feature, Setup automatically changes all associated child features to **Installed on First Use**, unless the child is already set to **Not Available**.

Not Available

Setup does not install the feature or any of its child features. If a user selects a menu command that refers to the feature, an error message instructs the user to rerun Setup and change the installation state in order to use the feature. Setup does not install some associated components, such as templates or converters, and does not create shortcuts for the feature. Use this option to minimize the use of local disk space and to reduce clutter by eliminating features that the user does not need.

When you select this option for a feature, Setup automatically changes all associated child features to **Not Available**.

See also

- For more information about the Setup command line, the Setup settings file, and Setup properties, see "Customizing How Setup Runs" on page 215.

- The Office Custom Installation Wizard allows you to fully customize the installation process, from modifying Setup properties to adding custom files and registry entries to the installation. For more information about the Office Custom Installation Wizard, see "Office Custom Installation Wizard" on page 250.

Office Custom Installation Wizard

The Microsoft Office Custom Installation Wizard allows you to customize the way that all users in your organization install Office on their computers.

Deploying a Custom Office Installation Throughout Your Organization

If you are deploying Microsoft Office throughout a large organization, it is probably the most efficient to first install Office on a network server and then to have users run Setup from your *administrative installation point*.

After you create an administrative installation point, you have many options for managing the deployment of Office. By using the Office Custom Installation Wizard, you can modify the administrative installation point to control how all the users in your organization install Office on their computers.

By using the Custom Installation Wizard, you can do the following:

- Define the path where Office is installed on users' computers.

- Define the default installation state for all features of Office applications. For example, you can choose to install Microsoft Word on the user's local hard disk and install Microsoft PowerPoint to run from the network.

- Add your own files and registry entries to Office Setup so that they are installed along with Office.

- Modify Office application shortcuts, specifying where they are installed and customizing their properties.

- Define a list of network servers for Office to use if the primary server is unavailable.

- Specify other products to install, or programs to run, on users' computers after Setup is completed.

- Configure Microsoft Internet Explorer 5 and Microsoft Outlook the way that you want.

After you fine-tune the options by using the wizard, your modifications become the default settings for anyone who runs Setup from your administrative installation point. You can even have users run Setup in quiet mode (with no user interaction) so that your modifications define precisely how Office is installed—no questions asked.

Toolbox

The Office Custom Installation Wizard includes a Help file that contains extensive reference information. To get access to Help topics without running the wizard, double-click **Custwiz.hlp**. For information about installing the wizard, see "Custom Installation Wizard" on page 774.

Transforming a Standard Office Installation

When you select modifications in the Office Custom Installation Wizard, the wizard alters the behavior of Office 2000 Setup to install Microsoft Office the way that you choose. The wizard can do this because Office 2000 Setup uses the new Windows installer to install and manage Office components.

The Windows installer uses two types of files to install Office:

- Installer *package* (*MSI file*)

  The package, or MSI file, contains a database that describes Office files and configuration information, plus instructions that determine how Setup installs the files.

- Installer *transform* (*MST file*)

  The transform, or MST file, contains modifications to be applied to the package as Setup installs Office.

The Custom Installation Wizard creates a new MST file based on your customizations. Setup reads the information in the MSI file, applies the changes specified in the MST file, and installs Office by using the combined set of instructions. The original MSI file is never altered. This arrangement allows you to create any number of MST files; so you can design any number of Setup scenarios by using the wizard, all from the same *administrative installation point*.

For example, you can use the Custom Installation Wizard to create unique MST files for your Accounting, Engineering, and Human Resources departments. You can install a customized set of features and settings for each department. Your settings become the default when users in each of these departments install Office by using the MST file that's customized for their department.

Using a Windows installer package

The Windows installer package is a relational database that contains all the information necessary to install Office 2000. The package associates product components with features and contains information about the installation process itself, such as installation sequence, destination folder paths, system dependencies, and installation options. The package also contains a number of properties that control the installation process.

After installation, the installer continues to use the package to add or remove components and replace missing or damaged files. When you set Office features to be installed on first use, the installer uses the package to copy the files the first time the user activates the feature.

Using a Windows installer transform

By using the Custom Installation Wizard, you can create a Windows installer transform that describes how to transform the package so that Setup installs Office the way you want. Like the package, the transform is a relational database with information about components, features, and Setup properties. But the transform contains only the changes that you want to apply to the package.

When you run Setup by using both the package and the transform, the installer applies the transform to the original package, and Setup uses your altered configuration to perform the installation. The installer does not change the package itself, but only temporarily applies the changes in memory before carrying out the package instructions.

Creating multiple custom installations of Office

To customize the Office installation, you use the Custom Installation Wizard to create a new transform that contains all of the changes you want to make to the Office installation. You then run Setup by using both the package and the transform.

Because the transform is typically much smaller than the package, you can easily create multiple custom installations by creating multiple transforms to use with the default package. In each transform, you can select a different set of installation options, add custom files or registry entries, and customize Setup properties.

For example, you can use the Custom Installation Wizard to create three MST files for three departments: Accounting, Engineering, and Services.

In the Accounting transform, you specify that Microsoft Access is to be installed to run on the user's computer and that Microsoft Word is to run on the network. In the Engineering transform, you choose to install the spreadsheet templates to run on the user's computer. And in the Services transform, you add a set of Word templates that are used to create corporate forms.

When users in the Accounting department run Setup, they use their department's MST file, and Setup installs their customized version of Office. Users in the Engineering and Services departments install different customized versions of Office by using the MST file created for their particular department.

How to Set Options in the Custom Installation Wizard

When you run the Office Custom Installation Wizard, you first identify the Windows installer *package* (*MSI file*) that you want to customize. Then you can either open an existing Windows installer *transform* (*MST file*) (if you want to work with those customizations as a starting point) or create a new MST file.

Start with the MSI and MST files

After the **Welcome** panel appears in the Custom Installation Wizard, you identify the MSI and MST files on the following panels.

- **Open the MSI File**

  Enter the name and path of the Office MSI file, Data1.msi, which is located in the root folder of the *administrative installation point*.

- **Open the MST File**

  If you are creating a new MST file, select **Do not open an existing MST file**.

  –or–

  If you are modifying an existing MST file, select **Open an existing MST file** and enter the name and path of the MST file.

- **Select the MST File to Save**

  Specify a file name for the MST file in which to save your customizations. You can save your changes in the same file you opened, or you save your changes in a new MST file.

If you plan to store multiple MST files in the same folder that contains the MSI file, give them unique file names. When users run Setup from your administrative installation point, the users specify in the Setup command line the name of the MST file designed for them.

Important   The Custom Installation Wizard is designed for use with the MSI and MST files included with Office 2000 applications and related products. If you use the Custom Installation Wizard to customize the MSI file of another product, some of the panels of the wizard might not appear and some of the Setup properties described in Help might not have any effect.

Specify your Setup options

After you specify the correct MSI and MST files, the Custom Installation Wizard guides you through the many installation options that you can customize and records your choices in the MST file.

In addition to customizing installation options, you can also set default application settings by using the Profile Wizard and the Custom Installation Wizard together. For example, you can set the default file format for saving Word documents for all the users in your organization.

First, you customize settings in Office applications and use the Profile Wizard to record them in an Office profile settings (OPS) file. Then, you use the Custom Installation Wizard to copy the *OPS file* into the MST file. Setup uses your OPS file to preset the default options on users' computers.

Toolbox

You can use the Custom Installation Wizard to specify that Setup runs the Profile Wizard separately, after Office installation is completed, to restore the settings in the OPS file. For information about installing these wizards, see "Custom Installation Wizard" on page 774 or "Profile Wizard" on page 779.

Save yourself some time

Most of the time, the installation scenarios that you create for various departments differ only slightly. If you need to make several MST files that are almost—but not quite—identical, create the first MST file by using the Office Custom Installation Wizard. You can then use the wizard to open your customized MST file, alter one or two options, and save these options in a new MST file.

Many of the customizations that you can make by using the wizard can also be done in other ways. This increases your flexibility for creating custom installations.

For example, suppose that the only difference between the Accounting department's installation configuration and the Engineering department's installation configuration is a different organization name for each department to use. You can use the wizard to create a single MST file and then use a different Setup command line to set the **COMPANYNAME** property for each department.

Record your changes in an MST file

After you click **Finish**, the Custom Installation Wizard writes all of your changes to the MST file. The original MSI file is never altered—so you can always go back to using the standard Office Setup program.

Note   Because MST files contain only the changes you want to make to the standard installation, MST files are typically much smaller than MSI files. If you add large files to your custom installation, however, these files are stored in the MST file and increase its size.

For a complete list of Setup command-line options that you can use when you run Setup by using your customized MST file, click **Help** on the final panel of the wizard. This topic also describes the format of the *Setup settings file*, which you can use to specify Setup properties or define the level of user interaction that Setup uses.

See also

- By using the Profile Wizard, you can customize Office application options and save them in an OPS file. You can then set these options for your users when you install Office on their computers. For more information about using the OPS file during Office installation, see "Profile Wizard" on page 255.

Profile Wizard

The Profile Wizard is a new tool for Microsoft Office 2000 that helps you deploy Office 2000 with specific *Office user profile* information.

Overview of the Profile Wizard

Microsoft Office is highly customizable. Users can change how Office functions by setting options or adding custom templates or tools. For example, the sales department can create a custom template for invoices or a custom dictionary with industry-specific terms.

Users can change everything from the screen resolution to the default file format for saving documents. These user-defined settings can be stored in an *Office user profile*. Office user profiles can contain most of the customizations that users make to the Office 2000 environment.

The Profile Wizard stores and retrieves Office 2000 customizations. By using the Profile Wizard, you can create and deploy a standard user profile when you deploy Office 2000 so that all of your users start off with the same settings.

When you save an Office user profile, you create an Office profile settings (OPS) file. You can include your *OPS file* in a Windows installer *transform* (MST), and the settings are distributed when Office 2000 is deployed. You can also use the Profile Wizard to help back up and restore user-defined settings from one computer to another.

Note   If an OPS file contains settings for an application that is not installed, those settings are still written to the registry.

Office profiles and multiple languages

Office user profiles generated by the Profile Wizard are independent of the operating system—including operating systems in other languages. For example, an OPS file created on Microsoft Windows 95 (U.S. English version) can be restored to a computer with Windows 2000 (Japanese version).

However, Office user profiles are specific to a particular Office language version. For example, if you create an OPS file in the U.S. English version of Office 2000, it cannot be restored to a computer with the German version of Office 2000 installed. There is some overlap between language families. For example, you can restore a U.S. English Office profile to an English or Australian version of Office 2000.

This Office language limitation exists because the different Office versions include localized folder names for the folders that contain the Office user profile information.

You can customize Profile Wizard to capture only certain user settings, and not all Office 2000 settings on the computer, or to run in quiet mode (without user interaction) as part of the Office Custom Installation Wizard. You can also run the Profile Wizard from the command line.

When a user receives a new computer, you can use the Profile Wizard to preserve user-defined Office 2000 settings from the old computer. Run the wizard on the old computer to create an OPS file, and then store the OPS file on the network. After the new computer arrives, run the wizard again to configure the new computer with the previous settings.

Toolbox

The Profile Wizard consists of three files: Proflwiz.exe, Proflwiz.ini, and Proflwiz.hlp. For information about installing the wizard, see "Profile Wizard" on page 779.

See also

- Office user profiles are different from system user profiles. For information about user profiles in a particular Windows operating system, see the appropriate Windows resource kit.

How to Distribute a Standard Office User Profile During Deployment

The Profile Wizard gives you control over which settings are deployed with Microsoft Office 2000. You can create and distribute a default user profile when you deploy Office 2000 so that all of your users start with the same settings.

For example, if you are an administrator in a large company, you can install Office 2000 on a test computer and then customize the toolbars, option settings, templates, custom dictionaries, and any other options. You then run the Profile Wizard to create an Office profile settings (OPS) file to capture all of these configuration options.

After testing the lab installation, you run the Office Custom Installation Wizard and include the *OPS file* that you created earlier. The OPS file settings are included in the Windows installer *transform* (*MST file*), so the customized settings are installed automatically when Office 2000 is deployed on client computers.

See also

- The Office Custom Installation Wizard allows you to control how all the users in your organization install Office on their computers. For more information, see the "Office Custom Installation Wizard" on page 250.

How to Distribute Unique Office User Profiles During Deployment

You can distribute different user profiles for different groups when you deploy Microsoft Office 2000. For example, a large corporation with several departments might want each department to specify how Office 2000 is installed on that department's computers. You can configure Office 2000 with the default corporate settings and then have each department update those settings with a unique user profile.

You can approach this task in two ways:

- Create a standard user profile, create separate department profiles, and then substitute the department profiles for the standard profile during deployment.

- Or you can create a standard user profile, create separate department profiles, and distribute both profiles during deployment.

The first approach is simpler, but it does involve keeping track of different versions of the customized installation—one customized by the corporate administrator and one customized by each department administrator. The second approach allows the department administrators to deploy Office 2000 without modifying the corporate installation.

Distribute a department-specific user profile

In this scenario, the corporate administrator creates a default Office profile settings (OPS) file first.

▶ To create a standard corporate user profile

1   Install and configure Office 2000 on a test computer, and then run the Profile Wizard to create the default *OPS file*.

2   Customize the Office 2000 installation to include the default OPS file.

   In the Office Custom Installation Wizard, the **Customize Default Application Settings** panel includes this option.

Before Office is deployed, the individual department administrators create a new OPS file based on the corporate version.

▶ To create a department-specific user profile

1   By using the corporate *transform* (*MST file*), install Office on a test computer.

2   Customize the Office 2000 environment to suit the department needs.

3   Run the Profile Wizard to create a new department-specific OPS file.

4   Customize the Office 2000 installation to include the new OPS file.

5   Deploy the customized Office 2000 installation to all department users.

Distribute both corporate and department settings

In this scenario, the corporate administrator customizes the Office 2000 installation to point to the Profile Wizard and OPS file with a relative path. Using a relative path allows each department to add the Profile Wizard and a departmental OPS file to their *administrative installation point*.

▶ **To customize the Office installation for department-specific user profiles**

1   Install and configure Office 2000 on a test computer, and then run the Profile Wizard to create a default OPS file.

2   Customize the Office 2000 installation to include the default OPS file.

In the Office Custom Installation Wizard, the **Customize Default Application Settings** panel includes this option.

3   Customize the Office 2000 installation to include the Profile Wizard as an application to be run at the end of the installation, and point to the Profile Wizard and OPS file with a relative path. Use the following syntax:

OPW\Proflwiz.exe /r *Department***.ops /q**

In the Office Custom Installation Wizard, the **Add Installations and Run Programs** panel includes this option.

4   Create separate administrative installation points on the network for each department.

5   Create an OPW folder at each administrative installation point, and copy the Profile Wizard to that folder.

When Office is deployed, the individual department administrators update the Office installation with their own customized versions.

▶ **To install a department-specific user profile**

1   By using the corporate transform (MST file), install Office on a test computer.

If the corporate administrator included an OPS file, this installation includes those settings.

2   Customize the Office 2000 environment to suit the department needs.

3   Run the Profile Wizard to create an OPS file based on the new settings, and name the file *Department*.ops.

4   Copy the new *Department*.ops file to the OPW folder on the department administrative installation point.

5   Deploy Office 2000 to department computers.

When Office 2000 is installed, the settings in the corporate OPS file are included. Immediately following the installation, the Profile Wizard automatically runs and the corporate settings are updated with the department administrator's changes.

How to Distribute a Standard Office User Profile in a Staged Deployment

In a staged deployment, some Microsoft Office 2000 applications are deployed in the initial stage, and the rest are deployed later. There are two general methods for handling a staged deployment, each yielding different results. You can take advantage of user profiles in either case.

Deploy the full set of user settings at each stage

In this scenario, you set up a test computer with all of the Office 2000 components, and create an Office profile settings (OPS) file based on all of the applications. You stage the deployment as follows:

Stage 1   Deploy the first set of applications (for example, Microsoft Excel, Microsoft Word, and Microsoft PowerPoint) with the full set of user profile settings.

Stage 2   Deploy the second set of applications (for example, Microsoft Outlook and Microsoft Internet Explorer) and repeat the full set of user profile settings.

This scenario represents the simplest way to stage a deployment and distribute default user settings. However, if users customize any of their Office settings between Stage 1 and Stage 2, they might lose those customizations during Stage 2.

Customize the Profile Wizard for a staged deployment

In this scenario, you customize the Profile Wizard to capture only the settings relevant to the set of applications that are installed in each stage. You stage the deployment as follows:

Stage 1   Create an *OPS file* based on only the Office 2000 applications scheduled for the first round of deployment, and then deploy Stage 1 applications.

Stage 2   Customize settings for the second round of Office 2000 applications, create a second OPS file, and then deploy Stage 2 applications.

This scenario ensures that both the default settings and any customizations made by the user are preserved. However, the administrator must invest time determining which settings to add at Stage 2 and then customizing the Profile Wizard to track only those settings.

Using the Profile Wizard with the Office Custom Installation Wizard

Although you can run Profile Wizard by itself to capture and restore user profile settings, it is a much more powerful tool when you use it in combination with the Office Custom Installation Wizard.

The Office Custom Installation Wizard helps you customize the Microsoft Office 2000 Setup program. When you customize the Office 2000 installation to include a default user profile, you save a step in your deployment process by distributing the profile during installation.

You have two choices for using the Profile Wizard and the Office Custom Installation Wizard together. Whichever method you choose, the Office Custom Installation Wizard uses the profile that you specify to modify how Office is installed.

Including an OPS file in the Custom Installation Wizard

When you add an Office profile settings (OPS) file to the Custom Installation Wizard, the *OPS file* is included in the Windows installer *transform* (*MST file*). This offers a couple of advantages:

- With the OPS file included in the MST file, you have only one file to keep track of.
- Because the profile is part of the customized Setup, users can install from any *administrative installation point*.

Setting the Profile Wizard to run after Office installation

When you add the Profile Wizard to the list of applications to run at the end of the Office installation, your OPS file is independent of your MST file. This option offers a number of advantages:

- You can update the OPS file without having to create a new MST file.
- If the OPS file is stored in a central place, users can install Office 2000 from any administrative installation point.

However, running the Profile Wizard separately has some limitations. If the OPS file is stored in an administrative installation point, the administrative installation point must be replicated around the network.

See also

- For more information about using the Office Custom Installation Wizard to add an OPS file or the Profile Wizard to your installation, see "How to Preset User Options in an OPS File" on page 235.

How to Run the Profile Wizard from the Command Line

You can run the Profile Wizard from the command line with no loss in functionality. Every option available in the wizard has a corresponding command-line switch.

Use the following syntax:

Proflwiz.exe [[/r] [/s] <*settings filename*>**] [/d] [/i** <INI *filename*>**] [/q] [/p] [/e]**

The following table describes these command-line options.

Switch	Action
/r	Restore settings from specified *OPS file*.
/s	Save settings to specified OPS file.
/d	Reset defaults settings before any restore.
/i	Use specified file instead of Proflwiz.ini.
/q	Run in quiet mode; suppress error messages and progress bar.
/p	Display progress bars; suppress error messages.
/e	Display error messages; suppress progress bars.
/?	Display syntax.

Note   When you use the Profile Wizard to restore the settings from the OPS file, and use the **Reset to defaults before restoring settings** option, be aware that any customizations you have made to the ResetToDefaults sections of the Proflwiz.ini file are ignored. The settings in the ResetToDefaults section of the Proflwiz.ini file are added to the OPS file when the OPS is written. If you want to use your customized ResetToDefaults settings, use the Office Custom Installation Wizard to include the OPS file as part of the Office 2000 Setup process.

The <*settings filename*> parameter is required if either the **/s** switch or the **/r** switch is used. If no additional switches are used, both progress bars and error messages are displayed.

You can use the **/r** switch and the **/d** switch together.

If the **/s** switch and the **/d** switch are specified in the same command line, the **/d** switch is ignored.

The **/p** and **/e** switches are mutually exclusive.

Customizing the Profile Wizard

You can customize the Profile Wizard to include only the settings you want to track. This is very helpful when you deploy Microsoft Office 2000 in stages with a default user profile.

For example, you can roll out Microsoft Excel, Microsoft Word, and Microsoft PowerPoint with one set of customizations now, and then roll out Microsoft Outlook and Microsoft Internet Explorer later. In this scenario, you can customize the Profile Wizard to track only the settings you need for each stage of your deployment.

To customize the performance of Profile Wizard, you edit the Proflwiz.ini file. Open the file in Notepad or another text editor, and then add or delete references to settings that you want to include or exclude. When you edit the Proflwiz.ini file, you can include or exclude specific applications, registry settings or Application Data folders, template files, and so on.

Each section of the Proflwiz.ini file contains comments documenting the usage and syntax for entries in that section. The default entries are designed to gather a complete set of user configuration data, including both files and Windows registry values, for Office 2000.

Note   Some settings in a user profile are shared among applications in Office 2000. When you customize the Proflwiz.ini file for a staged deployment, make sure that you change only nonshared settings or that you set any shared settings to work correctly for all the applications before you save the Office profile settings (OPS) file.

Preserving your customized settings

When Office is deployed in stages, it's easy to overwrite settings in previous user profiles. It's even easier to overwrite settings when you aren't the only administrator installing Office applications. The best way to control which settings are affected in a given deployment is to customize the Profile Wizard.

For example, you might invest a few late nights customizing Office 2000 in the lab. You run the Profile Wizard to capture your user profile settings. You don't configure Outlook because someone else is installing Outlook next month. Then, right on schedule, you deploy Excel, Word, and PowerPoint with a default user profile.

One month later, your colleague deploys Outlook. Like you, he customizes Office 2000 in the lab and uses the Profile Wizard to capture his user profile settings. But he doesn't customize the wizard to exclude settings for any of the other applications—the customized settings that you deployed and the customized settings that users have been working with for a month.

When your colleague installs Outlook, he accidentally changes your settings for Excel, Word, and PowerPoint. And, if he happens to use the **Reset to defaults** option, all of your *OPS file* settings are gone—along with any later user configurations—even if he didn't explicitly change them in his profile.

You can avoid this bleary-eyed scenario by editing the Proflwiz.ini file to exclude all settings except those needed by the Office applications that you are deploying at any given time.

Editing the Proflwiz.ini file

You can edit the Proflwiz.ini file to exclude selected settings when you run the Profile Wizard. You can also edit the Proflwiz.ini file to include additional files, folders, or registry subkeys and values when you create the OPS file.

Note If an OPS file is set to include an empty folder, that folder is created when the settings are restored.

The following table describes the contents of the Proflwiz.ini file. For a full description of each section, including examples of syntax, see the Proflwiz.ini file itself.

INI file section	Contents
[IncludeFolderTrees]	Folders and subfolders in the Application Data tree. Files in these folders and subfolders are included in the user profile.
[IncludeIndividualFolders]	Same as **[IncludeFolderTree]** but includes only folders, not subfolders.
[IncludeIndividualFiles]	Same as **[IncludeIndividualFolders]** but includes only files.
[ExcludeFiles]	Files excluded from the user profile. Allows exclusion of individual files within included folders.
[FolderTreesToRemoveToResetToDefaults]	Folder trees to be deleted prior to writing data from OPS file. Every file in the tree is deleted. Use this section with caution.
[IndividualFilesToRemoveToResetToDefaults]	Files in the Application Data tree to be deleted prior to writing data from OPS file.
[SubstituteEnvironmentVariables]	Environment variables to substitute in registry value data of the type **REG_EXPAND_SZ**.
[IncludeRegistryTrees]	Keys and subkeys in the **HKEY_CURRENT_USER** root of the Windows registry. Values for these keys and subkeys are included in the user profile.
[IncludeIndividualRegistryKeys]	Same as **[IncludeRegistryTrees]** but includes only specific keys, not subkeys.
[ExcludeRegistryTrees]	Keys and subkeys in the **HKEY_CURRENT_USER** root excluded from the user profile. Values and subkeys under these keys are excluded.

INI file section	Contents
[ExcludeIndividualRegistryKeys]	Same as **[ExcludeRegistryTrees]** but excludes only specific keys, not subkeys.
[ExcludeIndividualRegistryValues]	Same as **[ExcludeRegistryKeys]** but excludes only named values, not subkeys.
[RegistryTreesToRemoveToResetToDefaults]	Registry trees in the **HKEY_CURRENT_USER** trees to be deleted prior to writing custom values. All values and subkeys listed in this section are removed.
[IndividualRegistryValuesToRemoveToResetTo Defaults]	Registry values in the **HKEY_CURRENT_USER** subkey values to be deleted prior to writing custom values. All values and subkeys listed in this section are removed.

Note   When you use the Profile Wizard to restore the settings from the OPS file, and use the **Reset to defaults before restoring settings** option, be aware that any customizations you have made to the ResetToDefaults sections of the Proflwiz.ini file are ignored. The settings in the ResetToDefaults section of the Proflwiz.ini file are added to the OPS file when the OPS is written. If you want to use your customized ResetToDefaults settings, use the Office Custom Installation Wizard to include the OPS file as part of the Office 2000 Setup process.

Using Default Paths in Office Profiles

The Profile Wizard helps you distribute default settings to your users as you deploy Microsoft Office 2000. Among other types of settings, you can use the *OPS file* to set default paths for documents, templates, clip art, or other files on your users' computers.

For example, if you have a specific set of clip art files for your Marketing team to use, you can add a Marketing ClipArt folder and configure Office to look there for clip art by default. By distributing such settings when you deploy Office, you can cut down on support costs, because you'll always know where certain types of files are stored on each user's computer.

Default paths and the ORAPI database

Like previous versions of Office, Office 2000 uses many path settings to define user-specific configurations. These settings are stored in the Windows registry. However, if there are user-specific paths in the registry, these paths might be recorded literally in the OPS file and your settings might not apply to all users when the OPS file is distributed during Office 2000 deployment.

To handle path information for Windows registry settings with more flexibility, Office 2000 stores default paths as part of the Office Registry API (ORAPI) database. The path setting is not written to the Windows registry unless you or the user changes it from the default value. Some of these paths appear in the user interface, and they might even appear to be user-specific. However, because Office looks up the default value for each user, these settings function more like variables.

For example, in the **Options** dialog box (**Tools** menu) in Microsoft Word, the **File Locations** tab includes a **Location** setting for documents. The default value is the user's Personal folder (Microsoft Windows NT) or My Documents folder (Microsoft Windows 95/98).

In versions of Office earlier than Office 2000, the actual path and folder names were stored in the Windows registry. Office 2000 uses the ORAPI database instead, in effect making the value generic for all users. The information is written to the Windows registry only if the user or administrator changes the path or folder name from the default.

This means that even paths visible to the user in the user interface do not need special attention to be generalized for all users, as long as the default setting has not been changed.

Customizing a default path to apply to all users

When you create an Office profile settings (OPS) file on a test computer, you can customize a default file location, or you can customize any other setting that includes a path. However, you must also customize the actions of the Profile Wizard to generalize this setting so that it applies to all users. To generalize the setting, you use environment variables instead of a literal path.

For example, suppose you want to set the default location for saving files in Word to a folder called Engineering Documents located in each user's system profile folder. By using the user name AdminM on your test computer, you set this option on the **File Locations** tab in the **Options** dialog box (**Tools** menu). The following path is written to the Windows registry and saved in the OPS file:

C:\Winnt\Profiles\AdminM\Engineering Documents

Because this path points to your user name, this file location won't work for your users. To make the file location work for all of your users, you can replace the specific path with an environment variable, such as the **%USERPROFILE%** variable for Windows NT, resulting in the following path:

%USERPROFILE%\Engineering Documents

Note If the Profile folder is part of the desired path, as it is in this example, make sure that system user profiles are turned on for the client computers.

Defining environment variables in Windows 95/98

Windows 95/98 does not create the **%USERPROFILE%** environment variable automatically. You must create and define this variable manually so that it resolves to the correct location for each user.

To create the **%USERPROFILE%** environment variable for Windows 95/98 clients, use a Windows NT logon script for your users. The logon script processor does not directly support environment variables, but the Winset.exe utility allows you to create global environment variables from a batch file—including a logon script. When Windows 95/98 clients log on to the network, the environment variable **%USERNAME%** exists temporarily—long enough for your settings to be installed on users' computers.

Use the following syntax to create the environment variable when you log on:

<path>\Winset.exe USERPROFILE=%windir%\Profiles\%USERNAME%

If user profiles are not enabled on the Windows 95/98 computer, you must also include the commands to create the Profiles folder and the **%USERNAME%**. In this case, use the following syntax:

cd %windir%
md Profiles
md Profiles\"%USERNAME%"

When the Profile Wizard distributes the settings before or after Office installation, they are written to the Windows registry in unexpanded form and retain the type **REG_EXPAND_SZ**. Office 2000 then expands the environment variables whenever it encounters one of these Windows registry values.

Adding environment variables to the Proflwiz.ini file

One of the components of the Profile Wizard is the Proflwiz.ini file. You can customize the INI file to change what is stored in an Office profile settings (OPS) file. The Proflwiz.ini file includes a section for defining environment variables. You add environment variables to the SubstituteEnvironmentVariables section of the Proflwiz.ini file before you run the Profile Wizard to collect the user profile settings.

This section of the INI file already contains some environment variables, such as the Windows environment variables **%USERPROFILE%** and **%USERNAME%**. You can remove the default environment variables from this list. If you remove both **%USERPROFILE%** and **%USERNAME%** from the list, and you do not add any other environment variables, then no settings are generalized through environment variables.

When you run the Profile Wizard, it compares any Windows registry values of type **REG_EXPAND_SZ** with the strings stored in the environment variables listed in the Proflwiz.ini file. If a match is found, the Profile Wizard substitutes the environment variable name for the literal string.

The Profile Wizard checks for the longest possible string that matches the path, starting with the first element in the path, before substituting the environment variable name. If two variables resolve to paths with equal length strings, they are sorted by the order in which they appear in the Proflwiz.ini file.

For example, in the previous example of the Engineering Documents folder, the Profile Wizard matches the string C:\Winnt\Profiles\AdminM with the **%USERPROFILE%** environment variable. The Profile Wizard then records the value **%USERPROFILE%\Engineering Documents** instead of the actual path from the test computer. Now you can deploy Office 2000 with this setting to any Windows NT 4.0 or Windows 2000 computer with no additional adjustment.

Note   If you use environment variables to customize how the Profile Wizard works, you must also ensure that the appropriate environment variables are correctly set on all users' computers.

Tip   Customize default file locations after performing all of your other Office 2000 configurations. This step minimizes the risk of inadvertently overwriting a default path with a computer-specific path when you are customizing other Office 2000 features.

See also

- The Microsoft Office 2000 Resource Kit includes a copy of the ORAPI spreadsheet with all of the default settings for Office 2000. For more information about the ORAPI spreadsheet, see "Office Registry API" on page 332.

- You must edit the Proflwiz.ini file to add any environment variables that you plan to use in your user profile. For information about editing the Proflwiz.ini file, see "Customizing the Profile Wizard" on page 263.

- You can use a system policy to set a path with environment variables. For more information about environment variables and system policies, see "Using Environment Variables in System Policies" on page 288.

Removal Wizard

When you upgrade to Microsoft Office 2000, the Removal Wizard removes unnecessary or obsolete components from previously installed versions of Office and Office-related applications. The wizard components run behind the scenes during Office Setup, or you can run the Removal Wizard on its own.

Removing Components from Previous Versions of Office

The Microsoft Removal Wizard and the Office 2000 Setup program use the same logic and the same text file to remove unneeded or obsolete files and settings from users' computers.

The Removal Wizard consists of the following files:

Offcln9.opc   Text file that specifies files, registry, and INI file settings, and shortcuts associated with a particular language version of Office to be removed.

Oclean9.dll   Carries out instructions in Offcln9.opc to clean up the user's hard disk.

Offcln9.exe   Provides the user interface that lets you run the wizard as a stand-alone utility.

You can customize the OPC file so that only the components that you specify are removed—including non-Office applications.

Running the removal process during Office Setup

When users install Office 2000, the Office Setup program detects unneeded files, settings, and shortcuts from previously installed versions of Office and removes them. Because the removal function of Setup runs as part of the Windows installer package, Setup runs with administrative *permissions*. That way, Setup can remove prior versions of Office even for users who don't have administrative permissions.

Setup removes files according to instructions contained in one or more OPC files and can remove files for as many languages as you have OPC files. For example, a user might have a French version of Microsoft Word and an English version of Microsoft Excel. If the user has OPC files for both French and English, both the French and English components are removed.

Note   If you have an OPC file that instructs Setup to keep some Office files, while another OPC instructs Setup to remove those files, Setup removes the files.

The removal function of Setup detects the following components of prior versions of Office and Office-related products:

- Microsoft Office 4.*x*, Office 95, and Office 97
- Microsoft Team Manager 97
- Microsoft Outlook 97 and Outlook 98 (does not include Outlook Express)
- Microsoft FrontPage 1.1, FrontPage 97, FrontPage 98
- Microsoft Publisher 2.0, Publisher 95, Publisher 97, and Publisher 98
- Microsoft Project 4.0, Project 95, Project 97, Project 98

Note   Setup recognizes components at the application level. Therefore, the removal process detects and removes stand-alone versions of applications such as Word and Excel, as well as shared components such as Office Binder and Equation Editor.

Setup also detects the following as candidates for removal:

- Incompletely installed or uninstalled components that leave unusable files on the hard disk
- Files that begin with the tilde (~) character

Finally, Setup detects and removes temporary files, which are defined as files found in any of the following folders:

- Windows temporary folder (Windows\Temp or Windows\Tmp)
- Folders identified by the MS-DOS environment variable **%TEMP%** or **%TMP%**
- MS-DOS temporary folder (*drive*:\Temp or *drive*:\Tmp); Setup searches every drive on the computer.

Running the Removal Wizard as a stand-alone utility

After Office Setup removes files and settings from previously installed versions of Office or Office components, other unneeded files might remain on users' computers. For example, font files and dynamic-link library (DLL) files might not be removed. You can run the Removal Wizard as a stand-alone utility to remove all Office-related files from users' computers.

Note   Setup does not remove user files from the user's hard disk.

Situations in which it makes sense to run the Removal Wizard as a stand-alone utility include the following:

- Before you upgrade to Office 2000, to clean up all existing Office-related files.

- When you upgrade gradually. For example, if you upgrade to Word 2000 before upgrading to the rest of Office 2000, you can remove previously installed versions of Word only.

- When upgrading to Office 2000 replaces the need for a custom application on users' computers. You can use the wizard to remove the custom application.

Toolbox

The Removal Wizard gives you a great deal of control over how you clean up users' hard disks. For information about installing the wizard, see "Removal Wizard" on page 779.

Note In Microsoft Windows NT, the Removal Wizard needs administrator permissions to run. Therefore, if the user does not have administrator permissions, you must run the wizard with the proper permissions.

You can run the Removal Wizard in one of three modes, depending on the degree to which you want to clean up users' hard disks:

Aggressive mode   Removes all Office-related components, including components shared by more than one Office application. Before installing Office 2000, you might want to run the wizard in aggressive mode for users who are upgrading from a variety of Office versions.

Safe mode   Removes only components that are no longer needed. Components deleted in safe mode are not being used by any application.

Safe mode with user discretion   Runs in safe mode, but allows you to select which detected applications to keep and which to delete.

Caution   Never run the Removal Wizard in aggressive mode after you install Office 2000 because it removes all Office components, including those that might be needed by Office 2000 or an Office 2000-compatible application.

Tip   If you want to see a list of what files are deleted in the various modes, run the Removal Wizard to see the list or save the list in a text file. Then save the list as a text file and cancel the wizard. If you save the list as a text file, you can see which applications use which files.

See also

- You can use the Office Custom Installation Wizard to customize Setup so that it prompts users before removing components. For more information, see "Office Custom Installation Wizard" on page 250.

Customizing the OPC File

Whether Setup removes unneeded files from previously installed versions of Office automatically, or if you run the Removal Wizard to clean up users' computers, you can control what is detected for removal by customizing the OPC file.

Contents of the OPC file

The OPC file consists of two sections: Definitions and Commands. The Definitions section determines which commands in the Commands section to carry out.

The OPC file identifies files, registry entries, INI file entries, and **Start** menu items that were installed or modified by previously installed versions of Office and Office-related products. The OPC file also contains rules that describe which of these files or entries to remove, where they are located, and under what conditions they can be deleted.

When the Removal Wizard runs, it processes the OPC file. In safe mode, the wizard marks items for removal only if it does not detect a corresponding application. When the wizard runs in aggressive mode, it marks all items for removal.

Working with the OPC file

The default OPC file included with Office is Offcln9.opc and is used by both the Removal Wizard and Office Setup. By editing this file, or by modifying a copy of the OPC file, you can specify which components to remove from the users' computers. You can also use the OPC file to remove non-Office components, such as custom applications.

Toolbox

You can find information about the syntax of the OPC file and instructions for modifying the OPC file in the Word document OPC.doc. For information about installing OPC.doc, see "Office Information" on page 787.

Using Command-Line Options with the Removal Wizard

By using command-line options, you can specify the mode in which the Microsoft Removal Wizard runs, the OPC file it uses, the log file it creates, and so forth.

To run the Removal Wizard with command-line options, click **Run** on the **Start** menu, and then type **Offcln9.exe** followed by the command-line options you want.

The Removal Wizard command-line options use the following syntax:

Offcln9.exe [/a | /s [/q[/r]] [/l][!][*logfile*]]] [*opcfile*]

/a   Indicates aggressive mode; the Removal Wizard removes files associated with all previously installed versions of Office and Office-related applications. When you use this command-line option, the wizard does not allow you to select which files to keep.

/s   Indicates safe mode; the Removal Wizard removes only those files for which it does not detect an associated application. When you use this command-line option, the wizard does not allow you to select which files to keep.

/q   Indicates quiet mode; the Removal Wizard runs without prompting the user for information or displaying progress indicators. The wizard does not restart the user's computer; therefore, changes might not be completed until the user restarts the computer.

/r   Used with the **/q** option to restart the computer automatically if necessary. The user has no opportunity to save files before the computer restarts.

/l*logfile*   Generates a log with the file name *logfile*. If no log file name is specified, the Removal Wizard creates a default log file, Offcln9.log, in the current folder of the wizard.

opcfile   Indicates the name of the OPC file. If you don't specify a file name here, the Removal Wizard looks for Offcln9.opc, the default OPC file.

/l!*logfile*   Generates a log file in the same manner as **/l**, but the Removal Wizard does not perform the removal process. This option is useful to test the Removal Wizard before running it to remove files.

For example, the following command-line string runs the Removal Wizard in aggressive mode without user intervention, restarts the system automatically if needed, and creates the default log file:

Offcln9.exe /a /q /r /l

Tip   The Removal Wizard returns a code to indicate whether the wizard ran with any errors. If you create a batch file to run the wizard, you can include error-checking code so that the wizard returns **0** to indicate that errors occurred or returns **1** to indicate that no errors occurred.

How to Create a Custom Removal Routine

There are several ways that you can specify how the removal routine in the Microsoft Removal Wizard or Office Setup program cleans up users' computers:

- Customize the default OPC file (Offcln9.opc), which is used by Office Setup. When users run Office Setup, your custom removal routine automatically runs.

- Create your own OPC file and run the Removal Wizard with a command-line option indicating your custom OPC file name.

- In the Office Custom Installation Wizard, specify which Office components to keep on the **Remove Previous Versions** panel.

Use a custom OPC file and command-line options

Creating a custom OPC file and running the Removal Wizard with command-line options gives you the greatest amount of flexibility. For example, you can create a command that automatically does the following on users' computers:

- Runs the Removal Wizard without user intervention (quiet mode)

- Removes all files from previously installed versions of Office (aggressive mode)

- Empties temporary folders

- Restarts the computer automatically

In addition, suppose you want to remove an internal company tool that is being replaced by Office 2000 functionality. The internal tool, Chart.exe, resides on users' computers in the folder C:\Program Files\Internal\Chart. In addition, the folder contains support files—Chartsub.dll, Chartprt.dat, and Readme.txt.

The following procedure shows you how to modify the OPC file to accomplish all these aims.

▶ **To modify the OPC file for a custom removal routine**

1   Create a copy of the default OPC file (Offcln9.opc), and name it Newopc.opc.

2   Open Newopc.opc in a text editor.

In Microsoft Windows 95/98, this file is too large for Notepad, but it can be edited in WordPad.

3   In the definitions section, define the following values:

TEMPFOLDERCONTENTS = REMOVE

TEMPTWIDDLEFILESONLY = REMOVE

4 At the beginning of the Commands section (immediately before the **[TEMPTWIDDLEFILESONLY]** command) add the following lines:

[SAFE] "Internal charting tool"

C:\program files\internal\chart\chart.exe

C:\program files\internal\chart\chartsub.dll

C:\program files\internal\chart\chartprt.dat

C:\program files\internal\chart\readme.txt

This step ensures that the wizard detects the specified files.

5 Save and close Newopc.opc.

Toolbox

Information about the syntax of the OPC file and instructions for modifying the OPC file are included in the Word document OPC.doc. For information about installing OPC.doc, see "Office Information" on page 787.

Test and distribute your custom removal routine

Test your customized OPC file on a computer by using the **/l!***logfile* command-line option. This step generates a log of the files that are deleted by your customized OPC file.

To run your custom OPC file on users' computers, distribute Newopc.opc, along with the Removal Wizard (Offcln9.exe and Oclean9.dll). Instruct users to run the wizard by using the **Run** command on the **Start** menu with the following command line:

Offcln9.exe /a /q /r Newopc.opc

Tip   You can also create a batch file that includes the correct command-line string. Distribute the batch file to users as part of an e-mail message or logon script.

PART 3

Managing and Supporting Office 2000

Contents

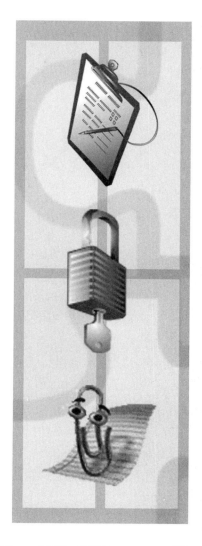

CHAPTER 7

Ongoing Configuration of Office on Users' Computers

With enhanced support for system policies and a clearer picture of how to lock down options, Microsoft Office 2000 gives administrators more control over their users' interaction with Office than ever before. Administrators who take advantage of these features can depend on a consistent configuration for all of their users and reduce the cost of supporting Office throughout their organization.

In This Chapter

Managing Users' Options with System Policies

The Microsoft Office 2000 Resource Kit offers enhanced support for system policies, including an expanded list of options that you can set, and a higher level of control for consistency and ease of use.

Setting the Standards for Your Organization

System policies help you control how your users work with Office 2000. By using system policies, you can configure Office 2000 to your own specifications. You can even use system policies to lock down Office options to varying degrees, depending on the level to which you want to control user options. By using system policies, you determine which options are available to your users.

You create a system policy file and store the file on your server. When users log on to client computers, the system policy file is downloaded, and the system policies are enforced. If you need to change a policy, you update the policy file on the server, and then the policy is automatically updated on each client computer the next time users log on.

Because of differences in how the Windows registry works, the Microsoft Windows 95/98 and Microsoft Windows NT operating systems require different formats for system policies. You can use the same System Policy Editor, however, to create policy files for client computers running any of these operating systems.

Note The Windows 3.1 and Macintosh operating systems do not support system policies on client computers.

See also

- System policies can be used to enforce a consistent user interface among all the Office users in your organization. For more information about using system policies to lock down options in Office 2000, see "Locking Down an Office Configuration" on page 291.
- The Office 2000 Resource Kit includes a new version of the System Policy Editor. For detailed instructions about setting system policies with the new version, see "Using the System Policy Editor" on page 296.

New and Improved Office 2000 System Policies

Office 2000 has enhanced and improved system policies, with more policies and a new version of the System Policy Editor.

As part of the enhanced support for system policies in Office 2000, policies are now stored in a separate HKCU\Software\Policies subkey in the Windows registry, rather than in the various Software subkeys, such as Software\Microsoft\Office\9.0 \Word or Software\Microsoft\Office\9.0\Excel.

Note Because the system policies are stored in a different part of the registry for Office 2000, system policies from previous versions of Office applications do not transfer to the new version. Use the new system policy templates to reset your system policies for Office 2000.

Other system policy enhancements in Office 2000 include the following.

Easily enforceable policies

When you set a policy for a user interface element, such as a menu command or toolbar button, that element appears dimmed in the user interface, so users cannot use or reset the option. Previously, users could change settings in the user interface, even if there were system policies set for that option.

Now, even if a user does manage to change a setting, that setting is changed back when the user quits and restarts the application, rather than when the user next logs on.

Safer policies

In Windows 2000, you can set an *access control list* (ACL) to lock the Policies subkey in the Windows registry. This step prevents users from changing policies by modifying settings in their registry.

More Excel and Word policies

Most of the settings in the **Options** dialog box (**Tools** menu) in Microsoft Word and Microsoft Excel can now be set by policy, except for settings that are stored in the document or that are not permanently stored. Many of the settings previously stored as binary files in the Word Settings subkey and the Excel Options subkey have now been incorporated into the Policies subkey.

More intuitive settings

The new version of the System Policy Editor allows you to set a policy as either enforced (selected) or not enforced (cleared). After you set the policy, you then specify the value for the enforced setting.

Policies that can be undone

In the previous version of the System Policy Editor, you could stop enforcing a system policy, but you could not return client computers to their original configuration. With Office 2000, however, you can set a policy and later clear the policy—and return client computers to their previous state, whether that state is the application default or a user's customized setting.

Policies that accept environment variables

The new version for the System Policy Editor and the Office 2000 system policy templates now accept environment variables. Environment variables take the place of actual file names, paths, and other changeable values. By using environment variables, you can use a variable instead of a specific path, which might not be valid for every client computer. When the policy is enforced, the variable is automatically expanded to the correct value for each client computer.

Options That Can Be Set Through a System Policy

You can set many Office 2000 options by using system policies. The following list describes some categories of options that can be set through policy:

- You can disable or enable any menu command and its corresponding toolbar button.
- You can disable or enable any shortcut key.
- You can specify settings for many dialog box items, including most of the options in the **Options** dialog box (**Tools** menu).

Policies affect application settings, but not document-specific settings. For example, in Word you can enable or disable most of the options on the **General** tab in the **Options** dialog box (**Tools** menu) by using system policies. However, you cannot use policies to alter anything on the **User Information** tab in the **Options** dialog box, or in the **Properties** dialog box (**File** menu).

See also

- All of the system policies for a particular application are listed in the corresponding policy template. For more information about the policies within each template, see "Office 2000 System Policy Reference" on page 306.

Working with System Policy Templates

A system policy represents a single option in an application. Each system policy corresponds to one or more Windows registry keys. A system policy template associates the option with the registry keys that the option affects.

When you create a system policy file, you base your file on one or more policy templates. The Office 2000 Resource Kit includes the following policy templates, which list the options you can control for each application.

Template file name	Includes
Office9.adm	Policies shared by Office 2000 components
Access9.adm	Policies for Access 2000
Excel9.adm	Policies for Excel 2000
FrontPg4.adm	Policies for FrontPage 2000
Outlk9.adm	Policies for Outlook
Pub6.adm	Policies for Publisher
Ppoint9.adm	Policies for PowerPoint 2000
Word9.adm	Policies for Word 2000
ClipGal5.adm	Policies for the Clip Gallery
Instlr1.adm	Policies for the Windows installer

Most policies in the system policy templates correspond to options that users can set in the **Options** dialog box (**Tools** menu) of each Office application. Some policies do not correspond to settings that users can select; these are organized by application or under the general Office heading.

The policies in the template are organized into a hierarchy to make them easier to find. In general, they are organized to correspond to the user interface. For example, items usually found in the **Options** dialog box (**Tools** menu) are listed under **Tools | Options** in the template.

In some cases, however, the templates do not exactly match the user interface. Some Office settings appear in the **Options** dialog box (**Tools** menu) for each component, but the corresponding policies are listed in the Office9.adm template. For example, the **Provide feedback with sound** option is common to Word, Excel, Microsoft PowerPoint, and Microsoft Access, so it is stored in the Office9.adm template rather than in the templates of the individual applications. Similarly, each component has a **Web Options** button on the **General** tab in the **Options** dialog box (**Tools** menu), so you can set options specifically for using Office with the Web. You set a policy for these options in the Office9.adm template under Web Options category rather than in the template for each application.

Note   The System Policy Editor can also work with three Windows template files (Common.adm, Windows.adm, and Winnt.adm). These files do not contain Office policies, but the Windows policies they contain may be useful in managing a workgroup. For more information, see the *Windows NT Server Resource Kit* or the *Windows NT Workstation Resource Kit*.

See also

- Before you create a new policy, you must specify which policy templates you want to use. For more information about adding a policy template, see "How to Set System Policies for Your Organization" on page 296.

- The system policy templates contain individual system policies organized by category. For detailed information about the contents of each template, see "Office 2000 System Policy Reference" on page 306.

Applying System Policies to Selected Users or Groups

You determine which users or groups are affected by a system policy. You can set policies for a single user, for a group of users, or for all users. You can also set policies for a single computer or for all computers. You make these choices in the System Policy Editor when you create a system policy file.

The Office 2000 policies you create and distribute are stored as entries in the HKEY_Current_User\Software\Policies subkey in the Windows registry.

Setting system policies for all users or all computers

You can set a policy for all of the users in your domain by double-clicking the **Default User** icon in the System Policy Editor. You can also set a policy for all client computers in your domain by double-clicking the **Default Computer** icon. When you double-click one of these icons, the **Properties** dialog box opens, and you can set the policies for that user or computer. You can set a policy for all users, for all computers, or for both.

Note   The full name of the **Properties** dialog box changes depending on the name of the icon you double-click in the main window of the System Policy Editor. The dialog box is referred to generically in this section as the "**Properties** dialog box."

Setting system policies for a particular user or computer

You can set a policy for a specific user account by adding the user to the policy file. For example, suppose that your network includes a Guest account and you want to limit a guest user's access to options. You can use a system policy for the Guest account. Similarly, if all your guest users can use the same computer, you can set a policy for that computer.

Note   The user name or computer name you specify in the System Policy Editor must already exist in the network system. You cannot create new user names or computer names from within the System Policy Editor.

Setting system policies for a group of users

You can also set policies for groups of users in your domain. For example, all of the users in your Accounting department may require the same options in Excel. If you create a Windows NT user group for the Accounting department, you can control the options for all users in Accounting by setting a policy for the Accounting group.

Note   The group names you specify in the System Policy Editor must already exist in the network system. You cannot create new groups from within the System Policy Editor.

Sometimes a user is a member of more than one group. To avoid potential conflicts between group policies, you can set relative priorities so that group policies are applied in a particular order. When a user who is a member of several groups logs on, the policy settings from the highest priority group are processed last so that those settings override the settings from lower priority groups.

Note   You must set group policies by installing the group policy capability on each client computer. For more information about group policies, see the *Windows NT Server Resource Kit* or the *Windows NT Workstation Resource Kit*.

See also

- The System Policy Editor provides a single interface for setting policies for users, groups, or computers. For detailed instructions, see "How to Set System Policies for Your Organization" on page 296.

Setting System Policies

After you have selected the policy templates you want to use, and specified which users or computers the policies affect, you are ready to set specific policies in the System Policy Editor. You can set a policy by opening the **Properties** dialog box for the desired user, group, or computer, and then selecting the policy you want to set.

Policies are organized by category within each policy template. The policy templates themselves are listed in order in the **Properties** dialog box. For example, if you add both the Excel9.adm and Word9.adm template files to the policy, both the Excel 2000 categories and the Word 2000 categories appear in the **Properties** dialog box.

Each policy has a check box to the left that indicates its current setting. When you select a policy, an edit control appears at the bottom of the dialog box so that you can provide additional information.

For example, if you select the **Save Excel files as** policy in the Transition category under **Tools | Options** in Excel, you use the list box at the bottom of the dialog box to indicate the file format you want to use.

System policy settings

A system policy can have one of three settings in the **Properties** dialog box:

Selected

The policy has been implemented. Another check box below the policy indicates whether the setting is enforced as on or off. When a user logs on, the Windows registry changes to conform to the policy.

For example, in Excel you can set a policy to determine whether the **Formula** bar is visible in normal view. You turn on the policy by selecting the **Show Formula bar in Normal view** check box. Then you use the **Check to enforce setting on; uncheck to enforce setting off** check box to determine which way the setting is enforced.

Cleared

The policy has not been implemented. If it was implemented previously, the previously specified settings are removed from the Windows registry. When you clear a policy, the option returns either to the application default state or to whatever setting the user had specified before you set the policy.

For example, if an Excel user has set the **Formula** bar to appear in normal view, and you apply a policy to turn off the **Formula** bar, that user no longer sees the **Formula** bar in normal view. If you then clear the policy, it reverts to the previous settings, so the user sees the **Formula** bar in normal view once again.

Unavailable

System policies can also be changed to an unavailable state, where the check box is shaded to indicate that the setting is unchanged from the last time the user logged on. When you first create a system policy, all of the settings are set to the unavailable (shaded) state. After you have selected a particular system policy and distributed the policy file, do not use the unavailable state to clear the policy. If you want to stop enforcing a policy, clear the policy check box.

Note   The unavailable state cannot clear a policy because when you enforce a policy, a value entry for that policy is added to the Policies subkey in the Windows registry. If you set the policy to the unavailable state, the value entry still exists in the Policies subkey and is still enforced. Even if a user changes the option in the user interface, the setting in the Policies subkey overrides the changes.

See also

- All of the system policies for a particular application are listed in the corresponding policy template. For more information about the templates, see "Office 2000 System Policy Reference" on page 306.

Using System Policies to Disable User Interface Items

One of the main reasons to use system policies is to prevent your users from changing items in the user interface. By using system policies, you can disable menu commands, toolbar buttons, and shortcut keys so that your users cannot use those options.

Disabling menu and toolbar items

You can use system policies to disable menu commands and their corresponding toolbar buttons. When you disable a menu command and toolbar button through a policy, users cannot use that command or button.

For your users, a menu command that is disabled through a policy appears on the menu, but it is shaded and unavailable. Similarly, a toolbar button that is disabled through a policy appears on the toolbar, but it is unavailable to users.

Several menu commands and toolbar buttons are listed in the Predefined category. These include several commands that administrators frequently disable, such as the **Hyperlink** command (**Insert** menu) and the **Macro** command (**Tools** menu). If you want to disable any other command in an Office 2000 application, use the Custom category. To disable a menu command and toolbar button in the Custom category, enter the control ID for that item in the System Policy Editor. You can look up the control ID for any command or button in Visual Basic for Applications (VBA).

Disabling shortcut keys

Many Office commands have corresponding shortcut keys. When you disable the menu command and toolbar button through a policy, users can still press the shortcut key to use that command. To make the option completely unavailable, you must also disable the shortcut key.

For example, suppose that you disable the **Insert Hyperlink** command in Excel and a user knows that the shortcut key for that command is CTRL+K; the user can still press the shortcut key to insert a hyperlink. To prevent your users from inserting hyperlinks altogether, you must disable the CTRL+K key combination, too.

To disable a shortcut key in the Predefined category of the policy template, select that shortcut key. You can also disable any shortcut key by using the Custom category. To disable a shortcut key in the Custom category, look up the *virtual key code* for the registry entry corresponding to the shortcut key and then enter the value in the System Policy Editor.

Note   Even when you disable both a menu command and its corresponding shortcut key, the command is still available through VBA. This is by design, so you can create macros that use the command.

See also

- You can disable either a predefined or custom menu or a toolbar item. For detailed instructions about disabling a menu or a toolbar button, see "How to Disable Menu Commands and Toolbar Buttons" on page 300.

- You can disable either a predefined or custom shortcut key. For detailed instructions about disabling a shortcut key, see "How to Disable Shortcut Keys" on page 303.

Using Environment Variables in System Policies

Windows 95/98, Windows NT 4.0, and Windows 2000 all include the capability to use environment variables in the Windows registry to take the place of actual file names, paths, or other changeable values. Environment variables in the Windows registry take the **REG_EXPAND_SZ** data type.

Although Windows system policies have used environment variables for some time, Office 97 did not recognize the data type **REG_EXPAND_SZ**, so you could not use environment variables in Office 97 system policies. However, you can use environment variables in Office 2000.

For example, the **Default file location** policy for Excel 2000 allows you to specify a default path to the location where you want users to store Excel files. If you want to store users' Excel files under their user names on the network, you can use a network drive and the following environment variable:

X:**%USERNAME%**

When you distribute the policy, the environment variable is written to each user's registry. Office 2000 recognizes that **%USERNAME%** is an environment variable and expands it to whatever the **%USERNAME%** variable is set to on the user's computer. So Office 2000 expands this example to X:*UserA* for User A, X:*UserB* for User B, and so on.

You could also use any other appropriately defined environment variable to set **Default file location** to a particular path or folder. Because Office 2000 recognizes the **REG_EXPAND_SZ** data type, you can use environment variables that exist by default in the operating system or that you set on your own.

Note Windows 95/98 does not create environment variables automatically. You must create and define variables manually so that they resolve correctly for each user. For example, to create the **%USERNAME%** environment variable for Windows 95/98 clients, use a Windows NT logon script.

See also

- Several Office 2000 system policies accept environment variables. For a list of these policies, see "Office 2000 System Policies That Accept Environment Variables" on page 330.

- You can use environment variables in place of directory paths or specific user information. For more information, see the *Windows NT Server 4.0 Resource Kit*.

System Policies and the Windows Registry

You use the System Policy Editor to create a system policy file, based on the system policy templates, and then store that file on a network server. When users log on to the network, the system policy file is downloaded to client computers, and then the Windows registry is updated to use the values specified in the system policy file.

Later, you can update client computers by using new system policies, and the Windows registry for each client computer is updated when the user next logs on.

Where are policies stored in the Windows registry?

In earlier versions of Office, system policies were stored in the Software subkey, under whatever subtree they affected (for example, HKEY_CURRENT_USER). System policies for Office 2000 are now consolidated in a separate Policies subkey under the HKCU\Software subkey in the Windows registry.

The Policies subkey mirrors most of the HKEY_CURRENT_USER\Software \Microsoft\Office\9.0 subkey. Placing all of the system policies together in the same subkey prevents Windows registry errors and also makes it possible for administrators to lock the Policy subkey in Windows NT.

The following example shows the hierarchy of the Policies subkey in the Windows registry.

```
HKEY_CURRENT_USER
    Software
        Policies
            Microsoft
                Office
                    9.0
                        Access
                        Binder
                        Common
                        Excel
                        Graph
                        Outlook
                        PowerPoint
                        Word
```

Locating the registry entry that corresponds to a system policy

Each system policy in a policy template corresponds to one or more entries in the Windows registry. If you want to find out exactly what entries in the Windows registry correspond to a particular policy, you can open the policy template in Notepad, and then look for that policy.

The policy template files are divided into categories, and each category lists the Windows registry subkey that contains the entries for that category. Each specific policy entry in the template lists the Windows registry value name that the policy affects and the specific Windows registry value data that is set when the policy is turned on or off.

For example, in the Word9.adm template, the following policy entry lists the Windows registry entries that are set when you disable the **Insert Hyperlink** shortcut key:

```
POLICY !!DisableShortcutKeys
KEYNAME Software\Policies\Microsoft\Office\9.0\Word\DisabledShortcutKeysCheckBoxes
    PART !!InsertHyperlinkKey CHECKBOX
    VALUENAME InsertHyperlink
    VALUEON 75,8
    VALUEOFF 0
    END PART
```

The double exclamation points (!!) in the template file indicate that there is a string reference at the bottom of the file. For example, if you see a line such as !!InsertHyperlinkKey in the template file, this means that text similar to the following will be at the bottom of the file:

```
[Strings]
InsertHyperlinkKey = "Ctrl+K (Insert | Hyperlink...)"
```

The following table lists the entries that appear in the policy template files when you open the files in Notepad.

Entry	Description
POLICY	Policy you are turning on or off. In the preceding example, the **Disable Shortcut Keys** policy includes several subpolicies, including the policy to turn off the **Insert Hyperlink** shortcut key.
KEYNAME	Registry subkey that is affected.
PART	Specific option you are setting with the policy. In the preceding example, there are several shortcut keys that you can disable individually.
VALUENAME	Registry value that is affected.
VALUEON	Registry value data that indicates when this policy is turned on (for example, the **Insert Hyperlink** shortcut key is disabled).
VALUEOFF	Registry value data that indicates when this policy is turned off (for example, the **Insert Hyperlink** shortcut key is enabled).

Locking Down an Office Configuration

The new administrative features in Microsoft Office 2000 include the ability to turn off options or features that you don't want people in your organization to use. Office 2000 gives you the ability to lock down a specific configuration of Office 2000 and control exactly how your users interact with the applications.

When to Lock Down an Office Configuration

Organizations might have several reasons for wanting to lock down a particular configuration of Office 2000. The following scenarios illustrate just a few.

Keep important information accessible

If your organization has a high employee turnover rate, you might not want your employees to add password-protection to their files. When you replace someone, your new employee probably needs ready access to all the previous user's files—without having to worry about lost or forgotten passwords. Disabling password-protection helps guarantee that important customer information is always accessible.

Reduce support costs

If you are training employees who are computer novices, you can raise everyone's confidence level instantly by locking down a uniform configuration of Office and disabling all user customization until your workforce becomes more skilled. Imposing default Office settings in this situation can help reduce your training and support costs.

Create a consistent user environment

If you have shifts of employees sharing the same computers, you can make the transitions easier for your users by locking down a consistent user interface on every computer. By establishing the same computer interface for everyone, you don't have to worry about reconfiguring the user interface before every shift change.

Limit the potential distractions of the Internet

Office 2000 includes a number of built-in hyperlinks to sites on the World Wide Web where users can get more information about features of Office 2000. However, if your users don't normally use the Internet for their work duties, you might not want to distract them with opportunities to browse the Web. You can disable Web connections in Office 2000 to help keep your users focused on their work.

How to Lock Down Options with System Policies

To lock down the options available in Office 2000, you use system policies. System policies are organized by application in system policy templates. Within the templates are categories (such as **Tools | Options** or **Disable items in user interface**), and within the categories are individual policies. You set a policy by selecting it in the System Policy Editor.

The following types of policies are useful for locking down options.

Disable command bar items

You can disable any menu command in the user interface, along with the corresponding toolbar button. To disable a standard command bar item, use the **Disable command bar buttons and menu items** policy in the Predefined category for a particular Office application. To disable any other command bar button, use the Custom category and enter the control ID for the item.

When you disable an item on a menu or toolbar, that item still appears on the menu or toolbar; but the item is shaded, which means the corresponding command is unavailable. When a user points to a disabled toolbar button, the ScreenTip indicates that the button has been disabled.

Prevent command bar customization

To ensure a consistent user interface across all of the computers in your organization, you can stop users from customizing menu bars or toolbars. To disable command bar customization, turn on the **Disable command bar buttons and menu items** policy in the Predefined category and select the **Tools | Customize** check box.

Disable shortcut keys

Many users memorize the keyboard shortcuts for various menu commands and toolbar buttons. If you want to completely lock down an option, you must disable the shortcut key as well as the corresponding menu bar and toolbar items.

You can disable any shortcut key by using the **Disable shortcut keys** policy under the Predefined or Custom category. When a user presses a shortcut key combination that has been disabled, the application does not respond.

Note   Even when you disable both a menu command and its corresponding shortcut key, the command is still available through Visual Basic for Applications. This is by design, so you can continue to create macros that use the command.

Disable dialog box items

You can prevent users from changing options in dialog boxes by locking down those options through a policy. For example, many of the settings in the **Options** dialog box (**Tools** menu) already appear in the policy templates, so you can easily disable an option that you don't want your users to change.

See also

- You use system policies to lock down many options in Office 2000. For detailed information about using system policies, see "Managing Users' Options with System Policies" on page 279 and "Using the System Policy Editor" on page 296.

- To make a feature completely unavailable, you must disable the menu command and any keyboard shortcuts corresponding to that feature. For more information about disabling menu bar commands, see "How to Disable Menu Commands and Toolbar Buttons" on page 300. For more information about disabling keyboard shortcuts, see "How to Disable Shortcut Keys" on page 303.

Disabling Password Protection

Several of the Office 2000 applications give users the ability to protect documents by setting a password. You can disable the command bar buttons and menu bar items that are used to set passwords in Access, Excel, and Word by setting a policy.

▶ **To disable password protection for Access, Excel, and Word**

1   In the System Policy Editor, double-click the **Default User** icon.

2   In the **Properties** box, click the plus sign (+) next to the application you want to change.

3   Click the plus sign next to **Disable items in user interface**, and then click the plus sign next to **Predefined**.

4   Select the **Disable command bar buttons and menu items** policy.

5   For Access, select the **Tools | Security | Set Database Password** check box in the **Settings for Disable command bar buttons and menu items** box.

For Excel, select the **Tools | Protection, Tools | Protection | Protect Sheet, Tools | Protection | Protect Workbook** and **Tools | Protection | Protect and Share Workbook** check boxes in the **Settings for Disable command bar buttons and menu items** box.

For Word, select the **Tools | Protect Document** check box in the **Settings for Disable command bar buttons and menu items** box.

Users of Word and Excel can still set password protection

In Word and Excel, users can still set passwords for a file by using the **Save As** command (**File** menu). Setting a policy to lock down the command bar buttons and menu bar items for password protection does not prevent users from taking advantage of this alternative.

For example, in Word, users can set a password for a document by clicking **Save As** on the **File** menu, and then in the **Save As** dialog box, clicking the **Tools** menu and then clicking **General Options**. The **Save** tab is displayed and includes two options that allow users to set a password for the file: **Password to open** and **Password to modify**. Excel makes similar options available through the **Save As** command (**File** menu).

See also

- You can use system policies and the System Policy Editor to lock down many other Office options. For more information about using the System Policy Editor, see "Using the System Policy Editor" on page 296.

Disabling Built-in Connections to the Web

Office 2000 takes advantage of Internet technology by including several built-in connections to information on the World Wide Web. For example, if a user queries the Office Assistant and it doesn't find the right information, the user can click **None of the above, look for more help on the Web** in the Answer Wizard to check for other information on the Internet.

If you don't want your users to use these built-in links to get to the Web, you can disable several of the connection points through system policies. For example, you can prevent users from installing the feature, or you can include the Web address in your *firewall* protection.

Toolbox

The built-in Web connections in Office 2000 are listed in a spreadsheet called WebEnt.xls. The spreadsheet also identifies which connections can be disabled and shows you how to disable them. For information about installing WebEnt.xls, see "Office Information" on page 787.

For example, you can disable the **Office on the Web** hyperlinks in Help by setting a system policy for each of the applications you want to limit in this way. The following procedure shows you how to disable this option for Excel.

▶ **To disable the Office on the Web connections in Excel**

1 In the System Policy Editor, double-click the **Default User** icon.

2 In the **Default User Properties** dialog box, click the plus sign (+) next to **Microsoft Excel 2000**.

3 Click the plus sign next to **Disable items in user interface**.

4 Click the plus sign next to **Predefined**.

5 Select the **Disable command bar buttons and menu items** check box.

6 Under **Settings for Disable command bar buttons and menu items**, select the **Help | Office on the Web** check box.

See also

- Several of the built-in Web connections in Office 2000 can be disabled through system policies. For information about using system policies, see "Using the System Policy Editor" on page 296.

- You can redirect the Answer Wizard Web connections to a place on your own Internet or intranet site. For more information about customizing Web connections in the Answer Wizard, see "Linking the Answer Wizard to the Web" on page 367.

Using the System Policy Editor

By using a few straightforward procedures, administrators can use the System Policy Editor and the Microsoft Office 2000 policy templates to control user settings across a network.

How to Set System Policies for Your Organization

By using the System Policy Editor, you can control which Microsoft Office 2000 options are available to your users. You can create system policies and easily distribute the settings from a central *administrative installation point*.

The Microsoft Office 2000 Resource Kit includes a new version of the System Policy Editor, as well as several system policy templates. You must install the System Policy Editor and these templates on your computer before you can create a system policy file.

Toolbox

The System Policy Editor consists of a file named Poledit.exe and several policy templates. For information about installing these files, see "System Policy Editor and Templates" on page 782.

When you create a system policy file for a client computer, you must run the System Policy Editor on the same operating system that the client computer is running. For example, to create a policy file for Windows NT 4.0 clients, you must run the System Policy Editor on either Windows NT 4.0 or Windows 2000. This limitation results from the fact that Windows 95/98 and Windows NT operating systems have different registries.

Note The System Policy Editor that comes with Windows 95 does not work with Office 2000. Be sure to install the latest version of the System Policy Editor from the Microsoft Office 2000 Resource Kit or from Windows NT Server version 4.0 with Service Pack 4.

Create a new policy file

When you use the System Policy Editor to create system policies, you first choose which templates you want to use and create a new policy file, and then you set policies for your users. You cannot add templates after you have created the policy file. Make sure to add in your policy file every policy template you plan to use.

▶ **To create a new policy file**

1 Start the System Policy Editor.

2 On the **Options** menu, click **Policy Template**, and then click **Add** to select the templates you want to use.

3 On the **File** menu, click **New Policy** to create a new policy file.

Add users, groups, or computers to the policy file

System policies can apply to all users, to a specific user, or to a group of users. They can also apply to a single computer or to all the computers on your network.

The **Default User** icon and the **Default Computer** icon are included in your policy file. To apply a system policy to all the users or all the computers on your network, start the System Policy Editor, and then double-click the **Default User** or **Default Computer** icon.

You can also add specific users, computers, or groups to your policy file by using the **Add User**, **Add Computer**, and **Add Group** commands on the **Edit** menu in the System Policy Editor. When you add a user, computer, or group, a new icon appears in the System Policy Editor. Use this icon to set policies for the new user, computer, or group.

Note   The group names or computer names you specify in the System Policy Editor must reference user groups or computers that already exist on the network. You cannot create new groups or computer names from within the System Policy Editor.

After you've selected the users, groups, or computers to whom your policy applies, you set the policy or policies you want by using the corresponding **Properties** dialog box in the System Policy Editor.

Sometimes a user is a member of more than one group. To avoid potential conflicts between group policies, you can set relative priorities so that group policies are applied in a particular order. To set group priorities, click **Group Priority** (**Options** menu) in the System Policy Editor.

Set the policy

In the System Policy Editor, when you double-click one of the user, group, or computer icons, the **Properties** dialog box appears, listing the available system policies. You scroll through the list of categories in the **Properties** dialog box to find the policy you want. You expand or collapse categories by clicking the plus sign (+) or minus sign (−), similar to expanding or collapsing folders in Windows Explorer.

When you find the policy you want, you set the policy by selecting the check box next to the policy name. After you select the policy you want, you must specify additional information under **Settings** to determine what is enforced by the policy. The following two examples show you how to set a simple policy (allowing background saves in Microsoft Word) and a more complex policy (controlling the recently used file list in Microsoft PowerPoint).

Allow background saves in Word

In Word, you can determine whether or not files can be saved in the background while you continue working. If you want to turn on this feature through a policy, you can use the **Allow background saves** policy to do so.

▶ To set a policy to allow background saves in Word

1   Start the System Policy Editor.

2   Double-click the **Default User** icon.

3   In the **Default User Properties** dialog box, click the plus sign (+) next to **Microsoft Word 2000**.

4   Click the plus sign next to **Tools | Options**.

5   Click the plus sign next to **Save**.

6   Select the **Allow background saves** check box.

7   Under **Settings for Allow background saves**, select the **Check to enforce setting on; uncheck to enforce setting off** check box.

Control the recently used file list in PowerPoint

In PowerPoint, you can control whether the user sees a list of recently used documents on the **File** menu and, if so, how many file names to display in that list. The following procedure shows how to set a system policy to display five recently used files for all users.

▶ To set a policy for the recently used file list in PowerPoint

1   Start the System Policy Editor.

2   Double-click the **Default User** icon.

3   In the **Default User Properties** dialog box, click the plus sign (+) next to **Microsoft PowerPoint 2000**.

4   Click the plus sign next to **Tools | Options**.

5   Click the plus sign next to **General**.

6   Select the **Recently used file list** check box.

7   Under **Settings for Recently used file list**, select the **Enable recently used file list** check box.

8   In the **Size of recently used file list** box, select **5**.

When you save and distribute this policy, all of your PowerPoint users see a recently used file list of five files on the **File** menu.

Save and distribute the policy file

After you set the policy values you want, you are ready to save and distribute the policy file. For Windows 95/98 clients, save the policy file as Config.pol. For Windows NT 4.0 or Windows 2000 clients, save the policy file as Ntconfig.pol. Then exit the System Policy Editor.

Next, you need to store the policy file on the network, where it can be downloaded to users' computers when they log on.

For networks running Windows NT Server, copy Config.pol or Ntconfig.pol to the Netlogon folder of the primary domain controller, as defined for your client computers. When your users next log on, the system policies are automatically downloaded to their computers and their registry settings are updated with the policy settings.

See also

- All of the system policies for a particular application are listed in the policy template for that application. For more information about the policy templates, see "Working with System Policy Templates" on page 282.

- For conceptual information about setting policies for specific users, groups, or computers, see "Applying System Policies to Selected Users or Groups" on page 284.

- You enable or disable options by selecting a policy and altering the settings for that policy. For conceptual information about setting policies, see "Setting System Policies" on page 285.

- In addition to the options you can set for Office 2000, you can set many system-level options through system policies. For more information about setting Windows NT 4.0 options with system policies, search for **Windows NT 4.0 Profiles** to find the "Guide to Microsoft Windows NT 4.0 Profiles and Policies" white paper on the Microsoft Web site at http://www.microsoft.com/.

How to Disable Menu Commands and Toolbar Buttons

You can disable any built-in or custom item on a menu or a toolbar by using the System Policy Editor. The policy disables both the menu command and the corresponding toolbar button at the same time.

Disable a predefined menu command and toolbar button

Several built-in menu commands and toolbar buttons are listed in the Predefined category of the system policy templates.

▶ **To disable a predefined menu command and toolbar button**

1   In the System Policy Editor, open the policy you want to modify.

2   Open the **Properties** dialog box for the group, computer, or user for which you want to set the policy.

3   Click the plus sign (+) next to the Office application that contains the item you want to disable.

4   Click the plus sign next to **Disable items in user interface**.

5   Click the plus sign next to **Predefined**.

6   Select the **Disable command bar buttons and menu items** check box.

7   Under **Settings for Disable command bar buttons and menu items**, select the check box next to the item you want to disable.

For example, to disable the **Hyperlink** command (**Insert** menu) and the **Insert Hyperlink** button (**Standard** toolbar) in Word, select the **Insert | Hyperlink** check box.

Disable a custom menu command and toolbar button

You can disable custom menu commands and toolbar buttons by using the System Policy Editor, even if the items are not predefined in the policy template.

Note   In order to disable a custom menu and toolbar item, you must know the control ID for the item.

▶ **To disable a custom menu command and toolbar button**

1   In the System Policy Editor, open the policy you want to modify.

2   Open the **Properties** dialog box for the user, group, or computer for which you want to set the policy.

3   Click the plus sign (+) next to the Office application that contains the item you want to disable.

4   Click the plus sign next to **Disable items in user interface**.

5   Click the plus sign next to **Custom**.

6   Select the **Disable command bar buttons and menu items** check box.

7   Under **Settings for command bar buttons and menu items**, click **Show**.

8   In the **Show Contents** box, click **Add**.

9   In the **Add Item** box, type the control ID for the menu and toolbar item.

Note   If you use the Custom category to disable a menu command or toolbar button that has already been disabled elsewhere in the policy file, the duplicate entry is ignored.

See also

- To disable a custom menu and toolbar item, you must know the control ID for the item. For information about finding control IDs, see "Control IDs for Menu Commands and Toolbar Buttons" on page 302.

- You can use system policies to control a range of items in the user interface. For conceptual information about disabling items in the user interface, see "Using System Policies to Disable User Interface Items" on page 286.

Control IDs for Menu Commands and Toolbar Buttons

You can look up control IDs for any item on a menu or toolbar in Microsoft Office 2000 applications by using Visual Basic for Applications (VBA). You enter the control ID into the System Policy Editor to disable that menu command and toolbar button. You can either look up a single control ID or use a macro to find a series of control IDs.

Note   Menu commands and their corresponding toolbar buttons share the same control ID. For example, the control ID for both the **Save** command (**File** menu) and the **Save** button (**Standard** toolbar) in Microsoft Word is 3.

Finding a single control ID

You can use the Immediate window in VBA to look up the control ID for a single item on a menu. For example, the following command displays the control ID for the **Save As** command (**File** menu):

```
? commandbars ("menu bar").controls ("file").controls ("save as…").id
```

Note   For Microsoft Excel, use "worksheet menu bar" instead of "menu bar" in the previous command.

You use the same command to find the control ID for a toolbar button. For example, the following command displays the control ID for the **Document Map** button (**Standard** toolbar) in Word:

```
? commandbars ("standard").controls ("document map"). id
```

Finding all the control IDs for a menu or toolbar

If you want to find the control IDs for all the items on a menu or toolbar, you can create a macro in VBA. For example, the following macro opens a series of message boxes to display the commands and corresponding control IDs for each item on the **File** menu for any Office 2000 application:

```
Sub EnumerateControls()
    Dim icbc As Integer
    Dim cbcs As CommandBarControls

    Set cbcs = Application.CommandBars("Menu Bar").Controls("File").Controls
    For icbc = 1 To cbcs.Count
        MsgBox cbcs(icbc).Caption & " = " & cbcs(icbc).ID
    Next icbc
End Sub
```

Note   To disable all of the items on a menu, you can enter each item individually in the System Policy Editor. Or, you can disable the entire menu by entering the control ID for the menu itself.

See also

- For more information about using Visual Basic for Applications, see the *Microsoft Office 2000/Visual Basic Programmer's Guide*.

How to Disable Shortcut Keys

You can use system policies to disable built-in and custom shortcut keys for commands in Microsoft Office 2000.

Disable a predefined shortcut key

Several built-in shortcut keys are listed in the Predefined category of the system policy templates.

▶ **To disable a predefined shortcut key**

1   In the System Policy Editor, open the policy you want to modify.

2   Open the **Properties** dialog box for the user, group, or computer for which you want to set the policy.

3   Click the plus sign (+) next to the Office application that contains the built-in shortcut key you want to disable.

4   Click the plus sign next to **Disable items in user interface**.

5   Click the plus sign next to **Predefined**.

6   Select the **Disable shortcut keys** check box.

7   Under **Settings for Disable shortcut keys**, click the check box next to the shortcut key you want to disable.

   For example, click the **Ctrl+K (Insert I Hyperlink)** check box to disable the shortcut key for the **Hyperlink** command (**Insert** menu) in Word.

Disable a custom shortcut key

You can disable any custom shortcut key by using the System Policy Editor, even if the item is not listed in the policy template.

Note   In order to disable a custom shortcut key, you must know the *virtual key codes* for the shortcut key.

▶ **To disable a custom shortcut key**

1 In the System Policy Editor, open the policy you want to modify.

2 Open the **Properties** dialog box for the user, group, or computer for which you want to set the policy.

3 Click the plus sign (+) next to the Office application that contains the custom shortcut key you want to disable.

4 Click the plus sign next to **Disable items in user interface**.

5 Click the plus sign next to **Custom**.

6 Select the **Disable shortcut keys** check box.

7 In the **Settings for Disable shortcut keys** box, click **Show**.

8 In the **Show Contents** box, click **Add**.

9 In the **Add Item** box, type the key and modifier key values for the shortcut key by using the following syntax:

key,modifier

For example, to disable the shortcut key ALT+K, type **75,16**

Note If you use the Custom category to disable a shortcut key that has already been disabled elsewhere in the policy file, the duplicate entry is ignored.

See also

- To disable a custom shortcut key, you must know the virtual key code for the shortcut key. For information about virtual key codes, see "Virtual Key Codes for Shortcut Keys" on page 305.

- You can use system policies to control a range of items in the user interface. For conceptual information about disabling items in the user interface, see "Using System Policies to Disable User Interface Items" on page 286.

Virtual Key Codes for Shortcut Keys

Each key and modifier key used in Windows has an associated *virtual key code*. You use these codes to identify the unique key you want to control.

In the System Policy Editor, you enter the values for keys and modifier keys by using the following syntax:

key,modifier

where *key* is the value of a key (for example, G) in Windows, and *modifier* is the value of either a modifier key (for example, ALT or SHIFT) or a combination of modifer keys in Windows.

If you have multiple modifier keys for the shortcut key, you add the values of the modifier keys together to determine the actual modifer key value you will enter in the System Policy Editor (for example, ALT+SHIFT = 16+4 = 20).

Use the following values to refer to keys in the System Policy Editor.

Key	Value
ALT	16
CONTROL	8
SHIFT	4
A–Z	A sequential number between 65 and 90, where A = 65, and Z = 90

Note   Office does not use the virtual key codes for ALT, CONTROL, and SHIFT. To refer to these keys in the Office environment, use the values of the modifier keys specified in the table.

See also

- You can look up additional virtual key codes in the *Windows NT Server Resource Kit* or on the Microsoft Developer Network Web site at http://msdn.microsoft.com/developer/. If you look up a virtual key code and find a hexadecimal value, however, you must convert the key code to a decimal value and enter that value in the System Policy Editor.

Office 2000 System Policy Reference

Look here for information about system requirements for using system policies and for details about the contents of each Microsoft Office 2000 policy template file.

Client Computer Requirements for Using System Policies

Client computers must meet the following requirements to use system policies:

- Operating system

  Windows 95/98 or Windows NT Workstation 4.0 or later. System policies are not supported for the Windows 3.1 and Macintosh operating systems.

- User profiles

  Client computers must have user profiles enabled.

- Group policies

  If you want to set group policies, the group policy capability must be installed on each client computer. For more information about group policies, see the resource kit for your Windows operating system.

- Network distribution

  For automatic downloading of policies over networks running Windows NT Server, Client for Microsoft Networks must be specified as the primary network logon client, and the domain must be defined on the client computers.

Note By default, Windows 95/98 and Windows NT Workstation 4.0 or later automatically download system policies from the appropriate network server. To change to manual downloading, see the resource kit for your client operating system.

System Policies in the Office 2000 Policy Template

The Office9.adm template contains policy settings that are common to all of the Microsoft Office 2000 applications. The following policies are available in the Office9.adm template.

USER SETTINGS

Microsoft Office 2000
   Tools | Customize | Options
      Menus show recently used commands first
      Show full menus after a short delay
      Large icons
      List font names in their font
      Show ScreenTips on toolbars
      Show shortcut keys in ScreenTips
      Menu animations
   Tools | AutoCorrect (Excel, PowerPoint and Access)
      Correct TWo INitial CApitals
      Capitalize first letter of sentence
      Capitalize names of days
      Correct accidental use of cAPS LOCK key
      Replace text as you type
   Tools | Options | General | Web Options...
      General
         Rely on CSS for font formatting
            Check to enforce CSS on; uncheck to enforce CSS off
            Use the CSS setting for Word as an E-mail editor
      Files
         Organize supporting files in a folder
         Use long file names whenever possible
         Update links on save
         Check if Office is the default editor for Web pages created in Office
         Download Office Web Components
            Download Office Web Components from
            Location:
      Pictures
         Rely on VML for displaying graphics in browsers
         Allow PNG as an output format
         Target monitor
            Screen size
            Pixels per inch
      Encoding
         Default or specific encoding
            Always save Web pages in the default encoding

Save this document as

Help | Office on the Web
    Office on the Web URL
Shared paths
    User templates path
    Shared templates path
    Shared themes path
    Web queries path
Assistant
    General
        Choose Assistant file
        Tip timeout
            Time tip bulb remains on (s)
    Options Tab
        Use the Office Assistant
        Respond to F1 key
        Help with wizards
        Display alerts
        Search for both product and programming help
        Move when in the way
        Guess Help topics
        Make sounds
        Using features more effectively
        Using the mouse more effectively
        Keyboard shortcuts
        Only show high priority tips
        Show the Tip of the Day at startup
    Help on the Web
        Feedback button label
        Feedback dialog text
        Feedback URL
Language settings
    User Interface
        Display menus and dialog boxes in
        Display help in
    Enabled Languages
        Show controls and enable editing for
            Afrikaans
            Albanian
            Arabic
            Armenian
            Assamese
            Azeri (Cyrillic)
            Azeri (Latin)
            Basque

Belarusian
Bengali
Bulgarian
Catalan
Chinese (Simplified)
Chinese (Traditional)
Croatian
Czech
Danish
Dutch
English (Australian)
English (Canadian)
English (U.K.)
English (U.S.)
Estonian
Faeroese
Farsi
Finnish
French
French (Canadian)
Frisian
Georgian
German
German (Austrian)
German (Swiss)
Greek
Gujarati
Hebrew
Hindi
Hungarian
Icelandic
Indonesian
Italian
Japanese
Kannada
Kashmiri
Kazakh
Konkani
Korean
Latvian
Lithuanian
Lithuanian (Classic)
Macedonian
Malay
Malayalam

Manipuri
Marathi
Nepali
Norwegian (Bokmal)
Norwegian (Nynorsk)
Oriya
Polish
Portuguese
Portuguese (Brazilian)
Punjabi
Romanian
Russian
Sanskrit
Serbian (Cyrillic)
Serbian (Latin)
Sindi
Slovak
Slovenian
Spanish
Swahili
Swedish
Tamil
Tatar
Telugu
Thai
Turkish
Ukranian
Urdu
Uzbek (Cyrillic)
Uzbek (Latin)
Vietnamese
Preferred Asian or right-to-left language
Installed version of Microsoft Office
Other
Do not adjust defaults to user's locale
Disallow Taiwan calendar
Customizable error messages
Base URL
Default button text
List of error messages to customize
Default save prompt text
Disable items in user interface
Tooltip for disabled toolbar buttons and menu items
Graph settings
Graph gallery path

List of error messages to customize
Custom Answer Wizard database path
Miscellaneous
Provide feedback with sound
Use system font instead of Tahoma
Do not track document editing time
Disable Clipboard Toolbar triggers
Do not emulate tabs with spaces when exporting HTML
Do not upload media files

System Policies in the Access 2000 Policy Template

The following policies are available in the Access9.adm template.

USER SETTINGS

Microsoft Access 2000
Tools | Options...
Web Options...
General
Hyperlink color
Followed hyperlink color
Underline hyperlinks
Tools | Macro
Security...
Security Level
Trust all installed add-ins and templates
Customizable error messages
List of error messages to customize
Disable items in user interface
Predefined
Disable command bar buttons and menu items
File | Open... | Tools | Find...
File | Send To | Mail Recipient
Insert | Hyperlink...
Tools | Online Collaboration
Tools | Security...
Tools | Security | Set Database Password...
Tools | Security | Database Security...
Tools | Security | User and Group Permissions...
Tools | Security | User and Group Accounts...
Tools | Security | User-Level Security Wizard...
Tools | Security | Encrypt/Decrypt Database...
Tools | Macro
Tools | Macro | Visual Basic Editor
Tools | Macro | Run Macro...

               Tools | Macro | Convert Macros to Visual Basic
               Tools | Macro | Create Menu from Macro
               Tools | Macro | Create Toolbar from Macro
               Tools | Macro | Create Shortcut Menu from Macro
               Tools | Add-Ins...
               Tools | Customize...
               Tools | Options...
               Help | Office on the Web
               Help | Detect and Repair...
               Web | Refresh Current Page
               Web | Start Page
               Web | Search the Web
               Web | Favorites
               Web | Go
               Web | Address
          Disable shortcut keys
               Ctrl+F (Find...)
               Ctrl+K (Insert | Hyperlink...)
               Alt+F11 (Tools | Macro | Visual Basic Editor)
     Custom
         Disable command bar buttons and menu items
               Enter a command bar ID to disable
         Disable shortcut keys
               Enter a key and modifier to disable
Miscellaneous
     Do not prompt to convert older databases
     Custom Answer Wizard database path

System Policies in the Excel 2000 Policy Template

The following policies are available in the Excel9.adm template.

USER SETTINGS

Microsoft Excel 2000
     Tools | Options...
         View
               Show Formula bar in Normal View
               Show Status bar in Normal View
               Show Formula bar in Full View
               Show Status bar in Full View
               Windows in Taskbar
               Comments
         Edit
               Edit directly in cell
               Allow cell drag and drop

Alert before overwriting cells
Move selection after Enter
Move selection after Enter direction
Fixed decimal to 2 places
Cut, copy, and sort objects with cells
Ask to update automatic links
Provide feedback with Animation
Enable AutoComplete for cell values
Extend list formats and formulas
Enable automatic percent entry
General
R1C1 reference style
Ignore other applications
Recently used file list
Entries on recently used file list
Prompt for workbook properties
Zoom on roll with IntelliMouse
Default Sheets
Sheets in new workbook
Font
Name,Size
Default file location
Alternate startup file location
Web Options...
General
Save any additional data necessary to maintain formulas
Load pictures from Web pages not created in Excel
Transition
Save Excel files as
Microsoft Excel menu or Help key
Help key
Microsoft Excel menus or Lotus 1-2-3 Help
Transition navigation keys
Chart
Show names
Show values
Right-to-Left
Default direction
Cursor movement
Show control characters
Tools | Macro
Record New Macro...
Store macro in Personal Macro Workbook by default
Security...
Security Level

> > > > > Trust all installed add-ins and templates
> > > > Customizable error messages
> > > > > List of error messages to customize
> > > > Disable items in user interface
> > > > > Predefined
> > > > > > Disable command bar buttons and menu items
> > > > > > > File | Open... | Tools | Find...
> > > > > > > File | Save as Web Page...
> > > > > > > File | Web Page Preview
> > > > > > > File | Send To | Mail Recipient
> > > > > > > Insert | Hyperlink...
> > > > > > > Tools | Protection
> > > > > > > Tools | Protection | Protect Sheet...
> > > > > > > Tools | Protection | Protect Workbook...
> > > > > > > Tools | Protection | Protect and Share Workbook...
> > > > > > > Tools | Online Collaboration
> > > > > > > Tools | Macro
> > > > > > > Tools | Macro | Macros...
> > > > > > > Tools | Macro | Record New Macro...
> > > > > > > Tools | Macro | Security...
> > > > > > > Tools | Macro | Visual Basic Editor
> > > > > > > Tools | Macro | Microsoft Script Editor
> > > > > > > Tools | Add-Ins...
> > > > > > > Tools | Customize...
> > > > > > > Tools | Options...
> > > > > > > Help | Office on the Web
> > > > > > > Help | Detect and Repair...
> > > > > > > Web | Refresh Current Page
> > > > > > > Web | Start Page
> > > > > > > Web | Search the Web
> > > > > > > Web | Favorites
> > > > > > > Web | Go
> > > > > > > Web | Address
> > > > > > Disable shortcut keys
> > > > > > > Ctrl+F (Find...)
> > > > > > > Ctrl+K (Insert | Hyperlink...)
> > > > > > > Alt+F8 (Tools | Macro | Macros...)
> > > > > > > Alt+F11 (Tools | Macro | Visual Basic Editor)
> > > > > > > Alt+Shift+F11 (Tools | Macro | Microsoft Script Editor)
> > > > > Custom
> > > > > > Disable command bar buttons and menu items
> > > > > > > Enter a command bar ID to disable
> > > > > > Disable shortcut keys
> > > > > > > Enter a key and modifier to disable
> > > > Miscellaneous

Chart gallery path
Custom Answer Wizard database path
Enable four-digit year display

System Policies in the FrontPage 2000 Policy Template

The following policies are available in the FrontPg4.adm template.

USER SETTINGS

Microsoft FrontPage 2000
   Disable items in user interface
      Predefined
         Disable command bar buttons and menu items
            File | Open... | Tools | Find...
            View | Toolbars | Customize...
            Format | Style
            Format | Style Sheet Links...
            Format | Position
            Insert | Advanced | ActiveX Control...
            Insert | Component | Office Spreadsheet
            Insert | Component | Office PivotTable
            Insert | Component | Office Chart
            Insert | Advanced | Java Applet...
            Insert | Component | Banner Ad Manager...
            Insert | Component | Hover Button...
            Insert | Component | Hit Counter...
            Insert | Component | Search Form...
            Insert | Component | Confirmation Field...
            Insert | Component | Marquee...
            Insert | Picture | Video...
            Insert | Advanced | Design-Time Control...
            Insert | Advanced | PlugIn...
            Insert | Advanced | Show Design-Time Controls
            Insert | Database | Results...
            Insert | Database | Column Value...
            Format | Dynamic HTML Effects
            Format | Page Transition...
            Format | Theme
            Format | Shared Borders...
            Tools | Security | Permissions...
            Tools | Security | Change Password...
            Tools | Add-Ins...
            Tools | Customize
            Tools | Web Settings...
            Tools | Macro | Macros...

> Tools | Macro | Visual Basic Editor
> Tools | Macro | Microsoft Script Editor
> Tools | Options
> Help | Office on the Web
> Help | Detect and Repair

> Custom
>> Disable command bar buttons and menu items
>> Enter a command bar ID to disable

System Policies in the Outlook 2000 Policy Template

The following policies are available in the Outlk9.adm template.

MACHINE SETTINGS

Microsoft Outlook 2000
> Outlook mail configuration
> Using Schedule+ as Outlook Calendar
> Prevent users from changing primary calendar application
> S/MIME password settings

USER SETTINGS

Microsoft Outlook 2000
> Tools | Options
>> Preferences
>>> E-mail options
>>>> Message handling
>>>> Advanced E-mail options
>>>>> Save Messages
>>>>> More save messages
>>>>> When new items arrive
>>>>> When sending a message
>>>> Tracking options
>>>>> Options
>>>> On replies and forwards
>>> Calendar options
>>>> Reminders on Calendar items
>>>> Calendar item defaults
>>>> Work week
>>>> First day of the week
>>>> First week of year
>>>> Working hours
>>>> Calendar week numbers
>>>> Meeting Requests using iCalendar
>>>> Free/Busy Options

          Internet Free/Busy Options
     Task options
        Color options
        Task reminder options
     Contact options
        Select the default setting for how to file new contacts
     Journal options
        Level of journaling
        Disable journaling of these Outlook items
        Automatically journal these items
        Automatically journal files from these applications
        Journal entry options
     Notes options
        Notes appearance
Mail Services (Corporate or Workgroup configuration)
     Synchronize
     Profile prompt
Mail Delivery (Internet Only configuration)
     Mail account options
     Dial-up options
Mail Format
     Message format/editor - Corporate or Workgroup configuration
     Message format/editor - Internet Only configuration
     Send pictures from the Internet
     Stationery Fonts
     Message format settings - Internet Only configuration
        HTML message format settings
        Text message format settings
     International Options
        English message headers and flags
        Encoding for incoming and outgoing messages
     Signature
        Don't add signature
Spelling
     General
Security
     Required Certificate Authority
     Minimum encryption settings
     S/MIME interoperability with external clients:
     Outlook Rich Text in S/MIME messages
Other
     Empty Deleted Items Folder
     AutoArchive
     Preview Pane
     Advanced

General
More Options
Appearance options - Notes
Appearance options - Tasks
Reminder Options
Reminders
More reminders
Advanced Tasks
Advanced Tasks
Right-to-left
Layout Options
Customizable error messages
List of error messages to customize
Disable items in user interface
Predefined
Disable command bar buttons and menu items
Disable shortcut keys
Custom
Disable command bar buttons and menu items
Disable shortcut keys
Miscellaneous
Resource scheduling
NetMeeting
Categories
Date format for importing cc:Mail (DB8 only)
Junk e-mail filtering
Auto-repair of MAPI32.DLL
Net Folders
Exchange settings
Exchange view information
Folder size display
OST Creation
Personal distribution lists (Exchange only)
Outlook Today settings
Outlook Today availability
URL for custom Outlook Today
Folders in the Messages section of Outlook Today
Folder Home Pages for Outlook special folders
Disable Folder Home Pages
Folder Home Page Security
Inbox Folder Home Page
Calendar Folder Home
Contacts Folder Home Page
Deleted Items Folder Home Page
Drafts Folder Home Page

> Journal Folder Home Page
> Notes Folder Home Page
> Outbox Folder Home Page
> Sent Items Folder Home Page
> Tasks Folder Home Page

System Policies in the PowerPoint 2000 Policy Template

The following policies are available in the Ppoint9.adm template.

USER SETTINGS

Microsoft PowerPoint 2000
> Tools | Options...
>> View
>>> Startup dialog
>>> New slide dialog
>>> Status bar
>>> Vertical ruler
>>> Windows in taskbar
>>> Popup menu on right mouse click
>>> Show popup menu button
>>> End with black slide
>> General
>>> Recently used file list
>>>> Enable recently used file list
>>>> Size of recently used file list
>>> Link Sounds File Size
>>>> Link sounds with file size greater than (Kb):
> Web Options...
>> General
>>> Slide navigation
>>>> Add slide navigation controls
>>>> Colors
>>> Show slide animation while browsing
>>> Resize graphics to fit browser window
> Edit
>> Replace straight quotes with smart quotes
>> When selecting, automatically select entire word
>> Use smart cut and paste
>> Drag-and-drop text editing
>> Auto-fit text to text placeholder
>> AutoFormat as you type
>> New charts take on PowerPoint font
>> Maximum number of undos
> Print

Background printing
Print TrueType fonts as graphics
Print inserted objects at printer resolution
Save
Allow fast saves
Prompt for file properties
Save AutoRecover info
Enable save AutoRecover info
AutoRecover save frequency (minutes):
Convert charts when saving as previous version
Save PowerPoint files as
Default file location
Spelling and Style
Check spelling as you type
Always suggest corrections
Ignore words in UPPERCASE
Ignore words with numbers
Check style
Style Options...
Case and End Punctuation
Check slide title case
Slide title case
Check body text case
Body text case
Check slide title punctuation
Slide title punctuation
Check body punctuation
Body punctuation
Slide title end puncutation other than period
Body text end puncutation other than period
Visual Clarity
Check number of fonts
Number of fonts should not exceed
Check title text size
Title text should be at least
Check body text size
Body text should be at least
Check number of bullets
Number of bullets should not exceed
Check number of lines per title
Number of lines per title should not exceed
Check number of lines per bullet
Number of lines per bullet should not exceed
Asian
True inline conversion for Japanese IME

Convert font-associated text
   for
Allow font subsetting
Tools | Macro
  Security...
    Security Level
    Trust all installed add-ins and templates
Slide Show | Online Broadcast | Set Up and Schedule...
  Broadcast Settings
    Send audio
    Send video
    Camera/microphone is connected to another computer
    Recording
      Record the broadcast
      Save it in the following location:
    Other Broadcast Settings
      Chat server URL
      Chat file CAB
      Override default chat client
      Media Player ActiveX download
      Transfer Control ActiveX download
      Media Player non-ActiveX download
      Event URL
      Mail to
      Help page URL
      Video/audio test page URL
  Server Options...
    Shared file location
    Local NetShow server on this LAN
    The server will access presentation files from
    Other NetShow Settings
      ConnectTimeout
      FECRedundancyRatio
      Netshow Server high bandwith
      Netshow Server low bandwith
      Multicast TTL
      Unicast rollover
      Location of audio ASD file
      Location of video ASD file
      Contact address
      Contact phone number
      Copyright
      Multicast address
      Read/write admin URL
      Read only admin URL

Drop dead time
Customizable error messages
List of error messages to customize
Disable items in user interface
Predefined
Disable command bar buttons and menu items
File | Open... | Tools | Find...
File | Save as Web Page...
File | Web Page Preview
File | Send To | Mail Recipient
Insert | Hyperlink...
Tools | Online Collaboration
Tools | Macro
Tools | Macro | Macros...
Tools | Macro | Record New Macro...
Tools | Macro | Security...
Tools | Macro | Visual Basic Editor
Tools | Macro | Microsoft Script Editor
Tools | Add-Ins...
Tools | Customize...
Tools | Options...
Help | Office on the Web
Help | Detect and Repair...
Web | Refresh Current Page
Web | Start Page
Web | Search the Web
Web | Favorites
Web | Go
Web | Address
Disable shortcut keys
Ctrl+F (Find...)
Ctrl+K (Insert | Hyperlink...)
Alt+F8 (Tools | Macro | Macros...)
Alt+F11 (Tools | Macro | Visual Basic Editor)
Alt+Shift+F11 (Tools | Macro | Microsoft Script Editor)
Custom
Disable command bar buttons and menu items
Enter a command bar ID to disable
Disable shortcut keys
Enter a key and modifier to disable
Miscellaneous
Custom Answer Wizard database path

System Policies in the Publisher 2000 Policy Template

The following policies are available in the Pub6.adm template.

USER SETTINGS

Microsoft Publisher 2000
    Tools | Options...
        General
            Preview fonts in font list
            Use Catalog at startup
            Show rectangle for text in web graphic region
            Default publication location
            Default picture location
        Edit
            Drag-and-drop text editing
            When selecting, automatically select entire word
            When formatting, automatically format entire word
            Automatically hyphenate in new text frames
            Use single click object creation
        User Assistance
            Preview Web site with Preview Troubleshooter
            Use Quick Publication wizard for blank publications
            Step through wizard questions
            Update personal information when saving
            Show tippages
            Remind to save publication
            Use helpful mouse pointers
        Print
            Automatically display Print Troubleshooter
    Spelling
        Check spelling as you type
        Ignore words in UPPERCASE
        Show repeated words

System Policies in the Word 2000 Policy Template

The following policies are available in the Word9.adm template.

USER SETTINGS

Microsoft Word 2000
   Tools | Options...
      View
         Show
            Highlight
            Bookmarks
            Status bar
            ScreenTips
            Animated text
            Horizontal scroll bar
            Vertical scroll bar
            Picture placeholders
            Field codes
            Field shading
            Left scroll bar
         Formatting marks
            Tab characters
            Spaces
            Paragraph marks
            Hidden text
            Optional hyphens
            Optional breaks
            All
         Print and Web Layout options
            Drawings
            Object anchors
            Text boundaries
            Vertical ruler (Print view only)
         Outline and Normal options
            Wrap to window
            Draft font
            Style area width
      General
         Blue background, white text
         Provide feedback with animation
         Confirm conversion at Open
         Update automatic links at Open
         Mail as attachment
         Recently used file list

Number of entries:
Help for WordPerfect users
Navigation keys for WordPerfect users
Asian fonts also apply to Latin text
Measurement units
Select units:
Show pixels for HTML features
Use character units
English Word 6.0/95 documents
Web Options...
General
Disable features not supported by browser
Files
Check if Word is the default editor for all other Web pages
Edit
Typing replaces selection
Drag-and-drop text editing
Use the INS key for paste
Tabs and backspace set left indent
Use smart cut and paste
Allow accented uppercase in French
When selecting, automatically select entire word
Picture editor
Enable click and type
IME Control Active
IME TrueInLine
Print
Printing options
Draft output
Update fields
Update links
Allow A4/Letter paper resizing
Background printing
Reverse print order
Include with document
Document properties
Field codes
Comments
Hidden text
Drawing objects
Options for Duplex Printing
Front of sheet
Back of the sheet
Save
Always create backup copy

Allow fast saves
Prompt for document properties
Prompt to save Normal template
Allow background saves
Save AutoRecover info
    Save AutoRecover info every (minutes)
Add Bi-Directional Marks when saving Text files
Save Word files as
Disable features not supported by Word 97
Spelling & Grammar
    Check spelling as you type
    Always suggest corrections
    Suggest from main dictionary only
    Ignore words in UPPERCASE
    Ignore words with numbers
    Ignore Internet and file addresses
    Use German post reform rules
    Combine aux verb/adj.
    Use auto-change list
    Process compound nouns
    Hebrew
    Arabic modes
    Check grammar as you type
    Check grammar with spelling
    Show readability statistics
    Writing style
File Locations
    Documents
    Clipart pictures
    AutoRecover files
    Tools
    Startup
Hangul Hanja Conversion
    Fast conversion
    Display recently used items
    Ignore Hangul ending
    Multiple words conversion
Right-to-left
    Document view
    Add control characters in Cut and Copy
    Add double quote for Hebrew alphabet numbering
    Numeral
    Movement
    Visual selection
    Control characters

```
        Diacritics
        Different color for diacritics
        Month names
    Tools | AutoCorrect...
      AutoCorrect
        Correct TWo INitial CApitals
        Capitalize first letter of sentence
        Capitalize names of days
        Correct accidental use of cAPS LOCK key
        Replace text as you type
      AutoFormat as you type
        Apply as you type
          Headings
          Borders
          Tables
          Dates
          Automatic bulleted lists
          Automatic numbered lists
          First line indent
          Closings
        Replace as you type
          Straight quotes with smart quotes
          Ordinals (1st) with superscript
          Fractions (1/2) with fraction character
          Symbol characters (--) with symbols
          *Bold* and _italic_ with real formatting
          Internet and network paths with hyperlinks
          Match parentheses
          Auto space
          Dash-like characters
        Automatically as you type
          Format beginning of list item like the one before it
          Define styles based on your formatting
    Tools | Macro
      Security...
        Security Level
        Trust all installed add-ins and templates
    Tools | Language
      Set Language...
        Detect language automatically
      Chinese Translation...
        Translation direction
        Use Taiwan, Hong Kong and Macao character variants
        Translate common terms
    Customizable error messages
```

List of error messages to customize
Disable items in user interface
Predefined
Disable command bar buttons and menu items
File | Open... | Tools | Find...
File | Save as Web Page...
File | Web Page Preview
File | Send To | Mail Recipient
Insert | Hyperlink...
Tools | Protect Document...
Tools | Online Collaboration
Tools | Macro
Tools | Macro | Macros...
Tools | Macro | Record New Macro...
Tools | Macro | Security...
Tools | Macro | Visual Basic Editor
Tools | Macro | Microsoft Script Editor
Tools | Templates and Add-Ins...
Tools | Customize...
Tools | Options...
Help | Office on the Web
Help | Detect and Repair...
Web | Refresh Current Page
Web | Start Page
Web | Search the Web
Web | Favorites
Web | Go
Web | Address
Disable shortcut keys
Ctrl+F (Find...)
Ctrl+K (Insert | Hyperlink...)
Alt+F8 (Tools | Macro | Macros...)
Alt+F11 (Tools | Macro | Visual Basic Editor)
Alt+Shift+F11 (Tools | Macro | Microsoft Script Editor)
Custom
Disable command bar buttons and menu items
Enter a command bar ID to disable
Disable shortcut keys
Enter a key and modifier to disable
Miscellaneous
Volume preference
Custom Answer Wizard database path
Alternate revision bar position in printed document
Disable MRU list in font dropdown

System Policies in the Clip Gallery 5.0 Policy Template

The following policies are available in the ClipGal5.adm template.

USER SETTINGS

Microsoft Clip Gallery 5.0
   Disable Clips Online access from Clip Gallery

System Policies in the Windows Installer Policy Template

The following policies are available in the Instlr1.adm template.

MACHINE SETTINGS

Windows Installer
   Always install with elevated privileges
   Disable Windows installer
   Disable browse dialog box for new source
   Disable patching

USER SETTINGS

Windows Installer
   Always install with elevated privileges
   Search order
   Leave transform at package source
   Pin transform at transform source
   Disable rollback

Office 2000 System Policies That Accept Environment Variables

The following tables list Microsoft Office 2000 system policies that accept environment variables, and the Windows registry entry that corresponds to each policy.

Office system policies that accept environment variables

Policy name	Registry entry
Microsoft Office 2000\Graph settings \Custom Answer Wizard database path	HKCU\Software\Policies\Microsoft\Office \9.0\Graph\AnswerWizard\AdminDatabase
Microsoft Office 2000\Graph settings \Graph gallery path	HKCU\Software\Policies\Microsoft\Office \9.0\Graph\Options\GalleryPath
Microsoft Office 2000\Shared paths \Shared templates path	HKCU\Software\Policies\Microsoft\Office \9.0\Common\General\SharedTemplates
Microsoft Office 2000\Shared paths \Shared themes path	HKCU\Software\Policies\Microsoft\Office \9.0\Common\General\WorkgroupThemes
Microsoft Office 2000\Shared paths \Web queries path	HKCU\Software\Policies\Microsoft\Office \9.0\Common\General\UserQueriesFolder
Microsoft Office 2000\Shared paths \User templates path	HKCU\Software\Policies\Microsoft\Office \9.0\Common\General\UserTemplates
Microsoft Office 2000\Tools | Options | General | Web Options…\Files\Download Office Web Components	HKCU\Software\Policies\Microsoft\Office \9.0\Common\Internet\LocationOfComponents

Access system policies that accept environment variables

Policy name	Registry entry
Microsoft Access 2000\Miscellaneous \Custom Answer Wizard database path	HKCU\Software\Policies\Microsoft\Office \9.0\Access\AnswerWizard\AdminDatabase

Excel system policies that accept environment variables

Policy name	Registry entry
Microsoft Excel 2000\Miscellaneous \Custom Answer Wizard database path	HKCU\Software\Policies\Microsoft\Office \9.0\Excel\AnswerWizard\AdminDatabase
Microsoft Excel 2000\Tools | Options…\General\Alternate startup file location	HKCU\Software\Policies\Microsoft\Office \9.0\Excel\Options\AltStartup
Microsoft Excel 2000\Tools | Options…\General\Default file location	HKCU\Software\Policies\Microsoft\Office \9.0\Excel\Options\DefaultPath
Microsoft Excel 2000\Miscellaneous \Chart gallery path	HKCU\Software\Policies\Microsoft\Office \9.0\Excel\Options\GalleryPath

PowerPoint system policies that accept environment variables

Policy name	Registry entry
Microsoft PowerPoint 2000\Miscellaneous \Custom Answer Wizard database path	HKCU\Software\Policies\Microsoft\Office\9.0 \PowerPoint\AnswerWizard\AdminDatabase
Microsoft PowerPoint 2000\Tools I Options…\Save\Default file location	HKCU\Software\Policies\Microsoft\Office \9.0\PowerPoint\RecentFolderList\Default

Word system policies that accept environment variables

Policy name	Registry entry
Microsoft Word 2000\Miscellaneous \Custom Answer Wizard database path	HKCU\Software\Policies\Microsoft\Office \9.0\Word\AnswerWizard\AdminDatabase
Microsoft Word 2000\ Tools I Options…\File Locations\AutoRecover files	HKCU\Software\Policies\Microsoft\Office \9.0\Word\Options\AUTOSAVE-PATH
Microsoft Word 2000\ Tools I Options…\File Locations\Documents	HKCU\Software\Policies\Microsoft\Office \9.0\Word\Options\DOC-PATH
Microsoft Word 2000\ Tools I Options…\File Locations\Clipart pictures	HKCU\Software\Policies\Microsoft\Office \9.0\Word\Options\PICTURE-PATH
Microsoft Word 2000\ Tools I Options…\File Locations\Startup	HKCU\Software\Policies\Microsoft\Office \9.0\Word\OptionsSTARTUP-PATH
Microsoft Word 2000\ Tools I Options…\File Locations\Tools	HKCU\Software\Policies\Microsoft\Office \9.0\Word\OptionsTOOLS-PATH

See also

- The ability to use environment variables in system policies is new in Office 2000. For more information, see "Using Environment Variables in System Policies" on page 288.

Office Registry API

Previous versions of Office relied on the Windows application programming interface (API) to control interactions between Office and the Windows registry. Office 2000 includes its own API, the Office Registry API (ORAPI). ORAPI makes Office 2000 more resilient than previous versions of Office because now applications can restore default registry value data, rather than allowing an error in the registry to make the application stop running.

Overview of ORAPI

Office 2000 uses the Office Registry application programming interface (ORAPI) to control interactions between Office applications and the Windows registry. In the past, a missing entry might bring an application to a halt, lowering productivity and wasting time and money while the application was reinstalled. ORAPI eliminates these costly delays. If a value is accidentally deleted from the registry, Office automatically looks up the default value and restores it to the registry; work can go on as usual.

Also, ORAPI reduces clutter in the Windows registry by storing default values in the application. Storing the default values in the application minimizes your hard disk use and speeds up registry access.

When an Office 2000 application needs a value, the following events occur:

1   The Office application calls ORAPI to read a value.

2   ORAPI searches for the value in the Windows registry.

3   If the value exists in the Windows registry, ORAPI returns the value to the application.

   −or−

   If the value is not set in the Windows registry, ORAPI locates the default value and returns the default value to the application.

System Policies Override ORAPI Defaults

System policies always take precedence when the Office Registry API (ORAPI) reads a value from or writes a value to the Windows registry.

When ORAPI reads a value from the Windows registry, it first checks to see whether a system policy has been set for the entry; if a policy has been set, ORAPI returns the policy value. If no policy has been set, ORAPI returns any value from the registry that the user has set for the entry. If the user has not set a value for the entry, ORAPI returns the default value for that entry.

When ORAPI writes a value to the Windows registry, it first checks to see whether a system policy has been set for the entry; if a policy has been set, ORAPI does not write the new value to the registry. If no policy has been set, ORAPI checks to see whether the entry is present in the registry. If the entry is present in the registry, ORAPI writes the new value for that entry to the registry. If the entry is not present in the registry, ORAPI checks to see whether the new value is the same as the default value. If the new value matches the default value, ORAPI does not write the new value to the registry. If the new value does not match the default value, ORAPI writes the new value to the registry.

If the Policies subkey does not exist in the Windows registry, the Policies subkey steps are skipped in the preceding sequences.

See also

- If you customize the Office 2000 installation to allow users' settings to migrate from a previous version of Office, their customized settings move to the new registry subtree. For more information about customizing the Office 2000 installation, see "Office Custom Installation Wizard" on page 250.

- System policies help you control which Office options your users can change. For more information about system policies, see "Managing Users' Options with System Policies" on page 279.

How to Read the ORAPI Spreadsheet

The ORAPI spreadsheet is a representation of the Office 2000 registry entries. The spreadsheet includes the default values for these registry entries, along with their locations in the registry. You can install the ORAPI spreadsheet and then look up any settings that you need.

Toolbox

The ORAPI spreadsheet (Regkey.xls) has been included as an Excel workbook in the Microsoft Office 2000 Resource Kit. For information about installing Regkey.xls, see "Office Information" on page 787.

The ORAPI workbook contains two worksheets:

- RegistryMain
- PathTree

The RegistryMain worksheet lists the default registry values that are used by Office 2000. The RegistryMain worksheet also lists the default value and data type for the entry, as well as which components of Office use that setting.

The PathTree worksheet lists all the registry subkeys that are used by Office 2000. The worksheet maps these subkeys to the RegistryMain worksheet by using the ID in the Registry Key Identifier column.

▶ **To find the default value and registry path for an entry in the registry**

1   Open the Regkey.xls spreadsheet.

2   Click the **RegistryMain** sheet tab.

3   In the Registry Key Identifier column, look up the registry entry whose default value you want to find.

4   Look in the Value-Name, Type, and Default-Value-Data columns to see the default value or values and data types for that entry.

5   In the Registry Key Identifier column, note the ID for the subkey.

6   Click the **PathTree** sheet tab.

7   In the Registry Key Identifier column, look up the subkey ID you found in the RegistryMain worksheet.

8   In the Path Node Location in Registry column, make a note of the path corresponding to the subkey ID.

Read the RegistryMain worksheet

The RegistryMain worksheet contains the registry entries used by Office 2000. Each entry includes a value name and default value data, as well as the correct data type for that value.

The worksheet is organized into columns. The following table lists the main columns in the worksheet and gives a brief explanation of what you find in each column. (The RegistryMain worksheet contains additional columns that are of interest to programmers.)

Column in RegistryMain	Explanation
Unique Identifier	Unique identifier for each entry in the ORAPI spreadsheet.
Registry Key Identifier	Registry path for the entry. Paths are not unique to particular registry entries: A subkey in the registry may contain multiple entries.
Value-Name	Name of the entry in the Windows registry.
Type	Default data type for the value in the entry.
Default-Value-Data	Default value data for the entry. **NO_DEFAULT** or **EMPTY_STRING** means that the entry has no default value.
Localized	Whether the entry has been localized for international versions of Office 2000.
Application Usage	Which Office applications use the entry.
Comments	Comments about the entry. Usually identifies the corresponding Office setting.

Note   ORAPI stores default information in English. Office 2000 substitutes localized entries in the Windows registry during installation. If a localized entry is corrupted or deleted, however, ORAPI returns the default English entry. Office 2000 continues to function, but some localized options may appear in English rather than in the localized language. You can restore localized entries by reinstalling Office 2000.

Read the PathTree worksheet

The PathTree worksheet helps you locate subkeys in the registry hierarchy. The Registry Key Identifier column lists the unique key identifier used to map a subkey to the entries on the RegistryMain worksheet. The Path Node Location in Registry column contains the paths to subkeys used by Office within the following Windows registry subtrees:

- HKEY_CLASSES_ROOT
- HKEY_CURRENT_USER
- HKEY_LOCAL_MACHINE

See also

- Some values in ORAPI take the **REG_EXPAND_SZ** data type, which allows you to use environment variables in the Windows registry. For more information about environment variables, see "Using Environment Variables in System Policies" on page 288.

CHAPTER 8

Helping Users Help Themselves

Microsoft Office 2000 provides you with online Help and several additional resources for finding technical support. You can also customize the Office 2000 Help system to provide your users with even more information about error messages, topics unique to your organization, and additional sources of user assistance on the Web.

In This Chapter

Office 2000 Help and Support

The Microsoft Office 2000 Help system offers more user assistance than any previous Office Help system. Besides providing hundreds of topics and thousands of index entries, the improved Office Assistant does a better job of answering users' questions and even lets you add your own Help content. Microsoft Web sites help you get up-to-date information and technical support whenever you need it.

Getting Help in Office 2000

Office 2000 includes an extensive Help system to help users find the information they need. In addition, the Microsoft.com Web site has several areas that offer additional articles, tools, and information about Office 2000.

Help available in every Office application

The Office 2000 Help system includes hundreds of Help topics and thousands of index entries. You can either browse or search for Help topics and index entries by using the new Office 2000 Help navigation pane.

Just like the **Microsoft** *Product* **Help** dialog box in Office 97 Help, the Help navigation pane in Office 2000 Help contains three tabs: **Contents**, **Index**, and **Answer Wizard** (which was labeled **Find** in previous versions of Office). The **Contents** tab allows you to browse a categorized list of Help topics. The **Index** tab allows you to browse an index of keywords and symbols. The **Answer Wizard** tab allows you to enter queries in natural language, such as "How do I print my document?"

The **Help** menu in every Office 2000 application includes a common set of Help options. You can use these options to get quick **What's This?** information about many interface objects, information for users switching to Office from other software applications, and links to Help content found either on users' computers or on the Web. In addition, the Office Assistant is available to offer suggestions as you work or to help you find information in the Help topics.

Running Office 2000 Help on a locked-down system

The first time a user opens an Office 2000 Help file, the HTML Help control creates an index of links between topics in the Help files. The index file is stored in the same folder and has the same name as the corresponding Help file (except it uses the file name extension .chw).

If the user does not have write *permissions* to the folders where the Help files are stored (for example, C:\Program Files\Microsoft Office\Office\1033), then these index files cannot be created. If the index files are not created, certain types of hyperlinks within the Help topics are not functional. For example, the Visual Basic for Applications and Access Help files contain many cross-links that cannot function without these index files.

To fix this problem, you can grant users write permissions to the folders where the Help files are stored. Alternatively, you can create the Help index files for your users. To create index files for your users, run the PrepHelp utility, which is available on the Office Update Web site at http://officeupdate.microsoft.com/. You must have write permissions to the folders where the Help files are stored to successfully run the PrepHelp utility.

Help available on Microsoft Web sites

The Microsoft.com Web site includes several areas where you can find useful information about Office 2000.

Office Update

The Office Update Web site at http://officeupdate.microsoft.com/ provides product updates, downloads (including utilities, add-ins, and templates), and user assistance for Office 2000, as well as the latest information about Office 2000.

Office Enterprise Center

The Office Enterprise Center Web site at http://www.microsoft.com/office/enterprise/focuses on information technology (IT) by providing a wide variety of Office 2000 materials.

Microsoft in the Enterprise

The Microsoft in the Enterprise Web site at http://www.microsoft.com/enterprise/ includes articles and information about managing your company's computing resources. This site addresses the spectrum of Microsoft products for the enterprise customer.

Microsoft TechNet

The Microsoft TechNet Web site at http://www.microsoft.com/technet/ is a Web resource for the IT community. Among the IT resources that you find here is the TechNet Reference section, which includes content about the Office family of applications.

TechNet also includes the Microsoft Year 2000 Resource Center, at http://www.microsoft.com/technet/topics/year2k/, which offers information about Microsoft products and how they will be affected by the arrival of the year 2000.

Microsoft Support Online

The Microsoft Support Online search page, at http://support.microsoft.com/support/, answers your questions about any Microsoft product, including Office 2000.

Microsoft Developer Network

The Microsoft Developer Network (MSDN™) Web site at http://msdn.microsoft.com/ contains a wealth of information for software developers and programmers.

The MSDN Web site contains several areas, including the Microsoft Scripting Technologies site at http://msdn.microsoft.com/scripting/.

Microsoft Seminar Online

The Microsoft Seminar Online Web site at http://www.microsoft.com/seminar/ provides online seminars on various topics directly to your desktop from the Internet.

Microsoft Press Online

The Microsoft Press Online Web site at http://mspress.microsoft.com/ keeps you up to date with the latest titles from Microsoft Press. The Microsoft Press Online Web site contains information about how to find many technical publications, including the *Microsoft Office 2000/Visual Basic Programmer's Guide*.

Microsoft Certified Technical Education Center

The Microsoft Certified Technical Education Center (CTEC) Web site at http://www.microsoft.com/ctec/ gives you thorough, in-depth instruction related to Office deployment, administration, and support. Many courses covering other Microsoft products are available as well.

Microsoft Solutions Framework

The Microsoft Solutions Framework Web site at http://www.microsoft.com/msf/ is designed to support enterprise organizations by providing information about best practices for IT strategy and project planning.

Microsoft Certified Solution Providers

The Microsoft Certified Solution Provider (MCSP) Web site at http://www.microsoft.com/mcsp/ helps you find Microsoft-certified IT professionals to assist you in evaluating the capabilities of Office 2000. You can also be referred automatically to a suitable MCSP resource by going to the Microsoft Software and Network Services page at http://www.microsoft.com/isapi/referral/obtain_servicesBasic.asp.

See also

- You can create your own custom Help content and present it to users through the Office 2000 Help system. For more information, see "Creating Your Own Help Topics" on page 358.

Getting Help from Microsoft Product Support Services

You have several options for getting technical answers from Microsoft Product Support Services.

Support Online at Microsoft.com

For quick answers to simple questions, use the Microsoft Support Online search page, at http://support.microsoft.com/support/, to search the Microsoft Knowledge Base and other technical resources for fast, accurate answers.

Telephone support from Product Support Services

If your question is urgent and complex, you can call Product Support Services to get assistance from a support engineer.

Standard no-charge support

During business hours, you can receive unlimited free support for usability issues with any of the Office 2000 applications except Microsoft Access.

With your purchase of Office 2000 Professional or Office 2000 Premium, Microsoft also offers free support for your first four developer support incidents. Developer assistance includes help with macros, syntax, and demonstrating basic principles when you develop with Office applications; external database connectivity issues; and installation and configuration of server extensions on a compatible server.

In the United States and Canada, you can contact a support engineer by telephone Monday through Friday, excluding holidays.

- In the United States:

  (425) 635-7056

  6:00 A.M.–6:00 P.M. Pacific time

- In Canada:

  (905) 568-229 for most Office 2000 questions

  (905) 568-3503 for questions about Microsoft Publisher 2000 and Microsoft FrontPage 2000

  8:00 A.M.–8:00 P.M. eastern time

Note   If Office 2000 was preinstalled on your personal computer, you are not eligible for free support from Microsoft. Contact your computer manufacturer for support. For more information, see your computer documentation.

Pay-per-incident support

If you need help after hours, or if you have used up your standard no-charge support options, you can purchase support on a per-incident basis. Support fees can be billed to your VISA, MasterCard, or American Express card.

In the United States and Canada, you can call a support engineer at the following locations with questions about using any Office 2000 application (except Access).

- In the United States:

  (800) 936-5700

  24 hours a day, 7 days a week, excluding holidays

  $35 US per incident
- In Canada:

  (800) 668-7975

  8:00 A.M.–8:00 P.M. eastern time, Monday–Friday, excluding holidays

  $45 CDN plus tax per incident

For questions about Access or developing software applications with Office 2000, you can reach a support engineer at the following locations.

- In the United States:

  (800) 936-5500

  24 hours a day, 7 days a week, excluding holidays

  $95 US per incident
- In Canada:

  (800) 668-7975

  8:00 A.M.–8:00 P.M. eastern time, Monday–Friday, excluding holidays

  $45 CDN plus tax per incident

E-mail support from Product Support Services

If your question isn't urgent, you can send an e-mail message to a Product Support Services engineer by means of a Web page and get an e-mail response back within one business day. You can attach files to your e-mail message. Submit questions on the Microsoft Support Online search page at http://support.microsoft.com/support/.

Note Except for having round-the-clock availability, standard no-charge support and pay-per-incident support through e-mail are subject to the same limitations and fees as telephone support.

TTY/TDD support

Teletypewriter/telecommunications device for the deaf (TTY/TDD) support is available Monday through Friday, excluding holidays, as follows:

- In the United States:

  (425) 635-4948

  6:00 A.M.–6:00 P.M. Pacific time
- In Canada:

  (905) 568-9641

  8:00 A.M.–8:00 P.M. eastern time

Fax support

FastTips is a fax-back service providing Knowledge Base articles and answers to common questions. Use your touch-tone telephone to call the following number:

(800) 936-4100

Then follow the prompts to hear recorded answers to your technical questions, obtain a catalog of available information, or order items by fax.

Business support services

There are a variety of support packages designed for businesses. To learn which package best meets your needs, go to the Microsoft Product Support Services Web site at http://www.microsoft.com/support/.

You can also call (800) 936-3500 for information about accounts for small to medium-sized businesses and (800) 936-3200 for large, enterprise businesses.

On-site, multivendor, or proprietary product support

Microsoft Certified Solution Providers (MCSPs) and Authorized Support Centers (ASCs) specialize in providing support packages for hardware, network, and software products from both Microsoft and other vendors.

For more information about MCSPs, call (800) 765-7768 or go to the Microsoft Certified Solution Provider Web site at http://www.microsoft.com/mcsp/.

For more information about ASCs, contact your Microsoft account representative, or go to the Microsoft Product Services Support Web site at http://www.microsoft.com/support/.

Support outside the United States and Canada

For information about support available in other countries, contact the Microsoft subsidiary that's nearest to you. For a list of Microsoft subsidiaries worldwide, click **About Microsoft** *Product* on the **Help** menu in any Office application. Then, in the **About Microsoft** *Product* dialog box, click **Tech Support**.

Note   Support outside the United States and Canada might vary. Microsoft support services are subject to then-current prices, terms, and conditions at Microsoft, which are subject to change without notice.

Office 2000 provides you with online Help and several resources for finding technical support. In addition, the Office 2000 Help system is customizable, so you can provide help tailored for your users' needs. You can customize error messages, create your own help content, and redirect users to Web pages for more information about a subject.

Customizing Built-in Error Messages

In Office 2000, you can customize error messages to provide additional or updated information about the error that triggered the message. When users can find the problem-solving information on their own, they are less likely to call your support staff.

Helping Users Out of the Error Message Box

Error messages, or alerts, are triggered when a user performs an action that the computer cannot successfully carry out. For example, if a user tries to print a document on a network printer without first installing the printer, the message "No printer available" is displayed. If the user does not know how to install a network printer, the user will probably click **OK** or **Cancel** and call your support staff.

In Office 2000, you can customize these error messages to provide users with more problem-solving information. You can link a custom button in the error message box to additional information by extending the error message to include comprehensive or updated information on a Web site.

For example, you can create a button in the "No printer available" error message box to connect the user to an intranet site that has instructions for installing a particular network printer.

Extending custom error messages on your network

Some of the Office 2000 error messages are extended by default. These messages connect users to the Office Update Web site so that they can get more information about the problem. You can redirect any of these extended error messages to point to a site on your intranet. Additionally, there are many error messages that are not extended by default, and you can also customize these messages for your users.

Whether you're creating new custom error messages or redirecting default error messages, you have to create your own Web pages and either modify the sample server-side script or create a new script to handle your custom error messages.

Expanding your use of custom error messages

Linking a custom error message to a Web page containing information about how to solve the problem is the simplest implementation of custom error messages. But if you create your own *Active Server Pages* (ASP) pages, you can develop more creative, custom solutions that can benefit you, your support staff, and your users.

Suppose your organization already has a system of Help pages available on your intranet site, and you've linked specific error messages to those pages by way of a **Help Desk** button in the error message boxes.

The following process describes what happens when an error in an Office application triggers an error message that you have customized:

1   When a user encounters the error message, the user clicks the **Help Desk** button to find out what to do.

2   The underlying ASP script checks the error message number, determines which Web page applies, and then redirects the user's browser to that Web page.

3   If the error message number does not match any of the predefined error message numbers listed in the ASP file, the ASP script connects the user to your generic Help page for more information.

Toolbox

You can look up detailed information about custom error messages (including error numbers and error categories) in an Excel workbook named Errormsg.xls. For information about installing Errormsg.xls, see "Customizable Alerts" on page 784.

The following scenarios represent what is possible when writing your own ASP pages to customize error messages.

Reducing calls to your support staff

Custom error messages can help reduce calls to your support staff. For example, you can link a "Server is down" error message to an ASP script that analyzes the occurrence of the error message and notifies your support staff to possible network problems.

When a server goes down, you can also link the error message to a Web page that provides users with status information about the server. So if users are able to get information that you are working on the server and that you expect it to be back on line by the end of the day, they will be less likely to flood your support staff with calls for technical assistance.

Forwarding error messages to your support staff

You can take it a step further and create an ASP script to collect and forward information about error messages to your support staff by means of e-mail or a pager. This use of customized error messages keeps your support staff informed about current issues and allows them to respond more quickly.

Creating Custom Error Messages

The task of creating and implementing your own custom error messages consists of the following four steps:

1 Gather error numbers, globally unique identifiers (GUIDs) for each application, and country codes

2 Create Web pages that are linked to your custom error messages

3 Create the *Active Server Pages* (ASP) page for your custom error messages

4 Activate the custom error messages

Note   This process documents the use of an ASP page. If you want to use a Common Gateway Interface (CGI) script, refer to your CGI reference manual for more information about CGI script.

At the end of this process, you have the following components:

- A functioning ASP page
- A set of Web pages that provides information about your custom error messages
- Updated Windows registries on users' computers
- Functioning custom error messages

To create custom error messages or to modify default error messages, you need to create a server-side script to handle the custom error messages. This script can be in either ASP or CGI code. You can create the server-side script by using the following tools:

ASP generator   If you are going to create a small number of custom error messages, you can use the ASP generator (an Excel workbook called ASPscrpt.xls) to create an ASP page. An ASP page is the best choice when you're running Microsoft Windows NT Server and Microsoft Internet Information Server (IIS).

Toolbox

The Office Resource Kit includes a file called ASPscrpt.xls to help you create your ASP script. Use this ASP generator to create the ASP file to handle your custom error messages. For information about installing ASPscrpt.xls, see "Customizable Alerts" on page 784.

Sample ASP script   There are also sample ASP pages and HTML files that you can modify to create your own ASP scripts.

Toolbox

The Office Resource Kit includes sample ASP scripts and HTML files to help you create custom error messages. Create your own ASP scripts and HTML files based on the files Alert.asp, Alert.htm, Alert2.asp, Alert2a.asp, and NYI.htm. For information about installing these files, see "Customizable Alerts" on page 784.

Microsoft Visual Basic Scripting Edition or a CGI-based scripting tool   You can also use Visual Basic Scripting Edition or a CGI-based scripting tool to create a server-side script. The script is used to process the error message numbers, GUID numbers, and country codes, and to return a Web page containing a solution for the user.

How to Set the Stage for Custom Error Messages

Before you're ready to write the *Active Server Pages* (ASP) script that will handle your custom error messages, you must do some preparation. First, you collect the information that identifies the error message you want to customize. Then, you create a Web page with your custom information on it. After you've completed these steps, you can write the ASP script.

Collect relevant information about each error message

Before you implement custom error messages, you need to gather the following information about each error message. This information is required by the server-side script to process the messages correctly.

Error message number   Each error message is assigned a unique number per application. For example, error message number 2202 in Access is "You must install a printer before you design, print, or preview." You need to know the error message number for each error message you plan to customize.

Toolbox

You can look up detailed information about custom error messages (including error numbers and error categories) in an Excel workbook named Errormsg.xls. For information about installing Errormsg.xls, see "Customizable Alerts" on page 784.

GUID   A globally unique identifier (GUID) identifies the application to which the error message belongs.

Country code   When custom error messages are localized, the ASP page uses the country code to determine the locale of Office 2000. Depending on your objective, the ASP page can use one or more of these country codes sent by Office 2000.

For example, if your organization uses only the U.S. English version of Office, you do not need to identify the country code. If you want to redirect all of the Word error messages to one page, you can fill in just the GUID. However, if you want to map a specific error message in a specific application, you must fill in both the error message number and the GUID.

Toolbox

The Office Resource Kit includes a file called ASPscrpt.xls to help you create your ASP script. The ASPscrpt.xls file also contains worksheets that list the GUIDs and country codes to use in creating your ASP script. For information about installing ASPscrpt.xls, see "Customizable Alerts" on page 784.

Create Web pages to provide information about custom error messages

You must create Web pages to provide your users with custom information about error messages they encounter. For example, when a user encounters the "No printer found" error message and then clicks the button linked to your Web site, you must create the Web pages that describe how to solve the printer error problem.

You can also use one general Web page to handle multiple error messages. Using a single page might be the best solution if you have a number of error messages that require the same information. A single page is also the best solution if you don't want to manage multiple ASP pages in a complicated implementation of custom error messages.

After you have created the HTML files, place them on your Web server and make a note of the paths so that you can reference them in your ASP file.

Toolbox

For simple implementations of customizable error messages, such as a general question and answer page, you can start with the following sample Web pages: Alert.asp, Alert.htm, Alert2.asp, Alert2a.asp, and NYI.htm. For information about installing these Web pages, see "Customizable Alerts" on page 784.

How to Write the ASP Script for Custom Error Messages

When a user clicks the custom button in an error message box, an *Active Server Pages* (ASP) page responds by displaying the Web page you created to provide information about the error. The ASP page directs the request sent when the user clicks the custom error button in the error message box.

Tip   ASP pages are designed to run on the Microsoft Windows operating system. For optimal performance, use Windows NT Server version 4.0 or later and Internet Information Server (IIS).

There are three ways to produce the ASP script. You can:

- Use the ASP generator to create or update an ASP page

  This method is the quickest and easiest way to create an ASP page. However, it doesn't allow complete customization and cannot handle large numbers of error messages. You need Excel 97 or later to use the ASP generator.

- Modify the sample ASP script

  This method requires knowledge of ASP scripting and Visual Basic Scripting Edition. It allows for both a quick start and complete customization. The sample script was created by using the file ASPscrpt.xls.

- Write your own script

  This method requires knowledge of ASP scripting and Visual Basic Scripting Edition. It allows for complete customization, but it requires development time.

Toolbox

The Office Resource Kit includes a file called ASPscrpt.xls to help you create your ASP script. Use this ASP generator to create the ASP file to handle your custom error messages. For information about installing ASPscrpt.xls, see "Customizable Alerts" on page 784.

Create or update an ASP page

The quickest way to create an ASP page is to use the ASP generator (ASPscrpt.xls). The template requires information about each error message you are going to customize. After entering this information, you run the macro and it creates the ASP script for you.

To use the ASP generator, you need the following:

- Excel 97 or later
- A network computer configured as a Web server running Windows NT Server 4.0 with Service Pack 3 or Windows 2000 Server.
- The ASP extensions that are included with Windows NT Server 4.0 with Service Pack 3 or included with the Windows NT Server 4.0 Option Pack installed on the network computer.

▶ **To generate an ASP file**

1   Start Excel, and open the file ASPscrpt.xls.

2   In the **Enter the default URL for error messages not listed below** box, type the URL of the default Web page.

The default Web page is a generic page used to handle all error messages that do not have a unique Web page assigned to them.

3   In the **Enter the physical, or actual, path of the base URL** box, type the path to the destination directory where the new ASP file is stored.

4   Fill in the **Country Code**, **Microsoft Installer GUID**, **Error Message Number**, and **URL to the Destination Web Page** columns for any error messages you want to customize.

Be sure to specify the correct URL of the Web pages that you want to link to the custom error message box.

5   Click **Go**.

The new ASP file is created and stored at the location you specified.

Modify the sample ASP script

You can also implement custom error messages by modifying a sample ASP script. The following ASP code from the sample file Alert.asp handles four custom printer-related error messages:

```
<% response.expires=0
alertNum=""&request.queryString("alrt")
LCID=request.queryString("HelpLCID")
GUID=request.queryString("GUID")

select case (alertNum & "GUID" & LCID)
case "197573{11111111-1111-1111-1111-111111111111}1033"
  response.redirect("http://helpdesk/office9alerts/printer.htm")
case "197574{11111111-1111-1111-1111-111111111111}1033"
  response.redirect("http://helpdesk/office9alerts/printer.htm")
case "197575{11111111-1111-1111-1111-111111111111}1033"
  response.redirect("http://helpdesk/office9alerts/printer.htm")
case "197576{11111111-1111-1111-1111-111111111111}1033"
  response.redirect("http://helpdesk/office9alerts/printer.htm")
case else
  response.redirect(http://helpdesk/office9alerts/FAQ.htm)
end select %>
```

To modify this sample script to work for your custom error messages, open the file in Microsoft FrontPage or another ASP editor and substitute the highlighted variables with your own values.

Toolbox

The Office Resource Kit includes sample ASP scripts and HTML files to help you create custom error messages. Create your own ASP scripts and HTML files based on the files Alert.asp, Alert.htm, Alert2.asp, Alert2a.asp, and NYI.htm. For information about installing these files, see "Customizable Alerts" on page 784.

The following values and variables are used in the sample ASP scripts:

Error Message ID   The number to the immediate right of the word case is the error message ID number.

GUID   The 32-character number to the right of the error ID number is the globally unique identifier (GUID). The ASP uses this number to determine which application to associate the error message with. There is only one GUID for each application.

Country Code   The number following the GUID is the country code. This number is used to identify the locale of Office 2000.

Response Redirect   This variable specifies the Web page associated with the error message.

All of the error messages in this sample script refer to the same Web page. You can easily assign different Web pages to each error by specifying other URLs. You can also add more error messages by repeating the case string.

Note   Two additional sample scripts, **Alert2.asp** and **Alert2a.asp**, provide examples of how you can extend the functionality of the ASP page. **Alert2.asp** prompts the user to enter an explanation of the problem that generated the error. After the user types their feedback and clicks **Submit**, they are redirected to **Alert2a.asp** which contains a message thanking them for their feedback.

Write your own ASP page

You can write your own ASP page by using Visual Basic Scripting Edition or JavaScript, both of which are supported by Windows NT Server and IIS. When you write your own ASP page, you can add additional functionality beyond helping users out of an error message box. A custom ASP script can take the variables it receives from the custom error message and reuse the information in new contexts.

For example, a custom ASP script can generate dynamic HTML or redirect a browser to go to a different page, depending on the values sent to the ASP script from the browser. It can also capture the values from an error message and write them to a log file. A network administrator can use the log file to help solve common network problems.

See also

- You can use Visual Basic Scripting Edition or JavaScript to create your own ASP page. The IIS Web site contains links to additional resources that can help you to start working with these scripting languages, as well as reference information useful to more advanced scriptwriters. For more information, go to the Microsoft Windows NT Server Web Services site at http://www.microsoft.com/ntserver/web/.

How to Activate Custom Error Messages

Custom error messages become active when the correct value settings are entered into the Windows registry. This means that after you have created the *Active Server Pages* (ASP) file, each computer on your network must be updated to activate custom error messages.

If you have already deployed Office 2000, the System Policy Editor allows you to add, remove, or modify a single custom error message, or to enable or disable all error messages simultaneously throughout your organization. If you have not yet deployed Office 2000, you can modify the registry during Office deployment by using the Custom Installation Wizard.

Enable custom error messages before deploying Office

If you have not yet installed Office 2000, you can use the Office Custom Installation Wizard to enable custom error messages.

Enable custom error messages for all applications

If you want to enable all custom error messages for all Office 2000 applications, use the Office Customize Wizard to modify the URL in the following registry subkey:

HKEY_CURRENT_USER\Software\Microsoft\Office\9.0\Common\General \CustomizableAlertBaseURL

Your new URL must point to the ASP page that you created to handle the custom error messages. The error message number, GUID, and country code will automatically be appended to this base URL for you so that the ASP script can correctly direct users to the defined HTML page. For the ASP page to function properly, you must type a question mark (?) at the end of the URL to allow for these parameters to be defined for use within the ASP page. The following is an example of a base URL:

http://localhost/mypage.asp?

If you have chosen to configure your ASP page to handle any additional parameters, such as the computer name, you will need to add an ampersand (&) to the end of the query string so that the default parameters are added when the link is activated. The following is an example of a base URL:

http://localhost/mypage.asp?ComputerName="Mamabear"&

When you change the URL, you can also update the custom button text by using the following registry subkey:

HKEY_CURRENT_USER\Software\Microsoft\Office\9.0\Common\General
\CustomizableAlertDefaultButtonText

Enable a single custom error message

If you want to enable a single error message, add an entry for that error message to the following registry subkey:

HKEY_CURRENT_USER\Software\Microsoft\Office\9.0*Application*\CustomizableAlerts

Each entry consists of a name and a value. The name is the numeric ID for the error message, and the value is the text you add to change the text that appears on the custom button for the error message.

For example, to add a custom error message for error message number 46 (a printer error) in Word, you can add the following registry subkey:

HKEY_CURRENT_USER\Software\Microsoft\Office\9.0\Word\CustomizableAlerts\46

Enable custom error messages after deploying Office

If you have already deployed Office 2000 and you want to enable custom error messages, use the System Policy Editor.

Note   When you enable custom error messages by using a system policy, the policy settings override any existing custom error messages registered in the HKCU\Software\Microsoft\Office\9.0\Application\Customizable Alerts subkey.

Enable custom error messages for all applications

If you want to enable all custom error messages for all Office 2000 applications, use the System Policy Editor to set the following policy:

Microsoft Office 2000\Customizable error messages\Base URL

Your new URL must point to the ASP page that you created to handle the custom error messages. The error message number, GUID, and country code will automatically be appended to this base URL for you so that the ASP script can correctly direct users to the defined HTML page. For the ASP page to function properly, you must type a question mark (?) at the end of the URL to allow for these parameters to be defined for use within the ASP page. The following is an example of a base URL:

http://localhost/mypage.asp?

If you have chosen to configure your ASP page to handle any additional parameters, such as the computer name, you will need to add an ampersand (&) to the end of the query string, to allow for the default parameters to be added when the link is activated. The following is an example of a base URL:

http://localhost/mypage.asp?ComputerName="Mamabear"&

Enable a single custom error message

If you want to enable a single error message, add an entry for that error message to the **List of error messages to customize** policy.

For example, to add a custom error message to Word, you set the following policy:

Microsoft Word 2000\Customizable error messages\List of error messages to customize

In the **Settings for List of error messages to customize** area, click the **Show** button. Click **Add**, and then type the name and value for the error message. The name is the numeric ID for the error message, and the value is the text you added to change the text that appears on the custom button for the error message.

See also

- The System Policy Editor is an effective and efficient way to update all of the client computers on your network. To learn how to use the System Policy Editor, see "Using the System Policy Editor" on page 296.

- By using the Custom Installation Wizard, you can specify exactly how Office 2000 is installed on your client computers. To learn how to use the Custom Installation Wizard, see "Office Custom Installation Wizard" on page 250.

How to Disable or Remove Custom Error Messages

You might decide to disable or remove one or more custom error messages. For example, if you don't want your users to have access to the Internet and you don't want to redirect them to an intranet site, you can disable or remove all custom error messages.

If you have not yet deployed Office 2000, you can use the Office Custom Installation Wizard to disable or remove custom error messages in your client installation. If you have already deployed Office 2000, you can use a system policy to disable or remove custom error messages.

Note If you disable a custom error message, the custom button in the error message box no longer appears. The error message will function as originally designed.

Disable custom error messages before deploying Office

If you have not yet installed Office 2000, you can use the Office Custom Installation Wizard to set up your installation so that none of the registry settings that enable custom error messages are created. Note, however, that the Office 2000 Setup program creates registry settings for some error messages by default and that these messages cannot be disabled.

Disable custom error messages for all applications

If you want to disable all custom error messages for all Office 2000 applications, use the Office Customize Wizard to delete the URL in the following registry subkey:

HKEY_CURRENT_USER\Software\Microsoft\Office\9.0\Common\General \CustomizableAlertBaseURL

The **CustomizableAlertBaseURL** entry is the master switch for custom error messages. If there is no URL listed in this entry, none of the error messages in Office are customizable.

When you remove the URL, be sure to remove any custom button text from the following registry subkey:

HKEY_CURRENT_USER\Software\Microsoft\Office\9.0\Common\General \CustomizableAlertDefaultButtonText

Disable all custom error messages for a single application

If you want to disable all custom error messages for a single application, such as Microsoft Word, use the Office Customize Wizard to remove any customized error message listed in the following registry subkey:

HKEY_CURRENT_USER\Software\Microsoft\Office\9.0*Application*\CustomizableAlerts

Remove a single custom error message

If you want to remove a single error message, delete the entry for that error message from the following registry subkey:

HKEY_CURRENT_USER\Software\Microsoft\Office\9.0*Application*\CustomizableAlerts

Each registry entry consists of a name and a value. The name is the numeric ID for the error message, and the value is the text you added to change the text that appears on the custom button in the error message box.

For example, to remove a custom error message for error message number 46 (a printer error) in Word, you would delete the following registry subkey:

HKEY_CURRENT_USER\Software\Microsoft\Office\9.0\Word\CustomizableAlerts\46

Disable custom error messages after deploying Office

If you have already deployed Office 2000, and you want to disable or remove custom error messages, you can use the System Policy Editor.

Disable custom error messages for all applications

If you want to disable all custom error messages for all Office 2000 applications, use the System Policy Editor to clear the following policy:

Microsoft Office 2000\Customizable error messages\Base URL

Disable all custom error messages for a single application

If you wan to disable all custom error messages for a single application, such as Microsoft Word, use the System Policy Editor to disable the application's **List of error messages to customize** policy.

For example, to remove custom error messages from Word, you would follow the policy path \\Default User\Microsoft Word 2000\Customizable error messages and clear the **List of error messages to customize** check box.

Remove a single custom error message

If you want to remove a single error message, delete the entry for that error message from the **List of error messages to customize** policy.

For example, to remove a specific custom error message from Word, use the following policy:

Microsoft Word 2000\Customizable error messages\List of error messages to customize

In the **Settings for List of error messages to customize** area, click **Show**, and then select the **Value Name** and click the **Remove** button.

See also

- If you don't want to enable custom error messages for your organization, you can disable them by using the Office Custom Installation Wizard to remove the URL entry from your users' registries. For more information, see "Office Custom Installation Wizard" on page 250.

- The System Policy Editor is another tool you can use to disable custom error messages by removing the URL entry from your users' registries. For more information, see "Using the System Policy Editor" on page 296.

Creating Your Own Help Topics

You can expand the scope of built-in Microsoft Office 2000 Help topics by creating your own Help topics through the use of Microsoft HTML Help Workshop and the Microsoft Answer Wizard Builder. Users gain access to your custom topics by using the Office Answer Wizard.

Customizing Help Content for Your Users

Microsoft Office allows you to create all sorts of custom solutions for users. But what if users want help with your custom features? Or what if you want your users to be able to look up information about using your organization's templates or filling in your organization's forms?

Whether you are documenting a new add-in or including topics specific to your organization, you can use Office 2000 to create your own Help content and distribute it to your users. When a user asks the Answer Wizard a question about the custom feature, the new Help content turns up in the Answer Wizard search, along with the rest of the Office 2000 Help topics.

For example, users might need assistance with a Visual Basic for Applications tool created by your IS department. If you have also created custom Help content for this feature, users can type a question in the Answer Wizard and find the answer, without knowing that they're searching for customized Help.

Creating custom content for use with the Office Help system involves three steps:

- Creating HTML-compatible Help files

  Custom Help topics can include HTML Help files that reside on a Web site, or compressed HTML (CHM) files that you distribute to users locally or over the network.

- Creating a new Answer Wizard (AW) file

  The Microsoft Answer Wizard Builder helps you build your own AW files, which are used by the Answer Wizard to locate topics in response to users' queries.

- Registering your custom Help files

  To make your custom Help content available to users, you copy the new AW file and Help files to each user's computer and update each user's Windows registry. The next time a user asks the Answer Wizard a question, your custom Help content becomes part of the answer.

How to Create Custom Help Content

Before you create a custom Answer Wizard (AW) file, you need to create HTML pages on a Web server, or you need to create compressed HTML (CHM) files that can be either distributed to your users' computers or stored on a network server.

In either case, the Answer Wizard Builder analyzes the words contained in these files and creates an index that can be searched by the Answer Wizard when a user enters a question.

If you don't have any Help files, you can use HTML Help Workshop and the Answer Wizard Builder to create both custom Help topics and an AW file to go with them.

Determine where to start

Where you start the process of creating custom Help depends on what you have to start with. If you already have Help topics in WinHelp format or CHM files, you can import them into HTML Help Workshop. Or if you have HTML Help topics already posted on a Web site, you can point the Answer Wizard Builder to the Web site.

Start with WinHelp

If your WinHelp files don't require any editing, you can import them directly into HTML Help Workshop; you then use HTML Help Workshop to create a CHM file from the separate WinHelp files. Then use the CHM file in the Answer Wizard Builder to create the AW file.

If you want to edit or update existing WinHelp files, you can either modify them by using your WinHelp tool, or you can edit the content in HTML Help Workshop.

Start with HTML files

If your Help content is currently on the Web, you can create an AW file by providing the Answer Wizard Builder with the URL to the Web site and the share location where the HTML files are hosted.

If you need to edit or update HTML files, modify them first by using an HTML editing tool (such as FrontPage) or HTML Help Workshop. You can also use HTML Help Workshop to create a new CHM file based on existing HTML files.

Start with compressed HTML files

If your users do not have access to the Web, you can use HTML Help Workshop to create CHM files and store them either on the network or on individual users' computers. You can use your existing CHM files in the Answer Wizard Builder or, if they need editing, modify them first by using HTML Help Workshop.

Start from scratch

If you don't have any existing content, you can create your own Help topics in HTML Help Workshop or in any other HTML authoring tool. Then just use the Answer Wizard Builder to create the AW file from the HTML or CHM Help content.

Choose a type of Help file

The format you choose for your Help files also depends on where you plan to store the files and how often you need to update the content.

Advantages of using HTML Help

HTML Help files are stored on a Web server. They offer the following advantages over other methods:

- You can update Help content directly on the Web server, without interrupting users.
- No disk space is required on the client side.
- If you already have a Web Help site, you can use its contents to create the custom AW file.
- You don't have to register Web-based help on your client computers—it's ready to use right away.

If you use HTML Help files, however, users must have access to the Web, and you must maintain the Web server and site. In addition, users might experience slow response times when they submit queries.

Advantages of using compressed HTML Help

CHM files are stored on a network share or locally on users' computers. They offer the following advantages over other methods:

- Users get faster results when the CHM file is stored locally.
- A single CHM file can contain multiple HTML files, so the administrator has fewer files to keep track of.
- Users don't need access to the Web.

If you use CHM Help files, however, you must redistribute them across the network or on each client computer whenever you update the content. You will also have to register these files on each client computer before they can be used.

Make custom Help work like Office Help

You can build your custom Help to work as a stand-alone Help system, using your own styles and window definitions in HTML Help Workshop. However, if you want your custom Help to work and look like the Office 2000 Help system, use CHM files with the Microsoft *cascading style sheets*, and add your custom Help content to the Answer Wizard. Using the Answer Wizard ensures that your Help uses the same window definitions and functionality as Office Help.

To make your Help look like Office Help, you use the styles in the Office cascading style sheet files. Attach the cascading style sheet files to your project, and use the styles in the cascading style sheet files when you create your Help text.

Note   To view the definitions for each style in a cascading style sheet file, open the file in Notepad. Each style is listed, along with the formatting specifications for that style, such as font and size.

To select the correct style sheet automatically based on the browser level, add the following code to the header in each HTML page:

```
<style>@import url(/Office.css);</style>
<link disabled rel="stylesheet" type="text/css" href="/MSOffice.css">
```

The user's Web browser determines which cascading style sheet file is used:

- Office.css for Microsoft Internet Explorer 4.0 or later
- MSOffice.css for Internet Explorer 3.*x*

Tip   To view the HTML code used in any of the Office Help CHM files, either open the file in HTML Help Workshop, or double-click the CHM file. When the file opens, right-click in a topic, and then click **View Source**.

Toolbox

HTML Help Workshop helps you create custom HTML-based Help content that can be used with the Office Help system. To help you create files that look like Office Help files, the Office Help cascading style sheet files are included. For information about installing HTML Help Workshop and supporting files, see "HTML Help WorkShop" on page 791.

How to Add Custom Help Content to the Answer Wizard

If you want your custom Help topics to work like Office 2000 Help, make sure your Help is accessible through the Answer Wizard. By using the Answer Wizard Builder, you can create an Answer Wizard Builder (AWB) project file to which you add your HTML Help topics. The Answer Wizard Builder project produces a new Answer Wizard (AW) file that is used like an index by the Office Help system to locate applicable information for users' queries.

If you significantly change your HTML Help files, by adding new topics or by renaming or deleting existing topics, then you must create a new AW file to replace the old one. To create a new AW file, you can use the original Answer Wizard project, or you can create a new project.

Toolbox

You can use the Answer Wizard Builder to help you create custom AW files for use with custom HTML Help topics and the Office Help system. For information about installing the Answer Wizard Builder, see "Answer Wizard Builder" on page 789.

Create an Answer Wizard Builder project

When you create an Answer Wizard Builder project, the Answer Wizard Builder indexes the HTML Help topics you specify. You can then optionally assign user questions to each topic.

▶ To create an Answer Wizard Builder project

1   If you installed the Answer Wizard Builder to the default directory specified during setup, click **Start**, point to **Programs**, and then click **Microsoft Answer Wizard Builder**.

2   In the **Create a New Answer Wizard Project Using** box, click **CHM File** or **Web Site**.

3   Enter the path to the CHM file, or enter the URL of the Web site and the share name of the Web server (plus the path to a particular folder, if necessary) in the appropriate text box, and then click **OK**.

The Answer Wizard Builder parses the CHM or HTML files and indexes the Help topics contained in them. When it is finished indexing the Help topics, the Answer Wizard Builder lists the file names of all the Help topics found at the location you specified in step 3.

Add user questions

Although the Answer Wizard Builder indexes your Help topics, you can improve the searching power of the Answer Wizard by assigning user questions to each topic. Questions that most closely reflect the questions that real users will probably ask are more likely to help you improve the usefulness of your topics. For example, you might select a topic about setting up a network printer and assign a question such as "What is the path to our department printer?"

Adding user questions is optional. They are an additional search mechanism designed to enhance the Answer Wizard, but are not required for the Answer Wizard to function normally.

Create a custom Answer Wizard file

When you are finished entering user questions (if you choose to add them), you must compile an AW file from the Answer Wizard Builder project.

▶ To build a new custom Answer Wizard file

• In the Answer Wizard Builder, click the **Build** button.

Tip   Store the new AW file in the same folder where you saved the AWB project file.

See also

- Not all language versions are supported by the Answer Wizard. For information about international considerations for the Answer Wizard, see "Recommended Operating Systems for International Use" on page 732.

How to Make Custom Help Content Accessible to Users

After you create custom Help content, you need to make your custom Help and Answer Wizard (AW) files accessible to your users by following these steps:

1 Determine whether you are going to store the custom Help files on each user's computer or on a network share.

2 Distribute the files to that location.

3 Update each user's Windows registry to point to the correct location.

  There are separate registry entries for AW files and compressed HTML (CHM) files. You do not need to register uncompiled HTML files.

Tip   You can store an AW file in any location as long as your users have access to the location. Storing the AW file on users' computers can improve access speed, especially if you have a congested network.

After the AW file and CHM or HTML files are in the desired location, the Windows registry of each client computer must be updated to reflect the location of the AW file and CHM files.

Note   If you need to update the contents of an AW file after you've registered the file, just replace the file with an updated version. You don't need to register the file again, as long as you use the same file name.

If you have not yet deployed Office 2000, you can use the Office Custom Installation Wizard to include the custom Help and AW files in your client installation. The Office Custom Installation Wizard also helps you update the registries for your client computers with paths to these new files.

If you have already deployed Office 2000, you must edit the registries for your client computers. You can use a system policy to register the AW file, but you must edit the registry manually to add a new CHM file.

Tip   The easiest way to administer customized Help is to set up the custom Help content on a Web site, store the AW file on a network share, and then set the locations through system policies. By having everything stored on network servers, and the file registration handled by system policies, you can avoid configuring the client computers individually.

Register a new Answer Wizard file before deploying Office

If you haven't yet deployed Office 2000, you can use the Office Custom Installation Wizard to register the AW file. On the **Add Registry Entries** panel of the Office Custom Installation Wizard, add a new entry in the registry in one of the Answer Wizard subkeys.

Values for the new entry take the **REG_SZ** data type. Use a unique name for the entry name and use the path where the AW file resides, including the AW file name, as the value.

There are separate Answer Wizard subkeys for each of the following Office 2000 applications:

- Word
- Excel
- Microsoft PowerPoint
- Access
- Microsoft Outlook
- Graph
- Binder

The Answer Wizard subkeys are stored in the following path in the Windows registry:

HKEY_CURRENT_USER\Software\Microsoft\Office\9.0\ApplicationName
\Answer Wizard

For example, if you create a new AW file called Plugins.aw for Word and place it in the C:\Program Files\Microsoft Office folder, you add a new entry called **PluginsAW** to the following subkey:

HKEY_CURRENT_USER\Software\Microsoft\Office\9.0\Word\Answer Wizard

Then you assign the following path as its value:

C:\Program Files\Microsoft Office\plugins.aw

Register a new Answer Wizard file after deploying Office

If you've already deployed Office 2000, you can use a system policy to change the registry settings on all the computers in your organization at one time. You use the **Custom Answer Wizard database path** system policy in the **Miscellaneous** category for each of the Office applications to add a custom AW file.

Note   The System Policy Editor allows only one AW file per Office application. If you need to add more AW files, you must manually create a separate registry entry for each new file.

For example, to add the file Plugins.aw to the Answer Wizard in Word, select the **Custom Answer Wizard database path** system policy under the **Miscellaneous** category for Word 2000, and then type **C:\Program Files\Microsoft Office\plugins.aw** in the **Custom Answer Wizard database path** box.

Note You must have your users restart the appropriate application in order to use a new AW file. For example, if you added a new AW file with topics for Excel, your users must restart Excel. Restarting the application is not necessary if you reset the list of AW files by calling AnswerWizard.ResetFileList in Visual Basic for Applications.

Register a new CHM file

You can use the Office Custom Installation Wizard to register a new CHM file before you deploy Office 2000, or you can register the CHM file manually after deployment. Either way, to register the CHM file, you create a new entry in the registry in the following subkey:

HKEY_LOCAL_MACHINE\Software\Microsoft\Windows\HTML Help

Values for the new entry take the **REG_SZ** data type. Use the CHM file name as the entry name and the path where the CHM file resides as the value. For example, if you create a new CHM file called Plugins.chm and place it in the C:\Program Files\Microsoft Office folder, add a new entry called **Plugins.chm** and assign the following path as its value:

C:\Program Files\Microsoft Office

See also

- The Office Custom Installation Wizard can install your new CHM and AW files, and even update registry settings on all client computers when you deploy Office 2000. For more information, see "Office Custom Installation Wizard Reference" on page 250.

- The System Policy Editor can save you time by helping you push registry settings out to all client computers on your network. For more information, see "Using the System Policy Editor" on page 296.

Disabling Links from Office 2000 Help to the Web

Many Office 2000 Help topics include links to more information on the Microsoft.com Web site. If you don't want your users connecting to the Microsoft.com site from Office 2000 Help, you can disable the links by removing them from the topics in compressed HTML (CHM) files. You can also modify these CHM files to disable some of the links or redirect these links to your intranet site.

The CHM files containing Web links are updated periodically to reflect new information available on the Web. You can choose whether to download the new CHM files. If you disable some of the links in these files, and then your users update the files with a new version from the Web, then the links might become active again. If you remove the files altogether, your users are not prompted to download new files.

Each Office 2000 application has its own CHM file that contains all of the links to the Web.

This file	Contains links to the Web from these Help files
Acweb9.chm	Access Help files
Olweb9.chm	Outlook Help files
Ppweb9.chm	PowerPoint Help files
Wdweb9.chm	Word Help files
Xlweb9.chm	Excel Help files

For example, if you don't want users to have access to the Microsoft.com site directly from Excel Help, you can delete the Xlweb9.chm file so that the links are broken. Or if you have an Excel Tips page on your internal Web site that you want users to connect to instead, you can modify the links in the Xlweb9.chm topics to point to your site.

Caution   To ensure proper functionality, do not modify any other CHM files included with Office 2000. The CHM files containing the Web links are designed to have customizable Web links without affecting Office Help functionality.

See also

- You use HTML Help Workshop to redirect or remove the links from the CHM files containing Web links. For more information about using HTML Help Workshop, see the Help system for HTML Help Workshop.

Linking the Answer Wizard to the Web

The new Help on the Web feature in Microsoft Office 2000 connects your users to information about Office 2000 on the Microsoft Office Update Web site. You can disable Help on the Web or customize it to point to a site on your intranet. You can also use Help on the Web to collect user feedback to improve your custom Answer Wizard files and Help topics.

Expanding Help on the Web

You can use the new Help on the Web feature to extend the Answer Wizard by providing additional or updated information for users whose queries are not satisfied by the Help topics returned by the Answer Wizard.

For example, suppose that one of your users asks the Office Assistant, "Why isn't my Exchange server responding?" Unless you've created custom Help content, the Answer Wizard returns a list of Help topics about Microsoft Exchange Server and Microsoft Outlook. But the final link returned by the Answer Wizard reads **None of the above, look for more help on the Web**.

Clicking this link connects users to a feedback form, which they can use to comment about their search. When they submit the feedback form, they are redirected to the Microsoft Office Update Web site, and their search is automatically repeated on the latest Office content. They find a list of Microsoft Knowledge Base articles about Exchange Server and Outlook, as well as information about typical server issues.

At the same time, their comments are collected and sent to Microsoft, where support engineers evaluate the data and use it to improve both Answer Wizard Help topics and the Office Update Web site.

If you want users to connect to information on your intranet instead (or if your users don't have access to the World Wide Web), you can customize the Help on the Web link to point to one of the sites on your intranet. For example, users might ask about the server that runs Microsoft Exchange Server and then click **None of the above, look for more help on the Web**. You can redirect their search to the intranet site, where you have a list of frequently asked questions (FAQs) about Exchange Server, including any current server issues.

To redirect the Help on the Web link, you just change the destination URL. You can also customize the text in the Office Assistant and some of the text in the Help topic pane. If you prefer not to use the Help on the Web feature at all, you can disable the link.

Depending on how creative you want to get and how many development resources are available to you, you can create *Active Server Pages* (ASP) pages that make the Help on the Web feature even more useful to your organization. The following examples show you a few of the many ways you can customize Help on the Web to suit your needs.

Directing users to a static page on your intranet site

If you don't want to create a custom ASP page, you can create a static Web page instead. For example, create a Web page that has a list of FAQs and a telephone number or e-mail address that users can use to contact your organization's support staff.

To implement this solution, all you have to do is create the Web page, delete the text in the Help pane, and supply the static Web page address as the destination URL.

Using queries to create or expand your custom Help files

If you aren't yet prepared to create a complete custom search system for your users, but you don't want to lose their questions, you can collect their comments without directing them to a Web site. You can keep track of the kinds of questions your users are asking and implement a method for handling them later.

If you've already created custom Help and Answer Wizard files for your organization, tracking users' queries and comments can help you find ways to expand your custom Help. By using their queries, you can research and write more topics and Answer Wizard questions for your custom Help file, as well as supplement the online Help system that comes with Office 2000.

To implement this solution, create an ASP page that logs users' queries and comments. Change the text in the Office Assistant to "Send us comments about your search," and change the text in the Help pane to inform them that their comments will be sent to you. Change the feedback URL to point to your ASP page, and you're done.

Continuing users' searches on your intranet site

You can set up Help on the Web so that it searches your intranet rather than Microsoft.com for more information. You can also collect users' feedback for your own use, rather than sending it to Microsoft.

To send users to your Web site, create an ASP page to capture users' questions and search your organization's Web site. Change the text in the Office Assistant and text in the Help topic pane to tell users where their questions are being sent and where their browsers are being redirected. Update the feedback URL to point to your ASP page.

Users can search your site for the latest information about internal tools. You can also collect comments about Office 2000 and send them on to Microsoft if and when you choose.

Sending questions to your support staff

You can use a custom ASP page and some of your coding experience to set up a complex system for handling user questions. For example, you can have users fill in the feedback form with all of their pertinent questions and comments and route the form to your support staff.

Then you can redirect your users to an ASP page with FAQs or provide a link to a Web site that they can use to search for more information. If they still can't find the answer, your support staff has had time to receive the query, research the answer, and supply a solution to the problem.

See also

- You can create custom Help content and integrate it with the Office Help system, including the Answer Wizard. For more information, see "Creating Your Own Help Topics" on page 358.

- You can disable Help on the Web and other entry points to the Web from Office 2000. For more information about locking down entry points to the Web, see "Disabling Built-in Connections to the Web" on page 295.

How to Customize Help on the Web

You can customize Help on the Web by changing any of the following items: the default URL, the text in the Office Assistant, and some of the text in the Help pane. You can also disable Help on the Web if you don't want to make this feature available to your users.

Change the default URL

By default, the Help on the Web link in the Office Assistant points to the Office Update site on the Microsoft Web site at http://officeupdate.microsoft.com/office/redirect/fromOffice9/AnswerWizard.asp. The default URL is http://officeupdate.microsoft.com/office/redirect/fromOffice9/AnswerWizard.asp. However, you can change the default URL to point to another Web site, such as your organization's home page or support Web site.

To change the default URL, set the **Feedback URL** policy.

▶ **To change the default URL**

1 In the System Policy Editor, double-click the **Default User** icon.

2 In the **Default User Properties** dialog box, click the plus sign (+) next to **Microsoft Office 2000**.

3 Click the plus sign next to **Assistant**.

4 Click the plus sign next to **Help on the Web**.

5 Select the **Feedback URL** check box.

6 Under **Settings for Feedback URL,** type the URL you want to use.

Note The maximum length of the text string for the feedback URL is 255 characters.

Customize the text in the Office Assistant

You can customize the text of the final Answer Wizard link, **None of the above, look for more help on the Web**. For example, you can include the name of your organization by changing the text to **None of the above, look for more help on the** *Organization* **Web site**.

To change the text in the Office Assistant, set the **Feedback button label** policy.

▶ **To change the text in the Office Assistant**

1 In the System Policy Editor, double-click the **Default User** icon.

2 In the **Default User Properties** dialog box, click the plus sign (+) next to **Microsoft Office 2000**.

3 Click the plus sign next to **Assistant**.

4 Click the plus sign next to **Help on the Web**.

5 Select the **Feedback button label** check box.

6 Under **Settings for Feedback button label,** type the text you want to use.

Note The maximum length of the text string for the feedback button label is 255 characters.

Customize the text in the Help window

You can customize some of the text in the Help window. By default, the following text appears in the middle of the Help window, just below the user question: "Click the **Send and go to the Web** button below to launch Microsoft Internet Explorer and send your question to a site that provides further assistance. You can switch back to Help at any time."

You can add the name of your Web site or organization to this text. To change the text in the Help window, you set the **Feedback dialog text** policy.

▶ To change the text in the Help window

1 In the System Policy Editor, double-click the **Default User** icon.

2 In the **Default User Properties** dialog box, click the plus sign (+) next to **Microsoft Office 2000**.

3 Click the plus sign next to **Assistant**.

4 Click the plus sign next to **Help on the Web**.

5 Select the **Feedback dialog text** check box.

6 Under **Settings for Feedback dialog text**, type the text you want to use.

Note   The maximum length of the text string for the feedback dialog text is 255 characters.

Disable Help on the Web

If you want to completely disable Help on the Web, you can do so by using a system policy. To disable Help on the Web, select the **Help | Office on the Web** option in the **Disable command bar buttons and menu items** policy for each application.

▶ To disable Help on the Web for Word

1 In the System Policy Editor, double-click the **Default User** icon.

2 In the **Default User Properties** dialog box, click the plus sign (+) next to **Microsoft Word 2000**.

3 Click the plus sign next to **Disable items in user interface**.

4 Click the plus sign next to **Predefined**.

5 Select the **Disable command bar buttons and menu items** check box.

6 Under **Settings for Disable command bar buttons and menu items**, select **Help | Office on the Web**.

Note   The Help on the Web feature is automatically disabled if there is no default Web browser on the user's computer or if there is no feedback URL defined in the Windows registry.

See also

- You use system policies to change or disable the Help on the Web feature. For more information about the system policies and the System Policy Editor, see "Using the System Policy Editor" on page 296.

- You can create custom Help content and integrate it with the Office Help system, including the Answer Wizard. For more information, see "Creating Your Own Help Topics" on page 358.

How to Customize the Answer Wizard Feedback Form

When your users click **None of the above, look for help on the Web** in the Answer Wizard, they are directed to a feedback form in Help. They use this form to enter comments about the problem that they are trying to solve and the kind of information they expected to find. When they submit their comments, they are directed to the Office Update Web site where their search is automatically run again to find any updated information.

Meanwhile, the data from the feedback form is submitted to the support staff at Microsoft, where the information is used to improve the next version of Answer Wizard topics, as well as the information available on the Office Update Web site.

The Answer Wizard feedback form is dynamic. It collects users' comments and also forwards pertinent information about the failed query. By default, the form sends the information to the Microsoft support staff for analysis. If you want to redirect information to your own organization's support staff, you can customize the form and create a custom *Active Server Pages* (ASP) file to handle the information from the form.

To customize the feedback form, change the following three options in the sample Answiz.asp file.

Option	Description
f_log=1	Set to **0** to disable logging of users' questions. Default is **1**.
f_redirect_to_MS=1	Set to **0** to disable sending of information to the Office Update Web site. Default is **1**.
where_if_not_MS="alert.htm"	Set to the URL of the page you want users to see after they submit the feedback form. This option is valid only if you have set the redirect option to **0**.

Toolbox

The Office Resource Kit includes a sample ASP file for customizing the Answer Wizard feedback form. For information about installing the Answiz.asp file and other sample HTML files, see "Help on the Web" on page 785.

Managing Security

Microsoft Office 2000 security features can help you protect information that is shared over your network or the Internet.

In This Chapter

Protecting Against Macro Viruses

Macro viruses can spread quickly when documents are shared, causing data corruption or loss. Microsoft Office 2000 provides advanced methods for protecting against macro viruses by using virus scanning applications and digital signatures.

Scanning for Viruses Before You Open an Office Document

Microsoft Word, Microsoft Excel, and Microsoft PowerPoint now allow virus scanning programs to check documents before you open them. When you open a document in Word, Excel, or PowerPoint, the document is checked by the virus scanning program before it is opened in the Office application.

Virus scanning programs that can check Office 2000 documents are registered on the computer when the programs are installed. This registration enables Word, Excel, or PowerPoint to determine how to pass the documents through the scanning program before the documents are opened.

When a virus scanning program is registered to scan Word, Excel, or PowerPoint documents, the **Security** dialog box indicates that scanning is registered. (To open the **Security** dialog box, point to **Macro** on the **Tools** menu, and then click **Security**.) If no virus scanning program is registered to scan Office documents, the **Security** dialog box indicates **No virus scanners installed**.

Documents that are password-protected cannot be checked by virus scanning programs because these documents are encrypted and cannot be read. Also, shared workbooks in Excel are encrypted and cannot be read. When you open a password-protected document or a shared workbook, the virus scanning program is bypassed.

Signing Macros Digitally to Verify the Source

Macro viruses are programs written in the macro languages of applications. These viruses can do serious harm to programs and data. Without proper precautions, macro viruses can be transmitted to a computer and stored in the Normal template or a global template when an infected document is opened in an Office application.

In Office 97, Microsoft Word, Excel, and PowerPoint can protect against macro viruses by warning that the document being opened contains macros. You can then choose to disable the macros or keep them enabled when you open the document.

Office 2000 expands on macro virus protection by allowing macros in documents to be digitally signed. A *digital signature* is binary data that is calculated by applying an algorithm to the original data (in this case, the macro code) and a numeric private key. The private key has a corresponding *public key*.

When a second algorithm is applied to the digital signature and the public key, the algorithm determines whether the data was signed by a user with access to the private key. Therefore, the digital signature can be used to prove that the data is really from the user or source that the digital signature claims to be from.

Using certificates to sign macros

A *certificate* is a set of data that completely identifies an entity and is issued by a *certificate authority* only after that authority has verified the entity's identity. The data set includes the public key tendered to the entity. The entity obtains a certificate that also includes the private key, so the certificate can be used to sign data.

A certificate that contains only a public key is called a public certificate. A certificate that contains public and private keys is called a private certificate or personal certificate. Certificates are automatically installed as needed and stored in the registry by the operating system.

VeriSign is an example of a certificate authority. You can also produce your own certificates by using Windows NT Certificate Services or by using the Selfcert.exe program. This program is installed with the Office Tools/Digital Signatures feature in Office Setup.

Note   Certificates created with Selfcert.exe are not verified by any authority, and any user with access to Selfcert.exe can create them. Therefore, it is recommended that users not trust self-signed certificates unless they know for sure that the certificate is valid. (You can determine who signed a certificate by viewing its properties.)

Not all certificates can be used for all security needs. Types of certificates include the following:

Identity   Proves user identity when the user is authenticated on a server computer.

E-mail   Digitally signs e-mail content to prove that it was produced by a specific user; encrypts the content so that it cannot be read or tampered with on a network.

Code-signing   Digitally signs code to prove that it was produced by a specific publisher; prevents code tampering.

When you sign Office macros, you must use a code-signing certificate. A public version of the certificate is stored with the digital signature in signed files. Personal certificates, which can be used to sign and encrypt the macros because they contain private keys, are also stored on the client computer.

Managing certificates with Internet Explorer

You can manage the certificates installed on a computer by using Microsoft Internet Explorer.

▶ **To manage certificates by using Internet Explorer 4.x**

1   On the **View** menu, click **Internet Options**, and then click the **Content** tab.

2   In the **Certificates** area, click **Personal** to manage the personal certificates installed on your computer.

3   To manage the list of trusted certificate authorities that is stored on your computer, click **Authorities**.

▶ **To manage certificates by using Internet Explorer 5**

1   On the **Tools** menu, click **Internet Options**, and then click the **Content** tab.

2   To display the **Certificate Manager**, click **Certificates**.

   Use the Certificate Manager to manage the personal certificates, public certificates, and list of trusted certificate authorities on your computer.

Using certificate timestamps

Certificates are given expiration dates after which the certificates are no longer valid. Expiration dates are chosen so that the amount of time between the issue date and expiration date of a certificate is too small for anyone to make the required computations to produce a private key from a public key and thereby falsify digital signatures.

If a macro is signed with a certificate after the certificate has expired, the signature is not considered valid. Certificate authorities provide a certified timestamp that can be applied as part of a digital signature when a document is signed. The timestamp proves when the document was signed and can be compared to the expiration date of the certificate to verify that the document was signed before the certificate expired.

You can specify the URL of a timestamp authority for Office to use in the following registry key:

HKEY_CURRENT_USER\Software\Microsoft\VBA\Security

Within this subkey, you specify values for the following entries:

- **TimeStampURL**   **String** value that provides the URL.
- **TimeStampRetryCount** . **DWORD** value that specifies how many times to attempt to connect to the timestamp URL.
- **TimeStampRetryDelay**   **DWORD** value that specifies how many seconds to wait between retries of the timestamp URL.

Signing macros by using the Visual Basic Editor

You sign Office 2000 macros in the Visual Basic Editor before saving the macro.

▶ **To sign a macro in the Visual Basic Editor**

1 With the macro open in the Visual Basic Editor, click **Digital Signature** on the **Tools** menu.

2 Click **Choose**.

3 In the **Select Certificate** dialog box, select the certificate you want to use.

   All personal certificates installed on your computer are listed.

Setting Security Levels in Office Applications

Microsoft Word, Microsoft Excel, and Microsoft PowerPoint can be set to a high, medium, or low security level.

High security   Macros must be signed by a trusted source. Otherwise, macros in documents are automatically disabled without notice when the documents are opened. Word is set to the high security level by default.

Medium security   Users are prompted to enable or disable macros in documents when the documents are opened. Excel and PowerPoint are set to the medium security level by default.

Low security   No macro checking is performed when documents are opened and all macros are enabled. This security level is not recommended because no protection is active when it is selected.

▶ **To set the security level in Word, Excel, or PowerPoint**

1   On the **Tools** menu, point to **Macro**, and then click **Security**.

2   Click the **Security Level** tab, and then select a security level.

Specifying trusted sources

When you open a document with signed macros in Word, Excel, or PowerPoint, and the certificate has not previously been trusted, you can choose to trust the source. If you choose to trust the source, all documents with macros signed by that source are trusted and are automatically enabled when documents are opened, regardless of the security level set for the application.

You can choose to trust all installed add-ins and templates so that any files that are installed with Microsoft Office or added to the Office templates folder are trusted even though the files are not signed.

▶ **To specify trusted sources in Word, Excel, or PowerPoint**

1   On the **Tools** menu in Word, Excel, or PowerPoint, point to **Macro**, and then click **Security**.

2   To view or remove sources that have been trusted, click the **Trusted Sources** tab.

3   To trust add-ins and templates that are installed with Office, select **Trust all installed add-ins and templates** check box.

Presetting trusted sources for all users in your organization

To preset trusted sources on users' computers, you can use the Profile Wizard to save your security settings. On a computer that has Office 2000 installed, open documents with macros signed by the sources you want to trust. Choose to trust the sources as you open each document.

Use the Profile Wizard to create an *OPS file* based on your configuration. Then use the Office Custom Installation Wizard to include your OPS file on the *administrative installation point*. When users run Office Setup from the administrative installation point, the sources that you specified as trusted sources are also specified as trusted sources on users' computers.

Tip   You can use a system policy to preset security levels in Word, Excel, or PowerPoint. In the System Policy Editor, set the **User\Microsoft** *application* **2000\Tools |Macro\Security\Security Level** policy. You can also set a system policy to specify whether to trust all installed add-ins and templates. In the System Policy Editor, set the **User\Microsoft** *application* **2000 \Tools | Macro\Security\Trust all installed add-ins and templates** policy. For more information about the System Policy Editor, see "Using the System Policy Editor" on page 296.

See also

- You can use Windows NT Certificate Services to create and manage certificates. Windows NT Certificate Services is available in the Microsoft Windows NT 4.0 Option Pack. For more information about Windows NT Certificate Services, see Windows NT 4.0 Option Pack online Help.

- For a list of certificate authorities that you can use, see the Microsoft SecurityAdvisor Web site at http://backoffice.microsoft.com/securitypartners/.

- You can use a virus scanning program and security levels with Microsoft Outlook 2000 in the same way you can with Excel, Word, and PowerPoint. For more information, see "Using Security Features in Outlook" on page 414.

- You can use the Profile Wizard to preset security levels and trusted sources. For more information, see "Profile Wizard" on page 255.

- You can use the System Policy Editor to preset security levels and specify whether to trust installed add-ins and templates. For more information, see "Using the System Policy Editor" on page 296.

Protecting Excel and Word Documents

Several features are available in Microsoft Excel and Microsoft Word to protect documents or portions of documents with passwords and to encrypt documents. These application-level security measures provide protection in addition to any security measures you implement at the operating system level.

Protecting Excel Workbooks

Microsoft Excel supports three levels of workbook file protection. The user who creates a workbook has read/write permission to a workbook and controls the protection level. The three levels of workbook protection are:

- File open protection

  Excel requires the user to enter a password to open a workbook.

- File modify protection

  Excel requires the user to enter a password to open the workbook with read/write permission. The user can click **Read Only** at the prompt, and Excel opens the workbook read-only.

- Read-only recommended protection

  Excel prompts the user to open the workbook as read-only. If the user clicks **No** at the prompt, Excel opens the workbook with read/write permission, unless the workbook has other password protection.

Excel encrypts password-protected workbooks by using the symmetric *encryption* routine known as 40-bit RC4. Because protected workbooks are encrypted, they are not indexed by Find Fast or by the Microsoft Office Server Extensions (OSE) search feature.

Note   Strong encryption such as RC4 is banned in France. If a user's locale setting in **Regional Settings** in Control Panel is set to **French (Standard)**, that user is not able to open an Office document that is password protected. Nor can the user save an Office document with RC4 encryption. The user can, however, use XOR encryption by saving an Office document with password protection.

In addition to protecting an entire workbook, you can also protect specific elements from unauthorized changes. This method is not as secure as using a password to protect the entire workbook because Excel does not use encryption when you protect only specific elements.

For example, cells that are hidden on a protected worksheet can be viewed if a user copies across a range on the protected worksheet that includes the hidden cells, opens a new workbook, pastes, and then uses the **Unhide** command to display the cells.

Tip   To ensure the strongest security on a workbook, use a password to protect the entire workbook.

The specific elements that you can protect in a workbook include the following:

- Structure of a workbook

  Worksheets and chart sheets in a protected workbook cannot be moved, deleted, hidden, unhidden, or renamed, and new sheets cannot be inserted.

- Windows in a workbook

  Windows in a protected workbook cannot be moved, resized, hidden, unhidden, or closed. Windows in a protected workbook are sized and positioned the same way each time the workbook is opened.

- Cells on a worksheet or items on a chart sheet

  Contents of protected cells on a worksheet cannot be edited. Protected items on a chart sheet cannot be modified.

- Graphic objects on a worksheet or chart sheet

  Protected graphic objects cannot be moved or edited.

- Formulas on a worksheet

  Protected formulas cannot be edited.

  Tip   You can also hide a formula so that it does not appear in the formula bar but the formula results appear in the cell.

- Scenarios on a worksheet

   Definitions of protected scenarios cannot be changed.

- Change histories of shared workbooks

   Protected change histories cannot be cleared by the user of a shared workbook or by the user of a copy of a workbook that is to be merged.

Caution   If a user assigns password protection to a workbook and then forgets the password, you cannot open the workbook, gain access to its data in another workbook through links, remove protection from the workbook, or recover data from the workbook. Advise your users to keep a list of passwords and corresponding workbook, worksheet, and chart sheet names in a safe place.

Protecting Word Documents

Microsoft Word supports three levels of document protection. The user who creates a document has read/write permission to a document and controls the protection level. The three levels of document protection are:

- File open protection

   Word requires the user to enter a password to open a document.

- File modify protection

   Word requires the user to enter a password to open the document with read/write permission. If the user clicks **Read Only** at the prompt, Word opens the document as read-only.

- Read-only recommended protection

   Word prompts the user to open the document as read-only. If the user clicks **No** at the prompt, Word opens the document with read/write permission, unless the document has other password protection.

Word encrypts password-protected documents by using the symmetric encryption routine known as RC4. Because protected documents are encrypted, they are not indexed by Find Fast or by the Microsoft Office Server Extensions (OSE) search feature.

Note   Strong *encryption* such as RC4 is banned in France. If a user's locale setting in **Regional Settings** in Control Panel is set to **French (Standard)**, that user is not able to open an Office document that is password protected. Nor can the user save an Office document with RC4 encryption. The user can, however, use XOR encryption by saving an Office document with password protection.

In addition to protecting an entire document, you can also protect specific elements from unauthorized changes. This method is not as secure as using a password to protect the entire document because Word does not use encryption when you protect only specific elements.

For example, field codes can be viewed in a text editor such as Notepad even if forms or sections of a document are protected.

The specific elements that you can protect in a document include the following:

- Tracked changes

  Changes made to the document can be neither accepted nor rejected, and change tracking cannot be turned off.

- Comments

  Users can insert comments into the document but cannot change the content of the document.

- Forms or sections

  Users can make changes only in form fields or unprotected sections of a document.

Caution   If a user assigns password protection to a document and then forgets the password, you cannot open the document, gain access to its data in another document through links, remove protection from the document, or recover data from the document. Advise your users to keep a list of passwords and corresponding document names in a safe place.

Using Security Features in Access

As a workgroup administrator, you might want to initiate or oversee workgroup-wide security practices for protecting Microsoft Access database applications. Access 2000 includes options for protecting databases and applications. These options are independent of any additional security measures at the operating system level.

Strategies for Securing an Access Database

Microsoft Access 2000 supports several levels and methods of file protection:

- User access restriction

  You can use startup options to restrict access to default menus and toolbars, the Database window, and special keys.

- File open protection

  You can set a password to control opening the database.

- Source code protection

  You can save an application as an *MDE file* to remove Visual Basic for Applications (VBA) source code and prevent changes to the design of forms, reports, and modules.

- Database *encryption*

  You can use database encryption to prevent unauthorized users from viewing the objects in an application with a disk editor or other utility program. You can use encryption with all other methods of protecting an application.

- *User-level security*

  You can use user-level security to apply the most powerful and flexible method of protecting an application. However, establishing user-level security is a complex process that might exceed your requirements.

The strategy that you use depends on the extent of security you need and how the application is used.

Restricting User Access with Startup Options

In an environment where strict security is not required, you can use Startup options to restrict access to default menus and toolbars, the Database window, and special keys. To perform the following procedure, the application must have a Startup form and a custom menu bar that contains only the commands you want to make available to users.

You can use this method to secure both MDB and ADP files. You can also use Startup options with other forms of security.

▶ **To restrict user access with Startup options**

1 On the **Tools** menu, click **Startup**.

2 To display the rest of the dialog box, click **Advanced**.

3 In the **Display Form** box, click the name of your Startup form.

4 In the **Menu Bar** box, click the name of your menu bar.

5 Clear the following check boxes: **Allow Full Menus**, **Allow Default Shortcut Menus**, **Display Database Window**, **Allow Built-in Toolbars**, **Allow Toolbar/Menu Changes**, and **Use Access Special Keys**.

After you have selected the Startup options you want, you must set the **AllowBypassKey** property to **False** in Visual Basic for Applications (VBA). This step prevents users from using the SHIFT key to bypass the settings in the **Startup** dialog box. You can also set the Startup options and properties used in this procedure by using VBA.

Note   A user familiar with Visual Basic for Applications can bypass this method of security by setting the **AllowBypassKey** property back to **True**. If you want a higher level of security, establish *user-level security* in addition to setting Startup options.

See also

• For information about creating a Startup form or custom menu bar, see Microsoft Access 2000 online Help.

• You can set many other Startup options and properties by using Visual Basic for Applications. For information about how to set VBA properties for Access, see Microsoft Access Visual Basic Reference Help.

• The highest level of security for an Access database is user-level security, which you can use with or in place of Startup options that restrict user access. For more information, see "Setting User-Level Security" on page 390.

Setting a Password to Prevent Opening a Database

Assigning a password to a database is an easy way to prevent unauthorized users from opening an application. Use this approach when you need to control which users can open the database, but not what they do after providing the correct database password.

Important   Before you set the database password, make a backup copy of the database. Also, close the database before you set the password; if the database is located on a server or in a shared folder, make sure no other user has it open.

▶ **To set a database password**

1   On the **File** menu, click **Open**.

2   Navigate to the folder that contains the database and select it in the file list, click the arrow next to the **Open** button, and then click **Open Exclusive**.

3   On the **Tools** menu, point to **Security**, and then click **Set Database Password**.

4   In the **Password** box, type the password. Passwords are case sensitive.

5   In the **Verify** box, type the password again to confirm it, and then click **OK**.

The password is now set. Each time a user tries to open the database, a dialog box appears that requests the database password.

Caution   If you or a user in your workgroup assigns password protection to a database and then forgets the password, you cannot open the database, gain access to its data from a *data access page* or from linked tables, remove protection from the database, or recover data from the tables. Keep a list of your passwords and their corresponding database names in a safe place.

When you set a database password, the **Set Database Password** command changes to **Unset Database Password**. To clear a database password, open the database in exclusive mode, click **Unset Database Password** (**Tools** menu, **Security** submenu), type the correct password in the **Password** box, then confirm it in the **Verify** box.

Administrator permissions

Any user who knows the database password and has access to the **Unset Database Password** command can change or clear the password, unless you remove the Administer permission on the database for all users and groups except the database administrator.

Similarly, if you want to prevent users from setting a password on a database, you must remove the Administer permission on the database for those users or groups. By default, the Users group, the Admins group, and the creator of the database all have Administer permission on the database.

You can remove the Administer permission without establishing *user-level security*, but users can restore the Administer permission by using the **User and Group Permissions** command on the **Security** submenu (**Tools** menu). To ensure that no unauthorized user can set, clear, or change a database password, you must establish user-level security in addition to removing the Administer permission.

System Policy Tip   You can use a system policy to disable the user interface for setting database passwords. In the System Policy Editor, set the **Microsoft Access 2000\Tools | Options\Disable items in user interface\Predefined\Disable command bar buttons and menu items** policy and select the **Tools | Security | Set Database Password** check box. For more information about the System Policy Editor, see "Using the System Policy Editor" on page 296.

Linked tables

If you use a password to protect an Access database that contains tables linked to another database, Access stores the password in an unencrypted form when the link is established. Any user who can open the database that contains the link can open the linked table. To avoid compromising the security of the password-protected database, implement user-level security instead to control access to sensitive data in the database.

See also

- Database passwords do not prevent an unauthorized user from using a disk editor or other utility program to read your data without opening the database. However, you can increase security by encrypting your database. For more information, see "Encrypting a Database" on page 389.

- You cannot synchronize a replicated database when a database password has been set. If you plan to replicate the database, establish user-level security instead, which does not interfere with *replica* synchronization. For more information, see "Setting User-Level Security" on page 390.

Protecting Source Code with an MDE or ADE File

If your primary security concern is protecting your Visual Basic for Applications (VBA) code and the design of your forms and reports, you can save your *MDB file* as an *MDE file*, or your *ADP file* as an *ADE file*. An MDE file is a Microsoft Access database file with all modules compiled and all editable source code removed. An ADE file is an Access project file with all modules compiled and all editable source code removed.

Saving your database as an MDE or ADE file creates a separate copy of the database that contains no VBA source code and is smaller than the original database. Your code is compiled and continues to run, but it can't be viewed or edited. Additionally, users can't view or modify the design of forms, reports, and modules. Users can still view and modify the design of your database's relationships, tables, queries, and macros after you have saved the database as an MDE file; however, you can establish *user-level security* if you want to protect the design of these objects.

Similarly, saving an ADP file as an ADE file doesn't protect the design of database diagrams, tables, views, stored procedures, and macros; but you can establish security on the server itself to protect any of these objects except macros.

Saving your database as an MDE or ADE file also prevents users from performing the following actions:

- Creating forms, reports, or modules.

- Adding or deleting references to object libraries or databases by using the **References** command (**Tools** menu).

- Using the Object Browser.

- Changing code by using the properties or methods of the Access or VBA *object models*.

- Importing or exporting forms, reports, macros, or modules.

   In an MDE database, tables and queries can be imported from or exported to other types of database files. In ADE files, only tables can be imported from or exported to other types of database files.

Note   The process of saving a database as an MDE or ADE file compiles all modules and compacts the destination database, so there is no need to perform these steps before saving a database as an MDE or ADE file.

▶ **To save a database as an MDE or ADE file**

1   Open the Microsoft Access database (MDB file) or Microsoft Access project (ADP file) you want to work with.

If the Access database is being shared on a network, first make sure that no other users have it open.

2   On the **Tools** menu, point to **Database Utilities**, and then click **Make MDE File** or **Make ADE File**.

3   In the **Save MDE As** or **Save ADE As** dialog box, enter a file name and the location where you want to save the file, and then click **Save**.

The original file is unchanged and a new copy is saved as an MDE or ADE file with the file name and location you specified.

Important   Be sure to keep your original Microsoft Access database (MDB file) or Microsoft project (ADP file) in a safe place. If you need to modify the design of forms, reports, or modules in your file, you must open the original file, modify the objects, and then save the file again as an MDE or ADE file. Also, databases saved as MDE or ADE files in Access 2000 cannot be opened or converted in later versions of Access. To convert or open it in later versions of Access, you must use the original file.

Saving as an MDE or ADE file doesn't create a run-time version of the file. To use an MDE or ADE file, users must have Access 2000 installed. If you have Microsoft Office 2000 Developer, you can save an MDE file and then use the Packaging and Deployment Wizard to create a Setup program that installs the run-time version of Access and your MDE file.

Modifying MDE and ADE files

If you need to modify the design of forms, reports, or modules in a database saved as an MDE or ADE file, you must open the original MDB or ADP file, modify the items, and then save it as an MDE or ADE file again.

Saving an MDB file that contains tables as an MDE file creates complications when you are reconciling different versions of the data if you need to modify the design of the database later. For this reason, saving a database as an MDE file is most appropriate for the front end of an application that has been split into a front-end/back-end database, in which the back end contains only tables and the front end contains the remaining objects.

An ADP file can only be a front end (client) to server tables, database diagrams, views, and stored procedures. That is, it can contain only connections to these objects, so this isn't an issue with an ADP file saved as an ADE file.

Using other forms of security with MDE files

Saving a database as an MDE file is a good way to protect the code and the design of forms and reports in a database application, without requiring users to log on and without having to manage the user accounts and *permissions* required by user-level security. However, an MDE file doesn't control how users gain access to tables, queries, or macros.

If you want more control over these database objects, establish user-level security for your MDB file before you save it as an MDE file. User-level security settings are preserved in the new MDE file. Alternatively, you can split your MDB file into a front-end/back-end database and establish user-level security for your front-end database to protect access to queries and macros and for your back-end database to protect access to your back-end tables. In this case, you would save only your front-end database as an MDE file to protect the design of forms, reports, and code.

After you have secured your MDB with user-level security, and you want to save it as an MDE file, you must meet the following requirements:

- Before starting Access, you must use the Workgroup Administrator program or the **/wrkgrp** command-line option to join the *workgroup information file* (.mdw) that was in use when the database was created.

- Your user account must have Open/Run and Open Exclusive permissions for the database.

- Your user account must have Modify Design or Administer permission for any tables in the database, or you must be the owner of any tables in the database.

- Your user account must have Read Design permission for all objects in the database.

You can also use a database password to control who can open an MDE file, but you must set the password in the original database before you save it as an MDE file. The database password is preserved in the new MDE database.

Saving an MDE file that references another database

If you try to save an MDB or ADP file that references another MDB, ADP, or add-in database (MDA file) as an MDE or ADE file, Access displays an error message and doesn't let you complete the operation. To save an MDB or ADP file that references another file, you must save all files in the chain of references as MDE or ADE files, starting from the first file referenced.

After you save the first file as an MDE or ADE file, use the **References** dialog box (**Tools** menu) to update the reference in the next file to point to the new MDE or ADE file before saving it as an MDE or ADE file, and so on.

For example, if Database1.mdb references Database2.mdb, which references Database3.mda, proceed as follows:

1   Save Database3.mda as Database3.mde.

2   Open Database2.mdb, and change its reference to point to the new Database3.mde.

3   Save Database2.mdb as Database2.mde.

4   Open Database1.mdb, and change its reference to point to the new Database2.mde.

5   Save Database1.mdb as Database1.mde.

See also

- Saving your database as an MDE file prevents all users (including database administrators) from modifying the design of forms, reports, and modules. If you want more control and flexibility in these areas, establish user-level security instead. For more information, see "Setting User-Level Security" on page 390.

- To save a replicated database as an MDE file, you must first remove replication system fields, tables, and properties. For more information about making a replicated database a regular database, see Microsoft Access 2000 online Help.

Encrypting a Database

If you want to protect your secured database from unauthorized access by someone who is using a disk editor or other utility program, you can encrypt the database. *Encryption* makes a database indecipherable, which protects it from unauthorized viewing or use. Encryption is particularly useful when you transmit a database electronically, or when your store it on floppy disk, tape, or compact disc.

Before you can encrypt or decrypt a Microsoft Access database, you must be either the owner of the database or a member of the Admins group of the *workgroup information file* that contains the accounts used to secure the database. You must also be able to open the database in exclusive mode. If the database is secured with *user-level security*, exclusive mode requires you to have the Open/Run and Open Exclusive *permissions*.

Note   Encrypting an unsecured database has no effect because anybody can open the database with Access or Visual Basic for Applications (VBA) and gain full access to all objects in the database.

The User-Level Security Wizard automatically encrypts your database. To encrypt or decrypt a database, start Access without opening a database, and then click the **Encrypt/Decrypt Database** command (**Tools** menu, **Security** submenu). When you encrypt a database by using the same file name as that of the original database, Access deletes the original unencrypted file after the encryption process is completed. If an error occurs during encryption, however, Access retains the original file.

Note   Encrypting a database slows its performance by up to 15 percent. Also, an encrypted database cannot be compressed by programs such as DriveSpace® or PKZIP.

Setting User-Level Security

User-level security is the most flexible and secure method of protecting sensitive data, code, and object design in a database application developed in Microsoft Access. In addition, user-level security is the only form of Access security that allows you to establish different levels of access to sensitive data and objects.

Unlike the security models of most other database systems, the primary form of security in Access is *user-level security* rather than *share-level security*. Access user-level security is similar to the security used in most network environments, such as Microsoft Windows NT Server versions 3.51 and 4.0. With user-level security, users are authenticated before they open a database. Users log on to the system with a name and a password, which are compared to a database of user account information in a *workgroup information file* or *system database*.

How user-level security works

When a user opens a secured database, Access determines the user's level of access to an object (including the database itself) by checking the set of *permissions* assigned to that user for that object. Different users and groups can have different permissions for the same objects. When a user tries to perform an action on an object—such as opening a form, running a query, or modifying the data in a table—Access checks to see whether the user, or any of the groups to which the user belongs, has the necessary permissions to carry out the operation.

In contrast, database systems that provide share-level security associate passwords with specific objects, and users must supply passwords to gain access to the objects. A user's level of access is determined by the kind of password that user has been given. For example, managers might be given an update password for a table, allowing them to change records, and general staff members might be given a read password, allowing them to view records but not modify them.

You can create a similar system with Access user-level security by creating a Managers group with Update Data permission and a Staff group with only Read Data permission and then assigning each user to the appropriate group. Users do not supply passwords when accessing the objects, because the members are identified as members of the appropriate group when they log on to a system that has Access user-level security.

Storing workgroup and permission information

Access stores information about users and groups in a database called a *workgroup information file*, commonly referred to as the *system database*. A workgroup information file stores the following information:

- Name of each user and group
- List of users that make up each group
- Encrypted logon password of each user
- *Security identifier* (SID) of each user and group

Each workgroup information file defines a workgroup and can be used by many Access databases. A workgroup is a group of users in a multiuser environment who share data and the same workgroup information file. You manage users, their passwords, and the groups they are assigned to in the **User and Group Accounts** dialog box (**Tools** menu, **Security** submenu).

Permissions that you assign to users and groups for the objects in a database are stored in hidden system tables within the database. Even if a new workgroup information file is created, the permissions associated with the objects in a database do not change. You assign permissions on the **Permissions** and **Change Owner** tabs in the **User and Group Permissions** dialog box; this information affects the objects in the open database, but not the workgroup information file.

The following illustration shows how these elements of Access user-level security are related.

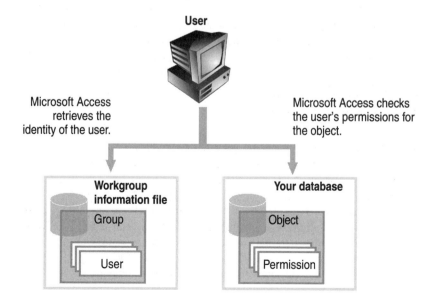

User

Microsoft Access retrieves the identity of the user.

Microsoft Access checks the user's permissions for the object.

Workgroup information file

Group

User

Your database

Object

Permission

The location of the workgroup information file is specified in the Windows registry. You can create a new workgroup information file or specify which file to use with the Workgroup Administrator program or the **/wrkgrp** command-line option.

Creating user and group accounts

You use the **User and Group Accounts** dialog box (**Tools** menu, **Security** submenu) to create new user and group accounts for your workgroup. When you create a new user or group account, you supply a name for the user or group as well as a *personal identifier* (PID). Access sends the user or group name and the associated PID to an *encryption* program to generate the SID for that account. If you send the same user name and PID back into the encryption program, you get the same SID. This gives you the ability to re-create user accounts if your workgroup information file becomes corrupted or is lost.

Access uses the SID to uniquely identify and validate users and groups. When a user requests access to objects, Access uses the user's or group's SID for identification (instead of the user name and password).

Saving names and personal identifiers

Be sure to write down the exact, case-sensitive names and PIDs that you use to create user and group accounts and keep them in a safe place. If your workgroup information file is damaged or lost and you need to re-create it, you must reenter the exact names and PIDs to re-create identical SIDs for the user and group accounts.

Use the Workgroup Administrator program to create an identical workgroup information file to contain these accounts by reentering the name, organization, and *workgroup ID* (WID) that you used when you created it originally.

An Access workgroup information file contains the following default user and group accounts:

- Admin
- Admins
- Users

Admin account

Admin is the default user account. Before user-level security is established, all users are automatically logged on using the Admin user account. Therefore, the Admin user owns and has full permissions on all objects created in the database. Because the Admin user's SID is identical across all installations of Access and Visual Basic, all objects that the Admin user owns or has permissions on are open to anyone using another copy of Access or Visual Basic for Applications (VBA).

When you establish user-level security, make sure that the Admin user does not own or have any permissions on objects that you want to secure. For assistance in securing objects, run the User-Level Security Wizard provided with Access.

Admins account

Admins is the workgroup administrator's group account. Before user-level security is established, the default Admin user is the only member of the Admins group. Members of the Admins group have the power to perform actions such as changing permissions, modifying user and group memberships, and clearing users' passwords.

Members of the Admins group that was in use when you created the database can also grant permissions on any object in that database. For example, if a user is a member of the Admins group, that user might not have permissions to open a particular table, but can nevertheless grant himself or herself permission to open that table. It is recommended that an Admins group have at least one member at all times.

Caution   Do not delete the last member of the Admins group. Only the owner of a database object has irrevocable permissions for that object. If the owner's account ever becomes corrupted or deleted, and cannot be re-created because you don't have that user's name and PID, there is no way to recover the permissions for that object. In other words, there is no member of the Admins group to fall back on.

Users account

Users is the default group account comprising all user accounts. Access automatically adds user accounts to the Users group when you create them. Any permissions assigned explicitly to the Users group are available to all users in all installations of Access and Visual Basic for Applications. This is true because, like the SID for the Admins group, the SID for the Users group is identical in all workgroup information files.

By default, the Users group has full permissions for all newly created objects. When you establish user-level security, make sure that the Users group does not own or have permissions on objects that you want to secure.

Creating a secure workgroup information file

The Access Setup program uses only the user's name and the company name provided during Setup to create the SID for the Admins group of the default workgroup information file. Because these two values are available from the Access **Help** menu, unauthorized users trying to breach security could re-create an identical Admins account by using the Workgroup Administrator program to create a new workgroup information file with these values, and then add themselves to the Admins group.

When establishing user-level security, use the Workgroup Administrator program or the User-Level Security Wizard to create a new workgroup information file, making sure to enter the WID, which is a value known only to you. This step ensures that the new workgroup information file contains a new Admins group with a unique, secure SID.

Because the SID of the Admins group is based on the exact, case-sensitive values you type in the **Name**, **Organization**, and **Workgroup ID** boxes, record and keep these values in a safe place. If the workgroup information file is lost or damaged, you can re-create it with an identical Admins group by reentering these three values. Members of this re-created Admins group can grant themselves permissions on all objects that were created when the original workgroup information file was in effect.

Setting security for replicated databases

Replicated databases use the same security model as nonreplicated databases. Users' permissions on database objects are determined at the time they start Access and log on. You must make sure the same security information is available at each location where a *replica* is used.

You can do this by making the identical workgroup information file available to users at each location where a replica is used. Although the workgroup information file cannot be replicated, it can be manually copied to each location.

Alternatively, you can create a new workgroup information file at each location and then re-create the required user and group accounts needed by entering the same user and group names with their associated PIDs.

Note Modifications to permissions are considered design changes and can be made only in the Design Master replica.

By default, Administer permission is granted to the Users group, the Admins group, and the creator of the database. If security is to be maintained, you must restrict this permission to selected users.

Setting permissions

Access permissions fall into one of two categories. *Explicit permissions* are those you explicitly grant to an individual user. When an explicit permission is granted to a user, no other users are affected. *Implicit permissions*, by contrast, are granted to a group. Because a group contains more than one user, all users in a group receive the permissions granted to the group. If a user is added to a group, that user automatically inherits all the implicit permissions of that group.

The easiest way to administrate a secure workgroup is to create new groups and assign permissions to the groups, rather than to individual users. Later you can change individual users' permissions by adding or removing them from groups. In a simple situation, you might want to use only the default groups to define permissions—assigning administrators to the Admins group and all other users to the Users group. If you do this, keep in mind that because the Users group is identical across all installations of Access, any permissions that you assign to the Users group are available to all users of Access.

For a higher level of security, revoke all permissions for the Users group, create your own groups, and assign permissions to them. There is no need to create an alternative to the Admins group, as long as you enter a secure WID when you create a new workgroup information file. By doing so, you ensure that the Admins group is unique to that file.

When a user tries to perform an operation on an object, the user's security level is determined by the least restrictive of the permissions explicitly granted to the user and the permissions implicitly granted to the groups to which the user belongs. For example, if a user has explicit Read permission for a table but no Write permission, and that same user also belongs to a group that has Write permission for the table, the user can write to the table because of the higher level of the implicit Write permission.

You can set permissions on all of the objects in the database except for modules and the links to *data access pages*. Access provides no form of security for data access page links other than control over who can open a database, but you can password-protect all of the modules stored in a database by locking the Visual Basic for Applications project.

Permissions for objects can be changed by:

- Members of the Admins group of the workgroup information file in use when the database was created.
- The owner of the object.
- Any user who has Administer permission on the object.

Permissions for a database can be changed only by the owner of the database or by members of the Admins group.

Revoking permissions

Even though users might not be able to perform an action at a given moment, they might be able to grant themselves permissions to perform the action. This is true if the user is a member of the Admins group of the workgroup information file in use when the database was created, or if the user is the owner of an object.

The following table summarizes the permissions that you can revoke or assign as they are identified in the **User and Group Permissions** dialog box.

This permission	Permits a user to perform these actions on database objects
Open/Run	Open a database, form, or report; or run a macro.
Open Exclusive	Open a database in exclusive mode.
Read Design	View tables, queries, forms, reports, and macros in Design view.
Modify Design	View and change the design of tables, queries, forms, reports, and macros; or delete these objects.
Administer	For databases, set database password, replicate a database, and change startup properties.
	For tables, queries, forms, reports, and macros, have full access to these objects and data, including ability to assign permissions.
Read Data	View data in tables and queries.
Update Data	View and modify data in tables and queries, but not insert or delete data.
Insert Data	View and insert data in tables and queries, but not modify or delete data.
Delete Data	View and delete data in tables and queries, but not modify or insert data.

Some permissions automatically include other permissions. For example, the Update Data permission for a table automatically includes the Read Data and Read Design permissions because they are needed to modify the data in a table. The Modify Design and Read Data permissions include the Read Design permission. For macros, the Read Design permission includes the Open/Run permission.

In most cases, you must assign Read Data and Read Design permissions for the table in the back-end database, and Modify Design permission for the table link defined in the front-end database so that users can access a linked table. If you want to restrict all access to the back-end tables but still allow users to view the data and relink the tables, remove all permissions on the back-end table and use queries in the front-end database with their **RunPermissions** property set to **Owner's.**

Note   When you edit an object and save it, the object retains its assigned permissions. However, if an object is saved with a new name, the associated permissions are lost, and you have to reassign them.

Why can't I revoke Administer permission for the Admins group?

In the Admins group, the Administer permission—the right to change permissions—cannot be revoked by using the Access user interface. Even if you clear the **Administer** check box on the **Permissions** tab in the **User and Group Permissions** dialog box (**Tools** menu, **Security** submenu) for the Admins group on an object, the permission remains. You can use DAO code to revoke the Administer permission, but this is not recommended because there is no way to grant the permission back again.

Instead, make sure that you are using a workgroup information file created with a secure WID, which ensures a unique and secure Admins group, and then make sure that only the appropriate users are assigned to the Admins group.

Ownership

Understanding the concept of ownership is crucial to understanding the Access security model. The user who creates an object owns that object. This ownership grants that user special privileges for that object; thus, that user can always assign or revoke permissions for that object. The owner of an object can always grant permissions on the object, even if a member of the Admins group has revoked his or her explicit permissions on it.

Before you establish user-level security, the default Admin user is the owner of the database and all the objects in it. To effectively manage security, you need to change the ownership of the database and all the objects in it. You can do this for all objects except the database itself on the **Change Owner** tab in the **User And Group Permissions** dialog box (**Tools** menu, **Security** submenu). However, you can't change the owner of a database on the **Change Owner** tab in the same way.

When you are using the Access user interface, the only way to transfer the ownership of all the objects and the database itself is to log on as the user who you want to own the database, create a new blank database, and then import all of the objects. However, when you run the User-Level Security Wizard to secure your database, it transfers ownership of the database and all of its objects by using code.

Transferring ownership of an object to another user can be achieved by logging on as that user and re-creating the object. To re-create an object, make a copy of the object, or import or export it to another database. To re-create an object, you must have Read Design permission for the object and, if the object is a table or query, you must also have Read Data permission.

Note These procedures don't change the ownership of queries whose **RunPermissions** property is set to **Owner's**. You can change ownership of a query only if you own the query, or if its **RunPermissions** property is set to **User's**.

See also

- You can set default permissions for all new objects in a database. This step reduces your administrative burden, because you do not need to keep checking to make sure that new objects are properly secured. For more information, see Microsoft Access online Help.

- For more information about using the Workgroup Administrator program or how the workgroup information file is specified in the registry, see Microsoft Access online Help.

Establishing Security with the User-Level Security Wizard

After you understand how the Microsoft Access *user-level security* model works, you can proceed with the steps to secure a database. Although you can perform individual steps yourself, the User-Level Security Wizard is the easiest and most reliable way to secure a database.

In Access 2000, the User-Level Security Wizard performs all the necessary steps for you and can even be run again on a secured database to modify previous settings. The User-Level Security Wizard performs the following actions to secure your Access database:

- Creates a new secure workgroup information file by using a secure *workgroup ID* (WID).

  You can also modify a workgroup information file previously created by running the User-Level Security Wizard or the Workgroup Administrator program. You can make the workgroup information file the default for the current installation of Access, or the wizard can create a Windows shortcut that uses the **/wrkgrp** command-line option to open your secured database by using the workgroup information file.

- Secures all selected database objects, and sets the *permissions* that are assigned to any new objects that users create after running the wizard.

- Secures the Visual Basic for Applications (VBA) project to protect access to all code modules (stand-alone modules, the modules behind forms and reports, and class modules) by setting a password.

  If the VBA project has been password-protected, you must unlock the project before running the wizard.

- Creates as many as seven predefined group accounts for the typical user roles.

  These groups include Backup Operators, Full Data Users, Full Permissions, New Data Users, Project Designers, Read-Only Users, and Update Data Users.

- Removes permissions on all objects for the default Users group.

  You can also grant permissions to the Users group for some objects. This option is useful for developers who don't want to require users to log on to the database and only want to secure certain objects.

- Creates and adds new user accounts to the workgroup information file, and allows you to assign passwords for each new user.

  If you choose to create a new workgroup information file, a new user account is created for you.

- Assigns users to the default Admins group account or to the selected predefined group accounts.

  At least one new user account must be assigned to the Admins group account to serve as the database administrator account. By default, the new user account created in the wizard is assigned to the default Admins group as the new database administrator account.

- Creates a backup copy of the current database, and secures the current database in place.

  The objects that you selected are secured by revoking all permissions on those objects for the default Users group. Ownership of the database and its objects is transferred to the new database administrator account. Finally, the secured database is encrypted.

- Formats a report that documents the values used to create the new workgroup information file and user accounts.

  Keep this report in a secure location in the event that you need to use these values to re-create the workgroup information file. This report also documents which objects have been secured.

▶ **To secure a database with the Access User-Level Security Wizard**

1 Open the database that you want to secure.

2 On the **Tools** menu, point to **Security**, and then click **User-Level Security Wizard**.

3 Follow the instructions in the wizard.

If you log on as a member of the Admins group, you can run the User-Level Security Wizard again on the new, secured database to create new users, modify permissions, and to assign users to groups.

Securing a front-end/back-end application

You can establish user-level security for a database that has been split into a back-end database that contains only tables and for a front-end database that contains the remaining objects as well as links to the tables in the back-end database.

▶ **To establish user-level security for a front-end/back-end database**

1   Assign users to the appropriate groups so that they have permissions to read, update, insert, or delete data in tables in the back-end database.

   –or–

   Remove all permissions for the tables and create queries in the front-end database that have the **RunPermissions** property set to **Owner's** and that use the tables in the back-end database. All users must be assigned to groups that have Open/Run permission for the **Database** object in the back-end database.

2   In the front-end database, grant users Modify Design permission for the table links.

3   When the users first install your database, have them run the Linked Table Manager (**Tools** menu, **Add-ins** submenu) from the front-end database to refresh the links to the tables in the back-end database in its new location.

Because users have Modify Design permission for the linked tables in the front-end database, they can reset the links to the back-end tables if the location of the back-end database changes. However, they can't make any modifications to the design of the tables in the back-end database.

Securing a database without requiring users to log on

If you want to secure some objects in a database, such as the code modules and the design of objects, but you do not care about establishing different levels of access for different groups of users, you might want to consider securing an application without requiring users to log on. You can do this by running the User-Level Security Wizard and granting the permissions you want available for all users to the Users group.

▶ **To secure your database without requiring users to log on**

1   Open the database that you want to secure.

2   On the **Tools** menu, point to **Security**, and then click **User-Level Security Wizard**.

3   When prompted by the wizard, click **Yes, I would like to grant some permissions to the Users group**.

4   Assign permissions to the Users group for objects that you want to make available to all users.

   Typical permissions include Read Data and Update Data permissions for tables and queries, and Open/Run permission for forms and reports. Don't give the Users group the permission to modify the design of tables and queries, and don't give users Administer permission for the database.

5   Distribute the database to users who are using the default workgroup information file that is created when Access is installed or to users who are using another file that allows users to start Access without logging on.

Important Do not distribute copies of the workgroup information file that was in use when you secured the database in this procedure. If you need to allow a user to administer your database, give a copy of the workgroup information file to that user only.

To perform administrative functions, you must use the workgroup information file that was in use when you secured the database, and you must log on as one of the members of that workgroup information file's Admins group in one of two ways:

- Temporarily define a password for the Admin user to reactivate the logon procedure, and then log on as a member of the Admins group.

  −or−

- Use the **/pwd** and **/user** command-line options to specify your password and user name when starting Access.

Removing User-Level Security

Securing a database is usually a one-way process. However, there might be instances when you want to remove security from your database. If you want to remove *user-level security*, perform the following procedure to reverse the process of securing your database.

Important Before you remove user-level security from the database, make a backup copy.

▶ **To remove user-level security**

1 Start Microsoft Access, and log on as a member of the Admins group.

   This can be the administrator account that you created when you secured the database, or it can be any member of the Admins group. Be sure that you're using your own secure workgroup information file when starting Access.

2 Open the database.

3 On the **Tools** menu, point to **Security**, and then click **User And Group Permissions**.

4 In the **User And Group Permissions** dialog box, assign full *permissions* to the Users group for the database and all the objects in the database.

   Because all users are automatically part of the Users group, this step has the effect of concealing security again.

5 Click the **Users** tab, click **Admin** in the **Name** box, and then click **Clear Password**.

   Clearing the password for the Admin user disables the **Logon** dialog box that is displayed when you start Access. All users are automatically logged on as the Admin user the next time they start Access. This step disables the **Logon** dialog box for all databases that are using the same workgroup information file.

6   Restart Access.

7   Create a new database, and then import all objects from the secured database.

You can accomplish this easily by using the **Import** command (**File** menu, **Get External Data** submenu).

The new database is completely unsecured. Anyone who can open the new database has full permissions on all its objects. The workgroup information file in use when the new database is created defines the Admins group for the new database.

Using the RunPermissions Property with User-Level Security

In order for Microsoft Access to display a table or query, it must read the design of that table or query. As a result, in order for a user to read and display the data in a table or query, that user must also have permission to read the design of the table or query.

If you don't want your users to see the design of your table or query, you can create a query and set its **RunPermissions** property to restrict their access to this information. The **RunPermissions** property determines whether Access uses the query user's *permissions* or the query owner's permissions when checking the *user-level security* permissions for each of the underlying tables in a query.

If the **RunPermissions** property is set to **User's**, the users of a query have only their own permissions to view data in underlying tables. However, if the owner of a query sets the **RunPermissions** property to **Owner's**, anyone who uses that query has the same level of permissions to view data in the underlying tables as the query's owner.

Displaying data from secured tables and queries

By using the **RunPermissions** property, you can create queries to display data to users who don't have access to the underlying tables. You can build different views of your data, which provides record-level and field-level security for a table.

For example, suppose that you have a secure database with an Employees table and a Salary table. By using the **RunPermissions** property, you can build several views of the two tables:

- One view that allows a user or group to view but not update the Salary field.

- A second view that allows a different user or group to view and update the Salary field.

- A third view that allows another user or group to view the Salary field for only a certain category of employees.

▶ To prevent users from viewing the design of underlying tables or queries

1 For the users or groups whose access you want to restrict, remove all permissions for the tables or queries whose design you want to secure.

2 Build a new query that includes all the fields you want to include from those tables or queries.

   You can exclude access to a field by omitting that field. You can also limit access to a certain range of values by defining criteria for your query.

3 On the query's property sheet, set the **RunPermissions** property of the new query to **Owner's**.

4 Grant appropriate data permissions for the new query to the users and groups that you want to be able to update data, but do not want viewing the design of the underlying table or query.

   Such permissions typically include Read Design, Read Data, Update Data, Delete Data, and Insert Data.

Modifying queries

By default, the user who creates a query is its owner, and only the owner of a query can save changes to it if the **RunPermissions** property is set to **Owner's**. Even members of the Admins group or users with Administer permission are prevented from saving changes to a query created by another user if the **RunPermissions** property is set to **Owner's**. However, anyone with Modify Design permission for the query can set the **RunPermissions** property to **User's** and then successfully save changes to the query.

Similarly, if a user is otherwise prevented from creating or adding to a table, you can create either a make-table or append query and set its **RunPermissions** property to **Owner's**.

Because the creator of a query owns it by default, having the **RunPermissions** property set to **Owner's** can create problems if you need to allow more than one user to work with the design of a query. To correct this, ownership of the query can be transferred to a group. To do this, create a group, change the owner of the query to this group on the **Change Owner** tab in the **User And Group Permissions** dialog box, and then add the users who need to modify the query to the new group. Any member of the new group can edit the query and save changes.

Security Issues for Data Access Pages

A *data access page* is the combination of a shortcut stored in the Microsoft Access database (MDB file) or Microsoft Access project (ADP file) and a corresponding HTML file located in your computer's file system.

Data access pages present security concerns in three areas:

- Security for the links to data access pages stored in the **Pages** object list in the Database window in an Access database or Access project

- Security for data access page files themselves

- Control over access to the database that a data access page is connected to

Security for data access page links

Access doesn't provide *user-level security* for the links to data access pages stored in the **Pages** object list in the Database window. When an Access database or Access project is opened with write access to the file, users can add, delete, or rename the links stored in the **Pages** object list in the Database window.

For this reason, the only way to prevent users from making changes to data access page links is to make the MDB or ADP file read-only. You can do this by using file-system access control (such as setting the read-only attribute) or by putting the file on a read-only network share.

Security for data access page files

Data access pages are HTML pages that contain <OBJECT> tag references to the Microsoft Office **Data Source** control and other Microsoft Office Web Components, as well as Extensible Markup Language (XML) and script. Data access pages are stored as files with the file name extension .htm either in the local file system, in a folder on a network share, or on an HTTP server. For this reason, Access has no control over the security of data access page files.

To secure a data access page file that is stored on a local or network file system, you must use the file access security available for your operating system. To secure data access page files that are stored on an HTTP server, you must use the security features available on the server itself. For example, if you are using Microsoft Internet Information Server (IIS), you can use the Internet Service Manager or FrontPage Server Administrator to control security settings for files stored on the server.

Controlling database access from data access pages

There are three primary concerns regarding securing access to a database from a data access page:

- Preventing unauthorized users from opening the database at all

- Controlling the level of access after a database is open

- Preventing malicious scripts from using the user's identity to gain access to other databases

For Access databases, there is the additional concern of controlling access to the Microsoft Access database (MDB file) through the file system.

Preventing unauthorized access to the database

You need to prevent unauthorized users from gaining access to the database, and you need to control the level of access after a user has logged on. If the database is protected with user-level security and you want to enable user-level security through a page, make sure that the connection information for a page specifies the correct workgroup information file and that this file is in a public network share accessible to all users.

▶ **To specify the workgroup information file to use**

1   Start Access, and open the data access page that you want to work with in Design view.

2   On the **View** menu, click **Field List**, and then click the **Database** tab.

3   Right-click the database name, and click **Connection**.

4   Click the **All** tab, and double-click **Jet OLEDB:System database**.

5   In the **Property Value** box, specify the path to the correct workgroup information file.

   In most cases, this is a UNC path (*ServerName**ShareName*) to the file on a network share.

6   Save your changes to the data access page.

You can also author a data access page against an Access database that is secured with a database password. However, a database password provides control only over who can open the database and requires that all users know a single password to open the database.

By default, a database password isn't saved with a data access page, so users are prompted to enter the database password when opening the page. (Similarly, if a database password is set for the database after you author the page, users of your page are prompted to enter the password before they can use the page.)

If you don't want to prompt users for the database password, you can embed the password in the page; however, the password is saved in an unencrypted format in the HTML code of the page itself, which makes the password easy to be discovered.

▶ **To save the database password with a data access page**

1   Start Access, and open the data access page that you want to work with in Design view.

2   On the **View** menu, click **Field List**, and then click the **Database** tab.

3   Right-click the database name, and click **Connection**.

4   Under **Enter information to log on to the server**, select the **Allow saving of password** check box.

5   Save your changes to the data access page.

Controlling the level of access to the database

To control the level of access after an Access database is opened from a data access page, you can use one of the following methods after establishing user-level security for the database:

- Define a user account that has the appropriate level of access you want to allow for any user of the data access page.

  Use the **Data Link Properties** dialog box to save this account name and password in the data access page connection information. Be sure to put the correct workgroup information file in a shared location and specify the path to the file in the **Data Link Properties** dialog box.

- Define the appropriate groups and access levels that you want to allow for users of the data access page.

  Create user account names and passwords to distribute to authorized users of the data access page, and assign those users to the appropriate groups. Use the **Data Link Properties** dialog box to prevent the password from being saved in the data access page connection information.

Important   Depending on the data access method that you choose for the data access page, where the database is located on the network relative to the IIS server used to publish the page, and how *authentication* is defined on the IIS server, you might not be able to control the level of access for individual users. That is, you might be able to control access based only on a single account used for all users who open the page.

Preventing unauthorized access from malicious scripts

A data access page uses the Microsoft Office **Data Source** control (MSODSC) to connect to its data source. When a data access page is open in Microsoft Internet Explorer or in an HTML-capable mail reader that uses Internet Explorer browsing components, such as Microsoft Outlook 98 or Outlook 2000, the MSODSC on the page is using the identity of the user to log on to the database.

A malicious user could exploit this fact to use script running against the MSODSC to gain access to databases on servers other than the one from which the page was downloaded. Attempts to use the MSODSC to access databases on servers other than the one the page originated from are referred to as *cross-domain data access*.

The mode of data access used by the MSODSC determines whether a data access page is considered inherently safe, or if cross-domain data access is possible from the page. The MSODSC can be configured to use one of two modes of data access: *two-tier data access* or *three-tier data access*.

In a two-tier data access mode, the client (first tier) makes a direct connection to the database server (second tier). Any page that uses two-tier data access is considered by Internet Explorer to be making a cross-domain access attempt. Depending on the security settings in Internet Explorer, when a user opens a page by using two-tier data access, one of three things occurs:

- The page is automatically disabled.
- The user is asked whether to allow data access.
- The page is automatically enabled.

Internet Explorer security settings also define different security zones. If a page is on a Web server in a trusted zone, the cross-domain attempt can be enabled automatically. In a controlled environment, such as a corporate intranet, your pages perform better if you use two-tier data access, and if you publish them from a server located in a trusted security zone. This method is the simplest way to provide security against unauthorized access from malicious scripts.

Three-tier data access includes a third, remote component between the client and database components. A page that uses three-tier data access to connect to a database is considered to be inherently safe regardless of what Internet Explorer security zone it is published from. These pages do not warn the user about *cross-domain data access* attempts when authentication settings have been left in the default configuration.

See also

- There are other strategies for maintaining secured data access pages. Both two-tier access and three-tier access are explained in more detail in the *Microsoft Office 2000/Visual Basic Programmer's Guide*.

Using Security Features in FrontPage

After a Web site is published, both the site and its server computer are exposed to a diverse community of users and a broad spectrum of interactions, all of which have some potential to compromise security. You can use the security features of Microsoft FrontPage 2000 with those of Microsoft Windows NT Server and Microsoft Internet Information Server (IIS) to control who can browse, author, or administer your Web sites.

Providing Security on a FrontPage-extended Web

Whether you are administering Web sites on an intranet or the Internet, the two main security issues are:

- Preventing unauthorized users from modifying a Web site or server computer.
- Preventing unwanted or bug-ridden programs and scripts from running on the server computer.

There are users who, with malicious intent, might try to gain access to a Web site. They might, for example, try to add to, change, or delete its content. Microsoft FrontPage provides a way to permit only certain users to browse, author, or administer a Web site.

A program or script can run on a server computer for a number of reasons. For example, marking a folder as executable can allow a program to run. HTML pages can themselves contain embedded controls, scripts, utilities, and other programs that can cause a program to run. And form handlers introduce the risk that users can submit commands from within form fields, thus causing programs to run. FrontPage has security settings that help prevent unauthorized programs from running on a server computer.

Authenticating users and setting permissions

The two main ways to provide security are to authenticate users and give them *permissions*. *Authentication* is the process a system uses to verify that a user has authorization to enter the system. For example, when a user logs on to a computer running Microsoft Windows NT Server, the operating system compares the user's name and password against an authorized list of user accounts that is maintained in Windows NT Server.

Permissions is the set of authorizations that specify what an authenticated user can do in a system. In the case of FrontPage, permissions specify which users can browse, author, and administer a *FrontPage-extended web*.

Just how FrontPage, Windows NT Server, and Microsoft Internet Information Server (IIS) work together to authenticate users and give them permissions forms the core of the FrontPage security strategy. That strategy enables you to:

- Set permissions based on a user's role: administrator, author, or browser.
- Set permissions on individual files and folders.
- Allow or prevent authors from uploading executable scripts and programs.
- Require authors to use the Secure Sockets Layer (SSL) protocol.
- Enable or disable authoring.
- Log authoring actions.

Applying role-based permissions in FrontPage

FrontPage provides the tools for setting permissions for three different categories of users. You can set permissions for:

- Web site visitors, to whom you give browsing permission.
- Authors, to whom you give authoring permission.
- Administrators, who can create, rename, and delete *subwebs*, as well as manage permissions.

Permissions are hierarchical: A user with administrative permissions has authoring and browsing permissions. A user with authoring permissions has browsing permissions.

By default, the permissions you set for a FrontPage-extended web are inherited by all the subwebs below it. You can, however, set unique permissions for a subweb that override the permissions inherited from the parent web.

By using FrontPage tools, you can set only role-based permissions and only on a FrontPage-extended web or nested subweb. You can't use FrontPage tools to set permissions on files and folders. You can, however, use Windows NT Server to manually set permissions on files and folders, but that requires you to override FrontPage permissions.

See also

- You can use FrontPage Server Extensions to provide security on UNIX operating systems. For more information, see the Front Page Server Extensions Resource Kit Web site at http://www.microsoft.com/frontpage/wpp/serk/.

Administering Security Through FrontPage Server Extensions

The key component that Microsoft FrontPage uses to provide security is a set of three programs that are collectively called Microsoft FrontPage Server Extensions. On a Web site that they support, called a *FrontPage-extended web*, they provide enhanced authoring, browsing, and administering functionality.

For example, authors can collaborate on Web sites, add hit counters without knowing any programming, and rename pages that FrontPage Server Extensions automatically relink. Web site visitors can fill out forms processed by a built-in form handler. You don't have to download, buy, or install a separate Common Gateway Interface (CGI)-compatible program to enable each function to work.

FrontPage Server Extensions also play a pivotal security role by working with Microsoft Windows NT Server and Microsoft Internet Information Server (IIS) to check the browsing, authoring, and administering *permissions* of visitors to a Web site. Based on the results of the check, they either permit or deny the action requested by the visitor.

Note   FrontPage Server Extensions do not work with Windows NT Server security if you use any Web server besides IIS, including the Netscape, O'Reilly WebSite, and FrontPage Personal Web Server (PWS) Web servers.

FrontPage Server Extensions consist of the following dynamic-link library (DLL) files:

- Admin.dll, which handles user requests for administrative actions
- Author.dll, which handles user requests for authoring actions
- Shtml.dll, which handles user requests for browsing actions

You add, modify, upgrade, or remove FrontPage Server Extensions by using any of the FrontPage Server Extensions administration tools: the Fpsrvadm and Fpremadm utilities, the FrontPage snap-in in *Microsoft Management Console* (MMC), or the FrontPage Server Extensions HTML Administration Forms.

Authenticating users through Windows NT Server

A user can be authenticated and gain access to the system and its resources, such as a FrontPage-extended web, only if the user has a user account on Windows NT Server. Typically, a system administrator creates a user account for each user and group that has access to the system. To gain access, the user supplies a user name and password when logging on to the system. Windows NT Server compares the user's name and password against the authorized list of user accounts that it maintains.

When an authenticated user runs an application, Windows NT Server forces the application to impersonate the user; that is, to run with the same permissions granted by Windows NT Server to the original user. That way, the application can invoke only other applications or system resources, such as files and folders that contain Web content, for which the original user has permissions.

Impersonation also works remotely. If a user can be authenticated on a remote computer, any application that the user runs on that computer (and has permission to run) impersonates the user. For example, when a user who has permission to author a FrontPage-extended web on a remote computer running Windows NT Server attempts to do so, the FrontPage authoring DLL file, Author.dll, runs as the impersonated user. (After a user is logged on and authenticated locally, the user does not need to log on to the remote computer again.)

To control access to individual files and folders, Windows NT Server, when running on an *NTFS* file partition, associates an access control list (ACL) with each file and folder. An ACL is a list that specifies which users and groups have access to its associated file or folder, and what permissions those users and groups have. An ACL is not a file, but rather a property of a file or folder.

The security that FrontPage Server Extensions provides is based on ACLs. Because only the NTFS file partition supports ACLs, be sure to use NTFS on a computer running Windows NT Server and not the *file allocation table* (FAT) file partition. (The FAT file system does not support ACL-based file permissions. Therefore, Windows NT Server cannot provide any security for a Web site on a FAT-partitioned system.)

Mediating authentication through IIS Web server

The IIS Web server is a Windows NT service, which is a special application that starts along with the operating system and runs in the background, without any user interface. IIS is a file and application server for the Internet and for intranets. It supports industry-standard Internet protocol services (such as HTTP protocol services), Web application development, server administration, management and control of Web server content, and security and *authentication*.

As part of the FrontPage security triad, IIS mediates authentication communication between FrontPage Server Extensions and Windows NT Server. When an authenticated user requests access to a Web resource, IIS impersonates that user. IIS supports four kinds of authentication.

Anonymous authentication   provides access to users who do not have Windows NT Server accounts on the server computer (for example, Web site visitors). IIS creates the anonymous account for Web services, IUSR_*computername*. When IIS receives an anonymous request, it impersonates the anonymous account.

Basic authentication   is an authentication protocol supported by most Web servers and Web browsers. Although Basic authentication transmits user names and passwords in easily decoded clear text, it has some advantages over more-secure authentication methods in that it works through a proxy server *firewall* and ensures that a Web site is accessible to almost any Web browser.

Windows NT Server Challenge/Response authentication   encrypts user names and passwords in a multiple transaction interaction between client and server, thus making this method more secure than Basic authentication. Disadvantages are that this method cannot be performed through a proxy server firewall, and some Web browsers (most notably, Netscape Navigator) do not support it. You can, however, enable both this method and Basic authentication at the same time.

Digest Access authentication   is similar to Basic authentication, except that a user's name and password are transmitted in a more-secure format. This method requires Microsoft Internet Explorer 5 on the client computer.

Applying the iron triangle

The central role of the ACLs—access control lists that specify what actions each authenticated user and group are permitted to perform on a file or folder—becomes clear when you view FrontPage Server Extensions, Windows NT Server, and IIS Web server as an integrated security system.

Windows NT Server creates and sets the initial permissions on the ACLs. But after FrontPage Server Extensions are installed on IIS, you can use administration tools such as Fpsrvadm and Fpremadm to modify the ACLs on FrontPage-extended web files and folders. That is, you can change the permissions on these files and folders. You can also use the FrontPage client **Permissions** command (**Tools** menu, **Security** submenu) to modify the ACLs. When you use this method, FrontPage displays the Windows NT Server user-account list by default.

Note   If the FrontPage **Security** command is unavailable, make sure that you entered **http://***webname* as the folder name when you opened the Web site, rather than opening the site as a file on your hard disk. You must manage security through IIS, and IIS uses NTFS to set permissions and enforce security settings. When you open a file from your NTFS drive, you bypass the server extensions security features within FrontPage.

The ACL in the root folder of a FrontPage-extended web is especially important. In this ACL, you add and set or modify permissions for users of the FrontPage-extended web. You specify **R** permission for browsing users, who can only read web files; **W** permission for authors, who also have **R** permission and can read and write to web files; and **P** permission for administrators, who also have **W** and **R** permissions and can change permissions by modifying ACLs.

If a user requests an administrative action on the FrontPage-extended web, Admin.dll checks the root folder that the ACL is in to see whether the user has **P** permission. If a user requests an authoring action, Author.dll checks the ACL to see whether the user has **W** permission. And if a user requests a browsing action, Shtml.dll checks the ACL to see whether the user has **R** permission.

The following example uses an author request to show from beginning to end how FrontPage, Windows NT Server, and IIS work together to provide security.

When using FrontPage, a user tries to perform an authoring action on a FrontPage-extended web. The FrontPage client or a Web browser sends a POST request to perform the authoring action on the web. IIS reads the request, interprets it as an authoring request, and directs the request to the FrontPage authoring DLL file, specifically, to Author.dll. Author.dll determines which web the user wants to act on, and then checks to see whether the user has **W** permission in the ACL of the web's root folder. If the user is authenticated, Author.dll impersonates the user and tries to access the file or folder specified by the author.

Windows NT Server checks the permissions of the impersonated user against the ACL of the specific file or folder that the user is trying to access. The user might have read, write, or delete permission. If the check is successful, Windows NT Server gives Author.dll access to the file or folder to perform the requested action. If the check fails, FrontPage displays a message specific to the operation that the user is trying to perform, such as "You do not have permission to delete the file."

See also

- You can use the FrontPage Server Extensions to provide security on UNIX operating systems. For more information, see the Front Page Server Extensions Resource Kit Web site at http://www.microsoft.com/frontpage/wpp/serk/.

Customizing Security

The Microsoft FrontPage built-in security management features allow you to set role-based *permissions* on *FrontPage-extended web*s (or nested *subwebs*). But setting permissions on a per-web basis might not give you the control you want. You can, in fact, set permissions at a finer level of granularity by setting permissions on files and folders.

Another way to customize security is to specify authoring restrictions. For example, you can prevent authors from uploading executable scripts and require authors to use the Secure Sockets Layer (SSL).

Setting permissions on files and folders

When you set permissions at the file or folder level, you bypass the security mechanisms in FrontPage and set permissions on the ACLs yourself.

Note   This is an advanced technique and must be done carefully to avoid weakening the security of the content on your Web server.

To set permissions on a file or folder of a FrontPage-extended web, open the FrontPage snap-in in Microsoft Management Console (MMC), right-click *computername*, and then click the **Properties** command. On the **Server Extensions** tab in the **Properties** dialog box, select the **Manage permissions manually** check box.

As a convenience, the FrontPage Server Extensions Configuration Wizard creates three empty local computer groups when you create a FrontPage-extended web. The groups are named *webname* Admins, *webname* Authors, and *webname* Browsers. If you decide to set permissions yourself on files or folders, it is recommended that you use these three groups in the ACLs and maintain these groups by using the Windows NT Server User Manager.

Refining security

In addition to setting permissions on ACLs, you can also perform the following actions to fine-tune security:

- Allow or prevent authors from uploading executable scripts and programs.
- Require authors to use the SSL protocol.
- Enable or disable authoring.
- Log authoring actions.

To perform any of these actions on a FrontPage-extended web, open the FrontPage snap-in in MMC and click the **Properties** command. On the **Server Extensions** tab in the **Properties** dialog box, select the appropriate check boxes.

See also

- You can use FrontPage Server Extensions to provide security on UNIX operating systems. For more information, see the Front Page Server Extensions Resource Kit Web site at http://www.microsoft.com/frontpage/wpp/serk/.

Using Security Features in Outlook

Outlook 2000 provides enhanced security features for sending and receiving secure e-mail messages over the Internet or local intranet.

Working with the Outlook 2000 Security Model

The Microsoft Outlook 2000 security model differs from that of Outlook 97 and previous Microsoft Exchange clients. Outlook 2000 supports *S/MIME* security, which allows users to exchange secure e-mail messages with other S/MIME e-mail clients over the Internet, as well as within an organization.

The new Outlook 2000 security model helps ensure the security of Outlook e-mail messages by using public key *encryption* to send and receive signed and encrypted e-mail messages. This feature includes *digital signing*, which allows users to verify the identity of senders and the integrity of messages, and message encryption, which protects the contents of messages from being read by anyone except their intended recipients. Users can exchange signed and encrypted e-mail messages with other e-mail clients that support S/MIME.

E-mail messages encrypted by the user's *public key* can be decrypted using only the associated *private key*. When a user sends an encrypted e-mail message, the recipient's *certificate* (public key) is used to encrypt it; likewise, when a user reads an encrypted e-mail message, Outlook 2000 uses the user's private key to decrypt it.

Digital certificates

S/MIME features rely on *digital certificates*, which associate the user's identity with a public key. The associated private key is saved in a secure store on the user's computer. The combination of a certificate and private key is called a *Digital ID*. Outlook 2000 fully supports X.509v3 standard digital certificates, which must be created by a *certificate authority*.

Outlook 2000 supports public Web-based enrollment to certificate authorities such as VeriSign and Microsoft Certificate Server. Outlook 2000 also works with Microsoft Exchange Key Management server to provide an integrated X.509v3-based public key infrastructure for corporate users. The sender only needs a X.509v3 certificate and private key to exchange digitally signed e-mail messages. For encrypted e-mail messages, the sender must also have each recipient's certificate.

Certificates can be exchanged by including them in a signed message. Certificates are stored in each Outlook user's Contacts. Microsoft Exchange Key Management Server automatically stores each user's certificate in the Global Address Book so that encrypted e-mail messages can be sent to other users in the organization.

See also

- Public key cryptography can help you maintain secure e-mail systems. For more information about the use of public key cryptography in Outlook, search for **Outlook security white paper** on the Microsoft Support Online Web site, at http://support.microsoft.com/support/, to find the "Microsoft Outlook 98 Security" white paper.

- S/MIME is based on RSA Labs Public Key Cryptography Standard documents. These documents were consolidated in the Internet Engineering Task Force process to become the Internet standard S/MIME. For more information, see the S/MIME Central Web site at http://www.rsa.com/smime/.

- If you are installing Outlook 2000 on a locked-down system, you must pay attention to where the e-mail messages and other storage files are located on the user's hard disk. For more information, see "How to Install Outlook 2000 on a Locked Down System" on page 198.

- Microsoft Exchange Key Management Server version 5.5 issues keys for Microsoft Exchange Server security only. Microsoft Exchange Key Management Server 5.5, Service Pack 1 supports both Exchange security and S/MIME security. For more information, see the *Microsoft Exchange Server version 5.5 Resource Guide* in the *Microsoft BackOffice Resource Kit, Second Edition*.

Working with Security Keys and Certificates

Occasionally, you must renew, import, or export a set of security keys and *digital certificates*. For example, you might need to change computers and take your *Digital ID* (the combination of your *certificate* and private *encryption* key) with you, or you might need to get someone's public security key in order to send them encrypted e-mail messages. Outlook provides ways to manage your security keys and certificates so that you can keep your e-mail messages secure.

Your Digital ID includes your digital certificate and public and private key set. Components for your Digital ID are stored in the Windows registry on your computer. The key set is encrypted using a password that you supply. If you use more than one computer, you must copy your Digital ID to each computer that you use.

Tip   Make a copy of your Digital ID for safekeeping. You can protect the file that contains the copy by encrypting it and by using a password.

Storing digital certificates

Certificates can be stored in three locations:

- Microsoft Exchange Global Address Book
- Lightweight Directory Access Protocol (LDAP) directory service
- Windows registry

Microsoft Exchange Global Address Book

Users who enroll in Exchange Advanced Security have their certificates stored in the Global Address Book. In Internet Only mode, users can open the Global Address Book by using the LDAP provider. In Corporate/Workgroup mode, however, users must use the Exchange MAPI provider to gain access to certificates in the Global Address Book.

The Exchange MAPI provider does not support certificate access to any LDAP provider. Only certificates generated by Microsoft Exchange Server Advanced Security or by Microsoft Exchange Key Management Server are published in the Global Address Book. Externally generated certificates are not published to the Global Address Book.

LDAP directory service

External directory services, certificate authorities, or other certificate servers may publish their users' certificates through an LDAP directory service. Internet Only mode in Outlook 2000 allows access to these certificates through LDAP directories.

Windows registry

If a user imports another user's certificate into Outlook 2000 (for example, by adding a contact or importing a file), the certificate is stored in the registry. It cannot be shared or published to a directory service directly.

Obtaining other users' certificates

In order to exchange secure e-mail messages with another user, you must have that user's *public key*. You gain access to the public key through the user's certificate. There are three ways to obtain another user's certificate:

- Digitally signed e-mail messages
- Directory services, such as the Exchange Global Address Book
- Imported files

Obtaining a certificate from a digitally signed e-mail message

When you receive a signed message from someone whose certificate you want to save, you can right-click the sender's name on the To line and then click **Add to Contacts**. The address information is saved in your Contacts, and the sender's certificate is saved in the registry.

Note   If you export a contacts list, the corresponding certificates are not included. You must add the certificates from a received e-mail message on each computer that you use.

Obtaining a certificate from a directory service

When you use Internet Only mode with a standard LDAP server, you can automatically retrieve another user's certificate from an LDAP directory when you send an encrypted e-mail message. You must be enrolled in *S/MIME* security and you must have a Digital ID for your e-mail account.

When you use Corporate/Workgroup mode with Microsoft Exchange Server, you can obtain certificates from the Global Address Book. You must be enrolled in Exchange Advanced Security.

Obtaining a certificate from a file

You can request that another user export a certificate to a file. To import a certificate for another user, click the **Import/Export Digital ID** button on the **Security** tab in the **Options** dialog box (**Tools** menu). You can also use the **Import** button on the **Certificates** tab in a contact item in your Contacts folder.

Renewing keys and certificates

A time limit is associated with each certificate and private key. When the keys given by the Microsoft Exchange Key Management Server approach the end of the designated time period, Outlook displays a warning message and offers to renew the keys. Outlook sends the renewal message to the server on your behalf.

How to Manage Security Settings

The **Options** dialog box (**Tools** menu) in Outlook allows you to view and change security settings, or to create a new security setting.

View security settings

If you enroll in Microsoft Exchange Server security, Outlook creates security settings that you can view and change.

▶ **To view Outlook security settings**

1   On the **Tools** menu, click **Options** and then click the **Security** tab.

2   In the **Default Security Setting** box, select the setting you want.

3   Click **Change Settings** to view a particular setting.

Change security settings

If you enroll in Microsoft Exchange Server security, you can view and change security settings in Outlook.

▶ **To create a new Outlook security setting for a user enrolled in Exchange Server security**

1   On the **Tools** menu, click **Options**, and then click the **Security** tab.

2   Click **Change Settings**.

3   Click **New**, and enter a name for the security setting.

4   In the **Secure Message Format** box, select **S/MIME** as your secure message format

   If you are using only Exchange 4.0 or 5.0 security in your organization, skip this step.

5   In the **Signing Certificate** area, click **Choose**.

6   Select a signing certificate and click **OK**.

   You can change the default algorithms by selecting a different value in the **Encryption Algorithm** box.

7   In the **Encryption Certificate** area, click **Choose**.

8   Select an encryption certificate and click **OK**.

   You can change the default algorithms by selecting a different value in the **Encryption Algorithm** box.

Tip   You can use the check boxes in the **Change Security Settings** dialog box to make a signing and encryption certificate setting the default setting for all secure e-mail messages or for a particular message format (S/MIME or Microsoft Exchange Server security). For an S/MIME security setting, you can send your certificates with a secure e-mail message. Select the **Send clear text signed message** check box (**Options** dialog box, **Tools** menu) to allow both signature verification and backward compatibility with non-S/MIME e-mail clients.

Create new security settings

If you obtained a *certificate* using Microsoft Exchange Server Advanced Security, Outlook creates a security setting for the certificates it issues. No additional steps are necessary.

When you have only one certificate installed on your computer, and that certificate was issued by Microsoft Certificate Server or another *certificate authority* such as VeriSign Inc, Outlook configures a default setting. Otherwise, you must create your own settings.

Before you can create a new security setting, you must have a *Digital ID*.

▶ **To get a Digital ID**

1   On the **Tools** menu, click **Options**, and then click the **Security** tab.

2   **Click the Get a Digital ID (Certificates)** button.

Then you can create a new Outlook security setting.

▶ **To create a new Outlook security setting**

1   On the **Tools** menu, click **Options**, and then click the **Security** tab.

2   Click **Setup Secure E-Mail**.

3   In the **Security Settings Name** box, enter a name for the security setting.

4   In the **Secure Message Format** box, select **S/MIME** as your secure message format

    If you are using only Exchange 4.0 or 5.0 security in your organization, skip this step.

5   In the **Signing Certificate** area, click **Choose**.

6   Select a signing certificate and click **OK**.

    You can change the default algorithms by selecting a different value in the **Encryption Algorithm** box.

7   In the **Encryption Certificate** area, click **Choose**.

8   Select an encryption certificate and click **OK**.

    You can change the default algorithms by selecting a different value in the **Encryption Algorithm** box.

Move certificates and keys between computers

If you have more than one computer, you can duplicate your security information in Outlook.

▶ To move certificates and keys between computers

1   On the **Tools** menu, click **Options**, and then click the **Security** tab.

2   In the **Digital IDs** section, click **Import/Export Digital ID**.

3   On the computer that contains your keys and certificates, click **Export your Digital ID to a file**.

4   Select exporting options, and then click **OK**.

   You must specify the Digital ID to export (if there is more than one on your computer), the file name to use, and a password. You can also select the **Delete Digital ID from system** check box if you want to remove the Digital ID from this computer permanently.

5   On the computer to which you want to import the security information, repeat steps 1 through 3, and then click **Import existing Digital ID from a file**.

6   Specify importing options, and then click **OK**.

   You must specify the file to import and enter the password that you set when you exported the file. You must specify a Digital ID name for the keys and certificates you are importing.

After importing the security information on your new computer, you can read and send secure messages.

Note   Outlook exports Microsoft Exchange Server security settings to an EPF file. S/MIME certificates and keys from external certificate authorities are exported to a PFX file.

Setting Consistent Security Options for All Users in the Workgroup

You can set several security options for Microsoft Outlook 2000 in the Windows registry. The following Outlook registry entries help you control security for your users.

Hiding the invalid signature message

By default, each time a user attempts to read a signed message that has an invalid signature, a dialog box appears warning the user about the signature and listing the cause of the failure. If you don't want users to see this message, you can hide this dialog box by setting the following registry entry:

HKEY_LOCAL_MACHINE\Software\Microsoft\Office\9.0\Outlook\Security\Options

To skip the warning dialog box, set the value of the last bit of the **DWORD** value to **1** (**0x00000001**). This entry is set to **0** by default. Do not alter the other bits in this value; they control other security options.

Specifying the minimum key length for encrypted e-mail messages

You can set a minimum key length for encrypted e-mail messages based on the desired security level. Outlook displays a warning message if an e-mail message does not meet this minimum key length. Standard key sizes are 40, 64, 128, and 168. To specify a minimum key length, enter a **DWORD** value in the following registry entry:

HKEY_LOCAL_MACHINE\Software\Microsoft\Office\9.0\Outlook\Security\MinEncKey

Note   International users cannot read e-mail messages encrypted using a key length greater than 40.

Specifying a certificate authority

You can limit users to *certificates* from a specific *certificate authority* only. For example, you can limit users to certificates from only the Microsoft Exchange Key Management Server. To limit users to a particular certificate authority, enter the certificate authority name as a **String** value in the following registry entry:

HKEY_LOCAL_MACHINE\Software\Microsoft\Office\9.0\Outlook\Security\RequiredCA

Tip   If you don't want your users to use *S/MIME* security, you can disable it. To disable S/MIME, set this registry entry to the name of the Microsoft Exchange Key Management Server In Key Management Server, set the **Issue V1 certificates only** option to disable users' ability to issue S/MIME (V3) certificates.

Specifying password time limits

You can specify the maximum amount of time that a password for a key set can be stored. Setting this value to **0** effectively removes the user's ability to save a password and requires that the password be entered each time a key set is requested. To set the maximum password time, set a **DWORD** value in the following registry entry:

HKEY_LOCAL_MACHINE\Software\Microsoft\Cryptography\Defaults\Provider \MaxPWDTime

You can also set the default value for the amount of time a password is saved. To set the default value for saving a password, specify a **DWORD** value in the following registry entry:

HKEY_LOCAL_MACHINE\Software\Microsoft\Cryptography\Defaults\Provider \DefPWDTime

Specifying the enrollment page address

When users sign up for a new *Digital ID* by clicking the **Get Digital ID** button on the **Security** tab in the **Options** dialog box (**Tools** menu), they are directed to a default external certificate authority enrollment page on the Microsoft Web site. If you prefer, you can set a registry entry to point to an internal certificate authority Web page instead.

Use one of the following registry entries to set a URL for the enrollment page:

- If you have *administrator privileges* on the user's computer, type the URL in this registry entry:

    HKEY_LOCAL_MACHINE\Software\Microsoft\Office\9.0\Outlook\Security \EnrollPageURL

- If you do not have administrator privileges on the user's computer, type the URL in this registry entry:

    HKEY_CURRENT_USER\Software\Microsoft\Office\9.0\Outlook\Security \EnrollPageURL

Note The EnrollPageURL entry in the HKEY_LOCAL_MACHINE subkey overrides the EnrollPageURL entry in the HKEY_CURRENT_USER subkey.

The EnrollPageURL registry entries use the following parameters to send information about the user to the enrollment Web page.

Parameter	Placeholder in URL string
User display name	%1
SMTP e-mail name	%2
User interface language ID	%3

For example, to send user information to the Microsoft enrollment Web page, set the EnrollPageURL entry to the following value, including the parameters:

www.microsoft.com/ie/certpage.htm?name=%1&email=%2&helplcid=%3

If the user's name is Jeff Smith, his e-mail address is someone@microsoft.com, and his user interface language ID is 1033, then the placeholders are resolved as follows:

www.microsoft.com/ie/certpage.htm?name=Jeff%20Smith&email=someone@ microsoft.com&helplcid=1033

System Policy Tip   You can use system policies to set security levels in Outlook. In the System Policy Editor, set the **Required Certificate Authority**, **Minimum encryption settings**, **S/MIME interoperability with external clients**, and **Outlook Rich Text in S/MIME messages** policies under User\Microsoft Outlook 2000\Tools | Options\Security. For more information about the System Policy Editor, see "Using the System Policy Editor" on page 296.

Setting Security for Outlook Folder Home Pages

In Microsoft Outlook 2000, you can associate a Web page with any personal or public folder. These Folder Home Pages use the following security modes:

- Use zone security and allow script access to Outlook object model
- Use zone security only

Use zone security and allow script access to Outlook object model

This mode, which is the default for Outlook 2000, gives scripts on a Web page access to the Outlook object model and also ensures that the Outlook Today ActiveX control is running continuously. For all other aspects of the Web page, the appropriate Microsoft Internet Explorer zone security settings are used.

For example, if the Internet Explorer zone security settings specify that ActiveX controls are not allowed to run, then no ActiveX controls run for a Folder Home Page except the Outlook Today ActiveX control.

Access to the object model allows scripts to manipulate all of the user's Outlook information on the computer. The primary security ramification of this mode is that it allows anyone who creates a public folder for a home page to include scripts that can manipulate data in user mailboxes. Although it provides the opportunity to create powerful public folder applications, access to the object model also exposes users to some security risks.

Use zone security only

This mode is activated directly through the Windows registry or indirectly through a system policy. In this mode, scripts on the Web page do not have access to the Outlook object model, and the Outlook Today ActiveX control is subject to the same Internet Explorer zone security settings as all other ActiveX controls.

For example, if the Internet Explorer zone security settings specify that ActiveX controls are not allowed to run, then the Outlook Today ActiveX control does not run on the computer.

System Policy Tip   You can tighten security by using a system policy to disable Folder Home Pages for all of your users. In the System Policy Editor, in the **Microsoft Outlook 2000\Miscellaneous\Folder Home Pages for Outlook special folders** category, select the **Disable Folder Home Pages** policy and then select **Disable Folder Home Pages for all folders** in the **Settings for Disable Folder Home Pages** area. For more information about the System Policy Editor, see "Using the System Policy Editor" on page 296.

Encryption Strengths for Secure E-mail Messaging

There are two classes of *encryption* key strengths available from Microsoft: 128-bit Domestic Only and 40-bit International.

The following table summarizes the capabilities of Domestic Only encryption.

Encryption algorithm	Key length
RSA	128 bit
3DES	168 bit
CAST	64 bit
DES	56 bit
RSA	40 bit
CAST	40 bit

The following table summarizes the capabilities of International encryption.

Encryption algorithm	Key length
RSA	40 bit
CAST	40 bit

Note   For signing, the Digital Signature Key lengths for Domestic and International encryption are RSA 1024-bit and RSA 512-bit, respectively.

Microsoft Office 2000 includes a technology that determines whether the user's installation is capable of 128-bit Domestic encryption operations. Microsoft provides *128-bit encryption* capabilities in Microsoft Internet Explorer 3.02, Internet Explorer 4.*x*, Internet Explorer Service Packs, Windows NT 4.0, and Windows NT 4.0 Service Packs. These are the programs that the Windows installer tests for certified 128-bit encryption capabilities during Office 2000 Setup.

If your system already has 128-bit encryption capabilities, Office 2000 installs new 128-bit encryption components during Setup. Systems that do not already have 128-bit encryption capabilities receive *40-bit encryption* components.

If 128-bit encryption capabilities are required, and if installation is allowed by US government restrictions, then the Outlook 2000 Domestic Security Pack installs 128-bit encryption components for Internet Explorer 4.*x* or later and Outlook 2000. The Domestic Security Pack is installed after the Office 2000 installation is completed.

Note   When users exchange e-mail messages internationally, Outlook uses the minimum encryption strength that is supported by the e-mail client application of both the sender and the recipient of the message.

See also

- You can upgrade to 128-bit encryption for Outlook 2000 by downloading the Outlook 2000 Domestic Security Patch. For more information, see the Outlook 2000 high encryption page on the Office Update Web site at http://officeupdate.microsoft.com/info/outlook2000highencrypt.htm.

Installation Modes and Feature Options for Secure E-mail Messaging

To get full security functionality in Microsoft Outlook 2000 under Windows NT 4.0 or Windows 2000, you must install Outlook 2000 with local administrative rights or with *elevated privileges*. (Full security functionality is automatically included with Windows 95/98.)

With full e-mail security, users can perform the following tasks:

- Read S/MIME V2 encrypted e-mail messages
- Send S/MIME V2 encrypted e-mail messages
- Read S/MIME V2 digitally signed e-mail messages
- Send S/MIME digitally signed e-mail messages
- Enroll in public S/MIME security
- Enroll in MS Exchange Advanced Security
- Read Exchange 4.0/5.0 secure e-mail messages
- Send Exchange 4.0/5.0 secure e-mail messages

Without administrative rights on Windows NT 4.0 or Windows 2000, e-mail security functionality is degraded to limited security or no security, depending on the circumstances.

With limited e-mail security, users can perform the following tasks:

- Read S/MIME V2 encrypted e-mail messages
- Send S/MIME V2 encrypted e-mail messages.
- Read S/MIME V2 digitally signed e-mail messages
- Send S/MIME digitally signed e-mail messages
- Enroll in public S/MIME security

With no e-mail security features, users can only read *S/MIME* V2 digitally signed e-mail messages; no other e-mail security features are available.

See also

- If you are installing Outlook 2000 on client computers for users who don't have local administrative rights, you can give them elevated privileges for the installation. For more information, see "Deploying Outlook 2000" on page 188.

Troubleshooting Outlook Security

Use the following tips to help resolve common problems with Outlook security.

When attempting to read signed e-mail messages, I receive an error message about an invalid signature.

This problem can occur for a variety of reasons, which are listed in the **Certificate** dialog box. The most common reason for this error is that the sender's *certificate* is not trusted.

Microsoft Outlook 2000 security uses trust-based certificates. If Outlook security does not trust the sender's certificate or the *certificate authority* that issued it, the signature is considered invalid. To correct the problem, you must edit the trust for the certificate.

▶ **To edit the trust for a certificate**

1   In the **Certificate** dialog box, click **Edit Trust**.

2   Click **Explicitly trust this certificate** to identify this certificate as trusted.

   You can also specify the certificate authority's certificate as trusted by selecting it from the list and changing its trust status.

I cannot view secure messages in the Outlook preview pane.

You can view only clear-signed messages in the preview pane. Outlook 2000 does not support viewing of encrypted and blob-signed (also known as binary-format signed) messages in the preview pane.

While sending secure e-mail messages, I receive an error message.

This error message indicates that either your e-mail address does not match the address on the certificate, or there is a problem with the certificate. If you have more than one e-mail account, the account you are using might have a different e-mail address than the one on the certificate. Also, the certificate might not be trusted, or the certificate might have expired or been revoked.

PART 4

Upgrading to Office 2000

Contents

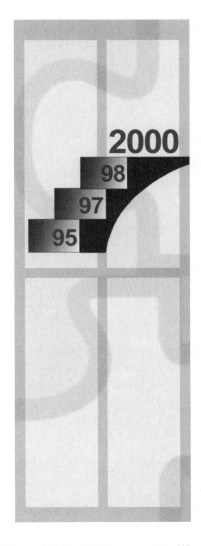

CHAPTER 10

Planning Your Move to Office 2000

You can have your entire organization upgrade to Microsoft Office 2000 at the same time, or you can have your organization upgrade one department at a time. The following topics describe how to plan and manage your upgrade to Office 2000.

In This Chapter

Before You Upgrade to Office 2000

Before you begin upgrading to Microsoft Office 2000 from a previous version of Office or from other applications, review the information in the following sections.

Getting Started with the Conversion Process

You can upgrade to Microsoft Office 2000 from the following applications:

- Office 98 (Macintosh)
- Office 95 and Office 97 (Microsoft Windows)
- Office 4.x (Windows and Macintosh)
- WordPerfect, Lotus 1-2-3, Harvard Graphics, and dBASE (Windows)

Before you start the conversion process, you must:

1   Determine which files you want to move to Office 2000, and then use a virus scanning program to scan the files for viruses.

2   Unbind all binder documents into component sections—if you have any.

3   Create backup copies of the files you want to convert.

4   Install the Office 2000 applications you want to deploy; follow the instructions in "Installing Office 2000 in Your Organization" on page 71.

See also

- Some Windows users might have to share documents and presentations with Macintosh users. For information about changes in graphics formats and fonts between operating systems, see "Moving Files Between the Windows and Macintosh Operating Systems" on page 435.

- You can incorporate your plan for solving year 2000 issues into your plan for upgrading to Office 2000. For information about what you can do to plan and manage your organization's transition into the year 2000, see "Meeting the Year 2000 Challenge" on page 449.

- The international features of Office 2000 with MultiLanguage Pack allow you to deploy it throughout your international organization. For information about multilingual support issues to consider if your organization is upgrading to Office 2000 with MultiLanguage Pack from localized versions of Office, see "Planning an International Move to Office 2000" on page 745.

File Formats in Microsoft Office 2000

A file format determines the way that information is stored in a document, workbook, presentation, or database. If Microsoft Office applications have the same file format, you can exchange files without installing special converters. Except for Microsoft Access, all Office 2000, Office 98 for the Macintosh, and Office 97 applications share the same file format.

Common file formats among versions of Microsoft Excel

Windows	2000	97	95	5.0
Macintosh		98		5.0

Common file formats among versions of Microsoft PowerPoint

Windows	2000	97	95
Macintosh		98	

Common file formats among versions of Microsoft Word

Windows	2000	97	95	6.0
Macintosh		98		6.0

See also

- For strategies to help you plan a gradual upgrade to Office 2000, see "Strategies for Sharing Files Among Different Versions of Office" on page 432 and "Strategies for Sharing Files with Other Applications" on page 433.

- For information about upgrading to Office 2000 from a previous version of Office, see "Getting Started with the Conversion Process" on page 429 and "Office 2000 Upgrading Reference" on page 455.

Strategies for Sharing Files Among Different Versions of Office

In many organizations, upgrading takes place gradually—one group of users at a time. During the upgrade process, users need to share files among Microsoft Office 2000 and previous versions of Office. There are several strategies that your workgroup can use to facilitate the sharing of files.

In Office 2000, you can open a file created in an earlier version of Microsoft Word, Microsoft Excel, or Microsoft PowerPoint—without losing any data or formatting. When you save a file created in a previous version of Office, however, not all of the new features in Word 2000, Excel 2000, and PowerPoint 2000 are supported.

By default, Word 2000, Excel 2000, and PowerPoint 2000 save new files in the Office 97-2000 format—that is, Office 97, Office 98 for the Macintosh, and Office 2000. If users in your workgroup use an earlier version of these applications, you can change the default file format for saving new files by using the **Options** dialog box (**Tools** menu) or the System Policy Editor. All files are saved in the default format unless you specify a different file format in the **Save As** dialog box (**File** menu).

Saving Office 2000 files in an earlier format

When you create a file in Office 2000, you can save that file in an earlier version of Office. For example:

- Word 2000 users can save files in Word 6.0/95 or Word 2.*x* format.
- Excel 2000 users can save files in Excel 5.0/95 or Excel 4.0 format.
- PowerPoint 2000 users can save files in PowerPoint 95 or PowerPoint 4.0 format.

Saving Office 2000 files in a dual file format

Word 2000, Excel 2000, and PowerPoint 2000 users can save files in a dual file format. For example:

- Word 2000 users can save files in Word 97-2000 & 6.0/95-RTF format.
- Excel 2000 users can save files in Microsoft Excel 97-2000 & 5.0/95 Workbook format.
- PowerPoint 2000 users can save files in PowerPoint 97-2000 & 95 Presentation format.

Saving Office 2000 files as Web pages

When you save a file in the Web Page format, Word 2000, Excel 2000, and PowerPoint 2000 work behind the scenes to create HTML tags for text, graphics, sounds, and videos that Web browsers can use for these features in a Web page.

All Word 2000, Excel 2000, and PowerPoint 2000 application features can import and export through HTML by using the Extensible Markup Language (XML).

See also

- For more information about sharing files with a specific version of Word, Excel, or PowerPoint, see "Office 2000 Upgrading Reference" on page 455.

- You can change the default file format that Word, Excel, and PowerPoint use when saving new files. For more information, see "How to Specify the Default Format in Which to Save Files" on page 438 and "Using the System Policy Editor" on page 296.

- You can save Word, Excel, and PowerPoint files in Web Page format. For more information, see "Transferring Files Between HTML and Office Document Formats" on page 592.

Strategies for Sharing Files with Other Applications

By installing the correct converters during Microsoft Office 2000 Setup, users of Microsoft Word, Microsoft Excel, and Microsoft PowerPoint can import data and formatting from files saved in other file formats.

Importing data and formatting into Word

If users select the appropriate converters in the Word Office Setup, they can import data and formatting from files saved in the following formats:

- Lotus 1-2-3 2.x–4.0
- Lotus Notes
- Excel 2000, 98, and 2.x–97
- Microsoft FoxPro 2.x/Borland dBASE IV, III, III+, and II
- Microsoft Works 4.x and 3.0
- Text with Layout
- WordPerfect 6.x and 5.x

Importing data and formatting into Excel

If users select the appropriate converters in the Excel Office Setup, they can import data and formatting from files saved in the following formats:

- Lotus 1-2-3
- Microsoft Multiplan®
- Works version 2.*x* (version 3.*x* or later can save worksheets in Excel)
- Quattro Pro versions 1.0 and 5.0

Importing data and formatting into PowerPoint

If users select the appropriate converters in the PowerPoint Office Setup, they can import data and formatting from files saved in the following formats:

- Harvard Graphics versions 3.0 and 2.3 (DOS)
- Lotus Freelance version 4.0 (DOS)
- Lotus Freelance for Windows versions 2.1 through 1.0

Note Converters only import PowerPoint presentations; they do not export presentations to other file formats. However, PowerPoint 2000 users can save a presentation as text or graphics to mimic the export function. Then, Harvard Graphics and Lotus Freelance users can open the text or graphics file.

See also

- For more information about sharing files with a specific version of Word, Excel, or PowerPoint, see "Office 2000 Upgrading Reference" on page 455.
- You can change the default file format that Word, Excel, and PowerPoint use when saving new files. For more information, see "How to Specify the Default Format in Which to Save Files" on page 438 and "Using the System Policy Editor" on page 296.
- You can save Word, Excel, and PowerPoint files in Web Page format. For more information, see "Transferring Files Between HTML and Office Document Formats" on page 592.
- For information about installing additional file converters, see "Microsoft Office Converter Pack" on page 793.

Moving Files Between the Windows and Macintosh Operating Systems

Microsoft Office 2000 users can share files with Office 98 for the Macintosh users. The following topics identify the graphics and font issues that a user encounters when moving files between the Microsoft Windows and Macintosh operating systems.

Changes in graphics formats between Windows and the Macintosh

Windows stores graphics in WMF format, while the Macintosh operating system stores graphics in PICT format. If you create a file in Microsoft Word 2000 or Microsoft PowerPoint 2000 (Windows) that contains a graphics image, and then you move the document or presentation to Microsoft Word 98 or PowerPoint 98 (Macintosh), Word and PowerPoint (Macintosh) convert the WMF graphics image to PICT format.

Although the original WMF image is retained in the Word or PowerPoint (Macintosh) file, the PICT image is the one that the user sees. In this conversion, there might be a slight loss of image quality because Windows-based and Macintosh computers have different graphics rendering systems—GDI (Windows) and QuickDraw GX (Macintosh).

Depending on how the Macintosh user manipulates the graphics, the graphics format changes.

If a Macintosh user disassembles a graphics image in Word or PowerPoint, the image becomes a group of drawing objects. When the group of drawing objects moves into a Windows environment, the image remains a group of drawing objects. That is, the image is not reassembled, and so the image quality decreases.

If a Macintosh user does not disassemble a graphics image in Word or PowerPoint, but instead modifies the image's attributes by cropping it, recoloring it, or changing its brightness or contrast, then Word and PowerPoint convert the WMF graphic to PICT format. However, Word and PowerPoint do not discard the original WMF image. When the file containing the graphics image is moved back to Word 2000 or PowerPoint 2000 (Windows), Word 2000 and PowerPoint 2000 display the original WMF graphic with no loss of image quality.

When a file that contains graphics originates in Word or PowerPoint (Macintosh), and then is moved to Word 2000 or PowerPoint 2000 (Windows), similar conversions are made.

Important   The Windows PICT filter does not convert PICT images that contain JPEG-compressed QuickTime® data. As a result, an Office 98 (Macintosh) image loses its clarity when the file containing the image is opened in an Office 2000 application.

Converting Macintosh fonts to Windows fonts

Font names are different for Macintosh and Windows environments. The following table identifies which Macintosh fonts you can convert to Windows fonts.

Replace this Macintosh font	With this Windows font
Avant Garde	Century Gothic
Bookman	Bookman Old Style
Helvetica	Arial
Helvetica Narrow	Arial Narrow
New Century Schlbk	Century Schoolbook
Palatino	Book Antiqua
Times	Times New Roman
Zapf Chancery	Monotype Corsiva
Zapf Dingbats	Monotype Sorts

To replace a Macintosh font in PowerPoint, click **Replace Fonts** (**Format** menu). In the **Replace** box, click the Macintosh font you want to replace; in the **With** box, click the Windows font that you want as the substitute font.

▶ **To specify fonts to use when converting files in Word**

1   On the **Tools** menu, click **Options**, and then click the **Compatibility** tab.

2   Click **Font Substitution**.

3   In the **Missing document font** box, click the font you want to replace.

4   In the **Substituted font** box, click the font you want to use.

Converting Files to Office 2000

You can convert a single file or a group of files to the Microsoft Office 2000 version of Microsoft Word, Microsoft Excel, and Microsoft PowerPoint.

How to Convert Files to Word 2000, Excel 2000, and PowerPoint 2000

Microsoft Word 2000, Microsoft Excel 2000, and Microsoft PowerPoint 2000 include converters, add-ins, and filters that work with Office 98, Office 97, Office 95, and Office 4.*x* file formats—as well as other word-processing, spreadsheet, presentation, and database applications.

When you open files saved in other file formats, Word 2000, Excel 2000, and PowerPoint 2000 automatically convert the file to the default file format for Office 2000—the 97-2000 format. To complete the conversion process, save the file in Office 97-2000 format.

During the conversion process, built-in converters, add-ins, and filters preserve most of the original content and formatting. However, Word 2000, Excel 2000, and PowerPoint 2000 contain new features not included in other versions of Office. Other word-processing, spreadsheet, and presentation applications might also have features that work differently from the features in Office 2000.

You can convert files either one at a time or several at a time. The file formats that Word 2000, Excel 2000, and PowerPoint 2000 convert automatically are listed in the **Files of type** box in the **Open** and **Save As** dialog boxes (**File** menu).

Note   In Excel 2000, the list of file formats varies, depending on which type of sheet is active—worksheet, chart, and so on. For most formats, Excel 2000 converts only the active sheet. To convert the other sheets, switch to each sheet and save it separately by using the **Save As** dialog box.

If the file type that you want to convert is not listed in the **Files of type** box, then you must save the file in a format that Office 2000 supports. For example, you can open the file in the original application, and then you can save the file in Rich Text Format (RTF) or plain text, both of which Office 2000 can open.

In Office 2000, you convert a Word, Excel, and PowerPoint file or a file created in another word-processing, spreadsheet, or presentation application by using the **Open** and **Save As** dialog boxes (**File** menu).

▶ **To convert a single file**

1   On the **File** menu, click **Open**.

2   In the **Files of type** box, select a format.

3   In the **File name** box, select the file you want to convert.

4   On the **File** menu, click **Save As**, and then enter a new name for your converted file.

Conversion tools are an important element in helping your organization make a smooth transition to Microsoft Word, Microsoft Excel, and Microsoft PowerPoint 2000 either from a previous version of Microsoft Office or another application.

For the latest information about new tools for the conversion process, you can connect to the Microsoft Office 2000 Resource Kit Web site at http://www.microsoft.com/office/ork. The Web site is updated frequently and is a helpful resource when you are planning your organization's transition to Office 2000.

See also

- During the conversion process, some features and formatting might be changed or lost. For more information about sharing files with an earlier version of Office, see "Office 2000 Upgrading Reference" on page 455.

How to Specify the Default Format in Which to Save Files

When users save a file in Microsoft Office 2000, the file is saved in the Office 97-2000 file format by default—that is, the Office 97, Office 98, and Office 2000 file format. If Office 2000 users need to share files often with users of other versions of Office or other applications, you can change the default format that Microsoft Word, Microsoft Excel, and Microsoft PowerPoint 2000 use for saving new files.

Users select a default file format by using the **Options** dialog box (**Tools** menu). You can set one default file format for your organization by using the System Policy Editor.

Change the default file format in Word, PowerPoint, or Excel

To specify a default format for Word 2000 or PowerPoint 2000, use the **Save** tab in the **Options** dialog box (**Tools** menu). In the **Save Word files as** or **Save PowerPoint files as** box, select a file format. If you want to disable Word 2000 features that Word 97 does not support, select the appropriate check box when saving documents.

To specify a default format for Excel 2000, use the **Transition** tab in the **Options** dialog box (**Tools** menu). In the **Save Excel files as** box, select a file format.

After you set the default file format, all new documents, workbooks, and presentations are saved in the default format unless you specify a different format in the **Save As** dialog box (**File** menu) when you save a file.

Use a system policy to set a default file format

In Microsoft Windows 95/98, Microsoft Windows NT Workstation 4.0, and Windows 2000 Professional, you can set system policies for a single user, a specific group of users, or all users in a workgroup. The Office policy templates include a system policy to change the default value for the **Save as type** option in the **Save As** dialog box (**File** menu). This policy allows you to set one default file format for all the users in your organization.

▶ **To set a policy for the Save as type option for Word, Excel, and PowerPoint**

1   In the System Policy Editor, double-click the **Default User** icon.

2   In the **Default User Properties** dialog box, click the plus sign (+) next to the application you want to change.

3   Click the plus sign next to **Tools | Options**.

4   For Word, click the plus sign next to **Save**, and then select the **Save Word files as** check box.

   –or–

   For Excel, click the plus sign next to **Transition**, and then select the **Save Excel files as** check box.

   –or–

   For PowerPoint, click the plus sign next to **Save**, and then select the **Save PowerPoint files as** check box.

5   In the **Save Word files as**, **Save Excel files as**, or **Save PowerPoint files as** box, select the file format you want to use as the default.

   When you save and distribute this policy, all new files are saved in this default format.

When you set a **Save as type** policy, you can customize a message for users. For example, you can create a custom message to alert users if they are about to save a file in a format that is not the default format in a **Save as type** policy.

▶ **To prompt users to save in the default file format**

1   In the System Policy Editor, double-click the **Default User** icon.

2   In the **Default User Properties** dialog box, click the plus sign (+) next to **Microsoft Office 2000**.

3   Click the plus sign next to **Custom error messages**.

4   Select the **Default save prompt text** check box.

5   Type the text you want to use as the custom error message.

    When you save and distribute this policy, the message appears when a user tries to save a file in a format that is not the default format you specified in a **Save as type** policy.

When you distribute your system policies, all the users in your workgroup save Office files in the same format.

See also

- You can set policies for other Office 2000 options by using the System Policy Editor and the Microsoft Office policy templates. For more information, see "Using the System Policy Editor" on page 296.

New Tools for the Conversion Process

Conversion tools such as the Microsoft Office Converter Pack help your organization make a smooth transition to Microsoft Word, Microsoft Excel, and Microsoft PowerPoint 2000 either from a previous version of Office or another application. In the future, you can find additional conversion tools on the Microsoft Office 2000 Resource Kit Web site at http://www.microsoft.com/office/ork/.

How to Use the Microsoft Office Converter Pack

Many organizations upgrade gradually to new applications. During the transition, users often need to exchange files among old and new versions of an application.

To make the upgrade process go smoothly, the Microsoft Office Converter Pack provides tools that allow Microsoft Word, Microsoft Excel, and Microsoft PowerPoint users to share files with previous versions of Office and other applications.

The Office Converter Pack includes add-ins, converters, and filters for Word 97, Word 95, and Word 6.0; Excel 97, Excel 95, and Excel 5.0; and PowerPoint 97, PowerPoint 95, and PowerPoint 4.0.

Note   The Office Converter Pack does not recognize Word 6.0 for Windows NT or Excel 5.0 for Windows NT. You cannot install converters or add-ins from the Office Converter Pack for these 32-bit versions of Word or Excel.

Components for users of previous versions of Office

The Office Converter Pack includes the 97-2000 and HTML converters, which are of particular interest to users of previous Office versions.

Word 2000 and PowerPoint 2000 users can open documents and presentations saved in previous versions of Word and PowerPoint by using the converters installed during Office 2000 Setup. However, to open files saved in 97-2000 format, Word 95 and Word 6.0 users and PowerPoint 95 and PowerPoint 4.0 users must first install the 97-2000 converters included in the Office Converter Pack.

When Office 2000 users save documents, workbooks, and presentations in Web Page format, the files are converted to HTML format. The add-ins and converters necessary for opening and saving files in HTML format are included with Office 2000 Setup. However, users of previous versions of Word, Excel, and PowerPoint must first install the HTML add-ins and converters included in the Office Converter Pack before they can open and save HTML files.

Components for Office 2000 users

The Office Converter Pack includes additional text converters and filters not included with Office 2000 Setup.

Word 2000 users can install the following text converters:

- Borland dBASE II, III, III+, and IV
- Lotus AmiPro 3.*x* for Windows
- Microsoft FoxPro 2.6
- Microsoft Windows Write 3.*x*
- Microsoft Word 3.*x*–6.0 for MS-DOS
- Microsoft Works 3.0 for Windows
- Revisable-Form-Text Document Content Architecture (RFT-DCA)
- WordPerfect 4.0 for MS-DOS
- WordStar 3.3–7.0 for MS-DOS and WordStar 1.0–2.0 for Windows

Word 2000, Excel 2000, and PowerPoint 2000 users can install the following graphics filters:

- AutoCAD
- Micrografx Designer/Draw graphics filter
- Targa graphics filter

Install Office Converter Pack components

To install the add-ins, converters, and filters included in the Office Converter Pack on users' computers, perform the following steps:

1   Specify the components that you want to install by editing the Convpack.ini file.

2   Distribute the Office Converter Pack program files, and then instruct users to copy the files to a folder on their hard disks.

3   Instruct users to run the Office Converter Pack Setup program by clicking the Setup icon or typing **setup –s** on the command line.

Toolbox

The Office Converter Pack provides tools that allow Word 2000, Excel 2000, and PowerPoint 2000 users to share files with previous versions of Office and other applications. For more information about installing the Office Converter Pack, see "Microsoft Office Converter Pack" on page 793.

Edit the Convpack.ini file

The Office Converter Pack includes several program files; however, the Convpack.ini file is the only file that you can modify.

The Convpack.ini file stores Setup options for the Office Converter Pack. By editing the INI file, you can select the components that you want to install on users' computers.

The default is to install the add-ins, converters, and filters listed in the Convpack.ini file. However, if an application is not installed on a user's computer, the Office Converter Pack does not install any components for that application. For example, if a user doesn't have Word 95 installed on their computer, the Office Converter Pack does not install any Word 95 components (such as the WordPerfect, WordStar, or Word 97-2000 converters) even though you might have specified text converters in the Word95 section of the INI file.

In the Convpack.ini file, you can also specify the mode in which you want users to run the Office Converter Pack Setup program:

- Quiet mode

  The Office Converter Pack is installed on user's computers with the options specified in the Convpack.ini file. Users are not prompted to select components for installation.

- Full user interface mode

  Users are prompted to select add-ins, converters, and filters for installation.

▶ **To modify the Convpack.ini file**

1   Open the Convpack.ini file in a text editor, such as Notepad.

2   In each section of the INI file, set the options that you want.

In all sections of Convpack.ini (except the ConvPack section), the default for each option is **Yes**, which installs or automatically registers the component. If you do not want to install or automatically register a particular add-in, converter, or filter, you must change the value of the option to **No**.

The following syntax is used in the Convpack.ini file:

option = *value*

ConvPack section

The ConvPack section of the Convpack.ini file determines the Setup mode for the Office Converter Pack. The two options in this section include the following.

- **Quiet**
- **PreventUninstall**

When the value of the **Quiet** option is set to **No** (the default), the Setup program runs in full user interface mode and users are prompted to select add-ins, converters, and filters for installation.

If you do not want the Setup program to prompt users to select components, set the value of the **Quiet** option to **Yes**. The components that you specify in the Convpack.ini file are installed automatically on users' hard disks when they run the Setup program.

Note   If a user does not have an application on their computer, the Office Converter Pack does not install any components for that application even though you might have specified components for installation.

When the value of the **PreventUninstall** option is set to **No** (the default), the **Uninstall Microsoft Office Converter Pack** submenu is added to the **Programs** menu in Windows. By clicking **Uninstall Microsoft Office Converter Pack**, users can remove Office Converter Pack components from their computers. Users are prompted to confirm the removal of any shared components.

If you do not want users to remove components, set the value of the **PreventUninstall** option to **Yes**. The Setup program does not add a submenu to the **Programs** menu. However, users can still remove Office Converter Pack components by clicking **Add/Remove Programs** in Control Panel.

Word sections

The following table identifies the options in the Word2000, Word97, Word95, and Word6 sections of the Convpack.ini file. The default value for each option is **Yes**. If you do not want Word users to install a particular converter, change the value of the option to **No**.

Option	Description
AmiPro2	Lotus AmiPro 2. 0 for Windows. Included in Word6 section only.
AmiPro3	Lotus AmiPro 3.x for Windows. Not included in Word6 section.
dBASE	Borland dBASE II, III, III+, and IV
FoxPro	Microsoft FoxPro 2.6
Excel	Microsoft Excel 2.x–Excel 97
HTML	Hyper Text Markup Language (import and export). Not included in Word6 section.
Lotus123	Lotus 1-2-3 versions 2.0–4.0
RFT-DCA	Revisable-Form-Text Document Content Architecture
Text	Text with Layout converter and recover text from any file
Word97-2000	Microsoft Word 97-2000. Included in Word6 and Word95 sections only.
Word6-95	Microsoft Word 6.0/95. Included in Word97 section only.
DOSWord	Microsoft Word 3.x–6.0 for MS-DOS
MacWord	Microsoft Word 5.x and 4.0 for the Macintosh
WordPerfect4	WordPerfect 4.0 for MS-DOS
WordPerfect5	WordPerfect 5.x for MS-DOS and Windows
WordPerfect6	WordPerfect 6.x for MS-DOS and Windows. Not included in Word6 section.
WordStar	WordStar 3.3–7.0for MS-DOS and WordStar 1.0–2.0 for Windows
Works3	Microsoft Works 3.0 for Windows. Not included in Word6 section.
Works95	Microsoft Works 4.x for Windows. Not included in Word6 section
Write	Microsoft Windows Write 3.x

Excel sections

The following table identifies the options in the Excel97, Excel95, and Excel5 sections of the Convpack.ini file.

Option	Description
RegisterHTMLAddIn	Registers the HTML add-in
HTML	HTML Language add-in
Lotus123	Lotus 1-2-3 version 4.0 add-in. Included in Excel5 section only.
QuattroPro1	Quattro Pro 1.0–5.0 for Windows add-in
RegisterQuattroPro7AddIn	Registers the Quattro Pro 7.0–8.0 for Windows add-in. Included in Excel5 and Excel95 sections only.
QuattroPro7	Quattro Pro 7.0–8.0 for Windows add-in

For Excel 97, Excel 95, and Excel 5.0, the default is to install and automatically register the HTML add-in. The **RegisterHTMLAddIn** option is set to **Yes**, and a semicolon appears in front of the **HTML** option. If you don't want users to install and automatically register the HTML add-in, change the **RegisterHTMLAddIn** option to **No**. Then delete the semicolon in front of the **HTML** option, and set the option to **Yes** or **No** depending on whether you want users to install the HTML add-in.

For Excel 95 and Excel 5.0, the default is to install and automatically register the Quattro Pro 7.0–8.0 for Windows add-in. If you don't want users to install and automatically register the add-in, change the **RegisterQuattroPro7AddIn** option to **No** in the Excel95 and Excel5.0 sections. Then delete the semicolon in front of the **QuattroPro7** option, and set the option to **Yes** or **No** depending on whether you want users to install the add-in.

PowerPoint sections

The following table identifies the options in the PowerPoint97, PowerPoint95, and PowerPoint4 sections of the Convpack.ini file. The default for each option is **Yes**. If you do not want PowerPoint users to install a particular converter, change the value of the option to **No**.

Note If you change the value of the **PowerPoint97-2000** option in the PowerPoint4 section to **No**, you must also update the Filters16 section by removing the semicolons that appear in front of the **EMF**, **JPEG**, **PICT**, and **PNG** options and setting these filter options to **Yes** or **No** depending on whether you want users to install these filters.

Option	Description
PowerPoint95	PowerPoint 95 converter for PowerPoint 4.0. Included in PowerPoint4 section only.
PowerPoint97-2000	PowerPoint 97-2000 converter for PowerPoint 95 and PowerPoint 4.0. Included in PowerPoint95 and PowerPoint4 sections only.
HTML	Hypertext Markup Language converter. Included in PowerPoint95 section only.
Harvard	Harvard Graphics 3.0 and 2.3 for DOS converters
Freelance	Lotus Freelance 4.0 for DOS and Lotus Freelance 1.0–2.1 for Windows

Filters16 section

The Office Converter Pack includes a set of 16-bit graphics filters for Word and PowerPoint users.

The following table identifies the options in the Filters16 section of the Convpack.ini file. The default for each option is **Yes**. If you do not want Word or PowerPoint users to install a particular filter, change the value of the option to **No**.

Note By default, the **PowerPoint97-2000** option in the PowerPoint4 section is set to **Yes** and a semicolon appears in front of the **EMF**, **JPEG**, **PICT**, and **PNG** options in the Filters16 section. If you don't want PowerPoint 4.0 users to install the 97-2000 converter, change the value of the **PowerPoint97-2000** option to **No** in the PowerPoint4 section. Then delete the semicolon in front of the **EMF**, **JPEG**, **PICT**, and **PNG** options in the Filters16 section, and set the options to **Yes** or **No** depending on whether you want users to install the filters.

Option	Description
BMP	Bitmap import filter (Bmpimp.flt, Iffbmp.dll)
DRW	Micrografx Designer & Draw import filter (Drwimp.flt)
DXF	AutoCAD import filter (Dxfimp.flt)
EPS	Encapsulated PostScript import filter (Epsimp.flt)
GIF	Graphics Interchange Format import filter (Gifimp.flt, Iffgif.dll)
HPGL	Hewlett-Packard Graphics Language import filter (Hpglimp.flt)
PCX	PC Paintbrush import filter (Pcximp.flt, Iffpcx.dll)
TGA	Truevision Targa import filter (Tgaimp.flt, Ifftga.dll)
TIFF	Tag image file format import and export filter (Tiffimp.flt, Ifftiff.dll)
WMF	Windows Metafile import filter (Wmfimp.flt)
WPG	WordPerfect graphics import (Wpgimp.flt) and export (Wpgexp.flt) filters
EMF	Windows Enhanced Metafile import filter (Emfimp.flt)
JPEG	JPEG File Interchange Format import and export filter (Jpegimp.flt, Iffjpeg.dll)
PICT	Macintosh PICT import filter (Pictimp.flt)
PNG	Portable Network Graphics import filter (Pngimp.flt)

Filters32 section

The Office Converter Pack includes a set of 32-bit graphics filters for Word and PowerPoint users.

The following table identifies the options in the Filters32 section of the Convpack.ini file. The default for each option is **Yes**. If you do not want Word or PowerPoint users to install a particular filter, change the value of the option to **No**.

Note By default, the **GIF** option is set to **Yes** and the **PNG** option is disabled. (A semicolon appears in front of the **PNG** option.) If you don't want users to install the GIF filter, change the **GIF** option to **No**. Then delete the semicolon in front of the **PNG** option, and set the option to **Yes** or **No** depending on whether you want users to install the PNG filter.

Option	Description
BMP	Bitmap import filter (Bmpimp32.flt)
CDR	CorelDRAW import filter (Cdrimp32.flt)
CGM	Computer Graphics Metafile import filter (Cgmimp32.flt, Cgmimp32.fnt, Cgmimp32.cfg, Cgmimp32.hlp)
DRW	Micrografx Designer & Draw import filter (Drwimp32.flt)
DXF	AutoCAD import filter (Dxfimp32.flt)
EMF	Windows Enhanced Metafile import filter (Emfimp32.flt)
EPS	Encapsulated PostScript import filter (Epsimp32.flt)
FPX	FlashPix™ and Microsoft Picture It!® import and export filter (Fpx32.flt)
GIF	Graphics Interchange Format import and export filter (Gifimp32.flt)
PNG	Portable Network Graphics import and export filter (Png32.flt)
JPEG	JPEG File Interchange Format import and export filter (Jpegim32.flt)
PCD	Kodak® Photo CD import filter (Pcdimp32.flt, Pcdlib32.dll)
PCX	PC Paintbrush import filter (Pcximp32.flt)
PICT	Macintosh PICT import filter (Pictim32.flt)
TGA	Truevision Targa import filter (Tgaimp32.flt)
TIFF	Tag Image File Format import and export filter (Tiffim32.flt)
WMF	Windows metafile import filter (Wmfimp32.flt)
WPG	WordPerfect graphics import (Wpgimp32.flt) and export (Wpgexp32.flt) filters

Distribute the Office Converter Pack

After selecting the components that you want users to install by editing the
Convpack.ini file, you are ready to distribute the Office Converter Pack program to
users.

An easy way to distribute the program is to copy the Convpack.ini file and other files
to a network location where users can download the files. When it's time for users to
install add-ins, converters, and filters, you can notify the users to copy the
Convpack.ini file and other files from the network location to a folder on their hard
disks.

Install add-ins, converters, and filters on users' computers

Users can install the add-ins, converters, and filters on their computers by running the Office Converter Pack Setup program.

▶ **To install add-ins, converters, and filters**

- Type **setup –s** on the command line.

  –or–

  In the Office Converter Pack folder, double-click the Setup icon.

  If the **Quiet** option in the ConvPack section of the INI file is set to **No** (the default), the Setup program runs in full user interface mode and users are prompted to select add-ins, converters, and filters.

  If you changed the value of the **Quiet** option to **Yes**, the components specified in the INI file are installed automatically on users' hard disks and users are not prompted to make selections.

Remove Office Converter Pack components

If users no longer need the add-ins, converters, and filters that they installed with the Office Converter Pack, they can remove the components by using one of the following methods.

- Clicking the **Uninstall Microsoft Office Converter Pack** submenu on the **Programs** menu in Windows.

  The submenu is available to users only if the **PreventUninstall** option in the Convpack section of the INI file is set to **No**.

- Clicking **Add/Remove Programs** in Control Panel.

Future Tools for the Conversion Process

Conversion tools are an important element in helping your organization make a smooth transition to Microsoft Word, Microsoft Excel, and Microsoft PowerPoint 2000 either from a previous version of Microsoft Office or another application.

For the latest information about new tools for the conversion process, you can connect to the Microsoft Office 2000 Resource Kit Web site at http://www.microsoft.com/office/ork. The Web site is updated frequently and is a helpful resource when you are planning your organization's transition to Office 2000.

Meeting the Year 2000 Challenge

The scope of year 2000 issues presents a major challenge for administrators in many organizations. With a few exceptions, Microsoft Office 2000 applications are ready for the year 2000. However, there are several additional steps you can take to prepare for and manage the transition to the next millennium.

Understanding Year 2000 Issues

Microsoft has expanded and emphasized testing for year 2000 related issues in all Microsoft products, including Microsoft Office 2000. All products meet (or meet with minor issues) the requirements of the Microsoft Year 2000 Compliance Statement before they are released to manufacturing.

Note   If date-related issues are identified after a product is released, Microsoft addresses them through standard Microsoft Technical Support channels at no additional cost.

Consistent with Microsoft's policy of compliance, Office 2000 is prepared for the year 2000 in the following ways:

- Office 2000 applications store and calculate dates by using a four-digit year format.
- Date fields contain only date functionality.
- Office 2000 applications carry out accurate leap-year calculations.

If your organization uses technology from vendors other than Microsoft, including custom Excel macros or Access reports, then the following date issues might present problems in the year 2000:

- Two-digit and four-digit date formats

    Some applications use a two-digit rather than a four-digit date format to represent the year. With a two-digit format, some applications cannot reliably determine which century to use for the year 00 calculations.

- Date fields that contain more than the date

    Date fields sometimes contain not only the date, but also special functions that begin or end on a specific date. Date functions vary among organizations, so no single tool can provide consistent date and function adjustments.

- Year 2000 leap-year anomaly

    The year 2000 is an unusual leap year that happens only once every 400 years. A typical leap year is divisible by 4. However, years that are divisible by 100 are not leap years unless they are also divisible by 400. Some software systems and applications use a simple set of rules to calculate a leap year and do not recognize the year 2000 as a leap year.

See also

- The *Microsoft Year 2000 Product Guide* includes additional information about year 2000 date-handling capabilities in Microsoft products. For more information, see the Microsoft Year 2000 Resource Center Web site at http://www.microsoft.com/year2000/.

Microsoft Year 2000 Readiness Disclosure Statement

The information in this document is being designated a year 2000 readiness disclosure and is found at the Microsoft Year 2000 Web site located at http://www.microsoft.com/year2000/.

This information is provided pursuant to the Year 2000 Information and Readiness Disclosure Act for the sole purpose of assisting the planning for the transition to the year 2000. This document contains information currently available concerning the behavior of Microsoft's products with respect to year 2000 processing and is updated regularly and subject to change. We therefore recommend that you check the information regularly for any changes.

The information in this document is provided "As Is" without warranty of any kind. Microsoft disclaims all warranties, either express or implied, including the warranties of merchantability and fitness for a particular purpose. Moreover, Microsoft does not warrant or make any representations regarding the use or the results of the use of the information contained herein in terms of its correctness, accuracy, reliability, or otherwise. No oral or written information or advice given by Microsoft Corporation or its authorized representatives shall create a warranty or in any way decrease the scope of this warranty disclaimer. In no event shall Microsoft corporation or its suppliers be liable for any damages whatsoever including direct, indirect, incidental, consequential, loss of business profits, punitive or special damages, even if Microsoft corporation or its suppliers have been advised of the possibility of such damages. Some states do not allow the exclusion or limitation of liability for consequential or incidental damages, so the foregoing limitation may not apply to you. The information in this document is found at the Year 2000 Web site and is intended to be read in conjunction with other information located at the Year 2000 Web site, including but not limited to Microsoft's year 2000 compliance statement, the description of the categories of compliance into which Microsoft has classified its products in its year 2000 product guide, and the Microsoft year 2000 test criteria.

Any statements made to you by Microsoft or contained herein in the course of providing year 2000 related fixes, year 2000 diagnostic tools, or remediation services (if any) are subject to the Year 2000 Information and Readiness Disclosure Act (112 Stat. 2386). In case of a dispute, this act may reduce your legal rights regarding the use of any such statements, unless otherwise specified by your contract or tariff.

How to Prepare for the Year 2000

To prepare your organization for the transition to the year 2000, you can take several steps to reduce potential errors and problems.

Educate and train users

You are better prepared for solving year 2000 problems when your users can recognize and respond to date-related issues. Educate users, and make sure to include anyone who uses macro languages such as Visual Basic for Applications or date-dependent applications such as Microsoft Access.

Customize how dates are interpreted by Office 2000

By default, Microsoft Office 2000 interprets dates formatted with two digits for the year to be between 1930 and 2029. If this range is not appropriate for your organization, you can customize the setting for all Microsoft Windows 98 and Windows 2000 users in your organization.

To customize this setting, double-click the **Regional Settings Properties** icon in Control Panel, and then click the **Date** tab. In the **When a two digit year is entered, interpret as a year between** box, enter the range that you want to use.

When you customize this setting, the following value entry is added to the Windows registry:

HKEY_CURRENT_USER\Control Panel\International\Calendars\TwodigitYearMax

Set a four-digit short date format

After verifying that there are no conflicting date settings in any applications, set the system short date on users' computers to represent the year with a four-digit format, rather than a two-digit format. To set the system short date, double-click the **Regional Settings Properties** icon in Control Panel, and then click the **Date** tab. In the **Short date style** box, select the date format you want.

Establish clear guidelines for date formats

The date format is typically not a problem for Microsoft Word or Microsoft PowerPoint users. However, Microsoft Excel and Access users must comply with the four-digit year requirement. In particular, users must use a four-digit format to represent the year in applications that use dates in calculations.

Excel 2000 has two new date formats: m/d/yyyy and Mmm yyyy. To specify one of these new date formats, click **Cells** on the **Format** menu, click the **Number** tab, click **Date**, and then select the format you want in the **Type** box.

Update existing files

Scan all existing files to see whether there are any potential problems with the way that dates are formatted. For example:

- In Excel workbooks, convert dates with a two-digit year to a four-digit year, and then confirm the accuracy of the conversion.

- After converting workbooks from Excel 95 or Excel 5.0 format to 97-2000 format, scan the workbooks to see whether they have functions that accept text dates with a two-digit year.

  The date algorithm in Excel 2000 is different from the one used in Excel 95 and Excel 5.0, so functions might produce different results from what they did in Excel 95 and Excel 5.0. (Text dates with a four-digit year and serial dates are not affected by the change in the algorithm.)

Toolbox

To expedite the task of scanning Excel workbooks for potential date format problems, you can use the Microsoft Excel Date Fix Wizard and the Microsoft Excel Date Migration Wizard. For information about installing these tools, see "Excel File Recovery and Date Tools" on page 775.

See also

- Many Excel 2000 and Excel 97 functions accept dates as arguments. For a complete list of these functions, see "Date Arguments in Microsoft Excel Functions" on page 453.

- There are other ways that you can reduce your organization's exposure to software problems related to the year 2000. For more information, see the Microsoft Year 2000 Resource Center Web site at http://www.microsoft.com/year2000/.

Date Arguments in Microsoft Excel Functions

The date algorithm in Microsoft Excel 2000 and Excel 97 is different from the date algorithm in earlier versions of Excel.

The following Excel functions accept dates as arguments:

ACCRINT	DURATION	RECEIVED
ACCRINTM	EDATE	TBILLEQ
AMORDEGRC	EOMONTH	TBILLPRICE
AMORLINC	INTRATE	TBILLYIELD
COUPDAYBS	MDURATION	WEEKDAY
COUPDAYS	MONTH	WEEKNUM
COUPDAYSNC	NETWORKDAYS	WORKDAY
COUPNCD	ODDFPRICE	XIRR
COUPNUM	ODDFYIELD	XNPV
COUPPCD	ODDLPRICE	YEAR
DATEVALUE	ODDLYIELD	YEARFRAC
DAY	PRICE	YIELD
DAYS360	PRICEDISC	YIELDDISC
DISC	PRICEMAT	YIELDMAT

CHAPTER 11

Office 2000 Upgrading Reference

Microsoft Office 2000 users can collaborate with users of other versions of Office, as well as other software applications. However, previous versions of Office do not support all Office 2000 features. As you plan your upgrading strategy, be sure to take advantage of new collaboration tools—and also be sure to take the differences between Office 2000 and earlier versions of Office applications into consideration.

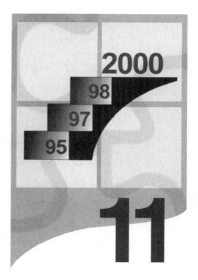

In This Chapter

Upgrading to Access 2000

In a multiuser environment, your strategy for upgrading to Microsoft Access 2000 depends on whether all users are upgrading to Access 2000 at the same time.

Strategies for Upgrading to Access 2000

If all the users in your organization are upgrading to Microsoft Access 2000 at the same time, you probably want to convert previous-version databases to Access 2000. You cannot open an Access 2000 database in a previous version of Access, but you can convert an Access 2000 database to Access 97.

If your organization is upgrading gradually to Access 2000, users of different versions of Access might need to share information. In this scenario, you can enable previous-version Access databases, or you can upgrade only parts of them. You can use the enabled Access database in Access 2000, but you must make any changes to the design of the database in the previous version of Access.

If users are upgrading gradually to Access 2000, but you want to make design changes in Access 2000, you can split an Access database into a front-end/back-end application. The back-end database contains the data, and it remains in the earliest version of Access that you are using. The front-end database is linked to the tables in the back-end database. To take advantage of new features, you can convert the front-end database to Access 2000.

How to Convert a Previous-version Database to Access 2000

If you want to make design changes to a previous-version Microsoft Access database in Access 2000, or if you want to take advantage of Access 2000 features when you use a database, you must convert the database to Access 2000.

Convert a previous-version Access database

You cannot convert an Access database into a file with the same name and location as the original database. Before you convert a previous-version Access database, perform the following tasks:

- Create a backup copy of the Access database.
- Close the Access database.

If the Access database that you are using is a multiuser database located on a server or in a shared folder, make sure that no one else has it open.

▶ To convert a previous-version Access database

1   In Access 2000, on the **Tools** menu, point to **Database Utilities**; point to **Convert Database**, and then click **To Current Access Database Version**.

2   In the **Database To Convert From** dialog box, select the database you want to convert, and then click **Convert**.

3   In the **Convert Database Into** dialog box, type a new name (without the .mdb extension) for the Access 2000 database file.

 –or–

 Select a different location for the Access 97 database file. (You can keep the same name for the database file or change it.)

4   Click **Save**.

Convert a secured Access database

Before you convert a secured database, you must join the *workgroup information file* that defines the user accounts, and the user account that you use to log on during conversion must have the following *permissions*:

- Your user account must have Open/Run and Open Exclusive permissions for the database.

- Your user account must have Modify Design or Administer permissions for all tables in the database, or you must be the owner of all tables in the database.

- Your user account must have Read Design permissions for all objects in the database.

▶ To join a workgroup information file

1 Quit Access 2000.

2 To start the Workgroup Administrator, open the folder for the language of Microsoft Office that you are using, and then double-click **Wrkgadm.exe**.

   Alternatively, you can use the MS Access Workgroup Administrator shortcut in the Program Files\Microsoft Office\Office folder.

3 In the **Workgroup Administrator** dialog box, click **Join**.

4 In the **Database** box, type the path and name of the workgroup information file that defines the Access workgroup you want to join, and then click **OK**.

   –or–

   Click **Browse**, and use the **Select Workgroup Information File** dialog box to locate the workgroup information file.

The next time you start Access 2000, it uses the user and group accounts and passwords in the workgroup information file for the workgroup that you join.

After you convert an Access database, you can make sure that it retains its security by recreating the workgroup information file in Access 2000. If you recreate the workgroup information file, you must have the exact, case-sensitive information, and you must define the accounts and groups exactly the same as the original workgroup information file.

If you cannot recreate the workgroup information file, you can use the Workgroup Administrator to join the secure database's previous-version workgroup information file. However, it is recommended that you convert the workgroup information file to Access 2000 before you join it. As long as you use the database with its original workgroup information, it retains all its security except permissions for the modules.

Protect Visual Basic for Applications code in a converted database

In Access 2000, you cannot protect your modules with *user-level security*. However, you can protect your modules, and the code behind your forms and reports, by protecting the Visual Basic for Applications (VBA) code with a password.

▶ To protect VBA code with a password

1   Open the Microsoft Access database that contains the VBA code you want to protect.

2   In the Database window, under **Objects**, right-click **Macro**, and then click **Visual Basic Editor**.

3   In the Visual Basic Editor, on the **Tools** menu, click *ProjectName* **Project Properties**.

4   Click the **Protection** tab.

5   Select the **Lock project for viewing** check box.

6   Enter a password in the **Password** box, and confirm the password by entering it again in the **Confirm password** box.

The next time you open the Access database or Access project, the Visual Basic for Applications code is protected. You or any user is required to enter the password to view and edit the Visual Basic for Applications code.

When you protect Visual Basic for Applications code with a password, consider the following:

• To remove the password, clear all information on the **Protection** tab in the **Project Properties** dialog box for the Access database file or Access project file.

• If you set a password but do not select the **Lock project for viewing** check box, anyone can view and edit the code; only the **Project Properties** dialog box is protected.

• Store the password in a safe place. If you forget the password, you cannot view or edit the VBA code.

Convert new toolbars and menu bars

Access 97 or later supports a new style of toolbars and menu bars. When you convert an Access version 2.0 or Access 95 database to Access 2000, any custom toolbars, as well as built-in toolbars, are automatically converted to the new style of toolbar.

Custom menu bars created with the Microsoft Access 95 Menu Builder or with macros that use **AddMenu** actions are interpreted as the new style of menu bars when you open a converted Access database. However, custom menu bars are not automatically converted, and therefore they cannot be edited by using the **Customize** dialog box.

▶ **To create a menu bar or shortcut menu from previous-version macros**

1   In the Database window, under **Objects**, click **Macros,** and then click the name of the macro for which you want to create a menu bar or shortcut menu.

To create the new style of menu bar or shortcut menu from macros that you previously used for custom menus, select only the top-level menu bar macro. You do not need to select the macro group for each menu that appears on the menu bar.

2   On the **Tools** menu, point to **Macro,** and then click **Create Menu From Macro** or **Create Shortcut Menu From Macro.**

Enable Name AutoCorrect in a converted Access database

The Name AutoCorrect feature automatically corrects common side effects that occur when you rename forms, reports, tables, queries, or fields, or controls on forms and reports. However, this feature is not enabled by default in a converted database.

▶ **To enable Name AutoCorrect in a converted Access database**

1   On the **Tools** menu, click **Options,** and then click the **General** tab.

2   To have Access maintain the information it needs to run Name AutoCorrect, but not take any action, select the **Track name AutoCorrect info** check box.

3   To have Access run Name AutoCorrect as name changes occur in the database, select the **Perform name AutoCorrect** check box.

4   To have Access keep a log of the changes it makes each time it runs Name AutoCorrect, select the **Log name AutoCorrect changes** check box. Access saves the changes in a table called name AutoCorrect Log. Each change is a record in the name AutoCorrect Log table.

5   Open each of the database objects in Design view, save the object, and close it.

Update code in a converted database

The DoMenuItem action is replaced in Access 2000 with the RunCommand action; the DoMenuItem action is still supported for backward compatibility. When you convert a database, the DoMenuItem action is automatically converted to the RunCommand action.

If your Access database uses add-ins or library databases created in previous versions of Access, you must convert them.

Access 2000 does not support the DAO 2.5/3.x compatibility library. If you attempt to convert an Access database in which the code contains older versions of DAO objects, methods, and properties that depend on the DAO 2.5/3.x compatibility library, you receive a message that there were compilation errors during the conversion of the database.

Before you convert an Access database, update the code so that it does not depend on the DAO 2.5/3.x compatibility library. If you still receive a message that there were compilation errors during conversion, open the converted database in Access 2000, remove the reference to the missing DAO 2.5/3.x compatibility library, and then set a reference to the Microsoft DAO 3.6 Object Library.

If you enable the database instead of converting it, you cannot remove or set references in Access 2000. You must make any changes to the code or the references in the previous version of Access.

▶ **To remove or set a reference while the Visual Basic Editor is open**

1   On the **Tools** menu, click **References**.

    The **References** command is available only when a Module window is open and active in Design view.

2   In the **References** *ProjectName* dialog box, select the check boxes for the type libraries you want to reference, and then clear the check boxes for the type libraries that you do not want to reference.

Convert a replica set to Access 2000

To convert a replica set created in Access 97 so that you can use it in Access 2000, you must convert each *replica* individually. For best results, synchronize your replica set before conversion. If your replica set is secured, it is also helpful to convert the System.mdw file, which contains permissions for the database. For the conversion to work, all members of the replica set must be using computers with Access 2000 installed.

Take a conservative approach when converting a replica set. The following procedure allows you to test a temporary second replica set before committing your original replica set to the conversion.

Caution   Do not synchronize the test Design Master you create by following this procedure with members of your working replica set. Otherwise, unintended changes to the data or structure of your working replica set might occur.

▶ **To convert a replica set to Access 2000**

1   Make a copy of the current Design Master created in Access 97, and put the copy on a different computer, or isolate it completely from any other members of the replica set.

2   In Access 97, make the isolated copy the new Design Master by pointing to **Replication** on the **Tools** menu, and then clicking **Recover Design Master**.

3   Create some replicas based on the new Design Master.

4   To convert the new Design Master to an Access 2000 database, on the **Tools** menu, point to **Database Utilities**, and then click **Convert Database**.

5   Repeat step 4 for all replicas in your replica set.

6   Synchronize the newly converted Design Master with the newly converted replicas.

7   Test the replica set.

If you want to change some objects, either you can make the changes in the original Design Master after you convert it or you can keep the copy to import the changed objects from the original Design Master.

After you are satisfied that the copy works, delete the new Design Master and all of its replicas. Make sure that all users who have access to the Design Master and replica databases have installed Access 2000. Then you can follow the same steps to convert the original Design Master to Access 2000 and convert all the original replicas.

Note   You cannot open the converted replicas again in Access 97.

See also

- For more information about the Name AutoCorrect feature or converting a database that contains code, see Microsoft Access online Help.

- For more information about workgroup information files and secured Access databases, see "Setting User-Level Security" on page 390.

How to Convert an Access 2000 Database Back to Access 97

After you convert a database from a previous version of Microsoft Access to Access 2000, you might need to make a copy of the database available for a user who is running Access 97. You can convert an Access 2000 database to an Access 97 database if it is not a member of a *replica* set. Any functionality that is specific to Access 2000 is lost when you convert the database to Access 97.

Converting an Access 2000 database to an Access 97 database makes the following changes to the converted database:

- Links to *data access pages* are lost.

- Data that relies on *Unicode* support in Access 2000 might not convert correctly. Access 97 uses characters from only a single *code page*—a numbered set of 256 characters. For example, an Access 97 database might use only ANSI characters. During conversion, the collating order of the original Access 2000 database determines which set of characters that the resulting Access 97 database can use; any characters that are not in this set are not converted correctly.

- An Access 2000 database containing a table with a **FieldSize** property of Decimal cannot be converted to Access 97. You must change the **FieldSize** property to another value such as Single or Double, or you must change the data type of the field to Currency before you can successfully convert the database.

Convert the database to Access 97

If the Access database is secure, remove *user-level security*. After you convert the database, you can secure the Access database in Access 97. If the Access database is protected with a password, you can convert the database without removing the password.

Important   If the Visual Basic for Applications (VBA) code is protected with a password, you must supply the password before you convert the database. To supply the password, open a module to start Microsoft Visual Basic. On the **Tools** menu, click *Database Name* **Properties,** and then enter the password in the **Password** dialog box.

▶ **To convert an Access 2000 database to Access 97**

1   Open the Access database that you want to convert.

If this is a multiuser database located on a server or in a shared folder, make sure that no one else has it open.

If you are converting a secured Access database, make sure that you have Open/Run and Open Exclusive *permissions* for the database and Read Design permissions for all objects in the database.

2   On the **Tools** menu, point to **Database Utilities**, click **Convert Database**, and then click **To Prior Access Database Version**.

3   In the **Convert Database Into** dialog box, type the name of the new previous-version database that you want to create in the **File name** box, and then click **Save**.

4   If the Access 2000 database is secured and you want the converted database to retain that security, open the database in Access 97 and reapply user-level security.

Note   If your Access 2000 database contains code, you might need to fix missing references after you convert the database to Access 97. Also, if your Access database uses add-ins or library databases created in Access 2000, you must convert them back to Access 97.

Fix missing references in the converted database

You can convert code that uses Data Access Objects (DAO) back to Access 97, but you might receive a message that your computer is missing at least one of the Access 97 object libraries.

▶ **To fix the missing references in a converted database**

1   Convert the Access 2000 database to Access 97. When you receive a message that your computer is missing at least one of the Access 97 object libraries, click **OK**.

2   Open the converted Access database in Access 97.

3   Open a module in the database.

4   On the **Tools** menu, click **References**.

5   In the **Available References** box, clear the check boxes next to any missing references, and then set a reference to the Microsoft DAO 3.51 Object Library.

Note   Unlike Access 2000, Access 97 is not designed to work with ActiveX Data Objects (ADO).

See also

• For more information about settings permissions in Access 2000, see "Setting User-Level Security" on page 390.

Enabling a Previous-version Access Database in Access 2000

You can enable a Microsoft Access database in a multiuser environment in which all users do not upgrade to Access 2000 at the same time. In this situation, a database must be used simultaneously with different versions of Access, and Access 2000 users can enable a database in a previous-version format.

When an Access 2000 user enables a database, Access maintains the original format so that a user of a previous version of Microsoft Access can continue to use the database. For example, if a shared database is created in Access version 2.0, you can use this database with Access 2.0, and you can enable it in Access 2000.

Access enables the previous-version database in Access 2000 without making any permanent changes to the previous-version database. An enabled database can still be opened with its original version of Access.

▶ **To enable a previous-version Access database in Access 2000**

1   On the **File** menu, click **Open**.

2   Click the previous-version Access database that you want to enable, and then click **Open**.

3   In the **Convert/Open Database** dialog box, click **Open Database**.

Modifying the design of objects

You can enable an Access 2.0 database, an Access 95 database, or an Access 97 database so that you can use them in Access 2000. When you use Access 2000 to enable a previous-version Access database, you can view database objects, and you can add, delete, or modify records. However, you cannot modify the design of objects.

To modify the design of existing objects or to add new objects, you must open the database with the version of Access used to create it. You cannot open an Access 2000 database with a previous version of Access.

Linking or importing tables

In a previous-version Access database, you cannot link or import an Access 2000 table. However, you can export an Access 2000 table to a previous-version Access database. You can also cut, copy, and paste data from an Access 2000 table to a table in a previous version of Access.

Converting toolbars and menu bars

Access 97 or later supports a new style of toolbars and menu bars. When you enable an Access 95 database in Access 2000, custom toolbars are converted to the new style, but the conversion is not saved. Custom menu bars are interpreted as the new style of menu bar, but the menu bar macros are not converted and continue to be supported.

Managing the size of an enabled database

Your Access database might increase in size when you enable it. If you have a database that has already been enabled in a previous version of Access, and if you enable it in Access 2000, the size of the Microsoft Visual Basic project increases even more.

In rare cases, you might have to enable an Access 2.0 database in Access 95, enable it again in Access 97, and then enable it in Access 2000. In this case, the Visual Basic project must store information in the format of each version.

See also

- Before you enable an Access database, you must update code that uses objects, methods, or properties that depend on the DAO 2.5/3.x compatibility library. Code that depends on this library causes compilation errors. For more information, see "How to Convert a Previous-version Database to Access 2000" on page 456.

- Instead of enabling, you can share front-end/back-end applications between Access 2.0, Access 95, Access 97, and Access 2000, provided that the back-end database is maintained in the oldest version of Access. For more information, see "Using an Access Database with Multiple Versions" on page 465.

- For information about enabling a secured Access database, see "How to Convert a Previous-version Database to Access 2000" on page 456.

Using an Access Database with Multiple Versions

In some situations, users of a shared Microsoft Access database might not upgrade to Access 2000 at the same time. You can allow users of different versions of Access to share an Access database—without having to alter the original database. You can upgrade parts of the database to Access 2000 so that Access 2000 users can take advantage of many new features, and you can still use the original unchanged database for users of previous versions of Access. Users of all versions of Access can share the same data.

You can use this strategy whether your Access database is in one file or your database is a front-end/back-end application. To use an Access database that is one file in several versions of Access, convert it to a front-end/back-end application. The data in the back end remains in the oldest version of Access, and you use a front end that has been converted to Access 2000.

To use a front-end/back-end application with several versions of Access, convert the front end of the application.

Using a one-file database with multiple versions of Access

To use an Access database that consists of one file in several versions of Access, convert the database to a front-end/back-end application. The data remains in the oldest version of Access, and you use a front end that is converted to Access 2000.

After you convert the front end, you can enhance it to support new features for users of Access 2000. Users of previous versions of Access can continue to use the previous-version database. For example, if the back-end tables are in Access version 2.0 format, you can use up to four versions of Access as identified in the following list:

- Access 2.0 (using the original database)
- Access 95 and Access 97 (using an enabled version of the original database, or a converted front-end database)
- Access 2000 (using a converted front-end database)

▶ **To use a one-file Access database with several versions of Access**

1   Convert the Access database to Access 2000, and specify a new name.

2   Use the Database Splitter Wizard (**Tools** menu, **Database Utilities** command) to split the converted database into a front-end/back-end application.

3   Delete the back-end database that the Database Splitter Wizard creates. You want your data to remain in the original database, so you are going to be using the original database as the back-end database. The back-end database must be in the oldest version of Access that you are using.

4   Run the Linked Table Manager (**Tools** menu, **Database Utilities** command) to link the new Access 2000 front-end database to the tables in the previous-version database.

Using a front-end/back-end application

If your Access database is already a front-end/back-end application, you need to convert only the front end to Access 2000.

After you convert the front end, you can enhance it to support new features for users of Access 2000.

▶ **To use a front-end/back-end application with several versions of Access**

1   Convert the front-end database to Access 2000, but leave the back-end database unchanged.

2   Run the Linked Table Manager (**Tools** menu, **Database Utilities** command) to link the new Access 2000 front-end database to the tables in the previous-version back-end database.

See also

- For information about optimizing linked tables, or more information about the Linked Table Manager, see Microsoft Access online Help.

Saving Design Changes to a Shared Access Database

You cannot save design changes to a Microsoft Access database while other users are sharing the Access database with you. The only way to ensure that changes are saved is by opening the Access database in exclusive mode.

In general, when you are working in a database in shared mode, and you try to make a design change to an item or to a database object that is not a table or a query, Access temporarily promotes you to exclusive mode for the Access database—if you are the only user of the Access database at that time. When you save all your design changes, and close all the Design view windows, Access returns the Access database to shared mode. In the interim, other users cannot open the Access database.

If another user has the Access database open in shared mode, and you try to make a major design change such as modifying a form, Access alerts you that you might not be able to save your changes. However, if another user has the Access database open in shared mode, and you try to make a minor design change such as changing printer settings, Access does not alert you that you might not be able to save your design changes. In both cases, wait until you are the only user of the Access database so that you can save your major design changes, and Access can save your minor design changes.

Saving major and minor design changes

If you are not the only user who has the Access database open, Access alerts you when you might not be able to save the following major design changes:

- Changes to database objects (except tables and queries) in Design view.

- Changes to a form property sheet in Form view.

- Compiling the project, modifying project properties, or adding or removing a reference in the Visual Basic Editor.

- Renaming, pasting, or deleting a database object.

- Saving a database object as another type of database object.

- Adding or modifying controls on a command bar.

- Editing custom groups in the Database window.

- Creating, renaming, moving, and deleting a *data access page*.

If you are not the only user who has the Access database open, Access does not alert you when you might not be able to save the following minor design changes:

- Changes to datasheet formatting properties such as line styles and fonts.

- Freezing, unfreezing, hiding, and showing datasheet columns.

- Adjusting datasheet column width and row size.

- Changes to the filter or sort order for a form or datasheet.

- Changes to the state of a subdatasheet (whether expanded or collapsed).

- Changes to the OLE/DDE link of an OLE object, or changes to the contents of an unbound object frame.

- Changes to printer settings.

- Changes to a command bar, such as the location, and whether the command bar is visible or not invisible.

- Changes to the layout of the database window.

Sharing Access database design and development

If you are going to share the design of an Access database, consider using the following strategies:

- Assign specific objects or groups of objects to each developer. For example, one developer can design forms, and another developer can design reports. Then, each developer can work on a private copy of the Access database. When your development team is ready to test, assemble, and produce the database, each developer can export each database object from a private copy of the database to a main Access database.

- Use a source code control program. For example, you can use a combination of Microsoft Visual SourceSafe® version 6.0, and the Source Code Control add-in that enables Visual Source Safe Code support in Access. This add-in is available from the Microsoft Office 2000 Developer. If you use Visual SourceSafe, it is a good idea to run the Performance Analyzer on a regular basis to maintain optimum performance. To run the Performance Analyzer, on the **Tools** menu, point to **Analyze**, and then click **Performance**.

See also

- For information about sharing an Access database on a network, see Microsoft Access online Help.

Troubleshooting Your Upgrade to Access 2000

Use the following tips to help resolve common problems when upgrading to Microsoft Access 2000.

An identifier causes an error.

Microsoft Access 97 or later supports some new Microsoft Visual Basic keywords, so you cannot use these keywords as identifiers in Access 2000. The following keywords are supported by Access 97 or later: **AddressOf**, **Decimal**, **DefDec**, **Enum**, **Event**, **Friend**, **Implements**, **RaiseEvent**, **WithEvents**. When you convert a previous-version Access database to Access 2000, existing identifiers that are the same as new Visual Basic keywords cause a compile error. To fix this problem, change existing identifiers so that they are not keywords.

A procedure causes an error.

In Access version 2.0, you can specify a name for a procedure that is the same as a module name. However, in Access 95 or later, a procedure and a module cannot have the same name. To fix this problem, rename the procedure or rename the module. Alternatively, you can avoid this error by using a fully qualified name for the procedure in your Visual Basic for Applications (VBA) code.

I receive an error that a table exceeds the limit of 32 indexes.

If your Access 2.0 database contains a table with 32 or more indexes and relationships combined, you might receive an error when you convert to Access 2000. To resolve this error, open your database in Access 2.0, and either modify your table design to reduce the number of relationships for the primary key table or remove some indexes from the foreign key table. Then try to convert your database again.

I receive an out-of-memory error when converting a large database.

Visual Basic for Applications (VBA) has a limit of 1,082 modules per Access database, which includes forms and reports with the **HasModule** property set to **Yes**. To fix this memory problem, reduce the number of objects in your Access database. Consider dividing your application into multiple databases. If you have modules with a large amount of code, consider using library databases to store the code.

My 16-bit API calls do not convert.

If an Access 2.0 module contains 16-bit application programming interface (API) calls, you might receive an error message when you convert the database to Access 2000. You must change the API **Declare** statements in the converted database to their 32-bit equivalents.

My code does not compile.

When you convert an Access 2.0 database to Access 2000, the conversion utility converts Access Basic code to Visual Basic for Applications (VBA) code. If all code does not successfully compile, you might receive an error message after you convert to Access 2000.

In the converted Access database, open a module in Design view, and then on the **Debug** menu, click **Compile** *ProjectName*. As Access compiles, it stops at any line of code that contains an error. You can then modify the syntax to resolve the compile error.

In rare instances, the conversion utility might fail to convert some syntax. For example, it might fail to modify a **DoCmd** statement into a **DoCmd** method. You might also receive compile error messages, if your Access 2.0 database contains syntax errors. For this reason, it is a good idea to compile all of your previous-version database modules before you convert them to Access 2000.

Access 2000 does not support the DAO 2.5/3.*x* compatibility library. If you attempt to convert a database in which the code uses objects, methods, or properties that depend on the DAO 2.5/3.*x* compatibility library, you receive a message that there were compilation errors during the conversion of the database. Before you convert the database, update the code so that it does not depend on the DAO 2.5/3.*x* compatibility library. If you still receive a message that there were compilation errors during conversion, open the converted database in Access 2000, remove the reference to the missing DAO 2.5/3.*x* compatibility library, and then set a reference to the Microsoft DAO 3.6 Object Library.

My converted Access 2.0 report has different margins

You might encounter problems when you try to print or preview an Access 2000 report converted from an Access 2.0 report that has margins set to zero (0). When you convert an Access 2.0 report with margins set to 0, the converted report margins are set to the minimum margin that is valid for the default printer. This prevents the report from printing data in the nonprinting region of the printer.

To resolve this problem, reduce the column width, column spacing, or number of columns in the report so that the width of the columns plus the width of the default margins is less than the width of your paper.

My ActiveX controls do not convert.

When you convert an Access database that contains ActiveX controls to Access 2000, you might receive a message that ActiveX controls are not converted. Access 2.0 supports 16-bit ActiveX controls, but Access 95 or later supports 32-bit ActiveX controls. Access can automatically update a 16-bit control to its 32-bit version only when a 32-bit version exists and is registered on your computer.

Time or date values in my query criteria return different results.

When you convert an Access 2.0 database to Access 2000, a query that contains criteria based on specific time values in Date/Time fields might return different results than the query in earlier versions. This query result might also occur when you link tables from an Access 2.0 database to an Access 2000 database. Only the time portion of Date/Time fields is affected.

A query that contains criteria specifying dates between 1900 and 1929 might also return different results. For example, a date criteria of **#01/01/15#** in Access 2.0 and Access 95 represents January 1, 1915, while the same date criteria in Access 97 or later represents January 1, 2015. To work around this difference, modify the data in your criteria to specify the century—for example, **#01/01/1915#**.

I receive an ODBC message when opening a form or report in a converted database.

The message "ODBC-connection to *datasourcename* failed" occurs when a table in your converted Access 1.*x* or 2.0 database is linked to an ODBC data source that uses a 16-bit driver and driver manager. Access 2000 can open only linked ODBC data sources that use the 32-bit versions of the appropriate ODBC driver and ODBC Driver Manager (Odbc32.dll). For example, the 32-bit version of Microsoft SQL Server ODBC driver (Sqlsrv32.dll).

To correct the situation, you must create a new, identically named 32-bit data source name (DSN) for each ODBC data source that is linked to the original Access 1.*x* or 2.0 database.

If you do not know the original name of the DSN, open the original database in the original version of Access, open the linked table in Design view, and then display the **Table Properties** sheet. The **Description** property of the table contains the definition of the ODBC connection string. The parameter following **DSN=** in the connection string is the name of the DSN. To view the complete DSN definition, in Microsoft Windows 95 or later, open Control Panel and double-click the **ODBC** icon [not the **ODBC (32bit)** icon]. To view the DSN definition, in the **Data Sources (Driver)** list, click the name of the DSN, and then click **Setup**.

▶ **To create a 32-bit ODBC data source, follow these steps**

1   Click the Windows **Start** button, point to **Settings**, and then click **Control Panel**.

2   Double-click the **ODBC (32bit)** icon (in Windows 95 or later) or the **ODBC Data Sources** icon (in Microsoft Windows NT Workstation version 4.0 or later).

3   Create the new DSN by entering identical values to the original DSN. For example, for Microsoft SQL Server, you must define at least **Data Source Name** and **Server**, but you might also need to define additional values such as the **Database Name**.

I receive a message that my computer is missing at least one of the Access 97 object libraries

▶ **To fix the missing references in a converted database, follow these steps**

1   Convert the Access 2000 database to Access 97. When you receive a message that your computer is missing at least one of the Access 97 object libraries, click **OK**.

2   Open the converted Access database in Access 97.

3   Open a module in the database.

4   On the **Tools** menu, click **References**.

5   In the **Available References** box, clear the check boxes that are next to any missing references, and then set a reference to the Microsoft DAO 3.51 Object Library.

Note   Unlike Access 2000, Access 97 is not designed to work with ActiveX Data Objects (ADO).

FAQs About Upgrading to Access 2000

Use the following tips to answer commonly asked questions about upgrading to Microsoft Access 2000.

When I convert an Access database to Access 2000, can I open it in a previous version of Access?

You cannot open an Access 2000 database in a previous version of Microsoft Access. However, you can convert an Access 2000 database to Access 97 file format.

Do macros in my previous-version database work in Access 2000?

In most cases, macros in previous-version databases work in Microsoft Access 2000.

Does code in my previous-version database work in Access 2000?

In most cases, code in previous-version databases works in Microsoft Access 2000. However, in some cases, you might have to update your code. For example, you must update code when it contains 16-bit API calls, or when it contains older versions of DAO objects, methods, and properties that depend on the DAO 2.5/3.*x* compatibility library.

What is ADO?

ActiveX Data Objects (ADO) are programming objects that represent the structure of your database and the data that it contains. In Visual Basic Editor, you can use ADO objects and an additional component of ADO called Microsoft ADO Extensions for DDL and Security (ADOX) to create or change tables and queries, secure your database, or access data from external data sources. You can also use ADO objects in code to manipulate data stored in your database. ADO and ADOX support access to any data source that has an ODBC driver or *OLE DB provider* created for that data source. This includes Access databases (MDB files) through the OLE DB Provider for Microsoft Jet 4.0, and SQL Server 6.5 and 7.0 databases through the Microsoft OLE DB Provider for SQL Server.

The Microsoft DAO 3.6 Object Library is also available in Microsoft Access 2000. A converted Access database contains a reference to this library.

Can I disable the dialog box that prompts me to choose between converting and enabling a database?

You cannot disable the dialog box that prompts you to choose between converting and enabling a database.

Can I convert a replica set?

You can convert a *replica* set to Access 2000, but you must convert each replica individually. For more information, see "How to Convert a Previous-version Database to Access 2000" on page 456.

Can I convert a secured database?

You can convert or enable a secured database as long as you use the information in the original *workgroup information file* to maintain security. If you cannot recreate the workgroup information file in Access 2000, it is recommended that you convert it. For more information, see "How to Convert a Previous-version Database to Access 2000" on page 456.

What are data access pages?

Data access pages are Web pages that you can use to add, edit, view, or manipulate current data in a Microsoft Access database or an SQL Server database. You can create pages that are used to enter and edit data, similar to Access forms. You can also create pages that display records grouped hierarchically, similar to Access reports.

What is an Access project?

A Microsoft Access project (ADP file) is a new type of Access file that provides efficient, native-mode access to a Microsoft SQL Server database through the OLE DB component architecture. Using an Access project, you can easily create a client/server application. Working with a Microsoft Access project is very similar to working with an Access database. The process of creating forms, reports, data access pages, macros, and modules is the same. When you connect to an SQL Server database, you can view, create, modify, and delete tables, views, stored procedures, and database diagrams by using the Microsoft SQL Server Design Tools.

See also

- For more information about new features in Microsoft Access 2000, see Microsoft Access online Help.

Upgrading to Excel 2000

Microsoft Excel 2000 users can collaborate with users of other versions of Excel and users of other applications. However, previous versions of Excel and some other applications do not support all Excel 2000 features.

Sharing Workbooks with Previous Versions of Excel

If your organization is upgrading gradually to Microsoft Excel 2000, users might have to share workbooks with users of Excel 98, Excel 97, Excel 95, and Excel 5.0.

Running macros created in previous versions of Excel

Excel 2000 supports Excel macro language (XLM) macros and Visual Basic for Applications (VBA) macros created in Excel 5.0 or later. However, before you can run the macros you created in the previous versions of Excel, you must modify the code according to the following conditions:

- For a macro that makes calls to a custom 16-bit dynamic-link library (DLL) file, you must provide a version 32-bit compatibility layer for the 16-bit DLL file, or you must recompile the DLL source code into a 32-bit version of the DLL file.

- For a macro that makes calls to a 16-bit Windows 3. *x* application programming interface (API) functions or subroutines, you must edit the application code to replace the calls with appropriate calls to the Microsoft Win32® API.

In most instances, these are the only modifications you need to upgrade XLM and VBA macros created in previous versions of Excel. If the converted macros don't perform as expected in Excel 2000, users can use the following resources to help troubleshoot compatibility issues:

- Click **Office on the Web** (**Help** menu).

- Start the Visual Basic Editor, and then click **Microsoft Visual Basic Help** (**Help** menu).

Excel 2000 includes Visual Basic for Applications version 6.0. This latest version of VBA provides new features and enhancements such as support for additional ActiveX controls. You might want to rewrite existing macros or create new macros to take advantage of the new features in Visual Basic for Applications 6.0. You can create new macros in Excel 2000 by recording macros in Visual Basic for Applications or writing macros by using the Visual Basic Editor.

Preventing macro viruses

When you open a workbook, Excel displays a message if the workbook contains a macro. Excel displays the message regardless of whether the macro in the workbook actually contains a macro virus.

You help prevent macro viruses in Excel 2000 when you allow Excel to run only a macro with a digital signature from a trusted source. A digital signature confirms that the macro is from a trusted developer who signed it and that the macro has not been altered.

▶ **To allow Excel 2000 users to run only signed macros**

1   On the **Tools** menu, point to **Macro**, and then click **Security**.

2   On the **Security Level** tab, click **High**.

When users open workbooks with macros, Excel automatically disables any unsigned macros.

System Policy Tip   You can use a system policy to set the security level option in the **Security** dialog box (**Tools** menu). In the System Policy Editor, set the **Microsoft Excel 2000\Tools|Macro\Security\Security Level** policy. For more information about the System Policy Editor, see "Using the System Policy Editor" on page 296.

Using templates created in previous versions of Excel

You can exchange templates with users of other versions of Excel. However, Excel 2000 templates take advantage of the new and enhanced features in the application. The unique features in Excel 2000 are lost when a template is saved in an older format such as Excel 97 or Excel 95 format.

When you open a template or load an add-in that was already installed when you installed Excel 2000, macros within the file are automatically enabled.

▶ **To display a message when opening an old template or loading an add-in**

1   On the **Tools** menu, point to **Macro**, and then click **Security**.

2   On the **Trusted Sources** tab, clear the **Trust all installed add-ins and templates** check box.

System Policy Tip   You can use a system policy to set the **Trust all installed add-ins and templates** option in the **Security** dialog box (**Tools** menu). In the System Policy Editor, set the **Microsoft Excel 2000\Tools|Macro\Security\Trust all installed add-ins and templates** policy. For more information about the System Policy Editor, see "Using the System Policy Editor" on page 296.

In addition to built-in templates, Excel 2000 supports templates created in other versions of Excel. If you have old templates that you want to use in Excel 2000, store the templates in the XLStart folder. Templates stored in this location appear on the **General** tab in the **New** dialog box (**File** menu).

Sharing workbooks with Excel 98 and Excel 97 users

Excel 2000 users can open files created in Excel 98 (Macintosh) and Excel 97 (Windows). Excel 2000 supports all data and text formatting created in these earlier versions.

Excel 2000 users can collaborate with Excel 98 and Excel 97 users by saving workbooks in either the Excel 97-2000 default file format or Web Page format. However, for Excel 98 and Excel 97 text formatting to display accurately in Excel 2000 workbooks in Web Page format, users must have Microsoft Internet Explorer version 4.0 or later.

Excel 98 and Excel 97 users can open and save Excel 2000 workbooks. However, when Excel 2000 workbooks include a PivotTable, the PivotTable features are not preserved in the earlier versions of Excel.

System Policy Tip   You can use a system policy to define the default value for the **Save as type** option in the **Save As** dialog box (**File** menu). In the System Policy Editor, set the **Microsoft Excel 2000\Tools | Options\Transition\Save Excel files as** policy. For more information about the System Policy Editor, see "Using the System Policy Editor" on page 296.

Note   For text and font formatting to display correctly in workbooks saved in Web Page format, users opening the workbooks must use *cascading style sheets* and have Internet Explorer 4.0 or later.

Sharing workbooks with Excel 95 and Excel 5.0 users

Excel 2000 users can open and save Excel 95 and Excel 5.0 workbooks. With the exception of sound notes in cells, Excel 2000 supports all data and formatting in these earlier versions of Excel.

Excel 2000 users can collaborate with Excel 95 and Excel 5.0 users by saving workbooks in Excel 5.0/95 Workbook format, Excel 97-2000 & 5.0/95 Workbook format, and Web Page format. If Excel 95 and Excel 5.0 users want to open and save Excel 2000 workbooks in HTML, the users must install the HTML add-in.

Toolbox

You can install the HTML add-in from the Microsoft Office Converter Pack. For information about installing this add-in, see "Microsoft Office Converter Pack" on page 793.

Tip   Excel 2000 users can open and save Excel 5.0 for the Macintosh workbooks when they save the workbooks as tab-delimited or comma-separated text files.

See also

- Saving a workbook in a dual file format is an ideal solution for organizations that are upgrading gradually to Excel 2000. For more information, see "Using a Dual File Format in Excel" on page 479.

- You can specify the default format in which Excel 2000 saves new workbooks. For more information, see "How to Specify the Default Format in Which to Save Files" on page 438.

- The Removal Wizard removes unnecessary and obsolete files, settings, and components that previous versions of Office and Office-related applications install. For more information, see "Removal Wizard" on page 269.

Using a Dual File Format in Excel

A dual file format saves two formats in a single file. This format is an ideal solution for organizations that are upgrading gradually to Microsoft Excel 2000. You can standardize your organization on the Microsoft Excel 97-2000 & 5.0/95 dual file format until all Excel 95 and Excel 5.0 users have upgraded. Selecting the dual file format ensures that all Excel users have a common file format with which to collaborate on shared workbooks during the transition period.

System Policy Tip   You can use a system policy to define the default value for the **Save as type** option in the **Save As** dialog box (**File** menu). In the System Policy Editor, set the **Microsoft Excel 2000\Tools | Options\Transition\Save Excel files as** policy. For more information about the System Policy Editor, see "Using the System Policy Editor" on page 296.

Saving two file formats in one compound document

When you save a workbook in the Excel 97-2000 & 5.0/95 dual file format, the workbook is saved in a single file. This file includes two data streams: one data stream for Excel 97-2000 and another data stream for Excel 5.0 and Excel 95. Excel first writes the Excel 5.0/95 data stream to the file and then writes the Excel 97-2000 data stream.

When Excel 95 or Excel 5.0 users open a workbook saved in a dual file format, Excel 95 or Excel 5.0 reads only the Excel 5.0/95 data stream; and the Excel 97-2000 data stream is disregarded. Consequently, if an Excel 95 or Excel 5.0 user saves the workbook, the Excel 97-2000 data stream and features are permanently lost.

Excel 95 and Excel 5.0 users are prompted to open the workbook as read-only, although they can open the file with read/write permission. To avoid losing work performed in Excel 2000, you can protect a workbook by requiring a write password or by making the workbook read-only.

Working with objects in a compound document

An Excel workbook saved in a dual file format is called a compound document. When an Excel 2000 user creates or inserts an object in a compound document, Excel 2000 detects the setting in the **Default Save** subkey in the Windows registry. If the Microsoft Excel 97-2000 & 5.0/95 dual file format is set as the default, Excel 2000 uses the dual file format for the object linking and embedding (OLE) object.

When not activated, OLE objects are represented in container applications as either an icon or a portion of the document, such as a worksheet range. This portion of a document is actually a Windows Metafile (WMF) graphic that represents a portion of the Excel 97-2000 data stream from the workbook file. In most cases, the graphic represents either the 97-2000 data stream or the 5.0/95 data stream of the object. If the graphic includes features unique to Excel 2000, users of previous versions of Excel might initially see a graphics image that differs from the actual embedded object after they activate the object.

For example, if a compound document contains an embedded object that uses the Excel 2000 merged cell feature, and an Excel 5.0 user activates the object, then the merged cells appear as unmerged cells. The Excel 2000 merged cell feature is permanently lost, and the graphic reverts back to the Excel 5.0 unmerged cell form either when the Excel 5.0 user saves the compound document or when the application saves the document automatically.

Deciding when to use a dual file format

The following examples identify some uses for dual file formats.

- A Microsoft Office 95 user receives a compound document from an Office 2000 user. The compound document includes an embedded object in Excel 97-2000 & 5.0/95 format. The Office 95 user does not want to alter the format of the embedded object, but needs to activate the object.

- It is recommended that the Office 95 user open the compound document as read-only.

- An Excel 2000 user wants to publish a workbook in Excel 97-2000 & 5.0/95 format or to an audience of Excel 2000 and Excel 95 users. However, the Excel 2000 user does not want any Excel 95 users to alter the workbook.

- The Excel 2000 user can enter a write-reservation password for saving the workbook and then distribute the password to only Excel 2000 users. The write-reservation feature allows Excel 95 users to open the workbook but not save it.

- An Excel 2000 user wants to send a workbook to Excel 5.0 or Excel 95 users by using a modem. The Excel 2000 user can save the workbook in Excel 5.0/95 format rather than in a dual file format because the resulting file is much smaller and is transmitted more quickly.

- When you save an Excel 2000 workbook in Excel 5.0/95 format, you might encounter some conversion limitations. For more information, see "Saving Workbooks in Excel 5.0/95 Format" on page 482.

- You can specify the default format for Excel 2000 to save new workbooks. For more information, see "How to Specify the Default Format in Which to Save Files" on page 438.

Saving Workbooks in Excel 98 and Excel 97

When Microsoft Excel 2000 users save workbooks in Excel 97-2000 format, all worksheet and chart data, formatting, macros, and other Excel 2000 features are preserved in Excel 98 (Macintosh) and Excel 97 (Windows). However, if an Excel 98 or Excel 97 user saves the workbook in an earlier file format, some formatting and data might be lost.

System Policy Tip   You can use a system policy to define the default value for the **Save as type** option in the **Save As** dialog box (**File** menu). In the System Policy Editor, set the **Microsoft Excel 2000\Tools | Options\Transition\Save Excel files as** policy. For more information about the System Policy Editor, see "Using the System Policy Editor" on page 296.

The following table describes new features in Excel 2000 that might affect your data or formatting in Excel 98 and Excel 97.

When this Excel 2000 feature	Is saved in Excel 98 or Excel 97 format
External data ranges	Auto-refresh, column formatting, filtering, and sorting do not work.
Indented format PivotTable reports	If edited, reports change to nonindented layout but maintain character and cell formatting.
OLAP PivotTable and PivotChart reports	Appear as read-only.
PivotChart reports	Appear as regular charts. Multiple-level category labels are modified, and value axis display units convert to literal values.

See also

- You can specify the default format in which Excel 2000 saves a new workbook. For more information, see "How to Specify the Default Format in Which to Save Files" on page 438.

Saving Workbooks in Excel 5.0/95 Format

If you save a Microsoft Excel 2000 workbook in Excel 5.0/95 Workbook format, you might lose some of the formatting, data, and features unique to Excel 2000.

System Policy Tip   You can use a system policy to define the default value for the **Save as type** option in the **Save As** dialog box (**File** menu). In the System Policy Editor, set the **Microsoft Excel 2000\Tools | Options\Transition\Save Excel files as** policy. For more information about the System Policy Editor, see "Using the System Policy Editor" on page 296.

Basic use features

The following table describes new features in Excel 2000 that might affect your data or formatting in previous versions.

When this Excel 2000 feature	Is saved in Excel 5.0/95 format
32,000 characters per cell	Characters beyond the 255th character are truncated.
65,536 rows per worksheet	Data in rows below row 16,384 are truncated.

Formatting features

The following table describes new features in Excel 2000 that might affect your data or formatting in previous versions.

When this Excel 2000 feature	Is saved in Excel 5.0/95 format
Angled text	Angled text is reformatted to horizontal orientation.
Conditional formatting	Conditional formatting is lost, and cells are reformatted as normal text.
Data validation	Lost in the conversion.
Indenting within cells	Indentation within a cell is lost, and data remains left-aligned.
Merge cells option on the **Alignment** tab in the **Cells** dialog box (**Format** menu)	Merged cells are split into their original configuration. Data appears in the upper-left cell.
New border styles	New border styles are converted to the nearest border style available in Excel 5.0 or Excel 95.
Partial page breaks	Partial page breaks are converted to full page breaks.
Sheet backgrounds	Lost in the conversion.
Shrink to fit option on the **Alignment** tab in the **Cells** dialog box (**Format** menu)	Text and data retain the same point size they had before **Shrink to fit** was selected.

Formula and function features

The following new functions are not supported in Excel 95 or Excel 5.0. Excel 95 and Excel 5.0 calculate the functions before saving the file and replace the formula with the resulting value.

AVERAGEA	MAXA	STDEVPA
GETPIVOTDATA	MINA	VARA
HYPERLINK	STDEVA	VARPA

The following table describes new features in Excel 2000 that might affect your data or formatting in previous versions.

When this Excel 2000 feature	Is saved in Excel 5.0/95 format
Defined labels	Lost in the conversion.
English language references in formulas	English language references are converted to A1 reference notations. However, names of named cells and ranges are preserved.

Chart features

The following table describes new features in Excel 2000 that might affect your data or formatting in previous versions.

When this Excel 2000 feature	Is saved in Excel 5.0/95 format
3-D bar shapes (cylinder, pyramid, and cone)	Converted to 3-D column charts (rectangular shape).
Angled text on axis and data labels	The text is formatted straight (0 degrees).
Bubble chart format	Converted to type 1 xy (scatter) charts.
Data tables on charts	Lost in the conversion.
Gradient fills	Gradient fills are converted to the nearest color and pattern.
Office Art objects	Office Art objects are converted to the nearest available shape and tool.
Pie-of-pie and bar-of-pie chart types	Charts are converted to type 1 pie charts.
PivotChart reports	Displayed as regular charts. Multiple level category labels are modified, and value axis display units are converted into literal values.
Shading in surface charts	Lost in the conversion.
Shadows on series and points	Lost in the conversion.
Time series axis	Special scaling information is lost, and the axis is converted to a normal category axis.

PivotTable features

The following table describes new features in Excel 2000 that might affect your data or formatting in previous versions.

When this Excel 2000 feature	Is saved in Excel 5.0/95 format
Calculated fields, calculated items, and formatting based on structure	Preserved until the user makes changes to or refreshes the PivotTable data. Then they are lost.
External data ranges	Auto-refresh, column formatting, filtering, and sorting do not work.
Indented format PivotTable reports	If edited, reports change to nonindented layout but maintain character and cell formatting.
OLAP PivotTable and PivotChart reports	Appear as read-only.
PivotChart reports	Appear as regular charts. Multiple level category labels are modified, and value axis display units convert to literal values.
PivotTable features	The following properties new in Excel 2000 are lost in the conversion:
	Page field placement across columns or down rows
	Server-based page fields
	Multiple selection on page fields
	Persistent grouping and sorting
	Data fields displayed as numbers
PivotTable properties sheet	All new properties are lost. These include:
	Page field placement across columns or down rows
	Alternate strings for NA and error cell display
	Server-based page fields
	AutoSort and AutoShow on fields
	Multiselect on page fields
	Persistent grouping and sorting
	Data fields displayed as numbers

Workgroup and Internet features

The following table describes new features in Excel 2000 that might affect your data or formatting in previous versions.

When this Excel 2000 feature	Is saved in Excel 5.0/95 format
Comments	Comments are converted to CellTips.
Hyperlink (**Insert** menu)	The HYPERLINK value is lost.
Multiuser workbooks	Sharing is disabled, and the change tracking history is lost in the conversion.
Revision marks and audit trail	Lost in the conversion; the change log is also lost.

Data access features

The following table describes new features in Excel 2000 that might affect your data or formatting in previous versions.

When this Excel 2000 feature	Is saved in Excel 5.0/95 format
Parameterized queries	Parameterized queries cannot be run or edited.
Report templates	Lost in the conversion.
Shared queries (connections without a data source name, or DSN)	Files that contain connections without DSN are supported in Excel 95 (with ODBC 2.0). In Excel 5.0 (with ODBC 1.0), the user is prompted for connection information.

Programming features

The following table describes new features in Excel 2000 that might affect your data or formatting in previous versions.

When this Excel 2000 feature	Is saved in Excel 5.0/95 format
ActiveX controls (formerly OLE controls or OCX)	Appear in the workbook but cannot be used.
New Excel 2000 objects, methods, and properties	Not all program elements are supported. For more information about compatibility issues, see "Sharing Workbooks with Previous Versions of Excel" on page 476.
Forms toolbar controls	Lost in the conversion.

See also

- You can specify the default format in which Excel 2000 saves new workbooks. For more information, see "How to Specify the Default Format in Which to Save Files" on page 438.

How to Share Files with Other Spreadsheet Applications

You can customize Microsoft Office 2000 Setup so that it installs most converters that users need to share files with other applications such as Lotus 1-2-3 and Quattro Pro. If users need to open files created in other applications, and the file type is not listed in the **Files of type** box in the **Open** dialog box (**File** menu), then users must save the files in a format that Microsoft Excel 2000 can open.

Share text files

Excel 2000 users can open and save files in the following text formats:

- Comma-separated values (.csv)
- Data interchange format (.dif)
- Lotus 1-2-3 space-delimited formatted text (.prn)
- Symbolic link (SYLK)
- Tab-delimited text (.txt)
- Text (.txt)
- *Unicode* text (.txt)

Because Excel 2000 is based on the Unicode text encoding standard, users can display text files correctly no matter what language the files were created in, as long as users' computers are running an operating system that supports the characters particular to that language.

Import files by using the Text Import Wizard

Excel 2000 users can use the Text Import Wizard to import text files and parse text across columns. You run the wizard by opening a text file and following the instructions that appear on the screen.

Open HTML files

When users open HTML files, the files are opened in the applications in which they were created, rather than in Excel. Excel 2000 users can open HTML files created in other applications in Excel by right-clicking the file in the **Open** dialog box (**File** menu) and then clicking **Open in Microsoft Excel** on the shortcut menu.

See also

- If Excel 2000 users share workbooks with users of other applications, you can change the default format in which Excel 2000 saves workbooks. For more information, see "How to Specify the Default Format in Which to Save Files" on page 438.

- Office 2000 includes several new international features that help simplify the task of administering and supporting Office internationally, such as Unicode. For more information, see "Overview of International Features in Office 2000" on page 725.

- Office 2000 includes new and enhanced HTML features for publishing workbooks to your intranet or the World Wide Web. For more information, see "Taking Advantage of Office Web Features" on page 565.

FAQs About Upgrading to Excel 2000

Use the following tips to answer commonly asked questions about upgrading to Microsoft Excel 2000.

Do previous versions of Excel have the same file format as Excel 2000?

Microsoft Excel 2000 has the same file format as Excel 98 (Macintosh) and Excel 97 (Windows), but it has a few enhancements because of the new features included in Excel 2000. The Excel 95 and Excel 5.0 file formats are different from Excel 2000. For more information, see "Sharing Workbooks with Previous Versions of Excel" on page 476.

Are the date algorithms in Excel 95 and Excel 5.0 the same as the ones in Excel 2000?

The date algorithms in Excel 95 and Excel 5.0 are different from Excel 2000 because Excel 95 and Excel 5.0 use a two-digit format to represent the year while Excel 2000 uses a four-digit format. The Microsoft Excel Date Migration Wizard scans Excel 2000 workbooks for potential date function problems with converted versions of Excel that use a two-digit format to represent the year.

Toolbox

You can use the Microsoft Excel Date Migration Wizard to scan Excel 2000 workbooks for potential date function problems. For information about installing this wizard, see "Excel File Recovery and Date Tools" on page 775.

How can I address year 2000 date confusion?

Excel 2000 has two new formats to help you eliminate year 2000 date confusion. In Excel 2000 you can specify a m/d/yyyy or a Mmm yyyy format for the date.

▶ **To specify a date format in an Excel 2000 workbook**

1   On the **Format** menu, click **Cells**.

2   In the **Category** box on the **Number** tab, click **Date**, and then select a format in the **Type** box.

To expedite changing all date formats from two-digit to four-digit years in existing Excel workbooks, users can run the Microsoft Excel Date Fix Wizard.

Toolbox

You can use the Microsoft Excel Date Fix Wizard to change date formats from two-digit to four-digit years in Excel 2000 workbooks. For information about installing this wizard, see "Excel File Recovery and Date Tools" on page 775.

How can I prevent users from saving presentations in an unapproved format?

You cannot prevent users from saving presentations in an unapproved format, but you can:

- Set a system policy by using the System Policy Editor, and create a custom message to alert users when they try to save a file that is not the default format in the system policy.

- Set a default file format by using the **Options** dialog box (**Tools** menu).

- Limit the number of converters that you distribute to users.

For more information, see "How to Specify the Default Format in Which to Save Files" on page 438 and "Using the System Policy Editor" on page 296.

Why does text look different when a user saves an Excel 2000 workbook in Web Page format?

For text and font formatting to display correctly, users must upgrade to Microsoft Internet Explorer 4.0 or later, and use *cascading style sheets*.

To use cascading style sheets, click **Options** on the (**Tools** menu), and then click the **General** tab. Click **Web Options**, and then click the **General** tab. Select the **Rely on CSS for font formatting** check box.

For more information about saving workbooks in Web Page format, see "Transferring Files Between HTML and Office Document Formats" on page 592.

How can Excel 95 and Excel 5.0 users open HTML files created by Excel 2000 users?

When Excel 2000 users select Web Page format in the **Save As** dialog box (**File** menu), files are saved in HTML format. Before Excel 95 and Excel 5.0 users can open the files, they must install the HTML add-in included in the Microsoft Office Converter Pack.

Toolbox

You can install the HTML add-in from the Microsoft Office Converter Pack. For information about installing this add-in, see "Microsoft Office Converter Pack" on page 793.

Why don't the values in a converted workbook match the values in the original workbook?

Excel 2000 calculates some operators and functions in a different order from other applications. To calculate formulas by using the same rules as another application such as Lotus 1-2-3, click **Options** (**Tools** menu), and then click the **Transition** tab. Under **Sheet options**, select the **Transition formula evaluation** check box.

Why are some formulas changed to text or values when a workbook is opened in Excel 2000?

When Excel 2000 opens a file created in another application, and encounters an operator or function that it cannot convert, Excel uses the result of the formula rather than the formula itself for the contents of the cell. Enter the formula again in your Excel workbook by using an equivalent operator or function.

Can users of earlier versions of Excel view code or modify macros created in Excel 2000?

Excel 97, Excel 95, and Excel 5.0 users can't view the code or modify macros that are digitally signed by using the Visual Basic Editor in Excel 2000. This is a new Excel 2000 security feature that is not included in other versions of Excel.

Can users disable XLM macros?

You can disable the Auto_Open macro when you open a workbook; however, other XLM macros still run because you can't disable them. You can disable only macros created in Visual Basic for Applications (VBA).

Users need to make sure that the source of a workbook is reliable before opening the workbook.

Why can't users of previous versions of Excel view macros in some Excel 2000 workbooks?

The macros might have been digitally signed from within the Visual Basic Editor in Excel 2000. This new security feature is not included in other versions of Excel.

Why can't users run a macro or load an add-in in a workbook?

If the security level for Excel 2000 is set to High, and users open a workbook or load an add-in that contains unsigned macros, the macros are disabled and users cannot run them.

Users can enable macros that are not digitally signed by changing the security level to Medium in the **Security** dialog box (**Macro** submenu on the **Tools** menu), closing the workbook or unloading the add-in, and then opening the workbook or loading the add-in again.

Note   Remember to change the security level back to High if you want Excel 2000 to automatically disable unsigned macros in the future.

If the security level for Excel is set to Medium or High, and you chose to disable macros because you do not trust the source of the macros, then you cannot run the macros. To run the macros, close the workbook or unload the add-in, and then open the workbook or load the add-in again. Then click **Enable Macros**.

What can Excel 2000 users do if a file does not convert properly?

If a file does not convert properly, Excel 2000 users can close the file without saving it, and then open the file again by using a different converter. The original file remains unchanged until it is saved in Excel 2000.

Upgrading to FrontPage 2000

Microsoft FrontPage 2000 is compatible with FrontPage 97 and FrontPage 98. With the exception of new features that are not supported in previous versions, you can work with Web pages created in one version of FrontPage on a web created in another version. Different versions of the FrontPage client application also work together with different versions of Microsoft FrontPage Server Extensions.

Upgrading from Previous Versions of the FrontPage Client

Microsoft FrontPage 2000 saves files in the same file format as every previous version of FrontPage—namely, HTML. You can open your existing FrontPage files in FrontPage 2000 without having to convert them. The key difference between versions is the different feature sets. Features added to a Web page in FrontPage 2000 do not work in previous versions that do not include that feature.

You can use FrontPage 2000 to open a web created with FrontPage 98 or FrontPage 97 and edit any of its features. Each version of FrontPage includes and supports nearly all of the features that are in previous versions.

The features in previous versions that FrontPage 2000 does not support are:

- Internet Database Connectivity (FrontPage 97 and FrontPage 98)
- Channel Definition File (FrontPage 98 only)
- Microsoft Personal Web Server

  FrontPage 2000 does not include Personal Web Server; however, if Personal Web Server is installed on your computer, it is updated to the latest version of Personal Web Server when you install FrontPage 2000.

Settings that migrate to FrontPage 2000

When FrontPage 2000 opens a file created in FrontPage 97 or FrontPage 98, it preserves any special settings or customized components that were saved with that file in its original version. The following components from FrontPage 97 and FrontPage 98 files migrate to FrontPage 2000:

- Customized themes (FrontPage 98 only)
- Customized templates
- Customized menus
- List of the most recently used Web sites (added to Web folders)

In addition, any program that uses FrontPage 97 or FrontPage 98 Automation interfaces works with FrontPage 2000.

Working with webs created in previous versions

You can use FrontPage 2000 to edit and publish to webs created with FrontPage 97 or FrontPage 98. For example, if you create a Web page in FrontPage 2000, you can publish it to a FrontPage 98-based web. However, new FrontPage 2000 features do not work on FrontPage 98-based or FrontPage 97-based webs. You can also update a web created in a previous version by opening, editing, and then saving it in FrontPage 2000.

Note   When you update a Web server to FrontPage 2000 Server Extensions, any FrontPage 97-based or FrontPage 98-based webs on the server are automatically upgraded to FrontPage 2000-based webs. The upgraded webs support all the new functionality in the FrontPage 2000 client.

Opening FrontPage 2000-based webs in previous versions

Although you can use FrontPage 98 or FrontPage 97 to open a web created in FrontPage 2000, you can work with only those features that the two versions have in common.

For example, a FrontPage 2000-based web can consist of several levels of *subwebs*. FrontPage 98—which supports only one level of subweb—can open only the first subweb level below the *root web*. If you open a multilevel FrontPage 2000-based web in FrontPage 98 or FrontPage 97, you cannot open subwebs that are two or more levels below the root web.

Upgrading from Previous Versions of FrontPage Server Extensions

Each version of Microsoft FrontPage is accompanied by a new version of Microsoft FrontPage Server Extensions, which supports the new features. FrontPage Server Extensions are always backward-compatible, supporting features from several previous versions of FrontPage. FrontPage 2000 Server Extensions support all the functionality of FrontPage 2000, FrontPage 98, and FrontPage 97.

When you install FrontPage 2000 or Microsoft Office 2000 on a computer, FrontPage 2000 Server Extensions are automatically installed. If there is an older version of FrontPage Server Extensions on the computer, it is updated.

Note   During the upgrade to FrontPage 2000 Server Extensions, the _vti_bin folder and its subfolders are deleted because they are not required for FrontPage 2000-extended webs.

Using previous-version clients with FrontPage 2000 Server Extensions

You can use FrontPage 97, FrontPage 98, or FrontPage 2000 to work on a web extended with FrontPage Server Extensions from any of those versions. Because each version of FrontPage adds more features, however, each version of FrontPage Server Extensions supports more features than its predecessor. To support all of the new features in FrontPage 2000, you must use FrontPage 2000 Server Extensions.

For example, if you use FrontPage 98 to edit a web that has been extended with FrontPage 2000 Server Extensions, you can use all the functionality of FrontPage 98 in that web—and no more. Even though the web is extended with FrontPage 2000 Server Extensions, FrontPage 98 cannot add functionality unique to FrontPage 2000.

Similarly, if you use FrontPage 2000 to edit a FrontPage 98-extended web, you can use only the FrontPage 2000 features that are supported by FrontPage 98 Server Extensions. The new FrontPage 2000 features do not work.

Note   Microsoft occasionally issues bug fixes and updates for the most recently released version of FrontPage Server Extensions; previous versions are not updated. However, updates to new versions of FrontPage Server Extensions work with FrontPage 97 and later clients.

Upgrading security

FrontPage 2000 Server Extensions and FrontPage 98 Server Extensions implement security differently. In FrontPage 2000, *permissions* are determined by the access control list (ACL) of the Web site root folder. In FrontPage 98, permissions on a *FrontPage-extended web* are determined by the ACLs of the files Shtml.dll, Admin.dll, and Author.dll.

When you upgrade a FrontPage 98-extended web to a FrontPage 2000-extended web, security settings are automatically upgraded to the new scheme.

If the anonymous account, IUSR_*computername*, or a Windows NT group of which the anonymous account is a member, has browsing, authoring, or administrative permissions on the FrontPage 98-extended web being upgraded, it is given only browsing permissions on the upgraded web.

Resetting custom permissions after you upgrade

You can set custom permissions on individual files and folders in a web extended with FrontPage 97 Server Extensions or FrontPage 98 Server Extensions. For example, you can manually adjust ACL settings in Windows NT Explorer. When you subsequently upgrade to FrontPage 2000 Server Extensions, however, those custom permissions are reset to their default values.

You cannot preserve custom permission settings when you upgrade to FrontPage 2000. Instead, you must record custom permissions settings before you upgrade to the new version, install FrontPage 2000 Server Extensions, and then reset the custom permission settings.

See also

- You can upgrade *FrontPage-extended web*s to use Microsoft Office Server Extensions (OSE) in addition to FrontPage 2000 Server Extensions. For more information, see "Installing Office Server Extensions" on page 637.

Upgrading to Outlook 2000

Microsoft Outlook 2000 users can exchange e-mail messages and scheduling data with users of previous versions of Microsoft e-mail and calendar applications, as well as interact with users of other applications. However, previous versions of Outlook or other applications do not support all Outlook 2000 features.

Planning Your Upgrade to Outlook 2000

Because Microsoft Outlook 2000 is compatible with earlier versions of Outlook and can share files with other Microsoft e-mail and calendar applications, upgrading strategies typically involve only preparation and distribution issues. When you decide how you want your upgrade to proceed, and you identify the applications required, upgrading to Outlook 2000 is a simple process.

Before you start the upgrade process, you must make the following decisions:

- Decide whether you want Corporate/Workgroup or Internet Mail Only support.
- Decide whether you want to use Microsoft Schedule+ as your calendar or the Outlook 2000 Calendar.
- Decide which browser you want to use.
- Decide which security settings you want for your users.

Perform the following tasks to prepare for the upgrade process.

- Clean up your existing e-mail folders.

    For example, delete any unnecessary e-mail messages or personal folders.

- Create a backup copy of your existing e-mail folders.

    This task prevents you from permanently losing data during the upgrade process.

Tip Although Microsoft Office 2000 works with Microsoft Internet Explorer 4.0, it is recommended that you upgrade to Internet Explorer 5, which is included with Office 2000. Because of the offline capabilities of Internet Explorer 5, it's much easier for Outlook 2000 users to download and store any folder home pages so that they can be modified offline.

You can easily upgrade to Outlook 2000 from previous Microsoft e-mail and calendar applications. You can install Outlook 2000 over an Outlook 97 or Outlook 98 installation. Like other Office 2000 applications, Outlook 2000 migrates user settings stored in the registry. In addition, if a Messaging Application Programming Interface (MAPI) profile already exists on a user's computer, Outlook 2000 continues to use the profile.

As an administrator, it is recommended that you plan upgrade strategies for the following scenarios:

- A one-time upgrade to Outlook 2000.
- A gradual upgrade to Outlook 2000.

If you plan a gradual upgrade, Outlook users might need to exchange e-mail messages and scheduling data with users of other Microsoft e-mail and calendar applications.

See also

- You can deploy Outlook separately from the rest of Office 2000. For more information, see "Installing Outlook 2000 After Installing Office 2000" on page 201.

Support for Mail, Fax, and Forms in Outlook 2000

When you upgrade to Microsoft Outlook 2000, you must decide which e-mail, fax, and form configurations are appropriate for your organization. For e-mail and fax support, you can choose between Corporate/Workgroup e-mail support and Internet Only e-mail support—with their corresponding fax solutions. You also must decide whether to include support for electronic forms in your Outlook 2000 installation.

Choosing e-mail support in Outlook 2000

Outlook 2000 has the following two separate configurations for e-mail support:

- Corporate/Workgroup e-mail support
- Internet Only e-mail support

Corporate/Workgroup e-mail support is designed to serve Microsoft Exchange Server, and other corporate and workgroup e-mail servers across a local area network (LAN). Internet Only e-mail support is designed to connect Outlook 2000 users to Simple Mail Transfer Protocol (SMTP), Post Office Protocol version 3 (POP3), Internet Mail Access Protocol version 4 (IMAP4), and Lightweight Directory Access Protocol (LDAP) Internet mail servers.

When you upgrade to Outlook 2000 from Outlook 97 or Outlook 98, you choose Corporate/Workgroup or Internet Only e-mail support for your users. As the administrator, you are upgrading the client side of the e-mail support, while user e-mail accounts continue to function as before.

Note   If you upgrade from Outlook 98 Internet Mail Only support to Outlook 2000 Internet Mail only, then user Internet e-mail accounts are maintained.

Enabling Outlook 2000 as your primary e-mail processing application

Outlook uses Messaging Application Programming Interface (MAPI) as the underlying architecture to define Outlook items for storage formatting, and for communicating between Exchange and other e-mail servers. When you upgrade to Outlook 2000, a MAPI folder is added to the C:\Program Files\Common Files\System\MAPI folder. If there is an existing MAPI folder in the Windows System folder, it is not removed. However, Outlook 2000 uses only the MAPI folder in the Program Files folder.

Applications such as Eudora and Netscape Communicator install their own version of Mapi32.dll in the Windows System folder, and they specify their own folders for all e-mail applications. New dynamic-link library (DLL) files overwrite the Outlook Mapi32.dll file, and they circumvent Outlook 2000 for e-mail processing.

Outlook 2000 detects when the Mapi32.dll file is overwritten, and displays a message advising the user to run Fixmapi.exe, which is a Windows utility located in the Windows System folder. Fixmapi.exe restores the original Mapi32.dll, and copies the third-party file to another folder. This step allows Outlook 2000 to process e-mail messages without altering the functionality of the third-party application.

Choosing fax support in Outlook 2000

Microsoft Fax, also known as At Work Fax, is part of Microsoft Windows 95 and other products released at the same time. You can use Microsoft Fax in Outlook 97 to send and receive faxes directly from Outlook 97. However, the Outlook 2000 high-performance Internet e-mail feature uses Microsoft Fax in Corporate/Workgroup configuration while Internet Only uses the WinFax Starter Edition.

Note WinFax Starter Edition is a special edition of WinFax that is designed to work exclusively with Outlook 2000. WinFax Starter Edition provides basic fax service for Outlook 2000 Internet e-mail users. WinFax Starter Edition users can upgrade to WinFax Pro.

When you upgrade from Outlook 98 Internet Mail Only to Outlook 2000 Corporate/Workgroup, users automatically get the At Work Fax feature. However, if you select Outlook Internet Mail Only support, users see the WinFax window when they start the fax feature.

Changing the location of data storage files

Outlook 97 and Outlook 98 store Personal Store, Offline Store, Personal Address Book (PAB), and Offline Address Book files in the Windows folder. Outlook 2000 stores these files in the user Application Data folder. When you upgrade to Outlook 2000, any existing files from Outlook 98 or Outlook 97 remain in the Windows folder.

Supporting forms in Outlook 2000

Previous versions of Microsoft Exchange Client and Outlook install run-time files for Electronic Forms Designer, which allow users to design 16-bit custom forms that run without error.

Outlook 2000 does not install Electronic Forms Designer run-time files by default. If your organization requires Electronic Forms Designer support, you must install Electronic Forms Designer manually. You can use the Microsoft Office Custom Installation Wizard to set the Electronic Forms Designer installation state for all users in your organization.

▶ **To set Electronic Forms Designer Runtime to install with Outlook 2000**

1   Start the Office Custom Installation Wizard.

2   On the **Set Feature Installation States** panel, click the plus sign next to **Microsoft Outlook for Windows**.

3   Click the down arrow next to **Electronic Forms Designer Runtime**, and then select **Run from My Computer**.

Note   You do not need to install Electronic Forms Designer Runtime support on all your computers. However, users with computers that have never had Outlook or Exchange Client installed must install Electronic Forms Designer Runtime support if you deploy EDP-based forms on those computers, and users want to use the forms.

See also

- You can customize the Outlook 2000 installation by using the Office Custom Installation Wizard. For more information, see "Office Custom Installation Wizard" on page 250.

How to Upgrade to Outlook 2000 Security

The first time a user attempts to read or send secure e-mail messages, Microsoft Outlook 2000 triggers a security upgrade feature. To upgrade from Outlook 97 or Exchange Client to Outlook 2000 security, the user's security file (EPF file) must exist on the computer, and the user must know the password. To upgrade from Outlook 98 security, the user must know the *Digital ID* password.

During the upgrade process, a Digital ID name is generated for the security keys of each user, which includes one signing key and one *encryption* key. The user must select a password to associate with the Digital ID name.

The Outlook 2000 upgrade feature attempts to save the security information in a secure store. If the EPF file cannot be found, or the user cannot remember the password, the upgrade feature can be canceled.

If you are using Microsoft Exchange Advanced Security, you can recover the security keys (that is, enroll again) by asking for a new security token from the administrator. The upgrade process must occur before you are security enabled to send and receive secure e-mail messages.

If you are using Microsoft Certificate Server, or a public Certification Authority such as VeriSign, Inc., and you forget your password, the following restrictions occur:

- You cannot access your keys.
- You cannot read encrypted e-mail messages sent to you previously.
- You must re-enroll to get new Digital IDs.

The following procedure describes how Outlook 2000 users can enroll in security by using Microsoft Exchange Key Management Server (KMS). Before you begin this procedure, contact the system administrator for a security token. The request for security enrollment uses this token.

▶ **To enroll in security or obtain a certificate using Microsoft Exchange KMS**

1   On the **Tools** menu, click **Options**, and then click the **Security** tab

2   Click **Get a Digital ID**, select **Set up Security for me on the Exchange Server**, and then click **OK**.

3   In the **Digital ID name** box, type the name you want to use, in the **Token** box, type your security token, and then click **OK**.

    A message is sent to Microsoft Exchange KMS. After you receive a reply, Outlook 2000 attempts to store your security keys in the secure store.

4   Select a password for your Digital ID.

    You are prompted for the password every time you access the keys. However, you can choose to have Outlook 2000 remember the password for a limited period of time.

5   Click **OK** to save your changes.

6   To add the *certificate* to the Root Store, click **Yes**.

    The dialog box provides the required information about the certificate. If you click **No**, you experience problems when you attempt to read and send secure messages, and you must repeat the entire enrollment process.

The following procedure describes how Outlook 2000 users can enroll in security by using public certificate authorities.

▶ **To enroll in security or obtain a certificate by using external certificate authorities**

1 On the **Tools** menu, click **Options**, and then click the **Security** tab.

2 Click **Get a Digital ID**, select **Get a S/MIME certificate from an external Certification Authority**, and then click **OK**.

A Microsoft Web page provides information about obtaining a certificate. The page lists a number of certificate authorities.

3 Select the link to the *certificate authority* that you want to use to obtain a certificate.

While your Web browser is storing your certificate and keys on your computer, you might be prompted to select the security level to associate with your keys.

4 When prompted, select a password for your Digital ID.

You are prompted for the password every time you access the keys. However, you can choose to have Outlook 2000 remember the password for a limited period of time.

5 To add this certificate to the Root Store, click **Yes**.

While storing the certificates, you might be prompted to save the root certificate. The dialog box provides the required information about the certificate. If you click **No**, you experience problems when you attempt to read and send secure messages. When you experience such problems, contact your certification authority to install another copy of the root certificate.

After the certificate and keys are installed, Outlook can access and use them.

See also

- There are several options to choose from when you set up security for your Outlook 2000 users. For more information about security, see "Using Security Features in Outlook" on page 414.

Sharing Information with Outlook 97 and Outlook 98

Microsoft Outlook 2000 shares information seamlessly with Outlook 97 and Outlook 98 because Outlook 2000 has the same storage formats, Messaging Application Programming Interface (MAPI) profiles, and message formats. Consequently, you can upgrade gradually to Outlook 2000 without losing e-mail and other message functionality. The few exceptions are described in the following sections:

Offline folder file format

The off-line folder (OST) file in Outlook 97 version 8.03 is different in Outlook 2000 and Outlook 98. When you upgrade to Outlook 2000 from versions of Outlook 97 prior to version 8.03, you must recreate the OST file.

HTML-based e-mail

In addition to Rich Text Format (RTF) and plain text (ASCII) format, Outlook 2000 and Outlook 98 support HTML-based e-mail. This format allows users to send messages in HTML format.

Outlook 97 supports only RTF and plain text format, but Outlook 2000 converts and stores HTML in RTF so that Outlook 97 users can read the messages. However, the original HTML might not be displayed correctly in RTF.

Online meetings

Outlook 2000 supports online meetings, which can be hosted by using Microsoft NetMeeting® or Microsoft Windows NT Server NetShow™ Services. Online meeting requests made by using the Outlook 2000 NetMeeting or NetShow Services features appear as in-person meeting requests to Outlook 97 and Outlook 98 users.

If your organization includes Outlook 97 or Outlook 98 users, and you schedule an online meeting by using Outlook 2000, you must identify the meeting format in the content of the message as either NetMeeting or NetShow Services.

Stationery and custom signatures

When you upgrade to Outlook 2000, the Outlook 98 Stationery feature is moved to a new location. Outlook 98 user signatures are preserved in Outlook 2000.

Upgrading from Microsoft Exchange Client

Because both Microsoft Outlook 2000 and Microsoft Exchange Client are MAPI-compatible applications, Outlook can completely replace Exchange Client. Except for changes in the user interface and other features, you can continue working with e-mail messages in Outlook in the same way that you work with e-mail messages in Exchange Client. Outlook 2000 uses the same profile and other configuration information, and Outlook can use all Exchange Client extensions and custom forms. This means that users can exchange e-mail messages, and they can share public folders with Exchange Client users. Some exceptions are described in the following sections.

Toolbox

Outlook is not designed to run on the same computer as Exchange Client, but the Office Resource Kit includes the SwitchForms utility that allows you to run both Outlook and Exchange Client on the same computer. For more information about installing SwitchForms, see "Microsoft Office Resource Kit for Office 97/98" on page 792.

Unless you specify a profile, when you run Outlook 2000 for the first time, it uses the default e-mail profile to open your Personal Address Book (PAB) and personal folders; and it connects to the Exchange server and any other services that you specify in that profile.

Whether you configure the profile to deliver e-mail messages to the Inbox on the Exchange Server or to the Inbox in personal folders, Outlook 2000 continues to accept new e-mail in the same Inbox folder. After you install Outlook, you work with the same Inbox, Outbox, Sent Items, Deleted Items, and any other personal folders used by the Microsoft Exchange Client profile.

Tip   To make the new user interface of Outlook 2000 look more like the Exchange Client user interface, you can view the Outlook folder list by using the **Folder List** command (**View** menu). Later, you can choose to hide the folder list and then use the Outlook Bar exclusively for quick access to Outlook functions and Windows folders.

Outlook 2000 starts with the same profile configuration as Exchange Client, except that a new information service is added to the Outlook 2000 default profile. This allows Outlook and any other Messaging Application Programming Interface (MAPI) application to use the Outlook Contacts folder as an e-mail address book. Outlook 2000 can also do the following:

- Recognize any folder views you define.
- Maintain the read or unread message status.

Toolbox

The Microsoft Office Resource Kit for Office 97/98 provides additional upgrading and file sharing information for Microsoft Exchange Client, including information about Exchange Client folders and views, client forms, and extensions. For more information, see "Microsoft Office Resource Kit for Office 97/98" on page 792.

Sharing Information with Microsoft Exchange Client

Microsoft Outlook 2000 recognizes all Microsoft Exchange Client message properties. Although Outlook users can share information with Microsoft Exchange Client users, Microsoft Exchange Client users might not be able to view or use portions of Outlook 2000 messaging information.

When you install and run Outlook, it recognizes and opens all the Exchange Client e-mail folders defined in the mail profile. Outlook 2000 also creates the Outlook-specific folders: Calendar, Contacts, Journal, Notes, and Tasks.

Outlook 2000 recognizes and maintains all specified folder views in Exchange Client, including custom views. While Outlook can create more advanced custom views than Exchange Client, Outlook and Exchange Client can share public folders that might include custom views.

Exchanging messages

In a mixed environment, it is recommended that Outlook users be aware that their co-workers who use Microsoft Exchange Client cannot take full advantage of many Outlook 2000 messaging features, including the following:

Enhanced standard message form

Microsoft Exchange Client users who view messages created in Outlook 2000 see the messages in the Microsoft Exchange Client standard message form, which does not support the advanced features of the Outlook standard message form, such as message expiration. As a result, some of the information in an Outlook message might not be viewable to Microsoft Exchange Client users.

Extended message properties

When a Microsoft Exchange Client user opens an Outlook 2000 message, extended Outlook message properties, such as voting buttons are ignored because they are not recognized by Microsoft Exchange Client. This means that some messages created in Outlook might appear different to Microsoft Exchange Client users. However, Outlook recognizes all Microsoft Exchange Client message properties.

Private items

When an Outlook 2000 user marks an item (such as an e-mail or calendar item) as "Private," other Outlook users cannot view the item. However, Microsoft Exchange Client users can view the item if they have been granted folder access privileges for the folder where the item is stored. Because Outlook folder-level privacy is absolute, the workaround for this functionality difference is to have Outlook users put private items in a separate folder, which they do not share or for which they have set restrictions.

Non-table views

Microsoft Exchange Client users can display Outlook 2000 table views—views that consist only of rows and columns—if the **Automatically generate Microsoft Exchange views** check box is selected in the **Folder Properties** dialog box for the Outlook folder. However, Microsoft Exchange Client cannot display Outlook non-table views (such as the day, week, and month views in the calendar), or card, icon, and timeline views.

When Outlook and Microsoft Exchange Client users access the same set of public folders, Microsoft Exchange Client users cannot display any non-table views created by Outlook users.

Saved views

Outlook 2000 and Microsoft Exchange Client use different formats to create saved views. Outlook supports both formats, so Outlook users can use any Microsoft Exchange Client view. By contrast, Microsoft Exchange Client does not support the Outlook format, so Microsoft Exchange Client cannot use Outlook views.

Outlook users can choose to maintain two copies of all saved table views in a folder automatically—one copy in Outlook format and one copy in Microsoft Exchange Client format. This workaround enables Microsoft Exchange Client users to use Outlook forms, although any Outlook-specific view features, such as formula fields, are not included in the Microsoft Exchange Client copy.

Custom field types

Microsoft Exchange Client users cannot view Outlook 2000 custom field types, such as formula and combination fields.

Attachments

Outlook 2000 can open attachments or objects within e-mail messages created by Microsoft Exchange Client users, and Exchange Client users can likewise open attachment or objects in Outlook 2000 messages. Both Outlook and Microsoft Exchange Client users can attach one message to another message.

Outlook users can also attach other Outlook items (such as a contact) to a message. However, Microsoft Exchange Client users receive these items as text-only attachments.

Sending and receiving vCards

Outlook 2000 allows users to send and receive contact information by using the Internet standard vCard format. Microsoft Exchange Client does not support this feature.

Using public folders

Outlook 2000 supports all of the custom public folder view features of Microsoft Exchange Server. In fact, Microsoft Exchange Server does not distinguish between Outlook and Microsoft Exchange Client when users open a public folder. For this reason, Outlook and Microsoft Exchange Client users can gain access to a common set of public folders.

Using other messaging and collaboration features

Some interoperability differences between Outlook 2000 and Microsoft Exchange Client features go beyond the basic capabilities of exchanging e-mail messages and using public folders.

Rules

Microsoft Exchange Client users use the Inbox Assistant to manage rules. By contrast, Outlook 2000 includes an enhanced Rules Wizard. The Outlook Rules Wizard allows users to manage Inbox Assistant rules (server-side rules) in addition to their Outlook rules (client-side rules). The Rules Wizard also allows users to convert Inbox Assistant rules into Outlook rules.

Each time that the Rules Wizard is started, it checks for active Inbox Assistant rules on the user's computer. If any Inbox Assistant rules exist, the Rules Wizard gives the user the option to convert them automatically to Outlook rules. After an Inbox Assistant rule has been converted to an Outlook rule, users can modify the Outlook rule by using the Rules Wizard.

Forms

Forms created by using the Outlook 2000 forms design environment can be used only by Outlook users. Forms created by using Electronic Forms Designer can be used by both Outlook and Microsoft Exchange Client users. Forms implemented using Exchange Server HTML interfaces can be used by Outlook, but not by Microsoft Exchange Client. Developers can create forms by using the tool that is appropriate for the mix of operating systems in a specific organization.

Microsoft Exchange Server provides an alternative means of creating forms to use in collaborative applications. It does this by using *Active Server Pages* (ASP) pages and the Microsoft Exchange Collaboration Data Objects (CDO) interface to script forms that are displayed as HTML in a Web browser. Outlook supports Microsoft Exchange Server HTML forms. These features provide Microsoft Exchange sites with an option for developing electronic forms that can be deployed across all operating systems.

WordMail

Microsoft Exchange Client users can choose either Microsoft Word 95 or Microsoft Word 97 for WordMail. Outlook 2000 users, however, must have Microsoft Word 97 installed to create messages using WordMail—although they can receive and read messages composed with either WordMail 95 or WordMail 97.

Voting

By using Outlook 2000, users can easily create and send ballot messages to other Outlook users, and then they can track the voting responses automatically in Outlook. An Outlook user specifies the voting choices when creating the message and then sends the message to other users. When recipients using Outlook receive a voting message, the selections they can vote for appear as buttons in the Outlook message However, when Microsoft Exchange Client users receive voting messages from Outlook users, they receive only the text of the Subject line and the body of the voting message. No voting buttons are displayed.

Microsoft Exchange Client preview pane

Outlook 2000 has a built-in preview pane. The Microsoft Exchange Client preview pane is not compatible with Outlook.

Task delegation

When an Outlook 2000 user delegates a task to a user who is running Microsoft Exchange Client, the recipient receives only an e-mail message that lists the description of the task, start and end dates, and other information as text in the body of the message.

Toolbox

The Microsoft Office Resource Kit for Office 97/98 provides additional file sharing information for Microsoft Exchange Client, including information about using public folders, converting rules to use with the Rules Wizard, and exchanging forms. For more information, see "Microsoft Office Resource Kit for Office 97/98" on page 792.

Upgrading from Microsoft Mail 3.x for Windows

Microsoft Outlook 2000 provides all the features of Microsoft Mail 3.x for Windows, and it provides many new features, such as:

- Integrated calendar functions with contact, journal, and task items.
- Multiple views of messages.
- Custom view capabilities.

- Message handling rules.
- Custom form creation.
- Advanced printing options.

Note Because Outlook runs only on Microsoft Windows 95/98 and Microsoft Windows NT Workstation 3.51 or later, Microsoft Mail 3.x for Windows users running Windows 3.11 or Windows for Workgroups must upgrade to Windows 95/98 or Windows NT Workstation before upgrading to Outlook 2000.

Outlook 2000 can serve as a complete replacement for Microsoft Mail 3.x for Windows. Except for changes in the user interface and other features, you can work with e-mail in Outlook in the same way that you work with Microsoft Mail 3.x for Windows.

Outlook 2000 uses the same MSMail.ini file and other configuration information; and Outlook can use all Microsoft Mail 3.x for Windows add-ins and custom forms. This means that you can share information with Microsoft Mail 3.x for Windows users by sending e-mail back and forth or by making messages available in shared folders. However, Outlook 2000 e-mail messages might not appear the same to users of Microsoft Mail 3.x for Windows.

Tip To make the Outlook user interface look more like the user interface of Microsoft Mail 3.x for Windows, you can view the Outlook folder list by using the **Folder List** command (**View** menu). Later, you can choose to hide the folder list and then use the Outlook Bar exclusively for quick access to Outlook features and Windows folders.

The Microsoft Mail information service allows Outlook 2000 to use Microsoft Mail 3.x post office. By default, Office 2000 setup installs the service the first time it is used. That means that a user can just add this service to the Messaging Application Programming Interface (MAPI) profile, and Office setup installs the service. However, as the administrator, if you want to automatically generate MAPI profiles with the Microsoft Mail information service, then you must customize the Setup.ini file so that this feature is installed locally on a user's computer during setup.

▶ To customize the Setup.ini file

1   Go to the folder where the setup.exe is stored, and open the Setup.ini file.

   By default, the Setup.ini file is stored in the C:\Windows folder, or equivalent.

2   Add the following line to the Options section of Setup.ini:

   ADDLOCAL="OutlookMAPISFS,OutlookMAPISFS95"

Setup uses information from your MSMail.ini file to configure the service. When Setup is finished, Outlook can use the same post office that Microsoft Mail 3.x for Windows uses.

When Outlook is run for the first time, it uses the Microsoft Mail 3.*x* post office and e-mail message file (MMF) defined in MSMail.ini. After Outlook is installed, you work with the same Inbox, Outbox, and Sent Mail folders used by Microsoft Mail 3.*x* for Windows, as well as any private folders in the MMF, and public folders in the Microsoft Mail 3.*x* post office.

Note   If you install both the Microsoft Mail and the Microsoft Exchange Server information services in the same profile, and you use the **Plan a Meeting** command (**Action** menu) in Outlook to check the free/busy information of other users, Outlook looks for this information by using the Microsoft Exchange Server information service only.

Importing Microsoft Mail files

After Outlook is installed, you must import the contents of the MMF. The MMF stores your e-mail messages, attachments, and personal address book (PAB). You can store the MMF in the post office folder in the MMF directory, or you can move the MMF to your hard disk or a network location.

If the MMF is in the post office, you must first connect to the post office with Microsoft Mail 3.*x* for Windows, and you then move the MMF either to your hard disk or to an accessible network location before importing the contents by using Outlook.

▶ **To move the MMF from the post office to a hard disk**

1   On the Microsoft Mail 3.*x* for Windows **Mail** menu, click **Options**.

2   Click **Server**.

3   Click **Local**, and then enter a file name for your MMF.

4   After the MMF is on your hard disk or stored on a network server, you can import its contents to an Outlook personal folder.

▶ **To import the MMF to a personal folder in Outlook**

1   On the Outlook **File** menu, click **Import and Export**.

2   Select **Import from another program or file**, and then click **Next**.

3   In the **Select file type to import from** box, select **Microsoft Mail File (.mmf)**, and then click **Next**.

4   In the **File name** box, enter the name of the MMF to import, and then click **Open**.

5   Enter the password (if requested), and then select both the **Import messages** and **Import personal address book entries** check boxes.

6   To store messages in existing personal folders, click **Put the messages into existing Personal Folders**, and then click the folder you want.

–or–

To create a new personal folders store, click **Put the messages into new Personal Folders,** and then enter the path name. To display the new folders in the folder list, click **Display new Personal Folders**. Outlook creates the new personal folders and adds them to your profile.

Outlook imports the messages and PAB entries from the MMF.

If you have used multiple information services such as AT&T or CompuServe for e-mail messages, you might have multiple PAB files in the MMF. When you import the MMF with the **Import and Export** command, you can choose which PABs to import.

When you import an MMF, consider the following:

- If there is a network failure, Outlook retries the network connection four times in the first two seconds, and then repeats this process every 10 minutes. A message is displayed during the 10-minute retry period.

- Any errors while importing the MMF are logged to a file in the client directory with the same file name as the MMF and the file name extension .log. You can view the .log file in Notepad or any other text editor.

Note   When you begin using Outlook, there is no easy way to transfer new messages back to an MMF or a mailbag file. You can copy the messages to a shared folder, and then you can retrieve them with your old client. However, this does not guarantee privacy.

Avoiding duplicate e-mail messages

In Microsoft Mail, you can keep a copy of all of the e-mail messages in your Inbox in the post office on the server. If you migrate to Microsoft Exchange Server, these messages might be duplicated because during migration the Inbox in the post office is copied to your Microsoft Exchange Server folders, and you also import the messages from the local MMF by using Outlook.

To avoid duplicate messages, on the Microsoft Mail 3.x for Windows **Mail** menu, click **Options**. In the **Server** dialog box, clear the **Copy Inbox on Postoffice for Dialin Access** check box.

Using Microsoft Mail custom commands, menus, and messages

Custom menu and command entries in MSMail.ini and Shared.ini are used by Outlook 2000 in the same way that Microsoft Mail 3.*x* for Windows uses them.

Custom menus

Custom menu add-ins allow you to add top-level menus to Microsoft Mail 3. *x* for Windows. This feature is fully supported in Outlook: Top-level menus specified in the MSMail.ini file are added to the Outlook menu bar.

Note   The **Tools** menu is not available by default in Microsoft Mail 3.*x* for Windows, but you can use the menu add-ins feature to add it. Outlook uses its native **Tools** menu and does not create a second **Tools** menu. Therefore, custom menus with the tag **Tools** in the Custom Menus section of the INI file are ignored.

Custom commands

Custom command extensions allow you to add new commands to Microsoft Mail 3.*x* for Windows. However, because the menus in Outlook 2000 and Microsoft Mail 3.*x* for Windows are different, Outlook handles command add-ins differently. When you define a command add-in for the Microsoft Mail 3. *x* (Windows) **Mail** menu, Outlook adds the command to its **Actions** menu. When you add a custom command to a Microsoft Mail 3.*x* (Windows) **Tools** or **Windows** menu, Outlook adds the custom command to its **Tools** menu.

Msmail[32].ini and Shared[32].ini parsing

Outlook 2000 supports both 16-bit and 32-bit extensions; it uses either 16-bit or 32-bit extensions, depending on where the extensions are located when Outlook starts up. During startup, Outlook first looks for extensions in the Windows registry under **HKEY_CURRENT_USER\Software\Microsoft\Mail\Microsoft Mail**, where extensions for Microsoft Mail 3.*x* for Windows NT Workstation are installed. Outlook for Windows 95/98 uses this same registry subkey.

Outlook then looks for Microsoft Mail 3.*x* extensions defined locally and shared extensions defined for the workgroup. To find these extensions, Outlook retrieves the shared extensions folder location from the Windows registry in the set of value entries **SharedExtsDir**, **SharedExtsServer**, and **SharedExtsPassword** under **HKEY_CURRENT_USER\Software\Microsoft\Exchange\Client\Options**. If these value entries do not exist in the registry, Outlook looks for the value entry **SharedExtensionsDir**, first in MSMail32.ini, and then in MSMail.ini, to retrieve the location of the shared extensions folder.

If Outlook 2000 finds the shared extensions folder, Outlook opens the Shared32.ini file in that folder and reads the Custom Menus, Custom Commands, and Custom Messages sections to retrieve the shared Microsoft Mail 3.x extension definitions. Outlook then reads the same sections from the MSMail32.ini file. If there are any duplicate extensions defined in these two files, Outlook 2000 uses the extensions in MSMail32.ini file.

If Outlook does not find Shared32.ini and MSMail32.ini, it looks for the Shared.ini and MSMail.ini files.

Outlook supports an enhancement to the version parameter of the extension registration entry. The version number can be followed by **,16** to indicate a 16-bit-extension dynamic-link library (DLL), or by **,32** to indicate a 32-bit-extension DLL. For example, to specify a 16-bit-extension DLL for a shared extensions directory, you can use **SharedExtsDir,16** as the entry.

If a version does not specify a 16-bit-extension or 32-bit-extension DLL, Outlook assumes an extension type based on the file in which the extension is found.

If the extension is found in this file	Outlook assumes this extension type
MSMail.ini	16-bit
MSMail32.ini	32-bit
Shared.ini	16-bit
Shared32.ini	32-bit

Note   In Microsoft Mail 3.x for either Windows 3.11 or Windows NT Workstation, specifying a 16-bit or 32-bit extension in the version number results in a syntax error.

Custom message types

Microsoft Mail 3.x custom message handlers allow you to use custom forms in place of the standard e-mail message form. Outlook 2000 provides complete support for Microsoft Mail 3.x custom message types.

Upgrading remote users

Outlook users running either the Microsoft Mail 3.x information service or the Microsoft Exchange information service can retrieve e-mail messages remotely by using a method that is different from the Microsoft Mail 3.x remote client. Before upgrading the remote client users in your workgroup to Outlook, you must install, configure, and test the new connection method. Also, remote users who upgrade to Outlook can move their MMF files to a personal folder file, and then import them to Outlook 2000.

Note   If you use Microsoft Mail 3.x for MS-DOS remote client, you cannot migrate your locally stored messages to Outlook personal folders. You must mail the messages to yourself, save them as text files, or print them.

Migrating to Microsoft Exchange Server

If you plan to migrate your workgroup from Microsoft Mail 3.*x* to Microsoft
Exchange Server, upgrading to Outlook 2000 is a good intermediate step because
Outlook works with both e-mail applications. Microsoft Mail 3.*x* users can use
Outlook 2000 while they continue to work with Microsoft Mail 3.*x* post office.

Later, when you upgrade the post office to Microsoft Exchange Server, these users
only need to change their profiles to continue to use Outlook. This allows you to
manage the upgrade of the user interface and the upgrade of the e-mail system
separately.

The process of migrating users from Microsoft Mail 3.*x* post offices to Microsoft
Exchange Server involves more than upgrading e-mail client software, and it is
beyond the scope of the Microsoft Office 2000 Resource Kit. The Microsoft Exchange
Server CD-ROM contains a document that takes you through all the planning and
implementation steps necessary to migrate users from Microsoft Mail 3.*x* to Microsoft
Exchange Server. The document title is "Migrating from Microsoft Mail for PC
Networks," and you can find it on the Microsoft Exchange Server CD-ROM in
Migrate\Docs\Msmailpc.doc.

This document discusses upgrading Microsoft Mail 3.*x* users to Exchange Client, and
the information also applies to Outlook, because you can use Outlook as a direct
replacement for Exchange Client. Review this document thoroughly if you plan to
move your workgroup to Microsoft Exchange Server.

See also

- Outlook 2000 and Microsoft Mail 3.*x* remote clients have different hardware
  requirements. For more information, see "Office 2000 Systems Requirements"
  on page 9.

- You can install Outlook 2000 separately from the rest of Office 2000. For
  more information, see "Installing Outlook 2000 After Installing Office 2000"
  on page 201.

- You can customize Outlook 2000 installation for your users. For more
  information about customizing the Setup Wizard, see "Customizing How
  Setup Runs" on page 215.

Sharing Information with Microsoft Mail 3.x

Microsoft Outlook 2000 can exchange messages with users of Microsoft Mail 3.*x* for
Windows. Outlook 2000 recognizes all Microsoft Mail 3.*x* message properties.
However, Microsoft Mail 3.*x* users might not be able to view or use portions of
Outlook 2000 messaging information.

Although Outlook 2000 works with Microsoft Mail post offices, the full set of Outlook 2000 features is available only when you use it with Microsoft Exchange Server. The following Outlook 2000 features require Microsoft Exchange Server:

- Opening e-mail folders as a delegate of another user
- Security for "Sent on behalf of" messages
- Deferred delivery and message expiration
- Digital signatures and *encryption*
- Public folders
- Full-text search

In addition, Microsoft Mail 3.*x* and Outlook 2000 cannot share the same message store. To use data from a Microsoft Mail 3.*x* message store, users must import the message store to an Outlook-compatible format. Microsoft Exchange Server includes a utility that imports Microsoft Mail 3.*x* message stores to Messaging Application Programming Interface (MAPI) format.

Exchanging messages

Microsoft Mail 3.*x* users cannot take full advantage of many Outlook 2000 messaging features, including the following.

This Outlook feature	Has these limitations in Mail 3.*x*
Enhanced standard message form	Mail 3.*x* users cannot view advanced features such as message expiration.
Extended message properties	Mail 3.*x* ignores extended message properties such as voting buttons.
Custom field types	Mail 3.*x* does not display custom field types.
Rich Text Format (RTF) in messages	Plain text replaces RTF in messages.
Attachments	Mail 3.*x* users cannot view messages with other attached messages. Other attached Outlook items are viewed as text-only.
Embedded hyperlinks	Mail 3.*x* views hyperlinks as text only.
Unlimited message size	Mail 3.*x* has size limitations, but it can save entire messages to file or print.
HTML-based e-mail messages	Mail 3.*x* displays HTML as plain text.
vCard feature	Mail 3.*x* does not support the vCard feature.

Toolbox

The Microsoft Office Resource Kit for Office 97/98 provides additional file sharing information for Microsoft Mail 3.*x*, including information about exchanging forms and delegating tasks. This archive edition is included in its entirety in the Microsoft Office 2000 Resource Kit. For more information, see "Microsoft Office Resource Kit for Office 97/98" on page 792.

Upgrading from Microsoft Schedule+ 7.x

Microsoft Outlook 2000 includes all the features of Microsoft Schedule+ 7.*x*, including appointments, events, contacts, and tasks. Outlook also provides the following features that are not available in Schedule+ 95:

- Integrated e-mail functions with journal and note items
- Additional views for calendar, contact, and task information
- Advanced custom view capabilities
- Task delegation
- Advanced printing options

Except for changes in the user interface and other features, you can work with your calendar, contact, and task information in Outlook in the same way that you work with them in Schedule+ 95. You can also freely exchange group scheduling information with Schedule+ 95 users; and you have the option to retain Schedule+ 95 as your primary calendar while using Outlook 2000 for e-mail and other functions.

To upgrade to Outlook 2000 from Schedule+ 95, install Outlook 2000, and then import the Schedule+ 95 data file. Schedule+ is not removed from your computer.

Toolbox

The Microsoft Office Resource Kit for Office 97/98 includes additional information and procedures for importing the Schedule+ 95 data file. This archive edition is included in its entirety in the Microsoft Office 2000 Resource Kit. For more information, see "Microsoft Office Resource Kit for Office 97/98" on page 792.

See also

- You can install Outlook 2000 separately from the rest of Microsoft Office 2000. For more information about installing Outlook, see "Installing Outlook 2000 After Installing Office 2000" on page 201.

Upgrading from Microsoft Schedule+ 1.0

You have the option to use either Microsoft Schedule+ or the Microsoft Outlook 2000 native Calendar as your calendar client.

Outlook 2000 includes all the features of Schedule+ 1.0 such as appointments, events, contacts, and tasks. Outlook also provides the following features that are not available in Schedule+ 1.0:

- Integrated e-mail functions with contact, journal, and note items
- Additional views for calendar, contact, and task information
- Advanced custom view capabilities
- Task delegation
- Advanced printing options

Except for changes in the user interface and other features, you can continue working with your calendar and task information in the same way that you work with Schedule+ 1.0. You can also freely exchange group scheduling information with Schedule+ 1.0 users. However, when Outlook 2000 and Schedule+ 1.0 share information, Outlook uses Schedule+ 95 to read and interpret Schedule+ 1.0 data.

To upgrade, install Outlook 2000, and then import the Schedule+ 1.0 data (CAL) file. Schedule+ is not removed from your computer.

Toolbox

The Microsoft Office Resource Kit for Office 97/98 provides additional information and procedures for importing the Schedule+ 1.0 data file. This archive edition is included in its entirety in the Microsoft Office 2000 Resource Kit. For more information, see "Microsoft Office Resource Kit for Office 97/98" on page 792.

Sharing Information with Microsoft Schedule+

Microsoft Outlook 2000 users and users of all previous versions of Microsoft Schedule+ can share calendar and group scheduling information such as calendar free/busy status information, and meeting request messages. However, Schedule+ users might not be able to view or use some Outlook 2000 message or calendar features.

Note   Outlook 2000 users with Corporate/Workgroup e-mail support have the option to substitute Microsoft Schedule+ 7.*x* for the Outlook Calendar.

For most organizations, viewing free/busy status and exchanging meeting requests are essential scheduling tasks. Outlook 2000 and Schedule+ share information completely in both of these key areas.

Exchanging meeting requests

Outlook 2000 and Schedule+ 1.0 and Schedule+ 7.*x* users can freely exchange meeting messages across the Microsoft Windows and Macintosh operating environments. Although Outlook 2000 users and Schedule+ 1.0 users can freely exchange meeting requests and responses, Schedule+ 1.0 does not recognize the advanced features of Outlook such as attachments, the meeting location field, and recurring meetings. As a result, when a Schedule+ 1.0 user receives a meeting message from an Outlook user, Schedule+ 1.0 ignores any Outlook-specific message features it does not recognize. For example, if an Outlook user sends a recurring meeting request to a Schedule+ 1.0 user, the Schedule+ user receives only the first meeting request.

Viewing free/busy status

When users publish their free/busy status, other users can view the free/busy status in Meeting Planner. By having appropriate permission, Outlook 2000 and Schedule+ 7.*x* and Schedule+ 1.0 users can view each other's free/busy status. Permission is not needed to view the free/busy status of other users.

In addition to designating free/busy status, Outlook 2000 users can designate tentative and out-of-office status that other Outlook users can view. However, when Schedule+ users view an Outlook calendar, tentative status appears as free status, and out-of-office status appears as busy status.

Outlook differs slightly from Schedule+ in how it handles unpublished free/busy status. When Schedule+ users choose not to publish their free/busy status, other Schedule+ users can still view the free/busy status in Meeting Planner—provided they have read permission. However, when Outlook users choose not to publish their free/busy status, no one can view their free/busy status in Meeting Planner, but they can open calendars to view unpublished free/busy status, provided they have read permission to the users' calendar.

Viewing free/busy details

Outlook 2000 users on Microsoft Exchange Server can view the free/busy details of Schedule+ users who are on Microsoft Exchange Server, but they cannot view the details of users on Microsoft Mail Server. Schedule+ 7.*x* users can view the free/busy details of Outlook users when all users are on Microsoft Exchange Server, and the necessary Windows 16-bit or 32-bit driver is installed. Schedule+ 1.0 users cannot view free/busy details for Outlook users.

Outlook users who have Read Only permission for other user calendars can see when those users are free or busy, and they can view the details of scheduled appointments and activities in Meeting Planner.

Delegating e-mail messages and scheduling tasks

In Outlook 2000, you can give others permission to read or modify your folders, and you can delegate your e-mail messages and scheduling tasks to other users. Delegates can create, send, and reply to messages; and they can request meetings and delegate tasks on your behalf.

A delegate relationship requires that both users run the same scheduling client. For example, Outlook users can be delegates only for other Outlook users. Outlook users who want to participate in delegate relationships must keep all their primary folders, such as Calendar and Inbox, on the server instead of on their local computers.

Schedule+ 7.x users can designate other users to be their *delegate owners*. As a delegate owner, a user has all the capabilities of a delegate and can also designate additional delegates for the owner's schedule. Like Schedule+ 7.x users, Outlook folder owners can enable their delegates to give other users the necessary permission for gaining access to the owner's folders. However, Outlook does not allow a delegate to designate additional delegates for the owner's folders. To designate a delegate in Outlook, you must be logged on as the folder (account) owner.

Note   When Outlook is a client for a Microsoft Mail server, Outlook users cannot give other Outlook users access to their folders.

Using direct booking

Outlook 2000 users with the appropriate permission can use the direct booking feature to book appointments directly into an Outlook or Schedule+ Calendar. However, Schedule+ 1.0 and Schedule+ 7.x users cannot book appointments directly into Outlook 2000 Calendars.

With direct booking, no meeting request is actually sent to a user or resource such as a conference room. The client software of the meeting organizer adds the meeting directly to the resource calendar. If the direct booking fails for an Outlook 2000 user, the user is informed, and no meeting request is sent. If the direct booking fails for a Schedule+ user, a meeting request is sent. If no one responds to the meeting request, the resource is not booked.

Because a directly booked resource is unlikely to receive many meeting requests, you are not required to assign a delegate to the resource or to have a continuously running computer logged into the account of the resource to process incoming meeting requests. However, if a user sends a meeting request to the resource instead of booking an appointment, the meeting request is not noticed until a user logs on to the account of the resource. With appropriate permission, an Outlook user can open the Calendar of a resource and modify it directly—if necessary.

Note   A Schedule+ user can read the calendar of an Outlook user, but cannot add to it or edit it—regardless of the *permissions* that the Outlook user grants.

Working with tasks

Outlook 2000 gives users new task features that are not available in Schedule+ 7.*x* or Schedule+ 1.0. For example, Outlook provides additional views for task items, making it easier for users to manage tasks in a way that best suits their needs. Also, Outlook enables users to delegate tasks to other users. When Outlook users delegate a task to other Outlook users, all of the task information (such as start date, end date, and status) is sent as a special task request message to the recipients, who can add it to their own task lists automatically.

After Outlook 2000 is installed, users can import their Schedule+ 7.*x* or Schedule+ 1.0 task data at any time by using the **Import and Export** command on the Outlook **File** menu. By default, Outlook imports Schedule+ task information into the Outlook Tasks folder. Users can choose to ignore or replace any duplicate entries encountered during the import process.

Working with contacts

Outlook 2000 provides a Contacts feature that helps users keep their business and personal contact information up to date. Although Schedule+ 7.*x* includes some contact features, many of the Outlook contact management enhancements, such as additional contact views, are not available in Schedule+ 7.*x*.

The enhanced Contacts feature enables Outlook users to include e-mail addresses with their contacts. Outlook users can import all Schedule+ 7.*x* contacts, as well as contacts stored in Microsoft Exchange Client personal address books (PABs). In addition, Outlook users can maintain contacts as their personal e-mail address books, so they do not need to maintain contact names and e-mail addresses in two separate places.

After installing Outlook 2000, users can import their Schedule+ contact data at any time by using the **Import and Export** command on the Outlook **File** menu. By default, Outlook imports Schedule+ contact information into the Outlook Contacts folder. Users can choose to ignore or replace any duplicate entries encountered during the import process. The Outlook Import Wizard also imports Microsoft Exchange Client PABs.

Using the Outlook driver for Schedule+

By using the Outlook driver for Schedule+ 7.*x*, Schedule+ users can open an Outlook Calendar from Schedule+, and they can view Outlook free/busy details. The Schedule+ users must have at least read-only permission for the calendars of the Outlook users, and the calendars must be stored on a Microsoft Exchange Server. Outlook users with the appropriate permission can open the calendars of Schedule+ 7.*x* users, and they can view the free/busy details of Schedule+ 7.*x* users— without using a special driver.

The Outlook driver for Schedule+ has 16-bit and 32-bit versions (no Macintosh version is available). Both the Schedule+ and Outlook users must be running Microsoft Exchange Server. The 16-bit driver is available only with the Microsoft Exchange Server 5.5 CD-ROM, and the 32-bit driver is available with the Microsoft Exchange Server 5.0 and 5.5 CD-ROMs.

Sharing Information with Microsoft Project 98 and Project 95

Microsoft Project 98 and Microsoft Project 95, and Microsoft Outlook 2000 work together to provide task scheduling for your users. Microsoft Project 95 users can assign tasks to Outlook 2000 users. However, if the Outlook recipients accept the tasks, Microsoft Project 95 does not add the tasks to Outlook Tasks automatically. Microsoft Project 98 offers additional integration with Outlook. Users can create Outlook reminders from within Microsoft Project 98, and they can add Microsoft Project items to the Outlook Journal.

To use the workgroup features of Microsoft Project with Outlook 2000, you must configure Microsoft Project 98 for a workgroup. These workgroup configurations allow team members to view the custom e-mail messages, such as team status reports, generated in Microsoft Project 98. Project managers can use the TeamAssign feature to send custom e-mail messages, and to assign project tasks to the team members who receive all messages in the Outlook Inbox.

After each team member accepts a task and sends the response to the project manager, the task is logged automatically in the Outlook Task list of the team member. Project tasks are grouped under a new category that corresponds to the project name. Each team member can keep track of the task status in the Outlook Task list.

When they use previous versions of Microsoft Project, project managers have to send TeamStatus messages to team members to request that the team members submit status reports. However, Microsoft Project 98 adds a new menu command called **New TeamStatus Report** to the Outlook **Tasks** menu. This feature allows team members to generate and submit TeamStatus reports without waiting for the project manager to ask for them.

When the team member chooses this command, a custom TeamStatus e-mail message is created and stored in the Outlook Inbox. If the team member is tracking the task status in the task list, the status information is added automatically to the TeamStatus report. Users can just open the report and send it to the project manager. In addition, they can use the TeamStatus message to track the task status, and to save and store the message in the Inbox until they are ready to submit it to the project manager.

See also

- You must configure Microsoft Project 98 for workgroups before you can take advantage of the interactions between Microsoft Project 98 and Outlook 2000. For more information, see the Microsoft Project 98 Resource Kit Web site at http://www.microsoft.com/project/prk/.

Upgrading to PowerPoint 2000

Microsoft PowerPoint 2000 users can collaborate with users of other versions of PowerPoint and users of other applications. However, previous versions of PowerPoint and some other applications do not support all PowerPoint 2000 features.

Working with PowerPoint 2000 Files and Graphics Formats

Microsoft PowerPoint 2000 users can save presentations in different file and graphics formats. If a presentation includes graphics, PowerPoint 2000 includes most of the graphics filters that users need to import and export graphics that are embedded in or linked to a presentation.

PowerPoint 2000 file formats

The following table identifies the file formats in which PowerPoint 2000 users can save presentations.

File format	Description
Presentation (.ppt)	Default PowerPoint 97-2000 file format.
Web Page (.htm)	HTML format that allows the file to be opened in a Web browser.
PowerPoint 95 (.ppt)	Format that PowerPoint 95 can open.
PowerPoint 97-2000 & 95 Presentation (.ppt)	Dual file format that PowerPoint 2000, PowerPoint 98, PowerPoint 97, and PowerPoint 95 can open.
PowerPoint 4.0 (.ppt)	Format that PowerPoint 4.0 can open.
Design Template (.pot)	Template format.
PowerPoint Show (.pps)	Slide show format.
Outline/RTF (.rtf)	Outline/Rich Text Format (RTF). Text in the presentation is saved, but graphics content is lost.

PowerPoint 2000 graphics formats

Saving PowerPoint 2000 presentations in a graphics format is an ideal solution for users who need to preserve the graphic design of a presentation and to share the presentation with users of applications for which there is no PowerPoint converter.

PowerPoint 2000 users can save presentations in the following graphics formats:

- Graphics Interchange Format (GIF) (.gif)
- JPEG File Interchange Format (.jpg)
- Portable Network Graphics (PNG) (.png)
- Device-independent bitmap (DIB) (.bmp)
- Windows Metafile (WMF) (.wmf)
- Tag Image File Format (TIFF) (.tif)

When a PowerPoint 2000 user saves a presentation in a graphics format, each slide becomes a separate image—including text. The text becomes a graphical text element that a user cannot edit but can move on the slide.

When saving a presentation in a graphics format, a user can export only the active slide or all the slides in the presentation. If the user exports only the active slide, PowerPoint saves the slide in the active folder with the file name that the user specifies. If the user exports all the slides in the presentation, PowerPoint saves each slide as a graphics file in a folder with the file name that the user types in the **File name** box of the **Save As** dialog box. Each slide is named Slide*x*, where *x* is the slide number.

PowerPoint 2000 graphics filters

If a presentation includes graphics, PowerPoint 2000 uses graphics filters to import and export graphics that are embedded or linked to the presentation.

When a PowerPoint 2000 user clicks the **From File** command (**Insert** menu, **Picture** submenu) to insert a graphic onto a slide, one of the following events occurs:

- If the graphic is in a format that PowerPoint recognizes (a native format), PowerPoint preserves the graphic in its original format.
- If the graphic is in a nonnative format but a compatible graphics filter has been installed, PowerPoint converts the graphic to a format that it can open.
- If the graphic is in a format PowerPoint does not recognize, PowerPoint displays a message and does not convert the graphic.

The following table identifies the PowerPoint 2000 graphics filters that you can install by using Microsoft Office 2000 Setup.

Graphics filter	Description
Computer Graphics Metafile (CGM) (Cgmimp32.flt)	Imports CGM images that conform to CGM:1992 version 1.0.
CorelDRAW (CDR) (Cdrimp32.flt)	Imports CDR images from CorelDRAW versions 3.0 through 6.0.
Encapsulated PostScript (EPS) (Epsimp32.flt)	Imports EPS images with embedded preview images in Tagged Image File Format, WMF format, and PICT format.
Enhanced Metafile (EMF) (Emfimp32.flt)	Converts EMF images to WMF format.
FlashPix (FPX) and Microsoft Picture It! (MIX) (Fpx32.flt)	Imports FPX and MIX images. Converts a multiple-resolution image to a single-resolution image. You can choose which resolution to import.
Graphics Interchange Format (Gifimp32.flt)	Imports GIF images in versions Gif87a and Gif89a.
JPEG File Interchange Format (Jpegimp32.flt)	Imports JPEG images that conform to JPEG File Interchange Format version 6.0. The filter does not support JPEG Tagged Interchange Format (JTIF) images.
Kodak Photo CD (PCD) (Pcdimp32.flt and Pcdlib32.dll)	Imports PCD images saved in Kodak Photo CD version 3.0. Converts a multiple-resolution image to a single-resolution image. You can choose which resolution to import.
Macintosh PICT (Pictim32.flt)	Imports Macintosh PICT images.
PC Paintbrush (PCX) (Pcximp32.flt)	Supports all versions of PCX images through ZSoft version 3.0.
Portable Network Graphics (Png32.flt filter)	Imports and exports PNG images conforming to the Portable Network Graphics Tenth Specification.
Tagged Image File Format (Tiffim32.flt)	Imports TIFF images and compressions that conform to TIFF Specification Revision versions 6.0 and 5.0.
Windows bitmap (Bmpimp32.flt)	Supports BMP, RLE, and DIB bitmaps.
Windows Metafile (Wmfimp32.flt)	Imports WMF images.
WordPerfect Graphics (WPG) (Wpgimp32.flt and Wpgexp32.flt)	Imports and exports WPG images saved in WordPerfect versions 1.0, 1.0e, and 2.0.

By default, Office 2000 Setup installs graphics filters in the following location:

Program Files\Common Files\Microsoft Shared\Grphflt

The following table identifies the additional PowerPoint 2000 graphics filters that you can install by using the Microsoft Office Converter Pack.

Graphics filter	Description
AutoCAD (Dxfimp32.flt)	Supports AutoCAD format 2-D graphics versions through Release 12, including AutoCAD for Windows.
Micrografx Designer/Draw graphics filter (Drwimp32.flt)	Supports Micrografx Designer 3.*x*, Charisma 2.1, and Draw files.
Targa graphics filter (Tgaimp32.flt)	Imports Truevision Targa images with up to 32 bits per pixel.

By default, the Setup program for the Microsoft Office Converter Pack installs graphics filters in the following location:

Program Files\Common Files\Microsoft Shared\Grphflt

Toolbox

You can install graphic filters from the Microsoft Office Converter Pack. For information about installing these filters, see "Microsoft Office Converter Pack" on page 793.

Sharing Presentations with Previous Versions of PowerPoint

Some Microsoft PowerPoint 2000 users might have to share presentations with users of PowerPoint 98, PowerPoint 97, or PowerPoint95.

Running macros created in previous versions of PowerPoint

PowerPoint 2000 supports macros that users create in PowerPoint 97 by using Visual Basic for Applications (VBA) version 5.0. PowerPoint 97 macros might not run correctly in all situations because some macros might depend on certain PowerPoint options or settings. For example, a PowerPoint 97 macro that inserts a drawing object does not run correctly when you are in PowerPoint 2000 Slide Sorter view.

If a macro is not able to run, a message appears. Users can look up messages in Visual Basic Help. Start the Visual Basic Editor, and then click **Microsoft Visual Basic Help** (**Help** menu).

In most instances, users do not need to make any modifications when upgrading PowerPoint 97 macros. However, when converted macros do not perform correctly in PowerPoint 2000, Online Support can help users troubleshoot compatibility issues. To access Online Support, on the **Help** menu, click **Office on the Web**.

PowerPoint 2000 includes Visual Basic for Applications version 6.0. This latest version of VBA provides new features and enhancements such as support for additional ActiveX controls. Users might want to rewrite existing macros, or they might want to create new macros to take advantage of the features in Visual Basic for Applications 6.0. In PowerPoint 2000, users create new macros by recording macros in VBA or writing macros by using the Visual Basic Editor.

Preventing macro viruses

To prevent users from inadvertently downloading macro viruses, PowerPoint displays a message when users open a presentation containing a macro. PowerPoint displays this message by default—regardless of whether the macros in the presentation actually contain a virus.

For additional security, you might want to specify that PowerPoint run only signed macros with digital signatures from trusted sources. A digital signature allows users to confirm that the macro originated from a trusted developer who signed it and that the macro has not been altered.

▶ **To set PowerPoint 2000 to run only signed macros**

1   On the **Tools** menu, point to **Macro**, and then click **Security**.

2   On the **Security Level** tab, click **High**.

When users open presentations, PowerPoint automatically disables any unsigned macros.

System Policy Tip   You can use a system policy to set the security level option in the **Security** dialog box (**Tools** menu). In the System Policy Editor, set the **Microsoft PowerPoint 2000\Tools|Macro\Security\Security Level** policy. For more information about the System Policy Editor, see "Using the System Policy Editor" on page 296.

Sharing templates with previous versions of PowerPoint

PowerPoint 2000 users can exchange templates with users of other versions of PowerPoint. However, the templates included with PowerPoint 2000 take advantage of the new and enhanced features in the application. The unique features in PowerPoint 2000 are lost when a template is saved in a previous format such as PowerPoint 97 format.

When PowerPoint 2000 users open a template or load an add-in that is already installed, macros within the file are automatically enabled.

▶ **To display a message when opening an old add-in or template**

1   On the **Tools** menu, point to **Macro**, and then click **Security**.

2   On the **Trusted Sources** tab, clear the **Trust all installed add-ins and templates** check box.

System Policy Tip   You can use a system policy to set the **Trust all installed add-ins and templates** option in the **Security** dialog box (**Tools** menu). In the System Policy Editor, set the **Microsoft PowerPoint 2000\Tools|Macro\Security\Trust all installed add-ins and templates** policy. For more information about the System Policy Editor, see "Using the System Policy Editor" on page 296.

PowerPoint 2000 includes general, design, and presentation templates. The templates are listed in the **New** dialog box (**File** menu), which is on the **General**, **Design Templates**, and **Presentations** tabs.

The templates contain professionally designed formats and color schemes that users can apply to any presentation to give it a unique look. Some templates also contain suggested text for specific subjects and occasions.

By default, Office 2000 Setup installs templates at the following location:

Program Files\Microsoft Office\Templates

Sharing presentations with PowerPoint 97 and PowerPoint 98 users

PowerPoint 2000 users can open presentations created in PowerPoint 98 (Macintosh) and PowerPoint 97 (Windows)—without losing any data and formatting. However, when PowerPoint 98 and PowerPoint 97 users save a PowerPoint 2000 presentation, some data and formatting might be lost. If PowerPoint 2000 users save presentations in the PowerPoint 97-2000 default file format or Web Page format, they can collaborate with PowerPoint 98 and PowerPoint 97 users.

For text formatting to display correctly in presentations saved in Web Page format, users opening the presentations must use *cascading style sheets* and Microsoft Internet Explorer version 4.0 or later.

System Policy Tip   You can use a system policy to define the default value for the **Save as type** option in the **Save As** dialog box (**File** menu). In the System Policy Editor, set the **Microsoft PowerPoint 2000\Tools | Options\Save\Save PowerPoint files as** policy. For more information about the System Policy Editor, see "Using the System Policy Editor" on page 296.

Sharing presentations with PowerPoint 95 users

PowerPoint 2000 users can open PowerPoint 95 presentations without losing any data and formatting. PowerPoint 2000 and PowerPoint 95 users can collaborate on presentations by using the following methods:

- PowerPoint 2000 users can save presentations in the formats that PowerPoint 95 users can open.

- PowerPoint 95 users can install converters included in the Microsoft Office Converter Pack so that they can open presentations saved in the HTML and PowerPoint 97-2000 formats.

Saving PowerPoint 2000 presentations for PowerPoint 95 users

PowerPoint 2000 users can collaborate with PowerPoint 95 users by saving presentations in the following formats:

- PowerPoint 95 format saves the presentation in a format that's native to PowerPoint 95.

  PowerPoint 95 users can open, edit, and save the presentation. However, some data and formatting are lost when PowerPoint 2000 presentations are saved in PowerPoint 95 format.

- PowerPoint 97-2000 & 95 format saves the presentation in a dual file format.

  The file includes two data streams: one data stream for PowerPoint 97-2000, and another data stream for PowerPoint 95. PowerPoint 95 users can open the presentation, but only PowerPoint 2000 users can edit and save the file. The dual file format also increases the file size, and increases the time it takes to save a file.

- Web Page format saves the presentation in HTML format.

  PowerPoint 95 users can open the presentation by using a Web browser.

System Policy Tip   You can use a system policy to define the default value for the **Save as type** option in the **Save As** dialog box (**File** menu). In the System Policy Editor, set the **Microsoft PowerPoint 2000\Tools | Options\Save\Save PowerPoint files as** policy. For more information about the System Policy Editor, see "Using the System Policy Editor" on page 296.

Installing converters for PowerPoint 95 users

PowerPoint 95 users can collaborate on presentations with PowerPoint 2000 users by installing converters included in the Microsoft Office Converter Pack.

The converter pack includes the following converters for PowerPoint 95 users.

- The Microsoft PowerPoint 97-2000 converter allows PowerPoint 95 users to read (but not edit) presentations saved in PowerPoint 97-2000 format.

- The HTML converter allows PowerPoint 95 users to open and edit presentations that PowerPoint 2000 users save in Web Page format.

Toolbox

You can install graphics filters from the Microsoft Office Converter Pack. For information about installing these filters, see "Microsoft Office Converter Pack" on page 793.

See also

- For more information about the new features in Visual Basic for Applications 6.0, see the *Microsoft Office 2000/Visual Basic Programmer's Guide*.

- PowerPoint 2000 users can select the default format in which to save new presentations. For more information, see "How to Specify the Default Format in Which to Save Files" on page 438.

Using a Dual File Format in PowerPoint

The dual file format is an ideal solution for your organization if you are upgrading gradually to Microsoft PowerPoint 2000. PowerPoint 2000 users can save files in the PowerPoint 97-2000 & 95 dual file format until all PowerPoint 95 users have upgraded to PowerPoint 2000. By using the dual file format, you can ensure that all PowerPoint users have a common file format with which to collaborate on presentations during the transition period.

System Policy Tip   You can use a system policy to define the default value for the **Save as type** option in the **Save As** dialog box (**File** menu). In the System Policy Editor, set the **Microsoft PowerPoint 2000\Tools | Options\Save\Save PowerPoint files as** policy. For more information about the System Policy Editor, see "Using the System Policy Editor" on page 296.

Saving two file formats in one compound document

When a PowerPoint 2000 user saves a presentation in the PowerPoint 97-2000 & 95 dual file format, the presentation is saved in a single file with two data streams: one data stream for PowerPoint 97-2000, and another data stream for PowerPoint 95. PowerPoint first writes the 95 data stream to the file and then writes the PowerPoint 97-2000 data stream.

When PowerPoint 95 users open a presentation saved in the dual file format, PowerPoint reads only the PowerPoint 95 data stream in the file and disregards the PowerPoint 97-2000 data stream. Consequently, if a PowerPoint 95 user saves the presentation, the PowerPoint 97-2000 data stream is permanently lost, which means that features unique to PowerPoint 2000 are lost.

PowerPoint 95 users can open a PowerPoint 2000 presentation with read/write permission, but they are prompted to open the presentation as a read-only file. To protect a PowerPoint 2000 presentation, and to avoid losing PowerPoint 2000 features, you can require a write password or make the presentation read-only.

Deciding when to use a dual file format

The following examples can help you make the best use of the dual file formats.

- A PowerPoint 2000 user wants to publish a presentation in PowerPoint 97-2000 & 95 format for an audience of PowerPoint 2000 and PowerPoint 95 users. However, the PowerPoint 2000 user does not want any PowerPoint 95 users to modify the presentation.

  The PowerPoint 2000 user can enter a write-reservation password when saving the presentation and then distribute the password only to other PowerPoint 2000 users. This password protection keeps the file available for PowerPoint 95 users, but it prevents them from modifying the file.

- A PowerPoint 2000 user must send a presentation to a PowerPoint 95 user by using a modem.

  The PowerPoint 2000 user can save the presentation in PowerPoint 95 format rather than in a dual file format because a file in PowerPoint 95 format is smaller and is transmitted more quickly.

See also

- When you save a PowerPoint 2000 presentation in PowerPoint 95 format, there are conversion limitations. For more information, see "Saving Presentations in PowerPoint 95 Format" on page 530.

- If PowerPoint 2000 users save files often in the PowerPoint 97-2000 & 95 dual file format, you can specify the format as the default file format for new presentations. For more information, see "How to Specify the Default Format in Which to Save Files" on page 438.

Saving Presentations in PowerPoint 98 or PowerPoint 97 Format

When a Microsoft PowerPoint 98 or PowerPoint 97 user saves a PowerPoint 2000 presentation in PowerPoint 98 or PowerPoint 97 format, some features unique to PowerPoint 2000 are lost.

System Policy Tip   You can use a system policy to define the default value for the **Save as type** option in the **Save As** dialog box (**File** menu). In the System Policy Editor, set the **Microsoft PowerPoint 2000\Tools | Options\Save\Save PowerPoint files as** policy. For more information about the System Policy Editor, see "Using the System Policy Editor" on page 296.

The following table identifies new features in PowerPoint 2000 that might affect your data or formatting in PowerPoint 98 or PowerPoint 97 format.

When this PowerPoint 2000 feature	Is saved in PowerPoint 98 or PowerPoint 97 format
Animated GIF pictures	Appear as static images without animation.
Automatically numbered lists	Appear as bulleted lists, not as numbered lists.
Graphic or picture bullets	Appear as regular font-based bullets.
Tables	Appear as a single grouping of shapes.
Voice narration	Bullet point animations do not synchronize to the voice narration. There is a long gap in the audio between slides.

See also

- Microsoft Office 2000 includes several new international features that help simplify the task of administering and supporting Office 2000 internationally. For more information, see "Overview of International Features in Office 2000" on page 725.

- PowerPoint 2000 users can select the default format in which to save new presentations. For more information, see "How to Specify the Default Format in Which to Save Files" on page 438.

Saving Presentations in PowerPoint 95 Format

If your organization is upgrading gradually, Microsoft PowerPoint 2000 users can collaborate by saving all presentations in PowerPoint 95 format. However, because of changes to the PowerPoint file format, saving a PowerPoint 2000 file in PowerPoint 95 format can result in lost data or changed formatting.

System Policy Tip   You can use a system policy to define the default value for the **Save as type** option in the **Save As** dialog box (**File** menu). In the System Policy Editor, set the **Microsoft PowerPoint 2000\Tools I Options\Save\Save PowerPoint files as** policy. For more information about the System Policy Editor, see "Using the System Policy Editor" on page 296.

Basic use features

The following table identifies new features in PowerPoint 2000 that might affect your data or formatting in PowerPoint 95 format.

When this PowerPoint 2000 feature	Is saved in PowerPoint 95 format
Animated chart elements	Display as static chart objects. PowerPoint 95 users must use Microsoft Graph to edit charts.
Animated GIF pictures	Appear as static images without animation.
Custom shows	Appear in the presentation, but they are not designated as a group.
Elevator effects	Convert to Wipe Up effects.
Native format movies and sounds	Convert to Windows Media Player and Sound Recorder objects.
Automatically numbered lists	Appear as bulleted lists.
Play options for CD tracking and movie looping	Lost in the conversion.
Tables	Appear as a single grouping of shapes.

Graphics features

The following table describes new features in PowerPoint 2000 that might affect your data or formatting in PowerPoint 95. In general, graphics features in PowerPoint 2000 are converted to their closest equivalent in PowerPoint 95.

When this PowerPoint 2000 feature	Is saved in PowerPoint 95 format
3-D effects	Convert to pictures.
AutoShapes	Convert to freeform shapes when there are no matching shapes.
Composite shapes	Convert to separate shapes and grouped lines.
Connectors	Lose the automatic connecting characteristic, and convert to freeform lines.
Curves	Convert to connected line segments that approximate curves.
Gradient fills	Lose the semi-transparency characteristic.
Graphic or picture bullets	Appear as regular font-based bullets.
Joins and endcaps of lines	Convert to mitered joins and round endcaps on AutoShapes. On freeform shapes, they convert to round joins and round endcaps.
Objects that are linked or embedded	Lose brightness, contrast, and color transformation settings.
Picture brightness, contrast, and color transformation	Render at current PowerPoint 95 settings.
Picture fills	Convert to picture objects.
Picture fills on shapes	Converts to a picture object with a solid fill that is the last applied foreground color.
Shadows, engraved	Convert to an embossed shadow effect.
Shadows, perspective	Convert to grouped shapes with a shadow.
Shapes or arcs with attached text that are new in PowerPoint 2000 and PowerPoint 97	Convert to freeform shapes or arcs, and text boxes.
Text box margins	Average to center the text block in the box.
Text effects	Convert to pictures.
Thick compound lines	Convert to picture objects.

Workgroup and Internet features

The following table identifies the workgroup and Internet features in PowerPoint 2000 that might affect your data or formatting in PowerPoint 95 format.

When this PowerPoint 2000 feature	Is saved in PowerPoint 95 format
Comments	Convert to Rich Text Format (RTF); and hidden comments appear in the presentation.
Hyperlinks that combine Play Sound with other action settings	Lost in the conversion.
Hyperlinks embedded within an object	Lost in the conversion.
Action settings embedded within an object.	Lost in the conversion.

Other features

The following table identifies other new features in PowerPoint 2000 that might affect your data or formatting in PowerPoint 95 format.

When this PowerPoint 2000 feature	Is saved in PowerPoint 95 format
Charts	Can only be edited with Microsoft Graph.
Clip Gallery	Does not launch when users double-click the clip art object. The clip art object converts to a picture object.
Macros	Do not convert because PowerPoint 95 does not include a macro language.
Unicode characters (two bytes per character)	Map to corresponding ANSI. Foreign language characters do not change.
Voice narration	Does not synchronize with bullet point animation. There is a long gap in the audio between slides.

See also

- If PowerPoint 2000 users share presentations often with PowerPoint 95 users, you can specify PowerPoint 95 format as the default file format for new presentations. For more information, see "How to Specify the Default Format in Which to Save Files" on page 438.

- Microsoft Office 2000 includes several new international features that help simplify the task of administering and supporting Office internationally. For more information, see "Overview of International Features in Office 2000" on page 725.

How to Share Files with Other Presentation Applications

You can customize Microsoft Office 2000 Setup to install most converters that Microsoft PowerPoint 2000 users need to share presentations with users of other applications. The file formats and graphics formats available to PowerPoint 2000 users are listed in the **Open** and **Save as** dialog boxes (**File** menu).

Open a presentation saved in another file format

To open a presentation created in another application, click **Open** (**File** menu), and then click the appropriate file format in the **Files of type** box. When PowerPoint 2000 recognizes the file format of a presentation, it converts the file, and then opens it. If PowerPoint does not recognize the format, it displays a message.

If a user needs to open a presentation created in another application, but the appropriate file type is not listed in the **Files of type** box, the user must first save the file in a format that PowerPoint 2000 can open. PowerPoint can open a file in the following formats:

- HTML (.htm)
- Rich Text Format (.rtf)
- Plain text (.txt)

PowerPoint can also open presentations saved in graphics formats such as Windows Metafile (WMF) (.wmf) format. If the application that users are importing the presentations from doesn't support WMF files, save the slides in a graphics file format that is built into PowerPoint or for which a graphics import filter is installed.

Toolbox

You can install graphic filters from the Microsoft Office Converter Pack. For information about installing these filters, see "Microsoft Office Converter Pack" on page 793.

Save a presentation in a format that other applications can open

To save a PowerPoint 2000 presentation in a format that other applications can open, click **Save As** (**File** menu), and then in the **Save as type** box, click the appropriate file or graphics format.

System Policy Tip   You can use a system policy to define the default value for the **Save as type** option in the **Save As** dialog box (**File** menu). In the System Policy Editor, set the **Microsoft PowerPoint 2000\Tools | Options\Save\Save PowerPoint files as** policy. For more information about the System Policy Editor, see "Using the System Policy Editor" on page 296.

If users want to save presentations in a format for which there's no converter, users can save the presentation in the following formats:

- Web Page (.htm)

  Saving a presentation in Web Page format preserves the content.

- Outline/RTF (.rtf)

  Saving a presentation in Outline/RTF format preserves text formatting.

- Plain text (.txt)

  Saving a presentation in plain text format preserves the content of the file, but not the graphics or the text formatting.

In addition to the Web Page, Outline/RTF, and plain text file formats, a PowerPoint 2000 user can save a presentation in a graphics file format. Saving a presentation in a graphics format saves each slide as a separate graphic image— including the text. The text converts to a graphical text element that cannot be edited as text, but can be moved on the slide.

Share a presentation with users who do not have PowerPoint

PowerPoint 2000 users can share a presentation with users who do not have a presentation application installed on their computer. PowerPoint 2000 users can:

- Save the presentation in Web Page format, which allows the other users to view, print, and edit the presentation by using a Web browser.

- Provide the other users with the Microsoft PowerPoint 97-2000 viewer (Pptvw32.exe).

  After installing the viewer on their local hard disk, users can view and print (but not edit) the presentation.

Toolbox

The Microsoft PowerPoint 97-2000 viewer allows users who don't have PowerPoint to view and print presentations. For information about installing the viewer, see "PowerPoint 97/2000 Viewer" on page 794.

See also

- PowerPoint 2000 users can save presentations in several graphics formats, depending on the graphics filters installed during Setup. For more information, see "Working with PowerPoint 2000 Files and Graphics Formats" on page 520.

- If PowerPoint 2000 users share presentations often with users of other applications, you can change the default format in which PowerPoint 2000 saves presentations. For more information, see "How to Specify the Default Format in Which to Save Files" on page 438.

- Office 2000 includes some new and enhanced features for publishing presentations on your intranet or the World Wide Web. For more information, see "Using HTML and Office Document Formats" on page 589.

FAQs About Upgrading to PowerPoint 2000

Use the following tips to answer commonly asked questions about upgrading to Microsoft PowerPoint 2000.

Do previous versions of PowerPoint have the same file format as PowerPoint 2000?

Microsoft PowerPoint 2000 shares the same file format as PowerPoint 98 (Macintosh) and PowerPoint 97 (Windows), but it has a few enhancements because of the new features included in PowerPoint 2000. PowerPoint 97-2000 format is different from the file format used in PowerPoint 95. For more information, see "Sharing Presentations with Previous Versions of PowerPoint" on page 523.

Can PowerPoint 2000 users share templates with previous versions of PowerPoint?

PowerPoint 2000 users can share templates with users of other versions of PowerPoint. However, the templates included with PowerPoint 2000 take advantage of the new and enhanced features in the application. The unique features in PowerPoint 2000 are lost when a template is saved in a previous format such as PowerPoint 97 or PowerPoint 95 format. For more information, see "Sharing Presentations with Previous Versions of PowerPoint" on page 523.

How can I prevent users from saving presentations in an unapproved format?

You cannot prevent users from saving presentations in an unapproved format, but you can:

- Set a system policy by using the System Policy Editor, and create a custom message to alert users when they try to save a file that is not the default format in the system policy.

- Set a default file format by using the **Options** dialog box (**Tools** menu).

- Limit the number of text converters you distribute to users.

For more information, see "How to Specify the Default Format in Which to Save Files" on page 438 and "Using the System Policy Editor" on page 296.

Why can't users of other versions of PowerPoint edit the charts in a converted presentation?

If users of other versions of PowerPoint are not able to edit charts in a converted presentation, PowerPoint 2000 users might have changed a default option in the **Options** dialog box before saving the presentation. To convert charts to a usable format when converting a presentation to a format that other versions of PowerPoint can use, click **Options** on the (**Tools** menu), and then click the **Save** tab. Click **Web Options**, and then click the **Convert charts when saving as previous version** check box. Then save the PowerPoint 2000 presentation again.

System Policy Tip   You can use a system policy to set the convert charts option in the **Options** dialog box (**Tools** menu). In the System Policy Editor, set the **Microsoft PowerPoint 2000\Tools | Options\Save\Convert charts when saving as previous version** policy. For more information about the System Policy Editor, see "Using the System Policy Editor" on page 296.

How can PowerPoint 95 users open HTML files created in PowerPoint 2000?

To open an HTML file created in PowerPoint 2000, PowerPoint 95 users must install the HTML add-in included in the Microsoft Office Converter Pack.

Toolbox

You can install the HTML add-in from the Microsoft Office Converter Pack. For information about installing this add-in, see "Microsoft Office Converter Pack" on page 793.

Where can users get additional graphics filters not included in PowerPoint 2000?

Users can install the following additional graphics filters by using the Microsoft Office Converter Pack:

- AutoCAD (Dxfimp32.flt)
- Micrografx Designer/Draw (Drwimp32.flt)
- Targa (Tgaimp32.flt)

Toolbox

You can install graphic filters from the Microsoft Office Converter Pack. For information about installing these filters, see "Microsoft Office Converter Pack" on page 793.

Why are graphics not automatically resized so that they display properly in a Web browser?

If graphics do not resize automatically in a Web browser, the PowerPoint 2000 user might have changed the default option that resizes graphics in a file saved in Web Page format.

▶ **To automatically resize graphics in a presentation**

1   On the **Tools** menu, click **Options**, and then click the **General** tab.

2   Click **Web Options**, click the **Resize graphics to fit browser window** check box, and then save the PowerPoint 2000 presentation again.

System Policy Tip   You can use a system policy to set the resize graphics option in the **Options** dialog box (**Tools** menu). In the System Policy Editor, set the **Microsoft PowerPoint 2000\Tools I Options\Web Options\Resize graphics to fit browser window** policy. For more information about the System Policy Editor, see "Using the System Policy Editor" on page 296.

Why can't PowerPoint 2000 users ungroup an imported graphic?

Check to see whether the image is a bitmap. You can't ungroup and convert bitmaps to a PowerPoint object.

Modify the image in a program such as Microsoft Photo Editor, and then insert the image in your presentation.

Why is AutoShape a different size?

When PowerPoint 2000 converts a PowerPoint 95 AutoShape to PowerPoint 2000 format, the AutoShape changes from an inset pen outline to a centered pen outline. Likewise, when a PowerPoint 2000 AutoShape is saved in PowerPoint 95 format, it is rendered with an inset, rather than centered, pen.

It is easiest to see the difference between the inset pen and the centered pen by outlining an AutoShape with a dashed line. The fill color of the AutoShape allows you to see the difference in pen position through the gaps of the dashed line.

Because the size of shapes drawn with a centered pen might be slightly larger than the same shape drawn with an inset pen, users might need to reduce the size of AutoShapes drawn in PowerPoint 95 to make them look exactly the same in PowerPoint 2000.

Why can't PowerPoint 97 users view macros in some PowerPoint 2000 presentations?

The macros might have been digitally signed from within the Visual Basic Editor in Microsoft PowerPoint 2000. This new security feature is not included in PowerPoint 97. Because PowerPoint 97 doesn't recognize digital signatures, it can't update the signature if you modify a signed Visual Basic for Applications macro. Therefore, to prevent modifications, you cannot view in PowerPoint 97 the code for macros that have been digitally signed in PowerPoint 2000.

Why can't users run a macro or load an add-in in a presentation?

If the security level for PowerPoint 2000 is set to High, and users open a presentation or load an add-in that contains unsigned macros, the macros are disabled and users cannot run them. Users can enable macros that are not digitally signed by changing the security level to Medium in the **Security** dialog box (**Macro** submenu on the **Tools** menu), closing the presentation or unloading the add-in, and then opening the presentation or loading the add-in again.

Note   Remember to change the security level back to High if you want PowerPoint 2000 to automatically disable unsigned macros in the future.

If the security level for PowerPoint is set to Medium or High and you chose to disable macros because you do not trust the source of the macros, you cannot run the macros. To run the macros, close the presentation or unload the add-in, and then open the presentation or load the add-in again. Then click **Enable Macros**.

Upgrading to Word 2000

Microsoft Word 2000 users can collaborate with users of other versions of Word and users of other applications. However, previous versions of Word and some other applications do not support all Word 2000 features.

Working with Word 2000 Text Converters and Graphics Filters

When Microsoft Word 2000 opens or saves a document, it uses text converters to change the file format of the document. If a document includes images, Word 2000 uses graphics filters to open and save images that are within or linked to the document.

To successfully convert documents and images to and from different formats, you must install the appropriate text converters and graphics filters included with Office 2000 Setup and the Microsoft Office Converter Pack.

Office 2000 Setup and the Microsoft Office Converter Pack install text converters and graphics filters in the following locations:

- Program Files\Common Files\Microsoft Shared\TextConv
- Program Files\Common Files\Microsoft Shared\Grphflt

Word 2000 text converters

The following text formats are native to Word 2000:

- HTML
- MS-DOS Text
- MS-DOS Text with Line Breaks
- Rich Text Format (RTF)
- Text Only
- Text with Line Breaks
- *Unicode* Text
- Word 97 for Windows, and Word 98 for the Macintosh
- Word 6.0/95 for Windows and the Macintosh (Asian versions require a converter)
- Word 4.*x*-5.1 for the Macintosh (import only)
- Word 2.0 and 1.0 for Windows (import only)

The following table identifies the text converters that you can install by using Office 2000 Setup.

Text converter	Description
Borland dBASE (Dbase32.cnv)	Opens files in dBASE IV, III+, III, and II.
Lotus 1-2-3 (Lotus32.cnv)	Opens documents in Word 4.0, 3.*x*, and 2.*x* format. An export converter is not available.
Lotus AmiPro (Ami332.cnv)	Opens and saves documents in Lotus AmiPro 3.*x* for Windows.
Lotus Notes (Msimp32.dll, Mscthunk.dll, Mswrd632.cnv, Mswrd832.cnv)	Opens Word 2000, Word 97, Word 95, and Word 6.0 documents in Lotus Notes versions 4.*x* and 3.*x*.
Microsoft Excel (Excel32.cnv)	Opens Excel workbooks saved in Excel 97-2000, Excel 98 (Macintosh), Excel 97, Excel 95, and Excel 2.*x*–5.0.
Microsoft FoxPro (Dbase32.cnv)	Opens files in FoxPro 2.6.
Microsoft Windows Write (Write32.cnv)	Opens and saves documents in Write 3.1 and 3.0 for Windows.
Microsoft Word 6.0/95 (Wrd6ex32.cnv)	Saves documents in Word 6.0/95 binary file format with a .doc extension. (A converter is needed for importing.)
Microsoft Word for MS-DOS (Doswrd32.cnv)	Opens and saves documents in Word 3.*x*–6.0 for MS-DOS.
Microsoft Word for the Macintosh (Macwrd32.cnv)	Saves documents in Word 5.*x* and 4.*x* for the Macintosh format. (A converter is not needed for importing.)
Microsoft Word for Windows 2.*x* (Wnwrd232.cnv)	Saves documents in Word 2.*x* format. (A converter is not needed for importing.)
Microsoft Works 3.0 for Windows (Works332.cnv)	Opens and saves documents in Works 3.0 for Windows format.
Microsoft Works 4.0 for Windows (Works432.cnv)	Opens and saves documents in Works 4.0 for Windows.
Recover Text (Recovr32.cnv)	Recovers text from damaged documents.
Revisable-Form-Text Document Content Architecture (RFT-DCA) (Rftdca.cnv)	Opens and saves documents in RFT-DCA format.
Text with Layout (Txtlyt32.cnv)	Saves documents with layout preserved.
WordPerfect 4.*x* for MS-DOS (Mpft432.cnv)	Opens and saves documents in versions 4.2 and 4.1. The converter also allows you to install WordPerfect fonts.
WordPerfect for MS-DOS and Windows (Wpft632.cnv and Wpft532.cnv)	Opens Word Perfect 6.*x* documents, and opens and saves Word Perfect 5.*x* documents.
WordStar for MS-DOS and Windows (Wrdstr32.cnv)	Opens documents in WordStar 3.3–7.0 for MS-DOS and WordStar 1.0–2.0 for Windows. Allows you to also save documents in WordStar 7.0 and 4.0 for MS-DOS.

Word 2000 graphics filters

When a document contains images, Word 2000 uses graphics filters to open and save images that are embedded or linked to the document.

When you click **From File** (**Insert** menu, **Picture** submenu) to insert an image into a document, one of the following events occurs:

- If the image is in a format that Word recognizes (a native format), Word preserves the image in its original format.
- If the image is in a nonnative format, and if a compatible graphics filter is installed, then Word converts the image to a format that is native to Word.
- If the image is in a format that Word does not recognize, Word displays a message and does not convert the image.

Some images in Word documents convert to different formats in Word 2000. This situation occurs when a Word document is saved in:

- A previous Word format, such as Word 95 for Windows format.
- A different text format, such as WordPerfect 5.*x* format.

When a file is saved in a previous Word format or a different text format, Word 2000 converts the nonnative images to Windows Metafile (WMF) format.

The following graphics formats are native to Word 2000:

- Graphics Interchange Format (GIF)
- Joint Photographic Experts Group (JPEG)
- Macintosh PICT (PCT)
- Portable Network Graphics (PNG)
- Windows bitmap (BMP)
- Run-length encoded (RLE)
- Device-independent bitmap (DIB)
- Windows Enhanced Metafile (EMF)
- Windows Metafile (WMF)

You can install graphics filters by using Office 2000 Setup. Some additional graphics filters are included in the Microsoft Office Converter Pack.

Toolbox

You can install graphics filters from the Microsoft Office Converter Pack. For information about installing these filters, see "Microsoft Office Converter Pack" on page 793.

Graphics filters included with Office Setup

The following table identifies the graphics filters you can install by using Office 2000 Setup.

Graphics filter	Description
Computer Graphics Metafile (Cgmimp32.flt)	Opens CGM images that conform to CGM:1992 version 1.0.
CorelDRAW (CDR) (Cdrimp32.flt)	Opens CDR images from CorelDRAW versions 3.0–6.0.
Encapsulated PostScript (Epsimp32.flt)	Opens EPS images with embedded preview images in Tagged Image File Format (TIFF), WMF format, and PICT format. If no preview is embedded, a generic title page is used.
Enhanced Metafile (Emfimp32.flt)	Converts EMF images to WMF format.
FlashPix (FPX) and Picture It! (MIX) (Fpx32.flt)	Opens FPX and MIX images. Converts a multiple-resolution image to a single-resolution image. You can choose which resolution to import.
Graphics Interchange Format (Gifimp32.flt)	Opens GIF images in versions Gif87a and Gif89a.
JPEG File Interchange Format (Jpegimp32.flt)	Opens JPG images that conform to JPEG File Interchange Format version 6.0. The filter does not support JPEG Tagged Interchange Format (JTIF) images.
Kodak Photo CD (PCD) (Pcdimp32.flt and Pcdlib32.dll)	Opens PCD images saved in Kodak Photo CD version 3.0. Converts a multiple-resolution image to a single-resolution image. You can choose which resolution to import.
Macintosh PICT (Pictim32.flt)	Opens images created or edited in Microsoft Office for the Macintosh.
PC Paintbrush (PCX) (Pcximp32.flt)	Supports all versions of PCX images through ZSoft version 3.0.
Portable Network Graphics (Png32.flt filter)	Opens and saves PNG images conforming to the Portable Network Graphics Tenth Specification.
Tagged Image File Format (Tiffim32.flt)	Opens TIFF images and compressions that conform to TIFF Specification Revision versions 6.0 and 5.0.
Windows bitmap (Bmpimp32.flt)	Supports BMP, RLE, and DIB bitmaps.
Windows Metafile (Wmfimp32.flt)	Opens WMF images.
WordPerfect Graphics (WPG) (Wpgimp32.flt and Wpgexp32.flt)	Opens and saves WPG images saved in WordPerfect versions 1.0, 1.0e, and 2.0.

Note Although some of the graphics formats listed in the table are native to Word, you can customize Setup to install some graphics filters. Some graphics filters are not used by Word, but by other Office applications (such as Microsoft Photo Editor). In addition, some of the Word 2000 text converters use the graphics filters.

Graphics filters included in the Microsoft Office Converter Pack

The following table identifies the additional graphics filters you can install by using the Microsoft Office Converter Pack.

Graphics filter	Description
AutoCAD (Dxfimp32.flt)	Supports AutoCAD format 2-D graphics versions through Release 12, including AutoCAD for Windows.
Micrografx Designer/Draw graphics filter (Drwimp32.flt)	Supports Micrografx Designer 3.*x*, Charisma 2.1, and Draw files.
Targa graphics filter (Tgaimp32.flt)	Opens Truevision Targa images with up to 32 bits per pixel.

Toolbox

You can install graphic filters from the Microsoft Office Converter Pack. For information about installing these filters, see "Microsoft Office Converter Pack" on page 793.

See also

- The Removal Wizard removes unnecessary and obsolete files, settings, and components installed by previous versions of Office and related applications. For more information, see "Removal Wizard" on page 269.

How to Customize the Way That Word 2000 Displays Documents

Alignment and layout of some items in Microsoft Word 2000 are different from those in previous versions of Word and other applications. For example, line breaks and page breaks in Word 2000 might appear different from those in Word 95 or WordPerfect.

You can customize the way that documents created in previous versions of Word and other applications are displayed in Word 2000 by using the **Compatibility** tab in the **Options** dialog box.

Changing the options on the **Compatibility** tab affects only the display of the current document when you are working with it in Word 2000. It does not permanently change any formatting in the document. If you convert the document back to its original file format, the formatting appears as it did before you opened it in Word 2000.

▶ **To customize the way that Word 2000 displays documents**

1   On the **Tools** menu, click **Options**, and then click the **Compatibility** tab.

2   In the **Recommended options for** box, click the file format of the document you are working with.

3   In the **Options** box, click the check boxes to select the options you want.

Sharing Macros and Templates with Previous Versions of Word

If your organization is upgrading gradually to Microsoft Word 2000, users might have to share macros and templates with users of previous versions of Word.

Rewriting macros in Visual Basic for Applications 6.0

Word 2000 includes Visual Basic for Applications (VBA) version 6.0. This latest version of VBA provides new features and enhancements such as support for additional ActiveX controls.

You might want to rewrite existing macros, or create new macros to take advantage of the features in VBA version 6.0. To create new macros in Word 2000, you can record macros in Visual Basic for Applications or write macros with the Visual Basic Editor.

Running macros created in previous versions of Word

Word 2000 supports macros created in Word 97 with Visual Basic for Applications version 5.0. Most WordBasic macros created in Word 95 and Word 6.*x* run in Word 2000.

Running Word 97 macros

If a Word 97 macro does not run in Word 2000, an error message appears. To look up error messages, start the Visual Basic Editor, and then click **Microsoft Visual Basic Help** (**Help** menu).

In most instances, you do not need to make any modifications when you are upgrading Word 97 macros to Word 2000. However, if the converted macros do not perform correctly in Word 2000, you can use online support to troubleshoot compatibility issues. To use online support, click **Office on the Web** (**Help** menu).

Running Word 95 and Word 6.x macros

Word 2000 automatically converts WordBasic code to the equivalent Visual Basic for Applications code whenever you:

- Open a Word 95 or Word 6.*x* template with WordBasic macros.
- Create a new document based on a Word 95 or Word 6.*x* template with WordBasic macros.
- Use the **Templates and Add-ins** command (**Tools** menu) to attach a Word 95 or Word 6.*x* template to a Word 2000 document.

While Word 2000 is converting macros, a message appears on the status bar.

If the converted macros do not perform correctly in Word 2000, you can use online support to troubleshoot compatibility issues. To use online support, click **Office on the Web** (**Help** menu).

It is important to remember that the conversion from WordBasic to VBA happens automatically in Word 2000 and that there is no undo feature. If you want to reuse the WordBasic macros in Word 95 or Word 6.*x*, you must make backup copies of your files before you start upgrading to Word 2000.

Preventing macro viruses

To prevent you from downloading macro viruses, Word 2000 displays a message to inform you that the document or template you are opening contains macros. Word displays this message by default regardless of whether the macros actually contain a virus.

For additional security, you might want to allow Word to run only macros with a digital signature from a trusted source. A digital signature confirms that the macro is from a trusted source and that the macro has not been altered.

▶ **To allow Word 2000 to run only signed macros**

1 On the **Tools** menu, point to **Macro**, and then click **Security**.

2 On the **Security Level** tab, click **High**.

When you open a document or template, Word automatically disables any unsigned macros.

System Policy Tip   You can use a system policy to set the security level option in the **Security** dialog box (**Tools** menu). In the System Policy Editor, set the **Microsoft Word 2000\Tools\Macro\Security\Security Level** policy. For more information about the System Policy Editor, see "Using the System Policy Editor" on page 296.

Sharing templates with previous versions of Word

Word 2000 users can share templates with users of previous versions of Word. However, the Word 2000 templates include new and enhanced features that are lost when users save Word 2000 templates in previous formats such as Word 97 or Word 95 format.

When users open templates or load installed add-ins from previous versions of Word, Word 2000 enables macros automatically. You can have Word 2000 alert users about previously installed templates and add-ins by using the **Security** dialog box.

▶ **To warn users about previously installed templates and add-ins**

1   On the **Tools** menu, point to **Macro**, and then click **Security**.

2   On the **Trusted Sources** tab, clear the **Trust all installed add-ins and templates** check box.

System Policy Tip   You can use a system policy to set the **Trust all installed add-ins and templates** option in the **Security** dialog box (**Tools** menu). In the System Policy Editor, set the **Microsoft Word 2000\Tools\Macro\Security\Trust all installed add-ins and templates** policy. For more information about the System Policy Editor, see "Using the System Policy Editor" on page 296.

Storing templates in Word 2000

Word 2000 includes global and document templates:

- Global templates, such as the Normal template, contain settings that are available to all documents.

- Each document template, such as the memo and fax templates, contain settings that are available only to documents based on that template.

The following factors determine on which tab each template appears in the **New** dialog box (**File** menu):

- The location of the stored template.

- The file location settings that you specify for the user templates and workgroup templates on the **File Locations** tab in the **Options** dialog box.

▶ **To specify template file location settings**

1   On the **Tools** menu, click **Options**, and then click the **File Locations** tab.

2   Specify the settings that you want to set for user and workgroup templates.

To eliminate confusion about where to store user and workgroup templates, instruct users to do the following:

- Store templates that they share on the network in the workgroup templates file location specified on the **File Locations** tab.

- Store other templates (such as custom templates) in the user templates file location specified on the **File Locations** tab. By default, this location is the Templates folder and its subfolders.

  If users save a template in a different location, the template does not appear on the **General** tab of the **New** dialog box.

Tip   To make it easy for users to locate templates, you can create custom tabs for templates in the **New** dialog box by creating a new subfolder in the Templates folder and then saving the templates in the subfolder. The name you give the subfolder appears on the new tab.

See also

- The *Microsoft Office 2000/Visual Basic Programmer's Guide* contains information about new features in Visual Basic for Applications version 6.0. For more information, see the Microsoft Press Web site at http://mspress.microsoft.com/.

- The Removal Wizard removes unnecessary and obsolete files, settings, and components installed by previous versions of Office and related applications. For more information, see "Removal Wizard" on page 269.

Sharing Documents with Word 98 and Word 97 Users

Microsoft Word 2000 users can open Word 98 and Word 97 documents; and Word 2000 supports all data and formatting in these earlier versions of Word.

When Word 98 and Word 97 users open Word 2000 documents, some data and formatting are lost because Word 98 and Word 97 do not offer the new and enhanced features that are in Word 2000.

Disabling features that Word 97 does not support

If Word 2000 users need to share documents with Word 97 users, you can disable the Word 2000 features that Word 97 does not support. To disable the new Word 2000 features, select the **Disable features not supported by Word 97** check box on the **Save** tab of the **Options** dialog box (**Tools** menu).

Note   You cannot disable Word 2000 features that Word 98 does not support.

When you select the **Disable features not supported by Word 97** check box, Word saves the document without any new Word 2000 features. Word 2000 removes the formatting that Word 97 does not support and then replaces it with formatting that Word 97 supports.

System Policy Tip   You can use a system policy to set the **Disable features not supported by Word 97** check box on the **Save** tab of the **Options** dialog box (**Tools** menu). In the System Policy Editor, set the **Microsoft Word 2000\Tools I Options\Save\ Disable features not supported by Word 97** policy. For more information about the System Policy Editor, see "Using the System Policy Editor" on page 296.

Opening documents in Word 98 or Word 97

The following table identifies features that might affect data or formatting when Word 98 and Word 97 users open Word 2000 documents.

When this Word 2000 feature	Is opened in Word 98 or Word 97
24-bit color	Colors are mapped to the closest match.
Floating tables	The tables appear in frames.
Frames	Frame properties are lost in the conversion. The frames are saved in individual documents.
Measurements such as pixels and percentages for images and tables	Measurements are preserved when the document is saved.
New character underline styles	Decorative underlines are changed to a single underline.
Table AutoFit	Column widths are preserved when the document is saved.
Table cell margins and spacing	Margins and spacing are lost in the conversion.
Tables within tables	Nested table cells are converted to tabbed text. Tab marks are used to separate the contents of each cell.
Text wrapping break	Text-wrapping breaks are converted to line breaks.
Text-wrapped objects in a table	The objects are moved outside of the table.

See also

- The Removal Wizard removes unnecessary and obsolete files, settings, and components installed by previous versions of Office and related applications. For more information, see "Removal Wizard" on page 269.

Sharing Documents with Word 95 and Word 6.0 Users

Microsoft Word 2000 users can open Word 95 and Word 6.0 documents; and Word 2000 supports all data and formatting in these earlier versions of Word.

When Word 95 and Word 6.0 users open Word 2000 documents, some data and formatting are lost because Word 95 and Word 6.0 do not offer the new and enhanced features in Word 2000. The following strategies can help users who are sharing documents among these versions of Word:

- Word 95 and Word 6.0 users can open Word 2000 documents by installing the Word 97-2000 text converter included in the Microsoft Office Converter Pack.

- Word 2000 users can save documents in one of the following file formats: HTML (Web Page), Rich Text Format (RTF), dual file format, and Word 6.0/95.

Note that Word 95 and Word 6.0 have a 32-megabyte (MB) size limit for document files. If users get a message when they try to save a large document in RTF, Word 97-2000 & 6.0/95-RTF, or Word 6.0/95 format, they can divide the document into smaller files.

System Policy Tip   You can use a system policy to define the default value for the **Save as type** option in the **Save As** dialog box (**File** menu). In the System Policy Editor, set the **Microsoft Word 2000\Tools | Options\Save\Save Word files as** policy. For more information about the System Policy Editor, see "Using the System Policy Editor" on page 296.

Opening documents in Word 95 and Word 6.0

If you are planning a one-time upgrade to Word 2000, and your workgroup includes a large number of Word 95 and Word 6.0 users, users can open Word 2000 documents directly in Word 95 and Word 6.0. However, Word 95 and Word 6.0 users must install the Word 97-2000 converter included in the Microsoft Office Converter Pack before they can open documents saved in Word 97-2000 format.

Toolbox

The Microsoft Office Converter Pack includes converters for Word 95 and Word 6.0 users. For information about installing these converters, see "Microsoft Office Converter Pack" on page 793.

The following table identifies features that might affect data or formatting when Word 95 and Word 6.0 users open Word 2000 documents.

When this Word 2000 feature	Is opened in Word 95 or Word 6.0
Animated text (**Animation** tab)	Animated text formatting is lost.
Character borders (**Borders** tab)	Character borders are lost.
Character shading (**Shading** tab)	Character shading is lost.
DOCPROPERTY field	The DOCPROPERTY field is retained in Word 95. In Word 6.0, the DOCPROPERTY field displays "Error! Bookmark not defined."
Document properties (**File** menu)	New document properties are preserved in Word 95, but they are lost in Word 6.0.
Embedded fonts	The embedded fonts are lost, and Word 6.0 or Word 95 assigns the closest font available.
Embossed and engraved characters (**Font** tab)	Embossed and engraved characters are converted to AutoColor.
EMF, PNG, and JPEG graphics	Graphics in these formats are saved in the document, but Word 2000 also creates WMF format versions. Word 6.0 or Word 95 displays the WMF version of the graphics; the original formats are preserved in the document for better fidelity if the document is reopened in Word 2000.
Floating OLE objects	Floating OLE objects are converted in a frame.
Floating pictures surrounded by wrapped text	Floating pictures are converted in a frame to WMF format.
Forms controls	Forms controls are displayed, but they cannot be modified.
Highlighting applied with the **Highlight** button (**Formatting** toolbar)	Highlighting is preserved in Word 95. (In Word 6.0, highlighting is lost.)
HYPERLINK field (**Insert** menu)	The field displays "Error! Bookmark not defined." When the document is reopened in Word 2000, the HYPERLINK field is re-established.
Multilevel and heading numbering	Lists are converted to plain text, and the numbering property is lost.
Page borders (**Page Border** tab)	Page borders are lost.
Paragraph borders (**Borders** tab)	Paragraph borders are converted to the border styles used in Word 95 and Word 6.0.
Password protection options in the **Save As** dialog box (**File** menu)	Word 95 and Word 6.0 users cannot open password-protected Word 2000 documents.
Protect Document settings (**Tools** menu)	The password is lost, but the protection state is retained.
Shadow and outline effects (**Font** tab)	Shadow and outline effects are lost.
Tracked changes to properties, paragraph numbers, and display fields (**Tools** menu)	Revision marks for properties, paragraph numbers, and display fields are lost, but other revision marks are retained.

When this Word 2000 feature	Is opened in Word 95 or Word 6.0
Unicode characters	Unicode characters can be lost. Unicode characters (2 bytes per character) are mapped to corresponding ANSI (Windows), or converted to question marks (?). Foreign language characters might be affected.
Vertical text in table cells	Vertical text is reformatted as horizontal text.
Vertically aligned text in table cells	Vertically aligned text is reformatted to align at the top of the cell.
Vertically merged table cells	Merged table cells are unmerged.

Saving documents in Web Page format

If users need to share Word 2000 documents with Word 95 users, they can save the documents in Web Page format, which converts the documents to HTML format. To save Word 2000 documents in HTML format, on the **File** menu, click **Save As**, and then in the **Save as type** box, click **Web Page**.

Word 95 users must install the HTML converter, and then they can use a Web browser to open and make changes to the converted document. The HTML converter is included in the Microsoft Office Converter Pack.

Toolbox

The Microsoft Office Converter Pack includes the HTML converter for Word 95 users. For information about installing this converter, see "Microsoft Office Converter Pack" on page 793.

Saving documents in Rich Text Format

Rich Text Format (RTF) is a native file format for Word 2000, Word 95, and Word 6.0. When a user saves a Word 2000 document in RTF, the formatting converts to text instructions that Word 95 and Word 6.0 can read. The document is also given a different file name extension (.rtf).

The advantages of saving documents in Rich Text Format include the following:

- Text and formatting are saved.
- Any version of Word, and other programs such as Microsoft FrontPage and Adobe PageMaker can read RTF documents.

The disadvantages of saving documents in Rich Text Format include the following:

- Because the RTF document has an .rtf file name extension, the file name does not appear in the **Open** dialog box until the user clicks **All Files (*.*)** in the **Files of type** box.
- RTF documents increase in size after conversion. For example, graphics convert from their compressed JPEG or PNG format in Word 2000 to bitmaps, which can be up to 10 times larger.
- Password protection is lost.

Saving documents in a dual file format

When you save a Word 2000 document in the Word 97-2000 & 6.0/95-RTF format, the dual file format document is a combination of binary and RTF formats. However, the file name extension (.doc) indicates that the document is a Word document. You can customize Setup to install the Word 97-2000 & 6.0/95-RTF text converter (Wrd6er32.cnv) the first time a user activates the feature.

The advantages of saving documents in Word 97-2000 & 6.0/95-RTF format include the following:

- Text and formatting are retained when the file is saved.
- Word 95 and Word 6.0 users can open and edit the documents, and then they can save the documents in either RTF or native binary format.

The disadvantages of saving documents in Word 97-2000 & 6.0/95-RTF format include the following:

- Macros and passwords are lost in the conversion.
- When Word 95 and Word 6.0 users make changes, and then save a dual file format document, the Word 2000 features are lost when the document is reopened in Word 2000.
- Dual file format documents are generally larger in size than documents in Word 6.0/95 format. For example, Word 2000 graphics convert from their compressed JPEG or PNG format in Word 2000 to bitmaps in dual file format documents, which can be up to 10 times larger.

See also

- When Word 2000 users share documents with users of other applications, you can change the default format in which Word 2000 saves documents. For more information, see "How to Specify the Default Format in Which to Save Files" on page 438.
- The Removal Wizard removes unnecessary and obsolete files, settings, and components installed by previous versions of Office and related applications. For more information, see "Removal Wizard" on page 269.
- Office 2000 includes new and enhanced features for publishing documents on your intranet or the World Wide Web. For more information, see "Using HTML and Office Document Formats" on page 589.

Saving Documents in Word 6.0/95 Format

If you are planning a gradual upgrade to Microsoft Word 2000, and your workgroup includes a large number of Word 95 and Word 6.0 users, users can save Word 2000 documents in Word 6.0/95 format.

Word 2000 includes the Word 6.0/95 text converter, which enables users to save documents in the Word 6.0/95 binary file format with a .doc extension. Office 2000 Setup installs the text converter (Wrd6ex32.cnv) as part of the default installation.

The advantages of saving documents in Word 6.0/95 format include the following:

- Word 2000, Word 95, and Word 6.0 users can open, edit, and save Word 6.0/95 format documents.

- Users running other programs that read Word 6.0/95 format (such as Microsoft FrontPage, Adobe PageMaker, and Corel WordPerfect) can open, edit, and save Word 6.0/95 format documents.

- Documents in Word 6.0/95 format are generally smaller in size than documents in Word 97-2000 & 6.0/95-RTF format.

The disadvantages of saving documents in Word 6.0/95 format include the following:

- Features unique to Word 2000, password protection, and Visual Basic for Applications (VBA) macros are lost when users save documents in Word 6.0/95 format.

- Word 6.0 and Word 95 have a 32-megabyte (MB) limit for document file size.

Note that Word 95 and Word 6.0 have a 32-MB size limit for document files. If you are saving a large document with lots of graphics from Word 2000 to Word 6.0/95 format and you get an error message, try to divide the Word 2000 document into smaller files.

System Policy Tip   You can use a system policy to define the default value for the **Save as type** option in the **Save As** dialog box (**File** menu). In the System Policy Editor, set the **Microsoft Word 2000\Tools I Options\Save\Save Word files as** policy. For more information about the System Policy Editor, see "Using the System Policy Editor" on page 296.

Table features

The following table identifies new features in Word 2000 that might affect data or formatting when users save documents in Word 6.0/95, Rich Text Format (RTF), or Word 97-2000 & 6.0/95-RTF format.

When this Word 2000 feature	Is saved in another format
Vertical text in table cells	Vertical text is reformatted as horizontal text.
Vertically aligned text in table cells	Vertically aligned text aligns at the top of the cell.
Vertically merged table cells	Merged table cells are exploded into unmerged cells.

Formatting features

The following table identifies new features in Word 2000 that might affect your data or formatting when users save documents in Word 6.0/95, RTF, or Word 97-2000 & 6.0/95-RTF format.

When this Word 2000 feature	Is saved in another format
Outline and heading numbered lists	Outline numbered lists and heading numbered lists are converted to normal text but retain their appearance. In Word 6.0 or Word 95, use the **Bullets and Numbering** command (**Format** menu) to format lists.
Multilevel bullets	Multilevel bullets are converted to regular text but retain their appearance. In Word 6.0 or Word 95, use the **Bullets and Numbering** command (**Format** menu) to format lists.
Page borders	Page borders are not converted.
Character shading	Character shading is lost.
Character borders	Character borders are lost.
Paragraph borders	Paragraph borders and shading unique to Word 2000 are lost.
Animated text	Animated text formatting is lost.
Embossed and engraved characters	Embossed and engraved character formatting is lost, and the text converts to white text.
EMF, PNG, and JPEG graphics	EMF, PNG, and JPEG graphics are converted to WMF format, which does not support graphics compression. This increases the file size of documents that contain graphics.
Floating pictures with text wrapping	Floating pictures are converted to WMF format in frames.
Floating OLE objects	Floating OLE objects are converted to OLE objects in frames.
Highlighting	Highlighting is preserved in Word 95 but lost in Word 6.0.

Workgroup and Internet features

The following table identifies new features in Word 2000 that might affect data or formatting when users save documents in Word 6.0/95, RTF, or Word 97-2000 & 6.0/95-RTF format.

When this Word 2000 feature	Is saved in another format
Password protection of documents	Password protection is lost. In Word 6.0 and Word 95, you can reapply document protection by clicking **Save As** (**File** menu), clicking **Options**, and then selecting the options you want on the **Save** tab.
HYPERLINK field	The HYPERLINK field is lost, but the last value of the field is retained as plain text. When Word 6.0 or Word 95 users save to RTF, "Error! Bookmark not defined" is displayed, and the field is preserved—even when the user saves a document in Word 6.0 or Word 95 format.
AUTOTEXTLIST field	The field is lost, but the last value of the AUTOTEXTLIST field is retained as plain text.
Tracked changes for properties, paragraph numbers, and display fields	Tracked changes for properties, paragraph numbers, and display fields are lost; but other tracked changes are retained and displayed with revision marks. (In Word 95 and Word 6.0, tracked changes are called revisions.)
Document protection for tracked changes, comments, and forms	The protection state is retained, but the password is lost. When users open the document in Word 6.0 or Word 95, the document has protection for forms, changes, or comments, but no password is required to turn off the change tracking feature. (In Word 6.0 and Word 95, comments are called annotations.)
New document properties	New document properties are preserved in Word 95 but lost in Word 6.0.

Other features

The following table identifies new features in Word 2000 that might affect data or formatting when users save documents in Word 6.0/95, RTF, or Word 97-2000 & 6.0/95-RTF format.

When this Word 2000 feature	Is saved in another format
Visual Basic for Applications macros	Visual Basic for Applications macros are lost.
ActiveX controls on forms	ActiveX controls can be used but not modified.
Unicode characters	Unicode characters might be lost. Unicode characters (2 bytes per character) are mapped to corresponding ANSI (Windows) or converted to question marks (?). International characters might be affected.

When this Word 2000 feature	Is saved in another format
DOCPROPERTY field	The DOCPROPERTY field is retained in Word 95. In Word 6.0, the field appears as "Error! Bookmark not defined."
Embedded fonts	Embedded fonts are lost. Word 95 and Word 6.0 assign the closest font available.
WordArt drawing objects, or drawings created by using the **Drawing** toolbar	Basic shapes such as lines and boxes are retained. Grouped objects and shapes are lost.

See also

- By default, Word 2000 saves documents in Word 97-2000 format. For more information about changing the default file format that Word 2000 uses to save documents, see "How to Specify the Default Format in Which to Save Files" on page 438.

How to Share Files with Other Applications

You can customize Microsoft Office 2000 Setup and the Microsoft Office Converter Pack to install most of the graphics filters and text converters that open and save documents from other applications.

Open a document saved in another file format

To open a file created in another application, click **Open** (**File** menu), and then in the **Files of type** box, click the appropriate file format.

When Word 2000 recognizes the file format of a document, it converts the file, and then opens it. If Word does not recognize the image or text file format, it displays an error message.

To view the list of installed text converters, click **Open** (**File** menu), and then in the **Files of type** box, view the list of text converters.

To view the list of the graphics filters installed, point to **Picture** (**Insert** menu), and then in the **Files of type** box, view the list of filters.

You can customize your Office 2000 Setup to install most of the text converters and graphics filters that your Word 2000 users need. However, you might need to use the Microsoft Office Converter Pack to install additional text converters and graphics filters. If a converter is not available, users must save files in a format that Word 2000 can open.

Toolbox

You can install graphics filters in the Microsoft Office Converter Pack. For information about installing these filters, see "Microsoft Office Converter Pack" on page 793.

The following list identifies text file formats that Word 2000 can open:

- HTML

    Converts text to HTML.

- MS-DOS text

    Converts files the same way as Text Only format. Use this format to share documents between Word, and applications that do not run on Microsoft Windows.

- Rich Text Format

    Converts formatting to instructions Word 2000 can read. No formatting is lost in the conversion.

- Text Only

    Converts all section breaks, page breaks, and new-line characters to paragraph marks. Saves text without formatting. Select this format only if the destination application cannot read any other available file formats.

- Text Only with Line Breaks, or MS-DOS Text with Line Breaks

    Converts all line breaks, section breaks, and page breaks to paragraph marks. Saves text without formatting.

- Text with Layout, and MS-DOS Text with Layout

    Converts a document to a text file format while preserving the page layout and line breaks. Inserts spaces in a converted document to approximate indents, tables, line spacing, paragraph spacing, and tab stops. Converts section breaks and page breaks to paragraph marks.

Save a document in a format that other applications can open

To save a document in a format other applications can open, click **Save As** (**File** menu), and then in the **Save as type** box, click the appropriate file format.

If a Word 2000 user wants to save a document in a format for which there is no converter, the user can save the file in one of the following formats:

- Web Page (.htm)

    Saving a document in Web Page format allows a user to reopen the file in Word without losing any formatting or contents.

- Rich Text Format (.rtf)

    Saving a document in RTF preserves text formatting in files.

- Plain text (.txt)

    Saving a document in plain text saves the content of files but not the text formatting.

The advantage of saving presentations in HTML format or RTF is that no formatting or content is lost. The advantage of saving a document in a text file format is that most other applications can open the file.

System Policy Tip   You can use a system policy to define the default value for the **Save as type** option in the **Save As** dialog box (**File** menu). In the System Policy Editor, set the **Microsoft Word 2000\Tools I Options\Save\Save Word files as** policy. For more information about the System Policy Editor, see "Using the System Policy Editor" on page 296.

Share a document with users who don't have Word

If Word 2000 users need to share a document with users who do not have a word-processing application, Word 2000 users can save the document in Web Page format (HTML), which allows users to view, print, and edit the document by using a Web browser.

See also

- If Word 2000 users share documents with users of other applications, you can change the default format in which Word 2000 saves documents. For more information, see "How to Specify the Default Format in Which to Save Files" on page 438.

- Office 2000 includes new and enhanced features for publishing documents on your intranet or the World Wide Web. For more information, see "Using HTML and Office Document Formats" on page 589.

FAQs About Upgrading to Word 2000

Use the following tips to answer commonly asked questions about upgrading to Microsoft Word 2000.

Do previous versions of Word have the same file format as Word 2000?

Microsoft Word 2000 has the same file format as Word 98 and Word 97, but it has a few enhancements because of the new features included in Word 2000. The Word 97-2000 format is different from the file format used in Word 95 and Word 6.0. For more information, see "Sharing Documents with Word 98 and Word 97 Users" on page 547 or "Sharing Documents with Word 95 and Word 6.0 Users" on page 549.

Can users share templates with previous versions of Word?

You can share macros and templates with users of other versions of Word. However, the templates included with Word 2000 take advantage of the new and enhanced features in the application. The unique features in Word 2000 are lost when a template is saved in a previous format such as Word 97 or Word 95 format. For more information, see "Sharing Macros and Templates with Previous Versions of Word" on page 544.

How can I prevent users from saving documents in an unapproved format?

You cannot prevent users from saving documents in an unapproved format, but you can:

- Set a system policy with the System Policy Editor, and create a custom message to alert users when they try to save a file that is not the default format in the system policy.
- Set a default file format with the **Options** dialog box (**Tools** menu).
- Limit the number of text converters that you distribute to users.

For more information, see "How to Specify the Default Format in Which to Save Files" on page 438 and "Using the System Policy Editor" on page 296.

Why does text look different when a user saves a Word 2000 document in Web Page format?

For text and font formatting to display correctly, users must upgrade to Microsoft Internet Explorer version 4.0 or later and use *cascading style sheets*.

▶ **To use cascading style sheets**

1 On the **Tools** menu, click **Options**, and then click the **General** tab.

2 Click **Web Options**.

3 Select the **Rely on CSS for font formatting** checkbox.

Where can users get graphics filters not included in Word 2000?

Word 2000 includes most of the graphics filters that users need to open and save images. The following graphics filters are included in the Microsoft Office Converter Pack.

- AutoCAD (Dxfimp32.flt)
- Micrografx Designer/Draw (Drwimp32.flt)
- Targa (Tgaimp32.flt)

Toolbox

You can install text converters and graphics filters from the Microsoft Office Converter Pack. For more information about installing these converters and filters, see "Microsoft Office Converter Pack" on page 793.

How can Word 95 users open documents saved in HTML format and Word 2000 format?

Before Word 95 users can open HTML and Word 97-2000 documents, they must install the HTML converter and Word 97-2000 converter included in the Microsoft Office Converter Pack.

Toolbox

You can install the HTML and Word 97-2000 converters from the Microsoft Office Converter Pack. For more information about installing these converters, see "Microsoft Office Converter Pack" on page 793.

Why does Word 2000 prompt for a converter when a user tries to open a file from another application?

Word 2000 users might have changed a default option in the **Options** dialog box.

▶ **To have Word select the correct converter**

1 On the **Tools** menu, click **Options**.

2 On the **General** tab, clear the **Confirm conversion at Open** check box.

Why do the graphics disappear in a converted document?

Graphics seem to disappear in a converted document when the graphics display feature is turned off or when the graphics filters needed to import the images are not installed.

▶ **To turn on the graphics display feature**

1 On the **Tools** menu, click **Options**.

2 On the **View** tab, clear the **Picture placeholders** check box.

To view the list of installed graphics filters, point to **Picture** (**Insert** menu), and then click **From File**. The **Files of type** box lists the graphics filters installed.

Most of the graphic filters that users need are included with Office 2000, but additional graphics filters are included in the Microsoft Office Converter Pack.

Toolbox

You can install graphic filters from the Microsoft Office Converter Pack. For more information about installing these filters, see "Microsoft Office Converter Pack" on page 793.

Why are the fonts different in the converted document?

Word 2000 substitutes fonts that are not installed on a user's computer.

▶ To customize the substitution of fonts

1   On the **Tools** menu, click **Options**.

2   On the **Compatibility** tab, click **Font Substitution**.

3   In the **Missing document font** box, click the font you want to replace.

4   In the **Substituted font** box, click the font you want to use.

Why are line breaks and page breaks different in the converted document?

Line breaks and page breaks in Word 2000 are treated differently from those in other versions of Word and other applications.

▶ To customize the display for a converted document

1   On the **Tools** menu, click **Options**, and then click on the **Compatibility** tab.

2   In the **Recommended options for** box, click **Custom**.

3   In the **Options** box, select the check boxes you want.

Note   The document is not permanently changed. The selected options only affect how Word displays the document while you are working with it in Word.

Can Word 2000 users run macros created in other versions of Word?

WordBasic macros created in Word 95 and Word 6.0 and Visual Basic for Applications (VBA) version 5.0 macros created in Word 97 run in Word 2000. For more information, see "Sharing Macros and Templates with Previous Versions of Word" on page 544.

Why can't users of previous versions of Word view macros in some Word 2000 documents?

The macros might have been digitally signed from within the Visual Basic Editor in Word 2000. This new security feature is not included in other versions of Word. Users of other versions of Word can run—but not modify—the macros.

Why can't users run a macro or load an add-in in a document?

If the security level for Word 2000 is set to High, and users open a document or load an add-in that contains unsigned macros, then the macros are disabled and users cannot run them. Users can enable macros that are not digitally signed by changing the security level to Medium in the **Security** dialog box (**Tools** menu, **Macro** submenu), closing the document or unloading the add-in, and then opening the document or loading the add-in again.

Note   Remember to change the security level back to High if you want Word 2000 to automatically disable unsigned macros in the future.

If the security level for Word is set to Medium or High and you chose to disable macros because you do not trust the source of the macros, you cannot run the macros. To run the macros, close the document or unload the add-in, and then open the document or load the add-in again. Then click **Enable Macros**.

What can Word 2000 users do if a file does not convert properly?

If a file is not converted correctly, Word 2000 users can close the file without saving it, and then open it again using a different text converter. For a list of text converters, see "Working with Word 2000 Text Converters and Graphics Filters" on page 539.

Office 2000 and the Web

Contents

CHAPTER 12

Integrating Office 2000 with Your Intranet

Microsoft Office 2000 makes communicating across your internet or the Internet easier than ever before. With new Web features in Office 2000, you can publish and manage online documents, create and publish your own Web sites, and use new HTML-based e-mail messages to communicate across your organization or around the world. And with the new broadcasting features in Microsoft PowerPoint 2000, you can broadcast presentations and multimedia shows in real time on your own network.

In This Chapter

Using Office with a Web Server

New Web features in Microsoft Office 2000 make it easy for users to publish and manage Office documents on an intranet—without the overhead normally associated with Web publishing. In addition, users can collaborate within documents and subscribe to an e-mail service that notifies them automatically when documents on a Web server change.

Taking Advantage of Office Web Features

Users in your organization probably browse sites and view documents on your intranet already, but typically, only a few users have write access to the servers. By using Microsoft Office 2000, the rich functionality of the Web environment can be more than a read-only experience for the majority of your users.

Office 2000 makes publishing and collaborating on intranet documents simple and intuitive. Microsoft Office Server Extensions (OSE) is a powerful new Web feature that you can install on any Web server running Microsoft Windows NT Server and Internet Information Server (IIS), or Windows NT Workstation and Peer Web Services. OSE allows Office 2000 users to:

- Create threaded discussions in published documents.
- Receive e-mail notification when documents change.
- Search and navigate documents published on Web servers.

Web features that require Office Server Extensions

A Web site extended with OSE is called an *OSE-extended web*. When you set up an OSE-extended web, Office 2000 users can work with documents on the server by using Web features installed on their computers.

The following features work only with an OSE-extended web:

- Web Discussions

  The Web Discussions feature creates threaded discussions that allow users to collaborate on Office documents. Users can add and view specific discussion items located within documents, or they can add and view general discussion items located in the discussion pane.

- Web Subscriptions

  The Web Subscriptions feature allows users to subscribe to an e-mail notification service. When documents on a Web server are created or modified, subscribers receive e-mail messages that identify changes.

Additional OSE features give users easy access to documents stored on the Web server:

- OSE Start Page

  This Web page provides users with a logical starting place on an OSE-extended web. The OSE Start Page also makes OSE features available to users of any Web browser that supports frames.

- Browse Web Folders

  The **Browse Web Folders** option is on the OSE Start Page and gives users a convenient view of files and folders on the Web server. You can modify the *Active Server Pages* (ASP) page to customize this view with graphics, annotations, or additional hyperlinks.

- Search Web Folders

  The **Search Web Folders** option is on the OSE Start Page and allows users to search for documents on the Web server by using author, keyword, or document properties. You can control the search criteria available to users on this page.

Web features that work with other supported Web servers

Even if you do not install OSE on your Web server, users can still take advantage of some of the Web features included in Office 2000. The features that do not require an OSE-extended web work with any Web server that runs Microsoft FrontPage Server Extensions or any Web server that supports the Distributed Authoring and Versioning (DAV) Internet protocol.

Note   Microsoft FrontPage 2000 includes FrontPage Server Extensions. DAV is an Internet protocol supported by IIS version 5.0.

When Office 2000 users connect to a supported Web server, the *Web Folders object*, which is available when the Web Publishing feature is installed, allows them to browse, publish, and manage the folders and files on the Web server from their computers. The Web Folders object contains shortcuts to files and folders on the Web server. Web Folders appears in My Computer, Windows Explorer, and the **Save As** and **Open** dialog boxes (**File** menu) in Office 2000 applications.

Which Office Web features does my browser support?

Microsoft Internet Explorer 5 fully supports all Web Publishing and Web Discussions features—including the features you can use with an OSE-extended web. Internet Explorer 5 is the only browser that supports offline caching and replication, which allow users to work on published documents when they are not connected to the network.

Internet Explorer version 4.0 fully supports Web Publishing and the OSE Start Page features. However, when you use Web Discussions with Internet Explorer 4.0, inline discussions are displayed in a separate frame.

Internet Explorer version 3.0, Netscape Navigator, and other frame-based browsers support many Office Web features—including Web Publishing and the OSE Start Page. However, users with these browsers must enable the **Collaboration** toolbar frame by using the OSE Start Page; and inline discussions are displayed in a separate frame.

See also

- You can take advantage of Web-based functionality in Office 2000 without a detailed understanding of the Web server and client architecture. For information about all of the OSE components, see "Architecture of Office Server Extensions" on page 709.

- OSE and Microsoft Web server products are not required for you to take advantage of Office 2000 Web-based functionality. For more information about using Office 2000 with other Web servers, see "Using Office with Other Web Servers" on page 585.

How to Install Web Features on Office Client Computers

During Office 2000 Setup, you can select the following features to install on client computers:

- Web Publishing

  Installs the *Web Folders object*. Users can view, open, and save documents on any supported Web server.

- Web Discussions

  Installs the Web Discussions and Web Subscriptions features. Users can collaborate on Microsoft Word, Microsoft Excel, Microsoft PowerPoint, HTML, and RTF documents that are published on Web servers.

▶ To install Web features during Office Setup

1   On the **Selecting Features** panel in Office Setup, expand the Office\Office Tools feature.

2   Select the Web features you want.

   To make these features available to users only when they need them, set the installation state for Web Publishing and Web Discussions to **Install on demand**.

Note   The Web Publishing feature is included with Microsoft Windows 2000, so Office 2000 Setup does not reinstall the feature during Office Setup.

For users of Windows 95 and Microsoft Windows NT 4.0, you might want to install the Windows Desktop Update included with Microsoft Internet Explorer 4.01. The Windows Desktop Update makes the Web Publishing feature stable. (The Windows Desktop Update is already included in the Windows 98 and Windows 2000 operating systems, and it is not required when using Internet Explorer 5.)

Note   When you install Office 2000 on a computer that more than one person uses, such as a Windows Terminal Server, do not specify a user name during Setup. If you specify a user name, all Web Discussions items are attributed to that user—regardless of who adds an item.

See also

- You can use the Custom Installation Wizard to add Web features to your Office installation. For more information, see "Office Custom Installation Wizard" on page 250.

- If you install the Microsoft Office 2000 MultiLanguage Pack, you can use localized client Web features supported by Office Server Extensions. For more information, see "Features of the MultiLanguage Pack" on page 727.

Managing Files on a Web Server Through Web Folders

By using the new Web features in Microsoft Office 2000, users can manage files on a Web server in the same way they manage files on any local hard disk or network server.

When you install the Web Publishing feature, Office adds an object named Web Folders to the Microsoft Windows environment. In Microsoft Windows NT 4.0 and Windows 95/98, Web Folders appears immediately after My Computer in the Windows Explorer hierarchical structure.

The *Web Folders object* contains shortcuts to Web sites. You can create, move, rename, and delete shortcuts in Web Folders. The shortcuts you add can include both a URL and a friendly display name. In Windows Explorer, publishing is as easy as dragging files to sites in Web Folders.

In Office 2000 applications, Web Folders gives users access to Web sites from My Computer, Windows Explorer, and the **Open** and **Save As** dialog boxes (**File** menu). With the Web Folders object installed, users can navigate within, open files from, and save files to Web sites.

Web Folders object

The Web Folders object viewed in the Open dialog box

My Network Places in Windows 2000

Windows 2000 Server and Windows 2000 Workstation do not display a Web Folders object. Instead, there is an object named My Network Places, which also replaces Network Neighborhood. My Network Places contains Web folder and universal naming convention (UNC) shortcuts, as well as connections to computers on your local area network (LAN).

In the **Open** and **Save As** dialog boxes (**File** menu) in the Office 2000 applications, My Network Places appears in the **Look in** box, where users can select any Web folder shortcut or UNC shortcut to open or save documents.

Note   There might be some files on your Web site that you want to hide from users, such as Common Gateway Interface (CGI) or *Active Server Pages* (ASP) scripts. To prevent files stored on an *NTFS*-formatted drive from appearing in Web Folders on client computers, apply NTFS permission settings to the files that you want to hide.

How to Add Shortcuts to Web Folders

You create a Web folder shortcut inside the *Web Folders object* by using the Add a Web Folder Wizard. A Web folder shortcut is not a folder, but it points to a folder that exists on a Web server—similar to a universal naming convention (UNC) shortcut that points to a file share on a server. When you open a Web folder shortcut, you can do the following:

- View and manage the contents of the folder.

- Create subfolders and files within the folder.

▶ **To add a Web folder shortcut to Web Folders**

1   In My Computer or Windows Explorer, open the Web Folders object, and then double-click **Add Web Folder.**

   −or−

   In the **Open** or **Save As** dialog box (**File** menu) of a Microsoft Office 2000 application, on the **Places** bar, click **Web Folders**, and then click **Create New Folder**.

2   Follow the instructions in the wizard.

Office applications create Web folder shortcuts automatically when you enter an HTTP URL in the **File name** box of the **Open** or **Save As** dialog box (**File** menu). URLs for automatically created Web folder shortcuts include only the server name and top-level directory. For example:

directory on *server*

In Microsoft Windows 2000, the URL is truncated to include *only* the server name. Because the name includes only the top-level directory, users can enter URLs for several subdirectories in the same root directory—without automatically creating extra Web folder shortcuts for each subdirectory.

Note   Web Folders only displays folder and file objects on a Web server when the server supports the Distributed Authoring and Versioning (DAV) Internet protocol or when the server is running Microsoft Office Server Extensions (OSE) or Microsoft FrontPage Server Extensions.

See also

- In Windows 2000, the Application Data subfolder in the user profile folder stores the Web folder shortcuts. Therefore, Web folder shortcuts travel with the user. For more information about support for traveling users, see "Supporting Users Who Travel Between Computers" on page 176.

How to Use FTP to Open and Save Documents

If your Web server does not support Microsoft Office Server Extensions (OSE), Microsoft FrontPage Server Extensions, or the Distributed Authoring and Versioning (DAV) Internet protocol, you cannot use the Web Publishing feature. However, users can still open and save files by using the FTP Internet protocol.

In Microsoft Office applications, the **Open** and **Save As** dialog boxes (**File** menu) support logging on to an FTP site and resolving FTP and HTTP addresses. This allows Office users to open or save documents on FTP sites as easily as they open and save documents on a hard disk.

To log on to an FTP site from within an Office application, users must have dial-up networking access through an Internet service provider (ISP) or through a proxy server on a local area network (LAN).

▶ **To add an FTP site to the Open or Save As dialog box**

1   On the **File** menu, click **Open** or **Save As**.

2   In the **Look in** box, click **Add/Modify FTP Locations**.

3   In the appropriate boxes, enter the full FTP path, logon name (or anonymous), and password.

After the initial connection to an FTP site, the Office applications keep track of the FTP address and logon credentials. The FTP site appears in the **Look in** box in the **Open** and **Save As** dialog boxes. Users can also edit or delete FTP site information.

▶ **To connect to an FTP site after the initial connection**

1   On the **File** menu, click **Open** or **Save As**.

2   In the **Look in** box, under **FTP Locations,** select an FTP site.

When you save Office documents to an FTP site, be sure to include the appropriate file name extension. For example, include the extension .doc for Microsoft Word documents.

How to Use the Web Publishing Wizard

If your Web server does not support Microsoft Office Server Extensions (OSE), you can use the Web Publishing Wizard to publish Web pages on the Internet or your intranet. This wizard automates the process of copying files from your computer to almost any Web server. You can use the Web Publishing Wizard to publish Web pages to Internet service providers (ISPs) such as CompuServe and America Online, as well as to servers on your intranet.

The Web Publishing Wizard is included in Microsoft Windows 98 and Microsoft Internet Explorer version 4.0.

▶ **To install the Web Publishing Wizard (Windows 98 only)**

1   In Control Panel, double-click **Add/Remove Programs**, and then click the **Windows Setup** tab.

2   Click **Internet Tools**, and then click **Details**.

3   Click **Web Publishing Wizard,** and then follow the instructions on the screen.

Tip   On a computer running either the Windows 95 or a Microsoft Windows NT operating system, you can install the Web Publishing Wizard from the Internet Explorer 4.0 Setup program, or you can download the wizard from the Microsoft Web site at http://www.microsoft.com/.

If you want to publish to an FTP site or a Web site on the Internet, and you have an account with an ISP, then you can use the Web Publishing Wizard to copy your Web page to the Internet. The wizard works the same way whether you are publishing to your intranet, an FTP site, or a Web site.

▶ **To start the Web Publishing Wizard**

• Click the **Start** button, point to **Programs**, point to **Internet Explorer**, and then click **Web Publishing Wizard**.

Note   The first time you run the Web Publishing Wizard, you must provide information about your ISP or intranet—including the protocol that sends files to the server, and the location of the server that stores the files.

Using the Office Server Extensions Start Page

By using the Microsoft Office Server Extensions (OSE) Start Page, users can work with OSE features from within a Web browser. Users open the OSE Start Page at the following address:

http://*computer_name*/msoffice/

where *computer_name* is the name of an *OSE-extended web*.

The OSE Start Page is located in the Default.asp file in the MSOffice *virtual directory*, which the OSE Configuration Wizard creates.

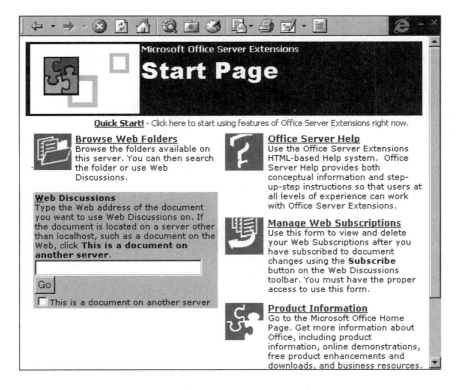

The OSE Start Page viewed in Internet Explorer 5

From the OSE Start Page, users can perform the following tasks:

- Open a document for browsing and discussions.

- Turn on the frame-based **Collaboration** toolbar (Microsoft Internet Explorer version 3.0, or Netscape Navigator version 3.0 or later).

- View a list of all folders on the OSE-extended web.

- Add shortcuts to Web Folders.

- View or delete Web Subscriptions.

- Start online Help, or start the OSE Quick Start guide.

- Connect to the Microsoft Office 2000 Web site at Microsoft.com.

- Search for documents on the Web server.

Note   Search criteria include text, date and time, document properties, and location. The **Search Web Folders** option is available only for Internet Information Server (IIS) servers. If your Web server is not an IIS server, users do not see a **Search Web Folders** option on the OSE Start Page.

Support for Internet Explorer 3.0 and Netscape Navigator

The OSE Start Page is particularly helpful for users of Microsoft Internet Explorer 3.0 or Netscape Navigator. These users do not have access to the **Discussions** toolbar from their Web browser. However, they can display a frame-based version of the toolbar from the OSE Start Page.

When users open documents on the Web server from the OSE Start Page, an *Active Server Pages* (ASP) script generates a frame set for discussion items that appear in a separate pane in these browsers. (Only Internet Explorer 5 or later supports inline discussions.)

Browsing Web folders

By using the **Browse Web Folders** option on the OSE Start Page, users can explore the files and folders on an OSE-extended web by using a Web browser. Users can view the contents of a Web folder as easily as they browse a Web site.

▶ To browse a Web file or folder from the OSE Start Page

1   In the **Address** box, type the following address:

2   **http://***computer_name***/msoffice/**

3   where *computer_name* is the name of an OSE-extended web.

4   Click **Browse Web Folders**.

When the content of a Web folder changes, underlying ASP scripts automatically update the file and folder lists, and the hyperlinks displayed on the page. This automatic update simplifies administration of the site.

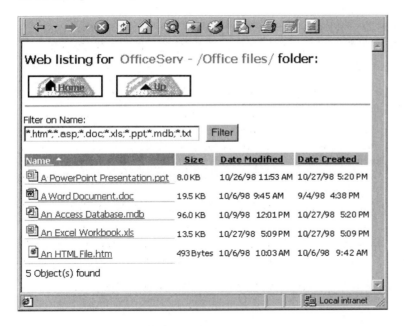

Browse Web Folders in Internet Explorer

Customizing the OSE Start Page

As the Web server administrator, you can use a standard authoring tool such as Microsoft FrontPage or Microsoft Word to modify the appearance and functionality of the OSE Start Page. If you know HTML source code, you can change the OSE Start Page with a text editor such as Notepad.

To enhance the OSE Start Page, you can add a company logo, links to other pages on your intranet, or additional text to help your users get the most out of OSE.

See also

- You can use the Custom Installation Wizard to add Web features to your Office installation, and even have Office Setup create a Favorites entry, desktop shortcut, or **Start** menu item for the OSE Start Page. For more information about using the wizard to modify your Office installation, see "Office Custom Installation Wizard" on page 250.

- You can customize the page displayed by using the **Browse Web Folders** option with themes, annotations on folders and files, or additional hyperlinks. For more information, see "Advanced Administration of Office Server Extensions" on page 685.

Collaborating on Documents Stored on a Web Server

Microsoft Office Server Extensions (OSE) provide powerful collaboration capabilities. Users can participate in discussions in Microsoft Word, Microsoft Excel, and Microsoft PowerPoint documents, as well as any HTML or Rich Text Format (RTF) file. The threaded discussions are maintained on either the Web server that has OSE installed or a remote SQL Server computer.

To participate in a discussion, users configure their computers to point to the *OSE-extended web*. All user discussion items are displayed in a shared document that users can view either in the original Microsoft Office 2000 application or in most Web browsers.

Because discussion items are stored separately from the shared document, users can modify the document without affecting the collaborative discussion. This separation also allows multiple users to create and edit discussion items simultaneously. Users can also add discussion items to read-only documents.

By using the **Collaboration** toolbar, users can view, search, or filter discussions by author, or date and time. Discussions print on a separate page when the document is printed. Users can view discussions offline, but they cannot add to them offline. Users can participate in discussions about documents that are stored on a server remote from the Web server that contains the OSE-extended web.

Adding discussion items to Office documents

Office 2000 applications support different levels of functionality for the OSE Web Discussions feature.

Discussions in Word

In Word, users can add general discussion items that refer to the entire document. General discussion items appear in a separate pane. Users can add inline discussions anywhere within a Word document.

When a user adds an inline discussion item to a Word document, a bookmark at the end of the paragraph attaches that discussion item to the relevant text in the document. A user can also add discussion items to tables in Word.

Note   If a table cell contains more than 40 characters, the discussion item is anchored with a bookmark at the end of the cell. If the table cell contains less than 40 characters, the discussion item is attached to the table. Discussion items cannot be attached to endnotes, footnotes, or comments.

Discussions in HTML and RTF

Both HTML and RTF documents support inline discussions. Users can:

- Attach discussion items to the end of any paragraph.
- Create general discussion items that refer to the entire document.

Discussions in Excel and PowerPoint

Excel workbooks and PowerPoint presentations have general discussion areas only. If a user is in Excel or PowerPoint, and then opens an HTML or RTF document containing inline discussions, Excel and PowerPoint display the inline discussions in the general discussion pane.

Discussions in Access

Microsoft Access does not support discussions from within the application. However, if a user creates a *data access page* in Access and then saves the page as an HTML file, the user can open the file in a Web browser and then create discussion threads.

Editing discussion items

The logon *authentication* account identifies a user, and only the user who adds a discussion item can edit or delete that item. However, if you allow anonymous authentication, users who log on anonymously can create discussion items that any other users can edit or delete.

If your OSE-extended web is located on a disk formatted with the *NTFS* file system, the OSE Configuration Wizard creates the *Admins* Windows NT group. The users who you add to this group can edit and delete discussion items in any document.

Modifying documents that contain discussion threads

Because discussion items are not stored in the document itself, users can modify the document independently from any discussions they create.

The following table explains how a modification to a document can affect the threaded discussion of the document.

When a document is modified in this way	The discussion data is affected this way
The change is made in an area without a discussion item attached.	Inline and general discussions are not affected.
The change is made in an area with a discussion item attached.	Inline discussions attached to modified text are deleted. General discussions are not affected.
The entire document is moved, renamed, or deleted.	All inline and general discussions are lost.

How to Participate in a Discussion on an OSE-extended Web

To participate in a discussion, users must specify an *OSE-extended web* for the discussion. If there is more than one OSE-extended web available on your network, users can maintain a list of the addresses of multiple OSE-extended webs. However, one of those servers must be specified as the current OSE-extended web. After users specify a server, they can contribute to discussions in Microsoft Office applications or in their Web browser.

Specify the current discussion server

Users can view and participate in discussions stored only in the database of their current OSE-extended web. Typically, a department establishes one OSE-extended web, and users specify that web as their current discussion web. Unless the OSE-extended web is renamed or more OSE-extended webs are set up, users never have to adjust this setting.

To view and participate in discussions stored on another server, a user must make that server the current server. A user collaborates on the same server through an Office application or in a Web browser.

Tip If you set up multiple OSE-extended webs, you can allow different departments to conduct independent and secure discussions in the same document. However, use this feature carefully to avoid confusing users about which discussion server to use for a document.

▶ **To specify the current discussion server or add discussion servers to the list**

1   On the **Tools** menu in Microsoft Word, Microsoft Excel, or Microsoft PowerPoint, click **Online Collaboration**, and then click **Web Discussions**.

   –or–

   In Microsoft Internet Explorer version 4.0 or later, on the **View** menu, click **Explorer Bar,** and then click **Discuss**.

   –or–

   In Internet Explorer 5, on the **Standard** toolbar, click the **Discussion** button.

2   On the **Collaboration** toolbar, click **Discussions**, and then click **Discussion Options**.

3   Select a server in the **Select a discussion server** box.·

   The server you select becomes the current server.

4   To add a new discussion server to the list, click **Add**.

Note   Users can connect to only one discussion server at a time—the current server. This restriction prevents users from opening two instances of an Office application or Web browser where each points to a different server.

Contribute to a discussion in an Office document

After users specify their current discussion server, they can collaborate on shared documents in Word, Excel, or PowerPoint.

▶ **To contribute to a discussion in Word, Excel, or PowerPoint**

1   Open a document, and then save it.

   –or–

   Create a new document, and then save it.

2   On the **Tools** menu, click **Online Collaboration**, and then click **Web Discussions**.

3   To begin a new inline discussion thread in Word, position the insertion point at the desired location in the document, click **Discussions** on the **Collaboration** toolbar, and then click **Insert in the Document**.

   –or–

   To insert a general discussion in Word, Excel, or PowerPoint, click **Discussions** on the **Collaboration** toolbar, and then click **Insert about the Document**.

4   Type the subject and text of the discussion item, and then click **OK**.

   Discussion text can include formatting and hyperlinks.

The discussion item is sent to the current OSE-extended web of the user, and then the discussion item is stored in the database. The following list identifies the properties that are stored with each discussion item.

- Date and time
- Display name

  This is the name you create during Office 2000 Setup. You can modify the display name on the **User Information** tab in the **Options** dialog box (**Tools** menu).

- Microsoft Windows NT account name

  If the user does not have a Windows NT account, the account name appears as Anonymous.

In a shared document, each discussion item is displayed with an action button. Clicking the action button displays a menu for users to reply, edit, or delete the item. Right-clicking the button displays the shortcut menu, where users can delete the entire discussion thread—if they have permission.

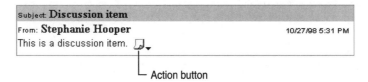

Action button

Contribute to a discussion in a Web browser

After users specify a current discussion server, they can collaborate on shared documents in a Web browser.

▶ **To contribute to a discussion in Microsoft Internet Explorer 4.0 or later**

1   On the **View** menu, click **Explorer Bar**, and then click **Discuss**.

   The **Discussions** toolbar appears at the bottom of the Microsoft Internet Explorer window.

2   Open the document in Web Folders.

   –or–

   Type the URL in the **Address** box.

The Discussions toolbar in Internet Explorer 4.0 or later

▶ **To contribute to a discussion in Internet Explorer 3.0, or in Netscape Navigator**

- On the OSE Start Page, type the URL of the document in the **Use Web Discussions by entering a document's location** box, and then click **Go**.

  The document opens and displays a frame-based **Collaboration** toolbar to view and contribute to discussions.

The frame-based Collaboration toolbar

Note   Microsoft Internet Explorer 3.0 and Netscape Navigator users can view and contribute to discussions, but all discussion items (including inline items) are displayed in a frame separate from the document. Only Internet Explorer 4.0 or later displays inline discussions directly in the document.

See also

- You can use the Custom Installation Wizard to point a user's computer to a specific OSE-extended web. For more information, see "Custom Installation Wizard" on page 774.

How to Subscribe to E-mail Notifications on an OSE-extended Web

The Web Subscriptions feature in Microsoft Office 2000 allows a user to subscribe to an e-mail notification service. The subscriber receives an e-mail message when a folder or document changes on an *OSE-extended web*. A user can choose to receive notification when:

- A new document is added to the folder.
- A document is modified, renamed, moved, or deleted.
- A discussion item is added to or deleted from a document.

A subscriber receives an update for a folder event when the event occurs on a document at the top level of a folder. If the event occurs on a document inside a subfolder, no update is sent.

Note   An OSE-extended web can store discussions about documents saved on other Web sites and servers. Users can subscribe to receive updates when discussion items are added or changed in remote documents. However, users cannot subscribe to receive updates for any other changes to remote documents.

For subscriptions, users can set the frequency they want to receive e-mail updates to one of the following options: **Within a few minutes, Once a day,** or **Once a week.** The administrator of the OSE-extended web defines the intervals in increments of minutes, hours, or days.

▶ **To create a Web Subscription**

1   On the **Tools** menu in Microsoft Word, Microsoft Excel, or Microsoft PowerPoint, click **Online Collaboration,** and then click **Web Discussions.**

2   –or–

3   On the **View** menu in Microsoft Internet Explorer version 4.0 or later, click **Explorer Bar,** and then click **Discuss.**

    –or–

    On the Standard toolbar in Microsoft Internet Explorer 5, click the **Discussion** tool.

    Click **Subscribe.**

    Select a file or folder, and then select the type of e-mail notifications you want to receive.

    In the **Address** box, type your e-mail address.

    In the **Time** box, select how often you want to receive e-mail notifications.

The OSE-extended web stores subscription information in a database and then processes the information in batches. The subscription message contains a link to the shared document and a link to cancel the subscription.

To view and delete subscriptions, a user clicks the **Manage Web Subscriptions** option on the Office Server Extensions (OSE) Start Page.

Working with Office Web Features Offline

Microsoft Office 2000 users can continue to work on shared documents even when they log off the network. When the Web Publishing feature is installed, a replication mechanism automatically maintains a list of recently opened Web server documents, and stores copies of them in a cache on the local hard disk.

To add files to the cache, users select a file in Windows Explorer, and then on the **File** menu, click **Make Available Offline.**

Note   Only Microsoft Internet Explorer 5 or later supports offline caching and replication.

A user can open and edit replicated files while offline. Then, the next time the user logs on to the network, all changes the user has made while offline are automatically replicated to the server. Also any changes that have occurred on the server while the user has been offline are replicated locally. A user can select a file in Windows Explorer, and then on the **File** menu, click **Synchronize** to manually update the local copy of a file with the server copy.

Working with cached documents

When a user logs off from the network, all necessary caching is performed to ensure that the entire set of documents is available offline.

While offline, users can continue working on documents as if they are still connected to the Web server. While offline users can:

- View, edit, and save new or cached documents—using HTTP URLs.
- View cached folders in Web Folders.
- Create new Web folders within Web folder shortcuts.
- View and filter Web Discussions.

Note When users work offline, they cannot edit discussion items or add new discussion items.

Reconciling differences on the Web server

When users reconnect to the network, any changes made locally are replicated back to the Web server. At the same time, any changes made by someone else in the shared versions of documents are replicated back to the local computer. And everyone is in sync once again.

But, if user A logs off and then changes a document locally, while user B is changing the document online, user A can resolve the conflict in one of two ways:

- In the **Conflict** dialog box, click **Resolve Conflict**, and then select either the local or the published copy.

  –or–

  Save the document with a different name, make changes to the local copy, and then merge the changes manually with the published document on the Web server.

Assigning Workgroup Properties to Web Documents

When users publish Microsoft Word and HTML documents on a FrontPage-extended web or an *OSE-extended web*, they can set the following workgroup properties on the documents:

- Category

  Indicates the type of document. Users select from a list of categories that are defined for the Web site. Documents can be assigned to multiple categories.

- Assigned to

  Indicates the owner of the document. Users select from a predefined list of Microsoft Windows NT account user names.

- Review status

  Indicates what stage of development the document is in.

You can set these workgroup properties in Word or in Microsoft FrontPage. The values of workgroup properties are stored in documents when they are saved. When a document is published to the Web, the workgroup properties are synchronized with the metastore on the FrontPage-extended web. The *metastore* is a small database maintained in each FrontPage-extended web that contains properties and settings of the Web site.

You can save a document that contains new values for the workgroup properties. In this case, the list of values available for the properties is extended to include the new values, and the metastore is updated.

Administrators can use workgroup properties to manage projects. For example, by using the FrontPage 2000 Category component, you can create a page that lists all the defined categories for the Web site and provides links to the documents that fall into each category. By using the FrontPage 2000 reporting feature, you can generate a list of all documents and their assigned users. You can also generate a report that summarizes the review status of all documents on the site.

Prompting users to assign workgroup properties in Word

The workgroup properties that you can set on published Web documents are similar to the properties that you can set in any Microsoft Office document. However, users can modify workgroup properties only in Word and FrontPage.

You can configure your Web site to have Word prompt users to assign workgroup properties to their documents. You can even configure the site to require users to assign workgroup properties before they can save a document.

On the **File** menu, Word users can click **Properties** to display the **Workgroup Properties** dialog box, and then they can set the properties.

Note   In addition to workgroup properties, standard document properties of Word are available through this dialog box. To display the **Properties** dialog box, in the **Workgroup Properties** dialog box, click the **Document Properties** button.

When a Word user selects the **Prompt for document properties** check box on the **Save** tab in the **Options** dialog box (**Tools** menu) and then saves a document to a site that is configured to prompt for workgroup properties, the **Workgroup Properties** dialog box appears first. After the user sets workgroup properties for the document, the **Properties** dialog box appears, and the user can set other document properties.

Adding new workgroup property values

FrontPage users can use the **Workgroup Properties** dialog box to set workgroup properties. FrontPage users can add the following new values:

- Categories to the **Category** box.
- Users to the **Assigned to** box.
- Status items to the **Review status** box.

Word users can add new workgroup property values by using the **Custom** tab in the **Properties** dialog box for a document.

You can also copy workgroup property values instead of recreating them each time you create a new FrontPage-extended web. When you copy a Word or HTML document from the existing web to the new web, all the **Category**, **Assigned to**, and **Review status** box items set for the document are transferred to the new web.

Note Any user who has author permission on a site can add new workgroup property values by publishing a document that contains new values for these properties.

See also
- You can use workgroup properties to manage Web projects with FrontPage. For more information, see "Publishing and Maintaining Web Sites with FrontPage" on page 633.

Using Office with Other Web Servers

When you connect to Web servers running Microsoft Internet Information Server (IIS) or Personal Web Server, you can use all of the Microsoft Office 2000 Web features. However, when you connect to a Web server that is not running IIS or Personal Web Server, you can still use a subset of the Office 2000 Web features.

Collaborating on documents stored on remote servers

Although OSE cannot be installed on a computer running Web server software other than IIS or Personal Web Server, users can still use Microsoft Office Server Extensions (OSE) collaboration features with that server if a single Microsoft Web server that has OSE installed is available on the network.

Web Discussions

You can configure the Web Discussions feature to allow users to discuss documents that are stored on a server that does not have OSE installed. In this scenario, you can use any Web server software on the Web server storing the remote documents. The discussion data is stored locally on the Web server with the *OSE-extended web* or in a remote Microsoft SQL Server database.

Web Subscriptions

The Web Subscriptions feature is partially supported for documents stored on a remote server. However, for remote documents, users can subscribe to e-mail notifications regarding only new or changed discussion items. Subscriptions cannot be created for changes in the content of remote documents.

Using the Web Publishing feature with other Web servers

The Web Publishing feature installs the *Web Folders object*, which can be used when an Office 2000 client is connected to any Web server that has Microsoft FrontPage Server Extensions installed or any Web server that supports the Distributed Authoring and Versioning (DAV) Internet protocol.

FrontPage Server Extensions can be installed on most popular Web servers, including those running the UNIX operating system.

The Web servers on which you can use FrontPage Server Extensions are listed below.

If you have this operating system	You can use FrontPage Server Extensions on any of these Web servers
Microsoft Windows NT Server, Intel x86 Microsoft Windows NT Workstation, Intel x86	Internet Information Server version 3.0 and later, including IIS 5.0 Netscape Commerce Server 1.12 Netscape Communications Server 1.12 Netscape Enterprise Server 3.0 Netscape FastTrack 2.0 O'Reilly WebSite 2.0 FrontPage Personal Web Server
Microsoft Windows 95	Microsoft Personal Web Server 2.0 and later FrontPage Personal Web Server Netscape FastTrack 2.0 O'Reilly WebSite
UNIX Digital UNIX 3.2c, 4.0 (Alpha) BSD/OS 2.1 (Intel x86) BSD/OS 3.0 (Intel x86) Linux 3.03 (Red Hat Software) (Intel x86) HP/UX 9.03, 10.01 (PA-RISC) IRIX 5.3, 6.2 (Silicon Graphics) Solaris 2.4, 2.5, 2.6 (SPARC) SunOS 4.1.3, 4.1.4 (SPARC) AIX 3.2.5, 4.1, 4.2 (RS6000, PowerPC) SCO OpenServer 5.0 (Intel x86)	Apache 1.2, 1.3 NCSA 1.5.2 (1.5a and 1.5.1 are not supported) Netscape Commerce Server 1.12 Netscape Communications Server 1.12 Netscape Enterprise Server 2.0, 3.0 Netscape FastTrack 2.0 Stronghold 2.0 or later

Using Office with a Netscape Web server

When a Web server sends a document to a Web browser, the Web server must send the document in the correct format. In most cases, this format is HTML; however, Office also allows documents to be sent in Office document format.

Some Web server applications, such as IIS, store Multipurpose Internet Mail Extensions (MIME) content type and file name extension mappings in the Windows registry. These MIME settings allow the Web server to send Office 2000 documents in the original document format—rather than as plain text.

By contrast, some Web servers, such as the Netscape Commerce Server and FastTrack Server, store MIME settings in a file named Mime.types. This different mapping convention sometimes prevents Netscape Web servers from delivering Office documents accurately.

To ensure that Office 2000 documents are delivered accurately, you must add Office MIME type information to the Mime.types files on your Netscape Web server.

Note Multiple copies of the file named Mime.types might be on your Web server. Use the file search capabilities included with Windows NT Server to locate all the files named Mime.types.

▶ **To update Mime.types files**

1 On your Web server, locate all the files named Mime.types.

2 Create a backup of each Mime.types file, and store the backups in a safe location.

3 In a text editor such as Notepad, open a Mime.types file.

4 Enter the following lines next to the other file name extension mappings in the Mime.types file:

   type=application/msword exts=doc

   type=application/x-msexcel exts=xls

   type=application/vnd.ms-powerpoint exts=ppt

5 Repeat steps 3 and 4 for each copy of the file named Mime.types.

See also

- Upgrading your Web server to run IIS or Personal Web Server significantly enhances your use of OSE. For more information about OSE features and deployment, see "Architecture of Office Server Extensions" on page 709.

- The Web Publishing feature of Office 2000 allows users to browse and publish to Web servers as easily as they work with file shares. For more information, see "Client Components of Office Server Extensions" on page 721.

- FrontPage Server Extensions enable extended capabilities on your Web sites. For information about installing FrontPage Server Extensions on Web servers other than IIS and Personal Web Server, see the "FrontPage 2000 Server Extensions Resource Kit" on page 790.

Installing Office Web Features for International Users

The Microsoft Office 2000 MultiLanguage Pack includes *plug-in language features* that allow users to change the language of the user interface. When you use Office Web features in an international environment, you can do the following:

- Conduct Web Discussions in any available language

  All collaboration data is sent over the wire in Universal Character Set Transformation Format 8-bit (UTF-8). UTF-8 is an ISO standard for transmitting character codes for all languages.

- Use localized versions of Web Folders

  When a user selects different languages for Office and for Microsoft Windows, the Web Folders interface is displayed in the Office language in Office applications, and in the Windows language in My Computer and Windows Explorer.

The *Web Folders object* name and corresponding ScreenTip are displayed in the language to which Windows is set when you install the Web Publishing feature. If Windows is set to a language that is not supported by the plug-in language features you are installing, then the Web Folders object name and corresponding ScreenTip appear in the Office *installation language* instead.

Note   The plug-in language features do not translate the user interface for the offline features that the Web Publishing feature makes available.

See also

- To use localized versions of Office Web features, you must install the Microsoft Office 2000 MultiLanguage Pack. For more information, see "Features of the MultiLanguage Pack" on page 727.

Using Office Documents in a Web World

Microsoft Office 2000 applications offer many features that help users publish, analyze, and collaborate on an intranet. There are common tools for Web browsing and publishing across all the applications and unique tools in each application that maximize the benefits of application-specific capabilities when users work on an intranet.

Using HTML and Office Document Formats

Many organizations publish both HTML and Microsoft Office documents on their intranets. In Office 2000, users create HTML and Office documents with the same tools. Office 2000 also includes a Microsoft Office Web Components feature, which allows users to manipulate Excel and Access data directly in their Web browsers.

When you develop an intranet, HTML often provides the most effective means for broadcasting information across different platforms. For example, many organizations distribute company policy manuals, directories, or product information forms in HTML.

Office document formats are typically more efficient for distributing information that is developed collaboratively and changes frequently. For example, a team of individual contributors might develop a business plan with detailed schedules and financial analyses by using Microsoft Word and Microsoft Excel. Office features such as revision marks and version tracking are critical in this context.

Office 2000 is a flexible and robust tool for creating content either in Office document formats or in HTML—or for going back and forth between these formats. Office documents can be saved in HTML format and then reopened in an Office application without losing any features supported by native Office document formats.

Deciding between Office document formats and HTML

Because Office 2000 includes extensive support for HTML, users might wonder whether every document stored on the server should be converted to HTML format. Although HTML does offer a convenient format for sharing across different operating environments, using a native Office document format provides Office-specific advantages.

Web servers can maintain documents in both formats, even when users use binary files exclusively. In fact, the binary format has superior formatting capabilities when viewed in Office applications and has property tags that allow for easier searching. Microsoft Office Server Extensions (OSE) features make publishing and sharing documents on Web servers as easy as collaborating on a network share, so users can save documents in the best format for their needs.

The following table summarizes common business tasks that you might perform on an intranet by using HTML or Office document formats, or both.

To accomplish this task	Use this format
Disseminating information quickly to large audience	HTML or an Office application.
Distributing information in a slide show	HTML or Microsoft PowerPoint 2000. When you save a PowerPoint presentation in HTML format, users can use outline and navigation controls to view slides in a Web browser.
Searching documents for specific content	HTML or an Office application. The OSE search feature allows users to search published documents. Office applications allow similar search flexibility.
Distributing documents for review	HTML or an Office application. OSE or Microsoft FrontPage Server Extensions simplify posting to a Web server. Documents can also be shared and routed in an Office document format.
Discussing documents	HTML or an Office application. OSE allows threaded discussions in both HTML and Office documents. Office documents can include embedded comments.
Authoring documents collaboratively	Office applications only. Word and Excel include change tracking and version tracking tools.
Analyzing data	HTML or an Office application. The Office Web Components feature allows interactive data manipulation in a Web browser. Excel and Microsoft Access include additional tools for analyzing data.
Gaining quick access to enterprise data	Office application recommended. Office includes data access tools such as Web queries, Microsoft Query, and ODBC. Data access through HTML requires advanced programming knowledge.
Creating documents with flexible, easy-to-use features	Primarily Office applications. Most HTML output is static; however, Office Web Components provide more options for interactive content.

Specifying HTML as the default file format for Word or PowerPoint

If you've decided to standardize on the HTML format for Word or PowerPoint documents, you can use a system policy to set HTML as the default format for your users.

▶ **To specify HTML as the default file format for Word**

1 In the System Policy Editor, double-click the **Default User** icon.

2 Click the plus sign (+) next to **Microsoft Word 2000**.

3 Click the plus sign next to **Tools | Options**.

4 Click the plus sign next to **Save**.

5 Select the **Save Word files as** check box.

6 Under **Settings for Save Word files as**, select **Web Page (*.htm, *.html)**.

▶ **To specify HTML as the default file format for PowerPoint**

1 In the System Policy Editor, double-click the **Default User** icon.

2 Click the plus sign (+) next to **Microsoft PowerPoint 2000**.

3 Click the plus sign next to **Tools | Options**.

4 Click the plus sign next to **Save**.

5 Select the **Save PowerPoint files as** check box.

6 Under **Settings for Save PowerPoint files as**, select **Web Page (*.htm, *.html)**.

See also

• OSE can be installed on a Web server on your intranet to support publishing and collaboration in Office and HTML documents. For more information, see "Installing Office Server Extensions" on page 637.

Transferring Files Between HTML and Office Document Formats

Microsoft Office 2000 offers improved support for HTML format, including the ability to save files back and forth between HTML format and standard Office document formats. You can open an HTML page in an Office 2000 application without losing the HTML coding. If you save a Microsoft Word document in HTML format and then reopen it in Word, you do not lose document properties or other Word-specific document information.

Starting with HTML files

When you open an HTML file in an Office application, the HTML code is preserved, even if Office 2000 doesn't recognize the code. You can make changes to the file and save it again as an HTML file without losing any of your HTML information. If you save the file as a standard Office file, however, the HTML tags are not preserved.

Note Scripting tags within the body section of an HTML file are preserved even if the file is saved in an Office document format.

Starting with Office documents

Office 2000 uses Extensible Markup Language (XML) and other methods to ensure that formatting, special characters, document properties, and similar information are preserved when you save an Office file in HTML format.

Visual Basic for Applications (VBA) macros are preserved when you save an Office file in HTML format. When you save an Office document in HTML format, any VBA macros in the document are stored in a separate file linked to the HTML file. When you open the HTML file in an Office application, the macros are available and run correctly.

Microsoft PowerPoint and Microsoft Excel files saved in HTML format use scripts to make slide shows and workbooks function similarly to the way they function in the original applications.

Limitations of transferring between HTML and Office document formats

Saving files back and forth between Office document formats and HTML format works in the following Office applications: Word, Excel, PowerPoint, and Access. As with any new feature, there are a few limitations.

Limitations in Word

The **Version** command (**File** menu) is only available in DOC format.

Limitations in Excel

The following limitations apply to Excel 2000 files saved in HTML format:

- Password protection must be turned off before saving a file in HTML format.

- Scenarios and custom views are available only in XLS format.

- Shared workbooks are available only in XLS format.

- Templates and add-ins can be saved only in XLS format.

- English language formulas are converted to sheet references when the file is saved in HTML format.

- Formulas that link to a cell in an HTML workbook do not work when the file is saved in HTML format (for example, =book1.htm!A1).

Limitations in PowerPoint

When you save a PowerPoint file to the Web (for example, by clicking the **Publish** button in **Save As Web Page** dialog box), select **Microsoft Internet Explorer 4.0 or later (high fidelity)** under **Browser support** if you plan to reopen the file later in PowerPoint. If you save to a lower-level browser, the file cannot be reopened as a PowerPoint presentation.

Limitations in Access

Only *data access pages* can be saved in HTML format. The database file itself (the MDB file) cannot be saved in HTML format.

Keeping Track of Supporting Files

An HTML document consists exclusively of plain text. Within this text are embedded tags that specify the formatting and functionality of the page. Pictures, animations, sounds, and other resources that appear to be part of the page when viewed in a browser are actually stored in supporting files that are referenced by the main HTML page.

In contrast, native Microsoft Office documents (such as Word DOC files and Excel XLS files) maintain all text and embedded elements within one file. When an Office document is saved as a Web page, the Office application saves the main document as an HTML file and automatically creates a folder containing all the supporting files that are referenced by the HTML file. The folder is created in the same folder where the main HTML file is saved and is named *name*_files, where *name* is the document name specified in the **Save** dialog box.

Note The word **files** in the supporting files folder name changes depending on the language setting specified in the Office application.

If you don't want supporting files stored in a folder, you can change an option in each application to specify that the files are stored at the same level as the HTML file. For example, if your users store their files on a server, and you have not given them permission to create folders on the server, they see an error message when they save an HTML file that contains embedded files.

To work around this error message, set the default to save the supporting files at the same level as the HTML file. In the **Options** box (**Tools** menu), click the **General** tab, and then click **Web Options**. In the **Web Options** box, click the **Files** tab, and clear the **Organize supporting files in a folder** check box.

System Policy Tip   You can use a system policy to determine whether supporting files are stored in a folder or at the same level as the HTML file. Use the **Organize supporting files in a folder** policy in the **Microsoft Office 2000\Tools | Options | General | Web Options...\Files** category to control this behavior for all applications in Office. For more information about system policies, see "Using the System Policy Editor" on page 296.

Within the supporting files folder is a file named Filelist.xml that contains an index of all the supporting files. This file list tracks which files are actually embedded in the file. If you remove an embedded file from your HTML file, the embedded file is automatically deleted from the file list and the supporting files folder.

Windows 2000 mirroring

Windows 2000 implements a special feature to make working with Office HTML files and supporting files folders easier. Often, users do not realize that the HTML file has an associated supporting files folder. They copy, move, delete, or rename the HTML file without changing the corresponding supporting files folder.

For example, a user copies the HTML file to a floppy disk to take home and work on the file there. When she gets home, she discovers that she has only the HTML file, and not the graphics that were linked to it, so she can't work on the layout of the file.

To remedy this potential inconsistency, Microsoft Windows 2000 detects when an HTML file has an associated supporting files folder and then automatically copies, moves, deletes, or renames the supporting files folder to synchronize with the change being made to the HTML file.

Integrating Office Documents with a Web Browser

Microsoft Office 2000 was designed to integrate seamlessly with most Web browsers by using a technology called ActiveX. ActiveX documents allow container applications, such as Web browsers, to open native Office files in place.

ActiveX technology combines the navigation capabilities of the Web browser with the ease and flexibility of Office, complete with toolbars and menu commands. For example, a user can open a fully functional Microsoft Excel workbook in Microsoft Internet Explorer. The Excel workbook is an *active document* in Internet Explorer.

Note The integration of Office and Internet Explorer is particularly tight, which ensures seamless browsing. These products are designed with consistent toolbars, caches, and Favorites lists.

Office 2000 behaves differently from previous versions of Office when Office documents are opened from hyperlinks. In previous versions, clicking the hyperlink opened the Office document in place in the Web browser window. In Office 2000, however, clicking the hyperlink starts an instance of the Office application. For example, if you click a hyperlink to an Excel 2000 workbook in Internet Explorer, Excel starts and the workbook opens in Excel.

If you prefer to have Office documents open in place in the Web browser, you can override the default behavior of Office 2000 for particular document types, as described in the following procedure.

▶ **To configure a document type to open in the same window as its hyperlink**

1 In Windows Explorer or My Computer, click **Folder Options** on the **View** menu, and then click the **File Types** tab.

2 In the **Registered File Types** box, select the file type you want to modify (for example, **Microsoft Excel Worksheet**) and then click **Edit**.

3 Select the **Browse in Same Window** check box.

Connecting Office Documents by Using Hyperlinks

Providing hyperlinks between related documents gives readers and authors easier access to relevant information. For example, the specifications for a new bicycle might include hyperlinks to descriptions of individual parts that make up the bicycle. Or an annual report distributed online as a Microsoft Word document might contain hyperlinks to a Microsoft Excel spreadsheet with year-end balances, so users can do their own detailed analyses.

Inserting hyperlinks in Office documents

Office 2000 includes a simplified dialog box that is shared across all Office 2000 applications to make it easy for any user to create and edit hyperlinks: the **Insert Hyperlink** dialog box (**Insert** menu).

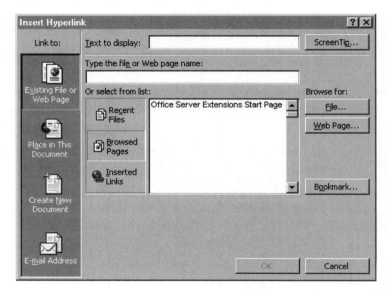

Office 2000 Insert Hyperlink dialog box

By using this dialog box, Office 2000 users can attach hyperlinks to a variety of objects, including text, graphics, tables, slides, cells, and custom database form fields. These hyperlinks can go to any of the following locations:

- Another location within the same document

- Another Office document

- An HTML document on the intranet

- An Internet e-mail address

- Any file with a recognized address through a fully qualified path, Uniform Resource Locator (URL), universal naming convention (UNC) path, or File Transfer Protocol (FTP) site

From the administrator's perspective, hyperlinks are generally simpler to support than OLE or dynamic data exchange (DDE) links. In the case of OLE or DDE links, Office applications maintain a connection to the linked source data, and administrators must manage the document to maintain this connection. Hyperlinks, by contrast, are primarily navigational tools.

The hyperlink feature in Office 2000 is designed for intranets with high-speed links and direct file access. Hyperlinks work on local area networks (LANs) or high-speed wide area networks (WANs) without HTTP or any special Web server software. (Office also supports hyperlinks to documents on the World Wide Web, although access time can be much slower.)

Using the Web toolbar

Using hyperlinks to navigate between Office documents is similar to navigating on the Web. To extend the similarity, Office includes the **Web** toolbar, which is shared across Office 2000 applications.

Office 2000 Web toolbar

The **Web** toolbar is similar to the navigation elements in standard Web browsers, with buttons for navigating forward, back, and to the home page. By using the **Search the Web** button, users can search the Web or an intranet. Users can enter a URL or a file path in the **Address** box. The **Favorites** menu on this toolbar provides easy access to frequently visited sites.

See also

- If you don't want your users navigating to the Web from within Office, you can disable the buttons on the **Web** toolbar. For more information, see "Locking Down an Office Configuration" on page 291.

Working with Content on an Intranet

Microsoft Office 2000 applications include many new features for creating and working with Web content.

Creating Web pages for an intranet

Every Office application has a **Save as Web Page** command on the **File** menu. This command saves the active document in HTML format. Also on the **File** menu is the **Web Page Preview** command, which opens the Web browser and shows a preview of what the document will look like when saved in HTML format and displayed in the Web browser.

Individual Office applications have new tools for creating and publishing documents to the Web or an intranet. For example, Microsoft Word 2000 can be used as a powerful HTML authoring tool. The **Web Layout** command (**View** menu) gives users a WYSIWYG view of Word documents created for the Web.

Microsoft PowerPoint 2000 makes it easy for users to share presentations over the Web. When a presentation is published in HTML format, the presentation appears in Web browsers with slide navigation controls, a **Full Screen Slide Show** tool, and optional speaker notes.

In Microsoft Excel 2000 and Microsoft Access 2000, Microsoft Office Web Components allow data to be displayed dynamically in HTML. Users can manipulate, modify, and format this data on the Web.

Collaborating on documents and sharing information

One of the most powerful uses of an intranet is collaboration. Typical examples of collaboration include the following:

- Collaborative authoring

  Often several authors work together to create a document—for example, a budget or extensive specifications for one product. Shared documents are typically stored on an intranet.

- Content review

  Peers or managers frequently review a document before the author publishes the final version. Office provides a set of tools for collaboration, making it as easy as opening a published document and going to work. Both Word and Excel support comments and change tracking. Microsoft Office Server Extensions (OSE) allow users to participate in threaded discussions in documents stored on a Web server.

- Shared workbooks

  Excel allows two or more users to edit the same workbook simultaneously by using the **Share Workbook** command (**Tools** menu).

Office also provides tools for tracking and reviewing changes in a document or for rolling them back to earlier versions. These tools can be used with documents published on an intranet to enhance workgroup functionality.

- Change tracking

  Word and Excel users can track all changes to a file with revision marks that are color-coded for each user. In Excel, a color border appears around the cell. In Word, the modified text appears in a different color or has special formatting such as underlining or strikethrough.

- Conflict resolution

  Office applications can track multiple changes to the same data, allowing the original author to roll back changes. The **Reviewing** toolbar lets users explore all revisions and comments and decide which changes to accept and which to reject.

- Merged files

  Many people distribute documents for review through e-mail. Because Office has the ability to merge files, users can consolidate multiple versions of a document into one master file.

- Offline caching

  Office 2000 includes a new feature that allows users to work offline on documents published on an intranet. While users are working online, documents are cached locally. When users reconnect, any changes made offline are synchronized with the online version. If there are conflicts, users are prompted to resolve them during synchronization.

Note   Offline caching is available only to users of Microsoft Internet Explorer 5 or later.

Publishing in multiple media

Although many documents are created for print, other documents are published directly on CD-ROM, on an intranet, or on the Web. Presentations are distributed in an increasing variety of formats, including 35mm slides, electronic presentations, or HTML documents. Office applications allow users to publish in multiple formats.

Finding Office documents on an intranet

After documents are published, users might spend a lot of time trying to locate key information or find related documents created by other groups. This challenge effectively limits the size of the audience for the publication—making publication on an intranet a useful alternative because hyperlinks and searching capabilities help users find what they need.

When OSE is installed on a Web server, users can go to the OSE Start Page, a Web page with several tools that assist in using OSE features. One of these tools can search the server for documents based on user-specified criteria, such as words and phrases, and Office document properties, such as title, author, and summary.

Note   The Web Find Fast feature in Office 97 has been replaced in Office 2000 with the OSE Search feature.

See also

- By having OSE installed on a Web server, users are offered many additional collaboration features. For more information about these OSE features, see "Using Office Server Extensions" on page 637.

- Another way to share Web data among your users is by using Excel Web queries. You can create a query (IQY file) to run against data published to the Web. For more information, see the *Microsoft Office 2000/Visual Basic Programmer's Guide*.

Adding Interactive Web Controls to Office Documents

Microsoft Office Web Components are a family of controls that can be used in Microsoft Internet Explorer to enable interactive browsing of Office data. Certain Office documents can be saved in *interactive HTML format*. The saved HTML file contains Office Web Components that are bound to the data in the document. The data can be manipulated and modified in Internet Explorer.

Spreadsheet component

The Spreadsheet Component displays data in a grid format similar to a Microsoft Excel worksheet. Values in the grid can be modified and formatted. The **Property** toolbox offers formatting, display, calculation, and search tools in the browser window.

PivotTable component

The PivotTable Component brings the functionality of PivotTables to Internet Explorer. Multidimensional data can be manipulated and modified in the browser window by using this component.

Chart component

Interactive charting is made possible with the Chart Component. A Chart component is bound to the data of a Spreadsheet or PivotTable Component. When a user modifies the bound data in Internet Explorer, the Chart component is updated to reflect the new data.

Data Source component and data access pages

The Data Source Component displays relational data in Internet Explorer. Data can be grouped by fields, and then browsed in the same way it can be in an Access form. *Data access pages* created in Microsoft Access use the Data Source component to provide interactive database control on published HTML documents.

Managing Office Web Components

The Microsoft Office Web Components are available in Office 2000 Standard, Office 2000 Professional, and Office 2000 Premium. They are not included in Office 2000 Small Business or in the standalone version of Excel 2000. Office Web Components are also available on the Office Update Web site at http://officeupdate.microsoft.com/.

Note   Office Web components require Microsoft Internet Explorer version 4.0 or later. You can view the data in Internet Explorer version 3.0, but the data is not interactive.

Installing Web Components during Office Setup

By default, Office Web Components are installed in the user's hard disk during Office Setup. You can determine whether the Office Web Components feature is available to users, or where they are installed (local hard disk or network server), by using the Office Custom Installation Wizard.

Specifying a path to download Office Web Components

By default, the Office Web Components download path is set to the Office installation server. If you want users to be able to install Office Web Components from another location, you can specify where they install the components from by setting a system policy. Use the **Download Office Web Components** policy to specify a server path for them to use.

▶ **To specify a path for users to download Office Web Components**

1   In the System Policy Editor, double-click the **Default User** icon.

2   In the **Default User Properties** dialog box, click the plus sign (+) next to **Microsoft Office 2000**.

3   Click the plus sign next to **Tools | Options | General | Web Options....**

4   Click the plus sign next to **Files**.

5   Select the **Download Office Web Components** check box.

6   Under **Settings for Download Office Web Components**, select the **Download Office Web Components from** check box.

7   In the **Location** box, type the path to the location on the file server you want to use.

Preventing users from downloading Office Web Components

If you don't want to make Office Web Components available to your users, you can choose not to install the components with Office. You can also keep users from downloading the components later by setting the **Download Office Web Components** system policy.

▶ **To prevent users from downloading Office Web Components**

1   In the System Policy Editor, double-click the **Default User** icon.

2   In the **Default User Properties** dialog box, click the plus sign (+) next to **Microsoft Office 2000**.

3   Click the plus sign next to **Tools | Options | General | Web Options....**

4   Click the plus sign next to **Files**.

5   Clear the **Download Office Web Components** check box.

Administering Office 2000 Web Options

You can control how your users interact with Office 2000 documents on the Web by setting both Office 2000 Web options and Web options specific to each application. Many of the Web options included in Office 2000 can be set through system policies.

Office 2000 system policies for Web options

The general Office 2000 Web options can be set through system policies found in the following category: **Microsoft Office 2000\Tools | Options | General | Web Options...\General**. Use the **Rely on CSS for font formatting** policy to specify whether to use *cascading style sheets* with your Web pages. If you use a cascading style sheet, you can cut down on the amount of formatting information you save with the file itself, thus paring down the file size. Cascading style sheets require Microsoft Internet Explorer version 3.0 or later, or a Web browser that supports cascading style sheets.

In addition to the general policies, you can set policies for how Office 2000 handles Web files. These system policies are found in the following category: **Microsoft Office 2000\Tools | Options | General | Web Options...\Files**. Use these policies to determine how Office 2000 stores files associated with your Web pages and when to update links in a document. The **Check if Office is the default editor for Web pages created in Office** policy also lets you set Office applications as the default HTML editors for Office-generated HTML files.

If you want to control how Office 2000 handles Web graphics, use the system policies in the following category: **Microsoft Office 2000\Tools | Options | General | Web Options...\Pictures**. These policies determine how Office handles graphics associated with your Web pages. Graphics are stored as bitmaps by default, but can be set to Vector Markup Language (VML) format or Portable Network Graphics (PNG) format instead. You can also use the **Target monitor** policy to optimize your Web pages for a particular monitor size and resolution.

Finally, the encoding policy enables multiple language support for your Web pages. You can use the default language, or you can specify a particular language to use. To specify encoding options, open the **Microsoft Office 2000\Tools | Options | General | Web Options...\Encoding** category and set the **Default or specific encoding** policy.

Access 2000 system policies for Web options

System policies specific to Microsoft Access 2000 are found in the **Microsoft Access 2000\Tools | Options\Web Options...\General** category. By using these policies, you can change the default colors and appearance of your hyperlinks.

Excel 2000 system policies for Web options

System policies specific to Microsoft Excel 2000 are found in the **Microsoft Excel 2000\Tools | Options\Web Options…\General** category. Use the **Save any additional data necessary to maintain formulas** policy to ensure that your formulas can find all the values they need, even from cells that aren't in your selected range. Use the **Load pictures from Web pages not created in Excel** policy to help control the layout of your Web pages, ensuring that your formulas continue to point to the correct cells in a spreadsheet.

PowerPoint 2000 system policies for Web options

System policies specific to Microsoft PowerPoint 2000 are found in the **Microsoft PowerPoint 2000\Tools | Options\Web Options…\General** category. You can specify slide navigation, slide animation, and graphic size options by using the system policies in this category.

Word 2000 system policies for Web options

Microsoft Word includes a system policy to disable features not supported by a particular browser level. You can also set Word as the default editor for all Web pages by using the policies in the **Microsoft Word 2000\Tools | Options\Web Options…** category.

See also

- By using system policies, you can change options once and apply them to all of your users. For more information, see "Using the System Policy Editor" on page 296.

Managing Communications on Your Intranet

Microsoft Office 2000 helps you and your users communicate over an intranet in new and sophisticated ways. By using Microsoft Outlook 2000 options, including the ability to send HTML-based e-mail messages, your organization can take advantage of your intranet to exchange enhanced and dynamic information.

Organizing and Sharing Information with Outlook 2000

Microsoft Outlook 2000 is a desktop information manager that organizes e-mail messages, calendars, contacts, tasks, documents, and files into a single, integrated environment. Outlook 2000 also helps users share information through Microsoft Exchange Server public folders, electronic forms, groupware, and the Internet.

Using electronic mail options

Outlook 2000 makes it easy for users in your organization to communicate internally or externally by using Exchange Server, Microsoft Mail, or other third-party mail systems. Support for Post Office Protocol version 3 (POP3), Internet Mail Access Protocol version 4 (IMAP4), and Simple Mail Transfer Protocol (SMTP) in Outlook 2000 allows users to communicate directly over the Internet.

In addition, Outlook 2000 automatically creates hyperlinks for any URL contained in an e-mail message or any other Outlook 2000 item. Using **Mail Recipient** command (**File** menu, **Send To** submenu), you can send the following Office 2000 files as HTML-based e-mail messages:

- Microsoft Word 2000 documents
- Microsoft Excel 2000 worksheets
- Microsoft PowerPoint 2000 slides
- Microsoft Access 2000 data pages

Scheduling meetings

Group scheduling with Exchange Server helps users schedule meetings and keep in touch with other members of their organization. In addition, Outlook 2000 includes the ability to perform group scheduling over the Internet. Users can publish and download free/busy information for scheduling meetings, as well as send and receive meeting requests and responses over the Internet by using the iCalendar Internet standard.

Sharing information in public folders

By using Outlook 2000 and Exchange Server, you can share information with other people in your organization. For example, you can publish in a public folder such items as:

- Calendars that identify holidays, trade shows, and so on.
- Contact lists.
- Project task lists.

Or you can create an online conversation to track ideas about a new project. Administrators can create custom views of the message, task, contact, schedule, or journal items in a public folder, and then each user can create personalized views of this shared information.

Toolbox

The Microsoft Office Resource Kit for Office 97/98 provides additional information about using public folders. This archive edition is included in its entirety in the Microsoft Office 2000 Resource Kit. For more information, see "Microsoft Office Resource Kit for Office 97/98" on page 792.

Developing solutions for collaborating over the Internet

Outlook 2000 takes the Internet beyond just Web pages and electronic mail and provides new ways for you to collaborate and share information across the Internet. For workgroups and enterprises, Outlook 2000, combined with Microsoft Exchange Server, is a complete solution for developing and deploying a wide variety of collaborative applications, from contact management solutions for workgroups to enterprise-wide workflow and tracking applications.

Outlook 2000 and Internet Standards

Microsoft Outlook 2000 provides a central point from which to communicate with others through the Internet.

As an administrator, you have many ways to set up your e-mail system to send and receive Internet e-mail messages by using Outlook 2000. If you use Microsoft Exchange Server, the Internet Mail Connector handles Internet e-mail messages. However, e-mail messages can be exchanged directly over the Internet by using any other e-mail service provider that is compatible with the Internet Mail Access Protocol (IMAP) and Simple Mail Transfer Protocol (SMTP) or Post Office Protocol version 3 (POP3) and SMTP. SMTP and POP3 are MAPI service providers that are installed by default with Outlook 2000.

With an Internet mail connection, your workgroup can use Internet messaging for the following activities in addition to sending and receiving messages:

- Connect to the Internet from a remote location and download messages.

  For example, a traveling salesperson can check for new e-mail messages while on the road.

- Use rules to process incoming and outgoing e-mail messages.

  For example, a user can have an Outlook file with all the messages from a specific Internet address in a separate folder.

- Send and receive group scheduling meeting requests.

  For example, a meeting organizer can send a meeting request to offsite clients or suppliers.

- Assign tasks, and then receive notification when tasks are updated or completed.

  For example, a manager can send a task request to an employee who works at home.

When a user types an Internet e-mail address in the **To** box, Outlook automatically resolves and formats the address by removing spaces and changing commas to periods.

Outlook 2000 automatically recognizes Internet addresses (URLs) in the body of e-mail messages and then converts them to hyperlinks. Outlook 2000 recognizes the following commonly used Internet URL protocols:

- file
- mailto
- http
- News
- nntp
- outlook
- ftp

When you type one of these Internet protocols in an e-mail message or other item, Outlook creates a hyperlink from the text. However, when the Internet address includes spaces, you must enclose the entire address in angle brackets (< >). For example:

<file://C:\My Documents\MyFile.doc>

Outlook 2000 contains advanced Internet messaging and collaboration standards and protocols. Outlook 2000 is closely integrated with the Web and provides mail functionality regardless of the Internet service provider or browser. Outlook provides the following standards to enable communication on the Internet:

- POP
- SMTP
- LDAP
- IMAP
- *S/MIME*
- NNTP
- Dynamic HTML
- vCard
- vCalendar

You can use Outlook 2000 as your primary Internet-messaging client or as an enhanced Microsoft Exchange client.

Support for creating and sharing vCards

Outlook 2000 supports vCard, which is the Internet standard for creating and sharing virtual business cards. Outlook users can save vCards in their Contacts folders. You can send or receive vCards as e-mail attachments, and you can import vCards as files. All contacts that are stored in Contacts folders can be shared in the vCard format with other users.

Support for iCalendar and vCalendar standards

Outlook 2000 has enhanced support for the iCalendar (iCal) standard for calendar information, including appointments, meeting requests, and displaying free/busy times. In Outlook 2000, you can save, import, and export vCalendar appointments.

▶ **To save an appointment as a vCalendar appointment**

1   On your Calendar, select an appointment.

2   On the **File** menu, click **Save As**.

3   In the **Save as type** box, select **vCalendar Format**.

To import or export information, use the **Import and Export** command (**File** menu).

HTML-based e-mail messages

Outlook 2000 allows you to format your e-mail messages in HTML format. A recipient can read an HTML-based e-mail message as long as the mail client of the recipient supports HTML.

HTML-based e-mail messages also allow you to communicate professionally by using:

- Colorful backgrounds
- Bulleted and numbered lists
- Hyperlinks
- Embedded images

When you send an HTML-based e-mail message, Outlook 2000 also sends a plain text version of the e-mail message so that all mail clients can read your message.

Support for POP3 and SMTP

Post Office Protocol version 3 (POP3) and Simple Mail Transfer Protocol (SMTP) are the two most commonly used protocols for sending and receiving e-mail messages over the Internet. Outlook 2000 provides support for POP3 and SMTP, including full support for the following:

- Multiple Internet e-mail accounts.
- Authenticated SMTP.
- Distributed Password Authentication (DPA).
- The ability to store messages on the server.

Support for IMAP4

Internet Mail Access Protocol version 4 (IMAP4) is an Internet standard for e-mail and server-based mail storage. IMAP4 provides a superset of POP3 and SMTP features, including the ability to store e-mail messages in multiple folders. Outlook 2000 supports IMAP4, including full support for multiple IMAP4 e-mail accounts.

Support for LDAP

Lightweight Directory Access Protocol (LDAP) is an Internet protocol that allows a user to find other e-mail users on the Internet or your organization's intranet. LDAP is currently being used as the primary means of searching global directories that are available on the Internet. Outlook 2000 fully supports LDAP, including specification of multiple LDAP Internet information accounts.

Support for S/MIME

The Secure Multipurpose Internet Mail Extensions (S/MIME) features of Outlook 2000 allow users to exchange encrypted and digitally signed messages with any S/MIME-compliant mail reader. Messages are encrypted or digitally signed by the sending client, and then they are decrypted by the recipient, thereby providing end-to-end secure communications across the Internet.

By using S/MIME features, you get the following security elements in your e-mail messages:

Identification   Digitally signed messages allow recipients to verify the identity of the sender.

Data Integrity   Digitally signed messages confirm that the messages have not been altered in transit.

Nonrepudiation   Digitally signed messages contain enough information to prevent the sender of the message from denying that he or she actually sent it.

See also

*   The S/MIME features rely on each user having a unique Digital ID. For more information about Digital IDs, S/MIME, and Outlook 2000, see "Using Security Features in Outlook" on page 414.

Sending Office Documents as HTML-based E-mail Messages

HTML-based e-mail messages allow users to send and receive e-mail messages that contain any of the features of a Web page that are viewed in a Web browser including Rich Text Format (RTF), embedded graphics and sounds, and hyperlinks. The following e-mail clients support sending and receiving HTML-based e-mail messages:

*   Microsoft Outlook Express
*   Microsoft Outlook
*   Netscape Messenger
*   Qualcomm Eudora Pro
*   Lotus Notes Mail

Several Microsoft Office 2000 applications support the **Mail Recipient** command (**File** menu, **Send To** submenu). This command converts the *active document* to HTML, and then sends it as an HTML-based e-mail message to specified recipients.

Note   You must have Outlook 2000 or Outlook Express 5.0 installed to use the **Mail Recipient** command in other Office 2000 applications.

The following table describes the **Mail Recipient** command in each Office 2000 application.

Application	Description
Word	The entire active document is sent as an HTML-based e-mail message.
Access	The active data page and its attached images and style sheets are sent as an HTML-based e-mail message. Access does not support HTML frame sets, so you cannot send multiple pages as an HTML-based e-mail message.
Excel	The active worksheet is sent as an HTML-based e-mail message. If the workbook contains multiple worksheets, you can send the entire workbook as a standard file attachment. You cannot send the entire workbook as an HTML-based e-mail message.
PowerPoint	The active slide is sent as an HTML-based e-mail message. If the presentation contains multiple slides, you can send the entire presentation as a standard file attachment. You cannot send an entire presentation as an HTML-based e-mail message.

Note   Office 2000 applications also support the **Mail Recipient (as Attachment)** command (**File** menu, **Send To** submenu), which opens a new mail message with the attached active document in the native format of the application.

If some of your users do not have e-mail clients that can read HTML-based e-mail messages, you can disable the **Mail Recipient** command in any Office 2000 application. Office 2000 automatically disables this feature when the local computer does not have Outlook 2000 or Outlook Express 5.0 installed.

System Policy Tip   You can disable the option to send Office files as HTML-based e-mail messages by setting a system policy. Use the **Disable command bar buttons and menu items** system policy in the **Disable items in user interface\Predefined** category for each application. Under **Settings for Disable command bar buttons and menu items**, select the **File I Send To I Mail Recipient** check box to disable this feature. For more information, see "Using the System Policy Editor" on page 296.

You can disable the **Mail Recipient** command in selected Office 2000 applications. When you do this, consider replacing the **E-mail** button (**Standard** toolbar) with the **Mail Recipient (As Attachment)** button.

Publishing Calendar Information on an Intranet or the Web

By using Microsoft Outlook 2000, you can publish your Calendar information to a site on your intranet or the Web. When you open your Calendar and then click **Save As Web Page** (**File** menu), Outlook 2000 creates a calendar in HTML—complete with links and graphics. This feature allows you to do the following:

- Post an internal calendar of events on your intranet.

- Publish a calendar to advertise sales or new products on the Web.

Note   When you save your Calendar as a Web page, you can use File, HTTP, and FTP protocols to specify the address to use.

Outlook 2000 supports the iCalendar (iCal) free/busy standard, which allows you to see when people outside your organization, or people using a different personal information management product that supports iCalendar, are free or busy. This support for the iCalendar standard allows you to schedule meetings with people across organizations, or across the Internet.

System Policy Tip   You can set free/busy options for all your users at one time by using system policies. In the System Policy Editor, set the policies in the **Microsoft Outlook 2000\Tools | Options\Preferences\Calendar Options\Free/Busy Options** category to control these options for your users. For more information, see "Using the System Policy Editor" on page 296.

▶ **To specify the location for an individual's free/busy information**

1   Open the contact, and then click the **Details** tab.

2   In the **Internet Free-Busy** area, in the **Address** box, type the location of the free/busy iCalendar file.

When you invite a contact to a meeting, Outlook retrieves the iCal free/busy information and displays the availability of that person.

You can publish free/busy information to an iCalendar file automatically by setting the free/busy options for Outlook.

Note   Before your users can publish their free/busy information in iCalendar format, you must set up Microsoft Posting Acceptor. Posting Acceptor is included with Microsoft Internet Information Server 4.0 (in the Windows NT 4.0 Option Pack), with Microsoft Site Server 3.0, or with Microsoft Visual Studio® 6.0.

▶ **To publish free/busy information to an iCalendar file**

1   On the **Tools** menu, click **Options**.

2   Click the **Preferences** tab.

3   In the **Calendar** area, click **Calendar Options**.

4   In the **Calendar Options** box, click the **Free/Busy Options** button.

5   Select the **Publish my free/busy information** check box, and then type the URL in the **Publish at this URL** box.

You can also schedule a specific meeting in iCal format by clicking on **Forward as iCalendar** on the **Actions** menu.

System Policy Tip If you want all of your users throughout your organization to send meeting requests using the iCalendar standard by default, you can set this option through a system policy. In the System Policy Editor, select the **Microsoft Outlook 2000\Tools I Options\Preferences\Calendar options\Meeting Requests using iCalendar** policy. Then under **Settings for Meeting Requests using iCalendar**, select **Send meeting requests using iCalendar by default**. For more information, see "Using the System Policy Editor" on page 296.

How to Use Outlook Web Features

Microsoft Outlook 2000 provides the following ways to manage information from the Internet or your intranet. Users can use the Contacts folder to do the following:

- Keep track of contacts' Web sites.
- Open the Web history folder from within Outlook 2000.
- Share a catalog of Web sites in a public folder.

Browse Web pages in Outlook

In Outlook 2000, you can select a Web page from the Favorites menu or use the **Web** toolbar to enter a URL and display a Web page in Outlook. Or you can send the Web page that you are currently viewing in Outlook as the body of an e-mail message by clicking **Send Web Page by E-Mail** on the **Actions** menu.

System Policy Tip If you do not want your users browsing the Web from Outlook 2000, you can disable commands on the **Web** toolbar by using a system policy. In the System Policy Editor, disable the commands in the **Microsoft Outlook 2000\ Disable items in user interface\Predefined** category that you do not want available to your users. For more information, see "Using the System Policy Editor" on page 296.

Create home pages for folders

Because you can view Web pages in Outlook 2000, it is easy to create a home page for a public folder. A folder home page can be used to provide the following:

- Information about the purpose and use of a public folder.
- A primary or secondary customizable view of the folder contents.

▶ **To add a folder home page in Outlook 2000**

1 In the Outlook Folder list, right-click the folder, and then click **Properties**.

2 In the **Properties** dialog box, click the **Home Page** tab.

3 Select all the options that you want to set up the home page.

System Policy Tip   You can specify folder home pages for your users by setting a system policy. You can also disable folder home pages through a system policy. In the System Policy Editor, set the policies in the **Microsoft Outlook 2000\Miscellaneous\Folder Home Pages for Outlook special folders** category to specify folder home pages options for your users. For more information, see "Using the System Policy Editor" on page 296.

Store URLs on the Outlook Bar

To keep track of interesting or important Web sites, you can add URLs to the Outlook Bar. You can also send a script in an e-mail message that automatically adds a URL to the Outlook Bar of every recipient.

Customizing the Outlook Bar

You can customize the Outlook Bar to include the shortcuts your users need either by customizing the Outlbar.inf file or by using the Outlook 2000 *object model* to programmatically create Outlook Bar shortcuts. For more information about programming the Outlook Bar, see the *Microsoft Office 2000/Visual Basic Programmer's Guide*.

If you have not deployed Outlook 2000, and you want to add a shortcut to a Web page when you deploy the application, you can customize the Outlbar.inf file. The Outlbar.inf file is stored in the Program Files\Microsoft Office\Office\1033 folder. After you customize the file, replace the existing Outlbar.inf file on your *administrative installation point* with your new Outlbar.inf file, and then deploy Outlook 2000.

Outlook Bar groups are stored in an FAV file located in the Application Data folder. When Outlook 2000 detects that the Outlook Bar needs to be refreshed (for example, during Setup), it follows instructions in the Outlbar.inf file and then installs Outlook Bar groups and shortcuts accordingly. If the user already has an FAV file (from Outlook 97/98), the new Outlook Bar shortcut does not appear until the Outlook Bar is recreated.

▶ **To add a URL to the Outlook Bar**

1   In Outlook 2000, use the **Address** box on the Web toolbar to go to the Web page that you want to add.

2   On the **File** menu, click **New**, and then click **Outlook Bar Shortcut to Web Page**.

When you click the URL in the Outlook Bar, the Web page appears in the right pane of the Outlook 2000 window.

System Policy Tip   If you do not want your users to create Outlook Bar shortcuts to Web pages, you can disable this command by using a system policy. In the **Microsoft Outlook 2000\Disable items in user interface\Predefined** category, select the **Disable command bar buttons and menu items** policy. Then in the **Settings for Disable command bar buttons and menu items** area, select **All folders: File | New | Outlook Bar shortcut to web page**. For more information, see "Using the System Policy Editor" on page 296.

Save Web page addresses in Contacts

Outlook 2000 can store an Internet address for each contact in the Contacts folder so that you can go directly to a contact's Web page from Outlook 2000. This feature is useful in individual contact lists, but it can also be used by a workgroup to keep track of important customer information.

For example, a sales department can maintain a list of customers in a public folder. The public folder can include a custom view that shows each customer name, business phone number, e-mail address, and Web site address.

▶ **To create a list of contacts' Web addresses in a public folder**

1   Create a new public folder, and then configure it to contain the information for your contacts.

2   Create or modify a view to show only the Full Name, Business Phone, E-mail address, and Web Page fields.

3   Add or import contacts to the public folder.

Toolbox

The Microsoft Office Resource Kit for Office 97/98 provides additional information about using public folders. This archive edition is included in its entirety in the Microsoft Office 2000 Resource Kit. For more information, see "Microsoft Office Resource Kit for Office 97/98" on page 792.

See also

- You can use public folders to facilitate communication between your users without filling up their Inboxes. For more information, see your Microsoft Exchange documentation.

- You can use the Outlook 2000 object model to automate tasks and customize options in Outlook 2000. For more information about programming Outlook 2000, see the *Microsoft Office 2000/Visual Basic Programmer's Guide*.

Broadcasting PowerPoint Presentations over the Network

Microsoft PowerPoint 2000 includes the Presentation Broadcasting feature, which allows users to broadcast streaming PowerPoint presentations in real time to network users. In addition to slides, presenters can broadcast video and audio simultaneously to deliver a live multimedia show online. The PowerPoint 2000 Presentation Broadcasting feature combines the functionality of PowerPoint, Microsoft Outlook, Windows NT Server NetShow™ Services, and Windows Media Player.

Installing Presentation Broadcasting and Scheduling Broadcasts

To install the Presentation Broadcasting feature on users' computers during Office Setup, select the Microsoft Office\Microsoft PowerPoint for Windows\Presentation Broadcasting feature and set the installation state to **Run from My Computer**.

Note   To install the Presentation Broadcasting feature on Microsoft Windows NT 4.0 computers, you must log on with *administrator privileges*.

After you install the Presentation Broadcasting feature on a client computer, you can schedule, modify, and present broadcasts. To take advantage of the Presentation Broadcasting feature, first you create a presentation in Microsoft PowerPoint, and then you schedule your presentation for broadcast.

▶ **To schedule a presentation for broadcast**

1   On the **Slide Show** menu, point to **Online Broadcast**, and then click **Set Up and Schedule**.

2   In the **Broadcast Schedule** dialog box, choose the option to set up and schedule a new broadcast.

3   In the **Schedule a New Broadcast** dialog box, click the **Description** tab and type any description information you want to display on the Lobby page.

4   On the **Broadcast Settings** tab, specify the broadcast settings you want.

You can modify broadcast settings for a scheduled broadcast before the broadcast begins. Available broadcast settings include the following:

- **Send audio**

  Select this option to include audio in a presentation. The audio is transmitted as you speak into a microphone. You can connect the microphone to the computer that you are broadcasting from, or you can connect it to another computer on the network. If you use both a microphone and video camera in a presentation, you must connect the microphone and camera to the same computer.

- **Send video**

  Select this option to include video in a presentation. You can connect the video camera to the computer you are broadcasting from, or you can connect it to another computer on the network. If you use both a video camera and a microphone in a presentation, you must connect the camera and microphone to the same computer.

  Note   Video capturing and transmission require significant CPU capacity. For the best performance, connect the camera to a computer with an Intel Pentium II 266 megahertz (MHz) or faster processor.

- **Viewers can e-mail**

  Select this option to allow viewers to send feedback e-mail messages during a broadcast. You can specify any valid e-mail address.

- **Enable Chat**

  Select this option to allow viewers to participate in a Chat session during a broadcast. You can specify a Chat server for all the users in your organization by using a system policy.

- **Record the broadcast**

  Select this option to save the broadcast for later viewing. The broadcast is saved as an Advanced Streaming Format (ASF) file on a shared network drive that you specify.

  Note   Do not specify a network location if you plan to save the recorded broadcast on a CD-ROM. If a location is not specified, the file is saved by default in the shared directory, which can be distributed or copied to a CD-ROM.

- **Specify a shared location**

  Click the **Server Options** button and enter a universal naming convention (UNC) path to a shared location that viewers connect to during the broadcast to download the presentation. This path must be entered in UNC format when scheduling the broadcast. However, you can change the path to a URL that points to the same location when you send the meeting request for the broadcast.

  Note   If the broadcast uses a NetShow server, that server must have write access to the shared location; otherwise, the broadcast fails.

- **Specify a NetShow server**

  When you have more than 15 viewers, you must specify a NetShow server. By using a third-party NetShow service provider, you can also broadcast presentations over the Internet.

After you specify settings for the broadcast, PowerPoint 2000 opens an Outlook 2000 online meeting request form for the broadcast. Enter the addresses of the viewers whom you want to invite to the broadcast, and then send the form.

Viewers can accept the meeting request when they receive it, and then they can click the event URL address in the request to connect to the lobby page and to the presentation broadcast. The lobby page displays the time remaining until the broadcast begins.

Note Viewers must have their clock set with the correct time and time zone or the time calculation might not be correct.

Broadcast information is saved in the presentation file, so it can be moved to any computer without losing the settings for the broadcast. However, broadcast settings are relative to the computer on which the presentation is saved. If you move a broadcast to a different computer, the domains and file paths might not be accessible.

Note The Presentation Broadcasting feature supports e-mail applications other than Outlook. However, only Outlook makes time information available and allows you to replace a presentation file with an updated version before the scheduled broadcast.

Using Chat with Presentation Broadcasting

Before you can enable Chat on a presenter's computer, you must change a setting in the Windows registry.

1 On the presenter's computer, locate the following registry subkey:

   HKEY_CURRENT_USER\Software\Microsoft\Office\9.0\Powerpoint\Broadcast

2 Add a new string value named **ChatURL**.

3 Set the value data for the new string to **mic://<Chatserver>/%23<Chatroom>**

   where *<Chatserver>* is the name of Chat server and *<Chatroom>* is the name of your Chat room.

   For example, if the Chat server is MyServer and the Chat room is NewChatRoom, then the value for the string is **mic://myserver/%23newchatroom**.

When the Broadcast subkey is set to the correct Chat room, the presenter can select the **Enable Chat** check box on the **Broadcast Settings** tab to allow Chat, or clear the check box to prevent Chat. If the presenter allows Chat, the audience sees an **Online Chat** button on the Event page. Clicking the button starts their Chat client and takes them to the specified Chat room.

> **Customizing HTML scripts for presentation broadcasts**
>
> The HTML files used for presentation broadcasts are located in the Program Files\Microsoft Office\Office\Broadcast folder. You can customize the HTML code in these files by using an HTML editor such as Microsoft FrontPage, or you can replace image files in this folder with your own images.
>
> For example, you can replace Nsnbg.gif to change the background displayed during presentation broadcasts, or you can replace Ns_logo.gif to add your own corporate logo. When you customize these files, save the original files in case you need to revert back to them.

See also

- You can set the installation state of the Presentation Broadcasting feature to be installed the first time a user activates the feature. For more information, see "Intelligent Installation—Office 2000 Setup Improvements" on page 74.

Using NetShow Services with Presentation Broadcasting

When you use Presentation Broadcasting to broadcast a Microsoft PowerPoint presentation to more than 15 viewers, you must also use Windows NT Server NetShow Services. NetShow Services consists of services that run on Microsoft Windows NT 4.0 with Service Pack 3 or later and Windows 2000. NetShow Services distributes streaming audio and video content that can be displayed on client computers by using Windows Media Player.

Presentation Broadcasting includes the Online Broadcasting Service, which must be installed on your NetShow server before it can be used for Presentation Broadcasts. The Online Broadcasting Service is not included on the Office Resource Kit CD-ROM, but is available as a self-extracting executable file from the Office Resource Kit Web site at http://www.microsoft.com/office/ork/.

To install the Online Broadcasting Service, run the executable file and follow the instructions on your screen. Configure the NetShow server, and then add users to the NetShow Administrators group by using User Manager.

Note   When you install NetShow Services on Windows NT 4.0, a local Windows NT group named NetShow Administrators is created. Accounts that are members of this group are permitted to administer NetShow functions.

System requirements for NetShow Services

You can use the Presentation Broadcasting feature with either Windows NT Server NetShow Services version 3.0 or 4.0, but you can use Presentation Broadcasting only with NetShow Encoder 3.0. NetShow Services 4.0 fully supports NetShow Encoder 3.0.

The following table identifies the recommended hardware for NetShow Services.

Component	Requirements
Processor	100 MHz (or faster) Intel Pentium
Free hard disk space	21 MB
RAM	64 MB

To run NetShow Services, you must have the following software installed on your server:

- Windows NT Server 4.0 with Service Pack 3, or Windows 2000 or later
- Microsoft Internet Explorer 4.01 or later
- TCP/IP protocol

When you use NetShow Services on a server running Windows NT 4.0, you must install the Online Broadcasting Service. Client computers interact with this add-in to perform presentation broadcasts.

Note Windows 2000 already includes the Online Broadcasting Service.

Using NetShow Encoder

NetShow Encoder is installed with installation of Presentation Broadcast. The Netshow encoder produces streaming audio and video from microphone and camera input of the machine and sends it either to Netshow Server over the network or to ASF file.

The following table identifies the recommended hardware for NetShow Encoder.

Component	Requirements
Processor	266 MHz (or faster) Intel Pentium II
RAM	32 MB
Audio	Creative Labs SoundBlaster 16, or a compatible sound card
Video	Video capture card that supports Video for Windows.

To run NetShow Encoder, you must have the following software on your computer:

- Windows 95/98, Windows 2000, or Windows NT Server 4.0 with Service Pack 3 with video and audio input (for audio/video broadcast) or audio input (for audio only broadcast).

NetShow Encoder encodes live or stored audio and video into an ASF stream, an ASF file, or both. NetShow Encoder can accept a live source, and it can compress the video source (live or stored) so that the resulting ASF stream or file fits within a target bandwidth.

By using NetShow Encoder, you can set the size of the display window and choose which codec to use to compress the output ASF stream. Even when you use live video and CD-quality audio as input, NetShow Encoder can create an ASF stream with a bit rate of 28.8 kilobits per second (Kbps).

What is a codec?

Codec stands for compressor/decompressor. It is an algorithm or scheme for recording digital video or audio. A codec can be used to transmit a video over the Internet; the video is compressed on the sending end, and decompressed on the receiving end. Windows NT Server NetShow Services provides a choice of codecs for NetShow Services content. Users can select a codec based on the audio or image quality, and the preferred image size.

NetShow Encoder does not deliver ASF information to clients. It delivers the ASF stream to a NetShow server that can either multicast or unicast the ASF stream over the network. If NetShow Encoder creates an ASF file, that file is saved to the directory specified during the configuration process.

NetShow Encoder must be configured before you use it to create content. The NetShow Encoder configuration contains the settings such as:

- Audio and video cards to use
- Audio and video codecs to use
- Where to send the ASF stream
- Size of the video display window
- Pixel format for video display

You can save a NetShow Encoder configuration as an ASF stream descriptor (ASD) file so that you can reuse it or, if necessary, provide the ASD file to a NetShow server. The NetShow server uses the information in the ASD file to prepare to stream the ASF information associated with that configuration. After you create a new encoder configuration or open an existing ASD file, you can start the encoder.

Running NetShow Encoder remotely

You can run NetShow Encoder remotely on a computer that is separate from the NetShow server. If you run NetShow Encoder remotely, however, you must enable remote application launching on the NetShow Encoder server so that NetShow Services can start NetShow Encoder.

▶ **To enable remote application launching on the NetShow Encoder server**

1 On the **Start** menu, click **Run**, and then type **DCOMCNFG**.

   This command runs the Distributed Component Object Model (DCOM) configuration utility.

2 Click the **Applications** tab.

3 In the **Applications** box, click **Microsoft NetShow 2.0 Real-Time Encoder Proxy**, and then click **Properties**.

4 Click the **Security** tab, click **Use Custom Launch Permissions,** and then click the middle **Edit** button.

5 In the **Access Permissions** dialog box, add the **Everyone** account, and then click **OK** until you return to the **Applications** tab.

6 In the **Applications** box, click **NetShow Real Time Encoder Callback Class**, and then click **Properties**.

7 Click the **Security** tab, click **Use Custom Access Permissions**, and then click the top **Edit** button.

8 In the **Permissions** dialog box, add the **Everyone** account, and then click **OK** in all dialog boxes to accept the changes.

If you create a custom ASD file, you must modify it to enable broadcast recording.

▶ **To modify an ASD file to enable broadcast recording**

1 Open an ASD file in a text editor, such as Notepad.

2 Locate the following line, which is created by default:

   ```
   Save Locally = 0x00000000
   ```

3 Change the line to read:

   ```
   Save Locally = 0x00000001
   ```

If you create a custom ASD file, the HTTP port specified in the ASD file must match the NetShow Encoder port specified in the registry of each client computer by using the Presentation Broadcasting feature. In an ASD file, the HTTP port is specified under the Encoder Configuration heading in the following line:

```
HTTP port = 0x00000050
```

In the registry on an Office client computer, the NetShow Encoder port is specified in the **REXPort** entry in the following subkey:

HKEY_CURRENT_USER\SOFTWARE\Microsoft\Office\9.0\PowerPoint\Broadcast

See also

- For more information about NetShow Services, or to download program files and documentation, see the Windows Media Web site at http://www.microsoft.com/windows/windowsmedia/.

Maintaining Presentation Broadcasting

A presentation broadcast on your network requires minimal ongoing maintenance. Two maintenance issues to consider are removing unnecessary files from shared broadcast folders and keeping client computer clocks synchronized with NetShow servers.

Cleaning up broadcast folders

Most Microsoft PowerPoint presentation files and streamed presentation broadcasts take a large amount of disk space. You can monitor the space these files use in the shared locations for broadcasts and archiving; and you can restrict broadcast file locations to a set of default folders so that you know which servers and folders to monitor.

For archive folders, ensure that ample disk space is available for users to archive broadcasts. Use the following usage rates to estimate the amount of disk space that users need.

Stream type and rate	Archive rate
Audio only at 28.8 kilobits per second (Kbps)	165 kilobytes (KB) per minute
Audio only at 56 Kbps	420 KB per minute
Audio and video at 100 Kbps	750 KB per minute

For example, a half-hour broadcast with audio and video takes about 22 megabytes (MB) of disk space.

Keeping client clocks synchronized with the server

The presentation broadcast lobby page has a remaining-time display that relies on the client system clock and on the scheduled start time of the broadcast. If the client system clock is not synchronized with the server clock, the remaining-time display on the lobby page is not accurate.

Typically, system clocks across a network vary by plus or minus five minutes. This error range can cause a discrepancy of up to ten minutes between a server and clients. If you do not have a solution in place to synchronize system clocks across your network, consider using the **net time** command in user logon scripts—to synchronize the server clock with client clocks when users log on.

Configuring Client Computers for Presentation Broadcasting

Most presentation broadcasts require significant disk space and network bandwidth, and you can configure client computers to limit Presentation Broadcasting use. To limit Presentation Broadcasting use you can:

- Set client computers to use default server resources.
- Restrict the types of broadcasts that users can distribute over your network.

Toolbox

To view a list of all registry entries, descriptions, and default settings for Presentation Broadcasting, see the workbook Presbrod.xls. For information about installing Presbrod.xls, see "Office Information" on page 787.

Setting default values for client computers

You can set default values in the Windows registry to maintain storage control of presentation broadcasts. The following table identifies the Presentation Broadcasting settings that you can adjust on users' computers.

Setting	Description
Presentation files location	Default file server path where Microsoft PowerPoint stores presentation files for broadcasts.
Viewing location	URL where viewers of a presentation broadcast point their Web browsers.

Setting	Description
Record	Options to enable recording by default and specify a default file server path for recorded broadcasts. If you do not set this option, PowerPoint saves the ASF file in the default presentations file folder, and you can copy the entire folder to a CD-ROM for distribution.
Chat information	Default Chat server and Chat room.
Encoder information	NetShow Encoder server name and IP port that NetShow Services connects to when reading the ASF stream. To ensure that client computers receive the entire stream, specify the time delay that NetShow Encoder waits before shutting down at the end of a broadcast.
Windows Media Player file locations	Location for media player files used during presentation broadcasts.
Test audio and video URLs	Location of Web sites that contain test audio and video used to set up a broadcast.
Help URL	Location of site where users go when they click the **Help** button during a broadcast.
E-mail address to include on broadcasts	Address added to the To line of a broadcast schedule form; can be used to send a copy of broadcast invitations to administrators whenever a broadcast is scheduled.

Tip   In Microsoft Outlook, the e-mail address is also added to the resources field of the broadcast schedule form, so you can automatically add a NetShow server account as a resource. Then, you set rules on the NetShow server account to accept or reject broadcast requests based on criteria such as how many users have scheduled the server within a specific time period. By using this method, you can automatically load-balance your NetShow server.

You can also specify the following values for client computers to control NetShow Services use, which is required when a presentation is broadcast to more than 15 viewers.

Setting	Description
NetShow server	Name of the NetShow server.
Presentation files location for NetShow server	Location from which the NetShow server picks up the presentation files for broadcast. This location can be different from the shared location specified for the broadcast. Using a different location can improve performance for broadcasts that are viewed by 1,000 users or more.

Setting	Description
Multicast IP address and port	IP address and port on which the NetShow server makes the broadcast stream available. The address and port combination must be unique on the NetShow server.
Bandwidth rates	Throughput rates for file transfers used before and during the broadcast.
Router Time to Live (TTL)	Number of routers a broadcast can travel through on your network before being terminated. Helps control network traffic and prevent router bottlenecks.
Timeout	Number of seconds that PowerPoint waits to connect to the NetShow server before timing out.
Error correction	The percentage of the streamed data that is used for error correction information. Error correction information ensures an accurate broadcast stream, but the more data you include, the more bandwidth is required.
Unicast enable	Option to allow viewing of one-to-one streamed broadcasts from the NetShow server if the network is not enabled for multicast (one-to-many) streams.
ASD location	URL for the ASD file that NetShow Encoder uses. The ASD file describes how to encode the stream.
Session delete time	Amount of time that a session remains on the NetShow server before it is deleted.
Administration URLs	URLs where required multicast files are located and log files are created.
Contact information and copyright	Contact address, e-mail address, and phone number to associate with the broadcast. Copyright notice attached to the broadcast.
About NetShow Services URL	URL where users are directed when they click **About NetShow Services** when setting up a broadcast.

System Policy Tip   You can use system policies to set default values for Presentation Broadcasting options for all users in your organization. In the System Policy Editor, set the policies available under **Microsoft PowerPoint 2000\Slide Show | Online Broadcast | Set Up and Schedule**. For more information about the System Policy Editor, see "Using the System Policy Editor" on page 296.

Restricting broadcast types

To conserve network bandwidth and resources, you can configure client computers to disable the following broadcast features.

- Audio

  When you disable the audio feature, it remains in the broadcast ASF stream but it is muted, so network bandwidth for audio is still required.

- Video

  When you disable the video feature, you substantially reduce the network bandwidth that presentation broadcasts use.

- Recording

  When you disable the recording feature, you conserve disk space and the extra processor capacity that is required to record broadcasts.

The Windows registry of each client computer stores the default values for these broadcast features.

See also

- The Office Custom Installation Wizard lets you set options on client computers during installation. You can use this feature to configure default settings for Presentation Broadcasting. For more information, see "Office Custom Installation Wizard" on page 250.

Managing Sites on Your Intranet with FrontPage

Many applications can help you create and publish specific kinds of information on the World Wide Web. However, Microsoft FrontPage 2000 helps you create and publish Web sites that include a variety of information as well as interactive features. In addition, FrontPage provides all the tools you need to manage and administer Web sites.

Creating Web Sites with FrontPage

Microsoft FrontPage 2000 provides a full range of Web authoring tools. You can use FrontPage to do any of the following tasks:

- Create Web pages
- Add dynamic graphics
- Create richly linked Web sites
- Manage and update Web sites

FrontPage also helps you create Web projects faster, because collaboration features allow more than one author to work on a Web site at the same time.

Creating professional-looking Web sites

By using FrontPage, you can create, format, and edit Web pages. The word-processor-style interface makes it easy to add, modify, rearrange, and remove page elements. As you add or modify text, images, tables, forms, and other elements, you view your pages as they appear in a Web browser.

Here's a small sampling of what you can do with FrontPage to create a Web site:

- Create and design pages quickly.

    You can use one of the built-in templates or wizards to create a Web page, or you can create your own template.

- Add and edit pictures and image maps—pictures you can click.

    You can insert pictures in almost any graphics format. FrontPage converts them into GIF or JPEG format.

- Create links easily.

    You can create links to a page within the same Web site, or you can create links to a file, an e-mail form, or another Web site.

- Apply a built-in theme.

    You can modify built-in themes or create your own. A theme is a set of unified design elements and color schemes that gives pages and navigation bars a consistent look throughout a Web site.

- Create a frames page.

    You can create a frames page with a separate, scrollable page within each frame. A frames page is divided into frames, much like how a window is divided into panes.

Collaborating with other Web authors

In many organizations, creating a Web site is a team effort. FrontPage allows team members to work on the same Web site without slowing each other down or overwriting each other's work.

For example, you can use FrontPage to do the following:

- Check in and check out pages.

  You can prevent two or more authors from modifying the same Web page at the same time.

- View the revision history for a Web page.

  You can use the revision history feature to keep a record of all the changes you make to a file.

- Customize and share themes and templates.

  You can use themes and templates to ensure a consistent look among pages of a Web site or even among different Web sites.

- Selectively disable FrontPage features that your Web browser and Web server do not support.

  You can prevent Web authors from inadvertently including nonfunctioning features.

- Customize HTML formatting.

  For example, you can specify the amount of white space between paragraphs, which helps to ensure a consistent look among Web pages.

In short, you can use FrontPage to define the environment in which Web authors work so that they produce professional-quality Web sites efficiently.

Working with other Office applications

When you install Microsoft Office 2000 Premium, FrontPage is installed with all the other applications. FrontPage supports the Microsoft Office 2000 MultiLanguage Pack, so you can install the entire package in one language and then add other languages as required.

All Office 2000 applications can save documents in HTML format and publish them to the Web. However, FrontPage provides powerful site-management capabilities that you can use on a Web site that any Office 2000 application publishes—if you install Microsoft FrontPage Server Extensions on the Web server. And Office users can save Office documents and Web pages to FrontPage-based Web sites as easily as they save files to a hard disk.

HTML is the native format of FrontPage documents, and HTML is becoming the common format for many applications. However, FrontPage is the only Office application that allows you to open an HTML document created in any other Office application, make and save changes (except to pictures created in the original application), and then reopen the file in its original application. You can also convert files from other Office applications to HTML format, edit the files in FrontPage, and then publish them to the Web.

FrontPage features are available to other Office 2000 applications, and Office 2000 application features are available to FrontPage. For example, you can include an Excel 2000 worksheet in a page that you create in FrontPage. Then you can double-click the worksheet in FrontPage to open Excel 2000 and edit the worksheet. After you finish making changes, you just quit Excel.

Effectively managing Web site content and structure

You use FrontPage to create the structure of a Web site as well as the site's individual Web pages. The links between pages, called hyperlinks, determine the structure. Often, pages are linked in a hierarchical structure that resembles an organization chart. This hierarchical structure can be many levels deep, and it can contain hundreds, or even thousands, of pages. Usually, such a complex Web site is divided into *subwebs*.

Keeping track of the links in a moderately sized Web site can be difficult, if not impossible. For example, if each page in a 20-page Web site has only one link to every other page in the site, the site has a total of 380 links. FrontPage keeps track of all the links. If a page is renamed, deleted, or moved to a different folder, FrontPage automatically updates the links to and from that page.

To help you manage Web sites even more effectively, the Reports view shows broken links and orphaned files, which are files that are not linked to any other file. The Reports view also shows new files, old files, and slow pages, which are large pages that take a long time to download.

Using Workgroup Properties to Manage Web Files

Building and maintaining a Web site often involves many people who contribute Web pages that are created in more than one Microsoft Office application. Keeping track of page status, and who is working on each page, represents a significant challenge for Web site administrators.

Microsoft FrontPage 2000 makes it easy to manage a Web project of any size because you can set one of three new workgroup properties for any Web page created in FrontPage or Microsoft Word 2000. You can set the value of the following three properties in your FrontPage or Word files:

- Assigned to
- Review status
- Category

Tracking page status and assigned author for any page

The Assigned to and Review status workgroup properties allow you to identify the status and assigned author for each page in a Web project. The Assigned to property assigns a particular person or group to a Web page. The Review status property specifies which phase the page is in.

In FrontPage and Word 2000, you can apply workgroup properties to each Web page. That way, you can keep track of the authorship and status of many of the Web pages that make up a FrontPage-based web.

▶ **To specify the Assigned to and Review status properties to a page in FrontPage**

1   On the **View** menu, click **Folders**.

2   In the right pane, right-click the file for which you want to specify workgroup properties, click **Properties**, and then click the **Workgroup** tab.

3   In the **Assigned to** box, select the name of the person to whom you want to assign the file.

4   In the **Review status** box, select the current status of the file.

Using categories to link new Web pages on the fly

In versions of Office earlier than Office 2000, a user can create a Web page by using any Office application and then save it to a FrontPage-based web. However, an administrator has to create links from an existing page in the FrontPage-based web, such as a home page, to the new page.

FrontPage 2000 dynamically generates a link from an existing page on a FrontPage-based web to a new page saved on the same web—at the moment a visitor opens the Web site in a browser.

To have FrontPage generate a link dynamically, you need to specify a value for the Category property for each page you save on a Web site. A category is a way to classify pages that contain related information. Examples of categories are Business, Expense Reports, and Goals/Objectives. In FrontPage and Word 2000, a category is a property of a page.

Here's how dynamic linking works. You select a page, perhaps a home page, on which you want links to related pages to appear dynamically. Then you specify the category of pages that you want the home page to link to. When a visitor opens the home page, FrontPage adds a link to each page that belongs to the specified category.

You can specify more than one category of pages for the home page to link to, in which case FrontPage generates a separate list of links for each category. The home page automatically links to any page you save to the Web site, providing that page belongs to a category that the home page recognizes. If you remove a page from the Web site, the home page link to the deleted page disappears automatically.

Note   Only FrontPage allows you to modify a category list.

▶ **To create a list of dynamically generated links to a specific category of pages**

1 Open the page to which you want to add links to other pages, and then switch to Page view.

2 On the **Insert** menu, point to **Component**, and then click **Categories**.

3 In the **Sort files by** box, click **Date Last Modified** to sort the list by file dates.

   −or−

   Click **Document Title** to sort the list alphabetically by title or by file name.

4 To include modification dates in the generated links, select the **Date the file was last modified** check box.

5 To include comments in the generated links, select the **Comments added to the file** check box.

See also

- You can use Word to set workgroup properties when publishing documents on a FrontPage-extended web. For more information, see "Using Office with a Web Server" on page 565.

Adding Interactive Elements to Web Pages in FrontPage

Programmers are not the only ones who can add sophisticated functionality to Web pages. Now, without knowing a shred of programming or HTML, Web authors can use FrontPage to add hit counters, search forms, interactive Web discussions, and other sophisticated functionality, including forms, hover buttons, and animations.

Inserting hover buttons, animations, and forms

Hover buttons, banner ads, page transition effects, marquees, animations, and scheduled images (pictures that are displayed for a specified period of time and then replaced) are just some of the elements that you can add to a Web page in seconds.

To add a form in FrontPage

1 Open the page that you want to insert a form into.

2 Select the location where you want to add the form.

3 On the **View** menu, click **Form**, and then select a form.

When you select the form, it is inserted into the page. After that, the form handler that is built into FrontPage takes care of how the inserted form actually operates.

Enhancing Web site performance with FrontPage Server Extensions

Microsoft FrontPage Server Extensions are the server-side components of FrontPage. The FrontPage Server Extensions are a set of three programs whose routines perform a range of useful tasks for those who administer, create, and visit *FrontPage-extended webs*.

Some of the interactive elements that you can add to FrontPage do not work by themselves. For example, hit counters, search forms, and full-text searches work only when the Web site is supported by FrontPage Server Extensions.

If you are the administrator for an intranet, you can add FrontPage Server Extensions yourself by downloading them from the Microsoft FrontPage Web site at http://www.microsoft.com/frontpage/. You can also install FrontPage Server Extensions from the FrontPage 2000 CD-ROM. FrontPage Server Extensions are automatically installed with Microsoft Windows 2000, and Office Server Extensions (OSE) in Office 2000 Standard, Office 2000 Professional, and Office 2000 Premium.

Web authors can publish to the World Wide Web if their Internet service providers (ISPs) have FrontPage Server Extensions installed on their servers. However, FrontPage Server Extensions are not required on a Web server that hosts a FrontPage-based web. Without FrontPage Server Extensions, authors can use FrontPage to publish and manage Web sites; but some features such as hit counters and search forms do not work without FrontPage Server Extensions. If you decide not to use FrontPage Server Extensions, you can turn off the interactive features that FrontPage Server Extensions support.

See also

- With OSE installed on a Web server, users are offered many collaboration features. For more information about OSE, see "Installing Office Server Extensions" on page 637.

Publishing and Maintaining Web Sites with FrontPage

Sending a Web page or an entire Web site into cyberspace has been a scary experience for some. "Where is it going?" and "What's happening to my document?" are just some of the questions Web authors ask when they publish to the Web. Now, Microsoft FrontPage not only simplifies maintaining a Web site but also takes the mystery out of Web publishing.

Adjusting the Web site for the Web server

By using FrontPage, you do not have to adjust your Web site because of the type of Web server where you are publishing your Web site. At the time you publish your Web site, FrontPage detects the Web server and then adjusts your Web site to make it compatible with that Web server. If the home page is missing a name that the Web server requires—usually either "default.htm" or "index.htm"—then FrontPage automatically modifies the name of the home page.

FrontPage has built-in support for File Transfer Protocol (FTP) that allows authors to publish on any Web server, whether or not Microsoft FrontPage Server Extensions are installed on that Web server. If the Web server has FrontPage Server Extensions installed, then FrontPage and the Web server use the Hypertext Transfer Protocol (HTTP) to transmit information between them.

Keeping hyperlinks up to date automatically

FrontPage automatically updates hyperlinks. If you move a page, rename it, or delete it, FrontPage keeps track of each folder that contains each page, as well as which pages and files a page is linked to. You can view the pages and files that are linked to a specific page in Hyperlinks view.

In addition, FrontPage updates pages directly on the Web server. That is, after you edit a page on your own computer, FrontPage makes all necessary changes to the pages that are dependent on the edited page. For example, if you change the name of a page, FrontPage immediately updates the hyperlinks to other pages, on the Web server.

Tracking the status of the publishing process

FrontPage has always made it easy to publish a Web page but FrontPage 2000 makes it easier because FrontPage 2000 provides a progress indicator. After you click the **Publish** button in the **Publish Web** dialog box, FrontPage displays the progress indicator in the middle of your screen. The progress indicator shows the names of the files, one at a time, being published to a Web site. After the last file is published, FrontPage displays the message, "Web site published successfully!" The message includes a link to the Web site.

Tools That Simplify Web Site Administration

After a Web site is published, you need to control who can view the site, who can edit the content, and who can administer the site. And, while a Web site is under construction, you need to prevent two or more authors from changing a file at the same time. Microsoft FrontPage provides several effective, and easy-to-use tools to help you administer Web sites.

Managing permissions

To help you manage access to webs on a Web server, FrontPage provides simple role-based administrative tools for setting *permissions*. For each FrontPage-extended web on a Web server, you can set permissions for users in the following three roles:

- Web site visitors

  These users have *browsing* permission to view and use a FrontPage-extended web after it has been published on a Web server.

- Authors

  These users have *authoring* permission, which is permission to open a FrontPage-extended web and modify its content.

- Administrators

- These users have *administering* permission, which is permission to add, upgrade, or remove Microsoft FrontPage Server Extensions from a FrontPage-extended web; create and delete *subwebs*; log authoring operations; set permissions for other users; and perform other administrative tasks.

FrontPage-extended web permissions are hierarchical, which means that a user with administrative permissions has authoring and browsing permissions. A user with authoring permissions has browsing permissions.

By default, the permissions you set for a web are inherited by all the subwebs below it. However, you can set unique permissions for a subweb that override the permissions it inherits from the parent web. You set permissions for a web in FrontPage by using FrontPage Server Extensions utilities, such as the command-line utility Fpsrvadm or the **Permissions** command on the **Tools** menu.

Determining the level of source control you need

The complexity of a Web project, and the number of people working on it, determine how much source control you need to manage the project effectively. When you use FrontPage, you can work with three levels of source control.

- Level 1 source control is built into FrontPage. If two users open and edit the same file at the same time, the user who saves the file first can do so as usual. However, if the other user tries to save the file, FrontPage displays a warning that the file has been modified. If the second user ignores the warning and saves the file, the changes that the first user made are overwritten. If the second user heeds the warning and does not save the file, the changes that the second user made are lost.

- Level 2 source control supports checking in and checking out the files on a Web site. When one person has a file checked out, no other person can check out or save changes to the same file.

- Level 3 source control requires you to use Microsoft Visual SourceSafe or any other configuration management application that provides both source control and version control. Visual SourceSafe is not included in Office 2000, but it provides you with the best source control. By using Visual SourceSafe, you can check in and check out files, recover previous versions of files, and much more.

Supporting sophisticated functionality

If the FrontPage Server Extensions are installed on a Web Server, Web authors can easily include sophisticated functionality in their Web sites. FrontPage Server Extensions support hit counters, full-text searches, e-mail form-handling, and other functions that an author can add to a Web site. You don't have to download, buy, or install a separate CGI-compatible program to enable each function to work. FrontPage Server Extensions work on Microsoft Windows NT and UNIX operating systems, and many popular Web servers such as Microsoft Internet Information Server (IIS), Apache, WebSite, and Netscape.

See also

- Each Office application offers unique tools for publishing documents to an intranet or the Web. For more information, see "Using Office Documents in a Web World" on page 589.

CHAPTER 13

Using Office Server Extensions

After you install Microsoft Office Server Extensions (OSE) on a Web server on your intranet, Microsoft Office 2000 users can publish documents, participate in discussions, and collaborate on team projects. OSE also offers a full set of security features and works well in environments ranging from small departments to large organizations or Internet service providers (ISPs).

In This Chapter

Installing Office Server Extensions

Microsoft Office Server Extensions (OSE) has its own Setup program and the OSE Configuration Wizard that guides you through the installation of OSE on your Web server. During installation, you can configure database, security, and e-mail server settings.

System Requirements for Office Server Extensions

Before installing Microsoft Office Server Extensions (OSE) on your Web server, make sure that you have installed the required hardware and software.

Hardware requirements

The following table identifies the minimum and recommended hardware requirements for OSE.

Component	Requirements
Processor	166 MHz Intel Pentium
	Recommended: 300 MHz or higher Intel Pentium
Free hard disk space	120 MB
RAM	64 MB

Software requirements

To run OSE, you must first install the following software on your server:

- Microsoft Windows 2000 Premium or Server edition.

  −or−

  Microsoft Windows NT Server version 4.0 with Service Pack 4 or later, or Windows NT Workstation version 4.0 with Service Pack 4 or later.

- Microsoft Internet Information Server (IIS) version 4.0 or later with the World Wide Web service installed (Windows NT Server or Windows 2000 Server).

  −or−

  Microsoft Personal Web Server (Windows NT Workstation or Windows 2000 Premium).

  Although configurations based on both IIS 4.0 and Personal Web Server are supported, only IIS 4.0 provides full support for the OSE server properties.

  Note Optionally, you can install the IIS Simple Mail Transfer Protocol (SMTP) service to use with the Web Subscriptions feature on your OSE-extended web. If you do not want to use the Web Subscriptions feature, or if you have a separate SMTP mail server, then you do not need to install the IIS SMTP service.

- Microsoft Internet Explorer version 4.01 or later.

- Microsoft Exchange Server or other SMTP mail server (optional).

  You can use the Internet Mail Service feature of Exchange Server as your SMTP mail server to support the Web Subscriptions feature. In fact, you can use any mail server that supports SMTP—including the IIS SMTP service.

Better security with the NTFS file system

OSE supports the *file allocation table* (FAT) file system, but a FAT-formatted drive provides very few security features. For better security, format a disk with the *NTFS* file system before you install OSE.

Windows NT provides a tool named Convert.exe that makes it easy for you to maintain the integrity of your data when you convert an existing volume from the FAT file system to the NTFS file system. To run the Convert.exe tool, on the **Start** menu, click **Run**, and then type the following command:

convert [*drive*] **/fs:ntfs**

Note   OSE does not support the *plug-in language features* of the Microsoft Office 2000 MultiLanguage Pack. OSE features are displayed in the installation language only. Multilanguage functionality is supported only on Microsoft Office 2000 client systems.

See also

- When you locate your OSE-extended web on a disk formatted with the NTFS file system, you can increase security on the server significantly. For more information about OSE security configurations, see "Securing Your OSE-extended Web" on page 664.

- You can use the Convert.exe tool to convert your existing FAT-formatted drive to NTFS file system. For more information about using the Convert.exe tool, see the *Microsoft Windows NT Server 4.0 Resource Kit*.

- You can use a SQL Server to support your OSE-extended web. For more information about Microsoft SQL Server, see the Microsoft SQL Server Web site at http://www.microsoft.com/sql/.

- For more information about the NTFS file system, search for **NTFS file attributes** on the Microsoft Web site at http://www.microsoft.com/.

How to Install Office Server Extensions

Microsoft Office Server Extensions (OSE) Setup is a separate application from Office 2000 Setup. If you have Microsoft Office 2000 Professional, the OSE Setup application is named Setupse.exe, and it is located in the root folder on Microsoft Office 2000 Disc 1. If you have Office 2000 Premium, the OSE Setup application is named Setupse.exe, and it is located in the root folder on Microsoft Office 2000 Disc 3. Like Office 2000 Setup, OSE Setup uses Windows installer technology.

If you have Office 2000 Premium, you can start OSE Setup by clicking **Install Microsoft Office Server Extensions** on the **Microsoft Office 2000** panel that appears when you insert Office Disc 3. If you have Office 2000 Professional, run Setupse.exe, which is located in the root folder on Office Disc 1.

Specify installation location

After entering your name and organization, and then accepting the licensing agreement, you specify the folder where OSE Setup installs OSE files. The default location is C:\Program Files\Microsoft Office.

OSE Setup installs the following items on your server:

- OSE Start Page and supporting content
- OSE Administration Home page and supporting content
- Microsoft FrontPage 2000 Server Extensions
- Microsoft Data Engine (MSDE)
- OSE files

Note   OSE also runs with Microsoft SQL Server version 6.5 or later, instead of MSDE. However, you cannot use MSDE if you have any version of Microsoft SQL Server installed on the local computer. If you have Microsoft SQL Server installed on your computer, and you wish to instead use MSDE, you must remove SQL Server before installing MSDE.

Install OSE files

When you click **Install Now**, OSE Setup copies the OSE files to your hard disk. If Setup detects any version of SQL Server installed on the local computer, OSE Setup does not install MSDE.

After OSE Setup, you must complete the OSE Configuration Wizard to configure the settings for OSE. When OSE Setup is completed, it starts the wizard. It is recommended that you complete the wizard immediately after OSE Setup because you cannot use OSE features until you complete the wizard. However, you can exit the wizard and complete it at a later time. Until OSE is fully configured, the wizard automatically runs every time you log on to your Web server interactively.

Use SQL Server with OSE

OSE can use MSDE or SQL Server to store Web Discussions and Web Subscriptions data. MSDE is included with OSE. If you want to use SQL Server, you must install it separately.

Using an existing SQL Server has the following advantages:

- OSE data can be administered along with data in other databases on your SQL Server. No new administration processes are needed.

- OSE data is protected by the backup strategy that you have in place on the SQL Server.

- The SQL Server reduces the processing time and storage required on your Web server that is running OSE.

Tip   If you do not have a SQL Server available on your network, and your only storage needs are for OSE, use MSDE to simplify your administrative tasks. MSDE can be easily installed by default along with OSE.

Prevent installation of Microsoft Data Engine

If MSDE is installed on a computer, you cannot use that computer to connect to a remote SQL Server. To connect to a remote SQL Server, to save hard disk space, or to free memory and CPU time on a Web server that is running OSE, you can prevent OSE Setup from installing MSDE.

▶ **To install OSE without MSDE**

- If you have Office 2000 Premium, insert Office Disc 3, open a command prompt, change to the CD-ROM drive, and then type the following command:

  setupse.exe /nd

  −or−

  If you have Office 2000 Professional, insert Office Disc 1, open a command prompt, change to the CD-ROM drive, and then type the following command:

  setupse.exe /nd

Note   If you have Microsoft SQL Server installed on the same computer on which you are installing OSE, you do not need to follow this procedure because OSE Setup detects the local SQL Server installation and does not install MSDE.

Run OSE Setup in quiet mode

In a text file, you can specify all the information that OSE Setup needs and then run OSE Setup in quiet mode. Quiet mode does not require any user interaction to complete OSE Setup, so it is convenient when you need to configure several Web sites at one time. By using quiet mode, you can develop a standard installation configuration that you can apply to several computers, while defining the OSE Setup parameters only once.

▶ **To run OSE Setup in quiet mode**

1   If you have Office 2000 Premium, insert Office Disc 3, open a command prompt, change to the CD-ROM drive, and then type the following command:

setupse.exe /q [LOGFILE=*logfilepath***] [BINROOT=***installpath***]**

–or–

If you have Office 2000 Professional, insert Office Disc 1, open a command prompt, change to the CD-ROM drive, and then type the following command:

setupse.exe /q [LOGFILE=*logfilepath***] [BINROOT=***installpath***]**

where *logfilepath* is the folder path to the log file containing installation settings, and *installpath* is the folder path where OSE files are installed.

Note   If you do not specify the **LOGFILE** switch, OSE Setup defaults to the Cfgquiet.ini file on the CD-ROM in the PFiles\MSOffice\Office folder. If you do not specify the **BINROOT** switch, OSE files are installed to the Windows NT disk in the C:\Program Files\Microsoft Office folder.

2   To confirm that OSE Setup is completed, run Task Manager, and then on the **Processes** tab, check for Setupse.exe.

3   Restart the computer.

The log file you use when running OSE Setup in quiet mode is a text file with sections that contain entries and values. The log file included on the CD establishes default settings for OSE, and you can copy the file to a writeable location and modify it to meet your needs. To create the log file, start with the Cfgquiet.ini file that is included with OSE, and modify the file with a text editor such as Notepad.

Cfgquiet.ini is located in the PFiles\MSOffice\Office folder on:

- Office Disc 1 in Office 2000 Professional
- Office Disc 3 in Office 2000 Premium

If you have already installed Office 2000, Cfgquiet.ini is located in the C:\Program Files\Microsoft Office\Office folder.

Toolbox

As a starting template to use when creating your log file, you can use Cfgquiet.ini, which is a fully commented example of a quiet mode log file. For information about installing Cfgquiet.ini, see "Office Information" on page 787.

See also

- OSE Administrator is a set of Web-based forms that you can use to administer OSE-extended webs. For more information about OSE Administrator, see "Maintaining Office Server Extensions" on page 653.

Configuring Office Server Extensions

After you run Microsoft Office Server Extensions (OSE) Setup, the OSE Configuration Wizard completes the configuration of your *OSE-extended web*. The wizard is started automatically when OSE Setup is completed. The wizard creates a *virtual directory* named MSOffice on your Web site, and when the wizard is completed, the OSE-extended web is ready for Office 2000 users to publish and collaborate.

OSE works with Microsoft FrontPage 2000 Server Extensions. OSE Setup installs FrontPage Server Extensions automatically, and the OSE Configuration Wizard completes the configuration. If you install the stand-alone FrontPage Server Extensions, you use the same wizard. However, with OSE, the wizard includes some additional panels to configure elements unique to OSE.

Although you must specify settings in the wizard before you run OSE for the first time, you can modify many of the settings later by using the OSE Administration Home page.

Modifying OSE settings

Although you can modify many OSE settings through the OSE Administration home page, you need to use other utilities to make certain types of modifications.

Changing SQL Server passwords   Administration pages cannot change SQL Server passwords—you must do this through SQL Server. For MSDE, you can use the OSE Configuration Wizard to change a password the first time you run MSDE.

Creating a new database   Administration pages cannot create a new database; they can only accept a database that has already been created. You can use the OSE Configuration Wizard to create a database in SQL Server 7.0 or in MSDE.

Creating Windows NT user groups   You can use the OSE Configuration Wizard to create Windows NT user groups, but you cannot create groups with the Administration pages. Outside of the Configuration Wizard, you must use the Windows NT User Manager to create or modify user groups.

Setting the IIS Directory Browsing flag   You can use the OSE Configuration Wizard to turn on the IIS Directory Browsing flag if it is off. Administration pages cannot reset this option. The flag can also be set by using the IIS Internet Service Manager.

Enabling Basic authentication and Allow Anonymous   The OSE Configuration Wizard can be used to turn on or turn off Basic *authentication* and Allow Anonymous on the MSOffice directory. Administration pages cannot reset these options. The setting can also be controlled by using IIS Internet Service Manager.

Setting collaboration access   By default, the OSE Configuration Wizard gives everyone collaboration access. Alternatively, you can use the wizard to limit access to specific Windows NT user groups. Collaboration access cannot be controlled by Administration pages. You can also use Windows NT or Windows 2000 to manually set or remove an *access control list.*

Storing collaboration information

Publishing, collaboration, and subscription data are stored in the Web collaboration database that is separate from your Web site content. You must set up a separate Web collaboration database for each OSE server that you deploy, because multiple OSE servers cannot successfully share the same collaboration database.

If you are using the Microsoft Data Engine (MSDE), the OSE Configuration Wizard automatically creates the Web collaboration database. The wizard also creates a System Administrator account for the database, using a password you specify. You must log on to the Web collaboration database as Administrator to create or grant access to user accounts.

If you are using a local installation of Microsoft SQL Server version 7.0, the OSE Configuration Wizard attempts to create the database and tables with the user name and password you specify. If you don't have appropriate *permissions* to create a new database, this step fails. You must then obtain the correct permissions before proceeding. After successfully creating the database, you must log on as Administrator to create or grant access to user accounts.

If you are using a remote SQL Server with your OSE-extended web, you must create a database on the SQL Server and then give a user account access to that database. When you run the wizard, you specify the name of the SQL database that you create, and the user account name and password.

Note   If you are using a local installation of SQL Server 6.5 or a remote SQL Server, you must use SQL Server administration tools to create a Web collaboration database on that server, and then you give a user account access to it.

On the **Web Collaboration Database** panel of the OSE Configuration Wizard, specify the information you need to gain access to the database:

- For MSDE databases, you need only specify the password.
- For Microsoft SQL Server databases, you must specify the name of the database, the user name, and the password. Note that Windows NT Authentication Security is not supported when communicating from the OSE Configuration Wizard to SQL Server.

In all cases, the default database name is *server*_Collab, where *server* is the name of your Web site. The default user name is the user name of the Microsoft Windows NT account currently logged on to the computer.

Managing user permissions and access to data

When you install an OSE-extended web on your network, you need to consider the security of the data that is published on the server in two primary areas:

- Who has permission to connect to the OSE-extended web through a Web browser?
- Which files on the OSE-extended web can authenticated users access?

Authenticating users who connect to the Web server

Internet Service Manager allows you to configure authentication for users who connect to your Web server. When you identify the users who you want to log on to your OSE-extended web, you have several authentication methods to choose from including *anonymous access*, which allows users to log on without providing any user name or password.

Controlling access to content on the Web server

When users are authenticated, they have access to the content in all files and folders on the Web site to which they are connected. To limit this access, your OSE-extended web must be located on a disk formatted with the *NTFS* file system. If the disk is formatted with the *file allocation table* (FAT) file system, you cannot enforce permissions at the folder and file levels.

When your Web site is located on an NTFS-formatted disk, the wizard can create four local Windows NT or Windows 2000 groups to make it easy to add administrators, authors, browsers, and collaborators. To have the wizard create the groups, on the **Create Windows Groups** panel, select **Create local machine Groups**. The wizard creates the following four user groups:

- *group_prefix* Admins
- *group_prefix* Authors
- *group_prefix* Browsers
- *group_prefix* Collaborators

where *group_prefix* is a prefix that you specify on the **Create Windows Groups** panel in the wizard. If you do not specify a prefix, the wizard default prefix is the text name of the Web site you are configuring.

The wizard adds these groups to the access control lists (ACLs) of the appropriate folders. This arrangement simplifies subsequent administration of permissions because you can add or remove user accounts from these groups when you want to grant or deny users permissions on your OSE-extended web—without modifying ACLs manually.

On the **Access Control** panel of the wizard, you enter the name of a Windows NT user account or group to which the wizard gives administrative permissions on the Web site. Also on the **Access Control** panel, select which users can participate in Web Discussions and create Web Subscriptions from the drop-down list in the middle of the panel. The user accounts or groups that you select determine how the wizard configures authentication on the MSOffice virtual directory it creates.

If you have users running Web browsers other than Microsoft Internet Explorer version 4.0 or later, you must select the **Allow Basic Authentication logins for Collaboration** check box. Basic authentication and anonymous access are the only authentication methods that you can use with Web browsers other than the more recent versions of Microsoft Internet Explorer.

If you want to allow users to browse the folders of your Web site by using the OSE Start Page, on the **Access Control** panel of the wizard, select the **Enable Directory Browsing on this web site** check box.

Specifying an SMTP mail server for Web Subscriptions

OSE maintains the user subscriptions in the Web collaboration database. When a user adds, modifies, deletes, or discusses a published document, OSE queues e-mail notifications for delivery to any corresponding subscriptions in the database. At the interval specified in each subscription, OSE submits the e-mail notification to a Simple Mail Transfer Protocol (SMTP) server.

On the **Mail Server** panel of the OSE Configuration Wizard, you specify the name of the mail server, the sender address, and the optional contact address to use in e-mail notifications. The sender address appears in the notification as the source of the e-mail notification. The optional contact address appears in the text of the e-mail notification and instructs users where to send questions about OSE or their subscriptions.

Note   OSE e-mail notifications must originate from an SMTP mail server. Both Windows 2000, and the Windows NT 4.0 Option Pack include an SMTP mail server. You can also use a Microsoft Exchange Server with the Internet Mail Service installed.

Configuring new Web sites on Internet Information Server

When you run only one Web site on your Web server, you need to run the OSE Configuration Wizard only once. You can perform all subsequent administration from the OSE Administration Home page and the Microsoft Internet Information Server (IIS) Internet Service Manager.

Note   The ability to have multiple Web sites is a feature of IIS for Windows NT Server. Personal Web Server for Windows NT Workstation supports only a single Web site.

If you add additional Web sites on your Web server, you must run the OSE Configuration Wizard for each new Web site.

▶ **To run the OSE Configuration Wizard for additional Web sites**

1   In the left pane of Internet Service Manager, select the new Web site.

2   On the **Action** menu, point to **Task**, and then click **Configure Server Extensions**.

Configuring multiple Web sites

By using IIS, a single computer can host multiple Web sites. Multiple Web sites on a single computer are also known as Web sites, webs, and multiple identities.

Each IIS Web site has a unique IP address and port combination. You can configure independent authentication methods, logging methods, and operator lists on each Web site. IIS Setup creates a default Web site with the description Default Web Site. Default Web Site is accessible through all local IP addresses on the computer, on port 80.

Typically, you do not need additional Web sites. However, in a complex Web server deployment there might be administrative or security needs that require creating multiple Web sites with Internet Service Manager.

If you have multiple Web sites on your Web server, the OSE Configuration Wizard prompts you with a list of all the Web sites that you have not configured with the wizard. Each time you run the wizard, you can configure one Web site. If you extend a server from the Internet Service Manager, you do not see a list of unextended Web sites—only the server you have selected is extended. The list of extended sites is displayed only during Setup.

Note that the OSE Configuration Wizard can only install OSE features on Web sites that use port 80. If you extend a Web site on another port, the wizard extends the Web site with FrontPage Server Extensions, but without OSE features.

See also

- Internet Service Manager is a utility included with IIS and Personal Web Server that allows you to configure the Web sites your server supports. For information about Internet Service Manager, see the online product documentation installed with the Windows NT Option Pack.

- You can use the OSE Administration Home page locally or remotely from a Web browser to adjust OSE settings. For more information, see "Using the Office Server Extensions Start Page" on page 573.

- There are several methods of applying security to your OSE-extended web. For more information about OSE security, see "How to Configure Security on Your OSE-extended Web" on page 678.

- The OSE Configuration Wizard automatically upgrades FrontPage 98 Server Extensions. For more information see, "Upgrading to FrontPage 2000" on page 491.

Office Server Extension Installation Scenarios

You have many choices for customization when you install Microsoft Office Server Extensions (OSE) on your Web server. Depending on your environment and user requirements, there are three general scenarios for OSE installation:

- Standard workgroup installation
- Secure workgroup installation
- Centrally managed installation

Standard workgroup installation

This scenario applies to you when:

- You do not have a SQL Server to use with OSE.
- You want users with access to your intranet to use the Web Discussions and Web Subscriptions features on your *OSE-extended web*.
- You want only specific users to add content to your Web server.
- You want Netscape Navigator users to use the Web Discussions and Web Subscriptions features.
- You want users to browse Web folder contents by using the OSE Home Page.
- You want users to create Web Subscriptions for entire folders.
- You want users to create Web Discussions for documents published on other Web sites—that is, Web sites other than your OSE-extended web.

When you configure OSE for a standard workgroup installation, do the following:

- In the OSE Configuration Wizard, accept the defaults on the **Create Windows Groups** and **Access** Control panels. Then, if you want users to gain access to collaboration features anonymously, on the **Access Control** panel, select **All users, including those without Windows accounts**, select **Allow Basic Authentication logins for Collaboration**, and then select **Enable Directory Browsing on this web site**.
- Use the User Manager application to:

    Add users to the Admins group that the wizard creates. By default, users in the local computer Administrators group have administrative access to the Web site.

    Add users to the Authors group that the wizard creates. By default, the Authors group does not have members.

- Use Microsoft FrontPage 2000 to modify permissions on the Web site.

Secure workgroup installation

This scenario applies to you when:

- You want to restrict access to Web Discussions, Web Subscriptions, and publishing documents on your Web site.

- You want to secure password transmissions.

- You do not want users to browse Web folder contents using the OSE Home Page.

- You do not want users to create Web Subscriptions to entire folders.

- You do not want users to create Web Discussions for documents published on Web sites other than your OSE-extended web.

When you configure OSE for a secure workgroup installation, do the following:

- In the OSE Configuration Wizard, accept the defaults on the **Create Windows Groups** panel. On the **Access Control** panel, select **Members of the** <*group_prefix*> **Groups** from the list, and then clear the **Allow Basic Authentication logins for Collaboration** and **Enable Directory Browsing on this web site** check boxes

- Click the **Start** button, point to **Programs**, point to **Microsoft Office Server Extensions**, click **OSE Administrator (HTML)** to open the OSE Administration Home Page, click **Configure Web Subscription Settings**, under **Allow Web Subscriptions to,** select **Documents only**, and then click **Submit**.

- Return to the OSE Administration Home Page, click **Configure Web Discussion Settings**, under **Allow Web Discussions on,** select **Documents located on this server only**, and then click **Submit**.

- Use the User Manager application to do the following:

  Add users to the Admins group that the wizard creates. By default, users in the local computer Administrators group have administrative access to the Web site.

  Add users to the Authors group that the wizard creates. By default, the Authors group does not have members.

  Add users to the collaborators group that the wizard creates. By default, the Collaborators group does not have members. Members of the Collaborators group can participate in Web Discussions and create Web Subscriptions.

- SQL Server user names and passwords that OSE uses are stored in the Microsoft Windows NT registry, in a log file named Owsconf.log. To provide increased security for user names and passwords, you must restrict remote registry access, and set the access control list (of the Owsconf.log file, which is located in C:\Winnt) to allow only the Administrators group and System account access.

Centrally managed installation

This scenario applies to you when:

- You want multiple Web sites on the Web server.

- You want your collaboration databases stored on Microsoft SQL Server version 6.5 or later computers.

When you configure OSE for a centrally managed installation, do the following:

- For SQL Server 6.5 on the local computer, or a remote SQL Server, you must create a database for each Web site that you are extending with OSE. You must also give a user account full access to each database and then provide the OSE Configuration Wizard with the user account and password.

  For SQL Server 7.0 on the local computer, the OSE Configuration Wizard creates the database automatically, but you need to give a user account full access to the database that the wizard creates. When there is both a remote SQL Server 7.0, and a SQL Server 7.0 on the local computer, the user must have database creation rights in the master database, even if the database already exists.

  Whenever users have database creation rights, they automatically have access to the OSE database.

- Run OSE Setup with the **/nd** switch to suppress installation of Microsoft Data Engine (MSDE).

- OSE Setup starts the OSE Configuration Wizard automatically, but you can configure only a single Web site each time that you run the wizard. You must run the wizard for each Web site you want to configure.

▶ To run the OSE Configuration Wizard

1   To start Microsoft Management Console with the OSE snap-in, click the **Start** button, point to **Programs**, point to **Microsoft Office Server Extensions**, and then click **Server Extensions Administrator**.

2   In the left pane, select the Web site that you want to extend with OSE.

3   On the **Action** menu, point to **Task**, and then click **Configure Server Extensions**.

Maintaining Office Server Extensions

An OSE-extended web is a Web site with Microsoft Office Server Extensions (OSE) installed. Web-based forms make the administration of your OSE-extended Web simple. You can access the Web-based forms locally or remotely from the Web server that is running OSE.

Managing Web Discussions on an OSE-extended Web

The Microsoft Office Server Extensions (OSE) Administration Home Page has several options to help you manage the Web Discussions feature on your *OSE-extended web*. When managing the Web Discussions feature, you can:

- Limit discussions to only documents on the OSE-extended web.

  With OSE, users can create discussions on any local server Web page that contains an Office, Rich Text Format (RTF), or HTML file. Users can also create discussions in files located on remote servers. However, you can limit discussions to the local server to prevent the database from becoming too large.

- Enable automatic deletion of discussion items.

  With OSE, discussions remain in the database permanently unless you delete them manually or enable the automatic deletion feature. You can specify a maximum length of time for a discussion item to remain in the database. When the discussion item surpasses that maximum length of time, it is automatically deleted from the database that the OSE-extended web uses.

- Delete all discussion items or selected discussion items in a particular document.

  With OSE, you can view the list of files being discussed, select a file, select one or all discussion items, and then delete the discussion or discussions from the database. Managing discussion items selectively helps you keep disk space available, and moderate discussions when necessary.

- Disable the Web Discussions feature.

  With OSE, you can disable the Web Discussions feature when you want to offer the Web Discussions feature to your users at a later time or if your Web server has limited disk space, memory, or processor speed.

How to Configure Web Discussions on an OSE-extended Web

The Configure Web Discussion Settings page has several options for you to specify a variety of settings for Web Discussions. You access the Configure Web Discussion Settings page from the Microsoft Office Server Extensions (OSE) Administration Home Page.

▶ **To open the Configure Web Discussion Settings page**

1   If you are logged on locally to the Web server with OSE installed, click **Start**, point to **Programs**, then point to **Microsoft Office Server Extensions**, and then click **OSE Administrator (HTML)**.

    −or−

    If you are connecting remotely to the Web server with OSE installed, enter the following URL in your Web browser:

    http://_site_name_**/msoffice/msoadmin/**

    where _site_name_ is the name of the OSE-extended web.

    When you are connected to the OSE Administration Home Page, you see the name of the server you are connected to at the bottom of the configuration and management pages.

    Note   You can view the OSE Administration Home Page only with Microsoft Internet Explorer 4.0 or later, or Netscape Navigator 3.0 or later.

2   Click **Configure Web Discussion Settings**.

Enable or disable Web Discussions

On the Configure Web Discussion Settings page, you can enable or disable the Web Discussions feature. You can also disable Web Discussions on documents that are not located on the OSE-extended web.

▶ **To enable or disable Web Discussions**

1   Next to **Web Discussions are,** click **On** to enable Web Discussions.

    −or−

    Click **Off** to disable Web Discussions.

2   Click **Submit**.

▶ **To enable or disable Web Discussions on remote documents**

1 Next to **Allow Web Discussions on**, click **Documents located on this server only**

   –or–

   Click **Documents located anywhere on the Web**.

2 Click **Submit**.

Delete discussion items

On the Manage Web Discussions page, you can view a list of all documents on which users are maintaining Web Discussions, and then you can delete specific discussion items or all of the discussion items on a document. You can also select when you want discussion items automatically deleted. For example, you might specify that all items older than 15 days should be deleted from a document. When deleting discussion items, note that top-level items continue to exist until all their component items are deleted.

▶ **To delete a specific discussion item in a document**

1 On the OSE Administration Home Page, click **Manage Web Discussions**.

2 Select the document in the list box, and then click **View** to open the document in your Web browser.

3 Point to **Explorer Bar** in the **View** menu, and then click **Discuss** to view the discussion items in that document.

4 Click the **Action** button at the end of the discussion item you want to delete, and then click **Delete**.

▶ **To delete all discussion items in a document**

1 On the OSE Administration Home Page, click **Manage Web Discussions**.

2 To delete all discussion items for a document, select the document, and then click **Delete**.

▶ **To configure automatic deletion of discussion items**

1 On the OSE Administration Home Page, click **Configure Web Discussion Settings**.

2 Select the **Enable automatic deletion of Web Discussion items** checkbox.

3 In the **Delete Web Discussion Items after** text box, type a number for the quantity of time.

4 In the drop-down list, select **day(s)**, **week(s)**, **month(s)**, or **year(s)**.

5 Click **Submit**.

Managing Web Subscriptions on an OSE-extended Web

On your *OSE-extended web*, you have several options to help you manage the Web Subscriptions feature. A user who subscribes to a file chooses to receive an e-mail notification when a file changes or when a discussion is added or deleted. You can view the details of each subscription; and you can filter the view of all active Web Subscriptions, delete specific Web Subscriptions, enable and disable the Web Subscriptions feature, and specify the time of day that you want the change notices sent to subscribers.

When you view the details of an active Web Subscription on your OSE-extended web, you see the following elements:

- Microsoft Windows NT account name of the subscriber
- URL of the folder or document subscribed to
- Event that triggers e-mail notification
- E-mail address where notifications are sent

When you filter your view of Web Subscriptions, you can analyze how users are using the Web Subscriptions feature. You can even select individual Web Subscriptions to delete. You have several options for deleting individual Web Subscriptions. You can delete a subscription by using the Windows NT account name of the subscriber, the URL of the folder or document subscribed to, or the e-mail address where notifications are sent.

When you enable Web Subscriptions, you can set the frequency that users receive e-mail notifications. When users create a subscription, they choose to receive updates **When a change occurs**, **Once a day**, or **Once a week**. You define these intervals more precisely on the OSE-extended web where they correspond to the **Immediate**, **Daily**, and **Weekly** intervals, respectively.

Consider changing the frequency for **Immediate** notifications under the following circumstances:

- Users are configuring a large number of subscriptions.
- The documents or discussions on your OSE-extended web change frequently.
- You don't want to overburden your Web server or Simple Mail Transfer Protocol (SMTP) mail server with many e-mail notifications.

Consider disabling Web Subscriptions under the following circumstances:

- You do not have an SMTP mail server that can generate the e-mail notifications.
- You do not want to burden your mail server with automatic e-mail notifications.
- You do not want to offer Web Subscriptions to users.

Tip If users do not need updates during the workday, you can schedule the e-mail notification for **Daily** and **Weekly** intervals at off-peak hours. This setting reduces traffic on your Web server, SMTP mail server, and network.

How to Configure Web Subscriptions on an OSE-extended Web

On the Configure Web Subscription Settings page, you have several options to configure user subscriptions. The Configure Web Subscription Settings page is accessible from the Microsoft Office Server Extensions (OSE) Administration Home Page.

▶ **To open the Web Subscription Settings page**

1   If you are logged on locally to the Web server with OSE installed, click **Start**, point to **Programs**, point to **Microsoft Office Server Extensions**, and then click **OSE Administrator (HTML)**.

–or–

If you are connecting remotely to the Web server with OSE installed, enter the following URL in your Web browser:

http://_site_name_**/msoffice/msoadmin/**

where _site_name_ is the name of the OSE-extended web.

When you are connected to the OSE Administrator Home Page, you see the name of the server you are connected to at the bottom of the configuration and management pages.

2   Click **Configure Web Subscription Settings**.

Note The OSE Administration Home Page can be viewed only with Microsoft Internet Explorer version 4.0 or later, or Netscape Navigator version 3.0 or later.

Enable or disable Web Subscriptions

On the Configure Web Subscription Settings page, you can enable or disable all Web Subscriptions.

▶ **To enable or disable Web Subscriptions**

1   Next to **Web Subscriptions are,** click **On** to enable Web Subscriptions.

–or–

Click **Off** to disable Web Subscriptions.

2   Click **Submit**.

Note If you disable Web Subscriptions, any changes you make to other Web Subscriptions settings are not saved when you click **Submit**.

Specify the SMTP mail server

When you enter the name of your Simple Mail Transfer Protocol (SMTP) mail server on the Configure Web Subscription Settings page, use the fully qualified domain name (FQDN). If you are using WINS on your network, you can also enter the computer name without the leading double backslashes (\\).

Correct	Incorrect
Mail.company.com	company.com
SMTP1	\\SMTP1

▶ **To specify an SMTP mail server**

1   In the **SMTP Mail Server** box, type the name of the mail server.

2   Click **Submit.**

Define intervals for e-mail notifications

Subscribers choose to receive e-mail notifications when documents change. They also select when they want to receive the e-mail notifications. Subscribers can receive e-mail notifications at one of the following time intervals:

- **When a change occurs**
- **Once a day**
- **Once a week**

On the Configure Web Subscription Settings page, you define the details of the time intervals for sending e-mail notifications.

▶ **To define the details of e-mail notification intervals**

1   Scroll to the **Times to Send Document Change Notifications** section of the Configure Web Subscription Settings page.

2   In the **Immediate notifications every** x **minutes** box, enter a value for x.

3   In the **Daily notifications at** box, enter a time of day.

4   In the **Weekly notifications on** box, enter a day of the week, and time of day.

5   Click **Submit.**

Note   The Office Server Extensions Notification Service caches the notification times. When you click **Submit**, the service automatically stops and then restarts so that the new times are read. The service might be unable to stop if it is busy processing notification records. In this case, try to stop and restart the service manually by using **Services** in Control Panel.

Monitor Web Subscriptions

In addition to specifying settings, you can also monitor all the subscriptions on your OSE-extended web from the OSE Administration Home Page.

▶ **To view and modify Web Subscriptions**

1   If you are logged on locally to the Web server with OSE installed, click **Start**, point to **Programs**, then point to **Microsoft Office Server Extensions**, and then click **OSE Administrator (HTML)**.

   −or−

   If you are connecting remotely to the Web server with OSE installed, enter the following URL in your Web browser:

   http://*site_name*/msoffice/msoadmin/

   where *site_name* is the name of the OSE-extended web.

   When you are connected to the OSE Administration Home Page, you see the name of the server you are connected to at the bottom of the configuration and management pages.

2   To view the list of Web Subscriptions, click **Manage Web Subscriptions**.

3   To sort the list in ascending order, click the column heading of the list you want to sort; and then click to sort the list in descending order.

4   To filter the list, click **Web Subscriptions where**, select **User, URL, or E-mail**, then specify a value, and then click **Update** to update the list with the filter applied.

5   To delete one subscription, select the subscription, and then click **Delete**.

   −or−

   To delete all the subscriptions in the filtered view, click **Delete All**.

Note   Subscribers are not notified automatically when you delete subscriptions. If you want subscribers to know when you delete their subscriptions, you must notify them.

How to Configure Database Settings on an OSE-extended Web

Each *OSE-extended web* uses a database to store Web Discussions and Web Subscriptions data. The database is configured when you run the Microsoft Office Server Extensions (OSE) Configuration Wizard, but you can reconfigure it on the Database Settings page, which you get to from the OSE Administration Home Page.

▶ **To open the Database Settings page**

1   If you are logged on locally to the Web server with OSE installed, click **Start**, point to **Programs**, point to **Microsoft Office Server Extensions**, and then click **OSE Administrator (HTML)**.

–or–

If you are connecting remotely to the Web server with OSE installed, enter the following URL in your Web browser:

http://*site_name*/msoffice/msoadmin/

where *site_name* is the name of the OSE-extended web.

When you are connected to the OSE Administration Home Page, you see the name of the server you are connected to at the bottom of the configuration and management pages.

2   Click **Database Settings**.

Note   The OSE Administration Home Page can be viewed only with Microsoft Internet Explorer 4.0 or later or Netscape Navigator 3.0 or later.

Verify the integrity of your Web site database

On the Database Settings page, you can verify the integrity of your Web site's database. The verification checks to see that the tables needed by OSE exist in the database.

▶ **To verify database integrity**

1   Open the Database Settings page.

2   Click **Verify Database Integrity**.

3   Click **Submit**.

Change the database in which you store OSE data

OSE can use the Microsoft Data Engine (MSDE) database included with OSE, or a local or remote Microsoft SQL Server to store Web Discussions or Web Subscriptions data. Each OSE-extended web can use a different database. Initially, you configure which database to use when you run the OSE Configuration Wizard.

▶ To change the OSE database

1   On the Database Settings page, specify the name of the SQL Server and the database you want to use.

2   In the **User Id** and **Password** boxes, specify a user ID and password.

OSE requires a user ID and password to connect to the database. You must configure the database by using the SQL Server Administration program to give access to the user ID and password you specify.

3   Click **Submit**.

Backing Up and Restoring Microsoft Data Engine Databases

Microsoft Office Server Extensions (OSE) includes a command-line utility named Osql.exe that can be used to back up and restore a Microsoft Data Engine (MSDE) database on a disk or tape.

▶ To back up an MSDE database

1   At a command prompt on the Web server with OSE installed, type the following and press ENTER.

osql –Usa –P*password*

where *password* is either the password you specified in the OSE Configuration Wizard when you extended your Web site with OSE or the password you specified on the Database Settings page if you changed the database that the Web site uses since the site was first extended with OSE.

Note   The switches for Osql.exe are case sensitive, and they must be entered as shown above.

2   To back up the MSDE database on a disk, at the **1>** prompt, type the following and press ENTER.

BACKUP DATABASE *database_name* **TO DISK** = *file_path*

where *database_name* is the name of the MSDE collaboration database and *file_path* is the full path to an existing folder and ends in a file name with a .dat extension.

By default, the OSE Configuration Wizard names the database *websitename*_collab, where *websitename* is the name of the Web site. Enclose *file_path* in single quotation marks (for example, **'C:\backup\mybackup.dat'**).

–or–

To back up the MSDE database on a tape device, type the following and press ENTER.

BACKUP DATABASE *database_name* **TO TAPE** = *tape_device*

where *database_name* is the name of the MSDE collaboration database and *tape_device* is the device name of your tape drive (for example, **\\.\tape0**).

By default, the OSE Configuration Wizard names the database *websitename*_collab, where *websitename* is the name of the Web site.

3   At the **2>** prompt, type **GO** and press ENTER.

▶ **To restore an MSDE database**

1 On the Web server with OSE installed, stop the Office Server Extensions Notification Service by using **Services** in Control Panel.

2 At a command prompt, type the following and press ENTER.

osql –Usa –P*password*

where *password* is either the password you specified in the OSE Configuration Wizard when you extended your Web site with OSE or the password you specified on the Database Settings page if you changed the database the Web site uses since the site was first extended with OSE.

Note The switches for Osql.exe are case sensitive, and they must be entered as shown above.

3 To restore the MSDE database from a disk, at the **1>** prompt, type the following and press ENTER.

RESTORE DATABASE *database_name* **FROM DISK =** *file_path*

where *database_name* is the name of the MSDE collaboration database and *file_path* is a full path to an existing backup file enclosed in single quotation marks (for example, **'C:\backup\mybackup.dat'**).

If a copy of the database already exists on the local machine, you can append the **WITH REPLACE** keywords to the command line to replace the existing files with the backup files.

By default, the OSE Configuration Wizard names the database *websitename*_collab, where *websitename* is the name of the Web site.

–or–

To restore the MSDE database from a tape device, type the following and press ENTER.

RESTORE DATABASE *database_name* **FROM TAPE =** *tape_device*

where *database_name* is the name of the MSDE collaboration database and *tape_device* is the device name of your tape drive (for example, **\\.\tape0**).

By default, the OSE Configuration Wizard names the database *websitename*_collab, where *websitename* is the name of the Web site.

4 At the **2>** prompt, type **GO** and press ENTER.

5 When the restoration is complete, start the Office Server Extensions Notification Service by using **Services** in Control Panel.

Administering Security with Office Server Extensions

When you set up an OSE-extended web, users have new opportunities to share information. In this environment, security is an important consideration. By using Microsoft Office Server Extensions, you have several strategies to secure data and control users' access to your OSE-extended web.

Securing Your OSE-extended Web

In addition to the direct methods of securing your *OSE-extended web*, you can:

- Prevent users from accessing confidential Web Discussions.
- Prevent Web Discussions on documents located on other Web sites.
- Control Microsoft Office Server Extensions (OSE) Directory Browsing.
- Allow users to subscribe to documents only.
- Monitor and delete inappropriate subscriptions.

Preventing access to confidential Web Discussions

To contribute to Web Discussions, users need read permission to the documents being discussed and collaboration access to the OSE-extended web that maintains the collaboration database. If you want to prevent some users from gaining access to confidential Web Discussions, you need to do the following:

- Remove the Everyone group from the *access control list* of the OSE root and Help folders (NTFS file system only).
- Remove *anonymous access* from the MSOffice *virtual directory*.
- Give collaboration access to users (NTFS file system only).

You can control access to Web Discussions when you first set up Office Server Extensions with the OSE Configuration Wizard, or you can use the following procedure to manage access manually after OSE has been installed.

▶ **To remove anonymous access from the MSOffice virtual directory**

1   On the **Start** menu, point to **Programs**, point to **Windows NT 4.0 Option Pack**, point to **Microsoft Internet Information Server**, and then click **Internet Service Manager**.

2   In the left pane, expand the OSE-extended web, and then select the **MSOffice** virtual directory.

3 On the **Action** menu, click **Properties**, and then click the **Directory Security** tab.

4 In the **Anonymous Access and Authentication Control** area, click **Edit**.

5 Clear the **Allow Anonymous Access** check box.

▶ **To remove the Everyone group from the access control list of the OSE root, and Help folders (NTFS file system only)**

1 In Windows Explorer, select the folder C:\Program Files\Microsoft Office\Office\Scripts*N\localeID*.

where *N* is the index of the OSE-extended web and *localeID* is the ID of the OSE locale (for example, the locale ID for English is 1033).

2 On the **File** menu, click **Properties**, and then click the **Security** tab.

3 Click **Permissions**.

4 In the **Directory Permissions** dialog box, remove the **Everyone** group.

5 Repeat this procedure for the C:\Program Files\Microsoft Office\Office\Scripts*N\localeID*\Help folder.

▶ **To give collaboration access to users (NTFS file system only)**

1 On the **Start** menu, point to **Programs**, point to **Administrative Tools**, and then click **User Manager for Domains**.

2 On the **User** menu, click **Select Domain**.

3 In the **Domain** box, specify the local computer name.

4 In the bottom pane of the User Manager window, select *website* **Collaborators**, where *website* is the name of the OSE-extended web.

5 On the **User** menu, click **Properties**.

6 In the **Local Group Properties** dialog box, add the users you want to give collaboration access.

Note   When you extend your Web site with OSE, you can choose to have the OSE Configuration Wizard create local Microsoft Windows NT groups. If you do not choose to have the wizard create the groups, and then you decide you want to give users collaboration access, you can add users to the access control lists (ACLs) of the OSE root and Help folders.

When you want to give specific users read permission, but restrict them from accessing Web Discussions; or when you want to give specific users access to different Web Discussions on the same documents, you need to:

• Create multiple OSE-extended webs.

• Set different security settings on each site.

You can also use the Browsers group to give users the ability to view information on the server, but to block their access to Web Discussions.

Preventing Web Discussions on documents located on other Web sites

Users with access to Web Discussions on an OSE-extended web can post discussion items about documents on your Web site, or anywhere on the Web. For policy reasons, you might want to restrict discussions to documents only on your Web site.

▶ **To prevent Web Discussions on documents located on other Web sites**

1   On the **Start** menu, point to **Programs**, point to **Microsoft Office Server Extensions**, and then click **OSE Administrator (HTML)**.

   –or–

   Type the following URL in the **Address** box of your browser:

   http://*website*/msoffice/msoadmin/

   where *website* is the name of the OSE-extended web.

2   Click **Configure Web Discussions Settings**.

3   Under **Allow Web Discussions on**, click **Documents located anywhere on the web**.

4   Click **Submit**.

Controlling browsing of OSE folders

To maintain security on your Web site, you can control OSE directory browsing. When you enable OSE directory browsing, users with the List permission on the ACL of the OSE-extended web root folder can click **Browse Web Folders** in the OSE Start Page to see the files and folders that the root folder contains. This ability is a security consideration because users can see the server folder structure, and the names and types of documents that you might not want them to see.

You can disable OSE directory browsing for the entire Web site, or for particular subfolders of the Web site. When you clear the **Directory browsing allowed** check box in the content root, you disable OSE directory browsing for the entire Web site; and when you clear the **Directory browsing allowed** check box in particular subfolders, you disable OSE directory browsing in those subfolders.

▶ **To disable OSE directory browsing for the entire Web site**

1   On the **Start** menu, point to **Programs**, point to **Windows NT 4.0 Option Pack**, point to **Microsoft Internet Information Server**, and then click **Internet Service Manager**.

2   In the left pane, click the OSE-extended web, or a subfolder of the Web site where you want to disable browsing.

3   On the **Action** menu, click **Properties**.

4   On the **Home Directory** tab, clear the **Directory browsing allowed** check box.

▶ **To allow specific users to browse specific files and folders (NTFS file system only)**

1 In Windows Explorer, select a file or folder to control browsing.

2 On the **File** menu, click **Properties**.

3 On the **Security** tab of the **Properties** dialog box, click **Permissions**.

4 To allow a user to browse the file or folder, add the user to the list in the **Directory Permissions** dialog box, and then give the user the Read permission.

–or–

To allow a user to view a file, add the user to the list in the **File Permissions** dialog box, and then give the user the Read permission.

Allowing users to subscribe to updates on documents only

The Web Subscriptions feature allows users to subscribe to a single document or to all the documents in a folder. Subscribers receive e-mail notifications when documents or discussions change. The updates include document names and the types of changes to the documents.

When users subscribe to a folder, they receive updates about all the documents in the folder—including documents that they do not have permission to view or alter. However, you can prevent users from creating subscriptions to folders, and you can limit subscriptions to documents only.

▶ **To set Web Subscriptions to documents only**

1 On the **Start** menu, point to **Programs**, point to **Microsoft Office Server Extensions**, and then click **OSE Administrator (HTML)**.

–or–

Type the following URL in the **Address** box of your browser:

http://*website***/msoffice/msoadmin/**

where *website* is the name of the OSE-extended web.

2 Click **Configure Web Subscription Settings**.

3 Next to **Allow Web Subscriptions to**, click **Documents only**.

4 At the bottom of the page, click the **Submit** button.

Monitoring and deleting inappropriate subscriptions

By using the Web Subscriptions feature, users can designate any Internet e-mail address to receive document updates. In addition, users who are no longer members of a specific workgroup might still have subscriptions to documents that are supposed to be accessible to only the current members of the workgroup. These scenarios represent possible security risks. To maintain a secure server environment, monitor and delete Web Subscriptions configurations on a regular basis.

▶ **To monitor and delete Web Subscriptions**

1   On the **Start** menu, point to **Programs**, point to **Microsoft Office Server Extensions**, and then click **OSE Administrator (HTML)**.

–or–

Type the following URL in the **Address** box of your browser:

http://*website*/msoffice/msoadmin/

where *website* is the name of the OSE-extended web.

2   Click **Manage Web Subscriptions**.

3   To delete one subscription, select the subscription, and then click **Delete**.

–or–

To delete all subscriptions, click **Delete All**.

Using Windows NT Security with Office Server Extensions

Microsoft Office Server Extensions (OSE) use the built-in security mechanisms of Microsoft Windows NT to implement security on an *OSE-extended web*. When you configure security on an OSE-extended web, you must understand the Windows NT security model. For example, if you plan to assign per-user *permissions* to documents and folders, you must understand NTFS file system *access control lists* (ACLs).

As a Windows NT administrator, you can assign a user different levels of access to system resources. A user with a Windows NT account must enter a user name and password to gain access to a file share, printer, server application, and so on. You can also define groups with multiple accounts and then assign privileges to many user accounts simultaneously.

Advantages of the NTFS file system

Microsoft Windows NT Server, Windows NT Workstation, and all versions of Windows 2000 support the NTFS file system. Microsoft Windows 95 and Windows 98 support only the *file allocation table* (FAT) and the newer FAT32 file systems to format disks.

The NTFS file system offers several advantages over the FAT and FAT32 file systems, including:

• Fault tolerance

• Optimization of available disk space

• Advanced security capabilities, including access control lists and auditing

Advanced security

The NTFS file system contains advanced security features that allow you to set permissions on a per-file and per-folder basis, which is particularly useful in a Web server environment. OSE uses the file and folder permissions feature to control administration, browsing, authoring, and collaboration on your Web site.

By using the Windows 95 and Windows 98 FAT and FAT32 file systems, you cannot set permissions on individual files or folders. Therefore, when you give a user access to a shared drive, that user can modify, rename, or delete any file or folder in the volume. As a deterrent to users who might modify a file, you can set the file to read-only, but any user can easily change that setting.

You can use OSE without the NTFS file system, but the advanced security features are not available to you until you format a disk with the NTFS file system.

Access control lists

An *access control list* (ACL) is a list of accounts and permissions associated with a file or folder.

You can give accounts the following types of access in a file ACL.

This type of access in a file ACL	Permits this access to the file
None	No access to a file.
Read (Windows NT 4.0) or **Read Data** (Windows 2000)	View data in a file.
Write (Windows NT 4.0) or **Write Data** (Windows 2000)	Change data in a file.
Execute (Windows NT 4.0) or **Execute Data** (Windows 2000)	Run a program file.
Delete	Delete a file.
Change Permissions	Change permissions on a file.
Take Ownership	Take ownership of a file. (For informational purposes, files are marked with a user account that owns the file. Owners also have all other permissions on the file.)

You can give accounts the following types of access in a folder ACL.

This type of access in a folder ACL	Permits this access to the folder
None	No access to a folder.
Read (Windows NT 4.0) or **List Folder** (Windows 2000)	View file names and subfolder names in a folder.
Write (Windows NT 4.0) or **Create Files** (Windows 2000)	Add files and subfolders to a folder.
Execute (Windows NT 4.0) or **Traverse Folder** (Windows 2000)	Change to subfolders.

This type of access in a folder ACL	Permits this access to the folder
Delete (Windows NT 4.0) or **Delete subfolders and files** (Windows 2000)	Delete subfolders.
Change Permissions	Change permissions on a folder.
Take Ownership	Take ownership of a folder. (For informational purposes, folders are marked with a user account that owns the file. Owners also have all other permissions on the folder.)

See also

- You can convert an existing FAT volume to an NTFS volume without losing data by using a tool named Convert.exe, which is included with Windows NT. For more information, see the *Microsoft Windows NT Server 4.0 Resource Kit.*

Using Internet Information Server Authentication

All users are authenticated when they attempt to gain access to the Web sites, folders, and files on your Web server. You configure the *authentication* methods available to users with Microsoft Internet Information Server (IIS) administration tools.

Types of authentication

IIS supports the following types of authentication:

- Anonymous

  Anonymous access allows users to log on to a server without having a Microsoft Windows NT account. Users do not have to enter a user name and password. All Web browsers support anonymous access.

- Basic

  Basic authentication requires all users to have a Windows NT account to log on to a server. Users must enter a user name and password. Most Web browsers support Basic authentication.

- Windows NT Challenge/Response

  By using Windows NT Challenge/Response authentication, the Web browser automatically passes on the encrypted user name and password for a Windows NT account. Users do not have to enter a user name and password when they log on to a server. Only Microsoft Internet Explorer supports Windows NT Challenge/Response authentication.

Anonymous

Anonymous access lets users who do not have Windows NT accounts connect to the server and use server resources. This type of access reduces the amount of time you spend managing accounts, and you do not have to identify the users who log on to your Web server.

During Setup, IIS creates a special anonymous account named IUSR_*computer_name* for Web services. By default, all Web client requests use this anonymous account to gain access to Web content.

When IIS receives an anonymous request to log on to a server or access a resource, it impersonates the IUSR_*computer_name* account. The request succeeds when the IUSR_*computer_name* account has permission to log on to the server, or use the requested resource. IIS stores resource access permission information in the resource *access control lists* (ACLs). When access is denied, the server prompts the user to enter a valid Windows NT user name and password.

Note   If you want to provide both restricted and unrestricted access areas on your server, you can enable both authenticated and anonymous logon methods at the same time. A user who wants to access the restricted areas of the server needs to provide a user name and password, while any user can access the areas that allow anonymous access.

Basic authentication

When you use Basic authentication, a client application such as the Web browser prompts a user for a Windows NT user name and password. Then the browser passes the user information through HTTP in encoded text for IIS to use for Basic authentication.

Basic authentication is fast, and when you use it with Secure Sockets Layer (SSL), you also have secure authentication because SSL encrypts the transmission. If you use Basic authentication without SSL, however, the user name and password are passed in clear, unencoded text, thereby compromising the security of the transmission.

With Basic authentication, a user must have the **Log On Locally** right on the IIS server. You use the Windows NT User Manager for Domains application to grant a user the **Log On Locally** right.

Note   A user who has the **Log On Locally** right can start an interactive session on the Windows NT or Windows 2000 server.

In the following situations, Basic authentication is the best option for providing access to your Web server:

- When your Web site must be accessible from Web browsers other than Internet Explorer.

- When users connect to your Web server over the Internet through a proxy server or *firewall*.

Windows NT Challenge/Response authentication

Windows NT Challenge/Response (also called NTLM) is a more secure authentication method than Basic authentication. A user is authenticated when the user first logs on to the network. When the same user then logs on to the Web server, a client application such as the Web browser uses the credentials from the network logon. If those credentials are not valid, Windows NT Challenge/Response authentication requests a valid user name and password.

Windows NT Challenge/Response authentication provides the following advantages over other types of authentication:

- Users logged on to a Windows NT domain do not need to be authenticated again to access another computer in the same Windows NT domain.

- User names and passwords are securely encrypted in transactions between clients and the Web server, which prevents network eavesdroppers from monitoring network traffic to break into the system.

Windows NT Challenge/Response authentication has the following limitations:

- Windows NT Challenge/Response authentication is designed for use on an intranet, and it does not function through a firewall or proxy server. If your network is protected by a firewall, you must use Basic authentication.

- Windows NT Challenge/Response authentication is only supported by Internet Explorer. You cannot use this type of authentication with any other Web browsers.

- Windows NT Challenge/Response authentication does not support delegation to secondary servers. For example, when a request comes in to IIS, the user credentials cannot be passed to a remote computer running Microsoft SQL Server.

Tip   You can configure IIS with both Basic authentication and Windows NT Challenge/Response authentication enabled. If a user's Web browser supports Windows NT Challenge/Response authentication, IIS uses that authentication method. Otherwise, IIS defaults to Basic authentication.

Authenticating HTTP requests

When IIS receives an HTTP request from a Web browser, a Microsoft Office 2000 application, or another client, IIS processes the request in the following sequence:

1 Tries the anonymous account, IUSR_*computer_name*.

2 Uses Basic authentication or Windows NT Challenge/Response authentication to authenticate a user.

3 Allows access to the file on the Web server. If the file is located on an NTFS volume, IIS allows access only when the authenticated account is on the ACL of the file and the folder in which the file is located.

Using IP address or domain name to restrict access

You can use an IP address or domain name to control which computers connect to your Web site. Each client computer on an intranet or the Internet has an IP address, and in IIS you can create lists of IP addresses and domain names to grant or deny access to specific computers. You can configure the access restrictions at the Web site, folder, *virtual directory*, and file levels.

Using Secure Sockets Layer

Secure Sockets Layer is a protocol that provides communications privacy, authentication, and message integrity for TCP/IP connections. By using the SSL protocol, clients and servers can communicate with almost no possibility of eavesdropping, tampering, or message forgery. SSL is typically used with Basic authentication to encrypt user name and password transmissions.

SSL ensures secure communication through a firewall, and it also provides security for remote administration of a Web server. You can specify that Office 2000 applications and Internet Explorer use SSL to open or publish documents on an *OSE-extended web*.

- In Internet Explorer version 4.0, you specify SSL use on the **Advanced** tab of the Internet Options dialog box (**View** menu).

- In Office 2000 applications, you enable SSL when you create a Web folder shortcut.

In IIS, you must install a security *certificate* to use SSL. Use the Key Manager utility included with IIS to obtain a certificate that is a collection of encoded data identifying the server.

Using authentication with delegation applications

A *delegation application* passes on part of the Web server work to a secondary server application running on a different computer. For example, a Web server acting as a delegation application can use a database server running on a different host computer.

The various types of authentication handle delegation applications differently. If you use Basic authentication, a user logs on locally, and Windows NT security allows the secondary server to honor the user credentials.

However, if you use Windows NT Challenge/Response authentication, a secondary computer does not honor user credentials. In this case, both the secondary server and Web server must be running on the same host computer.

See also

- IIS provides considerable flexibility for secure access to your Web server. For more information about authentication methods, obtaining a security certificate, or using IP addresses and domain names to restrict access, see the online Help for IIS.

Setting Permissions on Web Sites

You can configure the types of actions that users can perform after they are authenticated on your *OSE-extended web*. There are four categories of users.

Users in this category	Are allowed to
Browsers	View documents on the Web site. They cannot create or modify any content.
Collaborators	Participate in Web Discussions and create Web Subscriptions, in addition to having browser access. They cannot create or modify any content.
Authors	Create and modify Web site documents, in addition to having collaborator access.
Administrators	Modify *permissions* and other settings on the Web site, in addition to having author access.

Note   You can configure user permissions only if your Web site is located on an NTFS-formatted disk.

When you use the Microsoft Office Server Extensions (OSE) Configuration Wizard to install OSE on a Web site, the wizard creates a Microsoft Windows NT group for each category of users. The following list identifies the user group names:

- *group_prefix* Browsers
- *group_prefix* Collaborators
- *group_prefix* Authors
- *group_prefix* Admins

    where *group_prefix* is a text label you provide to the wizard that defaults to the name of the Web site.

When you want to add a user to a category, use the User Manager application to add that user Windows NT account to the Windows NT group. For example, if you add a user account to the *group_prefix* Browsers group, that account automatically gains browsing access to the Web site.

When OSE is installed on a Web site, the Microsoft FrontPage Server Extensions are automatically installed. A Web site with OSE installed is called an OSE-extended web. Each OSE-extended web maintains its own list of users in the four user categories.

You can create *FrontPage-extended web*s under the root OSE-extended web, and FrontPage-extended webs can be nested within other FrontPage-extended webs. Each FrontPage-extended web under the root OSE-extended web maintains its own list of Administrators, Authors, and Browsers groups—making a web a convenient way to differentiate user access while maintaining the other settings of the *root web*. User names associated with each group are stored separately in their respective webs. However, only one Collaborators group is used for the root OSE-extended web, and all the FrontPage-extended webs beneath it.

If you are just getting started using Microsoft Internet Information Server (IIS) and OSE, you probably do not need to worry about multiple Web sites. By default, IIS Setup creates one Web site with the description *Default Web Site*. When you install OSE, the default Web site becomes the root OSE-extended web.

The Configuration Wizard creates the four local Windows NT groups that correspond to the four categories of user privileges. By default, everyone has access to the Collaborators group, but you must add users to the other appropriate groups. Later, if you need to subdivide your OSE-extended web and give the same users different access to different content, you can create *subwebs*, or additional root OSE-extended webs. However, the OSE collaboration features work only with URLs that use the standard HTTP port (80). You cannot extend OSE-extended webs that use nonstandard ports, but you can extend any Web site with Microsoft FrontPage Server Extensions.

Enforcing permissions with NTFS access control lists

To grant Browsers, Collaborators, Authors, or Administrators permissions, the OSE Configuration Wizard adds the four Windows NT groups to the *access control lists* (ACLs) of the folders and files of the root OSE-extended web. The wizard also gives each group the appropriate type of access to folders and files. In addition, the Collaborators, Authors, and Administrators groups are added to the ACL of the MSOffice *virtual directory* that the Configuration Wizard creates. The following table shows the permissions that each of these groups has.

Windows NT group	Permissions on MSOffice virtual directory and files	Permissions on MSOAdmin folder and files
Collaborators	Read and execute	None
Authors	Read and execute	None
Administrators	Full control	Full control

You do not need to view or modify the ACLs directly because the wizard does this automatically. When you configure permissions with the FrontPage administration tools, you need only to specify that each user is in the Browsers, Authors, or Administrators category. The FrontPage tools do not manage the Collaborators group or recognize the Collaborators category. You can use the User Manager application to modify the Collaborators group membership and the other group lists.

The following administration tools modify the ACLs to assign permissions to FrontPage-extended web users.

- Fpsrvadm.exe
- Fpremadm.exe
- FrontPage Server Extensions Administrator snap-in
- FrontPage Server Extensions Administration forms

The administration tools automatically assign the following types of access to each of the Windows NT groups. (These settings are added to the ACL of the root folder of the Web.)

Windows NT group	Types of access
Browsers	Read, execute
Authors	Read, execute, write, delete
Administrators	Read, execute, write, delete, change permissions

Note   The Windows NT Administrators group and the system account have full control access to all files.

Granting permissions to computers

In addition to granting permissions to specific users, you can grant permissions to specific computers. Every computer on the Internet or an intranet uses the TCP/IP network protocol and has an IP address. By using the FrontPage client, you can use an IP address to identify a computer, and you can grant Browsers, Authors, or Administrators permissions to that computer.

Managing permissions more precisely

Permissions for content on an OSE-extended web typically apply to the entire OSE-extended web. For example, a user with authoring permission can change any page on the web, and a user with browser permission can view any page.

Although the OSE Configuration Wizard creates groups that make it easy to modify permissions on the FrontPage-extended web as a whole, it is often necessary to divide content on a server so that different users have different permissions in each area of the web.

You have two mechanisms for setting varied permissions on content.

- Divide the content into as many FrontPage-extended subwebs as there are sets of browsers, authors, or administrators.
- Set varying permissions on the folders and files of a single FrontPage-extended web. This option requires that you bypass the built-in FrontPage tools for setting permissions.

Using subwebs to set mixed permissions

When you use subwebs, you automatically achieve more controlled security than without subwebs because each subweb maintains separate security settings. Also, using subwebs to set mixed permissions on your content is usually the most efficient way to divide your content among different sets of browsers and authors.

Managing permissions manually

You can bypass the built-in security features of FrontPage, and manually set permissions on the content of a FrontPage-extended web. This option allows you to set permissions on a per-folder or per-file basis, and that gives you precise control of security for the FrontPage-extended web. However, if you set permissions manually, you must manage the ACLs yourself.

When you manage ACLs manually, you must modify the ACLs in the top-level folder of the FrontPage-extended web. At a minimum, you must give administrators Read, Write, and Change permissions on the top-level folder of the FrontPage-extended web or subweb.

Caution   Managing ACLs manually is an advanced technique, and mismanaging can result in weakened security for the content on your Web server.

See also

- For the procedure you need to use to manage permissions manually on a FrontPage-extended web, see "How to Configure Security on Your OSE-extended Web" on page 678.

- You can use several tools to manage permissions on FrontPage-extended webs. For more information about using the tools, see "Advanced Administration of Office Server Extensions" on page 685.

Using a Proxy Server with Office Server Extensions

If you plan to make your Web server available on the Internet, and if you want to limit inbound and outbound access to your intranet, then you need to use a proxy server such as Microsoft Proxy Server. A proxy server is also called a *firewall*.

By using a proxy server, you can control how remote clients—such as users connecting over the Internet—access your server applications. A proxy server can also help you control how users within your local network access external servers.

When you use a proxy server with Microsoft Office Server Extensions (OSE), the following requirements and limitations apply.

- You must use Basic *authentication* to secure logons to your *OSE-extended web*.

  To maximize security, use Basic authentication with Secure Sockets Layer (SSL) *encryption*. This combination prevents network eavesdroppers from viewing client/server conversations on your OSE-extended web.

  Note   IIS does not support Windows NT Challenge/Response authentication across a proxy server.

- OSE functions only with a proxy server that does not require authentication.

  Some proxy servers require clients to log on to the proxy server before establishing a connection to the Internet and an intranet. OSE does not function across proxy servers that require this type of authentication. You can configure Proxy Server to require clients to log on to the proxy server, but you must not configure the Proxy Server this way if you want to use it with OSE.

See also

- It is highly recommended that you use a proxy server if you are connecting your Web server to the Internet. For more information about Microsoft Proxy Server, see the Microsoft Proxy Server Web site at http://www.microsoft.com/proxy/.

How to Configure Security on Your OSE-extended Web

You can configure the following security elements on each OSE-extended web:

- Authentication
- Collaboration, browsing, authoring, and administration *permissions* (NTFS only)
- Individual file and folder permissions (NTFS file system only)

Configure authentication

When a Web client such as a Microsoft Office application or Web browser attempts to access a file or folder on a Web site, the server authenticates the client to determine whether the client has the credentials to connect to the server.

You can configure the Web server to allow *anonymous access* so that it does not require any credentials, or you can require user name and password information. If you require user name and password information, and the connecting client does not enter valid credentials, the Web server does not allow access.

▶ **To configure authentication for an entire Web site**

1 On the **Start** menu, point to **Programs**, point to **Windows NT 4.0 Option Pack**, point to **Microsoft Internet Information Server**, and then click **Internet Service Manager**.

2 In the left pane of Internet Service Manager, select the Web site.

3 On the **Action** menu, click **Properties**, and then click the **Directory Security** tab.

4 In the **Anonymous Access and Authentication Control** area, click **Edit**.

5 Select the authentication options you want, and then click **OK**.

Note All folders, virtual directories, and files in the Web site inherit the authentication settings configured at the Web site level unless the authentication is overridden at the file, folder, or virtual directory level.

You can also configure authentication for selected content on your Web site.

▶ **To configure authentication for a folder or virtual directory**

1 On the **Start** menu, point to **Programs**, point to **Windows NT 4.0 Option Pack**, point to **Microsoft Internet Information Server**, and then click **Internet Service Manager**.

2 In the left pane of Internet Service Manager, select the folder or virtual directory.

3 On the **Action** menu, click **Properties**, and then click the **Directory Security** tab.

4 In the **Anonymous Access and Authentication Control** area, click **Edit**.

5 Select the authentication options you want, and then click **OK**.

Note All files inherit the authentication settings configured at the folder and Web site level unless the settings are overridden at the file level.

▶ **To configure authentication for a file**

1 On the **Start** menu, point to **Programs**, point to **Windows NT 4.0 Option Pack**, point to **Microsoft Internet Information Server**, and then click **Internet Service Manager**.

2 In the left pane of Internet Service Manager, select the folder where the file is located, and then click the file in the right pane.

3 On the **Action** menu, click **Properties**, and then click the **File Security** tab.

4 In the **Anonymous Access and Authentication Control** area, click **Edit**.

5 Select the authentication options you want, and then click **OK**.

You can allow users to anonymously contribute to Web Discussions and create Web Subscriptions. To enable anonymous access to the Microsoft Office Server Extensions (OSE) Collaboration features, enable Anonymous Access on the MSOffice virtual directory. To do this, follow the previous instructions that describe how you configure authentication for a file.

If you enable Basic authentication, you must grant the **Log on Locally** right to user accounts that access your Web site.

▶ **To grant users the Log on Locally right**

1   On the **Start** menu, point to **Programs**, point to **Administrative Tools**, and then click **User Managers for Domains**.

2   In the **Policies** menu, click **User Rights**.

3   In the **Right** list, select **Log on locally**.

4   Add user accounts or groups to the **Grant To** list.

Configure user permissions

You can configure the types of actions that users can perform when they are authenticated on your OSE-extended web. The simplest way to configure these user permissions is to modify the memberships of the Windows NT groups that the OSE Configuration Wizard creates.

The OSE Configuration Wizard creates the following groups for each Web site:

- *group_prefix* Browsers
- *group_prefix* Collaborators
- *group_prefix* Authors
- *group_prefix* Admins

where *group_prefix* is a text label you provide for each Web site when you run the wizard. The default for the label is the Web site name.

▶ **To specify which users are Browsers, Collaborators, Authors, and Administrators (NTFS file system only)**

1   On the **Start** menu, point to **Programs**, point to **Administrative Tools**, and then click **User Managers for Domains**.

2   On the **User** menu, click **Select Domain**, type the name of your computer, and then click **OK**.

This step displays accounts and groups on the local computer.

3   Select the group of users you want to modify, and then on the **User** menu choose **Properties**.

4   In the **Local Group Properties** dialog box, use the **Add** and **Remove** buttons to add or remove user accounts.

Manage NTFS access control lists manually

You can set permissions manually on your Web site, and then you can manage *access control list* (ACL) settings manually in Windows NT Explorer—instead of using the FrontPage administration tools or using the Windows NT groups that the OSE Configuration Wizard creates. Setting permissions manually gives you the control to set permissions at the file and folder levels.

▶ **To configure file and folder ACLs (NTFS file system only)**

1   On the **Start** menu, point to **Programs**, point to **Windows NT 4.0 Option Pack**, point to **Microsoft Internet Information Server**, and then click **Internet Service Manager**.

2   In the left pane of **Internet Service Manager**, select the Web site for which you want to set ACLs manually.

3   On the **Action** menu, click **Properties**, click the **Publishing** tab, and then select the **Manage Permissions Manually** check box.

4   In My Computer or Windows NT Explorer, select the file or folder.

5   On the **File** menu, click **Properties**, click the **Security** tab, and then click **Permissions**.

6   In the **Name** box, select a user.

    –or–

    Click **Add** to add a user.

7   In the **Type of Access** box, select the type of access you want for the selected user.

You can grant a specific user or group collaboration access, and then you can manage permissions manually on the MSOffice virtual directory.

▶ **To grant a specific user or group Collaboration access**

1   In My Computer or Windows NT Explorer, select the folder:

    C:\Program Files\Microsoft Office\Office\Scripts\N\1033

    where *N* is the instance number of the Web site you are configuring.

2   On the **File** menu, click **Properties**, click the **Security** tab, and then click **Permissions**.

3   Add the user account or group to the ACL for the 1033 folder, grant it the Read permission, clear the **Replace permissions on Subdirectories** check box, and then clear the **Replace Permissions on Existing Files** check box.

4   Repeat Steps 1 through 3 for all files located in the 1033 folder, but not the MSOAdmin subfolder.

5   Repeat Steps 1 through 3 for the Help subfolder, and all files located in the Help subfolder.

You can grant a specific user or group administration access to OSE features, and then you can manage permissions manually on the MSOAdmin subfolder.

▶ To grant a specific user or group Administration access

1   In My Computer or Windows NT Explorer, select the folder:

C:\Program Files\Microsoft Office\Office\Scripts\N\1033\MSOAdmin

where *N* is the instance number of the Web site you are configuring.

2   On the **File** menu, click **Properties**, click the **Security** tab, and then click **Permissions**.

3   Add the user account or group to the ACL for the MSOAdmin folder, grant it the Read permission, clear the **Replace permissions on Subdirectories** check box, and then clear the **Replace Permissions on Existing Files** check box.

4   Repeat Step 3 for all files located in the MSOAdmin folder.

See also

- In Microsoft Internet Information Server (IIS), you can restrict access to a Web site by IP address or domain name. For more information, see IIS online Help.

- In addition to User Manager, several FrontPage administration tools allow you to modify permissions on FrontPage-extended webs, which are all webs used with OSE. For more information, see "Advanced Administration of Office Server Extensions" on page 685.

FAQs About Office Server Extensions Security

You can choose several methods to configure security on your Web server. The following frequently asked questions (FAQs) identify specific concerns you might have while you are configuring security settings for your *OSE-extended web*.

How do I prevent specific users from connecting to my OSE-extended web?

You use *authentication* to control access to your OSE-extended web. Users are authenticated when they connect to the server; each Web site, *virtual directory*, folder, and file on your server can have independent authentication settings. However, you typically configure authentication only at the Web site level.

Anonymous access is disabled by default, but if you enable it, any user can connect to the server. To prevent certain users from gaining access to your server, you can enable Basic authentication or Windows NT Challenge/Response authentication.

In addition to authentication, you can configure *permissions* settings on each OSE-extended web. When you configure permissions, you define which users can browse, author, or administer on that OSE-extended web or *subweb*. On *root webs*, you can configure who can collaborate on that OSE-extended web. Users can perform only the tasks you give them permission to perform.

Note   You can configure permissions only if the FrontPage-extended web is located on an NTFS-formatted disk.

How do I allow users to connect only to specific folders and files on my OSE-extended web?

You can enable different authentication methods for each file and folder on your OSE-extended web. By using authentication, you can require users to have a Microsoft Windows NT account to connect to a particular file or folder.

You can also grant or deny access to individual files and folders according to the IP address or domain name of the connecting client computer. For example, you can grant access to a particular client computer so that the user of that computer can access files and folders regardless of the user account logged in. Doing this is convenient when several users share a computer. Also, to protect your data, you can deny access to a computer in the domain *competitor.com*.

How do I give users different permissions on my OSE-extended web?

To vary user permissions across the content of your OSE-extended web, you can create a subweb of your existing web. A subweb inherits settings from its parent web, but you can change the user security settings of the subweb. In a subweb, you can give users browsing, authoring, and administrating permissions.

To divide content into more independent units, you can create multiple Web sites. Each Web site must have a unique IP address and port pair. Web sites can have unique security settings.

For the most detailed control of the content on your Web server, you can manually configure permissions for each file and folder. You use Windows NT Explorer to configure the access control list (ACL) for each file and folder on your web. An ACL identifies the type of access each user has for a specific file and folder.

Note   You can configure permissions only when the FrontPage-extended web is located on an NTFS-formatted disk.

Can I prevent specific computers from connecting to my Web server?

Yes. Each Web site, virtual directory, folder, and file on your server can have its own list of client computer IP addresses and domain names that are granted or denied access.

Why would I use SSL, and how do I configure it?

Secure Sockets Layer (SSL) encrypts a client/server connection, preventing a network eavesdropper from viewing the information that is passed between the client and server.

Use SSL when your clients are using Basic authentication, because Basic authentication sends user names and passwords between the client and server in an unencrypted and easily decoded format. (Windows NT Challenge/Response authentication encrypts user names and passwords without using SSL.)

To configure SSL, you must first obtain a security *certificate* for your server from a *certificate authority*. Use the Key Manager utility in Microsoft Internet Information Server (IIS) to get security certificates. After you have a certificate, users need to specify SSL when they connect to your server from a client application such as a Microsoft Office 2000 application or a Web browser.

Note   SSL client/server connections are established on server IP ports specifically reserved for SSL.

Do users need a Windows NT account to connect to my OSE-extended web?

Yes, unless you enable anonymous access. Anonymous access does not require a Windows NT account, and it allows any user to connect to your OSE-extended web.

Do I need NTFS to secure my OSE-extended web?

No, but without NTFS, you have fewer security options for your OSE-extended web. Without NTFS, security is limited to the various types of authentication and to the grant or deny lists that are based on a user IP address or domain name.

NTFS is a file system that you can use to format hard disks on computers running Windows NT. The NTFS file system provides strong and flexible security for files and folders. You can convert FAT-formatted hard disks to NTFS without any loss of data. NTFS is required if you want to assign users different permissions on a FrontPage-extended web, or on files and folders within a web.

See also

- Configuring authentication on your OSE-extended web allows you to restrict and give access to users and allows you to require encrypted client/server communications. For more information about authentication and encryption, see "Using Internet Information Server Authentication" on page 670.

Advanced Administration of Office Server Extensions

Most of the time, you can administer and maintain Microsoft Office Server Extensions (OSE) by using OSE Administrator. You can also use the administration tools for Microsoft FrontPage Server Extensions to perform maintenance and configuration tasks on an OSE-extended web.

Administering FrontPage Server Extensions

Microsoft Office Server Extensions (OSE) is installed on a Web site on a Web server with one of the following configurations:

- Microsoft Internet Information Server (IIS) on a computer running Microsoft Windows NT Server

  —or—

- Personal Web Server on a computer running Microsoft Windows NT Workstation

OSE includes Microsoft FrontPage Server Extensions, and OSE Setup automatically installs or upgrades FrontPage Server Extensions on the Web site.

A Web site that has FrontPage Server Extensions installed is called a *FrontPage-extended web*. If a FrontPage-extended web also has OSE installed, it is called an *OSE-extended web*. IIS supports multiple Web sites on a single computer, so it is possible to have multiple FrontPage-extended webs or multiple OSE-extended webs on an IIS computer. A FrontPage-extended web can have one or more *subwebs* below the *root web*. However, OSE can be installed only on the root web.

Using the following tools, you can perform several OSE maintenance tasks to administer FrontPage Server Extensions:

- Fpsrvadm

  Provides the complete set of FrontPage Server Extensions operations. Use Fpsrvadm from the command line or in batch files. Fpsrvadm must be run on the server.

- FrontPage Server Extensions *Microsoft Management Console* (MMC) snap-in

  Administers FrontPage Server Extensions on Microsoft Windows NT through a graphical user interface (GUI).

- Fpremadm

  Administers FrontPage Server Extensions from a Microsoft Windows-based computer other than the computer on which the Web server is running. Remotely performs all the operations that Fpsrvadm performs.

- FrontPage Server Extensions HTML Administration Forms

  Install and administer FrontPage Server Extensions remotely in a Web browser on any computer connected to the Internet. The forms are copied to your Web server during OSE Setup.

Administering a Web server remotely

You can create a new FrontPage-extended web, change user *permissions*, and do other administrative tasks when you do not have local access to the Web server on which you have installed OSE.

You can use FrontPage Server Extensions HTML Administration Forms, and the command-line utility Fpremadm to administer FrontPage Server Extensions remotely from any computer connected to your intranet or the Internet. However, remote administration can be less secure than direct administration.

Selecting the right tool for the task

The following table identifies the administrative tasks you can perform on an OSE-extended Web, and the FrontPage Server Extensions tools to use for each task.

Task	FrontPage snap-in	Fpsrvadm	Fpremadm	HTML Administration Forms
Install extensions	Yes	Yes	Yes	Yes
Upgrade extensions	Yes	Yes	Yes	Yes
Uninstall extensions	Yes	Yes	Yes	Yes
Full uninstall of extensions	Yes	Yes	Yes	Yes
Create a subweb	Yes	Yes	Yes	Yes
Merge a subweb	Yes	Yes	Yes	Yes
Check and fix extensions	Yes	Yes	Yes	Yes
Administer security	Yes	Yes	Yes	Yes
Enable authoring and administering	Yes	Yes	Yes	Yes
Disable authoring and administering	Yes	Yes	Yes	Yes
Recalculate web	Yes	Yes	Yes	Yes
Import a file	No	Yes	Yes	No
Recalculate hyperlinks	No	Yes	Yes	No
Delete a subweb	Yes	Yes	Yes	Yes

Task	FrontPage snap-in	Fpsrvadm	Fpremadm	HTML Administration Forms
Rename a subweb	No	Yes	Yes	Yes
Specify executable programs	Yes	Yes	Yes	Yes
Set e-mail options	Yes	No	No	No
Specify scripting language	Yes	No	No	No
Disable FrontPage permissions	Yes	No	No	No
Tune performance	Yes	No	No	No
Require SSL	Yes	No	No	No
Log authoring activity	Yes	No	No	No

Toolbox

The FrontPage Server Extensions Resource Kit contains additional information about administering FrontPage Server Extensions, including details about configuring settings for a FrontPage-extended web and about communicating between the FrontPage client and FrontPage Server Extensions. For information about installing the kit, see "FrontPage 2000 Server Extensions Resource Kit" on page 790.

Using FrontPage Server Extensions Tools

The following sections describe the administrative tasks that you can perform on an *OSE-extended Web* by using FrontPage Server Extensions tools.

Installing or upgrading FrontPage Server Extensions

You can use OSE Setup to install FrontPage Server Extensions. When you run OSE Setup, FrontPage Server Extensions are automatically installed on your computer. Then, you must configure FrontPage Server Extensions on each Web site that you want to support OSE.

The OSE Configuration Wizard allows you to install FrontPage Server Extensions on one of your existing Web sites. The wizard is started automatically at the end of OSE Setup. FrontPage Server Extensions create a root *FrontPage-extended web* on the Web site, and files and folders are added to the Web site.

Note   If you add more Web sites later, you must use a different tool to install FrontPage Server Extensions on the Web sites. Typically, after the first installation, the tool you use is the FrontPage Server Extensions MMC snap-in.

After FrontPage Server Extensions are installed on a Web site, you can upgrade them to a later version on the *root web* and on any *subweb* of that Web site.

Uninstalling FrontPage Server Extensions

You can uninstall FrontPage Server Extensions from a Web site to remove the server extensions from the root web and all the subwebs below the root web. The uninstall operation disables support for OSE on the Web site, but it does not delete web content. This operation leaves enough FrontPage meta-information in each content area to return each web to its previous state if you reinstall FrontPage Server Extensions.

Fully uninstalling FrontPage Server Extensions

You can perform a full uninstall operation to remove FrontPage Server Extensions from the specified port and Web site. If the root web has subwebs, full uninstall removes FrontPage Server Extensions from the subwebs. In contrast to the uninstall operation, full uninstall does not leave FrontPage meta-information in the web content area.

Creating a subweb

You can create a FrontPage-extended subweb in a specified folder on an existing FrontPage-extended web.

Merging a subweb into a parent web

You can merge a subweb into its parent FrontPage-extended web to convert the subweb into a folder on the parent web. When you merge a subweb with its parent, FrontPage Server Extensions are removed from the subweb, but subwebs that are part of the merged subweb do not merge.

Checking and fixing FrontPage Server Extensions

You can use the Check-and-Fix tool to troubleshoot FrontPage Server Extensions features such as hit counters and e-mail form handlers. If one of these features fails to work, use the Check-and-Fix tool to check FrontPage Server Extensions files in the FrontPage-extended web to determine whether or not anything is missing or corrupted. The Check-and-Fix tool performs the following functions:

- Opens each FrontPage-extended web.
- Locks each FrontPage-extended web for writing.
- Verifies read *permissions*.

- Verifies that the Service.cnf and Service.ick files have read/write access. If either file does not have read/write access, the Check-and-Fix tool includes this information in the summary, but it does not correct the problem.

- Updates Postinfo.html and _vti_inf.htm.

- Verifies that _vti_pvt, _vti_log, and _vti_bin are installed, and that _vti_bin is executable. If these folders are not installed or _vti_bin is not executable, the Check-and-Fix tool corrects the problem.

- Determines whether Web site roots or *metabase* settings are correct and up to date. If they are not, the Check-and-Fix tool corrects and updates them.

- Checks that the I_USR anonymous account does not have write access. If the anonymous account does have write access, the Check-and-Fix tool removes the write access.

- Warns you if you are running on a *file allocation table* (FAT) file system, which means that you can supply minimal security.

Administering security

You can add or remove permissions to administer, author, or visit a FrontPage-extended web, and set IP address restrictions.

Enabling web authoring and administration

You can enable FrontPage-extended web authoring and administering through the FrontPage client on a port and Web site.

Disabling web authoring and administration

You can disable FrontPage-extended web authoring and administering through the FrontPage client on a port and Web site.

Recalculating hyperlinks in a FrontPage-extended web

You can recalculate and repair all internal hyperlinks, and you can synchronize FrontPage content databases with the current state of a FrontPage-extended web. The hyperlink recalculating operation also:

- Restores pages in Include Page components.

- Recalculates FrontPage components such as Search Forms and Navigation Bars.

- Reapplies borders to any pages that use borders.

- Resets permissions on FrontPage form handler result pages.

- Recalculates text indexes.

Importing a file

You can import a file to a destination URL on a FrontPage-extended web.

Recalculating hyperlinks in a file

You can recalculate all hyperlinks in a file. This operation also refreshes pages in Include Page components and recalculates text indexes.

Deleting a subweb

You can delete a subweb that is out of date, seldom used, or no longer useful. For example, information published on an organization intranet might become obsolete when one of the following occurs:

- A project ends.

- New information is released.

- A subscriber posting content to an Internet service provider (ISP) Web server discontinues the service.

When you delete a subweb, you delete all of the contents and nested subwebs, as well as FrontPage Server Extensions. You also delete the meta-information files that make it easy to reinstall the server extensions on the subweb. You cannot undo the deletion of a subweb.

Renaming a subweb

You can rename a subweb, and FrontPage Server Extensions automatically recalculates the links in the subweb—after it is renamed.

Specifying whether web authors can load executable applications

You can specify whether or not executable applications or scripts can be uploaded to a FrontPage-extended web. You might want to prevent users from uploading scripts or applications because they can contain bugs or viruses.

Web authors using FrontPage can enable scripts to run in any folder on a web. You can prevent authors from enabling scripts to run in folders on Web sites.

▶ **To specify whether or not users can enable scripts in folders on all Web sites**

1   In the following registry subkey:

HKEY_LOCAL_MACHINE\SOFTWARE\Microsoft\Shared Tools
\Web Server Extensions\All Ports

Create the following entry, which takes the data type **String**:

NoMarkScriptable

2   To allow users to enable scripts, set the **NoMarkScriptable** value data to 0

–or–

To prevent users from enabling scripts, set the **NoMarkScriptable** value data to 1

▶ **To specify whether users can enable scripts in folders on a Web site**

1   In the following registry subkey:

HKEY_LOCAL_MACHINE\SOFTWARE\Microsoft\Shared Tools
\Web Server Extensions\Port X

where *X* is the Web site, create the following entry, which takes the data type
String:

NoMarkScriptable

2   To allow users to enable scripts, set the **NoMarkScriptable** value data to 0.

–or–

To prevent users from running scripts, set the **NoMarkScriptable** value data to 1.

Note   The values set for a specific Web site override the values set for all Web sites.

▶ **To specify whether users can enable scripts in folders on a FrontPage-extended web**

1   In an editor such as Notepad, open the Service.cnf file located in the _vti_pvt folder
of the web or subweb.

2   To allow users to enable scripts, include the following line:

vti_nomarkscriptable:BX|0

–or–

To prevent users from enabling scripts, include the following line:

vti_nomarkscriptable:BX|1

Note   The values set in the Service.cnf file override the values set for all Web sites and for a
specific Web site.

Setting the default language

You can set the default language to determine which language is used to pass error
messages from the Web server to the Web browser. FrontPage Server Extensions use
the default language setting for a FrontPage-extended web. This setting also affects
generated content such as the language in FrontPage Search Forms.

Selecting e-mail options

Authors can configure a form to send the contents of the form as an e-mail message.
To send e-mail messages from the Web server where the form is stored, you must
configure FrontPage Server Extensions to deliver the e-mail messages to a Simple
Mail Transfer Protocol (SMTP) mail server.

Specifying a scripting language

You can select the scripting language for the scripts that are automatically generated to enforce any data validation settings you apply to form fields. You can specify Microsoft Visual Basic Scripting Edition (VBScript) or Microsoft JScript as the scripting language.

Disabling FrontPage permissions settings

You can disable the FrontPage permissions model entirely, and then set permissions outside of FrontPage.

Optimizing performance of a FrontPage-extended web

You can adjust the cache size and full-text search index size to optimize the performance of a FrontPage-extended web.

Requiring Secure Sockets Layer

You can require the use of Secure Sockets Layer (SSL) for client connections to significantly improve security on a FrontPage-extended web.

Logging authoring activity

You can log authoring activity to keep track of which users make changes to a FrontPage-extended web.

See also

- When FrontPage Server Extensions are installed on a Web site, folders and files are added to the Web site. For information about these added folders and files, see "Special FrontPage Directories and Storage Locations" in the Appendixes section of the *FrontPage 2000 Server Extensions Resource Kit*.

- The Check-and-Fix tool verifies permission settings on files and folders. For information about which folder and file permissions this tool searches for, see "Files and Permissions on Internet Information Service" in the Appendixes section of the *FrontPage 2000 Server Extensions Resource Kit*.

How to Use Fpsrvadm.exe

The Fpsrvadm utility is a command-line application for Microsoft Windows NT and UNIX. This utility installs Microsoft FrontPage Server Extensions on Web sites and performs all administrative operations on *FrontPage-extended webs*. The Fpsrvadm utility administrative operations include:

- Updating FrontPage-extended webs
- Uninstalling FrontPage Server Extensions
- Verifying correct FrontPage Server Extensions configuration

You must run Fpsrvadm on the server computer that contains FrontPage Server Extensions. To administer FrontPage Server Extensions remotely, use the Fpremadm utility, or the HTML Administration Forms.

When you run Fpsrvadm, you supply an operation in the form-**operation** *CommandName*, and a set of command-line arguments in the form-*argument value*. For example, the following command upgrades FrontPage Server Extensions on port 80 of the Web site called sample.microsoft.com:

```
fpsrvadm.exe -operation upgrade -port 80 -multihost sample.microsoft.com
```

Each argument also has a short form. The short form of this command is the following:

```
fpsrvadm.exe -o upgrade -p 80 -m sample.microsoft.com
```

For example, here's how you would use Fpsrvadm to install FrontPage Server Extensions on the new Web site named example.microsoft.com:

```
fpsrvadm.exe -o install -p 80 -m example.microsoft.com -u AdminName
    -t msiis
```

The commands and arguments are defined as follows:

- **-o install** installs the FrontPage Server Extensions on the specified port of a Web site.
- **-p 80** gives the port number.
- **-m example.microsoft.com** is the domain name of the new Web site.
- **-u AdminName** is the name of the FrontPage-extended web administrator. By using the FrontPage client, this administrator can add authors and other administrators, and can create or delete FrontPage-extended *subwebs*.
- **-t msiis** is the server type. With Microsoft Office Server Extensions (OSE), this argument is always **msiis** for Microsoft Internet Information Server (IIS).

Toolbox

The command-line arguments and commands that you can use with Fpsrvadm are listed in the OSEAMain.xls workbook. For more information about installing OSEAMain.xls, see "Office Information" on page 787.

How to Use the FrontPage Server Extensions Snap-in

The FrontPage *Microsoft Management Console* (MMC) snap-in is a graphical application that is included with the Microsoft Windows NT operating system. You can use this snap-in to perform the following administrative tasks on FrontPage-extended webs:

- Create *subwebs*
- Configure FrontPage Server Extensions for webs
- Upgrade FrontPage Server Extensions on a web
- Convert folders into subwebs, and subwebs into folders
- Recalculate hyperlinks in a FrontPage-extended web

The FrontPage MMC snap-in adds commands, property sheets, and other tools to the Internet Information Server (IIS) snap-in. Commands are added to the **Action** and **Context** menus, and a **Publishing** property page is added to the Web site **Properties** dialog box. For overlapping functionality, the **IIS** command appears instead of a **FrontPage** command. In the console tree, IIS lists all IIS Web sites, regardless of whether they are FrontPage-extended webs.

Note   The FrontPage MMC snap-in replaces and improves upon the Fpsrvwin utility, which is the graphical administrative program included with IIS version 4.0. The FrontPage MMC snap-in allows you to perform similar and additional administrative tasks that you can perform by using the Fpsrvwin.exe, Fpsrvadm.exe, and Fpremadm.exe utilities.

FrontPage MMC snap-in administration tools give you several options to facilitate your administrative tasks. The tools are available at the following locations:

- **New** submenu

  From the **New** submenu, you can select commands to create a new web, add a new administrator, and so on—depending on the item you select in the console tree. You can select the computer object, a Web site, a subweb, or a folder in the console tree.

- **Task** submenu

  From the **Task** submenu, you can select commands to check and fix, remove, and upgrade FrontPage Server Extensions—depending on the item you select in the console tree. You can select the computer object, a Web site, a subweb, or a folder in the console tree.

- **Server Extensions** tab in the Web site **Properties** dialog box

  When you change the configuration of a FrontPage-extended web, you use the **Server Extensions** tab in the Web site **Properties** dialog box. For example, you can change version control, client scripting, e-mail, and security inheritance settings on the **Server Extensions** tab.

Extend a Web site with FrontPage Server Extensions

After you create a Web site, you can use the FrontPage Server Extensions to extend the site, and make it a *root web*. To use the FrontPage Server Extensions, you must install them on the Web server.

▶ To extend a Web site with FrontPage Server Extensions

1 In the console tree, right-click the Web site to which you want to add FrontPage Server Extensions.

2 Click **Task**, and then click **Configure Server Extensions**.

3 Follow the instructions in the Server Extensions Configuration Wizard.

Note   You must extend a Web site—that is, make it a root web—before you can create subwebs below it.

Add an administrator

You can add an unlimited number of administrators to your Web site.

▶ To add an administrator

1 In the console tree, right-click the FrontPage-extended web to which you want to add an administrator.

2 Click **New**, and then click **Server Extensions Administrator**.

3 Type a Windows NT account in the **New Administrator** dialog box.

Create a subweb

A subweb is a FrontPage-extended web that is located in a subfolder of the root web or a subfolder of another subweb. A FrontPage-extended web has one root web and can have an unlimited number of subwebs.

▶ To create a subweb

1 In the console tree, right-click the web under which you want to create a subweb.

2 Click **New**, and then click **Server Extensions Web**.

3 Follow the steps in the New Subweb Wizard.

Uninstall FrontPage Server Extensions

When you uninstall FrontPage Server Extensions from the root web, you remove the FrontPage Server Extensions from the root web, and all the subwebs below it. The uninstall process leaves the web content on the Web site, but FrontPage Server Extensions features such as hit counters and e-mail form handlers no longer work.

▶ **To remove FrontPage Server Extensions from a root web and its subwebs**

1   In the console tree, right-click the root web from which you want to remove FrontPage Server Extensions.

2   Click **Task**, and then click **Remove Server Extensions**.

Check and fix FrontPage Server Extensions

You can check and fix FrontPage Server Extensions on a Web site or subweb. This operation includes replacing missing folders and files, and verifying correct *permissions*. When you check a FrontPage-extended web that has subwebs, the subwebs are checked also.

▶ **To check and fix FrontPage Server Extensions**

1   In the console tree, right-click the FrontPage-extended web that you want to check and fix.

2   Click **Task**, and then click **Check Server Extensions**.

The **Check Web** window displays a status log for each web that you check.

Upgrade FrontPage Server Extensions

To take advantage of new features, you can upgrade a FrontPage-extended web to the latest version of FrontPage Server Extensions. You upgrade FrontPage Server Extensions on root webs only, but upgrading a root web also upgrades all subwebs below it.

▶ **To upgrade to the latest version of FrontPage Server Extensions**

1   In the console tree, right-click the root web that you want to upgrade.

   –or–

   To upgrade FrontPage Server Extensions for all root webs on your computer, right-click the computer object in the console tree.

2   Click **Task**, and then click **Upgrade Server Extensions**.

Delete a subweb

When you delete a subweb you delete all content, and all subwebs below the deleted subweb.

▶ **To delete a subweb**

1   In the console tree, right-click the subweb that you want to delete.

2   Click **Task**, and then click **Delete Server Extensions Web**.

Convert a folder to a subweb

When you have a folder that contains enough content to be its own Web site, you can easily convert that folder to a FrontPage-extended subweb. When you convert a folder to a subweb, you add FrontPage Server Extensions to the subweb.

▶ **To convert a folder to a subweb**

1   In the console tree, right-click the folder that you want to convert to a FrontPage-extended subweb.

2   Click **Task**, and then click **Configure Server Extensions**.

Convert a subweb to a folder

You can convert a FrontPage-extended subweb into a folder of its root web. When you convert a subweb into a folder, FrontPage Server Extensions are removed from the subweb, and the subweb is converted into a regular folder of the root web. Subwebs nested below the converted subweb are re-rooted.

The subwebs below the converted subweb might acquire different permissions settings if these subwebs are configured to inherit these settings from the root web. When there are no subwebs below the converted subweb, the pages within the converted subweb might lose some properties.

▶ **To convert a subweb into a folder**

1   In the console tree, right-click the FrontPage-extended subweb that you want to convert into a folder.

2   Click **Task**, and then click **Convert Server Extensions Web to Directory**.

Recalculate hyperlinks in a FrontPage-extended web

Any changes that are made to the structure of a web can change the links between different parts of that web. For example, if a page is moved from one folder to another or is renamed, then the hyperlinks to that page from every other page in the web need to be recalculated to re-establish logical links. FrontPage automatically recalculates hyperlinks when files are moved, renamed, or deleted. However, if you want to "force" a recalculation, you can do so.

▶ **To recalculate all hyperlinks in a FrontPage-extended web**

1   In the console tree, right-click the web whose hyperlinks you want to recalculate.

2   Click **Task**, and then click **Recalculate Web**.

Modify the content of a FrontPage-extended web or subweb

As an administrator, you can modify the theme, text, graphics, or other content of a FrontPage-extended web or subweb. If FrontPage is installed on the same host computer as a FrontPage-extended root web or subweb, then you can open the web directly from the console and change its content in FrontPage.

▶ **To modify the content of a FrontPage-extended web or subweb**

1   In the console tree, right-click the root web or subweb that you want to modify.

2   Click **Task**, and then click **Open With FrontPage**.

3   In FrontPage, modify the content, and then save your changes.

Note   If FrontPage is not installed on the host computer, the **Open With FrontPage** command does not appear on the **Task** menu.

Specify a default scripting language

In a FrontPage-extended web page, you can add components that embed code in the page. You can specify either Microsoft Visual Basic Scripting Edition (VBScript) or Microsoft JScript for the code that FrontPage generates. FrontPage queries FrontPage Server Extensions for the scripting language to use to generate the code.

▶ **To specify a default scripting language**

1   In the console tree, right-click the root web or subweb for which you want to specify a scripting language.

2   Click **Properties**, and then click the **Server Extensions** tab.

3   In the **Client scripting** box, select a scripting language.

Set permissions manually

After you select security settings for a root web, you can prevent anyone who is using the administrative tools for FrontPage Server Extensions from modifying them.

▶ **To set permissions manually**

1   In the console tree, right-click the root web for which you want to set permissions manually.

2   Click **Properties**, and then click the **Server Extensions** tab.

3   Select the **Don't Inherit Security Settings** check box.

4   Select the **Manage permissions manually** check box.

Enable or disable authoring

You can enable authoring for the users who need to access webs they are building, or updating. However, when a Web site is complete, and does not need updating, you can disable authoring to protect essential information that must remain unchanged. When you disable authoring, users can neither add to nor change web content.

▶ **To enable or disable authoring on a FrontPage-extended web**

1 In the console tree, right-click the web for which you want to enable or disable authoring.

2 Click **Properties**, and then click the **Server Extensions** tab.

3 To enable authoring, select the **Enable authoring** check box.

　　–or–

　　To disable authoring, clear the **Enable authoring** check box.

Log authoring activities

Users with permission to modify the content of a FrontPage-extended web can change text, graphics, links, structure, and so on. To keep track of who makes changes to a Web site, and which files are changed, you can log the following authoring actions that are stored in a log file:

- Time an authoring action is performed.
- User name of the author.
- Name of the FrontPage-extended web.
- IP address of the remote host.

The log file is stored in _vti_log/author.log in the root web. If a security breach occurs, you can analyze this log file to identify authoring activity on the FrontPage-extended web.

▶ **To log authoring actions**

1 In the console tree, right-click the root web for which you want to log authoring actions.

2 Click **Properties**, and then click the **Server Extensions** tab.

3 Select the **Don't Inherit Security Settings** check box.

4 Select the **Log authoring actions** check box.

Specify folders where authors can upload executable applications

You can specify whether or not authors can upload executable applications such as CGI scripts or *active server pages* to a root web. When you allow authors to upload executable applications to a root web, bugs and viruses in the uploaded applications can affect your Web server.

▶ **To specify whether or not authors can upload executable applications to a root web**

1   In the console tree, right-click the root web for which you want to control executable scripts or applications.

2   Click **Properties**, and then click the **Server Extensions** tab.

3   Select the **Don't Inherit Security Settings** check box.

4   To allow executable scripts or applications in the folder, select the **Allow authors to upload executables** check box.

   –or–

   To disallow executable scripts or applications in a folder, clear the **Allow authors to upload executables** check box.

Require Secure Sockets Layer for authoring

You can require authors to use Secure Sockets Layer (SSL) to significantly improve security on your FrontPage-extended web. SSL encrypts information, which means that network eavesdroppers cannot read information transmitted between a Web browser and a Web server. It is especially useful to require SSL if client applications connect to the server with Basic *authentication*, which does not encrypt user names and password if SSL is not used.

▶ **To require SSL for authoring**

1   In the console tree, right-click the root web for which you want to require the use of SSL.

2   Click **Properties**, and then click the **Server Extensions** tab.

3   Select the **Don't Inherit Security Settings** check box.

4   Select the **Require SSL for authoring** check box.

Customize performance settings of a FrontPage-extended web

To optimize the performance of your FrontPage-extended web, you adjust cache sizes and the full-text search index size, which is the amount of disk space used to store search indexes for the web. The speed with which a FrontPage-extended web responds to a client request depends on the number of pages and other files the web contains—compared to the cache size and full-text search index size settings.

▶ To customize performance settings of a FrontPage-extended web

1   In the console tree, right-click the web that you want to customize.

2   Click **Properties**, and then click the **Server Extensions** tab.

3   In the **Performance** box, click the page range closest to the actual number of pages in the web.

4   Click **Use custom settings**, enter the cache sizes you want, and then enter the full-text search index size you want.

Set and configure e-mail options

When you set e-mail options in a FrontPage-extended web, you allow e-mail messages to be sent from the Web to readers. To configure the e-mail options, you must specify the e-mail address of the Web server, a contact address, a Simple Mail Transfer Protocol (SMTP) host, an e-mail-encoding scheme, and an e-mail character set.

▶ To configure FrontPage-extended web e-mail options

1   In the console tree, right-click the web for which you want to configure e-mail options.

2   Click **Properties**, and then click the **Server Extensions** tab.

3   In the **Options** box, click **Settings**, and then enter the settings you want.

See also

- There are four utilities you can use to perform administrative tasks on a FrontPage-extended web: the FrontPage MMC snap-in, FrontPage HTML Administration Forms, Fpsrvadm, and Fpsrvrem. For information about which tool to use for a specific task, see "Using FrontPage Server Extensions Tools" on page 687.

How to Use the HTML Administration Forms and Fpremadm.exe

You can use HTML Administration Forms to install and administer Microsoft FrontPage Server Extensions remotely with a Web browser. When you install FrontPage Server Extensions during Microsoft Office Server Extensions (OSE) Setup, the forms are copied to your Web server. When you install the forms on your Web server, your home page for the HTML Administration Forms is Fpadmin.htm.

The HTML Administration Forms are not active when they are first installed because remote administration of FrontPage Server Extensions is a potential security risk. Before you activate the forms, you can evaluate the security implications of remote administration, and then you can decide whether you want to use the HTML Administration Forms to administer FrontPage Server Extensions remotely.

Fpremadm is the utility that actually lets you administer FrontPage Server Extensions remotely. The Fpremadm utility interface is based on the administration utility Fpsrvadm.exe and performs all of the same commands. Fpremadm requires Microsoft Internet Explorer installed on the client computer.

Fpremadm uses Fpadmdll.dll, which is the same server-side ISAPI program as the HTML Administration Forms. Because of this, before you can use Fpremadm, you must install and activate the HTML Administration Forms on the server you want to administer.

Fpremadm uses the same command-line syntax as the Fpsrvadm utility. For example:

```
fpremadm.exe -adminusername UserAccount -adminpassword
-targetserver https://sample.microsoft.com:1439/fpadmin/scripts/fpadmdll.dll
-o upgrade -p 8234 -m sample.microsoft.com
```

Note the use of a secured connection and a nonstandard port.

Fpremadm also includes the following arguments that set up the connection to the remote server.

Argument	Description
-targetserver	URL of the server-side administration program, Fpadmdll.dll.
-adminusername	User name to authenticate access to the administration program. Used to log on and access Fpadmdll.dll. (Not the same as the **username** argument.)
-adminpassword	Password to authenticate access to the administration application. Used to log on and access Fpadmdll.dll.

Note   If you are using Windows NT Challenge/Response *authentication*, you can omit the **adminusername** and **adminpassword** arguments.

Administer FrontPage Server Extensions remotely

The HTML Administration Forms and Fpremadm use a similar architecture to perform remote FrontPage Server Extensions administration. Both communicate with Fpadmdll.dll on the server computer, and both in turn run the FrontPage Server Extensions administration utility Fpsrvadm.exe.

Client and server communicate through HTTP by using WinInet. Fpremadm passes its command line to Fpadmdll.dll. Fpadmdll.dll, in turn, passes the incoming command and arguments to the Fpsrvadm utility, which carries out the command.

You can use the HTML Administration Forms from a Web browser on any computer. On the Web server computer, Fpadmdll.dll acts as the form handler for FrontPage Server Extensions HTML Administration Forms. The form handler, Fpadmdll.dll, passes a command and arguments to the Fpsrvadm utility.

Administer security on a remote Web server

Administering remotely makes your Web server less secure than local administration because an unauthorized user can potentially access your Web server from the Internet and modify settings or delete webs. To prevent unauthorized access, use the following precautions:

- Require a user to log on to your Web server with a secure administrator account to access Fpadmdll.dll.

  When you require a secure administrator account, you prevent unauthorized access to your Web server.

- Require a secure connection such as Secure Sockets Layer (SSL) to communicate with Fpadmdll.dll.

  When you require a secure connection, network eavesdroppers cannot read a user name and password.

- Require the use of a nonstandard HTTP port to access Fpadmdll.dll. The standard HTTP port is 80, and the secure, nonstandard HTTP port is 443.

  When you require a nonstandard HTTP port, it is difficult for network eavesdroppers to identify the URL of the HTML Administration Forms, and the remote administration programs.

- Allow only specific IP addresses to access HTML Administration Forms or Fpadmdll.dll.

  When you allow only specific IP addresses access, you prevent unauthorized computers from accessing your HTML Administration Forms or Fpadmdll.dll. Typically, only IP addresses that are associated with the owner of a FrontPage-extended web should have access.

Activate remote administration

When you use either the Fpremadm utility or the HTML Administration Forms to administer your Web server remotely over your network or the Internet, you need to activate the HTML Administration Forms because they make remote administration services available.

Also, you should run the HTML Administration Forms over a secure port, which requires that you install a security *certificate* on your server. Use the Key Manager application included with Microsoft Internet Information Server (IIS) to make a security certificate request, submit the request to a key authority, and then use the Key Manager application to install the certificate that the key authority returns.

After you install a security certificate, you should enable the HTML Administration Forms either as a separate Web site or as a *virtual directory* on an existing Web site. Using a separate Web site with a separate IP address makes the forms harder to discover and allows you to enable additional security settings, such as distinct nonstandard port numbers. However, using a separate Web site with its own IP address can be a disadvantage because the number of IP addresses available for you to use might be limited.

When the HTML Administration Forms are located on an NTFS-formatted drive, you can set *permissions* on the *access control list* (ACL) of the folder where the forms are located—to control access to the folders. Before you activate the HTML Administration Forms for remote use, determine which individual Microsoft Windows NT accounts that you want to access the HTML Administration Forms. Each individual account that you want to access the forms must be a member of the Administrators group for that computer. You can give access to individual accounts, or you can use the Windows NT User Manager to create a new group account. A group account for administrators allows you to add and remove users from the Administrators group instead of changing the ACL of the HTML Administration Forms folder.

▶ To set or modify the access control list of the HTML Administration Forms folder

1   In Windows Explorer, locate the HTML Administration Forms, and then select the ISAPI folder.

The default location is C:\Program Files\Common Files\Microsoft Shared \Web Server Extensions\Version 4.0\Admin.

2   On the **File** menu, click **Properties**, click the **Security** tab, and then click **Permissions**.

3   Use the **Add** and **Remove** buttons to update the list of authorized users and groups in the **Name** box.

Remove all users and groups that are not authorized. In particular, remove any groups, the IUSR_*computer_name* anonymous account, and any wide-access accounts such as EVERYONE.

4   In the **Name** box, type the SYSTEM account for the computer.

This account is required to give IIS access to the file during the security validation process.

5   For each user or group in the **Name** box, set **Type of Access** to **Read**.

6   Select **Replace Permissions on Subdirectories and Replace Permissions on Existing Files**, and then click **OK**.

You can create a Web site that is used to access only the HTML Administration Forms.

▶ To create a Web site for the HTML Administration Forms

1   Start the IIS Internet Service Manager application, and then open the IIS folder.

2   Right-click the computer object, point to **New**, and then click **Web Site**.

3   In the **Description** box, type a name for the site, and then click **Next**.

4   Select an IP address for the site, and then click **Next**.

5   In the **Enter the path for your home directory** box, type the path to the HTML Administration Form files, clear the **Allow anonymous access to this web site** check box, and then click **Next**.

6   Select the **Allow Read Access** check box, then select the **Allow Execute Access** check box, and then click **Finish**.

When you create a Web site for the HTML Administration Forms, you can require SSL on connections to that Web site so that user name and password information are encrypted.

► To require SSL on connections to the HTML Administration Forms Web site

1   In the left pane of Internet Service Manager, right-click the icon for the new Web site, then click **Properties**, and then click the **Web Site** tab.

2   In the **SSL Port** box, type a nonstandard port number. The standard HTTP port is 80 and the standard secure HTTP port is 443. Use a port number other than 80 and 443.

3   Click the **Directory Security** tab, and then click the **Secure Communications Edit** button.

4   Select the **Require Secure Channel** check box, and then click **OK**.

After you set the ACL, create a Web site for the HTML Administration Forms and require SSL. You can use the HTML Administration Forms for remote administration through a URL such as:

https://*computer_name*:*port_number*/fpadmin.htm

where *computer_name* is mapped to the DNS entry for the IP address assigned to the HTML Administration Forms Web site and where *port_number* corresponds to the port number of the HTML Administration Forms Web site.

You can create a virtual directory to enable access to the HTML Administration Forms on an existing Web site—instead of creating a Web site dedicated to the forms.

► To create a virtual directory on an existing Web site for the HTML Administration Forms

1   Start the IIS Internet Service Manager, open the IIS folder, and then open the computer object.

2   Right-click the Web site icon, then point to **New**, and then click **Virtual Directory**.

3   In the **Alias** box, type the alias name for the HTML Administration Forms, and then click **Next**.

4   In the **Enter the physical path of the directory containing the content you want to publish** box, type the path to the HTML Administration Form files, and then click **Next**.

5   Select the **Allow Read Access** check box, then select the **Allow Execute Access** check box, and then click **Finish**.

▶ **To configure authentication on the HTML Administration Forms virtual directory**

1   In the left pane of Internet Service Manager, right-click the icon for the new virtual directory, then click **Properties**, and then click the **Directory Security** tab.

2   In the **Password Authentication Method** box, click the **Edit** button.

3   Clear the **Allow Anonymous** check box.

4   Select either or both **Basic Authentication** and **Windows NT Challenge/Response** check boxes, and then click **OK**.

5   Under **Secure Communications**, click **Edit**.

6   Click **Require Secure Channel**.

To activate the forms for remote administration, use a URL such as https://computername/fpadmin/fpadmin.htm.

See also

• Fpremadm.exe uses parameters and commands that are almost identical to Fpsrvadm.exe. For a full description of all the commands available through Fpsrvadm.exe, see "How to Use Fpsrvadm.exe" on page 692.

• There are four utilities you can use to perform administrative tasks on a FrontPage-extended web: the FrontPage MMC Snap-in, FrontPage HTML Administration Forms, Fpsrvadm, and Fpsrvrem. For information about which tool you can use to perform a specific task, see "Using FrontPage Server Extensions Tools" on page 687.

Customizing AutoNavigation View

On the Microsoft Office Server Extensions (OSE) Start Page, users click **Browse Web Folders** to view the folder and file contents of the *OSE-extended web*. The Folder.asp file generates the view called *AutoNavigation view*. Folder.asp is located in the Msoffice *virtual directory* on the OSE-extended web. By default, the physical folder of the Msoffice virtual directory is C:\Program Files\Microsoft Office\Office\Scripts\1033.

You can use HTML code to modify the Folder.asp file and to customize AutoNavigation view for your users. To customize the view, you can add sounds, pictures (such as logos), and any other HTML element you want.

You can also use Microsoft Visual Basic Scripting Edition (VBScript) to modify the AutoNavigation object. However, before you can modify the object, you must create it by using the Folder.asp file as a starting place or template. To create the object, type the following line in the Folder.asp file:

Set OfficeWebFolder= CreateObject("OfficeWebServer.WebFolderItems.1")

After you create the object, you can use the following methods and properties to modify the object.

Method	Parameters	Description
Init	Server, Request	Setup
Item	An Index (long)	Returns item #X in an array of **IOfficeWebFolderItem** objects

Property	Property type	Description
ActiveItem	IofficeWebFolderItem	Returns an **IofficeWebFolder** item representing the current folder.
ActiveURL	String	Returns or sets the URL of the folder being viewed.
Count	Long	Returns the number of files in the active directory.
CurrentPageURL	String	Returns the URL of the page being viewed.
Filter	String	Sets a filter for files to display; can use the asterisk (*) and question mark (?) characters. Defaults are HTML, HTM, MHTML, SHTML, TXT, DOC, XLS, PPT, and MDB files.
ShowFolders	Boolean	Determines whether folders are displayed; default is **True**.
ShowFiles	Boolean	Determines whether files are displayed; default is **True**.
ShowHidden	Boolean	Determines whether hidden files are displayed; default is **False**.
SortBy	Property*	Sorts results by the passed property; default is **Name**.
SortAscending	Boolean	Sets sorting order for display; default is **True**.

Within the **OfficeWebFolder** object, you can gain access to **OfficeWebFolderItem** objects by using the following method.

Method	Parameters	Description
Value	Property	Returns the value of the property for the current item.

Valid properties for the **SortBy** and **Value** methods are **Name, Size, DateCreated, DateLastWritten, DateLastAccessed, Icon, URL, ParentName, ParentURL**, and **isdirectory**.

The following code demonstrates the syntax to use with the AutoNavigation view object model:

```
OfficeWebFolder.Init Server, Request
   OfficeWebFolder.ActiveURL = "/mydocs/temp"
   OfficeWebFolder.SortBy = "Size"
   First_Name = OfficeWebFolder.Item(1).Value("Name")
   First_Size = OfficeWebFolder.Item(1).Value("Size")
```

You can gain access to the properties of an OfficeWebFolder.Item directly with the following code:

sItemName = OfficeWebFolder.Item(1).Name

You can also gain access to the properties indirectly:

sItemName = OfficeWebFolder.Item(1).Value("Name")

Consider using the AutoNavigation object model to do the following:

- Create pages that can recursively search a directory hierarchy, and display all files greater than a certain size.
- Allow users to create a custom view for their own directory.

Architecture of Office Server Extensions

Microsoft Office Server Extensions (OSE) consist of several client and server components that work together to enable OSE features. When you understand the client and server components, it is easier for you to deploy and troubleshoot OSE.

Server Components of Office Server Extensions

Microsoft Office Server Extensions (OSE) use several components to provide Microsoft Office 2000 users with Web Discussions, Web Subscriptions, and a secure Web publishing environment. These server-based components are:

- Microsoft Internet Information Server (IIS) (Windows NT Server and Windows 2000 Server) or Personal Web Server (Windows NT Workstation and Windows 2000 Professional)
- NTFS file system
- Microsoft FrontPage Server Extensions
- Microsoft Data Engine (MSDE) or Microsoft SQL Server
- Custom Automation objects
- *Active Server Pages* (ASP) pages
- OSE Notification Service and Simple Mail Transfer Protocol (SMTP) mail server

The following diagram identifies server component interactions on a single Web server running OSE.

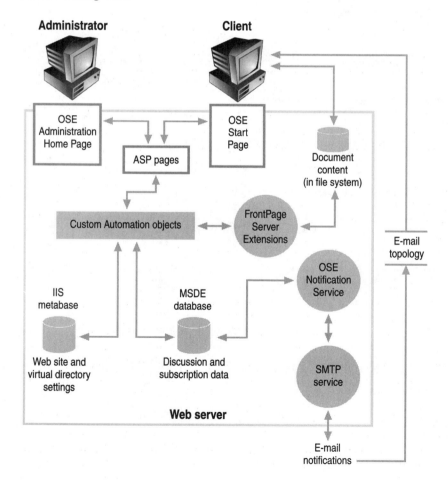

Some of the server components can be distributed across separate servers. The following diagram identifies server component interactions using more than one server.

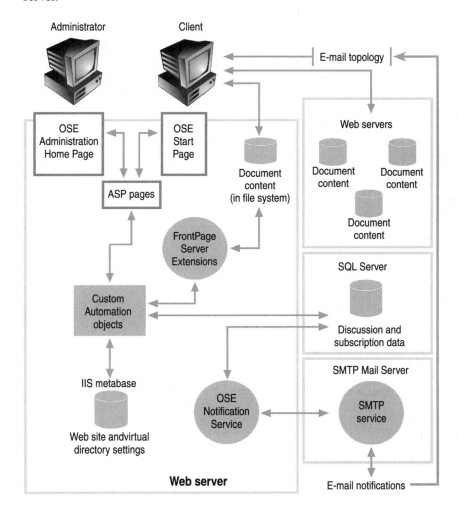

Using Office Server Extensions on Windows NT or Windows 2000

Microsoft Office Server Extensions (OSE) requires either Microsoft Windows NT Server running Internet Information Server (IIS) or Windows NT Workstation running Personal Web Server.

Using IIS on Windows NT Server or Windows 2000 Server

With Windows NT Server, OSE uses the following IIS elements:

- HTTP Web service
- Logon authentication
- IIS Metabase
- Web site space configuration (through the IIS Metabase)
- Virtual directory space configuration (through the IIS Metabase)
- Administration tools (Microsoft Management Console [MMC] or Web-based)
- Simple Mail Transfer Protocol (SMTP) mail service (optional)

HTTP Web service

HTTP is a simple and fast way to send data to and retrieve data from a Web server. The HTTP Web service is the primary component of IIS, and it runs as a Windows NT service. The service gives users access to a server through HTTP, which is the protocol that Web browsers and Office 2000 use so that users can view and publish documents.

To use the HTTP Web service, you must enable the TCP/IP network protocol on the Windows NT Server computer and all client computers. To connect to a server, the client application specifies a server and a port. The server is typically specified in a Uniform Resource Locator (URL), which contains the textual name of the server. The Internet Protocol (IP) address identifies the server location on the network. A Domain Name System (DNS) server maps the textual name to the IP address.

Note   With IIS and HTTP, users can connect simultaneously to multiple, uniquely numbered ports. However, to use OSE features, your Web sites must be configured to use port 80 only.

Logon authentication

When a client connects to your server to use a service such as HTTP, the server must authenticate the client. You use IIS to configure authentication on your server. Except when using anonymous authentication, each user must have a Windows NT account to log on to a server and to use IIS services.

To authenticate users, you must configure at least one Windows NT Server computer as the Primary Domain Controller (PDC) on your network. The PDC computer maintains the Security Accounts Management (SAM) database that contains the user Windows NT accounts, passwords, and *permissions* for network resources. User Manager for Domains is an application that runs on the Windows NT computer, and manages the SAM database.

During installation, IIS automatically creates an *anonymous account.* An anonymous account is a local computer account with the name IUSR_*computer_name*, where *computer_name* is the name of the computer running Windows NT Server. Anonymous users do not need an account to use IIS services.

The anonymous account is one Windows NT account that represents all users who log on to your server anonymously. The permissions you give to the anonymous account are given to anonymous users.

Important Anonymous authentication allows users to log on without a Windows NT account. However, this openness makes your server accessible to anyone on the network. If security is a priority, turn off anonymous authentication.

Web sites

In IIS, a Web site describes a self-contained area on the server that can be accessed by using either a unique IP address or server name, and port combination. You can configure the following properties for a Web site:

- IP address and port combination
- Operators (users who are allowed to configure Web site settings)
- Home directory
- Access permissions
- Authentication methods
- Number of allowable connections
- Logging format

During installation, IIS creates the Default Web Site. Users can access this Web site through port 80 by using the local IP addresses that you configure your server with. The Default Web Site home directory defaults to the path inetpub\wwwroot on the drive where you install IIS.

When you first establish an intranet for your organization or add a Web server to your department, it is easiest to keep the default configuration of a single Web site. As your needs expand and more users connect to your Web server, you can separate content and add more Web sites to the server for more flexible security and administration.

Virtual directories

Virtual directories allow you to hide the directory structure on your Web server and to reconfigure the structure while maintaining the same access addresses for users.

IIS implements virtual directories as a layer of indirection between the addresses users use and the physical directory structure of a Web site. Each virtual directory has an alias and a physical mapping. Users type in the alias when they connect to the server. The physical mapping identifies where IIS retrieves content when clients request the alias. The physical mapping is a local directory path, a network directory path, or a URL to which the client is redirected.

Each virtual directory belongs to a single Web site. The access permissions, authentication methods, and other settings from the Web site become the default settings for the virtual directory. However, you can configure permissions, authentication, and the other settings to override the default settings.

Each time you create a new Web site, you must run the OSE Configuration Wizard to add Microsoft FrontPage Server Extensions and an OSE-specific virtual directory to the new Web site. The wizard creates a virtual directory named MSOffice. The directory contains the *Active Server Pages* (ASP) pages and supporting files for Web Discussions, Web Subscriptions, OSE Directory Browsing and the OSE Start Page. The physical path for MSOffice is *office_install_root\ScriptsN\LCID*, where *ScriptsN* is the Web site instance number and *LCID* is the OSE language code. For example, the U.S. English OSE installation on the default Web site has N = 1 and LCID = 1033.

By default, the wizard turns on Basic authentication on the MSOffice virtual directory to allow the widest possible access to the OSE features. The wizard also creates two subfolders under MSOffice called Help and MSOAdmin. The Help folder contains the OSE Web-based Help pages and is accessible to all OSE users. The MSOAdmin folder contains the ASP pages, and supporting files for administering Web Discussions and Web Subscriptions. The MSOAdmin folder is accessible only to the Windows NT Administrators for the local computer, the Admins group the wizard optionally creates, and the System account. The Windows NT Administrators, the Admins group, and the System account likewise have Full Control access to MSOffice and its subfolders. Other users (collaborators and authors) have Read/Execute access to MSOffice and Help.

Metabase

The *metabase* is a database that stores *metadata* in a compressed format. IIS stores and maintains the Web site and virtual directory properties in the metabase. Metadata is data that describes other data. The metabase is similar to the Windows registry, but only IIS services use the metabase.

Note   Although the metabase can be modified programmatically, the primary means of browsing through and modifying the metabase is through performing IIS administration.

IIS administration

By using Internet Service Manager (ISM) and HTML-based forms, you can administer Web sites, virtual directories, and other IIS elements.

ISM is a snap-in extension to Microsoft Management Console.

▶ **To launch ISM after you install IIS**

1 Point to **Programs** on the **Start** menu.

2 Point to **Windows NT 4.0 Option Pack.**

3 Point to **Microsoft Internet Information Server.**

4 Click **Internet Service Manager.**

You access HTML-based forms through a Web browser.

▶ **To load the home page of the HTML-based forms**

• In the Address bar of your Web browser, type http://computer_name/iisadmin (where computer_name is the name of the IIS server).

Tip   You can use the IIS administration HTML forms on your server to administer a remote IIS server.

IIS SMTP mail service

The Web Subscriptions feature of OSE sends e-mail notifications to users who subscribe to documents or folders on the OSE-extended web. You specify the mail server for the OSE-extended web, and the SMTP mail server sends the e-mail notification.

If the SMTP service was not installed on your server when you installed IIS, rerun Windows NT Option Pack Setup to install the SMTP service. To configure the SMTP service, use either the Internet Service Manager application or the SMTP service's HTML-based administration forms.

Using Personal Web Server on Windows NT Workstation or Windows 2000 Professional

If your server runs Windows NT Workstation, you must run Personal Web Server (PWS) as your Web server software.

PWS is included with the Windows NT 4.0 Option Pack and is a scaled down version of IIS. Although PWS offers the same features as IIS, PWS supports only one Web site. PWS includes Personal Web Manager to simplify administration tasks, but you can also install and use Internet Service Manager with PWS.

OSE features and administration work identically with IIS and PWS.

Implementing advanced security with the NTFS file system

NTFS is a file system that you can use to format Windows NT Server and Windows NT Workstation hard disks. Windows 95 supports only the *file allocation table* (FAT) file system, and Windows 98 supports the FAT and FAT32 file systems.

NTFS offers several advantages over FAT and FAT32, including:

- Fault tolerance
- More efficient use of available disk space
- Advanced security capabilities, including access control and auditing

The advanced security features of NTFS allow you to set permissions on a per-file and per-folder basis. This access control is extremely useful in a Web server environment. OSE uses the file and folder permission feature to control access, browsing, and authoring on your Web site.

With the Windows 95 and Windows 98 FAT and FAT32 file systems, you cannot set permissions on individual files or folders. If you give a user access to a shared drive, that user can modify, rename, or delete any file or folder in the FAT or FAT32 volume. As a deterrent to users who might modify a file, you can set the file to read-only, but any user can change that setting.

You can use OSE without the NTFS file system, but the advanced security features are not available to you.

Using Office Server Extensions with FrontPage Server Extensions

Microsoft Office Server Extensions (OSE) requires Microsoft FrontPage Server Extensions, and OSE installs them during Setup. FrontPage Server Extensions use the Common Gateway Interface (CGI) and standard HTTP commands. With FrontPage Server Extensions, you do not need file sharing, FTP, or telnet access. FrontPage Server Extensions do not require proprietary file system sharing calls between the client and server.

FrontPage Server Extensions provide the following advanced features:

- Security administration

  FrontPage Server Extensions use NTFS permissions to let you control who can browse, author, or administer the Web site.

- Web site content maintenance

  FrontPage Server Extensions automatically maintain links, navigation bars, and themes across all documents on a Web site.

- Web site enhancements

  The FrontPage Server Extensions provide discussion groups, hit counters, search forms and many other enhancements to your Web sites.

- Trigger events

  OSE relies on FrontPage Server Extensions for notification of changed documents on the Web site to implement the Web Subscriptions feature.

FrontPage-extended webs

FrontPage Server Extensions support the creation and management of *FrontPage-extended webs*, which contain all the Web pages, images, scripts, and other files that make up a Web site. With FrontPage, users create, modify, and delete FrontPage-extended webs.

A FrontPage-extended web offers the following features:

- Hyperlink map recalculations

  FrontPage Server Extensions recalculate the entire hyperlink map when you copy a file from one Web server to another.

- Full-text index searches

  The FrontPage full-text index allows visitors to search for pages containing particular words or phrases.

- Site structure updates

  FrontPage Server Extensions update the site structure when you create or change the structure of a FrontPage-extended web.

- Design theme selections

  The design theme feature is an option that allows you to select a set of design elements, including background colors, stylized borders, navigation buttons, and so on. When you apply a new design theme to one page, FrontPage Server Extensions update all the pages in the FrontPage-extended web.

- Tasks list

  The Tasks list contains all the tasks needed to complete the FrontPage-extended web. Each task in the list links to the pages where tasks are performed.

- Unique security settings

  The security settings features of FrontPage-extended webs allow you to give specific administrators, authors, and Web site visitors access to specific FrontPage-extended webs.

Root webs and subwebs

A *root web* is a FrontPage-extended web that functions as the top-level content folder of a Web site. A root web can have many levels of subfolders, but there is only one root web for each Web site.

A *subweb* is a FrontPage-extended web that is contained within the root web or another subweb. Subwebs allow you to break up a Web site so that different users and groups can browse and maintain different areas of the Web site. You can configure unique security settings for each subweb.

FrontPage sets no limit on how deeply you can nest subwebs, although there may be a limit to the number of subdirectories supported by your operating system. You can use subwebs to set up your Web site in a way that matches the structure of your organization. For example, you can set up a root web that contains a manager subweb, contractor subweb, and customer subweb for each department in your organization. Then you can configure the permissions to allow only the department members to browse the subweb for the group in their department.

Working with Other Components of Office Server Extensions

Microsoft Office Server Extensions (OSE) use the following additional components to store and retrieve information:

- Microsoft Data Engine (MSDE) or SQL Server
- Custom Automation objects
- Active Server Pages (ASP) pages
- OSE Notification Service and SMPT mail server

Microsoft Data Engine or SQL Server

Microsoft Office Server Extensions (OSE) stores Web Discussions and Web Subscriptions data by using either the Microsoft Data Engine (MSDE) that is installed by default during OSE Setup or a Microsoft SQL Server version 6.5 or later database that can be local or remote.

If you already have a SQL Server installed on your Web server or available on your network, you can use that server to store your OSE data. To gain access to the SQL Server, you must specify the server name, user name, and a password that OSE uses.

The following list identifies the advantages of storing OSE data in an existing SQL Server:

- You can use the same administration that you already established for your SQL Server.

- Your OSE data is protected when your SQL Server has an existing backup strategy.

- You have fewer processing and storage burdens on the Web server running OSE.

Use MSDE when you need to store only OSE data and when you do not have a SQL Server established on your network.

Custom Automation objects

OSE supports features controlled by custom Automation objects. The custom Automation objects are installed on the Web server running OSE, and they perform the following functions:

- Read and write to the Internet Information Server (IIS) *metabase*—using the Active Directory Services Interface (ADSI).

- Read and write to MSDE or a SQL Server database—using ActiveX Data Objects (ADO).

- Receive requests from Active Server Pages (ASP) pages.

- Receive event notifications from Microsoft FrontPage Server Extensions—when documents are changed or discussion items are added.

- Respond to HTTP client requests—with Web pages or other response data.

- Prepare and queue e-mail notifications—in MSDE or the SQL Server database.

Active Server Pages

Active Server Pages (ASP) pages are script files located on a Web server. ASP pages create HTML tags dynamically to:

- Track user state and session information.

- Connect to various COM-based objects, such as the OSE custom Automation objects.

ASP pages are installed with OSE, and they process client requests and use custom Automation objects to return the appropriate response to the client computer. The OSE Start Page and Administration Home Page are examples of some of the ASP pages.

OSE Notification Service and SMTP mail server

The Office Server Extensions Notification Service is a Microsoft Windows NT service that OSE Setup installs. The notification service queries MSDE or the SQL Server database for queued e-mail notification at immediate, daily, and weekly intervals. The Office Server Extensions Notification Service delivers the e-mail notification to the Simple Mail Transfer Protocol (SMTP) mail server you specify when you configure OSE.

SMTP is an Internet standard protocol for formatting and transporting e-mail messages. If you use the Web Subscriptions feature of OSE, you must use a mail server with SMTP support, such as the Microsoft Exchange Server or the SMTP service in IIS. The mail server runs on either the Web server that is running OSE or a remote mail server.

The subscription notification process uses the following sequence of events to send e-mail notification to subscribers:

1 When a document changes, the FrontPage Server Extensions notify an OSE custom Automation object. This object is called the Event Sink.

2 When a user adds a discussion item to a document, an OSE custom Automation object responsible for managing discussion items notifies the Event Sink.

3 The Event Sink queries the MSDE database or SQL Server database to determine the subscription status for the file that has changed and for the folder that contains the changed file. If the file and folder do not have subscribers, no further action takes place. If the folder or file have subscribers, the procedure continues to the next step.

4 The Event Sink prepares e-mail notifications in SMTP format and then consolidates the notices into one e-mail message for each subscriber.

5 At the scheduled time, the notification service retrieves the e-mail message from the database, and sends the e-mail message to the SMTP mail server.

6 The SMTP mail server sends the e-mail message to the subscriber mailbox.

See also

- You need only a minimal understanding of HTTP, TCP/IP, IP addressing, URLs, and DNS to use OSE because OSE handles these components automatically. For more information about these subjects, see the *Microsoft Windows NT Server 4.0 Resource Kit*.

- Security is an important consideration when you deploy new server software such as OSE. For a complete discussion of OSE security issues, see "Using Windows NT Security with Office Server Extensions" on page 668 and "How to Configure Security on Your OSE-extended Web" on page 678.

- Windows NT includes the Convert.exe utility that you can use to convert an existing file allocation table (FAT) volume to NTFS —without losing data. For more information, see the *Microsoft Windows NT Server 4.0 Resource Kit*.

Client Components of Office Server Extensions

Microsoft Office 2000 client computers include Microsoft Office Server Extensions (OSE) client components as part of the Web Publishing feature. With these components, users have Web-based functionality even when they are not connected to an OSE-extended web.

The Web Publishing feature includes the following OSE client components:

- Namespace Extension
- Internet Publishing Provider

These additional components are included when Microsoft Internet Explorer 5 is installed:

- Synchronization Manager
- Internet Explorer 5 cache

The following diagram shows how the OSE components interact on a client computer to provide extended Web functionality in Office 2000.

Namespace Extension

The Namespace Extension adds the *Web Folders object* to the Windows environment. The Web Folders object is a container for shortcuts to your Web sites, and it appears immediately below My Computer in the Windows Explorer hierarchical structure.

Through the Web Folders object, users have access to Web sites from within My Computer, Windows Explorer, or the **Open** and **Save As** dialog boxes in Office 2000 applications. The Namespace Extension allows users to browse, open, and save documents on a Web site as easily as they work with files on a local hard disk.

Internet Publishing Provider

The Internet Publishing Provider provides access to files and folders on Web servers. The Namespace Extension and Office 2000 applications use the Internet Publishing Provider interface to upload, download, move, copy, or delete files and folders.

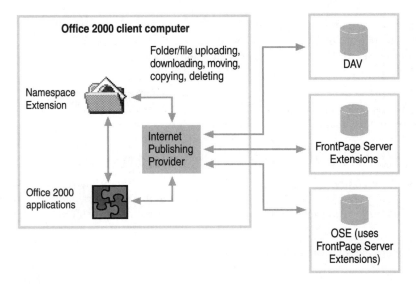

The Internet Publishing Provider supports two types of client/server communication:

- FrontPage Server Extensions—a subset of OSE.
- Distributed Authoring and Versioning (DAV)—an emerging standard Web server protocol.

Synchronization Manager and Internet Explorer 5 cache

When installed on an Office 2000 client computer, Microsoft Internet Explorer 5 supports offline caching—also called replication. A user can work offline from the network on cached copies of published documents. When a user goes online again, the Synchronization Manager copies the locally modified document to the server and reconciles differences in the local and published copies. To enable caching, the Internet Publishing Provider interacts with the Synchronization Manager and the Internet Explorer 5 cache.

The Synchronization Manager ensures that local up-to-date copies of recently used server-based files and other documents that users mark for offline replication are stored locally in the Internet Explorer 5 cache. When a user works offline, Internet Publishing Provider retrieves a document for a user from the Internet Explorer 5 cache by requesting it from the Synchronization Manager.

PART 6

Using Office 2000 in a Multinational Organization

Contents

Você sabe aonde
pode chegar?

¿Hasta dónde
quieres
llegar hoy?

Jusqu'ou
irez-vous?

CHAPTER 14

International Features of Office 2000

Microsoft Office 2000 is designed to accommodate users from all over the world. Because international features are built in, the tasks of deploying, administering, and supporting Office internationally are now greatly simplified.

In This Chapter

Overview of International Features in Office 2000

Microsoft Office 2000 with MultiLanguage Pack offers you the best of all worlds—core functionality that works around the world, as well as language-specific features designed for your international users.

Using Many Languages in One Office

In previous versions of Microsoft Office, Office is localized to work with different languages, so there is a separate version of Office for every language. Office 2000, however, combines support for all languages into a single product. Office 2000 with MultiLanguage Pack is built on core code that you can run internationally. Language-specific features are stored separately, primarily in dynamic-link library (DLL) files. These features "plug into" the core Office 2000 code; your users can install and run these features when they need them.

This plug-in language capability means you can install Office 2000 with MultiLanguage Pack on your computer, but view the Office 2000 user interface and online Help in German, or even view Help in German while displaying the user interface in English.

Installing the Microsoft Office 2000 MultiLanguage Pack

Plug-in language capability in Office 2000 is provided by the MultiLanguage Pack. The MultiLanguage Pack and Office 2000 are installed from different CD-ROMs; the MultiLanguage Pack has its own Setup program.

The procedure for installing the MultiLanguage Pack is the same as the procedure for installing Office 2000. You can create an *administrative installation point* for the MultiLanguage Pack, and you can use the Office Custom Installation Wizard to customize installations of the MultiLanguage Pack for different groups of users.

When you install the MultiLanguage Pack, you can make language files available to users on demand, instead of copying files to users' computers. (You can also choose to copy the language files to users' hard disks.) The MultiLanguage Pack works with the Windows installer to install the necessary files only when users run Office 2000 with a particular language configuration.

Installing localized versions of Office 2000

The MultiLanguage Pack lets you change the user interface and Help to any of dozens of languages and provides proofing tools for more than 80 languages. However, using Office 2000 with MultiLanguage Pack is not the same as using a localized version of Office 2000.

Because not all features have plug-in language capability, Office 2000 is localized in many languages for users who want to use all Office features in their own language. Localized versions of Office 2000 are compatible with Office 2000 with MultiLanguage Pack; that is, users of one language version can easily share documents created in other language versions.

Note   Localized versions of Office 2000, except the Thai and Indic language versions, are based on the same international core code as Office 2000 with MultiLanguage Pack. The Thai and Indic language versions are based on a separate, shared code base that also supports Vietnamese. The Indic languages supported include Devanagari-based languages (Hindi, Konkani, Marathi, Nepali, and Sanskrit) and Tamil.

Toolbox

You can look up information about which Office 2000 features cannot change the language of their user interface and online Help in the Microsoft Excel workbook Intlimit.xls. For information about installing Intlimit.xls, see "International Information" on page 786.

See also

- You can deploy Office 2000 with MultiLanguage Pack across your entire organization, or you can deploy a combination of Office 2000 with MultiLanguage Pack and localized versions of Office 2000. For more information, see "Deploying Office in a Multinational Setting" on page 151.

- Your decision to deploy Office 2000 with MultiLanguage Pack or a localized version is determined in part by your users' operating system. For information about operating system compatibility and international features of Office 2000, see "Configuring Users' Computers in an International Environment" on page 732.

Features of the MultiLanguage Pack

The Microsoft Office 2000 MultiLanguage Pack provides features that allow users to change the language of their Office user interface and online Help. It includes the Microsoft Office 2000 Proofing Tools; the Proofing Tools provide spelling checkers, grammar checkers, and other tools for editing in a variety of languages.

Features available in the MultiLanguage Pack Setup program

The MultiLanguage Pack Setup program installs features that allow you to change the language of the user interface and Help. You can also install features from the Proofing Tools.

The MultiLanguage Pack Setup program installs the following features:

- User interface dynamic-link (DLL) files

- Online Help DLL files

- Localized templates and wizards

- Asian user interface fonts

The MultiLanguage Pack Setup program includes the Proofing Tools, which installs the following features:

- Spelling checker

- Grammar checker

- Thesaurus

- Hyphenator

- AutoCorrect list

- AutoSummarize DLL file

- Word breaker (for languages that don't use blank spaces to divide words)

- Grammar, hyphenation, spelling, and thesaurus dictionaries

In addition, the Proofing Tools provide the following utilities that are particularly useful for users who work with Asian languages:

- Translator for Simplified Chinese and Traditional Chinese translator
- Korean converter for Hangul and Hanja

Toolbox

Information about user interface and Help features, as well as a list of proofing tools that are available for each language, is included on the LPK and PTK Language Components worksheets in the Excel workbook Multilpk.xls. For information about installing Multilpk.xls, see "International Information" on page 786.

Features available on the MultiLanguage Pack CD-ROM

Besides the features that are installed with the MultiLanguage Pack Setup program, you can install other features provided on the MultiLanguage Pack CD-ROM. These features are in folders in the Extras folder on the MultiLanguage Pack CD-ROMs.

The following table lists the features available in the Extras folder.

Feature	Folder	Description
Excel add-ins	XLAddins*language*	Allows users to run certain localized add-ins, such as Update Add-in Links.
Excel object libraries	95olbs*language*	Allows Excel 2000 to run multilingual macros created in Microsoft Excel 95 and 5.0
Microsoft Internet Explorer user interface language	Ie5*language*	Allows users to change the language of the user interface in Internet Explorer 5
Input method editors	Ime*language*	Allows users to type Asian text
Microsoft Jet 4.0 user interface language	Jet*language*	Allows users to change the language of the user interface for Microsoft Access 2000 database engine and other applications that use Microsoft Jet 4.0
Outlook At Work fax patch	AWFAXpat*language*	Provides localized patch for the Outlook At Work fax feature.
Outlook forms	EFDSupp*language*	Allows users to open forms with localized Electronic Forms Design files.

Note Global Input Method Editors (Global IMEs) allow users running non-Asian versions of the Microsoft Windows operating system to type Asian text in Microsoft Word, Microsoft Outlook, and Internet Explorer.

Installation path for MultiLanguage Pack features

MultiLanguage Pack features can be installed on the user's hard disk, either all at one time or on demand, or they can be run from a server. When MultiLanguage Pack features are installed on a user's hard disk, files are stored in the following folders, where *LCID* is the *locale ID* of the language.

The Program Files\Microsoft Office9\Office*LCID* folder contains the following features:

- User interface DLL files and other resources
- Online Help files
- Localized templates and wizards
- Default AutoCorrect lists

The Program Files\Common Files\Microsoft Shared\Proof folder contains the following features:

- Hyphenator (Mshy*.dll and Mshy*.lex files)
- Spelling checker (Msp*.dll, Mssp*.dll, and Mssp*.lex files)
- Thesaurus (Msth*.dll and Msth*.lex files)
- Grammar dictionary (Msgr*.lex files)

The Program Files\Common Files\Microsoft Shared\Proof*LCID* folder contains the following feature:

- Grammar checker (Msgr*.dll files)

Features that provide a user interface in more than one language have the same file name, but are stored in separate LCID folders. Other features, such as grammar and spelling dictionaries, have unique names and are stored in the same folder.

For example, the file for the English grammar checker is Msgr2en.dll; the Msgr2en.dll file for the English user interface is stored in the 1033 folder, but the Msgr2en.dll file for the Japanese user interface is stored in the 1041 folder. However, the file for the English grammar dictionary is Msgr2en.lex and the file for the Japanese grammar dictionary is Msgr2jp.lex; both files are stored in the Program Files\Common Files\Microsoft Shared\Proof folder.

See also

- There are special procedures for installing MultiLanguage Pack features that are in the Extras folder of the MultiLanguage Pack CD-ROM. For more information, see "MultiLanguage Pack Extras" on page 160.

How to Remove MultiLanguage Pack Files

In a busy international organization, a user might need a set of MultiLanguage Pack features for a particular language installed on a computer for short-term use. When a user no longer needs to work with files in that language, or if a *traveling user* moves on, these MultiLanguage Pack files remain on the computer, taking up disk space.

Office 2000 does not automatically remove unneeded MultiLanguage Pack files. But you can remove these files if you want.

▶ **To remove MultiLanguage Pack files**

1 Rerun the MultiLanguage Pack Setup program.

   –or–

   In Control Panel, double-click the **Add/Remove Programs** icon and then double-click **Microsoft Office 2000 MultiLanguage Pack Disc** *n*.

2 Click **Add or Remove Features**, select the MultiLanguage Pack features you want to remove, and then click **Not Available**.

3 Click **Update Now**.

Tip If you can't run the MultiLanguage Pack Setup program, you can recover disk space by deleting unnecessary LCID folders. LCID folders are in the Program Files\Microsoft Office9\Office folder and the Program Files\Common Files\Microsoft Shared\Proof folder. For a list of languages and corresponding LCIDs, see Office Help.

Office Features Set by the Installation and Editing Languages

Microsoft Word, Microsoft Excel, Microsoft Access, and Microsoft FrontPage use the *installation language* setting to govern default behavior. The installation language setting is the *locale ID* (LCID) assigned to the value entry **InstallLanguage**, which Office Setup creates in the following registry subkey:

HKEY_CURRENT_USER\Software\Microsoft\Office\9.0\Common\LanguageResources

For example, if the value of **InstallLanguage** is **1041** (Japanese), Word creates its initial Normal.dot file based on Japanese settings and automatically enables commands for Asian text layout.

When a user enables languages for editing, the user is actually turning on language-specific features in Office 2000 applications.

For example, Word automatically detects the language a user is typing based on the languages that the user enabled for editing. If the Proofing Tools features are installed, Word uses the spelling checker, AutoCorrect list, and so on for the languages it detects.

Some Office 2000 applications also display commands and dialog box options based on enabled languages. For example, if you enable an Asian language in Word, you can configure Asian text layout in the **Format** menu.

See also

- You can deploy Office 2000 so that its default settings are based on a particular language. For more information, see "Customizing Language Features" on page 170.

Configuring Users' Computers in an International Environment

All of the international features of Microsoft Office 2000 work on Microsoft Windows 95/98, Microsoft Windows NT 4.0, and Windows 2000. However, some of these operating systems are better able to handle multiple languages. You can also set up browsers, fonts, and printers to take better advantage of international features.

Recommended Operating Systems for International Use

The Microsoft Windows 95/98, Microsoft Windows NT 4.0, and Windows 2000 operating systems provide support for the international features of Microsoft Office 2000. However, if your users work with a set of different languages that includes Asian or right-to-left languages (Arabic, Farsi, Hebrew, and Urdu), then Windows 2000 provides the best support for displaying and editing documents and for changing the language of the user interface.

Toolbox

Information about the languages supported by each operating system, and the limitations of that support, is included in an Access database named Wwsuppt.mdb. For information about installing Wwsuppt.mdb, see "International Information" on page 786.

Displaying the user interface in other languages

The ability of Office 2000 to display the user interface and online Help in some languages depends on the capabilities of the operating system. Windows 95 and Windows 98 provide fairly broad support within a single language category. Windows NT 4.0 has more flexibility, and Windows 2000 provides support for all possible Office user interface languages.

For example, on a computer running the English version of Windows 95/98, Microsoft Word can display the user interface in any European language. On a computer running Windows NT 4.0, Word can also display the user interface in Asian languages, and on Windows 2000, right-to-left languages are also supported.

Some *code page*s provide support for groups of languages; other code pages provide support for only a single language. Therefore, make sure a user's *system locale* (which governs the code page of the system) is set to a locale that supports the primary language the user needs.

Note   Only Windows NT 4.0 and Windows 2000 support changing the system locale. With Windows 95/98, users must run the appropriate localized version of the operating system.

For example, if your users work primarily in Japanese, set their system locale to Japanese (or have them run a Japanese version of Windows 95/98). If your users work primarily in French, their system locale can be any Western European system locale (or they can run any Western European version of Windows 95/98).

The following tables are a guideline for getting the best support for displaying the Office 2000 user interface and online Help in Access, Excel, PowerPoint, and Word when your users run Windows 95/98 or Windows NT 4.0.

The following table is a guideline for getting the best support for displaying the Office 2000 user interface and online Help in Windows 95/98.

Users running this language version of Windows 95/98	Can display the user interface and online Help in these languages
English, Western European, or Eastern European	English, Western European, and Eastern European
Asian	English and the matching Asian
Right-to-left (Arabic or Hebrew)	English, Western European, Eastern European, and the matching right-to-left

The following table is a guideline for getting the best support for displaying the Office 2000 user interface and online Help in Windows NT 4.0.

Users running this language version of Windows NT 4.0	Can display the user interface and online Help in these languages
English, Western European, or Eastern European	English, Western European, and Eastern European, and Asian
Asian	English, Western European, Eastern European, and Asian
Right-to-left (Arabic or Hebrew)	English, Western European, Eastern European, and the matching right-to-left

The following table is a guideline for getting the best support for displaying the Office 2000 user interface and online Help in Windows 2000.

Users running this language version of Windows 2000	Can display the user interface and online Help in these languages
Any	English, Western European, Eastern European, Asian, and right-to-left

Note   Eastern European languages are supported by the Central European, Baltic Rim, Cyrillic, Greek, and Turkish code pages.

Limitations of displaying the user interface in other languages

For some applications and features in Office 2000, the native *code page* of the operating system must support the user interface language. For these applications and features, text in the user interface, including text typed by the user—such as Contacts in Outlook or file names in Binder—must be supported by the operating system's code page.

When you use Outlook and some Office features, such as Binder and the Office Shortcut Bar, you can change the user interface language as long as the language has code page support from your operating system.

In FrontPage, you can change the user interface language to most languages as long as the language has code page support from your operating system. However, you cannot change the user interface to a right-to-left language.

When you change the user interface to a language that does not have code page support, Outlook and FrontPage display the user interface in English.

Toolbox

You can look up information about which Office 2000 features cannot change the language of their user interface and online Help in the Microsoft Excel workbook Intlimit.xls. For information about installing Intlimit.xls, see "International Information" on page 786.

Displaying online Help in other languages

When you change the online Help language in Office 2000, the Help content is displayed in the new language, but the Help user interface is still displayed in the Office user interface language. However, some elements of the Help user interface (such as the **Contents** tab, the **Options** menu, and toolbar ScreenTips) are always in English.

Furthermore, when you change the Help content language, the language must have code page support from your operating system. Otherwise, the Help topics listed in the **Contents** tab will be unintelligible. In this case, you can use the **Answer Wizard** and **Index** tabs to find Help topics. However, if you want to use these tabs, you must display online Help in a language that the Answer Wizard supports.

Note   Windows 2000 supports all languages used by Office 2000.

If you change the Help language to a language that is not supported by the Answer Wizard, the language must have code page support. In this case, Help displays the **Full Text Search** tab to allow you to find Help topics.

The Answer Wizard supports the following languages:

Arabic	Finnish	Polish
Chinese (Simplified)	French	Portuguese (Brazilian)
Chinese (Traditional)	German	Portuguese (Iberian)
Czech	Italian	Russian
Danish	Japanese	Spanish
Dutch	Korean	Swedish
English	Norwegian	Thai

Displaying documents in other languages

Users running Office 2000 can display documents in a wider range of languages than when they display the Office 2000 user interface and online Help. For example, German users running Office 2000 on German language version of Windows 98 can view Japanese documents even though they cannot switch to a Japanese user interface.

All language versions of Windows 2000 support displaying documents in all languages. The following table is a guideline for getting the best support for displaying Office 2000 documents in Windows 95/98 or Windows NT 4.0.

Users running this language version of Windows 95/98 or Windows NT 4.0	Can display documents in these languages
English, Western European, Eastern European, or Asian	All languages, except right-to-left, Thai, Vietnamese, and Indic
Right-to-left (Arabic or Hebrew)	All languages, except Thai, Vietnamese, and Indic
Thai	All languages, except right-to-left, Vietnamese, and Indic
Vietnamese	All languages, except right-to-left, Thai, and Indic

Note   Eastern European languages are supported by the Central European, Baltic Rim, Cyrillic, Greek, and Turkish code pages. The Indic languages supported include Devanagari-based languages (Hindi, Konkani, Marathi, Nepali, and Sanskrit) and Tamil. Text in Thai and Vietnamese is supported by the South Asian English version of Office 2000 only.

Editing documents in other languages

Typically, if a user's operating system prevents the display of a certain language, users are not able to edit documents in that language. However, in the case of Asian documents, even though users can display documents, they might not be able to edit them.

Input of Asian characters requires an *Input Method Editor* (IME). Non-Asian operating systems don't commonly support IMEs, and Asian operating systems usually support the IME for their native language only. For example, this limitation means that users running the Korean language version of Windows 98 can't use the IME for Japanese.

The Microsoft Office 2000 MultiLanguage Pack overcomes this limitation to some degree by providing Global IMEs for Japanese, Korean, Simplified Chinese, and Traditional Chinese. The Global IMEs allow users to edit Asian text in Word and Microsoft Outlook, regardless of the language version of their operating system.

Adding international support to Windows 95/98

If your international organization includes Windows 95/98 users who work with Office 2000 documents in several languages, you can add international capabilities to the operating system. Adding multilingual support allows users to display foreign language characters that Windows 95/98 does not otherwise support, and adding keyboard support allows users to input characters not found on the U.S. keyboard.

▶ **To add multilingual support**

1   In Control Panel, double-click **Add/Remove Programs**, and then click the **Windows Setup** tab.

2   Select the **Multilanguage Support** check box.

    To install support for selected languages, double-click **Multilanguage Support** and then select the languages you want.

Note   Support for right-to-left languages (Arabic, Farsi, Hebrew, and Urdu) can be added only to a right-to-left language version of Windows 95/98.

To enter text in a given language, users need to use the appropriate keyboard layout.

▶ **To add keyboard support**

1   In Control Panel, double-click **Keyboard**, and on the **Language** tab, click **Add**.

2   In the **Add Language** dialog box, choose a setting from the **Language** list.

3   To change the keyboard layout for a language, click the **Properties** button, and in the **Language Properties** dialog box, choose a setting from the **Keyboard layout** list.

4   To be able to switch between keyboards by clicking an indicator on the taskbar, select the **Enable indicator on taskbar** check box.

See also

- Windows NT 4.0 and Windows 2000 provide multilingual support, but you must select the keyboard layout you want to use. For information about adding keyboard support, see online Help for the appropriate operating system.

- The MultiLanguage Pack provides a keyboard layout program that makes it easier for users to type languages not represented on the physical keyboard. For information about the MultiLanguage Pack, see "Features of the MultiLanguage Pack" on page 727.

Recommended Web Browsers for International Use

The Web browser installed on users' computers can affect how well Microsoft Office 2000 supports switching to different user interface languages. In addition, browsers that support *Unicode* allow users to create multilingual Web pages.

Supporting multilingual dialog boxes

Microsoft Internet Explorer 5 allows Office 2000 applications to display certain dialog boxes in any user interface language that the operating system supports. Dialog boxes such as **New** and **Open** from the **File** menu depend on the *code page* of the operating system to display text.

A minimum installation of Internet Explorer 5 allows users to switch to different user interface languages regardless of the code page. Without Internet Explorer 5, users might see meaningless characters in dialog boxes after changing user interface languages.

Note If users are switching between languages that use the same code page—for example, all Western European languages—they don't need to install Internet Explorer 5 to display all dialog boxes properly.

If you want users to be able to change their user interface language across code pages, but you don't want a full-featured installation of Internet Explorer 5 on users' computers, you can customize Office Setup with a minimum installation of Internet Explorer 5.

▶ **To customize Office Setup with a minimum installation of Internet Explorer 5**

- In the **Customize IE5 Installation Options** pane of the Office Custom Installation Wizard, select the **Upgrade to Internet Explorer 5** option, and in the **Internet Explorer 5 upgrade mode** box, select **Minimum**.

Note After installing Internet Explorer 5, users must turn Microsoft Active Desktop off before they can change their user interface language.

Using Unicode in multilingual Web pages

Unicode allows users to create multilingual Web pages that not only use multiple *scripts* but also produce smaller files that are easy to parse on your intranet. You need Internet Explorer version 4.01 or later, or Navigator 4.03 or later for your browser to interpret Unicode Web pages. If you want to maintain compatibility with earlier browsers, avoid using Unicode.

Note   The Unicode format commonly used on the Internet is called Universal Character Set Transformation Format 8-bit (UTF-8). UTF-8 is the only Unicode format that is commonly supported by Web browsers and by FrontPage Server Extensions.

You can set Office 2000 applications to save the current HTML document in Unicode. Click **Options** (**Tools** menu), and then click **Web Options** on the **General** tab. On the **Encoding** tab, select **Unicode (UTF-8)** in the **Save this document as** list.

Note   To save HTML documents in the Unicode format by default, select the **Always save Web pages in the default encoding** check box in the **Web Options** dialog box.

Using Unicode in multilingual URLs

In addition to allowing users to create HTML documents in UTF-8 encoding, Office 2000 and Internet Explorer 5 can send UTF-8 encoded URLs to Web servers.

UTF-8 encoding allows users to use URLs that include non-ASCII characters, regardless of the language of the user's operating system and browser, or the language version of Office. Without UTF-8 encoding, a user's Web server must be based on the same code page as that of the user's operating system in order for the Web server to interpret non-ASCII URLs. However, for a Web server to interpret UTF-8 encoded URLs, the Web server must have UTF-8 support.

Note   To use UTF-8 encoded URLs, you must have Microsoft Internet Information Server (IIS) version 4.0 or later or another Web server that supports UTF-8.

If your organization has code page-based Web servers that do not support UTF-8 and you have non-ASCII URLs, you should turn off UTF-8 URL encoding in Internet Explorer 5. Otherwise, when users try to use a UTF-8 encoded URL that includes non-ASCII characters, the code page-based Web server that doesn't support UTF-8 cannot interpret the URL.

▶ **To prevent sending URLs in UTF-8 encoding**

1   In Internet Explorer 5, on the **Tools** menu, click **Internet Options**.

2   In the **Internet Options** dialog box, click the **Advanced** tab.

3   In the **Settings** box under **Browsing**, clear the **Always send URLs as UTF-8** check box.

See also

- In addition to optimizing international capabilities on the client side, you can also add multilingual support on your international Web servers. For information about international server requirements, such as multilingual URLs, see "Installing Office Web Features for International Users" on page 588.

- Documents that use Unicode are easier for users who work in different languages to share. For more information about Unicode, see "Sharing Multilingual Documents" on page 746.

- To display localized server messages, you must install a localized version of Microsoft FrontPage Server Extensions. For information about the latest release of FrontPage Server Extensions in a particular language, see the Microsoft Front Page Web site at http://www.microsoft.com/frontpage/.

Administering Fonts in an International Office

Microsoft Office 2000 provides fonts that allow users to view and edit documents in different languages, across different *scripts*. Some of these fonts are installed with Office 2000; others are available in the Microsoft Office 2000 MultiLanguage Pack. Some international fonts supplied with Office 2000 might update Windows fonts that users already have.

Understanding how Office 2000 uses fonts for different languages can help you administer fonts for users across your international organization.

International fonts included with Office 2000

Office 2000 and the MultiLanguage Pack include fonts necessary for working with the international features of Office. These additional fonts allow you to:

- Display the user interface and online Help in various languages.

- Input text in various languages, except for languages that require Input Method Editors (IMEs).

Note The MultiLanguage Pack also includes several Global IMEs that work with Word, Outlook, and Internet Explorer.

In addition to the fonts in the MultiLanguage Pack, which support particular character sets, Office 2000 also includes a complete *Unicode* font, which supports all characters in all of the languages supported by Office. This Unicode font is especially useful when you cannot apply multiple fonts—for example, when you work with multilingual data in Access data tables.

The following table lists the fonts provided by the MultiLanguage Pack, along with the *code pages* and the languages they support.

Font (file)	Code page	Supported languages
BatangChe (BatangCh.ttf)	1250, 1251, 1252, 1253, 1254, 1257, 949	All European languages, Korean
MingLiU (Mingliu.ttf)	932, 936, 950	English, Simplified Chinese, Traditional Chinese, Japanese
MS UI Gothic (Msuigoth.ttf)	1250, 1251, 1252, 1253, 1254, 1257, 932	All European languages, Japanese

The following table lists the fonts provided by Office 2000, along with the code pages and the languages that the fonts support.

Font (file)	Code page	Supported languages
Arial Unicode MS (Arialuni.ttf)	All	All
Batang (Batang.ttf)	250, 1251, 1252, 1253, 1254, 1257, 949	All European languages, Korean
PMingLiU (PMingliu.ttf)	932, 936, 950	English, Simplified Chinese, Traditional Chinese, Japanese
MS Mincho (Msmincho.ttf)	1250, 1251, 1252, 1253, 1254, 1257, 932	All European languages, Japanese
SimSun (Simsun.ttf)	936	English, Simplified Chinese, Traditional Chinese

Updating Windows fonts to big fonts

Many of the fonts that are included with Windows 95/98, Windows NT 4.0, and Windows 2000 are stored as big font files. Big font files include Tahoma, which is the default Office 2000 user interface font for all languages except Asian languages. The big font files include *glyphs* for multiple character sets and accommodate many languages. When you install Office 2000, Office updates existing Windows fonts to big fonts and installs additional fonts.

Following are big fonts that Office Setup installs or updates:

- Arial
- Arial Black
- Arial Bold
- Arial Narrow
- Bookman Old Style
- Courier New
- Garamond
- Impact

- Tahoma
- Times New Roman
- Trebuchet (Central and Eastern European languages only)
- Verdana®

Installing fonts that support multiple languages

If your users frequently share documents or e-mail messages across different *scripts*, you can install fonts that support those scripts.

In most cases, Office Setup automatically installs or updates fonts to display characters in multiple scripts. For example, a document formatted in Arial font can display Western European, Cyrillic, Turkish, Baltic, Central European, Greek, Arabic, or Hebrew text.

For Asian languages or Unicode characters, however, you must install the appropriate fonts on users' computers.

Important Do not change the default user interface font. The Office 2000 user interface is designed to fit Tahoma and certain Asian fonts. Using a different user interface font might truncate user interface labels in some languages.

Installing Asian fonts

Office 2000 provides Asian fonts for four languages: Japanese, Korean, Simplified Chinese, and Traditional Chinese. If users need to edit or read documents in these languages, they must install the appropriate Asian fonts.

▶ To install Asian fonts

1 On the **Selecting Features** panel in Office Setup, select the Office Tools\International Support feature.

2 For each of the Asian fonts you want to use, select the font and set the installation state to **Run from My Computer**.

Installing the Unicode font

Some documents, such as Access data tables, can display only one font at a time. But these documents can display multilingual text in more than one script if you use the Unicode font. The Unicode font provided by Office 2000 allows users to input and display characters across scripts and across *code pages* that support the various scripts.

Installing a Unicode font on users' computers presents some disadvantages. First, the Unicode font file is much larger than font files based on code pages. Second, some characters might look different from their character equivalents in code pages. For these reasons, do not use the Unicode font as your default font. However, if your users share documents across many different scripts, the Unicode font might be your best choice.

▶ **To install the Unicode font**

1   On the **Selecting Features** panel in Office Setup, select the Office Tools\International Support feature.

2   Select the Universal Font feature, and set the installation state to **Run from My Computer**.

See also

- You can install a utility that adds code page information to the properties shown when you right-click a font file in Windows 95/98, Windows NT 4.0, or Windows 2000. For more information about the font properties extension utility, see the Microsoft Typography Web site at http://www.microsoft.com/typography/.

Printing Documents in an International Setting

Using the international features of Office 2000 in documents creates some special requirements for printing. You must ensure that your printers are configured for the correct paper size and for font substitution.

Specifying the correct paper size

Many printers allow you to load both A4 and letter-size paper. If users in Europe exchange documents with users in the United States, having both A4 and letter size paper in your printers accommodates everyone's documents.

Even if your printers are stocked only with the paper commonly used in your part of the world, most Office documents are printed with no loss of text. Word documents and Microsoft PowerPoint presentations are automatically scaled to fit the printer's default paper size. Outlook messages are printed according to locally defined default print parameters. FrontPage documents are printed according to the browser's page layout settings.

Note   For Access reports and Microsoft Publisher documents, users must open reports and documents and manually change the paper size.

In some circumstances, you might not want documents scaled to fit the printer's default paper size. For example, if your printer has A4 set as its default paper size but the printer also has letter-size paper, then Word cannot detect that both sizes are available. Because the printer can supply the correct size paper, you might want to turn off the resizing option that is available in Word.

System Policy Tip   You can use a system policy to turn off the **Allow A4/Letter paper resizing** option on the **Print** tab (**Options** menu) in Word. In the System Policy Editor, set the **Microsoft Word 2000\Tools | Options\Print\Printing options\Allow A4/Letter paper resizing** policy. For more information about the System Policy Editor, see "Using the System Policy Editor" on page 296.

Setting TrueType fonts to print correctly

To display characters in multiple *scripts*, Office uses big fonts. In addition to being bold or italic, big fonts can also be Cyrillic, Greek, or one of several other scripts.

However, big fonts are also TrueType® fonts, and many laser printers substitute built-in printer fonts when printing documents that use TrueType fonts. Built-in printer fonts cannot render text in multiple scripts, so characters in other scripts do not print properly.

For example, your laser printer might substitute its own internal version of Arial, which accommodates only Western European characters. Word uses the big font version of Arial to display Greek and Russian characters in documents, but if users print those documents, the Greek and Russian characters are printed as unintelligible Western European character strings.

To work around the problem, set the option in your printer driver to send TrueType fonts as graphics.

Tip   Some non-Asian printers cannot properly print Asian documents because the size of the Asian font is too large for the printer's memory. You might need to install additional memory in these printers.

See also

- Unicode might affect the way that Office 2000 documents are printed. For information about Office 2000 support of Unicode, see "Taking Advantage of Unicode Support in Office 2000" on page 748.

CHAPTER 15

Upgrading an International Organization to Office 2000

When you deploy Microsoft Office 2000 with MultiLanguage Pack, international users can upgrade easily from previous localized versions of Office. Migration of user settings from previous localized versions, Unicode support, and multilingual features of Office 2000 make for a smooth international upgrade, whether your organization makes the transition gradually or all at once.

In This Chapter

Planning an International Move to Office 2000

When users upgrade from a localized version of Microsoft Office to Office 2000 with MultiLanguage Pack, their settings in the localized version migrate to the new Office installation. Office 2000 support of Unicode allows users who work in different language versions of Office to use the same documents. By understanding how user settings of localized versions of Office migrate and how Office 2000 supports Unicode, you can help your upgrade to Office 2000 go smoothly.

Migrating Settings from Previous Localized Versions to Office 2000

If your organization is upgrading from a previous localized version of Microsoft Office to Office 2000 with Microsoft MultiLanguage Pack, you can customize the Office Setup program so that users' settings and preferences migrate from the previous localized version to the new installation of Office 2000.

Because user settings in the previous localized version of Office are designed to work with that language version, the settings cannot migrate across language versions of Office. Therefore, if you are deploying Office 2000 with MultiLanguage Pack and you want to migrate user settings, you must set the *installation language* of Office 2000 to match the language of users' previous localized version of Office. Then, when users run the Office Setup program, their settings migrate to Office 2000.

Note   You can also migrate user settings from a previous localized version of Office to the matching language version of Office 2000.

If a standard deployment throughout your organization is important and you don't want to deploy multiple settings for the installation language, leave the installation language set to English and disable migration of user settings. In this case, user settings cannot migrate across language versions of Office, and settings from previous non-English versions of Office are lost.

See also

- When you deploy Office 2000, you can specify the installation language, which sets the default behavior of Office 2000 applications. For information about customizing the installation language during deployment, see "Customizing Language Features" on page 170.

- You can disable migration of user settings in the Office Custom Installation Wizard. For information about using this wizard, see "Office Custom Installation Wizard" on page 250.

Sharing Multilingual Documents

Localized versions of Office 95 and earlier were based on character encoding standards that varied from one *script* to another. When users working in one language version of Office exchanged documents with a user who worked in another language version of Office, text was often garbled because of the difference between character encodings.

Therefore, users opening Office 2000 documents in a localized version of Office 95 or earlier might encounter some limitations in the languages that they can display. However, Office 2000 is based on an international character encoding standard— *Unicode*—that allows users upgrading to Office 2000 to more easily share documents across languages.

Sharing documents across languages

Multilingual documents can contain text in languages that require different *scripts*. A single script can be used to represent many languages.

For example, the Latin or Roman script has character shapes—*glyphs*—for the 26 letters (both uppercase and lowercase) of the English alphabet, as well as accented (extended) characters used to represent sounds in other Western European languages.

The Latin script has glyphs to represent all of the characters in most European languages and a few others. Other European languages, such as Greek or Russian, have characters for which there are no glyphs in the Latin script; these languages have their own scripts.

Some Asian languages use *ideographic scripts* that have glyphs based on Chinese characters. Other languages, such as Thai and Arabic, use *complex scripts*, which have glyphs that are composed of several smaller glyphs or glyphs that must be shaped differently depending on adjacent characters.

A common way to store text is to represent each character by using a single byte. The value of each byte is a numeric index—or *code point*—in a table of characters; a code point corresponds to a character in the *code page*. For example, a byte whose code point is the decimal value 65 might represent a capital letter *a*.

This table of characters is called a code page. A code page contains a maximum of 256 bytes; because each character in the code page is represented by a single byte, a code page can contain as many as 256 characters. One code page with its limit of 256 characters cannot accommodate all languages because some languages use far more than 256 characters. Therefore, different scripts use separate code pages. There is one code page for Greek, another for Cyrillic, and so on.

Single-byte code pages cannot accommodate Asian languages, which commonly use more than 5,000 Chinese-based characters. Double-byte code pages were developed to support these languages.

One drawback of the code page system is that the character represented by a particular code point depends on the specific code page on which the code point resides. If you don't know which code page a code point is from, you cannot determine how to interpret the code point.

For example, unless you know which code page it comes from, the code point 230 might be the Greek lowercase zeta (ς), the Cyrillic lowercase zhe (ж), or the Western European diphthong (æ). All three characters have the same code point (230), but the code point is from three different code pages (1253, 1251, and 1252, respectively). Users exchanging documents between these languages are likely to see incorrect characters.

Introducing a worldwide character set

Unicode was developed to create a universal character set that can accommodate all known scripts. Unicode uses a unique, two-byte encoding for every character; so in contrast to code pages, every character has its own unique code point. For example, the Unicode code point of lowercase zeta (ζ) is the hexadecimal value 03B6, lowercase zhe (ж) is 0436, and the diphthong (æ) is 00E6.

Unicode 2.0 defines code points for approximately 40,000 characters. More definitions are being added in Unicode 2.1 and Unicode 3.0. Built-in expansion mechanisms in Unicode allow for more than one million characters to be defined, which is more than sufficient for all known scripts.

Currently in the Microsoft Windows operating systems, the two systems of storing text—code pages and Unicode—coexist. However, Unicode-based systems are replacing code page-based systems. For example, Microsoft Windows NT, Office 97 and later, Microsoft Internet Explorer version 4.0 and later, and Microsoft SQL Server version 7.0 are all based on Unicode.

Taking Advantage of Unicode Support in Office 2000

In a *code page*-based environment, each *script* has its own table of characters. Documents based on the code page of one operating system rarely travel well to an operating system that uses another code page. In some cases, the documents cannot contain text that uses characters from more than one script.

For example, if a user running the English version of Windows 95 with the Latin code page opens a plain text file created in the Japanese version of Windows 95, the *code points* of the Japanese code page are mapped to unexpected or nonexistent characters in the Western script, and the resulting text is unintelligible.

The universal character set provided by *Unicode* overcomes this problem. Office 97 was the first version of Office to support Unicode in all applications except Microsoft Access and Microsoft Outlook. In Office 2000, Access and Microsoft Publisher gain Unicode support. Microsoft FrontPage 2000 also supports Unicode on Web pages, but text typed into dialog boxes and other elements of the user interface are limited to characters defined by the user's code page.

Note   Outlook 2000 supports Unicode in the body of mail messages. However, Outlook data—such as Contacts, Tasks, and the To and Subject lines of messages—are limited to characters defined by the user's code page.

Office 2000 also provides the conversion tables necessary to convert code page-based data to Unicode and back again for interaction with previous applications. Because Office 2000 provides fonts to support many languages, users can create multilingual documents with text from multiple scripts.

Unicode support in Office 2000 means that users can copy multilingual text from most Office 97 documents and paste it into any Office 2000 document, and the text is displayed correctly. Conversely, multilingual text copied from any Office 2000 document can be pasted into a document created in any Office 97 application (except Access).

In addition to document text, Office 2000 supports Unicode in other areas, including document properties, bookmarks, style names, footnotes, and user information. Unicode support in Office 2000 also means that you can edit and display multilingual text in dialog boxes. For example, you can search for a file by a Greek author's name in the **Open** dialog box.

Note   Windows NT 4.0 and Windows 2000 provide full support for Unicode. Some support is provided in Windows 95/98.

Using Unicode values in Visual Basic for Applications

The Microsoft Visual Basic environment does not support Unicode. Only text supported by the operating system can be used in the Visual Basic Editor or displayed in custom dialog boxes or message boxes.

You can use the **ChrW()** function to manipulate text outside the code page. The **ChrW()** function accepts a number that represents the Unicode value of a character and returns that character string.

Using ASCII characters in shared file names

In Windows 95/98, Unicode characters in file names are not supported, but they are supported in Windows NT and Windows 2000. In Windows 95/98, file names must use characters that exist in the code page of the operating system.

If users in your organization share files between language versions of Windows, they can use ASCII characters (unaccented Latin script) to ensure that the file names can be used in any language version of the operating system.

Printing and displaying Unicode text

Not all printers can print characters from more than one code page. In particular, printers that have built-in fonts might not have characters for other scripts in those fonts. Also, new characters such as the euro currency symbol might be missing from a particular font.

Although the Office applications contain many workarounds to enable printing on such printers, it is not possible in all cases. If text is not printing correctly, updating the printer driver might fix the problem. If the latest driver doesn't fix the problem, you can create a registry entry that works around the printing problems of most printers; the printing quality, however, might be lowered.

▶ **To set the registry so that extended characters are printed correctly**

1   Go to the following registry subkey:

HKEY_CURRENT_USER\Software\Microsoft\Office\9.0\Word\Options

2   Add a new entry to the subkey, consisting of the value name **NoWideTextPrinting** and the binary value data of **1**.

In addition to printers, not all video display drivers support Unicode. Even when your text prints correctly, it might not display correctly on the screen. If your documents are displaying unintelligible characters, upgrade to a display driver that supports Unicode.

Compressing files that contain Unicode text

Unicode characters are encoded in two bytes rather than a single byte, or in a mixture of one and two bytes in some Asian languages. Generally, Office 2000 files with multilingual text are 30 to 50 percent larger than files created in previous, non-Unicode versions of Office.

Note   If a file contains text from only English or Western European languages, there is little or no increase in file size because Office 2000 applications can compress the text.

When Microsoft Word 2000 users open and save an English or Western European file from a previous, non-Unicode version of Word, Word converts the contents to Unicode. The first time the file is saved, Word analyzes the file and notes regions that can be compressed, resulting in a file that is temporarily twice the size of the original file. The next time the file is saved, Word performs the compression, and file size returns to normal.

For Microsoft PowerPoint files, text is typically a small percentage of file size, so Unicode does not significantly increase file size. In fact, PowerPoint 2000 employs the same graphics compression used in PowerPoint 97, so PowerPoint 2000 files are smaller than PowerPoint 95 files of equivalent content.

Copying multilingual text

You can use the Clipboard to copy multilingual text from one Office application to another. Text in RTF, HTML, and Unicode formats can successfully be pasted into Office applications

Multilingual text in RTF, HTML, and Unicode

When you copy text from an Office 2000 document, the RTF or HTML formatting data, as well as the Unicode text data, is stored on the Clipboard. This allows applications that do not support Unicode to use font information to identify a code page for interpreting the content. For example, both Word 95 and Word 6.0 accept Word 2000 text from the Clipboard as RTF format.

All language versions of Word 95 and Word 6.0 can display text in most European languages. However, Asian and right-to-left language versions cannot display other Asian or right-to-left languages.

Word 97 can accept RTF and Unicode text from the Clipboard and display content in all European and most Asian languages.

Microsoft Access 2000 and Microsoft Excel 2000 support copying multilingual Unicode, RTF, or HTML text to the Clipboard. However, Access and Excel cannot accept RTF content, but they can accept HTML-formatted text or Unicode text from the Clipboard.

Multilingual code page-based single-byte text

If users paste single-byte (ANSI) text into an Office 2000 document from a code page that is different from the one their operating system uses, they are likely to get unintelligible characters in their text. This problem occurs because Office cannot determine which code page to use to interpret the single-byte text.

For example, you might paste text from a non-Unicode text editor that uses fonts to indicate which code page to use. If the text editor supplies only RTF and single-byte text, the font (and code page) information is lost when the text is pasted in an application that does not accept RTF. Instead, the application uses the operating system's code page, which maps some characters' code points to unexpected or nonexistent characters.

Upgrading Reference for Localized Versions of Office

Just as file compatibility affects how users share files between numbered versions of Microsoft Office, file compatibility also affects how users share files across different language versions of Office, such as the Japanese version of Office 95 and Office 2000 with the Microsoft Office 2000 MultiLanguage Pack. There are several strategies that you can use to share files across language versions of Office.

Sharing Office Files Across Language Versions

When all users in an international organization have upgraded to Microsoft Office 2000, sharing files across languages is easy, whether the files are from Office 2000 with the Microsoft Office 2000 MultiLanguage Pack or localized versions of Microsoft Office 2000. But even during a gradual upgrade to Office 2000, you can still share files with older localized versions of Office.

If you are upgrading gradually to Office 2000, you can save Office 2000 files in formats that allow users of previous localized versions of Office to open the files, yet preserve the Office 2000 multilingual features. These file formats vary by Office application.

However, if you save Office 2000 files in the format of the previous localized version, multilingual features of Office 2000 are lost. For example, Microsoft Word 2000, Microsoft Excel 2000, and Microsoft PowerPoint 2000 can display multiple Asian languages in the same file. When these files are saved in a previous version of Office, the multi-Asian language feature is lost and only one of the languages is displayed properly.

Unicode allows you to share multilingual files between Office 2000 and Office 97 without any loss of text. Older versions of Office might not properly display multilingual text from an Office 2000 file. This is because versions of Office prior to 97 are based on *code pages*.

In addition, your operating system can determine whether you can display Asian or right-to-left (Arabic, Hebrew, Farsi, or Urdu) text between different versions of Office.

To display a right-to-left language, you must be running a right-to-left language version of your operating system. To display Asian languages, see the following:

- Office 2000 provides files—including fonts—that extend an operating system's ability to support Asian languages.

- The Office 97 Asian support files—including fonts—extend an operating system's ability to support Asian languages.

- To display or edit Asian text in an older version of Office, you must run a language version of the operating system that matches the Asian language with which you want to work.

Note   Office 2000 upgrades fonts commonly used in Word and PowerPoint templates so that the fonts support multiple scripts. These fonts are Times New Roman, Courier New, Arial, Arial Narrow, Arial Black, Bookman Old Style, Garamond, and Impact.

See also

- If your organization is upgrading from a previous version of Office, there are several strategies for making a smooth transition, beyond considerations for multilingual support. For more information, see "Before You Upgrade to Office 2000" on page 429.

- The Unicode standard provides unique character values for every language that Office supports and makes it even easier to share multilingual documents. For more information, see "Sharing Multilingual Documents" on page 746.

- For some languages, you need to have an operating system and fonts that allow you to display and edit the text. For more information, see "Configuring Users' Computers in an International Environment" on page 732.

Sharing Access Databases Across Language Versions

Microsoft Access 2000 can open databases created in any previous localized version of Access. For some languages, Access 2000 users who are running Microsoft Windows NT version 4.0 might need to install language support that comes with Windows NT 4.0.

Note   Users of previous localized versions of Access cannot open Access 2000 databases.

Opening databases from previous localized versions in Access 2000

If only part of your organization is upgrading to Access 2000, you might want to leave existing databases in the format of your previous version of Access so that all users can open the databases.

However, if you are using Access 2000, you might not be able to open older databases if the language version of your operating system differs from that of the operating system on the computer used to create the database. Access databases are saved in a particular sort order, and the default sort order matches the sort order used by the operating system on the computer used to create the database.

For example, a database created in Access 95 on a computer running the Arabic version of Microsoft Windows 95 uses the Arabic sort order by default and cannot be opened on a computer running the English version of Windows 95/98 or the English version of Windows NT 4.0.

Note   Windows 2000 includes international sort order support for multiple languages. Users running Access 2000 on Windows 2000 can open databases from previous versions of Access in the native sort order.

There are two ways to work around this problem. One solution is to install national language support (NLS) files that extend the ability of the operating system to support additional sort orders. The other solution is to recompact the database by using a sort order that is supported by multiple operating systems.

Supporting the default sort order on Windows NT 4.0

In Windows NT 4.0, you can install a language pack that includes NLS files that support the default sort order of the database.

▶ **To install language pack files**

1   At your installation source for Windows NT 4.0, go to the Langpack folder.

2   Right-click on the .inf file for the language you want, and then click **Install**.

Using the General sort order on Windows 95/98

In Windows 95/98, you cannot add the NLS files that support foreign language sort orders. Instead, you must compact the database by using a sort order that is supported by the operating systems on all computers concerned. The most commonly supported sort order is General.

The General sort order allows users running a variety of language versions of Windows 95/98 to open a database. However, this might not work well for your organization if you store data in Spanish and Asian languages, which do not support the General sort order. For such databases, it might be preferable to convert the database to Access 2000 format.

For example, Access 2000 users running the English version of Windows 95 might need to open an Access 95 database that originated on a computer running the Japanese version of Windows 95. In this scenario, it might be better to convert the database to Access 2000 format than to attempt to share it across language versions of the operating system.

Note   For a list of languages that support the General sort order, see Access Help.

▶ **To compact the original database by using the General sort order**

1   Open the database in the original, localized version of Access.

You must open the database on a computer running the same language version of the operating system as that used to create the database, or you can open the database on a computer running Windows NT 4.0 or Windows 2000 with language support for the original sort order.

2   Change the sort order to **General**, and recompact the database.

Steps for changing sort order and compacting the database vary with different versions of Access. For more information, see Access Help.

Opening forms and reports from previous localized versions

Access 2000 can open and read the English and European-language content of forms and reports from any previous localized version of Access. However, if the database is based on a *code page* other than Latin 1 (code page 1252), and if you are using Access 2000 with an English or a Western European version of the operating system, some text might be rendered incorrectly.

For example, a database created in Access 95 on the Greek version Windows 95 is based on the Greek code page. When an Access 2000 user running the English version of Windows 95 opens the database, the operating system maps *code points* to the new code page, so some Greek characters might appear as accented European characters, question marks, open boxes, or other unintelligible characters.

Converting databases from previous localized versions of Access

If Access 2000 users don't need to share a database from a previous localized version of Access with users of the older version, convert the database to Access 2000 format. If the database was saved in the default sort order on a computer running a non-English version of the operating system, convert it by opening it in Access 2000 and saving it in Access 2000 format. Access converts the data to *Unicode*.

By using the original language sort order

When you convert an older database to Access 2000, Access uses the sort order to determine which code page to use for converting the data to Unicode. Access 2000 associates the General sort order with the Western European code page, so if non-Western European data is stored in the General sort order, the data is corrupted when Access 2000 converts it.

Therefore, if the older database is based on a non-English version of the operating system, and it is saved in the General sort order, you must recompact it in the original language sort order before converting it to Access 2000. Otherwise, Access 2000 cannot properly convert the data to Unicode.

▶ To convert a localized database to Access 2000

1   Open the database in the original, localized version of Access.

You must open the database on a computer running the same language version of the operating system as that used to create the database, or you can open the database on a computer running Windows NT 4.0 or Windows 2000 with language support for the original sort order.

2   Change the sort order to match the language of the operating system, and recompact the database.

Note   Steps for changing sort order and compacting the database vary with different versions of Access. For more information, see Access Help.

3 Start Access 2000, but do not open the database.

4 On the **Tools** menu, point to **Database Utilities**, point to **Convert Database**, and then click **To Current Access Database Version**.

5 In the **Database to Convert From** dialog box, select the database you want to convert, and click **Convert**.

By specifying the code page for the General sort order

If you don't have the necessary language version of the operating system, or if the data in the older database is in a language that had no sort order in earlier versions of Access, you can still convert the database to Access 2000.

For example, databases in earlier versions of Access that are based on Vietnamese, Farsi, or a Baltic version of the operating system (Estonian, Latvian, or Lithuanian) default to the General sort order because previous versions of Access did not support sort orders for those languages. To convert these databases, you must create a registry entry to prevent Access 2000 from corrupting the non-Western European data.

▶ **To convert non-Western European databases that use the General sort order**

1 If you are converting an Access version 1.*x* or 2.0 database, go to the following registry subkey:

HKEY_LOCAL_MACHINE\Software\Microsoft\Jet\4.0\Engines\Jet 2.x

−or−

If you are converting an Access 95 or 97 database, go to the following registry subkey:

HKEY_LOCAL_MACHINE\Software\Microsoft\Jet\4.0\Engines\Jet 3.x

2 In the Jet 2.x or Jet 3.x subkey, create a new entry named **ForceCp** and set the value to **ANSI** to use the computer's default code page.

You can specify a different code page by setting the value to the code page number, such as **1257** for Windows Baltic Rim.

3 Convert the database to Access 2000.

4 Delete the **ForceCP** registry entry so that Access 2000 reverts to using the sort order of a database to determine the code page.

Removing conflicting data to solve indexing problems

Access 2000 upgrades some sort orders so that they differ from previous versions of Access. In the new sorting, characters that were considered different in older databases might be considered the same in Access 2000. As a result, the converted database might contain conflicting data, making it impossible to create a unique index for some tables. To create a unique index on the affected tables, you must remove the conflicting data.

A similar problem might occur when changing the sort order of a database. Characters might be different in one language but equivalent in another language. For example, the Western European lowercase *i* and uppercase *I* are considered equivalent when sorting alphabetically. But in Turkish a lowercase *i* might be dotted or not dotted, and the two *i* characters are not considered equivalent when sorting alphabetically in Turkish. Because they are considered equivalent in the General sort order, however, these characters can create conflicting data when you upgrade a Turkish database to Access 2000.

See also

- If your organization is upgrading from a previous version of Access, there are several strategies for making a smooth transition, beyond cross-language considerations. For more information, see "Upgrading to Access 2000" on page 455.

- The Unicode standard provides unique character values for every language that Office supports and makes it even easier to share multilingual documents. For more information, see "Sharing Multilingual Documents" on page 746.

- For some languages, you need to have an operating system and fonts that allow you to display and edit the text. For more information, see "Configuring Users' Computers in an International Environment" on page 732.

Sharing Excel Workbooks Across Language Versions

Just as with nonlocalized versions of Microsoft Excel, localized Excel 97 can open and read Excel 2000 workbooks directly. However, for Excel 95 and Excel 5.0 users to share Excel 2000 workbooks, Excel 2000 users must save their workbook in the dual Excel 97-2000 & 5.0/95 format, which is readable by the four latest versions of Excel.

Users of Excel 2000 and previous localized versions can share workbooks as follows:

- In Excel 2000, you can open and edit any workbook created in a previous localized version of Excel, regardless of the language, provided the operating system supports the language of the file.

- In localized Excel 97, you can open and edit Excel 2000 workbooks, regardless of the language, provided the operating system supports the language of the file.

- In localized Excel 95 and Excel 5.0, you need an operating system that supports the language of the file and the workbooks must be saved in the dual Excel 97-2000 & 5.0/95 format.

Opening workbooks from previous localized versions in Excel 2000

When you open Excel 95 or Excel 5.0 workbooks in Excel 2000, Excel 2000 converts the text to *Unicode*. Because Excel 2000 and Excel 97 both support Unicode, Excel 2000 does not need to convert Excel 97 text.

Localized versions of Excel 2000 can display text in workbooks from previous versions of Excel as shown in the following table.

This language version of Excel 2000	Can display text in these languages
U.S./European	English, European, Asian
Asian	English, Asian
Right-to-left language (Arabic, Hebrew)	English, European, and a compatible right-to-left language

Note   English and European-language versions of Excel 2000 can display Asian text from Excel 97 workbooks, but not from Excel 95 and Excel 5.0 workbooks.

Opening Excel 2000 workbooks in localized Excel 97

Excel 97 can directly open and read Excel 2000 workbooks. However, to display Asian or right-to-left (Arabic, Hebrew, Farsi, or Urdu) text that doesn't match the language version of Excel 97, you must have the appropriate language support installed on your computer.

For Asian text, you can install the Office 97 Asian support files, but for right-to-left text, you must use a compatible right-to-left language version of Excel 97.

Localized versions of Excel 97 can display Excel 2000 text as shown in the following table.

This language version of Excel 97	Can display text in these languages
U.S./European	English, European, Asian (Asian requires the Office 97 Asian support files)
Asian	English, European, matching Asian and nonmatching Asian (nonmatching Asian requires the Office 97 Asian support files)
Right-to-left language (Arabic, Hebrew)	English, European, and a compatible right-to-left language

Opening Excel 2000 workbooks in localized Excel 95 and Excel 5.0

Depending on the language, any language version of Excel 95 and Excel 5.0 can open and read Excel 2000 workbooks that are saved in the dual Excel 97-2000 & 5.0/95 format.

Localized versions of Excel 95 and Excel 5.0 can display Excel 2000 text as shown in the following table.

This language version of Excel 5.0/95	Can display text in these languages
U.S./European	English, European
Asian	English and the matching Asian language
Right-to-left language (Arabic, Hebrew)	English, European, and a compatible right-to-left language

Running macros from previous localized versions of Excel

When Excel 2000 opens localized workbooks from Excel 95 or Excel 5.0, it translates commands written in Microsoft Visual Basic to English as long as the necessary object library files are installed. If the macro includes procedures written in more than one language, you must install an object library for each language used in the macro.

▶ **To install object library files for multilingual macros**

1   In the Extras\95olbs folder of the Microsoft Office 2000 MultiLanguage Pack CD-ROM, double-click **InstOLB.exe**.

2   In the **Object Library Installer** dialog box, choose the languages for which you want to install object library files.

3   If the path shown in the dialog box is not where the file Excel.exe is stored, click **Browse** and enter the correct path.

4   Click **Install**.

Note   All Excel 97 macros are compiled in English, so Excel 2000 does not need to translate them.

See also

- If your organization is upgrading from a previous version of Excel, there are several strategies for making a smooth transition, beyond cross-language considerations. For more information, see "Upgrading to Excel 2000" on page 476.

- The Unicode standard provides unique character values for every language that Office supports and makes it even easier to share multilingual documents. For more information, see "Sharing Multilingual Documents" on page 746.

- For some languages, you need to have an operating system and fonts that allow you to display and edit the text. For more information, see "Configuring Users' Computers in an International Environment" on page 732.

Sharing FrontPage Files Across Language Versions

Microsoft FrontPage 2000 allows you to work with more languages and characters than you can with previous versions. It can display and store several new languages, such as Thai, that are supported by *code pages*, as well as all Unicode 2.0 characters. In addition, FrontPage 2000 recognizes more HTML 4.0 *character entity references* than do previous versions.

Character entity references make up a set of HTML characters that are represented by easy-to-remember mnemonic names. For example, the character entity reference **å** specifies lowercase *a* topped by a ring. It's easier to remember **å** than it is to remember **&229;**.

In FrontPage 2000, you can open and edit any document created in FrontPage 97 or FrontPage 98, regardless of the language used in the document, provided the operating system supports the language of the file.

Note   FrontPage 2000 and Internet Explorer 5 encode URLs in UTF-8, a Unicode format. To use FrontPage 2000 to edit FrontPage-based webs that include non-ASCII URLs, you must either have a Web server that supports UTF-8 or turn off UTF-8 encoding.

The enhanced language features in FrontPage 2000 affect file sharing between FrontPage 2000 and previous versions in the following ways:

- If you use FrontPage 2000 to create a document in a language new to FrontPage, such as Thai, you cannot open or edit that document in FrontPage 97 or FrontPage 98. If you try to open it, FrontPage 97 and FrontPage 98 display an error message.

- If you use FrontPage 2000 to create a document that contains a *Unicode* character, such as **Β** for the Greek capital letter beta, you cannot display that character in FrontPage 97 or FrontPage 98. If you save the document in FrontPage 97 or FrontPage 98, the Unicode character is deleted.

- If you use FrontPage 2000 to create a document that contains an HTML 4.0 character entity reference, then you cannot edit that character in FrontPage 97 or FrontPage 98. The character entity reference appears as **δ** and is not deleted if you save the document in FrontPage 97 or FrontPage 98.

See also

- The Unicode standard provides unique character values for every language that Office supports and makes it even easier to share multilingual documents. For more information, see "Sharing Multilingual Documents" on page 746.

- For some languages, you need to have an operating system and fonts that allow you to display and edit the text. For more information, see "Configuring Users' Computers in an International Environment" on page 732.

Exchanging Outlook Messages Across Language Versions

You can configure Microsoft Outlook 2000 to send messages in a format that your previous e-mail client applications can display properly. To display some languages, however, users of previous localized versions of Outlook might need to install additional fonts and operating system files (such as *code pages*). If your organization uses Microsoft Exchange Server, the necessary code page extensions must be installed on the server as well as on users' computers.

For users of non-Asian language versions of Outlook 97 to display Asian text properly, they must have Microsoft Office 97 Service Release 2 (SR-2) installed. In addition, only users of a right-to-left language version of Outlook 98 or earlier can open and read right-to-left text in Outlook 2000 messages.

Note   Outlook data that is not in the body of the message—such as Contacts, Tasks, and the To and Subject lines of messages—are limited to characters defined by the sender's code page. Such characters might be unintelligible for a recipient whose operating system uses a different code page.

Previous localized versions of Outlook also save messages in RTF, so Outlook 2000 users can display multilingual text in e-mail messages sent from these previous versions, provided that the operating system supports the language of the text.

Configuring message formats

Outlook 2000 sends messages in three formats: HTML, RTF, and plain text. You can limit e-mail messages to a format that can be read by most of the applications used in your organization.

For example, if all the users in your organization use Outlook 98 or later as their e-mail client application, and they exchange mail primarily within the organization, you can configure Outlook 2000 to send messages in HTML format. In this scenario, Outlook 2000 users get the benefits of the new HTML format, and other users can still read the RTF or plain text version. (Outlook 2000 provides RTF or plain text versions of messages for client applications that do not support HTML format.)

Note   If you use Microsoft Exchange Server and have Outlook 2000 configured to send messages in HTML format, the HTML is converted to RTF on the server. These RTF conversions are larger-than-normal RTF messages and might cause network bandwidth and storage problems.

Alternatively, if the fidelity of text formatting is important in your organization, you can configure Outlook 2000 to send messages in RTF. All versions of the Outlook and Exchange client applications support RTF. In this scenario, however, Outlook 2000 users lose the features that HTML format provides.

Finally, if users in your organization frequently exchange e-mail messages outside your organization, or if your organization includes e-mail client applications that do not support messages formatted in HTML or RTF, you can configure Outlook 2000 to send messages in plain text. All e-mail client applications support plain text.

▶ **To configure the message format in Outlook 2000**

1   On the **Tools** menu, click **Options**, and then click the **Mail Format** tab.

2   In the **Send in this message format** box, select the format you want to use.

System Policy Tip   You can use a system policy to set the format of outgoing Outlook 2000 messages. In the System Policy Editor, set the **Microsoft Outlook 2000\Tools | Options\Mail Format\Message format/editor - Corporate or Workgroup configuration** policy. For more information about the System Policy Editor, see "Using the System Policy Editor" on page 296.

Specifying character encoding

In addition to configuring the format that Outlook 2000 uses to send messages, you need to specify the character encoding (also known as the code page) of the message being sent. Use an encoding that supports the characters being sent and that the recipient's e-mail application can interpret. For example, if all users' e-mail applications support Unicode, UTF-8 encoding is a good choice. Otherwise, use an encoding based on the sender's code page, such as Western European (ISO).

Note   An Outlook 2000 user's default character encoding for outgoing messages is the Internet encoding that corresponds to the user's code page. For example, JIS encoding for a Japanese code page, ISO-8859-1 encoding for a Western European code page, or KOI8-R encoding for a Cyrillic code page.

▶ **To specify character encoding in Outlook 2000**

1   On the **Tools** menu, click **Options**, and then click the **Mail Format** tab.

2   Click **International Options**, and select a character encoding in the **Use this encoding for outgoing messages** box.

3   If you want message flags and Forward and Reply headers to be in English, select the **Use English for message flags** and **Use English for message headers on replies and forwards** check boxes.

If you clear these check boxes, message flags and headers match the language of the Outlook user interface, and e-mail applications that run in another language might not display the text properly.

System Policy Tip   You can use a system policy to set character encoding for Outlook 2000 messages. In the System Policy Editor, set the **Microsoft Outlook 2000\Tools | Options\Mail Format\International Options** policies. For more information about the System Policy Editor, see "Using the System Policy Editor" on page 296.

When users click **Send To** on the **File** menu in Office applications to create e-mail messages, the content of the message is saved in HTML format. The character encoding setting for outgoing messages in Outlook determines the character encoding for the message.

Configuring fonts for incoming international messages

For Outlook 2000 users who expect to receive e-mail messages that include text in other languages, you can specify fonts that properly display the text in incoming messages.

▶ **To specify fonts for incoming messages**

1   On the **Tools** menu, click **Options**, and then click the **Mail Format** tab.

2   Under **Stationery and Fonts**, click **Fonts**, and then click **International Fonts**.

3   For every language that you want to configure, select the language's *script* in the **Font settings** box, and then select a setting in the **Fixed-width font** box.

    The scripts that appear in the list correspond to languages that the user has enabled for editing.

See also

- You can use the Microsoft Office Language Settings tool to enable languages for editing. For more information, see "Customizing Language Features" on page 170.

- You can install a Global Input Method Editor (IME) that allows users to input Asian text in Outlook messages, even if they are running a non-Asian version of their operating system. For more information, see "MultiLanguage Pack Extras" on page 160.

- If Outlook 2000 users exchange secure e-mail messages internationally, you need to consider the differences in encryption strength within and outside the United States. For more information, see "Encryption Strengths for Secure E-mail Messaging" on page 424.

- If your organization is upgrading from a previous version of Outlook, there are several strategies for making a smooth transition, beyond considerations for multilingual support. For more information, see "Upgrading to Outlook 2000" on page 495.

- For some languages, you need to have an operating system and fonts that allow you to display and edit the text. For more information, see "Configuring Users' Computers in an International Environment" on page 732.

Sharing PowerPoint Presentations Across Language Versions

Just as with nonlocalized versions of Microsoft PowerPoint, localized PowerPoint 97 can open and read PowerPoint 2000 presentations directly, but localized PowerPoint 95 must have the PowerPoint 97 converter for PowerPoint 95 installed, or PowerPoint 2000 presentations must be saved in PowerPoint 97-2000 & 95 format.

PowerPoint 4.0 users can open PowerPoint 2000 presentations if they install the PowerPoint 97 converter for PowerPoint 4.0.

Users of PowerPoint 2000 and previous localized versions can share presentations as follows:

- In PowerPoint 2000, you can open and edit any presentation created in a previous localized version of PowerPoint, regardless of the language, provided the operating system supports the language of the file.

- In localized PowerPoint 97, you can open and edit PowerPoint 2000 presentations, regardless of the language, provided the operating system supports the language of the file.

- In localized PowerPoint 95, in addition to an operating system that supports the language of the file, you need the following to open PowerPoint 2000 presentations:

  You must have the PowerPoint 97 converter for PowerPoint 95 converter installed.

  –or–

  The file must be in PowerPoint 97-2000 & 95 format.

- In localized PowerPoint 4.0, in addition to an operating system that supports the language of the file, you must have the PowerPoint 97 converter for PowerPoint 4.0 installed to open PowerPoint 2000 presentations.

Opening presentations from previous localized versions in PowerPoint 2000

When you open PowerPoint 95 or PowerPoint 4.0 presentations in PowerPoint 2000, PowerPoint 2000 converts the text to Unicode. Because PowerPoint 2000 and PowerPoint 97 both support *Unicode*, PowerPoint 2000 does not need to convert PowerPoint 97 text.

PowerPoint 2000 can display English and European text in presentations from any language version of PowerPoint 97, PowerPoint 95, and PowerPoint 4.0. If PowerPoint 2000 users have enabled the appropriate language in Microsoft Office Language Settings, PowerPoint 2000 can display text in any language provided the operating system supports the language of the file.

Note   Some unknown characters might appear when you open an English or European-language version of PowerPoint 95 or PowerPoint 4.0 presentation in the Korean, Simplified Chinese, or Traditional Chinese versions of PowerPoint 2000. To correct this problem, click **Options** on the PowerPoint 2000 **Tools** menu, and then click the **Asian** tab. Clear the **Convert font-associated text** check box.

Opening PowerPoint 2000 presentations in localized PowerPoint 97

PowerPoint 97 can directly open and read PowerPoint 2000 presentations. However, to display Asian or right-to-left (Arabic, Hebrew, Farsi, or Urdu) text that doesn't match the language version of PowerPoint 97, you must have the appropriate language support installed on your computer.

For Asian text, you can install the Office 97 Asian support files, but for right-to-left text, you must use a compatible right-to-left language version of PowerPoint 97.

Localized versions of PowerPoint 97 can display PowerPoint 2000 text as shown in the following table.

This language version of PowerPoint 97	Can display text in these languages
U.S./European	English, European, Asian (Asian requires the Office 97 Asian support files)
Asian	English, European, matching Asian and nonmatching Asian (nonmatching Asian requires Office 97 Asian support files)
Right-to-left language (Arabic, Hebrew)	English, European, and a compatible right-to-left language

Note   Layout for the Asian text in PowerPoint 97 might be different than it is in PowerPoint 2000.

Opening PowerPoint 2000 presentations in localized PowerPoint 95 and PowerPoint 4.0

Depending on the language, PowerPoint 95 can open and read PowerPoint 2000 presentations by using the PowerPoint 97 converter for PowerPoint 95 or if they are saved in the PowerPoint 97-2000 & 95 format. Similarly, PowerPoint 4.0 can open and read PowerPoint 97 and 2000 presentations by using the PowerPoint 97 converter for PowerPoint 4.0, depending on the language.

Note The PowerPoint 97 converter for PowerPoint 4.0 cannot be used with Asian versions of PowerPoint 4.0. Therefore, users of Asian versions of PowerPoint 4.0 cannot open PowerPoint 2000 presentations.

Localized versions of PowerPoint 95 and PowerPoint 4.0 can display PowerPoint 2000 text as shown in the following table.

This language version of PowerPoint 4.0/95	Can display text in these languages
U.S./European	English, European
Asian (PowerPoint 95 only)	English, European, and the matching Asian language
Right-to-left language (Arabic, Hebrew)	English, European, and a compatible right-to-left language

See also

- If your organization is upgrading from a previous version of PowerPoint, there are several strategies for making a smooth transition, beyond cross-language considerations. For more information, see "Upgrading to PowerPoint 2000" on page 520.

- The Unicode standard provides unique character values for every language that Office supports and makes it even easier to share multilingual documents. For more information, see "Sharing Multilingual Documents" on page 746.

- For some languages, you need to have an operating system and fonts that allow you to display and edit the text. For more information, see "Configuring Users' Computers in an International Environment" on page 732.

Sharing Publisher Files Across Language Versions

Microsoft Publisher 2000 can open and read publications created in any localized version of Publisher. However, previous localized versions of Publisher cannot open Publisher 2000 publications.

When you open Publisher 97 or earlier publications in Publisher 2000, Publisher 2000 converts the text to *Unicode*. Because Publisher 2000 and Publisher 98 both support Unicode, Publisher 2000 does not need to convert Publisher 98 text.

Publisher 2000 does not support editing right-to-left (Arabic, Hebrew, Farsi, or Urdu) text. However, users running a right-to-left language version of Microsoft Windows can edit English or Western European text in Publisher 2000.

Sharing Word Documents Across Language Versions

Just as with nonlocalized versions of Microsoft Word, localized Word 97 can open and read Word 2000 documents directly, but localized Word 95 or Word 6.0 must have the Word 97-2000 converter installed, or the Word 2000 documents must be saved in Rich Text Format (RTF).

RTF allows you to exchange multilingual documents between Microsoft Office versions. In Office 2000, RTF supports *Unicode* and it also allows Word 95 and Word 6.0 to use all Unicode characters that occur in single-byte *code pages*. As long as the Word 95 or Word 6.0 user does not save the file, the Unicode is preserved when the RTF file is reopened in Word 2000.

Users of Word 2000 and previous localized versions can share documents as follows:

- In Word 2000, you can open and edit any document created in a previous localized version of Word, regardless of the language, provided the operating system supports the language of the file.

- In localized Word 97, you can open and edit Word 2000 documents, regardless of the language, provided the operating system supports the language of the file.

- In localized Word 95 and Word 6.0, in addition to an operating system that supports the language of the file, you need the following to open Word 2000 documents:

  You must have the Word 97-2000 converter installed.

  –or–

  The file must be in RTF.

Opening documents from previous localized versions in Word 2000

When you open Word 95 or 6.0 documents in Word 2000, Word 2000 converts the text to Unicode. Because Word 2000 and Word 97 both support Unicode, Word 2000 does not need to convert Word 97 text.

Word 2000 can display English and European-language text in documents from any language version of Word 97, Word 95, and Word 6.0. If Word 2000 users have enabled the appropriate language, Word 2000 can display text in any language provided the operating system supports the language of the file.

For all languages except French, German, and Spanish, Word 2000 field codes such as Author, Date, and Time are stored in English. When a localized version of Word 95 or Word 6.0 document is opened in Word 2000, the document's field names are translated to English so that English versions of Word 2000 can use the fields.

Opening Word 2000 documents in localized Word 97

Word 97 can directly open and read Word 2000 documents. However, to display Asian or right-to-left (Arabic, Hebrew, Farsi, or Urdu) text that doesn't match the language version of Word 97, you must have the appropriate language support installed on your system.

For Asian text, you can install the Office 97 Asian support files, but for right-to-left text, you must use a compatible right-to-left language version of Word 97.

Localized versions of Word 97 can display Word 2000 text as shown in the following table.

This language version of Word 97	Can display text in these languages
U.S./European	English, European, and Asian (Asian requires the Office 97 Asian support files)
Asian	English, European, matching Asian, and nonmatching Asian (nonmatching Asian requires the Office 97 Asian support files)
Right-to-left language (Arabic, Hebrew)	English, European, and a compatible right-to-left language

Note Layout for the Asian text in Word 97 might be different than it is in Word 2000.

Opening Word 2000 documents in localized Word 95 and Word 6.0

Depending on the language, Word 95 and Word 6.0 can open and read Word 2000 documents by using the Word 97-2000 converter, or Word 95 and Word 6.0 can open and read Word 2000 documents that are saved in RTF.

Localized versions of Word 95 and Word 6.0 can display Word 2000 text as shown in the following table.

This language version of Word 6.0/95	Can display text in these languages
U.S./European	English, European
Asian	English, European, and the matching Asian language
Right-to-left language (Arabic, Hebrew)	English, European, and a compatible right-to-left language

Running macros from previous localized versions of Word

When Word 2000 opens older localized documents, it converts WordBasic to Visual Basic for Applications (VBA) and translates the commands to English. Converted macros use the form WordBasic.732. However, strings—including user-created strings and WordBasic strings—are not translated. If a command is a WordBasic command, the language of the arguments accepted by that command can be either English or the localized language.

In Word 2000 and Word 97, you can write macros that work in all language versions of Word 2000 and Word 97. Be sure to use enumerations in your VBA code, and do not refer to objects by the names used in the user interface, because these names are different in each language version.

See also

- If your organization is upgrading from a previous version of Word, there are several strategies for making a smooth transition, beyond cross-language considerations. For more information, see "Upgrading to Word 2000" on page 539.

- The Unicode standard provides unique character values for every language that Office supports and makes it even easier to share multilingual documents. For more information, see "Sharing Multilingual Documents" on page 746.

- For some languages, you need to have an operating system and fonts that allow you to display and edit the text. For more information, see "Configuring Users' Computers in an International Environment" on page 732.

Appendix

Contents

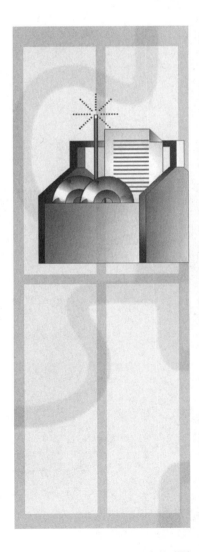

Overview of Tools and Utilities

The Microsoft Office 2000 Resource Kit includes a comprehensive set of information, tools, and converters designed to help administrators and IT professionals deploy, support, and maintain Office 2000.

You can install most of the core tools and support documents in the Office Resource Kit by running one integrated Setup program, which is included on the Office Resource Kit CD-ROM, and is also available through the Office Resource Kit Web site at http://www.microsoft.com/office/ork/. Some utilities and information files, which are not included in the integrated Setup program, must be installed separately.

After you install the Office Resource Kit, you have access to the tools and documentation. On the **Start** menu, point to **Programs**, point to **Microsoft Office Tools**, and then point to **Microsoft Office 2000 Resource Kit Tools** or **Microsoft Office 2000 Resource Kit Documents**.

In This Appendix

Tools Information

The Microsoft Office 2000 Resource Kit Tools folder contains installation tools that make customizing, configuring, and deploying Office 2000 in your organization easy and convenient. A number of other useful tools assist you with system administration, international deployments, and user support. All tools described in this section are installed automatically when you install the Office Resource Kit from the Office Resource Kit CD-ROM or through the Office Resource Kit Web site at http://www.microsoft.com/office/ork/.

Custom Installation Wizard

The new functionality and user interface of the Microsoft Office Custom Installation Wizard represent a great improvement over the Network Installation Wizard included in the Microsoft Office 97 Resource Kit.

Using the Custom Installation Wizard, you can record changes to the master installation in a Windows installer *transform* (MST file), without altering the original *package* (MSI file). Because the original package is never altered, you can create a different transform for every installation scenario you need. When you run Setup with both the package and the transform, the installer applies the transform to the original package, and Setup uses your altered configuration to perform the installation.

The Custom Installation Wizard takes advantage of other Office 2000 customization tools as well. For example, you can include an Office profile settings (OPS) file, created with the Profile Wizard, to preset user options in Office applications. You can also run the Microsoft Internet Explorer Administration Kit from within the Custom Installation Wizard to customize the way Office Setup installs Internet Explorer 5.

Installing the Custom Installation Wizard

The Custom Installation Wizard is automatically installed on your computer when you install the Office Resource Kit. To locate the tool, click the **Start** menu, point to **Programs**, point to **Microsoft Office Tools**, point to **Microsoft Office 2000 Resource Kit Tools**, and then click **Custom Installation Wizard**.

See also

- For more information about using the Custom Installation Wizard, see "Office Custom Installation Wizard" on page 250, and "Profile Wizard" on page 255.

Excel File Recovery and Date Tools

The Microsoft Office 2000 Resource Kit includes Microsoft Excel date and file utilities that can help you with such tasks as converting year dates from two to four digits, searching for functions that accept date arguments, and recovering corrupted data.

Excel File Recovery Macro

Use this add-in to gain access to Excel workbooks that appear to be corrupted. This utility extracts and copies salvageable data into a new Excel workbook.

Excel Date Migration Wizard

The Date Migration Wizard is an add-in for Excel 97 or Excel 2000 that you can use to scan workbooks for worksheet functions that accept date arguments. Dates entered as text may produce different results than they did in previous versions. The unexpected results that may occur are due to a change in the date algorithm in Excel 97 and Excel 2000.

Excel Date Fix Wizard

The Excel Date Fix Wizard has three primary functions. You can use it to change the year component of all date formats from two digits to the more precise and unambiguous four digits. You can use it to modify serial numbers related to dates so that they fall within a specific century. Finally, you can use the wizard to create a report of workbooks that contain dates for easy reference.

Excel Date Watcher

The Date Watcher add-in interactively flags date entry problems that calculate differently between older versions of Excel and Excel 2000.

Installing the Excel Tools

The Excel tools are automatically copied to your computer when you install the Office Resource Kit. The following table lists the file names for the tools.

File name	Description
Cleaner.xla	Excel File Recovery Macro
Datefix.xla	Excel Date Fix Wizard
Datescan.xla	Excel Date Migration Wizard
Datewtch.xla	Excel Date Watcher

To install an add-in, start Excel, click **Add-Ins** on the **Tools** menu, and then click the **Browse** button. In the **Browse** dialog box, change to the folder where you installed the files (the default location is \Program Files\ORKTools\ToolBox\Tools\Excel Tools). Finally, select the add-ins you want to install. These items are added to the list in the **Add-Ins** dialog box.

See also

- For more information about the Date Migration Wizard and Date Fix Wizard, see the following documents located in the Excel Tools folder.

File name	Description
Datemigw	Describes how to use the Excel Date Migration Wizard.
Datefixw	Describes how to use the Excel Date Fix Wizard.
Datewtch	Describes how to use the Excel Date Watch Wizard.

Microsoft Internet Explorer 5 Administration Kit

The Microsoft Internet Explorer Administration Kit allows administrators to customize, distribute, and maintain Internet Explorer 5 from one central location. You can start the Internet Explorer Administration Kit directly from the Microsoft Office Custom Installation Wizard to customize how Internet Explorer 5 is installed with Office 2000.

Installing Internet Explorer 5 Administration Kit

The Internet Explorer Administration Kit is automatically installed on your computer when you install the Office Resource Kit. To locate the kit, click the **Start** button, point to **Programs**, point **Microsoft IEAK**, and then click **Internet Explorer Customization Wizard**. To get reference and support information for the kit, click **IEAK Help**. To manage system settings or configure user options, click **IEAK Profile Manager**.

Language Version

Microsoft Office 2000 includes international features that you can tailor to fit the needs of your organization. When you install Office, an *installation language* setting governs the default behavior. For example, if the installation language is Japanese, Office applications display commands that allow you to work with Asian text. Under a non-Asian installation language setting, these commands are hidden. The installation language is set when you install Office 2000 and can only be changed with the Language Version utility.

Installing the Language Version

The Language Version utility is automatically installed on your computer when you install the Office Resource Kit. To locate the tool, click the **Start** button, point to **Programs**, point to **Microsoft Office Tools**, point to **Microsoft Office 2000 Resource Kit Tools**, and then click **Language Version**.

See also

- For more information about the Language Version utility, see "Deploying Office in a Multinational Setting" on page 151.

Terminal Server Tools

If you plan to deploy Microsoft Office 2000 in a Windows Terminal Server environment, you can use the Motionless Office Assistant on the Terminal Server computer. The Motionless Office Assistant uses no animation, and this reduces the amount of incidental display information transmitted between the server and the client computers. By minimizing the network traffic between the server and the clients, the Motionless Office Assistant can help to improve the performance of the client computers.

Installing the Motionless Office Assistant

The file for the Motionless Office Assistant is automatically installed on your computer when you install the Office Resource Kit. To make the Motionless Office Assistant the only Office Assistant on the Terminal Server computer, set all the Office Assistants to **Not Available** when you install Office, and then install the Motionless Office Assistant on the Terminal Server computer.

To install the Motionless Office Assistant, run Office Resource Kit Setup on the Terminal Server computer. If you want to install only the Motionless Office Assistant from the Office Resource Kit, then set all the features to **Not Available** except for **Terminal Server Tools**.

Other support information for Windows Terminal Server

The Office Resource Kit includes two additional files that provide support for Windows Terminal Server deployments.

File name	Description
Outlfeat.xls	Provides information about deploying Microsoft Outlook on Windows Terminal Server.
Termsrvr.mst	Provides the transform (MST file) used to install Office on a Terminal Server computer

See also

- For more information about installing the Motionless Office Assistant, see "How to Install Office Disc1 on a Windows Terminal Server" on page 93.

Profile Wizard

The Profile Wizard helps you to create and distribute a default user profile, including standard locations for files and templates. You can preset options so that users don't have to customize their settings. You can also change default values to match your organization's needs or to ensure that users have access to shared templates. When you deploy a standard user profile, all of your users start with the same Office configuration.

When you save an *Office user profile*, you create an Office profile settings (OPS) file. You can include your *OPS file* in a Windows installer *transform* (MST file), and the settings are distributed when Office 2000 is deployed. You can also use the Profile Wizard to help back up and restore user-defined settings from one computer to another.

Installing the Profile Wizard

The Profile Wizard is automatically installed on your computer when you install the Office Resource Kit. To locate the tool, click the **Start** button, point to **Programs**, point to **Microsoft Office Tools**, point to **Microsoft Office 2000 Resource Kit Tools**, and then click **Profile Wizard**.

See also

- For more information about the Profile Wizard, see "Office Custom Installation Wizard" on page 250, "Profile Wizard" on page 255, and other topics related to installation.

Removal Wizard

Although version removal functionality is integrated into Microsoft Office 2000 Setup and the Office 2000 Custom Installation Wizard, a standalone version of the Removal Wizard is included as well. You can use this tool to exert a detailed level of control over which files to remove and which to retain. For example, if you are upgrading gradually to Office 2000, you can use the Removal Wizard to remove previously installed versions of the specific applications you choose to upgrade.

Applicable Office versions are Office 97, Office 95, and Office 4.*x*—in English and all other languages in which these versions were localized. A companion file list allows you to review and edit the detailed list of files that can be removed. The Removal Wizard does not remove user files from your hard disk.

Installing the Removal Wizard

The Removal Wizard is automatically installed on your computer when you install the Office Resource Kit. To locate the tool, click the **Start** button, point to **Programs**, point to **Microsoft Office Tools**, point to **Microsoft Office 2000 Resource Kit Tools**, and then click **Removal Wizard**.

Files for localized versions of the Removal Wizard are included on the Office Resource Kit CD-ROM in the PFiles\ORKTools\ToolBox\Tools\RmvWiz\ folder. This folder contains subfolders for each supported language (indicated by the 4-digit language codes).

Files for localized versions are also available on the Office Resource Kit Web site. For more information, connect to http://www.microsoft.com/office/ork/ and click **Toolbox** in the left navigation pane. Follow the instructions to download the files.

See also

- For more information about the Removal Wizard, see "Removal Wizard" on page 269.

Systems Management Server Package Definition Files

The sample *package definition file*s (PDFs) can be used by the Microsoft Systems Management Server to install Office or Office applications remotely. PDFs are included for each of the Office 2000 product configurations, as well as for the standalone versions of Microsoft Access, Excel, FrontPage, Outlook, PowerPoint, Word, Publisher, and the MultiLanguage Pack.

Two versions of each PDF are included in the Microsoft Office 2000 Resource Kit—one version for SMS 1.2 and a second version for SMS 2.0. PDFs created for SMS 1.2 run in the SMS 2.0 product, but files created for SMS 2.0 reference features are not supported by SMS 1.2. Each PDF is accompanied by a respective INI file. The following table lists the PDFs included with the Office Resource Kit.

Component	PDFs (SMS 1.2)	PDFs (SMS 2.0)
Office Premium	off9pre.pdf off9spec.ini	off9pre.sms
Office Professional	off9pro.pdf off9spec.ini	off9pro.sms
Office Small Business	off9sbe.pdf off9spec.ini	off9sbe.sms
Office Standard	off9std.pdf off9spec.ini	off9std.sms
Access	acc2000.pdf accspec.ini	acc2000.sms

Component	PDFs (SMS 1.2)	PDFs (SMS 2.0)
Excel	xl2000.pdf xlspec.ini	xl2000.sms
FrontPage	fp2000.pdf fpspec.ini	fp2000.sms
Outlook	outl2000.pdf outlspec.ini	outl2000.sms
PowerPoint	ppt2000.pdf pptspec.ini	ppt2000.sms
Word	word2000.pdf wordspec.ini	word2000.sms
MultiLanguage Pack	lpk9_cd$x$.pdf lpk9_cd$x$.ini	lpk9_cd$x$.sms
Publisher	pub2000.pdf pubspec.ini	pub2000.sms
Office Disc 2	off9cd2.pdf off9cd2.ini	off9cd2.sms

You must edit the names of the Language Pack PDF and SMS files depending upon the specific MultiLanguage Pack CD-ROM you are installing. For example, to install MultiLanguage Pack CD-ROM 2, you would replace the x in the file name with a 2, changing the SMS 2.0 file name to lpk9_cd2.sms.

Additional PDF and SMS files for other applications will be made available through the Office Resource Kit Web site.

Installing the Systems Management Server Package Definition Files

The PDFs are automatically installed on your computer when you install the Office Resource Kit. To locate a file, click the **Start** button, point to **Programs**, point to **Microsoft Office Tools**, point to **Microsoft Office 2000 Resource Kit Tools**, and then click **Package Definition Files**.

See also

- For more information about Systems Management Server, see "Deploying Office with Systems Management Server" on page 106.

System Policy Editor and Templates

The Microsoft Office 2000 Resource Kit includes an updated version of the System Policy Editor and a number of system policy template files that provide the means for controlling the installed configuration of Office 2000.

System Policy Editor

Office 2000 applications have many options that users can customize to alter the user interface and behavior of the application. As a network administrator, you can set many of these options remotely by using Windows system policies. System policies allow you to provide greater consistency among client computers and to centralize support and maintenance efforts. For Office 2000, you can set and control the use of a much broader range of options than you could in Office 97.

System Policy Templates

The Office Resource Kit includes system policy templates for each of the Office 2000 applications. Each template contains settings for all configurable options for the application. You can edit the templates to change default settings and prevent users from changing certain settings. The following table lists the policy templates included with the Office Resource Kit.

Application	Policy template
Office 2000 (common settings)	Office9.adm
Access	Access9.adm
Clip Gallery	Clipgal5.adm
Excel	Excel9.adm
FrontPage	Frontpg4.adm
Outlook	Outlk9.adm
PowerPoint	Ppoint9.adm
Publisher	Pub9.adm
Windows installer	Instlr1.adm
Word	Word9.adm

Installing the System Policy Editor and Templates

The System Policy Editor and Templates are automatically installed on your computer when you install the Office Resource Kit. To locate the editor, click the **Start** button, point to **Programs**, point to **Microsoft Office Tools**, point **to Microsoft Office 2000 Resource Kit Tools**, and then click **System Policy Editor**. By default, the templates are installed in the \Program Files\ORKTools\ToolBox\Tools\Policy folder.

See also

- For more information, see "Managing Users' Options with System Policies" on page 279 and "Using the System Policy Editor" on page 296.

Unbind Binders Utility

If your workgroup is upgrading gradually to Office 2000, some users may have to share Microsoft Office 2000 binders with users of previous versions of Office, which cannot read binders created in Office 2000. You can use the Office 2000 Unbind Binders Utilities to separate Office 2000 binder files into their component files. The component files can then be converted and opened in earlier versions of Office.

Installing the Unbind Binders Utility

The Unbind Binders Utility is automatically installed on your computer when you install the Office Resource Kit. To locate the tool, click the **Start** button, point to **Programs**, point to **Microsoft Office Tools**, point to **Microsoft Office 2000 Resource Kit Tools**, and then click **Unbind Binders Utility**.

Supplemental Documentation

The Documents folder contains a broad collection of reference information and spreadsheets, along with sample files that you can adapt for use within your own organization. All files described in this section are installed automatically when you install the Office Resource Kit from the Office Resource Kit CD-ROM or through the Office Resource Kit Web site at http://www.microsoft.com/office/ork/.

Customizable Alerts

A custom error message, also known as a *custom alert*, is a message capable of linking to an external source (such as a Web page). Some message dialog boxes can contain a button with customized text that, when clicked, goes to a specified URL. This functionality allows you to add your own information to the message. For example, you can acknowledge a problem, give the estimated time when you expect it to be fixed, and provide a phone number or e-mail address to contact for assistance.

The Microsoft Office Resource Kit includes a spreadsheet that can help you create ASP scripts to handle custom messages, as well as a number of ASP and HTM files containing examples. The following table lists the sample files.

File name	Description
Alert.asp	Sample ASP page for an error message
Alert.htm	Sample HTML page for an error message
Alert2.asp	Sample ASP page with a response form
Alert2a.asp	Sample ASP page with embedded JavaScript
ASPscrpt.xls	Spreadsheet used to create or update ASP script
Errormsg.xls	ID numbers for all error message in Office 2000
Nyi.htm	Sample HTML page for a "Not yet implemented" error

Installing the files

Sample files for customizable alerts are automatically installed on your computer when you install the Office Resource Kit. To locate the files, click the **Start** button, point to **Programs**, point to **Microsoft Office Tools**, point to **Microsoft Office 2000 Resource Kit Documents**, and then click **Customizable Alerts**.

See also

- For more information, see "Customizing Built-in Error Messages" on page 345.

Help on the Web

The new Office on the Web feature in Microsoft Office 2000 connects your users to current information about Office 2000 on the Web. By default, when users ask a question of the Answer Wizard, they can click **None of the above, look for more help on the Web**. When they click this topic, they are connected to a feedback form, where they can comment about their search. When they submit their feedback, they are redirected to the Microsoft Product Services Support Web site, and their search is repeated on the latest Office content.

You can disable Help on the Web or customize it to point to your intranet. You can also use Help on the Web to collect user feedback that can help you create custom Answer Wizard files and Help topics. The following table lists the sample files.

File name	Description
Answiz.asp	Sample Help Desk ASP file
Answiz.htm	Sample HelpDesk HTM file
Fishng2_0.jpg	Sample image in JPG format
Fr_bkg.gif	Sample image in GIF format
Nyi.htm	Sample HTM file
Posredir.inc	Sample INC file (for use with Answiz.asp)

Installing the files

The Help on the Web samples are automatically installed on your computer when you install the Office Resource Kit. To locate the files, click the **Start** button, point to **Programs**, point to **Microsoft Office Tools**, point to **Microsoft Office 2000 Resource Kit Documents**, and then click **Help on the Web**.

See also

- For more information, see "Linking the Answer Wizard to the Web" on page 367.

International Information

Information about the language settings and international capabilities of Microsoft Office 2000 is available in several files included with the Microsoft Office 2000 Resource Kit. The following table lists the files and describes their contents.

File name	Description
IntLimit.xls	Lists the limitations of plug-in language compatibility by component.
MultiLPK.xls	Lists components of the MultiLanguage Pack and the Proofing Tools Kit by language.
WWFeatre.xls	Lists the effect of various language settings on each Office application.
WWSupport.xls	Lists support, by language of operating system, of different language features of Office applications.

Installing the files

The language settings files are automatically installed on your computer when you install the Office Resource Kit. To locate a file, click the **Start** button, point to **Programs**, point to **Microsoft Office Tools**, point to **Microsoft Office 2000 Resource Kit Documents**, and then click **International Information**.

See also

- For more information, see "Using Many Languages in One Office" on page 725 and "Recommended Operating Systems for International Use" on page 732.

Office Information

A collection of files included with the Microsoft Office 2000 Resource Kit provides details and settings information about a variety of components. The following table lists the files and describes what they contain.

File name	Description
Cfgquiet.ini	Contains default settings for the Microsoft Office Server Extension log file.
FileList.xls	Lists all files provided with Office 2000.
Formats.doc	Lists supported data formats and installed *OLE DB providers.*
IE5Feats.xls	Notes the Office features that degrade with previous versions of Microsoft Internet Explorer.
Opc.doc	Explains the syntax in files used by the Removal Wizard so that administrators can customize the removal of applications.
Oseamain.xls	Lists command-line arguments and commands that you can use with Fpsrvadm.exe.
Presbrod.xls	Lists the registry entries, descriptions, and default settings for Presentation Broadcasting.
Pubregkey.xls	Contains registry key values for Publisher.
RegKey.xls	Lists default registry key values.
SetupRef.xls	Lists Office Setup command-line options, properties, and *settings file* formats.
StopWord.doc	Contains the list of words not indexed by the Find Fast utility.
WebEnt.xls	Lists all entry points to the Web from within Office and describes how to disable them.

Installing the files

These files are automatically installed on your computer when you install the Office Resource Kit. To locate a file, click the **Start** button, point to **Programs**, point to **Microsoft Office Tools**, point to **Microsoft Office 2000 Resource Kit Documents**, and then click **Office Information**.

Outlook Information

The file Outlook.prf lists all of the profile settings supported for Microsoft Outlook. It is automatically installed on your computer when you install the Microsoft Office 2000 Resource Kit.

Installing the sample file

To locate the file, click the **Start** button, point to **Programs**, point to **Microsoft Office Tools**, point to **Microsoft Office 2000 Resource Kit Documents**, and then click **Outlook Information**.

Publisher Information

The support information for Microsoft Publisher is contained in two separate files.

File name	Description
PubFile.xls	Lists all files included with Publisher.
PubRegKy.xls	Lists the registry keys for Publisher.

Installing the sample files

These files are automatically installed on your computer when you install the Office Resource Kit. To locate a file, click the **Start** button, point to **Programs**, point to **Microsoft Office Tools**, point to **Microsoft Office 2000 Resource Kit Documents**, and then click **Publisher Information**.

Other Information and Utilities

The Microsoft Office 2000 Resource Kit contains additional tools and information that you can elect to install or deploy to your clients. These tools are not automatically installed by the Office Resource Kit Setup program—you must install each one separately before you can use it. The optional tools and documents are available on the Office Resource Kit CD-ROM or through the Office Resource Kit Web site at http://www.microsoft.com/office/ork/.

Answer Wizard Builder

Users sometimes submit queries to the Answer Wizard (the intelligence engine behind the Office Assistant) that the Answer Wizard cannot answer because the question is unique to your organization. For example, a user might ask for the path to a printer on your local network, or ask for the location of a form on your intranet. To provide this type of information, you can build your own Answer Wizard content that answers questions specific to your organization.

Installing the Answer Wizard Builder

The Answer Wizard Builder must be installed separately from the other utilities—it is not installed by the Office Resource Kit Setup program. To install the Answer Wizard Builder, run Setup.exe from the \Pfiles\ORKTools\ToolBox\Tools\AnsWiz folder on the Office Resource Kit CD-ROM.

Follow the instructions to install the Answer Wizard Builder on your computer. To distribute the utility for others to install, you need to deploy all of the files from the folder through a network installation point.

The Answer Wizard Builder is also available on the Office Resource Kit Web site. For more information, connect to http://www.microsoft.com/office/ork/ and click **Toolbox** in the left navigation pane. Follow the instructions to download the tool.

See also

- For more information, see "Creating Your Own Help Topics" on page 358.

FrontPage 2000 Server Extensions Resource Kit

The Microsoft FrontPage 2000 Server Extensions Resource Kit is a guide to installing and administering the FrontPage server extensions on a Web server. It contains an overview of the server extensions, a detailed discussion of server extensions security on Windows and UNIX platforms, a guide to server extensions installation, and descriptions of all server extensions administrative tools and techniques. The Server Extensions Resource Kit has a set of appendixes, including complete descriptions of server extensions configuration files and registry settings.

Installing the FrontPage 2000 Server Extensions Resource Kit

The FrontPage 2000 Server Extensions Resource Kit must be installed separately from the other utilities—it is not installed by the Office Resource Kit Setup program. To install the FrontPage 2000 Server Extensions Resource Kit, copy the FPSERK folder from \PFiles\ORKTools\ on the Office Resource Kit CD-ROM to your computer. In the FPSERK folder, double-click the file Default.htm to open the FrontPage 2000 Server Extensions Resource Kit.

To distribute the kit for others to install, you need to deploy all of the files from the folder through a *distribution point*.

The FrontPage 2000 Server Extensions Resource Kit is also available on the Office Resource Kit Web site. For more information, connect to http://www.microsoft.com/office/ork/ and click **Toolbox** in the left navigation pane. Follow the instructions to download the files.

HTML Help WorkShop

You can use the HTML Help Workshop to create Help topics that provide information and assistance specific to your organization. You can also integrate those topics with the Office 2000 Help system, or combine them with custom Answer Wizard databases to create a complete assistance solution.

Installing HTML Help WorkShop

The HTML Help Workshop must be installed separately from the other applications—it is not installed by the Office Resource Kit Setup program. To install the HTML Help WorkShop, run Htmlhelp.exe from the \PFiles\ORKTools\ToolBox\Tools\HTMLHelp\ folder on the Office Resource Kit CD-ROM.

Follow the instructions to install the HTML Help Workshop on your computer. To distribute the workshop for others to install, you need to deploy all of the files from the folder through a *distribution point*.

The HTML Help Workshop is also available on the Office Resource Kit Web site. For more information, connect to http://www.microsoft.com/office/ork/ and click **Toolbox** in the left navigation pane. Follow the instructions to download the workshop.

Installing the custom style sheets

Also included are two *cascading style sheets* so that you can build your own custom help topics using Microsoft styles. The two style sheets are listed in the table below.

File name	Description
Office.css	Cascading style sheet for HHW (for use with Internet Explorer version 4.0 or later).
MsOffice.css	Cascading style sheet for HHW (for use with Internet Explorer version 3.0).

The style sheets can be found in the \PFiles\ORKTools\ToolBox\Tools\HTMLHelp\ folder on the Office Resource Kit CD-ROM.

The style sheets are also available on the Office Resource Kit Web site. For more information, connect to http://www.microsoft.com/office/ork/ and click **Toolbox** in the left navigation pane. Follow the instructions to download the files.

See also

- For more information about HTML Help, see "Creating Your Own Help Topics" on page 358.

Microsoft Office Resource Kit for Office 97/98

The Microsoft Office 2000 Resource Kit includes the complete contents of the Resource Kit for Office 97 for Windows and Office 98 for the Macintosh, in case you need to refer back to earlier information or tools.

In some cases, the previous Office Resource Kit contains information no longer covered in the Office 2000 Resource Kit. In particular, procedures for converting files from earlier versions of certain applications are no longer included in the current version. If you are looking for information about working with older products, and you don't find it in the Office 2000 Resource Kit, check the Resource Kit for Office 97/98. The conversion information included still applies to the Office 2000 products.

The Office Resource Kit for Office 97/98 can be found in the \PFiles\ORKTools\ORK97folder on the Office Resource Kit CD-ROM.

The archive edition of the Office Resource Kit is also available on the Office Resource Kit Web site. For more information, connect to http://www.microsoft.com/office/ork/.

Microsoft Office Converter Pack

The Microsoft Office Converter Pack bundles together a collection of file converters and filters that can be deployed to users. The Converter Pack can be useful to organizations that use Office 2000 in a mixed environment with previous versions of Office, including Office for the Macintosh, or other Office-related productivity applications. Many of these converters and filters have been previously available, but this is the first time they are packaged together for convenient deployment.

You can customize the Converter Pack to deploy any number of these converters that your organization needs. You can also choose to deploy them with no user interaction, with full user interaction, or you can include the converters with your deployment of Office 2000.

Installing the Microsoft Office Converter Pack

The Office Converter Pack must be installed separately from the other applications—it is not installed by the Office Resource Kit Setup program. To install the Office Converter Pack, run Setup.exe from the \PFiles\ORKTools\ToolBox\Tools\OCP\ folder on the Office Resource Kit CD-ROM.

Follow the instructions to install the Office Converter Pack on your computer. To distribute the utilities for others to install, you need to deploy all of the files from the folder through a *distribution point*.

The Converter Pack is also available on the Office Resource Kit Web site. For more information, connect to http://www.microsoft.com/office/ork/ and click **Toolbox** in the left navigation pane. Follow the instructions to download the utilities.

See also

- For more information, see "How to Use the Microsoft Office Converter Pack" on page 440.

MultiLanguage Pack Support Files

The Microsoft Office 2000 MultiLanguage Pack contains files that allow users to switch the language of their Office user interface and online Help. It also includes a Proofing Tools Kit, with files such as spelling dictionaries and AutoCorrect lists to use when editing documents in different languages.

For information about installing and using the MultiLanguage Pack support files, see "Overview of International Features in Office 2000" on page 725.

PowerPoint 97/2000 Viewer

The Microsoft PowerPoint 97/2000 Viewer allows you to share PowerPoint 97 or PowerPoint 2000 presentations with users who do not have PowerPoint installed on their systems. The PowerPoint Viewer allows users to view and print PowerPoint presentations, but it does not allow them to edit the presentations.

Installing the PowerPoint 97/2000 Viewer

To install the PowerPoint 97/2000 Viewer, distribute the file Pptvw32.exe to users and instruct them to run the file from their local hard disk. The Pptvw32.exe file is located in the \PFiles\ORKTools\ToolBox\Tools\PPTView\ppview97.exe folder on the Office Resource Kit CD-ROM.

The PowerPoint 97/2000 Viewer is also available on the Office Resource Kit Web site. For more information, connect to http://www.microsoft.com/office/ork/ and click **Toolbox** in the left navigation pane. Follow the instructions to download the file.

Readme.doc

For notes on last-minute updates to the tools and documentation, see the Readme.doc file, located in the root folder of the Microsoft Office 2000 Resource Kit CD-ROM.

Updated information is also available on the Office Resource Kit Web site. Connect to http://www.microsoft.com/office/ork/ and click **Toolbox** in the left navigation pane.

Glossary

A

access control list (ACL) Contains entries that identify which groups or users have access to a particular object, including the type and scope of that access.

Acme Setup Setup technology used in previous versions of Microsoft Office. Acme Setup relies on tables of information in text files to copy program files, set registry entries, and perform other tasks necessary for installing Office on a user's computer.

active document In Microsoft Internet Explorer, a document from any application that supports ActiveX document interfaces. These interfaces allow the document to be activated and edited in Internet Explorer.

Active Server Pages (ASP) Technology that allows Web developers to combine scripts and HTML code to create dynamic Web content and Web-based applications.

add-in Software that extends an application by adding functionality that is not in the main application. For example, the Microsoft Office 2000 MultiLanguage Pack includes several localized Excel add-ins.

ADE file Microsoft Access project (ADP) file with all modules compiled and all editable source code removed.

administrative installation point Network share from which users install Office. Created by running Setup with the **/a** command-line option; contains all the Office files.

administrator privileges Highest level of permissions that can be granted to an account in Windows NT User Manager. An administrator can set permissions for other users and create groups and accounts within the domain.

Admins group **1.** In Office Server Extensions, the group account created by the OSE Configuration Wizard. Used to establish and maintain user permissions for access to Web Discussions. **2.** In user-level security for Access databases and MDE files, the default administrators group that can establish and maintain group and user permissions for access to database objects.

ADP file Microsoft Access project file. Provides efficient, native-mode access to a Microsoft SQL Server database through the OLE DB component architecture. Acts as a front-end to the SQL database.

advertise Windows installer method for making an application available to the user without installing it. When the user attempts to use the application, the application is installed and run. *See also* assign, publish.

advertisement In Systems Management Server, a notification to a target group of computers that a program is available to be run.

anonymous access Allows users without Windows NT accounts to connect to the server and use server resources. All Web browsers support anonymous access.

ANSI SQL-92 standard   Standard for Structured Query Language approved by the ANSI committee. Includes requirements to support international languages.

assign   Windows installer method for advertising an application. When you assign an application, the installer creates shortcuts and **Start** menu icons, and the application appears to be installed. The application is actually installed the first time the user attempts to use it. *See also* advertise, publish.

authentication   **1.** Process used to validate the user account that is attempting to gain access to the network or to a resource within the network. **2.** Process used to validate the source of a certificate delivered by a Web site. If the security level enabled on the recipient's computer cannot authenticate the digital signature of the certificate, the certificate is ignored or the user is prompted.

AutoNavigation view   Customizable view for OSE-extended web sites. Resembles the table of contents in a printed book..

B

bridgehead server   Server that handles directory replication between sites. Automatically updates other servers within a site.

C

cascading style sheets   Implementation of extended fonts and styles in HTML through the use of an external file usually indicated with a file name extension of .css.

certificate   Set of data issued by a certificate authority to completely identify an entity; issued only after that authority has verified the entity's identity.

certificate authority   A mutually trusted organization that issues certificates. Before issuing a certificate, the certificate authority requires you to provide identification information. Verisign, Inc. is a recognized certificate authority.

character entity reference   A set of HTML characters that are represented by easy-to-remember mnemonic names.

child feature   In Office Setup, an Office feature that is contained within another feature in the tree. For example, Help for Word Perfect is a child feature of the Microsoft Word for Windows Help feature.

code page   Ordered set of characters in which a numeric index (code point) is associated with each character of a particular writing system. There are separate code pages for different writing systems, such as Western European and Cyrillic. *See also* Unicode.

code point   Numeric value in Unicode encoding or in a code page; corresponds to a character. In the Western European code page, 65 is the code point for the letter A; however, in another code page, the code point 65 might correspond to a different character.

complex script   Writing system based on characters that are composed of multiple glyphs or whose shape depends on adjacent characters. Thai and Arabic use complex scripts. *See also* glyph.

Component Object Model (COM)   Methodology behind the design and development of Automation and ActiveX.

concurrency   **1.** In multitasking operating systems, allows more than one thread or process to run at the same time. For example, Explorer runs concurrently in Windows when other applications are running in the foreground. **2.** In multiuser database systems, such as a shared Access database, describes the availability of data to users sharing the database. Determined by a system of locking that regulates how users work with records in the database.

cross-domain data access Access to a database or Web site from an external domain without security authentication.

customizable alert Error message that can be linked to an external source (such as a Web page). Also known as a customizable error message.

D

data access page HTML pages created with the Microsoft Access Data Source component. Data access pages provide interactive database control for published HTML documents.

database engine Application designed to manage and organize a database. Usually incorporates a structured query language (SQL) or other means of manipulating or sorting content to assemble information from raw data elements.

database replication Method of keeping multiple Access databases synchronized. Requires special considerations for database design and connectivity between all instances of the database.

delegate owner User who has permissions to view and modify the schedule of another Schedule+ or Outlook user. A delegate owner can also designate other delegates.

delegation application Application designed or designated to share processing of a task submitted from another computer. For example, an OSE-extended web site can incorporate the use of a remote SQL Server to return information at a user's request.

Design Master Original copy of an Access database. Usually refers to the master copy when the database has been configured for replication. Changes to data structure and macros can be accomplished only in the Design Master.

digital certificate File issued by a certificate authority. Can be used to verify the user's identity for digitally signed or encrypted e-mail. Associates the user's identity with a public encryption key.

Digital ID Combination of a digital certificate and a public and private encryption key set.

digital signature Confirms that an e-mail message, macro, or program originated from a trusted source who signed it. Also confirms that the message, macro, or program has not been altered.

distribution point Server location for storing Systems Management Server package files. Clients contact distribution points to obtain programs and files after they have received notification of the availability from an advertisement. *See also* advertisement.

E

elevated privileges In Windows NT 4.0, method for giving an installation program administrator rights to install software into system areas. Can be accomplished by logging on with administrator rights, advertising the program, giving administrator rights to all Windows installer programs, or using Systems Management Server. *See also* advertise

encryption Method used to scramble the content of a file or data packet to make the data unreadable without the decryption key.

encryption, 40-bit Medium level of encryption. Uses a 40-bit key to scramble the contents of a file or data packet to make the data unreadable without the decryption key.

encryption, 128-bit High level of encryption. Uses a 128-bit key to scramble the contents of a file or data packet to make the data unreadable without the decryption key.

executable mode Configuration in which Microsoft Access and Microsoft Excel run to support display of text, macro behavior, and other features specific to a particular Asian or right-to-left language.

Execute mode Windows NT installation mode that installs Office for only the Windows Terminal Client user running Setup. *See also* Install mode.

explicit permissions **1.** Permission assigned to a user to grant or deny access to a specific resource on the network. **2.** In Access user-level security, set of permissions granted or denied to a user to access database objects in a shared Access database or MDE file.

F

file allocation table (FAT) Common file format of file cataloging for DOS and Windows operating systems; physical method of storing and accessing files from a hard drive. The FAT contains a list of all files on the physical or logical drive.

firewall Security system meant to protect your internal network from unauthorized external access. Used to block users from viewing inappropriate sites on the Internet. Also known as a proxy server.

FrontPage-extended web Web site in which FrontPage Server Extensions have been installed to provide support for forms and other interactive elements.

G

glyph Shape of a character as rendered by a font. For example, the italic "*a*" and the roman "a" are different glyphs representing the same alphabetical character.

I

ideographic script Writing system that is based on characters of Chinese origin, where the characters represent words or syllables that are generally used in more than one Asian language.

IExpress Installation technology that compresses a number of files into a self-extracting executable file.

implicit permissions **1.** Permission granted to a group of users so that all users have the same permission level for a specific resource on the network. **2.** In Access user-level security, the set of permissions granted or denied to a group of users to access database objects in a shared Access database or MDE file.

Input Method Editor (IME) Software utility that converts keystrokes to characters in an ideographic script (Korean, Chinese, Japanese, and so on).

Install mode Windows NT installation mode that installs Office for all Windows Terminal Client users who connect to a Windows Terminal Server computer. *See also* Execute mode.

installation language Locale ID (LCID) assigned to the value entry InstallLanguage in the Windows registry. This entry, which is created by Office Setup, determines default behavior of the installation process.

interactive HTML format Means of displaying and modifying Office documents in Internet Explorer by using most of the functionality of the original Office application.

J

job Systems Management Server object that handles distribution of packages to client computers. You configure jobs in the Jobs window in Systems Management Server versions 1.2 and 2.0.

L

locale ID (LCID) A 32-bit value defined by Windows that consists of a language ID, sort ID, and reserved bits. Identifies a particular language. For example, the LCID for English is 1033, and the LCID for Japanese is 1041.

M

machine group In Systems Management Server version 1.2, a set of computers with similar configurations and features. Used to stagger the distribution of Office 2000.

MDB file Microsoft Access database file.

MDE file Microsoft Access database file with all modules compiled and all editable source code removed.

metabase Database used exclusively by Internet Information Server (IIS). Composed of metadata in a compressed format. Design is similar to that of the Windows registry.

metadata Data that describes the structure of other data. Created and maintained by Internet Information Server (IIS) and stored in the metabase.

metastore Small database maintained within each FrontPage-extended web. Contains properties and settings of the Web site.

Microsoft Management Console (MMC) In Windows NT version 4.0 and Windows 2000, a utility designed to manage servers and services through a common user interface. MMC snap-ins include FrontPage Server Extensions, Internet Information Server (IIS), and SQL Server.

MSI file Windows installer package used by the Microsoft Office Custom Installation Wizard to run Office Setup from an administrative installation point. *See also* package.

MST file Windows installer transform that temporarily modifies the behavior of the package (MSI file) to customize Office installation. Created to modify or restrict Office 2000 Setup from an administrative installation point. *See also* transform.

multidimensional data source Data structure that contains Online Analytical Processing (OLAP) data. Consists of dimensions that organize the types of data into hierarchies, and data fields that measure the quantities being tracked in the database. Can be used to create dynamic PivotTable and PivotChart reports in Excel and Access.

N

NTFS file system (NTFS) Designed exclusively for use with the Windows NT operating system. NTFS allows for stronger security and more flexible file management methods than does FAT. *See also* file allocation table (FAT)

O

object model In object-oriented programming languages, the design of an object and the classes required to create and enable an instance of the object by using methods, properties, and events to interact with the object.

Office user profile Collection of user-defined settings for Office 2000 created by using the Profile Wizard. Contains most of the customizations that users make to the Office 2000 environment. *See also* OPS file.

OLE DB provider Data access component that provides access to data for applications and services that support the OLE DB standard. Makes data available in tabular form from both relational and nonrelational data sources. Excel and Access can use OLE DB providers to access data, and the ActiveX Data Objects (ADO) programming model can be used from any Office application to work with data exposed by an OLE DB provider.

Online Analytical Processing (OLAP) Technology that allows users to perform multidimensional analysis on large volumes of data. Supported by Excel 2000. *See also* multidimensional data source.

OPS file Settings file created by the Profile Wizard; a binary file.

OSE-extended web In Office Server Extensions, allows the Web site you create to use extended features, such as collaboration, advanced navigation, and search.

P

package 1. In Windows installer, MSI file used by the Microsoft Office Custom Installation Wizard to run Office Setup from an administrative installation point. 2. In Systems Management Server, defines the files that comprise the software application to be distributed, and includes package configuration and identification information.

package definition file (PDF) Used by Systems Management Server to distribute applications to selected clients.

permissions 1. In server management, user rights granted by an administrator for a given project, Web site, file, or folder. The highest level of flexibility and security is available only on an NTFS-formatted disk under Windows NT 4.0 or Windows 2000. 2. In Access 2000 user-level security, user or group rights granted or denied by an administrator to control access to database objects.

personal identifier (PID) In Access 2000, unique identifier used when creating a user-level security user or group account. Personal identifiers are case-sensitive alphanumeric strings that can be 4–20 characters long.

plug-in language features User interface, online Help, and editing tools that users can install with Office 2000 to run Office in their own language, and to create documents in many other languages.

private key One of a pair of keys used for encryption. A message encrypted with the public key must be decrypted with the private key. Part of a Digital ID.

private property In Windows installer, a type of Setup property in the package (MSI file). Private property names are a mix of uppercase and lowercase letters, and can be specified only on the **Modify Setup Properties** panel of the Custom Installation Wizard.

public key One of a pair of keys used for encryption. A message encrypted with the public key must be decrypted with the private key. Part of a Digital ID.

public property In Windows installer, a type of Setup property in the package (MSI file). Public property names are all uppercase and can be specified in the Setup command line, in the settings file, or on the **Modify Setup Properties** panel of the Custom Installation Wizard. With few exceptions, all properties used to manage the installation process are public properties.

publish Windows installer method for advertising an application. When you publish an application, the installer does not create shortcuts or Start menu icons, but the application is configured to be installed the first time another application activates it. *See also* advertise, assign.

R

reconciling Process of retrieving and updating a user profile.

replica Copy of an Access database distributed and maintained through replication.

replica set Set of replicated databases. Includes the Design Master and all replicas.

roaming user User who travels or who uses more than one computer on a regular basis. Works at multiple sites using different computers or transports a portable computer that must adapt to different locales.

roaming user profiles Account information established for roaming users within the given domain of a network. Automatically configures the computer when the user logs on. Available only under Windows NT version 4.0 or later.

root web FrontPage-extended web that functions as the top-level content folder of a Web site.

S

script **1.** In HTML documents, code or applets written in Microsoft Visual Basic Scripting Edition (VBScript) or JScript that manipulate elements on the page, such as responding to user actions or animating graphics. **2.** In character sets, a set of characters from a particular writing system, such as Arabic, Cyrillic, Hebrew, or Latin.

security identifier (SID) Computer-generated, nonreadable binary string that uniquely identifies a user or group.

Setup settings file Text file (Setup.ini) in which you enter properties and values to customize the installation process. You can edit the Setup settings file to specify the same properties that you use on the Setup command line. Every command-line option has a corresponding setting in the settings file.

share-level security Provides security for objects or resources within a database by requiring a user to enter a password to gain access to an object or to perform an operation. In Access 2000, the only form of share-level security is a database password, which is required before a user can open the database.

Secure Multipurpose Internet Mail Extensions (S/MIME) Method of security that allows users to exchange encrypted and digitally signed messages with any S/MIME–compliant mail reader. Messages are encrypted or digitally signed by the sending client and decrypted by the recipient.

Systems Management Server Installer Add-on utility that allows you to create installation scripts by comparing preinstallation and postinstallation computer images. Designed for administrators who need to maintain consistent desktop clients.

subweb Microsoft FrontPage-extended web that is contained within the root web or another subweb.

system database Database used to store group and user account names and the passwords used to authenticate users when they log on to an Access database or MDE file secured with user-level security. *See also* workgroup information file.

system locale In Windows NT 4.0 and Windows 2000, the setting that determines the code page and default user locale. *See also* user locale, code page.

Systems Network Architecture (SNA) Set of seven-layered protocols developed by IBM to connect mainframe computers. Dependent on the fundamental protocol synchronous data link control (SDLC).

T

three-tier data access One of two modes of data access used by the Microsoft Office Data Source control to determine whether a data access page is considered safe. With three-tier data access, the data access page is considered inherently safe, and cross-domain data access is allowed. *See also* two-tier data access.

transform Windows installer MST file that temporarily modifies the behavior of the package (MSI file) to customize Office installation. Created to modify or restrict Office 2000 Setup from an administrative installation point. *See also* package.

traveling user Uses more than one computer on a regular basis. Traveling users might have different language requirements or need access to different configurations of the same application (local or remote). *See also* roaming user.

two-tier data access One of two modes of data access used by the Microsoft Office Data Source control to determine whether a data access page is considered safe. With two-tier data access, a data access page is considered unsafe. Cross-domain data access is allowed only when the data access page is published from a Web site that is registered as a member of the Trusted sites security. *See also* three-tier data access.

U

Unicode Universal character set that can accommodate all known scripts. Unlike code pages, Unicode uses a unique two-byte encoding for every character.

user locale Setting that determines formats and sort orders for date, time, currency, and so on. Also known as regional settings.

user-level security Sets security for objects or resources within an Access database or MDE file by establishing a level of access for groups or individual users. User names and passwords are authenticated against a database of user and group account information in an Access workgroup information file or system database.

V

virtual directory Acts as a layer of indirection between the addresses that users enter and the physical folder structure of a Web site. The physical mapping identifies where IIS retrieves content when clients request the alias.

virtual key code Hardware-independent number that uniquely identifies a key on the keyboard.

W

Web Folders object Container for shortcuts to Web sites. Appears in My Computer, Windows Explorer, and the **Open** and **Save As** dialog boxes in Office 2000 applications.

Windows installer shortcut Application shortcut that uses the globally unique identifier (GUID), rather than a fixed path, to point to the application. Used to advertise an application and to support the **Installed on First Use** installation option in Office 2000 Setup. *See also* advertise.

workgroup ID In Access, a case-sensitive alphanumeric string 4–20 characters in length. Specified when you create a new workgroup information file. Prevents other users from creating an identical copy of the file.

workgroup information file In Access, synonym for the system database. Used to store group and user account names and the passwords used to authenticate users when they log on to an Access database or MDE file secured with user-level security. *See also* user-level security.

Index

I

M

N

S

U

END-USER LICENSE AGREEMENT FOR MICROSOFT SOFTWARE

(Book Companion CD)

IMPORTANT—READ CAREFULLY: This Microsoft End-User License Agreement ("EULA") is a legal agreement between you (either an individual or a single entity) and Microsoft Corporation ("Microsoft") for the Microsoft software product identified above, which includes computer software and may include associated "online" or electronic documentation ("SOFTWARE PRODUCT"). By installing, copying, or otherwise using the SOFTWARE PRODUCT, you agree to be bound by the terms of this EULA. If you do not agree to the terms of this EULA, do not install, copy or use the SOFTWARE PRODUCT.

SOFTWARE PRODUCT LICENSE

The SOFTWARE PRODUCT is protected by copyright laws and international copyright treaties, as well as other intellectual property laws and treaties. The SOFTWARE PRODUCT is licensed, not sold.

1. **GRANT OF LICENSE.** This EULA grants you the following rights:

- **Installation and Use.** You may install and use an unlimited number of copies of the SOFTWARE PRODUCT.

- **Reproduction and Distribution.** You may reproduce and distribute an unlimited number of copies of material, or portions of the material from the SOFTWARE PRODUCT; provided that all reproduced material shall be an unmodified copy, including all copyright and trademark notices, and shall be accompanied by a copy of this EULA. Use of some material from the SOFTWARE PRODUCT may be governed by a supplemental EULA. The material from the SOFTWARE PRODUCT may not be redistributed as a standalone product or included with your own product for any commercial purposes.

2. **DESCRIPTION OF OTHER RIGHTS AND LIMITATIONS.**

- **Limitations on Reverse Engineering, Decompilation, and Disassembly.** You may not reverse engineer, decompile, or disassemble the SOFTWARE PRODUCT, except and only to the extent that such activity is expressly permitted by applicable law notwithstanding this limitation.

- **Separation of Components.** Except for the rights described above, the SOFTWARE PRODUCT is licensed as a single product. Its component parts may not be separated for use on more than one computer.

- **Support Services.** Microsoft may provide you with support services related to the SOFTWARE PRODUCT ("Support Services"). Use of Support Services is governed by the Microsoft policies and programs described in the user manual, in "online" documentation, and/or in other Microsoft-provided materials. Any supplemental software code provided to you as part of the Support Services shall be considered part of the SOFTWARE PRODUCT and subject to the terms and conditions of this EULA. With respect to technical information you provide to Microsoft as part of the Support Services, Microsoft may use such information for its business purposes, including for product support and development. Microsoft will not utilize such technical information in a form that personally identifies you.

- **Software Transfer.** You may permanently transfer all of your rights under this EULA, provided the recipient agrees to the terms of this EULA.

- **Termination.** Without prejudice to any other rights, Microsoft may terminate this EULA if you fail to comply with the terms and conditions of this EULA. In such event, you must destroy all copies of the SOFTWARE PRODUCT and all of its component parts.

3. **INTELLECTUAL PROPERTY RIGHTS.** All ownership, title and intellectual property rights in and to the SOFTWARE PRODUCT (including but not limited to any images, photographs, animations, video, audio, music, text and "applets" incorporated into the SOFTWARE PRODUCT), and any copies you are permitted to make herein are owned by Microsoft or its suppliers. All ownership, title, and intellectual property rights in and to the content which may be accessed through use of the SOFTWARE PRODUCT is the property of the respective content owner and may be protected by applicable copyright or other intellectual property laws and treaties. This EULA grants you no rights to use such content. For each copy of the SOFTWARE PRODUCT you are authorized to use above, you may also reproduce one additional copy of the Software Product solely for archival or restoration purposes.

4. **U.S. GOVERNMENT RESTRICTED RIGHTS.** All SOFTWARE PRODUCT provided to the U.S. Government pursuant to solicitations issued on or after December 1, 1995 is provided with the commercial rights and restrictions described elsewhere herein. All SOFTWARE PRODUCT provided to the U.S. Government pursuant to solicitations issued prior to December 1, 1995 is provided with RESTRICTED RIGHTS as provided for in FAR, 48 CFR 52.227-14 (JUNE 1987) or FAR, 48 CFR 252.227-7013 (OCT 1988), as applicable.

5. **EXPORT RESTRICTIONS.** You agree that you will not export or re-export the SOFTWARE PRODUCT, any part thereof, or any process or service that is the direct product of the SOFTWARE PRODUCT (the foregoing collectively referred to as the "Restricted Components"), to any country, person or entity subject to U.S. export restrictions. You specifically agree not to export or re-export any of the Restricted Components (i) to any country to which the U.S. has embargoed or restricted the export of goods or services, which currently include, but are not necessarily limited to Cuba, Iran, Iraq, Libya, North Korea, Sudan and Syria, or to any national of any such country, wherever located, who intends to transmit or transport the Restricted Components back to such country; (ii) to any person or entity who you know or have reason to know will utilize the Restricted Components in the design, development or production of nuclear, chemical or biological weapons; or (iii) to any person or entity who has been prohibited from participating in U.S. export transactions by any federal agency of the U.S. government. You warrant and represent that neither the U.S. Commerce Department, Bureau of Export Administration nor any other U.S. federal agency has suspended, revoked or denied your export privileges.

6. **APPLICABLE LAW.** If you acquired this SOFTWARE PRODUCT in the United States, this EULA is governed by the laws of the State of Washington. If you acquired this SOFTWARE PRODUCT in Canada, unless expressly prohibited by local law, this EULA is governed by the laws in force in the Province of Ontario, Canada; and, in respect of any dispute which may arise hereunder, you consent to the jurisdiction of the federal and provincial courts sitting in Toronto, Ontario. If this SOFTWARE PRODUCT was acquired outside the United States, then local law may apply.

7. **QUESTIONS.** Should you have any questions concerning this EULA, or if you desire to contact Microsoft for any reason, please contact the Microsoft subsidiary serving your country, or write: Microsoft Sales Information Center/One Microsoft Way/ Redmond, WA 98052-6399.

8. **DISCLAIMER OF WARRANTIES. To the maximum extent permitted by applicable law, Microsoft and its suppliers provide the SOFTWARE PRODUCT and any (if any) support services related to the SOFTWARE PRODUCT ("Support Services")** *AS IS AND WITH ALL FAULTS*, **and hereby disclaim all warranties and conditions, either express, implied or statutory, including, but not limited to, any (if any) implied warranties or conditions of merchantability, of fitness for a particular purpose, of lack of viruses, of accuracy or completeness of responses, of results, and of lack of negligence or lack of workmanlike effort, all with regard to the SOFTWARE PRODUCT, and the provision of or failure to provide Support Services. ALSO, THERE IS NO WARRANTY OR CONDITION OF TITLE, QUIET ENJOYMENT, QUIET POSSESSION, CORRESPONDENCE TO DESCRIPTION OR NON-INFRINGEMENT, WITH REGARD TO THE SOFTWARE PRODUCT. THE ENTIRE RISK AS TO THE QUALITY OF OR ARISING OUT OF USE OR PERFORMANCE OF THE SOFTWARE PRODUCT AND SUPPORT SERVICES, IF ANY, REMAINS WITH YOU.**

9. **EXCLUSION OF INCIDENTAL, CONSEQUENTIAL AND CERTAIN OTHER DAMAGES. TO THE MAXIMUM EXTENT PERMITTED BY APPLICABLE LAW, IN NO EVENT SHALL MICROSOFT OR ITS SUPPLIERS BE LIABLE FOR ANY SPECIAL, INCIDENTAL, INDIRECT, OR CONSEQUENTIAL DAMAGES WHATSOEVER (INCLUDING, BUT NOT LIMITED TO, DAMAGES FOR LOSS OF PROFITS OR CONFIDENTIAL OR OTHER INFORMATION, FOR BUSINESS INTERRUPTION, FOR PERSONAL INJURY, FOR LOSS OF PRIVACY, FOR FAILURE TO MEET ANY DUTY INCLUDING OF GOOD FAITH OR OF REASONABLE CARE, FOR NEGLIGENCE, AND FOR ANY OTHER PECUNIARY OR OTHER LOSS WHATSOEVER) ARISING OUT OF OR IN ANY WAY RELATED TO THE USE OF OR INABILITY TO USE THE SOFTWARE PRODUCT, THE PROVISION OF OR FAILURE TO PROVIDE SUPPORT SERVICES, OR OTHERWISE UNDER OR IN CONNECTION WITH ANY PROVISION OF THIS EVALUATION LICENSE, EVEN IN THE EVENT OF THE FAULT, TORT (INCLUDING NEGLIGENCE), STRICT LIABILITY, BREACH OF CONTRACT OR BREACH OF WARRANTY OF MICROSOFT OR ANY SUPPLIER, AND EVEN IF MICROSOFT OR ANY SUPPLIER HAS BEEN ADVISED OF THE POSSIBILITY OF SUCH DAMAGES.**

10. **LIMITATION OF LIABILITY AND REMEDIES. Notwithstanding any damages that you might incur for any reason whatsoever (including, without limitation, all damages referenced above and all direct or general damages), the entire liability of Microsoft and any of its suppliers under any provision of this EULA and your exclusive remedy for all of the foregoing shall be limited to the greater of the amount actually paid by you for the SOFTWARE PRODUCT or U.S.$5.00. The foregoing limitations, exclusions and disclaimers shall apply to the maximum extent permitted by applicable law, even if any remedy fails its essential purpose.**

11. **NOTE ON JAVA SUPPORT.** THE SOFTWARE PRODUCT MAY CONTAIN SUPPORT FOR PROGRAMS WRITTEN IN JAVA. JAVA TECHNOLOGY IS NOT FAULT TOLERANT AND IS NOT DESIGNED, MANUFACTURED, OR INTENDED FOR USE OR RESALE AS ONLINE CONTROL EQUIPMENT IN HAZARDOUS ENVIRONMENTS REQUIRING FAIL-SAFE PERFORMANCE, SUCH AS IN THE OPERATION OF NUCLEAR FACILITIES, AIRCRAFT NAVIGATION OR COMMUNICATION SYSTEMS, AIR TRAFFIC CONTROL, DIRECT LIFE SUPPORT MACHINES, OR WEAPONS SYSTEMS, IN WHICH THE FAILURE OF JAVA TECHNOLOGY COULD LEAD DIRECTLY TO DEATH, PERSONAL INJURY, OR SEVERE PHYSICAL OR ENVIRONMENTAL DAMAGE. Sun Microsystems, Inc. has contractually obligated Microsoft to make this disclaimer.

Si vous avez acquis votre produit Microsoft au CANADA, la garantie limitée suivante vous concerne:

RENONCIATION AUX GARANTIES. Dans toute la mesure permise par la législation en vigueur, Microsoft et ses fournisseurs fournissent le Produit Logiciel et tous (selon le cas) les services d'assistance liés au Produit Logiciel ("Services d'assistance") TELS QUELS ET AVEC TOUS LEURS DÉFAUTS, et par les présentes excluent toute garantie ou condition, expresse ou implicite, légale ou conventionnelle, écrite ou verbale, y compris, mais sans limitation, toute (selon le cas) garantie ou condition implicite ou légale de qualité marchande, de conformité à un usage particulier, d'absence de virus, d'exactitude et d'intégralité des réponses, de résultats, d'efforts techniques et professionnels et d'absence de négligence, le tout relativement au Produit Logiciel et à la prestation ou à la non-prestation des Services d'assistance. DE PLUS, IL N'Y A AUCUNE GARANTIE ET CONDITION DE TITRE, DE JOUISSANCE PAISIBLE, DE POSSESSION PAISIBLE, DE SIMILARITÉ À LA DESCRIPTION ET D'ABSENCE DE CONTREFAÇON RELATIVEMENT AU PRODUIT LOGICIEL. Vous supportez tous les risques découlant de l'utilisation et de la performance du Produit Logiciel et ceux découlant des Services d'assistance (s'il y a lieu).

EXCLUSION DES DOMMAGES INDIRECTS, ACCESSOIRES ET AUTRES. Dans toute la mesure permise par la législation en vigueur, Microsoft et ses fournisseurs ne sont en aucun cas responsables de tout dommage spécial, indirect, accessoire, moral ou exemplaire quel qu'il soit (y compris, mais sans limitation, les dommages entraînés par la perte de bénéfices ou la perte d'information confidentielle ou autre, l'interruption des affaires, les préjudices corporels, la perte de confidentialité, le défaut de remplir toute obligation y compris les obligations de bonne foi et de diligence raisonnable, la négligence et toute autre perte pécuniaire ou autre perte de quelque nature que ce soit) découlant de, ou de toute autre manière lié à, l'utilisation ou l'impossibilité d'utiliser le Produit Logiciel, la prestation ou la non-prestation des Services d'assistance ou autrement en vertu de ou relativement à toute disposition de cette convention, que ce soit en cas de faute, de délit (y compris la négligence), de responsabilité stricte, de manquement à un contrat ou de manquement à une garantie de Microsoft ou de l'un de ses fournisseurs, et ce, même si Microsoft ou l'un de ses fournisseurs a été avisé de la possibilité de tels dommages.

LIMITATION DE RESPONSABILITÉ ET RECOURS. Malgré tout dommage que vous pourriez encourir pour quelque raison que ce soit (y compris, mais sans limitation, tous les dommages mentionnés ci-dessus et tous les dommages directs et généraux), la seule responsabilité de Microsoft et de ses fournisseurs en vertu de toute disposition de cette convention et votre unique recours en regard de tout ce qui précède sont limités au plus élevé des montants suivants: soit (a) le montant que vous avez payé pour le Produit Logiciel, soit (b) un montant équivalant à cinq dollars U.S. (5,00 $ U.S.). Les limitations, exclusions et renonciations ci-dessus s'appliquent dans toute la mesure permise par la législation en vigueur, et ce même si leur application a pour effet de priver un recours de son essence.

DROITS LIMITÉS DU GOUVERNEMENT AMÉRICAIN

Tout Produit Logiciel fourni au gouvernement américain conformément à des demandes émises le ou après le 1er décembre 1995 est offert avec les restrictions et droits commerciaux décrits ailleurs dans la présente convention. Tout Produit Logiciel fourni au gouvernement américain conformément à des demandes émises avant le 1er décembre 1995 est offert avec des DROITS LIMITÉS tels que prévus dans le FAR, 48CFR 52.227-14 (juin 1987) ou dans le FAR, 48CFR 252.227-7013 (octobre 1988), tels qu'applicables.

Sauf lorsqu'expressément prohibé par la législation locale, la présente convention est régie par les lois en vigueur dans la province d'Ontario, Canada. Pour tout différend qui pourrait découler des présentes, vous acceptez la compétence des tribunaux fédéraux et provinciaux siégeant à Toronto, Ontario.

Si vous avez des questions concernant cette convention ou si vous désirez communiquer avec Microsoft pour quelque raison que ce soit, veuillez contacter la succursale Microsoft desservant votre pays, ou écrire à: Microsoft Sales Information Center, One Microsoft Way, Redmond, Washington 98052-6399.

Register Today!

Return this
Microsoft® Office 2000 Resource Kit
registration card today

Microsoft *Press*
mspress.microsoft.com

0-7356-0555-6

Microsoft® Office 2000 Resource Kit

FIRST NAME

MIDDLE INITIAL

LAST NAME

INSTITUTION OR COMPANY NAME

ADDRESS

CITY

STATE

ZIP

( )

E-MAIL ADDRESS

PHONE NUMBER

U.S. and Canada addresses only. Fill in information above and mail postage-free.
Please mail only the bottom half of this page.

For information about Microsoft Press®
products, visit our Web site at
mspress.microsoft.com

Microsoft·*Press*

|||||||